The Csound Book

Edited by Richard Boulanger

The Csound Book

Perspectives in Software Synthesis, Sound Design, Signal Processing, and Programming

The MIT Press
Cambridge, Massachusetts
London, England

This book was set in Times Roman by Graphic Composition, Inc., on the Miles 33 typesetting system.

Printed and bound in the United States of America.

Library of Congress Cataloging-in-Publication Data

The Csound book : perspectives in software synthesis, sound design, signal processing, and programming / edited by Richard Boulanger.

p. cm.

Discography: p.

Includes bibliographical references (p.) and index.

ISBN-13 978-0-262-52261-8 (alk. paper)

ISBN-10 0-262-52261-6 (alk. paper)

1. Computer music—Instruction and study. 2. Computer composition. I. Boulanger, Richard Charles, 1956–

MT723.C77 1999

786.7'413453042—dc21 99-14922

CIP

10 9 8

This book is dedicated to the memory of Dr. Robert Cooper
Through his music and his evangelization of Csound, so many young musicians came to see the light.

Book Contents

Please note that any material referenced in the text as being included on the CD-ROM can now be found at http://mitpress.mit.edu/thecsoundbook.

CD-ROM Contents

CD-ROM Chapters

CD-ROM Tutorials

CD-ROM Music

Spare Luxury One

Robin Whittle

He Will Come

Shamil Gainetdinov

Impossible Planet

Luca Pavan

Incantation

Jean Piché

Shamantra

Vladimir Volkov

Featured Student Compositions and Etudes

Berklee College of Music and NYU Students of *Richard Boulanger*

Eloy Anzola, Severeine Baron, David Bax, Daniel Birczynski, Andreas Bjørck, Brian Cass, John Chen, Eun Suk Choi, Jean-Luc Cohen, Robert Elkins, Tobias Enhus, Matthew Fordham, James Forrest, Julie Friedman, Flavio Gaete, David Hanft, Chris Hobson, Glenn Ianaro, Ken Ichiyanagi, Nathan Jenkins, Yong-Jin Jeong, Jacob Joaquin, Jeff Knorr, Jahwan Koo, Samara Krugman, Kyogu Lee, David Linnenbank, Yuan Liu, Arran Lowe, Malte Luebe, Matthew Mariano, Luis Maurette, Matt Moldover, Patrick Montgomery, Joo Won Park, Nathan Pease, Bobby Pietrusko, Greg Rippin, Alan Rosenblith, Jen Scatturo, Larry "Big" Thunder Schertzer, Pawel Sek, Freddy Sheinfeld, Matthew Thies, Chuck Van Haecke, Michael Ward-Bergeman, Elaine Walker, Blake Williams, Jeremy Zuckerman

Glasgow Students of *Eduardo Reck Miranda*

Stuart Brown, Susanne Hein, Kenny McAlpine, Mark Newton, Neal Wade

Louisiana State University Students of *Stephen Beck*

Michael Alderson, Michael Blandino, John Endicott, Aaron Johnson, William Price, Charles Urban

Bowling Green State University Students of *Burton Beerman*

Matt Harder, Adam Zygmunt

University of Washington Students of *Richard Karpen*

Sean Costello, Elizabeth Hoffman

MIT Media Lab Students of *Barry Vercoe*

Kopyc, Joe Kung, Beth Leibowitz, Madanes, Tom Maglione, Majoros, Maney, Schaphor, Skupinsk, Sprouse, Theodoso

Instrument Anthologies and Libraries

Chapter Instruments from The Csound Book

Richard Boulanger

Selections from The Cook Collection

Steven Cook

Selections from The Comajuncosas Anthology

Josep M. Comajuncosas

The Amsterdam Catalog of Csound Computer Instruments

John-Philipp Gather

Selections from The Harrington Anthology of DX7-FM Instruments

Jeff Harrington

Selections from The Lyon Anthology

Eric Lyon

Selections from The Mikelson Anthology

Hans Mikelson

Selections from the Risset *Catalog*

Selections from the *Rossing Psychoacoustic CD* in Csound

David Sumy

Selections from The Smaragdis Anthology

Paris Smaragdis

Selections from The Varo Anthology of DX7-FM Instruments

Jonathan Varo

Selections from The Csound Mailing List

Csound Application and Sources

Csound for DOS and Windows
John ffitch

Csound for Macintosh
Mike Berry, Dave Madole, and Matt Ingalls

Csound for LINUX
Dave Phillips

DirectCsound and CsoundAV
Gabriel Maldonado

Active X Csound and Java Csound
Michael Gogins

The Canonical Csound Sources and Executables
John ffitch

Csound for Linux (Developer's Version)
Nicola Bernardini

MacCsound, CsoundLib, and csound
Matt Ingalls

Csound Front-Ends and Utilities

Blue
Steven Yi

Cecilia
Alexandre Burton and Jean Piché

Cmask
Andre Bartetzki

CsEdit
Roger Klaveness

Csound Reference Materials

Selections from The Csound Book

Selections from the Csound Catalog

Catalog Instruments

Comanjuncosas, Cook, Lyon, Mikelson, Smaragdis, Varga, Amsterdam, Risset, Dodge & Jerse, Harrington-Pinkston DX7, Varo-Pinkston DX7, Pavan's Deutsch & Noorden Psychoacoustics, Sumy's Rossing Psychoacoustics

Foreword

Barry Vercoe

It is indeed a pleasure to peruse this volume, to see so many composers and authors joined in a similar purpose of making their insights and experiences public and to feel that the computer music community will surely benefit from such broad-based disclosure. It is never easy to have more than one living composer present at a single concert of their collected works, and to the extent that these contributions represent composing time lost and thoughts and insights given away free, the richness and evenness of this volume suggests that these composer/authors must all have been ensemble performers first. Of course, every ensemble has its taskmaster, and I stand in awe of what Richard Boulanger has done to bring this one to the concert stage.

This field has always benefited most from the spirit of sharing. It was Max Mathews's willingness to give copies of **Music 4** to both Princeton and Stanford in the early 1960s that got me started. At Princeton it had fallen into the fertile hands of Hubert Howe and the late Godfrey Winham, who as composers imbued it with controllable envelope onsets (**envlp**) while they also worked to have it consume less IBM 7094 time by writing large parts in a BEFAP assembler (**Music4B**). Looking on was Ken Steiglitz, an engineer who had recently discovered that analog feedback filters could be represented with digital samples. By the time I first saw Music4B code (1966–1967) it had a **reson** filter—and the age of subtractive digital sound design was already underway.

During 1967–68 I wrote a large work (for double chorus, band, string orchestra, soloists and computer-generated sounds), whose Seattle Opera House performance convinced me that this was a medium with a future. But on my arrival back at Princeton I encountered a major problem: the 7094 was to be replaced by a new machine called a 360 and the BEFAP code would no longer run. Although Godfrey responded by writing a Fortran version (**Music4BF**, slower but eternally portable), I took a gamble that IBM would not change its assembler language again soon, and wrote **Music 360**. Like Max Mathews, I then gave this away as fast as I could, and its super efficiency enabled a new generation of composers with limited budgets to see computer music as an affordable medium.

But we were still at an arm's length from our instrument. Punched cards and batch processing at a central campus facility were no way to interact with any device, and on my move to the Massachusetts Institute of Technology in 1971 I set about designing the first comprehensive real-time digital sound synthesizer, to bring the best of Music 360's audio processing into the realm of live interactive performance. After two years and a design complete, its imminent construction was distracted by a gift from Digital Equipment Corporation of their latest creation, a PDP-11. Now, with a whole computer devoted exclusively to music, we could have both real-time processing and software flexibility, and **Music 11** was the result.

There were many innovations in this rewrite. First, since my earlier hardware design had introduced the concept of *control-rate* signals for things like vibrato pitch motion, filter motion, amplitude motion and certain envelopes, this idea was carried into the first 1973 version of Music 11 as **k-rate** signals (familiar now to Csound users). Second, envelopes became more natural with multi-controllable exponential decays. Indeed, in 1976 while writing my *Synapse,* for Viola and computer, I found I could not match the articulation of my soloist unless I made the steady-state decay rate of each note in a phrase be a functional inverse of the note length. (In this regard string and wind players are different from pianists, who can articulate only by early release. Up to this time we had all been thinking like pianists, that is, no better than MIDI.) My **envlpx** opcode fixed that.

This had been my second gamble that a particular machine would be sufficiently common and long-lived to warrant assembler coding, and Music 11's efficiency and availability sustained a decade of even more affordable and widespread computer music. Moreover, although the exported code was not real-time, our in-house experiments were: Stephen Haflich connected an old organ keyboard so that we could play the computer in real-time; if you played something reasonably metric, the computer would print out the score when you finished; if you entered your score via our graphical score editor, the machine would play it back in real-time (I made extensive use of this while writing *Synapse*); if you created your orchestra graphically using Rich Steiger's **OEDIT**, Music 11 would use those instruments. Later, in 1980, student Miller Puckette connected a light-sensing diode to one end of the PDP−11, and an array-processing accelerator to the other, enabling one-dimensional conducting of a real-time performance. Haflich responded with a two-dimensional conducting sensor, using two sonar cells from a Polaroid camera. This was an exciting time for real-time experiments, and the attendees at our annual MIT Summer Workshops got to try many of these.

Meanwhile, my interest had shifted to tracking live instruments. At IRCAM in Paris in 1982, flutist Larry Beauregard had connected his flute to DiGiugno's 4X audio processor, enabling real-time pitch-following. On a Guggenheim at the time, I extended this concept to real-time score-following with automatic synchronized accompaniment, and over the next two years Larry and I gave numerous demonstrations of the computer as a chamber musician, playing Handel flute sonatas, Boulez's *Sonatine* for flute and piano and by 1984 my own *Synapse II* for flute and computer—the first piece ever composed expressly for such a setup. A major challenge was finding the right software constructs to support highly sensitive and responsive accompaniment. All of this was pre-MIDI, but the results were impressive even though heavy doses of tempo rubato would continually surprise my **Synthetic Performer**. In 1985 we solved the tempo rubato problem by incorporating *learning from rehearsals* (each time you played this way the machine would get better). We were also now tracking violin, since our brilliant, young flutist had contracted a fatal cancer. Moreover, this version used a new standard called MIDI, and here I was ably assisted by former student Miller Puckette, whose initial concepts for this task he later expanded into a program called **MAX**.

On returning to MIT in 1985 it was clear that microprocessors would eventually become the affordable machine power, that unportable assembler code would lose its usefulness, and that ANSI C would become the *lingua franca.* Since many parts of Music 11 and all of my Synthetic Performer were already in C, I was able to expand the existing constructs into a working **Csound** during the Fall of that year. Once it was operating, I received additional help from students like Kevin Peterson and Alan Delespinase and later from Bill Gardner, Dan Ellis and Paris Smaragdis. Moreover, thanks to the internet and ftp/public, my continuing wish to share the system even as it gained further maturity would take even less of my time.

The step to **Real-time Csound** was a simple one. With the right constructs already in place owing to my long-time interest in interactive performance, and computers now fast enough to do floating-point processing on a set schedule, I only had to use the DAC output pointer to implement blocking I/O on a fine time-grid to achieve tight interactive control. I took that step in 1990, and demonstrated it during the ICMC paper *Real-time Csound: Software Synthesis with Sensing and Control* (Vercoe and Ellis 1990). For me, the only reason for real-time is controllable performance, and Dan Ellis illustrated this by controlling a Bach synthesis by tapping arbitrary drum patterns on the table that held the microphone. The sensing also introduced Csound's new **Spectral Data Types** (see my chapter in this volume). With a sufficiently powerful machine (at the time a DECstation), both sensing and controlled high-fidelity synthesis had finally become possible.

But not all of us can command such a powerful central processor and today's interest in deft graphical control and graphical audio monitoring can often soak up the new cycles faster than technology creates them. At the 1996 ICMC in Hong Kong, I demonstrated an alternative architecture for both software and hardware with

Extended Csound. This is the first stage of an orderly progression towards multiprocessor fully-interactive performance. In the current version, Csound is divided between two processors, a host PC and a DSP-based soundcard. The host does all compiling and translation, disk I/O, and graphical-user-interface (GUI) processing, such as Patchwork (editing) and Cakewalk (sequencing). The DSP does all the signal processing, with sole access to the audio I/O ports; it also traps all MIDI input with an on-chip MIDI manager, such that each MIDI note-on results in an activated instrument instance in less than one control period.

The tightly-coupled multi-processor performance of Extended Csound has induced a flurry of new opcodes, many of them tailored to the internal code of the DSP I am using (a floating-point SHARC™ 21060 from Analog Devices). The new opcodes extend the power of Csound in areas such as real-time pitch-shifting, compressor-limiting, effects processing, mixing, sampling synthesis and MIDI processing and control. Since this volume is not the place for details, the curious can look at my paper in the 1996 ICMC Proceedings. I expect to be active in this area for some time.

Meanwhile, the fully portable part of Csound is enjoying widespread use, and this volume is a testament to the ingenuity of its users. Some are familiar names (Stephen Beck, Richard Dobson, Brian Evans, Michael Clarke, John ffitch, Richard Karpen, Jon Nelson, Jean Piché and Russell Pinskton) whom we have come to lean on out of both habit and dependency; some are newer lights (Elijah Breder, Per Byrne Villez, Michael Gogins, Andrew Horner, Alan Lee, Dave Madole, David McIntyre, Hans Mikelson, Michael Pocino, Marc Resibois, and Erik Spjut) we are attending to with growing interest; others are fresh faces (Bill Alves, Mike Berry, Martin Dupras, Rajmil Fischman, Matt Ingalls, Eric Lyon, Gabriel Maldonado, and Paris Smaragdis) likely to leave long-term images. The range of topics is broad, from sound design using various synthesis and modeling methods to mathematical and signal processing constructs we can learn from, and from compositional strategies using existing Csound resources to some powerful lessons on what to do when what you need is not already there. The whole is amply supported by CD-ROM working examples of ports to other machines, user-interfaces, personal approaches to composing, and most importantly, compositions that speak louder than words.

I am impressed and somewhat humbled by the range of thought and invention that Csound has induced. Gathering all this energy into one place creates a singularity that defies real measurement, but I am certain the effects of this volume will be much felt over both distance and time. On behalf of the readers, my thanks to all the contributors. Finally, my hat off to Richard Boulanger for all that composing time lost (you should have known better), and my best wishes to Csound users as you continue to redefine your own voice.

Preface

Max V. Mathews

The synthesis of music by a computer was born in 1957 when an IBM704 in New York City slowly computed a 17-second "piece" composed in what was probably the first audible example of a new musical scale with my program, **Music 1**. The program was limited, but many limitations were overcome in a sequence of successor programs culminating in **Music 5**, which was finished in the 1960s. Subsequently, others have written programs that both added powerful new features and ran on the many new computers that rapidly developed. Today, **Csound**, written by Barry Vercoe is, in my opinion, the best and most popular software synthesis program. In addition to new features, it is written in the **C** language, which is universally available and likely to remain so in the future. Thus, music written in Csound can be expected to have a long technical lifetime in the sense that it can be played on future computers.

Until recently, general-purpose music programs all had one major restriction—they could not be used for live performance because computers were not fast enough to synthesize interesting music in real-time, that is to say it took more than one second to synthesize a second of sound. Special purpose computers called digital synthesizers overcame this limitation. But real-time synthesizers brought with them a new major problem—rapid obsolescence. The commercial lifetime of a new synthesizer is only a few years and therefore music written for such machines cannot be expected to be playable in a decade.

Live performance with a general purpose program like Csound is now possible, either running native on a fast PC, or when ported to a DSP such as Vercoe's **Extended Csound**—a superbly efficient version that makes rich complex music in real-time on today's fast processor chips and that can be expected to run even faster on tomorrow's chips. Because of the universality of the C language, not only can Csound be compiled and run on general purpose processors such as a Macintosh G3 or a Pentium II, but it can be run on digital-signal-processing (DSP) chips that have

C compilers. Thus a parallel processor using a multiplicity of DSP chips can provide almost unlimited musical power for a reasonable cost.

One of the crucial factors contributing to the success of the **Music 5** language was my book, *The Technology of Computer Music,* which described the program in detail so it could be used and modified; it was intended both as a tutorial and as a reference. *The Csound Book,* conceived of and edited by Richard Boulanger, fulfills these same needs for Csound.

A measure of the growth and richness of today's computer music is the sizes of these two books. *The Technology of Computer Music* contained only 137 pages and had only one author. *The Csound Book* has more than 700 pages that were contributed by over 50 authors. It is my belief that this book, plus the Csound programs, instruments and utilities on the accompanying CD-ROM, provide the essential tools for the next generation of composers and performers of computer music.

Acknowledgments

In one way or another, I have been working on *The Csound Book* for over fifteen years (including over 9000 email messages between collaborators, contributors, my student assistants and myself). Without the help and support of the following people, this book would have never become a reality. So . . .

Thanks to my mentors Tom Piggott, Robert Perry, and Hugo Norden for showing me the way and starting me on the path. Thanks to my computer music teachers, collaborators and friends—Bruce Pennycook, Dexter Morrill, F. Richard Moore, Mark Dolson, Hal Chamberlain, and Max Mathews—each of you opened my eyes, ears, and mind a little wider. And thanks to my artistic soulmates Marek Choloniewski and Lee Ray—you have been a constant source of friendship and opened my heart a little wider.

Thanks to my colleagues in the Music Synthesis Department at the Berklee College of Music, but most importantly to Berklee vice president Dave Mash who taught me how to teach music through technology. Thanks especially to my Csound students at Berklee, whose enthusiasm and creativity continue to be a source of energy—their technical questions and their musical answers keep me growing and keep me going.

In particular, I would like to recognize my thirteen most dedicated student assistants: David Bax, Brian Cass, Luigi Castelli, Young Jun Choi, Flavio Gaete, Nate Jenkins, Jacob Joaquin, Andy Koss, Samara Krugman, Bobby Pietrusko, Sandro Rebel, Yevgen Stupka, and Chuck Van Haecke.

Yevgen, all the authors owe you a debt of gratitude for the months of dedicated work you did on the block diagrams. They add a level of consistency to the entire manuscript and conceptual clarity to the concepts presented. Flavio, thank you for the hundreds of hours you put into the initial layout and editing—especially the orchestras. Samara, thanks for straightening out the references, and for converting and reformatting the entire book and reference manual. Bobby, thanks for the final read and then for spending the last weeks of summer (two years in a row) fixing ALL the "little" things you found. Chuck, thanks for rendering and formatting the hundreds of orchestras for the CD-ROM; and Brian thanks for taking over and finishing when Chuck left to tour with a Blues band. Andy, thanks for entering the figure captions and for your recommendations and suggestions on the preliminary CD-ROM and cover designs; and David, thanks for getting the CD-ROM off to such a good start. Sandro, thanks for running all the scores. Nate, thanks for the help proofing and correcting the figure text. Luigi, thanks for all your help with the instrument anthologies; and again Bobby, thanks for debugging and fixing all the busted ones. Young, thanks for all the help finishing the CD-ROM.

Finally, Jacob, thank you for all your work on *The Csound CD-ROM* and *The Csound FrontPage.* After graduating from Berklee, the fact that you took a year off before graduate school to work solely on this project is something for which I and the entire Csound community owe you a great deal. You single-handedly transformed a huge collection of "Csound stuff" into a coherent and beautiful interactive experience—a true "on-line" extension of *The Csound Book.* I would not have made it without you. In fact, without the dedicated and generous contributions of all these students from the Berklee College of Music, this book and CD-ROM would have taken forever to finish and would not have been half as beautiful.

Thanks to all the authors, developers, and composers who so generously contributed their knowledge and expertise to this project. I have learned so much from each of you and am so happy and honored to help you share your discoveries and insights with the world. Thank you Matt Ingalls for your incredible CsoundLib, MacCsound, and csound—for Max/MSP; and Joo Won Park for CsoundMax; Young Jun Choi for *Instant Csound;* Steven Yi for Blue; Flavio Tordini for his Csound Editor; Dave Perry for *Visual Orchestra;* Michael Gogins for *Silence, ActiveX Csound,* and *JCsound;* Alexandre Burton and Jean Piché for *Cecilia;* John Gauther for *The Amsterdam Catalog;* Gabriel Maldonado for your wonderful *Direct X Csound* and *VMCI;* Mike Berry, Dave Madole, and especially Matt Ingalls for your Macintosh *PPCsound* port and support; Dave Phillips for all your work on the LINUX port; and finally Hans Mikelson for your fabulous Csound E-Zine and your incredible *Instrument Anthology.* Thank you to these and all the other developers whose Csound "launchers," front-ends, and utilities have made the language so much more teachable, learnable, and usable.

I would like to thank the Csound documentation team lead initially by Jean Piché and including John ffitch, Rasmus Ekman, Kevin Conder, Matt Ingalls, Mike Berry, Servando Valero, Gabriel Maldonado, Jacob Joaquin, and especially David Boothe. David, you have worked to produce and, more important, to maintain, the definitive reference document that is printable, portable, linked and beautifully indexed. Your *Canonical Public Csound Reference Manual* in both PDF and HTML formats has become the de facto standard.

Thanks, of course, to all the Csound opcode developers. I doubt that Barry Vercoe himself would recognize the 1999 version of Public Csound with all the cool new stuff that YOU have put in there! Most important, on behalf of the entire Csound community, I would like to acknowledge and thank my dear friend John ffitch for maintaining, improving and extending Csound and for so generously sharing his code, his time, and his expertise with virtually anyone who posts a question to the Csound mailing list. While people like me speculate on the many ways of improving Csound, John ffitch just does it. In so many ways, Public Csound is truly John ffitch's program.

Thanks to Douglas Sery of the MIT Press for his encouragement, advice and support. Several years ago he contacted me about doing a Csound book and along the way, whenever I would fumble or drop the ball, he was there to pick it up and toss it back. His faith in me and belief in this project are largely responsible for its successful completion. Also at MIT Press, thanks to Chryseis Fox for such a beautiful layout and design. Thank you to Michael Sims for all his editorial input and guidance. And thank you Ori Kometani for your cover art, which at a glance captures the essence of Csound—a language that transforms letters and numbers into beautiful sonically animated waveforms!

Thanks to Mike Haidar for initiating and shepherding the Extended Csound Project at Analog Devices that resulted in my working closely with Scotty Vercoe, Sreenivasa Inukoti, and Barry Vercoe from 1995–1997 on a DSP-based version of Csound—and loving every minute of it! Thanks also to Bill Verplank and the Interval Research Corporation for supporting my research in alternate controllers and sound design at Berklee that resulted in my working closely with you, Perry Cook, Rob Shaw, Paris Smaragdis, and Max Mathews—another computer music dream team I got to play with!

Finally, thank you Barry Vercoe . . . for Csound. As a gifted young composer, you chose to put aside your manuscript paper and pencil to develop a tool that gave voice to a world of young and aspiring composers—including me. On behalf of every musician and teacher who has discovered the science of sound and the mathematical basis of music through Csound, I thank you.

At home here, I thank my parents for their love, faith, and support; my three sons Adam, Philip, and Adrien for keeping me in touch with reality and bringing me back to earth . . . and to music. And last, but not least, I extend my most heartfelt gratitude and ever lasting love to my wife, my song, my Susan—who understands me deeply and supports me completely. As a matter of fact, taking a summer course in Csound back in 1979 and working with Vercoe was Sue's idea. About an MIT promotional brochure, she said "Rick . . . what's this?" I said "Oh, just some sort of computer music course at MIT." She said, "Honey, you've got to go!" And choosing that road has made all the difference.

Introduction

Welcome to the world of computer-based software synthesis, signal processing, programming, sound-design, and composition. Welcome to world of Csound.

As a student composer in the 1970s, I was fascinated with electronic music instruments and multitrack recording technology, but I was always limited in what sounds and music I could produce by the limits of the synthesizer or recorder I could afford. Then I discovered the world's most powerful synthesizer—Csound—and I discovered that this synthesizer/resynthesizer/signal-processor/algorithmic-composer/sequencer/swiss-army-knife-of-a-computer-music-program, which runs on virtually any PC, is completely free!

Even today, I am still running out of voices on my digital multitimbral synthesizers, running out of effects on my digital multiverb signal processors and running out of tracks on my digital multitrack recorder. But, in the software synthesis world of Csound, there are no such limitations. In fact, the only limitations are the size of your hard disk, the amount of RAM in your PC, the speed of your CPU—and of course, the limits of your imagination.

Quite obviously, since Csound is a software synthesizer, which runs native on your personal computer, a faster CPU, a larger hard drive, and more RAM will improve the performance of the software. But most personal computers today are powerful enough for you to make extraordinary music.

There is one small catch, however: the Csound synthesizer has no presets. So, in order to make interesting sounds and music with Csound, you have to know how synthesizers make sounds, how signal-processors transform sounds, and, in fact, how computers make music. In the world of Csound, ignorance is the only obstacle.

This book is the key to learning Csound. Each chapter is written by one of the world's leading computer music educators, programmers, sound-designers, and composers. And each focuses on his or her particular specialty—illustrating specific concepts through actual working Csound instruments and C code. These pioneers will take you along the paths that they have traveled. They will guide you and help you understand and explore the world of Csound; and through their algorithms, sounds, and music, they will point out many new and wonderful places along the way—both technically and artistically.

As you will soon discover, the world of Csound is vast and ever expanding. I have found it to be a constant source of wonder, enlightenment, and fulfillment. On behalf of all of the authors, I welcome you to the world of Csound and I wish you the joy of endless discovery . . .

. . . and may your journey be a long one.

How to Use This Book

The Csound Book is not meant to be "read" from cover to cover. Although I have organized the chapters into thematic sections such as Software Synthesis, Signal Processing, Programming, Composition, MIDI, and Real-time, the material in each section does not necessarily progress from beginning to advanced. The best way to "read" *The Csound Book* will depend on your level of experience with synthesizers, signal processors, and computers. I assure you that there is something for both the beginner and the expert in every section, but given the breadth and scope of what is covered here, it is quite easy for beginners to lose their way. Below, I have outlined several of the paths I take with my students at Berklee. I hope you will find these suggestions helpful as you begin your journey into the world of Csound.

In my *Csound* class at Berklee I typically assign the following:

1. Read and do the exercises in chapter 1, *Introduction to Sound Design in Csound,* to familiarize yourself with the syntax of the language.
2. Read and modify my original Csound *Sound Design TOOTorials* on the CD-ROM, to review the chapter 1 basics.
3. Read Kim Cascone's CD-ROM chapter, *Recontextualizing Ambient Music,* for a compositional perspective.
4. Read and modify the instruments in my *Mastering Csound* CD-ROM Tutorial especially focusing on the MIDI versions of these tutorial instruments. Then try to MIDIfy some of the Cascone, TOOTorial, and chapter 1 instruments.
5. Read Mikelson's chapter, *Modeling a Multieffects Processor in Csound,* for a commercial DSP perspective.
6. Read Karpen's chapter, *Csound Phase Vocoder and Extensions,* for a glimpse at Csound's analysis and re-synthesis capabilities.

7. Compose three short etudes: a score-based composition (focused on a single software synthesis technique), a sample-based composition (driven by a MIDIfile), and a DSP-based composition (featuring filtering, reverberation, and analysis/resynthesis).

Even in my non-Csound classes at Berklee, I have found some of the more general chapters from *The Csound Book* to be an excellent source of both sound examples and theoretical material. In my *Intro* and *Advanced Synthesis* classes, I assign the Fischman *Survey* chapter. It provides an excellent theoretical and practical overview of classic synthesis techniques. I follow this with Pinkston's and Evans's *FM* chapters, and then on to Webman and Mikelson's *FX* chapters. These clearly reveal the mechanics of some "classic" analog synthesizer and studio processors. Then I use Lee's *Granular,* and the Comajuncosas and Mikelson *Wave Terrain* chapters to showcase innovative "non-commercial" techniques.

In my *Desktop DSP* class, I start by assigning Spjut's *Intro to Signal Processing* chapter. To me, this is one of the clearest and most concise overviews of DSP theory and application ever written. I follow this with Pinkston's *Delay* chapter, Karpen's, *Phase Vocoder* chapter, Lyon's *Reverb* chapter and Mikelson's *Multieffects* chapters. These all show how a general-purpose system like Csound can help one to fully understand the inner workings of today's commercial software and hardware. Furthermore, these chapters show how Csound is capable of producing sounds and effects far beyond anything commercially available. Finally, I conclude the semester with Klapper's *LPC* and Villez and Clark's *FOF* chapters to introduce some underutilized classic techniques and some fresh new algorithms.

In my *Alternative Composition and Aesthetics* seminars, I present the music and method of Biancini, Bush, Cascone, Clarke, Endrich, Evans, ffitch, Gogins, Hunkins, Ingalls, Nelson, Pavan, Pierce, and Sofia. (OK, sometimes I talk about my music, too.) To me, each of these inspiring composers has a totally original perspective on musical form and a unique approach to the substance and structure of organized sound and silence. It is wonderful to introduce such diversity of musical viewpoints to young composers.

In my *Physical Modeling* classes I work through Beck's *Viability,* Dobson's *Legato,* Horner and Ayer's *Horn,* Pinkston's and Evans's *FM,* ffitch's *Noise,* Comajuncosas's *Analog and Physical Modeling,* and Mikelson's *Keyboards, Waveguides and Chaos.* This collection quite literally covers it all.

For my *Directed Studies* classes I get my most advanced students into programming and research. With some, I focus on *Adding Opcodes* and assign the Katsianos, ffitch, Resibois, and Maldonado chapters. With others, I concentrate on *Interface Issues* and look to Ingalls, Gogins, Piché, and Burton. For a research perspective that touches upon medicine, perception, and even mind models, I introduce Barrass, Batista, Rossiter, Ballora, and Pennycook. And for those interested in *3D and Internet Audio* I assign the Casey, Furse, McIntyre, and Breder chapters.

Another approach entirely, is to simply study the instruments. In this case you could jump directly into the chapters focused on specific synthesis techniques or you could choose to study and modify the Csound instruments in the: Amsterdam, Comajuncosas, Lyon, Pinkston, Mikelson, Risset, and Smaragdis anthologies. These inspiring and diverse collections represent a wealth of knowledge and hold all of Csound's secrets. Once you begin to check out the instruments on the CD-ROM, you will soon discover that Csound is capable of making the most amazing sounds of any commercial synthesizer or signal processor. And although this book and CD-ROM seem to emphasize sound design, do remember that what this noisy world needs most . . . is music. Above all else, turn your Csound into Cmusic.

Software Synthesis

Csound Fundamentals

1 Introduction to Sound Design in Csound

Richard Boulanger

Csound is a powerful and versatile software synthesis program. Drawing from a toolkit of over 450 signal processing modules, one can use Csound to model virtually any commercial synthesizer or multieffect processor. Csound transforms a personal computer into a high-end digital audio workstation—an environment in which the worlds of sound-design, acoustic research, digital audio production, and computer music composition all join together in the ultimate expressive instrument. As with every musical instrument, however, true virtuosity is the product of both talent and dedication. You will soon discover that Csound is the ultimate musical instrument. But you must practice! In return, it will reward your commitment by producing some of the richest textures and most beautiful timbres that you have ever heard. In the audio world of Csound, knowledge and experience are the key . . . and your imagination the only limitation.

The goal of this chapter is to get you started on Csound's road of discovery and artistry. Along the way we'll survey a wide range of synthesis and signal processing techniques and we'll see how they're implemented in Csound. By the end we'll have explored a good number of Csound's many possibilities. I encourage you to render, listen to, study and modify each of my simple tutorial instruments. In so doing, you'll acquire a clear understanding and appreciation for the language, while laying down a solid foundation upon which to build your own personal library of original and modified instruments. Furthermore, working through the basics covered here will prepare you to better understand, appreciate and apply the more advanced synthesis and signal processing models that are presented by my colleagues and friends in the subsequent chapters of this book.

Now there are thousands of Csound instruments and hundreds of Csound compositions on the CD-ROM that accompanies this text. Each opens a doorway into one of Csound's many worlds. In fact, it would take a lifetime to explore them all. Clearly, one way to go would be to render all the orchestras on the CD-ROM, select the ones that sound most interesting to you and merely sample them for use in your own compositions. This library of presets might be just the collection of unique sounds you were searching for and your journey would be over.

I believe, however, it would be better to read, render, listen to, and then study the synthesis and signal processing techniques that fascinate you most by modifying existing Csound orchestras that employ them. Afterward you should express this understanding through your own compositions—your own timbre-based soundscapes and sound collages. Through this active discovery process you will begin to develop your own personal Csound library and ultimately your own voice.

To follow the path I propose, you'll need to understand the structure and syntax of the Csound language. But I am confident that with this knowledge, you'll be able to translate your personal audio and synthesis experience into original and beautiful Csound-based synthetic instruments and some unique and vivid sound sculptures.

To that end, we'll begin by learning the structure and syntax of Csound's text-based orchestra and score language. Then we'll move on to explore a variety of synthesis algorithms and Csound programming techniques. Finally we'll advance to some signal processing examples. Along the way, we'll cover some basic digital audio concepts and learn some software synthesis programming tricks. To better understand the algorithms and the signal flow, we'll block-diagram most of our Csound instruments. Also, I'll assign a number of exercises that will help you to fully understand the many ways in which you can actually work with the program.

Don't skip the exercises. And don't just read them—do them! They are the key to developing real fluency with the language. In fact, you may be surprised to discover that these exercises teach you more about how to work with Csound than any of the descriptions that precede them. In the end, you should have a good strong foundation upon which to build your own library of Csounds and you will have paved the way to a deeper understanding of the chapters that follow.

So, follow the instructions on the CD-ROM; install the Csound program on your computer; render and listen to a few of the test orchestras to make sure everything is working properly; and then let's get started.

What Is Csound and How Does It Work?

Csound is a sound renderer. It works by first translating a set of text-based *instruments,* found in the *orchestra file,* into a computer data-structure that is machine-resident. Then, it *performs* these user-defined instruments by interpreting a list of *note* events and *parameter* data that the program reads from: a text-based *score file,* a sequencer-generated *MIDI file,* a real-time *MIDI controller,* real-time *audio,* or a non-MIDI devices such as the ASCII keyboard and mouse.

Depending on the speed of your computer (and the complexity of the instruments in your orchestra file) the performance of this score can either be auditioned in real-time, or *written* directly into a file on your hard-disk. This entire process is referred to as *sound rendering* as analogous to the process of image rendering in the world of computer graphics.

Once rendered, you will listen to the resulting soundfile by opening it with your favorite sound editor and playing it either through the built-in digital-to-analog converter (DAC) on your motherboard or the DAC on your PC sound card.

Thus, in Csound, we basically work with two interdependent and complementary text files, the orchestra file and the score file. These files can be given any name you would like. Typically, we give the two files the same name and differentiate between them by a unique three letter extension—*.orc* for the orchestra file and *.sco* for the score file. Naming is up to you. In this chapter I have called the files *etude1.orc* and *etude1.sco, etude2.orc* and *etude2.sco, etude3.orc* and *etude3.sco,* etc. These etude orchestras contain six instruments each (*instr 101–106, instr 107–112, instr 113–118,* etc.). From these multi-instrument orchestras I have also created a set of single instrument orchestras to make it easier for you to isolate and experiment on individual instruments. These are named after the instrument number itself (*101.orc* and *101.sco, 102.orc* and *102.sco, 117.orc* and *117.sco,* etc.). Naming the corresponding score file the same as the orchestra file will help you keep your instrument library organized and I highly recommend you do the same. In fact, all the scores and orchestras in *The Csound Book* and on the accompanying CD-ROM follow this naming convention.

The Orchestra File

The Csound orchestra file consists of two parts: the *header* section and the *instrument* section.

The Header Section

In the header section you define the sample and control the rates at which the instruments will be rendered and you specify the number of channels in the output. The orchestral header that we will use throughout the text is shown in figure 1.1.

```
sr        =     44100
kr        =     4410
ksmps     =     10
nchnls    =     1
```

Figure 1.1 Csound's default orchestral "header."

The code in this header assigns the sample rate (*sr*) to 44.1K (44100), the control rate (*kr*) to 4410 and *ksmps* to 10 (*ksmps* = *sr/kr*). The header also indicates that this orchestra should render a mono soundfile by setting the number of channels (*nchnls*) to 1. (If we wanted to render a stereo sound file, we would simply set *nchnls* to 2).

The Instrument Section

In Csound, instruments are defined (and thus designed) by interconnecting modules or *opcodes* that either generate or modify signals. These signals are represented by *symbols, labels,* or *variable names* that can be patched from one opcode to another. Individual instruments are given a unique instrument number and are delimited by the **instr** and **endin** statements. A single orchestra file can contain virtually any number of instruments. In fact, in Csound everything is an instrument—your 8000 voice sampler, your 4000 voice FM synth, your 2000 voice multimodal waveguide synth, your 1000 band EQ, your 500 channel automated mixer, your 250 tap delay-line, fractal-flanger, convolution-reverb, vector-spatializer, whatever . . . To the Csound program each of these different pieces of synthesis, signal processing, and studio gear are merely *instr 1, instr 2, instr 3, instr 4,* etc.

The Orchestra Syntax

In the Csound orchestra file, the syntax of a generic opcode statement is:

```
Output   Opcode        Arguments         Comment (optional)
```

In the case of the **oscil** opcode, this translates into the following syntax:

```
output oscil  amplitude,  frequency,  function #   ; COMMENT
a1     oscil  10000,      440,        1            ; OSCILLATOR
```

Sound Design Etude 1: A Six Instrument Orchestra

The Orchestra File

In our first orchestra file, *instr 101* uses a table-lookup oscillator opcode, **oscil**, to compute a 440 Hz sine tone with an amplitude of 10000. A block diagram of *instr 101* is show in figure 1.2. The actual Csound orchestra code for this instrument is shown in figure 1.3.

The block diagram of *instr 101* clearly shows how the output of the oscillator, labeled *a1,* is "patched" to the input of the **out** opcode that *writes* the signal to the hard-disk.

Csound renders instruments line-by-line, from top to bottom. Input arguments are on the right of the opcode name. Outputs are on the left. Words that follow a semicolon (**;**) are considered to be comments and are ignored.

In *instr 101,* as show in figure 1.3, the input arguments to the oscillator are set at 10000 (amplitude), 440 (frequency) and 1 (for the function number of the waveshape template that the oscillator reads). The oscillator opcode renders the sound 44100 times a second with these settings and writes the result into the variable named *a1.* The sample values in the local-variable *a1* can then be read as inputs by subsequent opcodes, such as the **out** opcode. In this way, variable names are similar to patch cords on a traditional analog synthesizer. Audio and control signals can be routed virtually anywhere in an instruments and used to: set a parameter to a new value,

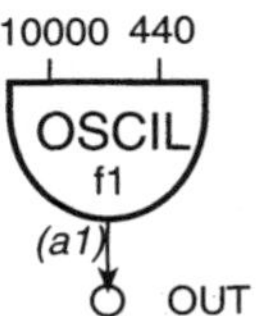

Figure 1.2 Block diagram of *instr 101,* a simple fixed frequency and amplitude table-lookup oscillator instrument.

```
        instr     101                  ; SIMPLE OSCIL
a1      oscil     10000, 440, 1
        out       a1
        endin
```

Figure 1.3 Orchestra code for *instr 101,* a fixed frequency and amplitude instrument using Csound's table-lookup oscillator opcode, **oscil**.

dynamically control a parameter (like turning a knob), or serve as an audio input into some processing opcode.

In figure 1.4, you can see that *instr 102—instr 106* use the same simple instrument design as *instr 101* (one signal generator writing to the **out** opcode), but replace the **oscil** opcode with more powerful synthesis opcodes such as: **foscil**—a simple 2-oscillator FM synthesizer, **buzz**—an additive set of harmonically-related cosines, **pluck**—a simple waveguide synthesizer based on the Karplus-Strong algorithm, **grain**—an asynchronous granular synthesizer and **loscil**—a sample-based wavetable synthesizer with looping.

Clearly the single signal-generator structure of these instruments is identical. But once you render them you will hear that their sounds are quite different. Even though they each play with a frequency of 440 Hz and an amplitude of 10000, the underlying synthesis algorithm embodied in each opcode is fundamentally different—requiring the specification of a unique set of parameters. In fact, these six signal generating opcodes (**oscil, foscil, buzz, pluck, grain,** and **loscil**) represent the core synthesis technology behind many of today's most popular commercial synthesizers. One might say that in Csound, a single opcode is an entire synthesizer. Well . . . maybe not an exciting or versatile synthesizer, but, in combination with other opcodes, Csound can, and will, take you far beyond any commercial implementation.

The Score File

Now let's look at the Csound score file that performs this orchestra of instruments. Like the orchestra file, the score file has two parts: *tables* and *notes.* In the first part, we use Csound's mathematical function-drawing subroutines (**GENS**) to generate function-tables (*f-tables*) and/or fill them by reading in soundfiles from the hard-disk. In the second part, we type in the *note-statements.* These note-events perform the instruments and pass them performance parameters such as frequency-settings, amplitude-levels, vibrato-rates, and attack-times.

The GEN Routines

Csound's function generating subroutines are called **GENS**. Each of these (more than 20) subroutines is optimized to compute a specific class of functions or wavetables. For example, the **GEN5** and **GEN7** subroutines construct functions from segments of exponential curves or straight lines; the **GEN9** and **GEN10** subroutines generate composite waveforms made up of weighted sums of simple sinusoids; the **GEN20** subroutine generates standard window functions, such as the Hamming window and

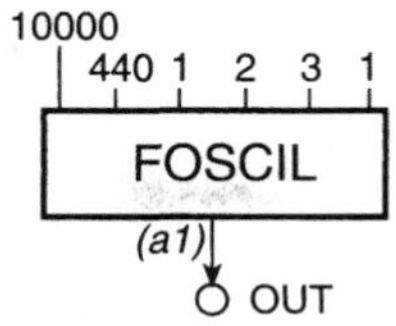

10000
440 1 2 3 1
FOSCIL
(a1)
OUT

```
        instr    102                 ; SIMPLE FM
a1      foscil   10000, 440, 1, 2, 3, 1
        out      a1
        endin
```

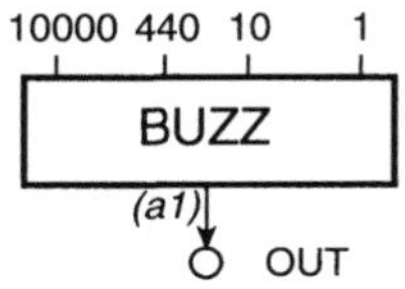

10000 440 10 1
BUZZ
(a1)
OUT

```
        instr    103                 ; SIMPLE BUZZ
a1      buzz     10000, 440, 10, 1
        out      a1
        endin
```

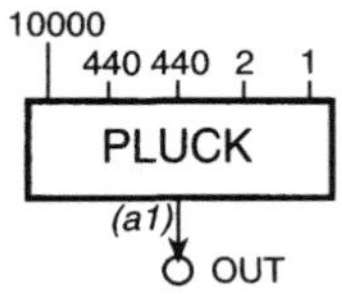

10000
440 440 2 1
PLUCK
(a1)
OUT

```
        instr    104                 ; SIMPLE WAVEGUIDE
a1      pluck    10000, 440, 440, 2, 1
        out      a1
        endin
```

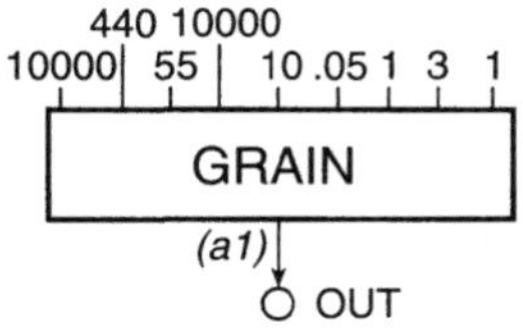

440 10000
10000 55 10 .05 1 3 1
GRAIN
(a1)
OUT

```
        instr    105                 ; SIMPLE GRANULAR
a1      grain    10000, 440, 55, 10000, 10, .05, 1, 3, 1
        out      a1
        endin
```

Figure 1.4 Block diagrams and orchestra code for *instr 102–instr 106,* a collection of fixed frequency and amplitude instruments that use different synthesis methods to produce a single note with the same amplitude (10000) and frequency (440).

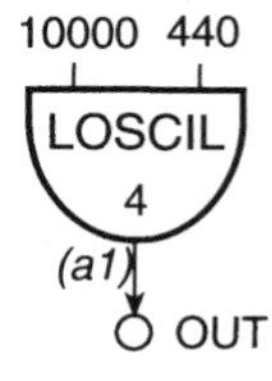


```
        instr      106                  ; SIMPLE WAVETABLE
a1      loscil     10000, 440, 4
        out        a1
        endin
```

Figure 1.4 continued

the Kaiser window, that are typically used for spectrum analysis and grain envelopes; the **GEN21** subroutine computes tables with different random distributions such as Gaussian, Cauchy and Poison; and the **GEN1** subroutine will transfer data from a prerecorded soundfile into a function-table for processing by one of Csound's opcodes such as the looping-oscillator **loscil**.

Which function tables are required, and how they are used by the instruments in your orchestra, is totally up to you—the sound designer. This can be a matter of common sense, preference or habit. For instance, since *instr 106* used the sample-based looping oscillator, **loscil**, I needed to load a sample into the orchestra. I chose **GEN1** to do it. Whereas in *instr 102,* since I was using the **foscil** opcode I could have chosen to frequency modulate any two waveforms, but decided on the traditional approach and modulated two sinewaves as defined by **GEN10**.

The Score Syntax

F-Statements

In the score file, the syntax of the Csound function statement (*f-statement*) is:

```
f number  loadtime  table-size  GEN Routine  parameter1  parameter... ; COMMENT
```

If we wanted to generate a 16 point sinewave, we might write the following f-statement:

```
f   111   0   16   10   1        ; A SINEWAVE
```

As a result, the f-table (*f 111*) would generate the function shown in figure 1.5.

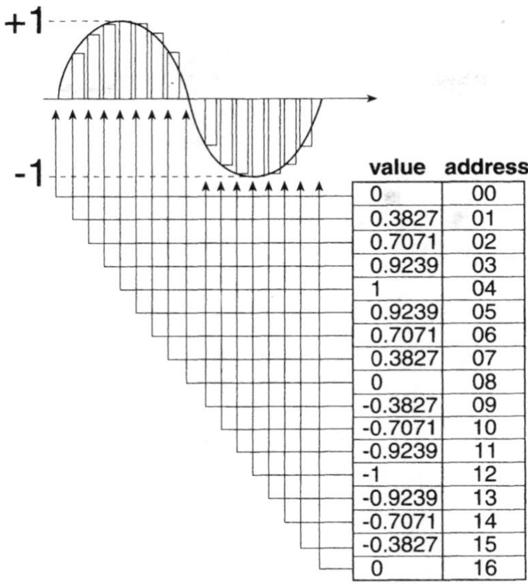

value	address
0	00
0.3827	01
0.7071	02
0.9239	03
1	04
0.9239	05
0.7071	06
0.3827	07
0	08
-0.3827	09
-0.7071	10
-0.9239	11
-1	12
-0.9239	13
-0.7071	14
-0.3827	15
0	16

Figure 1.5 A 16 point sine function defined by **GEN10** with the arguments: *f 111 0 16 10 1.*

```
f 1 0 4096 10 1
f 2 0 4096 10 1 .5 .333 .25 .2 .166 .142 .125 .111 .1 .09 .083 .076 .071 .066 .062
f 3 0 4097 20 2 1
f 4 0 0    1  "sing.aif" 0 4 0
```

Figure 1.6 Function tables defined in the score file *etude1.sco.*

As you can see, a sinewave drawn with 16 points of resolution is not particularly smooth. Most functions must be a power-of–2 in length (64, 128, 256, 512, 1024, 2048, 4096, 8192), and so, for wavetables, we typically specify function table sizes between 512 and 8192. In our first score, *etude1.sco,* we define the following functions using **GEN10, GEN20,** and **GEN1** as shown in figure 1.6.

All four functions are loaded at time *0.* Both *f 1* and *f 2* use **GEN10** to fill 4K tables (*4096* values) with one cycle of a sinewave (*f 1*) and with the first 16 harmonics of a sawtooth wave (*f 2*). **GEN20** is used to fill a 4K table (*f 3*) with a *Hanning* window for use by the **grain** opcode. Finally, *f 4* uses **GEN1** to fill a table with a 44.1K mono 16-bit AIFF format soundfile of a male vocalist singing the word *la* at the pitch A440 for 3 seconds. This sample is used by the **loscil** opcode. (Note that the length of *f 4* is specified as 0. This tells the **GEN1** subroutine to read the actual length of the file from the *header* of the soundfile "sing.aif." In this specific case the length would be 132300 samples—44100 samples-per-second * 3 seconds.)

The Note List

In the second part of the Csound score file we write the notes. As in the orchestra file, each *note-statement* in the score file occupies a single line. Note-statements (or *i-statements*) call for an instrument to be made active at a specific time and for a specific duration. Further, each note-statement can be used to pass along a virtually unlimited number of unique parameter settings to the instrument and these parameters can be changed on a note-by-note basis.

Like the orchestra, which renders a sound line-by-line, the score file is read line-by-line, note-by-note. Notes, however, can have the same *start-times* and thus be performed simultaneously. In Csound one must always be aware of the fact that whenever two or more notes are performed simultaneously, or whenever they overlap, their amplitudes are added. This can frequently result in *samples-out-of-range* or clipping. (We will discuss this in detail shortly.)

You may have noticed that in the orchestra an opcode's *arguments* were separated by commas. Here in the score both the f-table arguments and i-statement parameter fields (or *p-fields*) are separated by any number of spaces or tabs. Commas are not used.

In order to keep things organized and clear sound designers often use tab-stops to separate their p-fields. This practice keeps p-fields aligned in straight columns and facilitates both reading and debugging. This is not required—just highly recommended.

The First Three P-Fields

In all note-statements, the meaning of the first three p-fields (or columns) is reserved. The first three p-fields (as in fig. 1.7 on page 15) specify the *instrument number,* the *start-time* and the *duration.*

```
;    P1               P2              P3
i    INSTRUMENT #     START-TIME      DURATION
```

The function of all other p-fields is determined by you—the sound designer. Typically, *p4* is reserved for amplitude and *p5* is reserved for frequency. This convention has been adopted in this chapter and throughout this text. In our first score, *etude1.sco,* as shown in figure 1.7, a single note with a duration of 3 seconds is played consecutively on *instr 101—instr 106.* Because the start-times of each note are spaced 4 seconds apart there will be a second of silence between each audio event.

```
; P1                    P2                P3
; INSTRUMENT #          START-TIME        DURATION
i 101                   0                 3
i 102                   4                 3
i 103                   8                 3
i 104                   12                3
i 105                   16                3
i 106                   20                3
```

Figure 1.7 Simple score used to play instruments 101 through 106 as shown in figure 1.2 and 1.4.

Exercises for Etude 1

- Render the Csound orchestra and score files: *etude1.orc* & *etude1.sco.*
- Play and listen to the different sound qualities of each instrument.
- Modify the score file and change the duration of each note.
- Make all the notes start at the same time.
- Comment out several of the notes so that they do not play at all.
- Cut and Paste multiple copies of the notes. Then, change the start times (*p2*) and durations (*p3*) of the copies to make the same instruments start and end at different times.
- Create a canon at the unison with *instr 106.*
- Look up and read about the opcodes used in *instr 101–106* in the *Csound Reference Manual.*

```
k/ar oscil  k/amp, k/cps, ifn[, iphs]
ar   foscil xamp, kcps, kcar, kmod, kndx, ifn[, iphs]
ar   buzz   xamp, xcps, knh, ifn[, iphs]
ar   pluck  kamp, kcps, icps, ifn, imeth[, iparm1, iparm2]
ar   grain  xamp, xpitch, xdens, kampoff, kpitchoff, kgdur, igfn, iwfn, imgdur
            [; igrnd]
ar   loscil xamp, kcps, ifn[, ibas[, imod1, ibeg1, iend1[, imod2, ibeg2, iend2]]]
```

- In the orchestra file, modify the frequency and amplitude arguments of each instrument.
- Change the frequency ratios of the carrier and modulator in the **foscil** instrument.
- Change the number of harmonics in the **buzz** instrument.
- Change the initial function for the **pluck** instrument.

- Change the density and duration of the **grain** instrument.
- Make three copies of *f 4* and renumber them (*f 5, f 6, f 7*). Load in your own samples ("yoursound1.aif," "yoursound2.aif," "yoursound3.aif"). Create multiple copies of *instr 106* and number them *instr 66, instr 67* and *instr 68.* Edit the instruments so that they each read a different soundfile at a different pitch. Play the different samples simultaneously.
- In the file *etude1.orc* duplicate and renumber each duplicated instrument. Set different parameter values for each version of the duplicated instruments. Play all twelve instruments simultaneously. Adjust the amplitudes so that you have no *samples-out-of-range.*

Theory: Sound, Signals, and Sampling

To better appreciate what's going on in Csound, it might be best to make sure we understand the acoustic properties of sound and how sound is represented in a computer.

The experience of sound results from our eardrum's sympathetic response to the compressions and rarefactions of the air molecules projected outward in all directions from a vibrating source. This vibrating pattern of pressure variations is called a *waveform.* Looking at figure 1.8a, we can see that the air molecules would be *compressed* when the waveform is above the x-axis (positive) and *rarefacted* when below (negative). In fact, figure 1.8 shows a single cycle of a square wave in both the time and frequency domains.

The time domain representation (a) plots time on the x-axis and amplitude on the y-axis. The frequency domain representation (b) plots frequency on the x-axis and amplitude on the y-axis.

We *experience* sound in the time-domain as pressure variations, but we *perceive* sound in the frequency domain as spectral variations. The ear acts as a *transducer,* converting the mechanical motion of the eardrum (through the *ossicles:* the *hammer, anvil,* and *stirrup*) to the *oval window* membrane, which causes a traveling wave to propagate in the fluid of the *cochlea* and stimulate the hair cells on the *basilar membrane.* These hair cells are like a high resolution frequency analyzer that transmits this complex set of frequency information to the brain through nerves attached to each of the hair cells. With this extremely sensitive set of sensors, transducers, and transmitters we actively and continuously analyze, codify, classify, and perceive the complex frequency characteristics of soundwaves as we resonate with the world around us.

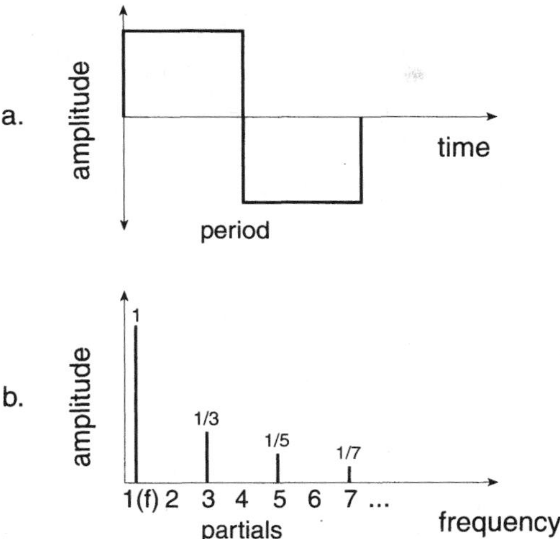

Figure 1.8 A time domain (a) and frequency domain (b) representation of a square wave.

Typically we employ a different transducer (a microphone) to convert acoustic waveforms into signals that we can visualize and manipulate in the computer. The process is referred to as *sampling* and is illustrated in figure 1.9.

When sampling a waveform we use a microphone first to convert an acoustic pressure wave into an *analogous* electrical pressure wave or an *analog* signal. Then, we pass this signal through an *anti-aliasing* lowpass filter to remove the frequency components above 1/2 the *sampling-rate.* In fact, a digital system can not accurately represent a signal above 1/2 the sampling rate (this reflective frequency barrier is known as the *Nyquist* frequency). So then, after we lowpass filter out the highs that we can't accurately represent, we proceed to measure or sample the amplitude of the signal with an analog-to-digital converter (ADC).

If you have a 16-bit linear system, you would sample the analog waveform with 16 bits of precision (in a range from –32768 to 32767 or 2^{16}) taking a new measurement at the sample-rate (44100 times per second as defined by our default header). In essence we have *quantized* this continuous analog signal into a series of little snapshots (or steps)—we are taking thousands of little samples from the signal. You can clearly see the quantization of the sinewave in figure 1.5, where each address corresponds with the amplitude of the signal at that point in time.

To hear a sound from our computer, we convert the digital signal (this sequence of samples) back into an analog signal (a continuously varying voltage) using a digital-to-analog converter (DAC) followed by a *smoothing* lowpass filter. Clear? Well, enough of the basics for now. More later, but let's get back to Csound.

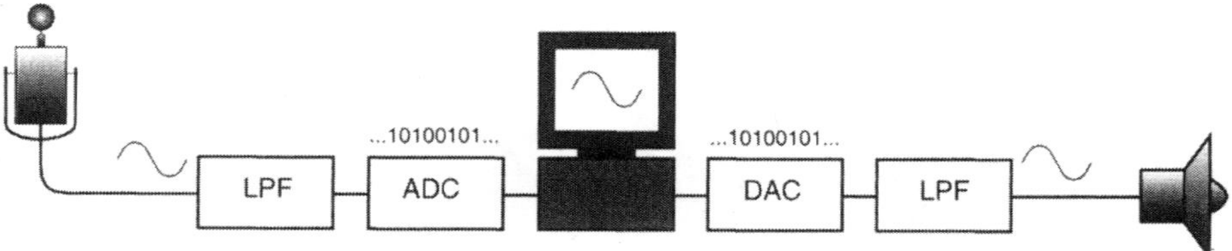

Figure 1.9 Digital recording ("sampling") and playback.

Sound Design Etude 2: Parameter Fields in the Orchestra and Score

In our second orchestra, we modify *instr 101–106* so that they can be updated and altered from the score file. Rather than setting each of the opcode's arguments to a fixed value in the orchestra, as we did in *etude1.orc,* we set them to "*p*" values that correspond to the p-fields (or column numbers) in the score. Thus each argument can be sent a completely different setting from each note-statement.

In *instr 107,* for example, p-fields are applied to each of the **oscil** arguments: amplitude (*p4*), frequency (*p5*) and wavetable (*p6*) as shown in figure 1.10. Thus, from the score file in figure 1.12, we are able to re-use the same instrument to play a sequence of three descending octaves followed by an A major arpeggio.

In our next p-field example, shown in figures 1.13, 1.14, and 1.15, our rather limited *instr 102* has been transformed into a more musically versatile *instr 108*—an instrument capable of a rich and varied set of tone colors.

In the score excerpt shown in figure 1.15, each of the **foscil** arguments has been assigned to a unique p-field and can thus be altered on a note-by-note basis. In this case *p4* = amplitude, *p5* = frequency, *p6* = carrier ratio, *p7* = modulator ratio, *p8* = modulation index and *p9* = wavetable. Thus, starting 7 seconds into *etude2.sco, instr 108* plays six consecutive notes. All six notes use *f 1* (a sine wave in *p9*). The first two notes are an octave apart (*p5* = 440 and 220) but have different *c:m ratios* (*p7* = 2 and .5) and different modulation indexes (*p8* = 3 and 8), resulting in two different timbres. Clearly, p-fields in the orchestra allow us to get a wide variety of pitches and timbres from even the simplest of instruments.

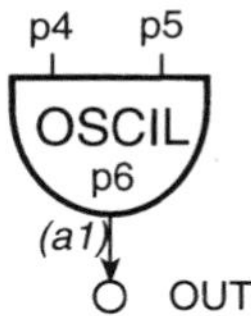

Figure 1.10 Block diagram of *instr 107,* a simple oscillator instrument with p-field substitutions.

```
        instr       107             ; P-FIELD OSCIL
a1      oscil       p4, p5, p6
        out         a1
        endin
```

Figure 1.11 Orchestra code for *instr 107,* a simple oscillator instrument with p-field arguments.

```
; P1    P2      P3      P4      P5      P6
; INS   STRT    DUR     AMP     FREQ    WAVESHAPE
i 107   0       1       10000   440     1
i 107   1.5     1       20000   220     2
i 107   3       3       10000   110     2
i 107   3.5     2.5     10000   138.6   2
i 107   4       2       5000    329.6   2
i 107   4.5     1.5     6000    440     2
```

Figure 1.12 Note-list for *instr 107,* which uses p-fields to "perform" six notes (some overlapping) with different frequencies, amplitudes, and waveshapes.

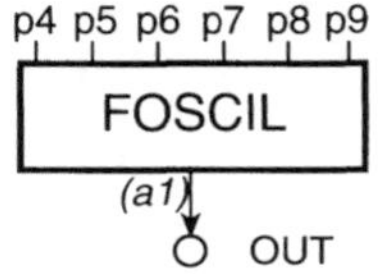

Figure 1.13 Block diagram of *instr 108,* a simple FM instrument with p-fields for each parameter.

```
        instr     108                   ; P-FIELD FM
a1      foscil    p4, p5, p6, p7, p8, p9
        out       a1
        endin
```

Figure 1.14 Orchestra code for *instr 108,* a simple FM instrument with p-field substitutions.

```
; P1    P2    P3    P4     P5     P6  P7     P8     P9
; INS   STRT  DUR   AMP    FREQ   C   M      INDEX  WAVESHAPE
i 108   7     1     10000  440    1   2      3      1
i 108   8.5   1     20000  220    1   .5     8      1
i 108   10    3     10000  110    1   1      13     1
i 108   10.5  2.5   10000  130.8  1   2.001  8      1
i 108   11    2     5000   329.6  1   3.003  5      1
i 108   11.5  1.5   6000   440    1   5.005  3      1
```

Figure 1.15 Note-list for *instr 108* in which nine p-fields are used to "play" an FM synthesizer with different start-times, durations, amplitudes, frequencies, frequency-ratios, and modulation indices.

Exercises for Etude 2

- Render the Csound orchestra and score: *etude2.orc & etude2.sco.*
- Play and listen to the different sound qualities of each note and instrument.
- Modify the score file and change the start-times, durations, amplitudes and frequencies of each note.
- Look up and read about the opcodes used in *instr 107–112* in the *Csound Reference Manual* and focus your study and experimentation on one synthesis technique at a time.
- Explore the effect of different C:M ratios in *instr 108.*
- Without changing the C:M ratio, explore the effect of a low and a high modulation index.
- Compare the difference in timbre when you modulate with a sine (*f 1*) and a sawtooth (*f 2*).
- Using *instr 109,* compose a 4-part chord progression in which the bass and tenor have more harmonics than the alto and soprano.
- Using *instr 109* and *112* simultaneously, play the same score you composed for *instr 9* by doubling the parts.

- Using *instr 110,* experiment with the various **pluck** methods. (See the *Csound Reference Manual* for additional arguments).
- Using *instr 110,* experiment with different initialization table functions—*f 1* and *f 2*. Also try initializing with noise and compare the timbre.
- Explore the various parameters of the **grain** opcode.
- Create a set of short etudes for each of the instruments alone.
- Create a set of short etudes for several of the instruments in combination. Remember to adjust your amplitude levels so that you do not have any *samples-out-of-range.*
- Lower the sample-rate and the control rate in the header. Recompile some of your modified instruments. Do you notice any difference in sound quality? Do you notice a change in brightness? Do you notice any noise artifacts? Do you notice any aliasing? (We will discuss the theory behind these phenomena a little later.)

Amplitudes and Clipping

As stated previously, if you have a 16-bit converter in your computer system (which is still quite common in 1999), then you can express 2^{16} possible raw amplitude values (i.e., 65536 in the range –32768 to +32767). This translates to an amplitude range of over 90 dB (typically you get about 6 dB of range per bit of resolution). If you have been doing the exercises you have probably noticed that note amplitudes in Csound are additive. This means that if an instrument has an amplitude set to 20000 and you simultaneously play two notes on that instrument, you are asking your converter to produce a signal with an amplitude of ±40000. The problem is that your 16-bit converter can only represent values up to about 32000 and therefore your Csound job will report that there are *samples-out-of-range* and the resulting soundfile will be clipped as show in figure 1.16.

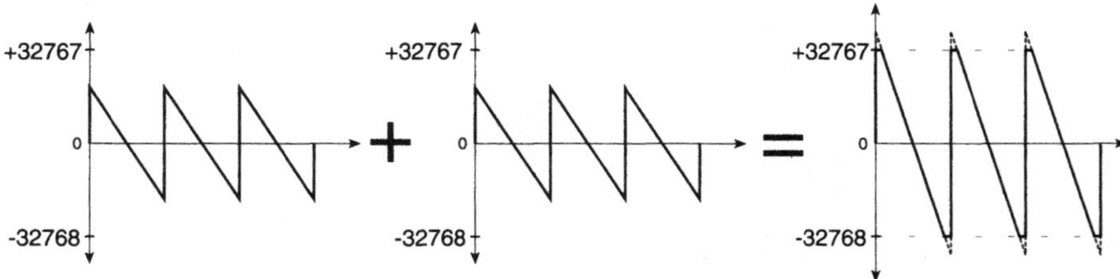

Figure 1.16 Clipping as a result of adding two high-amplitude waveforms together.

Dealing with amplitudes is one of the most problematic aspects of working with Csound. There is no easy answer. The problem lies in the fact that Csound amplitudes are a simple mathematical representation of *the signal.* These measurements take no account of the acoustical or perceptual nature of *the sound.*

Simply put, two times the linear displacement of amplitude will not necessarily be perceived as two times as loud. A good book on acoustics will help you appreciate the complexity of this problem. In the Csound world, remember that whenever two or more notes are sounding their amplitudes are added. If the numbers add up to anything greater than 32000 your signal will be clipped. Csound has some opcodes and tools that will help you deal with this samples-out-of-range problem but none of the current opcodes or value converters truly solve it. Most of the time you will just have to set the levels lower and render the file again (and again and again) until you get the amplitudes into a range that your system can handle, with the mix your ears desire.

Data Rates

As you have seen in the first two etude orchestras, we can set and update parameters (arguments) with floating-point constants either directly in the orchestra or remotely through parameter-fields. But the real power of Csound is derived from the fact that one can update parameters with *variables* at any of three update or data-rates: **i**-rate, **k**-rate, or **a**-rate, where:

- **i**-rate variables are changed and updated at the note-rate.
- **k**-rate variables are changed and updated at the control-rate (*kr*).
- **a**-rate variables are changed and updated at the audio-rate (*sr*).

Both **i**-rate and **k**-rate variables are scalars. Essentially, they take on one value at a given time. The **i**-rate variables are primarily used for setting parameter values and note durations. They are evaluated at *initialization-time* and remain constant throughout the duration of the note-event.

The **k**-rate variables are primarily used for storing and updating envelopes and sub-audio control signals. These variables are recomputed at the control-rate (4410 times per second) as defined by *kr* in our orchestra header. The **a**-rate variables are arrays or vectors of information. These variables are used to store and update data such as the output signals of oscillators and filters that change at the audio sampling-rate (44100 times per second) as defined by *sr* in our orchestra header.

One can determine and identify the rate at which a variable will be updated by the first letter of the variable name. For example, the only difference between the two

```
; OUTPUT    OPCODE  AMP,     FRQ,     FUNC   ; COMMENT
ksig        oscil   10000,   1000,    1      ; 1000 HZ SINE - F 1
asig        oscil   10000,   1000,    1      ; 1000 HZ SINE - F 1
```

Figure 1.17 Two **oscil** opcodes with *asig* versus *ksig* outputs.

oscillators shown in figure 1.17 is that one is computed at the audio-rate and the other at the control-rate. Both use the same opcode, **oscil** and both have the same arguments. What is different, then, is the sample resolution (precision) of the output signal.

Given our default header settings of *sr* = 44100 and *kr* = 4410, the output *ksig* would be rendered at a sample-rate of 4K and the output *asig* will be rendered at a sample-rate of 44.1K. In this case, the resulting audio would sound quite similar because both would have enough sample resolution to accurately compute the 1000 Hz sinewave. If, however, the arguments were different and the waveforms had additional harmonics, such as the sawtooth wave defined by *f* 2 in figure 1.18, the **k**-rate setting of 4410 samples-per-second would not accurately represent the waveform and *aliasing* would result. (We will cover this in more detail later.)

You should note that it is left up to you, the sound designer, to decide the most appropriate, efficient and effective rate at which to render your opcodes. For example, you could render all of your low frequency oscillators (LFOs) and envelopes at the audio-rate, but it would take longer to compute the signals and the additional resolution would, in most cases, be imperceptible.

Variable Names

In our instrument designs so far we have been using *a1, asig, k1* and *ksig*—in many cases interchangeably. What's with these different names for the same thing? Csound is difficult enough. Why not be consistent?

Well, when it comes to naming variables, Csound only requires that the variable names you use begin with the letter **i**, **k**, or **a**. This is so that the program can determine at which rate to render that specific line of code. Anything goes after that.

For instance, you could name the output of the **loscil** opcode below **a**1, **a**sig, **a**sample, or **a**coolsound. Each variable name would be recognized by Csound and would run without error. In fact, given that the lines of code each have the same parameter settings they would all sound exactly the same when rendered—no matter what name you gave them. Therefore, it is up to you, the sound designer, to decide on a variable naming scheme that is clear, consistent and informative.

```
a1         loscil 10000, 440, 4  ; SAMPLE PLAYBACK OF F 4 AT A440
           out    a1

asig       loscil 10000, 440, 4  ; SAMPLE PLAYBACK OF F 4 AT A440
           out    asig

asample    loscil 10000, 440, 4  ; SAMPLE PLAYBACK OF F 4 AT A440
           out    asample

acoolsound loscil 10000, 440, 4  ; SAMPLE PLAYBACK OF F 4 AT A440
           out    acoolsound
```

Theory: Aliasing and the Sampling Theorem

Let's review a bit more theory before getting into our more advanced instrument designs. As we stated earlier, the undersampled sawtooth (*ksig*) in figure 1.18 is an example of aliasing and a proof of the *Sampling Theorem.* Simply put, the Sampling Theorem states that, in the digital domain, to accurately reconstruct (plot, draw, or reproduce) a waveshape at a given frequency you need twice as many samples as the highest frequency you are trying to render. This hard upper limit at 1/2 the sampling rate is known as the *Nyquist frequency.* With an audio-rate of 44100 Hz you can accurately render tones with frequencies (and partials) up to 22050 Hz—arguably far above the human range of hearing. And with a control-rate of 4410 Hz you can accurately render tones up to 2205 Hz. This would be an extremely fast LFO and seems a bit high for slowly changing control signals, but you should realize that certain segments of amplitude envelopes change extremely rapidly and high-resolution controllers reduce the *zipper-noise* sometimes resulting from these rapid transitions.

Figure 1.19 illustrates graphically the phenomena known as *aliasing.* Because a frequency is undersampled an alias or alternate frequency results. In this specific case our original sinewave is at 5 Hz. We are sampling this wave at 4 Hz (remember that the minimum for accurate reproduction would be 10 Hz–2 times the highest frequency component). What results is a 1 Hz tone. As you can see from the figure, the values that were returned from the sampling process trace the outline of a 1 Hz sinewave, not a 5 Hz one. The actual aliased frequency is the difference between the sampling frequency and the frequency of the sample (or its partials).

To totally understand and experience the results of this phenomena it would be informative to go back to the earlier instruments in this chapter and experiment with different rate variables (I would recommend that you duplicate and renumber all the instruments and then change all the *asig* and *a1* variables to *ksig* and *k1* variables.

```
; OUTPUT    OPCODE  AMP,     FRQ,    FUNC   ; COMMENT
ksig        oscil   10000,   1000,   2      ; 1000 HZ SAW - F 2
asig        oscil   10000,   1000,   2      ; 1000 HZ SAW - F 2
```

Figure 1.18 An "under-sampled" sawtooth wave (given $kr = 4410$ and a frequency setting of 1000), resulting in an "aliased" *ksig* output.

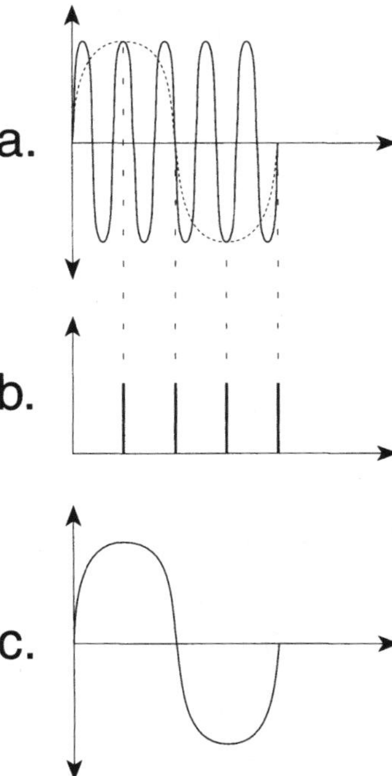

Figure 1.19 Aliasing. A 5Hz sine (a) is "under-sampled" at 4 times a second (b) resulting in the incorrect reproduction of a 1Hz sine (c).

You'll be surprised and even pleased with some of the lo-fi results.) For now let's move on.

Sound Design Etude 3: Four Enveloping Techniques

It is often stated that a computer is capable of producing any sound imaginable. Mathematically, this is true. But why is it that computerized and synthesized sounds are often so sterile, monotonous, and dull? To my ear, what makes a sound interesting

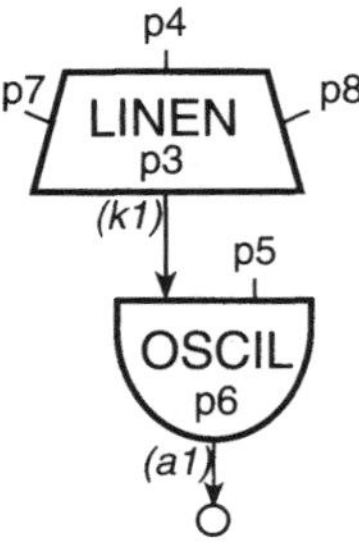

Figure 1.20 Block diagram of *instr 113,* an example of one opcode's output controlling the input argument of another. In this case we are realizing dynamic amplitude control by modifying the amplitude argument of the **oscil** opcode with the output of another—the **linen**.

```
     instr    113              ; SIMPLE OSCIL WITH ENVELOPE
k1   linen    p4, p7, p3, p8     ; P3=DUR, P4=AMP, P7=ATTACK, P8=RELEASE
a1   oscil    k1, p5, p6         ; P5=FREQ, P6=WAVESHAPE
out  a1
     endin
```

Figure 1.21 Orchestra code for *instr 113,* a simple oscillator instrument with amplitude envelope control.

and engaging is the subtle, dynamic and interdependent behavior of its three main parameters—pitch, timbre, and loudness. What makes Csound a truly powerful software synthesis language is the fact that one can literally patch the output of any opcode into virtually any input argument of another opcode—thereby achieving an unsurpassed degree of dynamic parameter control. By subtly (or dramatically) modifying each of your opcode's input arguments, your synthetic, computerized sounds will spring to life.

Up to this point we have essentially *gated* our Csound instruments—simply turning them on at full volume. I'm not sure that any acoustic instrument works like that. Clearly, applying some form of overall envelope control to these instruments would go a long way toward making them more musical. And by adding other dynamic parameter controls we'll render sounds that are ever more enticing.

In *instr 113,* shown in figure 1.20 and 1.21, Csound's **linen** opcode is used to dynamically control the amplitude argument of the oscillator, thus functioning as a typical attack-release (AR) envelope generator.

In *instr 115,* shown in figures 1.22 and 1.23, a **linen** is again used to apply a dynamic amplitude envelope. This time the enveloping is done by multiplying the output of the **linen** opcode (*k1*) with the output of the **buzz** opcode (*a1*). In fact, the multiplication is done in the input argument of the **out** opcode (*k1 * a1*). Here we

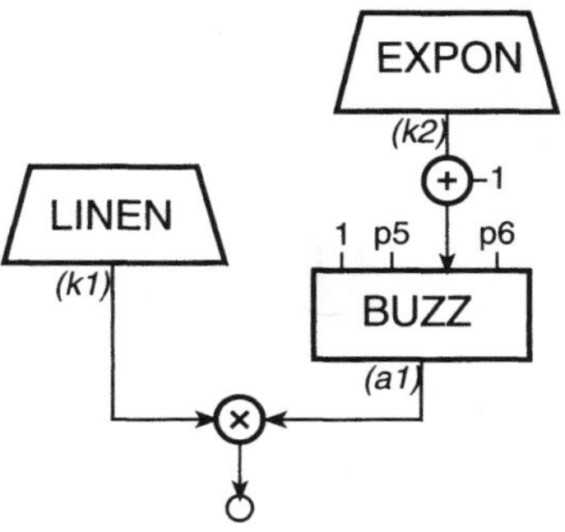

Figure 1.22 Block diagram of *instr 115* showing amplitude control by multiplying two outputs and dynamic control of an argument.

```
      instr     115                 ; SWEEPING BUZZ WITH ENVELOPE
k1    linen     p4, p7, p3, p8
k2    expon     p9, p3, p10
a1    buzz      1, p5, k2+1, p6
      out       k1*a1
      endin
```

Figure 1.23 Orchestra code for *instr 115,* an instrument with dynamic amplitude and harmonic control.

not only see a different way of applying an envelope to a signal (multiplying it by a controller), but we also see that it is possible to perform mathematical operations on variables within an opcode's argument.

In figure 1.22, it can also be seen that an **expon** opcode is used in this instrument to move exponentially from the value in *p9* to the value in *p10* over the duration of the note (*p3*), thereby sweeping the number of harmonic-cosines that **buzz** produces. The effect is much like slowly closing a resonant lowpass filter and is another simple means of realizing dynamic timbre control.

If you've been looking through the *Csound Reference Manual* you probably noticed that many opcodes, such as **oscil**, have both **k**-rate and **a**-rate versions. In *instr 117,* shown in figure 1.24, we use an audio-rate **linen** as an envelope generator. To do this, we patch the output of the **grain** opcode into the amplitude input of the **linen**, as can be seen in boldface in figure 1.25. Clearly this approach uses the linen to put an envelope on the signal coming from the granular synthesizer. In fact, we stuff the signal into an envelope before sending it out.

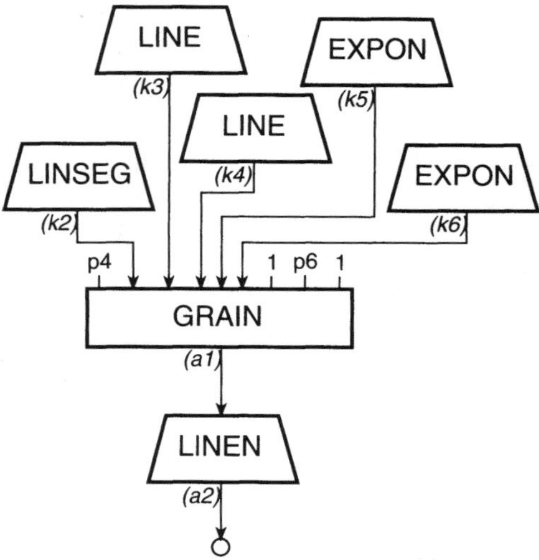

Figure 1.24 Block diagram of *instr 117* showing amplitude control by passing the signal (*a1*) through an **a**-rate envelope (*a2*).

```
        instr       117                  ; GRAINS THROUGH AN ENVELOPE
k2      linseg      p5, p3/2, p9, p3/2, p5
k3      line        p10, p3, p11
k4      line        p12, p3, p13
k5      expon       p14, p3, p15
k6      expon       p16, p3, p17
a1      grain       p4, k2, k3, k4, k5, k6, 1, p6, 1
a2      linen       a1, p7, p3, p8
        out         a2
        endin
```

Figure 1.25 Orchestra code for *instr 117,* a granular synthesis instrument with dynamic control of many parameters. Note that the output of **grain** (*a1*) is "patched" into the amplitude argument of an a-rate **linen** to shape the sound with an overall amplitude envelope.

Envelopes

I have to admit that as a young student of electronic music I was always confused by the use of the term *envelope* in audio and synthesis. I thought of envelopes as thin paper packages in which you could enclose a letter to a friend or a check to the phone company and could never quite make the connection. But the algorithm used in *instr 117* makes the metaphor clear. Here we see that the **linen** opcode completely packages or folds the signal into this odd-shaped AR container and then sends it to the output. Figure 1.26 is another way to visualize the process. First, we see the raw bipolar audio signal. Then, we see the unipolar attack-decay-sustain-release (ADSR)

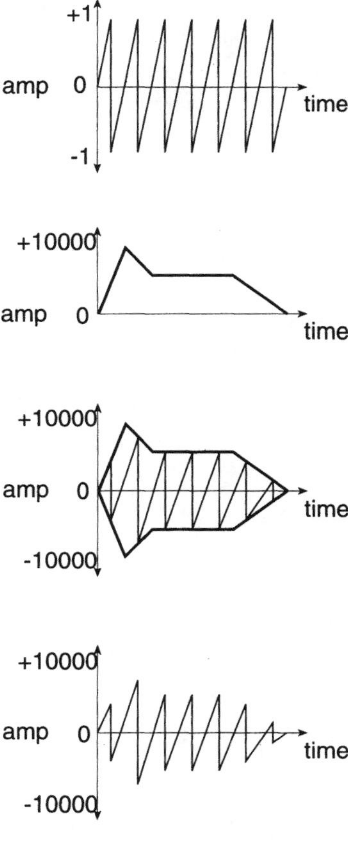

Figure 1.26 "Enveloping" a signal.

amplitude envelope. Next, we see the envelope applied to the audio signal. In the final stage we see the bipolar audio signal whose amplitude has been proportionally modified by the contour of the ADSR.

Another way of looking at figure 1.26 would be that our bipolar signal is scaled (multiplied) by a unipolar ADSR (Attack-Decay-Sustain-Release) envelope that symmetrically contours the unipolar signal. The result is that the unipolar signal is enveloped in the ADSR package. Let's apply this new level of understanding in another instrument design.

In *instr 118,* shown in figure 1.27 and 1.28, we illustrate yet another way of applying an envelope to a signal in Csound. In this case, we are using an oscillator whose frequency argument is set to *1/p3.* Let's plug in some numbers and figure out how this simple expression will help us compute the correct sub-audio frequency that will transform our periodic oscillator into an aperiodic envelope generator.

For example, if the duration of the note was 10 seconds and the frequency of our oscillator was set to 1/10 Hz it would take 10/10 Hz to completely read 1 cycle of the function table found in *p7.* Thus, setting the frequency of an oscillator to 1 divided by the note-duration, or *1/p3,* guarantees that this periodic signal generator will compute

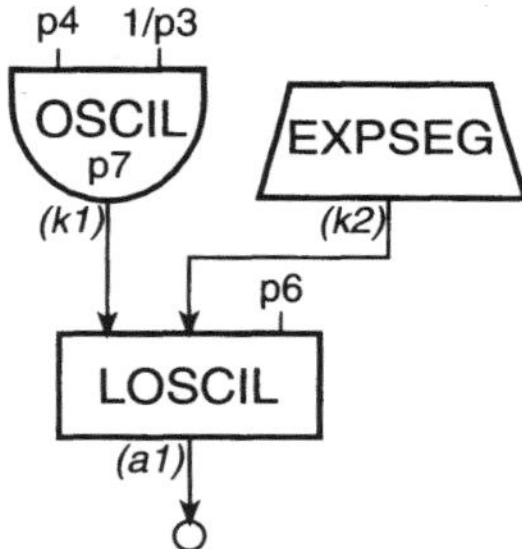

Figure 1.27 Block diagram of *instr 118,* an instrument with an oscillator for an envelope generator.

```
       instr      118                ; LOSCIL WITH OSCIL ENVELOPE
k1     oscil      p4, 1/p3, p7
k2     expseg     p5, p3/3, p8, p3/3, p9, p3/3, p5
a1     loscil     k1, k2, p6
       out        a1
       endin
```

Figure 1.28 Orchestra code for *instr 118,* a sample-playback instrument with an oscillator-based envelope and dynamic pitch modulation.

```
f 6 0 1024 7 0 10 1 1000 1 14 0                 ; LINEAR AR ENVELOPE
f 7 0 1024 7 0 128 1 128 .6 512 .6 256 0        ; LINEAR ADSR ENVELOPE
f 8 0 1024 5 .001 256 1 192 .5 256 .5 64 .001   ; EXPONENTIAL ADSR
```

Figure 1.29 Linear and exponential envelope functions using **GEN5** and **GEN7.**

```
    instr    119               ; RETRIGGERING FOSCIL WITH OSCIL ENVELOPE
k1  oscil    p4, 1/p3 * p8, p7   ; P8=RETRIGGER RATE PER NOTE DURATION
k2  line     p11, p3, p12
a1  foscil   k1, p5, p9, p10, k2, p6
    out      a1
    endin
```

Figure 1.30 Orchestra code for *instr 119,* an FM instrument with an oscillator envelope in which *p8* determines the "retriggering" frequency.

only 1 period, or read only 1 complete cycle of its f-table during the course of each note event.

In *instr 118* the envelope functions called by *p7* (*f 6, f 7* and *f 8*) use **GEN7** and **GEN5** to draw a variety of unipolar linear and exponential contours. It is important to note that it is *illegal* to use a value of 0 in any exponential function such as those computed by the **GEN5** subroutine or by the **expseg** opcode. You will notice therefore, that *f 8,* which uses **GEN5**, begins and ends with a value of .001 rather than 0.

The enveloping technique employed in *instr 118* (using an oscillator as an envelope generator) has several advantages. First, you can create an entire library of preset envelope shapes and change them on a note-by-note basis. Second, since the envelope generator is in fact an oscillator, you can have the envelope loop or retrigger during the course of the note event to create interesting LFO-based amplitude-gating effects. In *instr 119,* shown in figure 1.30, *p8* determines the number of repetitions that will occur during the course of the note. If *p8* is set to 10 where *p3* is 5 seconds, the instrument will retrigger the envelope 2 times per second. Whereas if the duration of the note was 1 second (*p3* = 1), then the envelope would be re-triggered 10 times per second.

Theory: Unipolar and Bipolar Functions

Typically we think of an oscillator as something that makes a sound by playing different waveshapes or samples. We have seen, however, that Csound's table-lookup oscillator is capable of reading any unipolar or bipolar function at any rate. Clearly this signal generator can be used equally as a control source or an audio source.

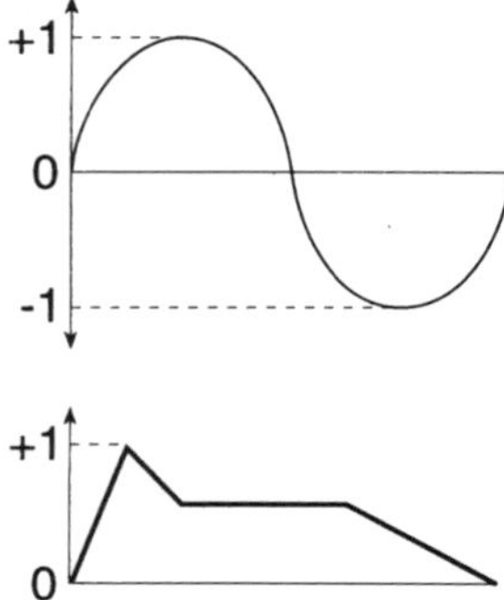

Figure 1.31 A bipolar (−1 to +1) and a unipolar (0 to +1) function.

```
f 1 0  512  10   1                       ; NORMALIZED BIPOLAR SINE
f 2 0  512  7    0 6 1 500 1 6 0         ; NORMALIZED UNIPOLAR ENVELOPE
f 3 0  512  -10  .3 .013 .147 .026       ; NON-NORMALIZED BIPOLAR SUM-OF-SINES
f 4 0  512  -7   440 256 220 256 440 ; NON-NORMALIZED UNIPOLAR ENVELOPE
```

Figure 1.32 Two normalized functions (*f 1* and *f 2*) and two non-normalized functions (*f 3* and *f 4*).

Unlike commercial synthesizers, in Csound the function of an opcode is defined by the use and by the user. So far, we have been using several of Csound's **GEN** routines to compute unipolar and bipolar functions and it is important that we make sure we understand the difference.

Most audio waveforms, such as those created with **GEN10** are bipolar—having a symmetrical excursion above and below zero. On the other hand, most envelope functions, such as those we have created using **GEN5** and **GEN7**, are unipolar—having an excursion in one direction only, typically positive. In Csound, by default, all bipolar functions are normalized in a range of −1 to +1 and all unipolar functions are normalized in a range from 0 to +1 as shown in figure 1.31. If you wish to bypass Csound's default normalization process you must use a minus sign (−) before the **GEN** number as shown in *f 3* and *f 4* in figure 1.32.

Exercises for Etude 3

- Render the third Csound orchestra and score: *etude3.orc* & *etude3.sco*.
- Play and listen to the different sound qualities and envelope shapes of each note and each instrument.

- Modify the orchestra file and change the variable names to more meaningful ones. For instance, rename all **a**1 variables **a**sig1 and **k**1 variables **k**env1.
- In the *Csound Reference Manual,* look up the new opcodes featured in *instr 113–119:*

```
k/ar linen    k/xamp, irise, idur,idec
k/ar line     ia, idur1, ib
k/ar expon    ia, idur1, ib
k/ar linseg   ia, idur1, ib[, idur2, ic[...]]
k/ar expseg   ia, idur1, ib[, idur2, ic[...]]
```

- Modify the attack time (*p7*) and release times (*p8*) of the **linen** opcodes in *instr 113–117.*
- Add a pitch envelope to *instr 113, 114,* and *115* by adding a **linseg** to each instrument and adding it's output to *p5.*
- Experiment with the dynamic controls of the **grain** parameters found in *instr 117.*
- Substitute **oscil**-based envelopes for the **linen**-based envelopes in *instr 113–117.*
- Use **GEN5** and **GEN7** to design several additional envelope functions. Try to imitate the attack characteristics of a piano—*f 9,* a mandolin—*f 10,* a tuba—*f 11,* a violin—*f 12* and a male voice singing "la"—*f 13.* Apply these envelopes to your newly designed versions of *instr 113–117.*
- Following the examples of the figures you have studied so far, draw block diagrams for *instr 112, 113, 114,* and *119.*

Sound Design Etude 4: Mixing, Chorusing, Tremolo, and Vibrato

Next, we improve the quality of our instruments by first mixing and detuning our oscillators to create a *fat* "chorused" effect. Then, we crossfade opcodes to create a hybrid synthesis algorithm unlike anything offered commercially. (The synthesis approach is sometimes referred to as *modal synthesis.*) Finally, we animate our instruments by introducing sub-audio rate and audio rate amplitude and frequency modulation (AM and FM). We also employ several of Csound's display opcodes to visualize these more complex *temporal* and *spectral envelopes.* And we'll learn a little more about the language as we go.

Self-Commenting Instrument Design

In *instr 120,* shown in figures 1.33 and 1.34, we mix together three detuned oscillators that all use the same **envlpx** opcode for an amplitude envelope. Using the **display** opcode this envelope is plotted on the screen with a resolution set to trace the envelope shape over the entire duration of the note (*p3*) and thus display the complete contour.

Although *instr 120* is still rather simple in design, it does serve as a model of the way that more complex instruments are typically laid out and organized in Csound. In figure 1.34 you can see that variables are initialized at the top of the instrument and given names that help us to identify their function (resulting in a self-commenting coding style). Clearly you can read that the attack time is assigned to *iatk* from the score value given in *p7* (*iatk* = *p7*) and that the release time is assigned to *irel* from the score value given in *p9* (*irel* = *p9*). Most importantly, by looking at where they are patched in the **envlpx** opcode you can see and remember which arguments correspond with which particular parameters, thereby making the opcode easier to read.

You should note that in Csound the equals sign (=) is the *assignment operator.* It is in fact an opcode. Assigning plain-English mnemonics and abbreviated names to variables at **i**-time at the top of your instrument, *the initialization block,* makes an instrument much easier to read and is highly recommended.

Spectral Fusion

Next we will look at *instr 122,* as shown in figures 1.35 and 1.36. This instrument uses independent **expon** opcodes to crossfade between a **foscil** and a **buzz** opcode that are both fused (morphed/mixed/transfigured) with a **pluck** attack creating a beautiful hybrid timbre. This instrument employs Csound's **dispfft** opcode to compute and display a 512 point Fast Fourier Transform (FFT) of the composite signal updated every 250 milliseconds. Although the **display** and **dispfft** opcodes are a wonderful way to look into the behavior of your instrument, it is important to note that when you are using your instruments to make music you should always remember to comment out these **display** and **print** opcodes. They significantly impact the performance of your system. These opcodes are informative and educational but really function as debugging tools and you should think of them as such.

Rather than simply mixing or crossfading opcodes as we have done in *instr 120* and *instr 122,* another popular approach is to *modulate* one audio opcode with the frequency and amplitude of another. In *instr 124,* as shown in figures 1.37 and 1.38

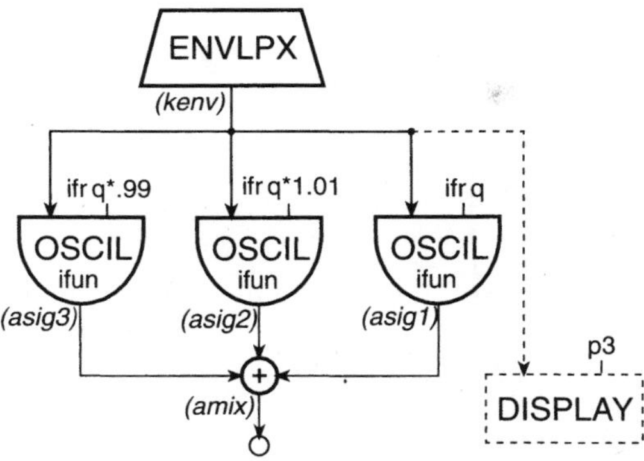

Figure 1.33 Block diagram of *instr 120* illustrating three chorusing oscillators with a common envelope and display.

```
         instr    120          ; SIMPLE CHORUSING
idur     =        p3                     ; INITIALIZATION BLOCK
iamp     =        ampdb(p4)
ifrq     =        cpspch(p5)
ifun     =        p6
iatk     =        p7
irel     =        p8
iatkfun  =        p9
kenv     envlpx   iamp, iatk, idur, irel, iatkfun, .7, .01
asig3    oscil    kenv, ifrq*.99, ifun  ; SYNTHESIS BLOCK
asig2    oscil    kenv, ifrq*1.01, ifun
asig1    oscil    kenv, ifrq, ifun
amix     =        asig1+asig2+asig3     ; MIX
         out      amix
         display  kenv, idur
         endin
```

Figure 1.34 Orchestra code for *instr 120,* a chorusing instrument in which p-fields are given **i**-time variable names. Also an **envlpx**, which is displayed, is used as a common envelope.

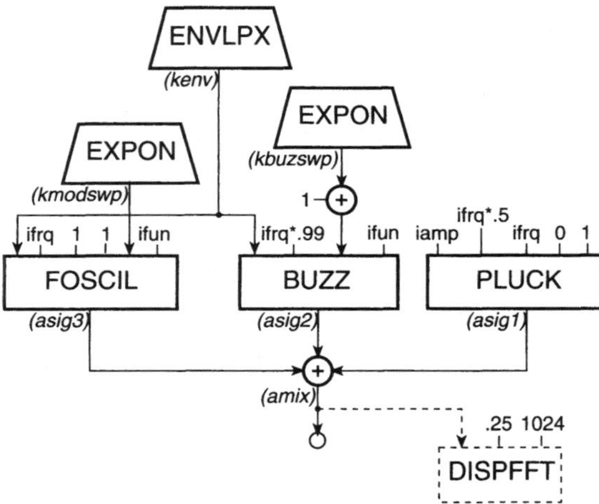

Figure 1.35 Block diagram of *instr 122* illustrating the FFT display of 3 mixed (fused) and crossfaded (morphed) opcodes.

```
            instr       122             ; SIMPLE SPECTRAL FUSION
idur        =           p3
iamp        =           ampdb(p4)
ifrq        =           cpspch(p5)
ifun        =           p6
iatk        =           p7
irel        =           p8
iatkfun     =           p9
index1      =           p10
index2      =           p11
kenv        envlpx      iamp, iatk, idur, irel, iatkfun, .7, .01
kmodswp     expon       index1, idur, index2
kbuzswp     expon       20, idur, 1
asig3       foscil      kenv, ifrq, 1, 1, kmodswp, ifun
asig2       buzz        kenv, ifrq*.99, kbuzswp+1, ifun
asig1       pluck       iamp, ifrq*.5, ifrq, 0, 1
amix        =           asig1+asig2+asig3
            out         amix
            dispfft     amix, .25, 1024
            endin
```

Figure 1.36 Orchestra code of *instr 122,* an instrument that demonstrates the fusion of three synthesis techniques—**pluck**, **foscil**, and **buzz**.

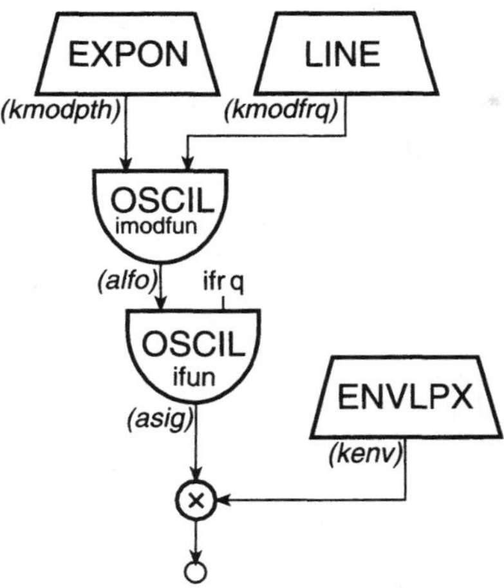

Figure 1.37 Block diagram of *instr 124,* a dynamic amplitude modulation instrument.

```
          instr     124      ; SWEEPING AMPLITUDE MODULATION
idur      =         p3
iamp      =         ampdb(p4)
ifrq      =         cpspch(p5)
ifun      =         p6
iatk      =         p7
irel      =         p8
iatkfun   =         p9
imodp1    =         p10
imodp2    =         p11
imodfr1   =         p12
imodfr2   =         p13
imodfun   =         p14
kenv      envlpx    iamp, iatk, idur, irel, iatkfun, .7, .01
kmodpth   expon     imodp1, idur, imodp2
kmodfrq   line      cpspch(imodfr1), idur, cpspch(imodfr2)
alfo      oscil     kmodpth, kmodfrq, imodfun
asig      oscil     alfo, ifrq, ifun
          out       asig*kenv
          endin
```

Figure 1.38 Orchestra code for *instr 124,* an amplitude modulation instrument with independent amplitude envelope and variable LFO.

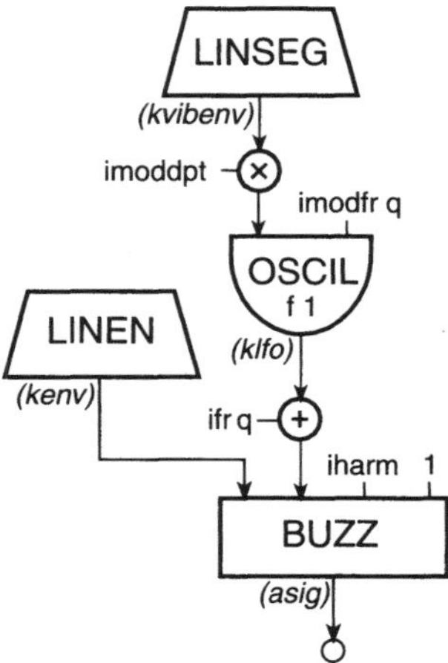

Figure 1.39 Block diagram of *instr 126,* an additive instrument with delayed vibrato.

for example, an **a**-rate **oscil** (*asig*) is amplitude modulated with the output of a dynamically swept **a**-rate **oscil** (*alfo*) whose frequency is dynamically altered with a **line** opcode and whose amplitude is controlled by an **expon**. This simple oscillator combination can produce a wide range of dynamically evolving harmonic and inharmonic timbres.

Next, in *instr 126,* shown in figures 1.39 and 1.40, we present a simple vibrato instrument that uses a **linseg** opcode to delay the onset of the modulation resulting in a more natural vibrato effect. Even the relatively simple designs of *instr 124* and *instr 126* can lend themselves to an extraordinarily diverse and rich palate of colors. Take time to explore and modify them.

Value Converters

In the initialization block of *instr 120,* shown in figure 1.34 (and in all the instruments in this etude for that matter), you might have noticed that two of Csound's *value converters* **ampdb** and **cpspch** were used (*iamp = ampdb(p4)* and *ifrq = cpspch(p5)*). These allow us to express frequency and amplitude data in a more familiar and intuitive format than having to use the straight Hz and linear amplitudes we have used thus far.

The **cpspch** value converter will read a number in *octave-point-pitch-class* notation and convert it to Hz (e.g., 8.09 = A4 = 440 Hz). Octave-point-pitch-class is a

```
            instr     126            ; SIMPLE DELAYED VIBRATO
idur        =         p3
iamp        =         ampdb(p4)
ifrq        =         cpspch(p5)
iatk        =         p6
irel        =         p7
ivibdel     =         p8
imoddpt     =         p9
imodfrq     =         p10
iharm       =         p11
kenv        linen     iamp, iatk, idur, irel
kvibenv     linseg    0, ivibdel, 1, idur-ivibdel, .3
klfo        oscil     kvibenv*imoddpt, imodfrq, 1
asig        buzz      kenv, ifrq+klfo, iharm, 1
            out       asig
            endin
```

Figure 1.40 Orchestra code for *instr 126,* a **buzz** instrument with delayed vibrato.

notation shorthand system in which octaves are represented as whole numbers (8.00 = Middle C or C4, 9.00 = C5, 10.00 = C6, etc.) and the 12 equal-tempered pitch classes are numbered as the two decimal digits that follow the octave (8.01 = C#4, 8.02 = D4, 8.03 = D#4, etc.). The scale shown in figure 1.41 should make the system extremely clear to you. And by adding more decimal places, it is also possible to specify microtones as shown in figure 1.42.

As you can see, **cpspch** converts from the **pch** (octave point pitch-class) representation to a **cps** (cycles-per-second) representation. If you are writing tonal or microtonal music with Csound you might find this value converter particularly useful.

Similarly, the **ampdb** value converter will read a decibel value and convert it to a raw amplitude value as shown in figure 1.43.

You should note that although the logarithmic dB or decibel scale is linear in perception, Csound doesn't really use dB. The **ampdb** converter is a direct conversion with no scaling. Regrettably, you will still have to spend a great deal of time adjusting, normalizing, and scaling your amplitude levels, even if you are using Csound's **ampdb** converter, because the conversion is done prior to the rendering.

Exercises for Etude 4

- Render the fourth Csound orchestra and score: *etude4.orc* & *etude4.sco.*
- Play and listen to the dynamic timbre and modulation effects of each note and each instrument.

NOTE #	Hertz (Hz)	CPSPCH	MIDI NOTE NUMBER
C4	261.626	8.00	60
C#4	277.183	8.01	61
D4	293.665	8.02	62
D#4	311.127	8.03	63
E4	329.628	8.04	64
F4	349.228	8.05	65
F#4	369.994	8.06	66
G4	391.955	8.07	67
G#4	415.305	8.08	68
A4	440.000	8.09	69
A#4	466.164	8.10	70
B4	493.883	8.11	71
C5	523.251	9.00	72

Figure 1.41 A chromatic scale beginning at middle C specified by using Csound's **cpspch** value converter.

NOTE #	CPSPCH
C4	8.00
C4+	8.005
C#4	8.01
C#4+	8.015
D4	8.02
D4+	8.025
D#4	8.03
D#4+	8.035
E4	8.04
E4+	8.045
F4	8.05
F4+	8.055
F#4	8.06
F#4+	8.065
G4	8.07
G4+	8.075
G#4	8.08
G#4+	8.085
A4	8.09
A4+	8.095
A#4	8.10
A#4+	8.105
B4	8.11
B4+	8.115
C5	9.00

Figure 1.42 An octave of equal-tempered quartertones specified using the **cpspch** value converter.

```
ampdb(42)    =    125.9
ampdb(48)    =    251.2
ampdb(54)    =    501.2
ampdb(60)    =    1000
ampdb(66)    =    1995.3
ampdb(72)    =    3981.1
ampdb(78)    =    7943.3
ampdb(84)    =    15848.9
ampdb(90)    =    31622.8
ampdb(96)    =    63095.7 ; WARNING: SAMPLES OUT OF RANGE!!!
```

Figure 1.43 Amplitude conversion uses the **ampdb** value converter.

- Modify *instr 120* so that you are chorusing three **foscil** opcodes instead of three **oscil** opcodes.
- As shown in *instr 126,* add a delayed vibrato to your three **foscil** version of *instr 120.*
- Block diagram *instr 121* (which was not discussed in this section) and add delayed vibrato plus some of your own samples to this wavetable synthesizer.
- Modify *instr 122* so that you are creating different hybrid synthesizers. Perhaps you could add a **grain** of **loscil**?
- Block diagram *instr 123* (which was not discussed in this section) and change the rhythms and pitches. Try audio-rate modulation. Finally, make and use your own set of amplitude modulation functions.
- Modify *instr 124* so that you are not sweeping so radically. Add chorusing and delayed vibrato.
- Block diagram *instr 125* (which was not discussed in this section). Change the modulation frequency and depth using the existing functions. Modulate some of your own samples.
- Modify *instr 126* so that these synthetic voices sing microtonal melodies and harmonies.
- Block diagram *instr 127* (which was not discussed in this section). Have fun modifying it with any of the techniques and bits of code you have developed and mastered so far.
- In the *Csound Reference Manual,* look up the new opcodes featured in *instr 120–127:*

```
k/ar envlpx   k/xamp,irise,idur,idec,ifn,iatss,iatdec[,ixmod]
     print    iarg[, iarg, ...]
     display  xsig, iprd[, inprds][, iwtflg]
     dispfft  xsig, iprd, iwsiz[, iwtyp][, idbouti][, iwtflg]
```

- Create a new set of attack functions for **envlpx** and use them in all the instruments.
- Add **print**, **display**, and **dispfft** opcodes to *instr 123–127.* (But do remember to comment them out when you are making production runs with your instruments.)

Theory: Filter Basics

The next sound design etude is an introductory exploration of a number of Csound's filter opcodes. But before we get too far along it might help if we review some filter basics. Four of the most common filter types are: *lowpass, highpass, bandpass* and *bandreject* as illustrated in figure 1.44. In this figure, a signal consisting of 12 harmonic partials of equal strength (a) is first filtered by a one-pole lowpass (b), a one-pole highpass (c), a two-pole bandpass (d), and a two-pole bandreject filter (e). The dotted spikes are in the filter's *stop band* and the solid spikes are in the *pass band.* The cutoff frequency is the –3 dB point in each of the *spectral envelope curves* outlined by the solid line.

In Csound these filters would correspond with the **tone** (b), **atone** (c), **reson** (d) and **areson** (e) opcodes. Notice that the cutoff frequency of the filter is indicated by the dashed line at −3 dB. Why −3 dB? Well, since the slope of a filter is in fact continuous, the cutoff frequency (f_c) of a filter is somewhere on the curve and has been defined as the point in this frequency continuum at which the pass band is attenuated by −3 dB.

Sound Design Etude 5: Noise, Filters, Delay Lines, and Flangers

The next set of instruments employ a number of Csound signal modifiers in various parallel and serial configurations to shape and transform noise and wavetables. In *instr 128,* shown in figures 1.45 and 1.46, we dynamically filter white noise produced by Csound's **rand** opcode. Separate **expon** and **line** opcodes are used to independently modify the cutoff frequency and bandwidth of Csound's two-pole **reson** (bandpass) filter. Also, an **expseg** amplitude envelope is used and displayed.

A Cascade Filter Network

In *instr 129* through *132,* shown in figure 1.47, a white noise source (**rand**) is passed through a series of one-pole lowpass filters (**tone**). The significant contribution made

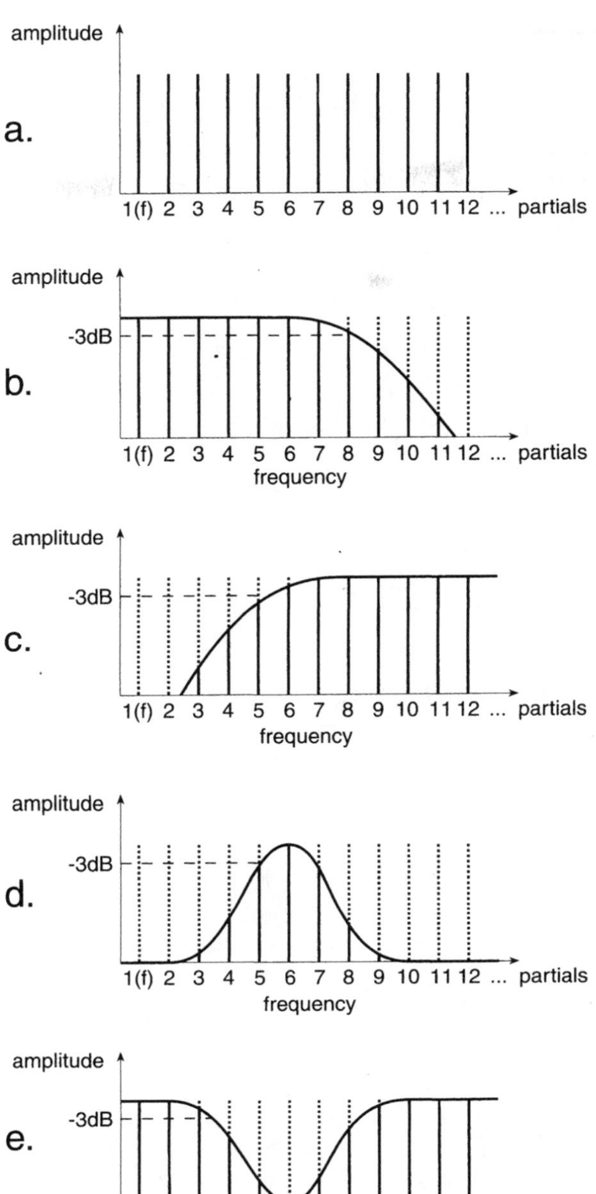

Figure 1.44 A source signal (a) modified by the four basic filters: **tone**—a one-pole lowpass (b), **atone**—a one-pole highpass (c), **reson**—a two-pole bandpass (d), and **areson**—a two-pole bandreject (e).

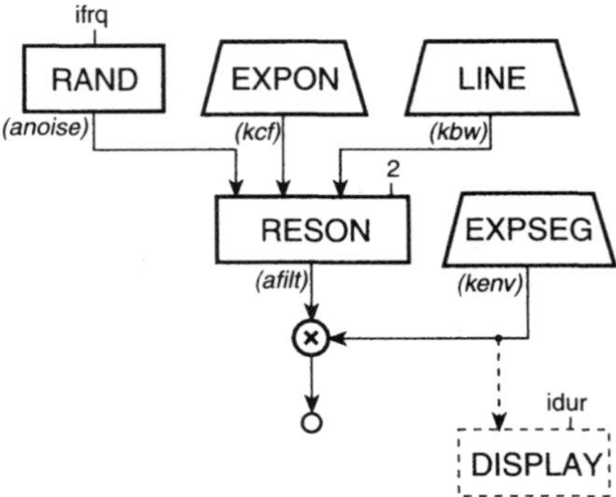

Figure 1.45 Block diagram of *instr 128*, a bandpass-filtered noise instrument.

```
        instr   128             ; BANDPASS-FILTERED NOISE
idur    =       p3
iamp    =       p4
ifrq    =       p5
iatk    =       p6
irel    =       p7
icf1    =       p8
icf2    =       p9
ibw1    =       p10
ibw2    =       p11
kenv    expseg  .01, iatk, iamp, idur/6, iamp*.4, idur-(iatk+irel+idur/6), iamp*.6, irel, .01
anoise  rand    ifrq
kcf     expon   icf1, idur, icf2
kbw     line    ibw1, idur, ibw2
afilt   reson   anoise, kcf, kbw, 2
        out     afilt*kenv
        display kenv, idur
        endin
```

Figure 1.46 Orchestra code for *instr 128*, a bandpass filtered noise instrument with variable cutoff frequency and bandwidth.

by each additional pole should be quite apparent from this set of examples. In fact, each pole increases the slope or steepness of a filter by adding an additional 6 dB per octave of roll-off at the cutoff frequency. A *cascade* filter design such as this makes the slope proportionally steeper with each added **tone** thus resulting in a more "effective" filter. Thus, in our cascade design *instr 129* would have a slope corresponding to an attenuation of 6 dB per octave; *instr 130* would have a slope of 12 dB per octave; *instr 131* would have a slope of 18 dB per octave; and *instr 132* would have a slope of 24 dB per octave. The **dispfft** opcode should clearly show the progressive effect on the spectrum of the noise source in each instrument.

```
          instr     129          ; ONE-POLE LOWPASS
anoise    rand      ifrq
afilt     tone      anoise, kcut
          dispfft   afilt, idur, 4096

          instr     130          ; TWO-POLE LOWPASS
anoise    rand      ifrq
afilt2    tone      anoise, kcut
afilt1    tone      afilt2, kcut
          dispfft   afilt1, idur, 4096

          instr     131          ; THREE-POLE LOWPASS
anoise    rand      ifrq
afilt3    tone      anoise, kcut
afilt2    tone      afilt3, kcut
afilt1    tone      afilt2, kcut
          dispfft   afilt1, idur, 4096

          instr     132          ; FOUR-POLE LOWPASS
anoise    rand      ifrq
afilt4    tone      anoise, kcut
afilt3    tone      afilt4, kcut
afilt2    tone      afilt3, kcut
afilt1    tone      afilt2, kcut
          dispfft   afilt1, idur, 4096
```

Figure 1.47 Orchestra code excerpts from *instr 129–132,* which pass white noise through a cascade of one-pole lowpass filters.

Displays

For several examples now, we have been using Csound's **display** and **dispfft** opcodes to look at signals. But what exactly is being displayed? And how are these opcodes different?

As you know, signals can be represented in either the time or the frequency domain. In fact, these are complementary representations illustrating how the signal varies in either amplitude or frequency over time. Csound's **display** opcode plots signals in the time domain as an amplitude versus time graph whereas the **dispfft** opcode plots signals in the frequency domain using the Fast Fourier Transform method. Both allow us to specify how often to update the display and thereby provide the means of watching a time or frequency domain signal evolve over the course of a note. We used **display** in *instr 128* to look at the shape of the **expseg** amplitude envelope and see the way that the amplitude varied over the entire duration of the note.

In *instr 129–132* we used the **dispfft** opcode to look at the way that the frequencies were attenuated by our filter network. By specifying that the FFT be 4096 we divided our frequency range into 2048 linearly spaced frequency bins of about 21.5 Hz (44100/2048 = 21.533), but we could have divided the spectrum anywhere from 8 bands (each 5512 Hz wide) to 2048 bands (each 21.5 Hz wide). We will continue using these opcodes to look into the time domain and frequency domain characteristics of the sounds that our instruments produce. In particular, the **dispfft** opcode will help us better understand the effect that Csound's different filters are having on the signals we put into them.

In the early days of analog synthesis the filters defined the sound of these rare and now coveted "classic" instruments. The **tone** and **reson** filters we have used thus far were some of Csound's first filters. They are noted for their efficiency (they run fast) and equally noted for their instability (they blow up). In fact it has always been good advice to patch the output of these filters into Csound's **balance** opcode in order to keep the samples-out-of-range under control.

Over the years, however, many new filters have been added to the Csound language. Today in Csound the *Butterworth* family of filters (**butterlp, butterhp, butterbp** and **butterbr**) sound great and are becoming more common in virtually all instrument designs. This is due in part to the fact that the Butterworth filters have: more poles (they're steeper and more effective at filtering), a flatter frequency response in the pass-band (they are smoother and cleaner sounding) and they are significantly more stable (meaning that you do not have to worry so much about samples-out-of-range). In *instr 133,* shown in figures 1.48 and 1.49 we use a parallel configuration comprised of a 4-pole **butterbp** and a 4-pole **butterlp** filter pair as a way to model the classic resonant-lowpass filter commonly found in first generation analog synthesizers.

As you can see and hear from the previous set of examples, dynamic parametric control of Csound's filter opcodes, combined in various parallel and serial configurations, opens the door to a wide world of subtractive sound design.

An Echo-Resonator

Let's shift our focus now to another set of Csound's signal modifiers—**comb** and **vdelay**.

A **comb** filter is essentially a delay line with feedback as illustrated in figure 1.50. As you can see, the signal enters the delay line and its output is delayed by the length of the line (25 milliseconds later in this case). When it reaches the output, it is fed back to the input after being multiplied by a gain factor.

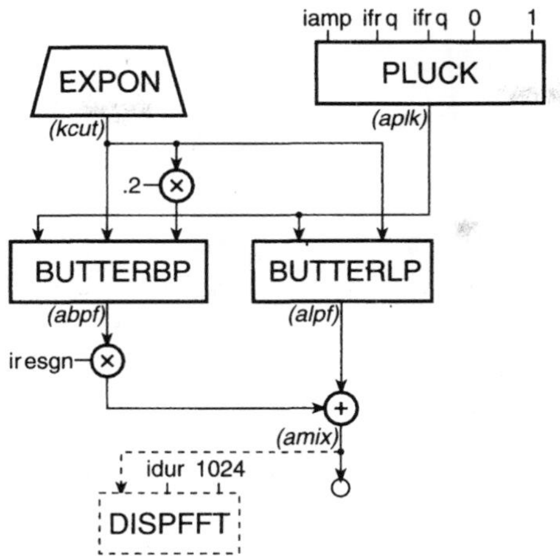

Figure 1.48 Block diagram of *instr 133,* a parallel **butterbp** and **butterlp** configuration resulting in a "classic" resonant-lowpass design.

```
        instr      133         ; LOWPASS WITH RESONANCE
idur    =          p3
iamp    =          ampdb(p4)
ifrq    =          p5
icut1   =          p6
icut2   =          p7
iresgn  =          p8
kcut    expon      icut1, idur, icut2
aplk    pluck      iamp, ifrq, ifrq, 0, 1
abpf    butterbp   aplk, kcut, kcut*.2
alpf    butterlp   aplk, kcut
amix    =          alpf+(abpf*iresgn)
        out        amix
        dispfft    amix, idur, 1024
        endin
```

Figure 1.49 Orchestra code for *instr 133,* a "classic" resonant-lowpass filter design.

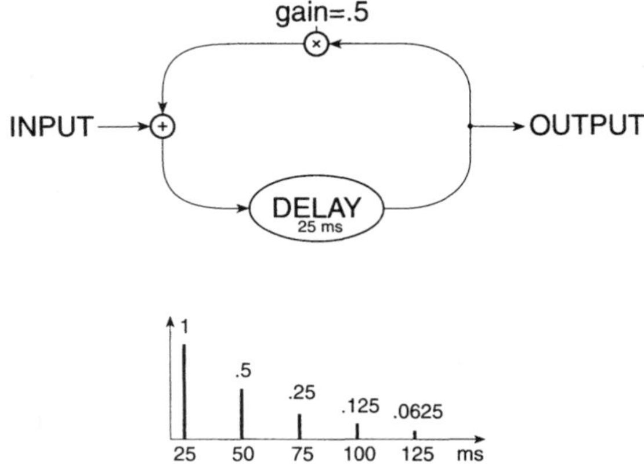

Figure 1.50 Flowchart of a **comb** filter and its impulse response.

The time it takes for the signal to circulate back to the input is called the loop-time. As demonstrated in *instr 135,* shown in figures 1.51, 1.52, and 1.53, a **diskin** opcode is used to read (in both forward and reverse) and transpose samples directly from disk into a **comb** filter. When the loop-time is long, we will perceive discrete echoes; but, when the loop-time is short, the **comb** filter will function more like a *resonator.*

As shown in figure 1.50, the *impulse response* of a **comb** filter is a train of impulses spaced equally in time at the interval of the loop-time. In fact, the resonant frequency of this filter is 1/loop-time. In *instr 135* this is specified in milliseconds. In the score comments you will see where I have converted the period of the loop, specified in milliseconds, into the frequency of the resonator, specified in Hz.

Although we can vary the loop time in *instr 135* on a note-by-note basis, the **comb** opcode will not allow you to dynamically vary this parameter during the course of a note event; the **vdelay** opcode will allow you to dynamically vary this parameter. Variable delay lines are the key to designing one of the more popular studio effects—a *flanger.*

In *instr 136,* as shown in figures 1.54 and 1.55, noise cascades through a series of variable delay lines to make a flanger. By patching the output from one **vdelay** opcode into the input of another, the strength and focus of the characteristic resonance is emphasized (just as in our **tone** example in *instr 132* as shown in figure 1.47 above). Furthermore, this resonant peak is swept across the frequency spectrum under the control of a variable rate LFO whose frequency is dynamically modified by the **line** opcode.

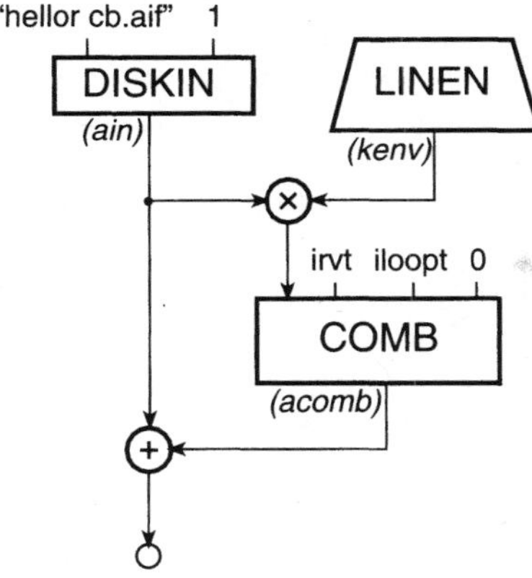

Figure 1.51 Block diagram of *instr 135,* a soundfile delay/resonator instrument using a **diskin** to read directly from disk without the use of an f-table and a **comb** to delay or resonate.

```
        instr   135         ; DISKIN ECHO-RESONATOR
idur    =       p3
iamp    =       p4
irvt    =       p5
iloopt  =       p6
kenv    linen   iamp, .01, idur, .01
ain     diskin  "hellorcb.aif", 1
acomb   comb    ain*kenv, irvt, iloopt, 0
        out     ain+acomb
        endin
```

Figure 1.52 Orchestra code for *instr 135,* an echo-resonator instrument using the **comb** opcode.

```
; INS  ST  DUR  AMP  IRVT  LOOPTIME    RESONANT FREQUENCY
i 135  0   5    .4   10    .5         ; 1/.5       =    2 Hz
i 135  5   5    .3   5     .25        ; 1/.25      =    4 Hz
i 135  10  5    .3   5     .125       ; 1/.125     =    8 Hz
i 135  15  5    .2   2     .0625      ; 1/.0625    =   16 Hz
i 135  20  5    .2   2     .03125     ; 1/.03125   =   32 Hz
i 135  25  5    .2   2     .015625    ; 1/.015625  =   64 Hz
i 135  30  5    .04  2     .001       ; 1/.001     = 1000 Hz
```

Figure 1.53 Score code for *instr 135,* the looptime (*p6*) sets the period and resonant frequency of this recirculating delay line.

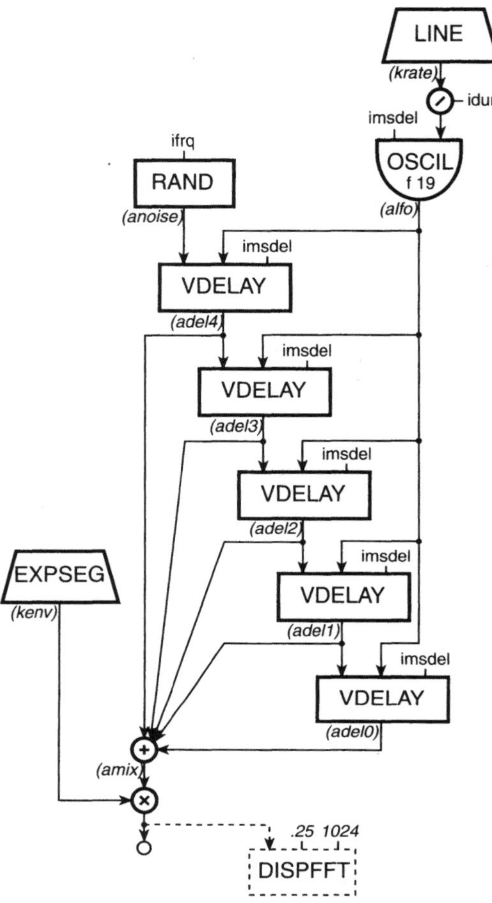

Figure 1.54 Block diagram of *instr 136,* a **vdelay** "flanger."

Score Statements and Note-List Shortcuts

Admittedly, creating and editing text-based note-lists is not fun. Granted, the note-list does offer you the most exacting and direct control over the behavior of your instruments, but it is still one of the most unmusical and tedious aspects of working with Csound.

As stated at the beginning of this chapter, Csound does read MIDI files and this may prove a more intuitive way of generating notes and playing your Csound instru-

```
        instr   136          ; VDELAY FLANGER
idur    =       p3
iamp    =       p4
ifrq    =       p5
iatk    =       p6
irel    =       p7
irat1   =       p8
irat2   =       p9
imsdel  =       p10
kenv    expseg  .001, iatk, iamp, idur/8, iamp*.3, idur-(iatk+irel+idur/8),
                iamp*.7, irel, .01
krate   line    irat1, idur, irat2
alfo    oscil   imsdel, krate/idur, 19
anoise  rand    ifrq
adel4   vdelay  anoise, alfo, imsdel
adel3   vdelay  adel4, alfo, imsdel
adel2   vdelay  adel3, alfo, imsdel
adel1   vdelay  adel2, alfo, imsdel
adel0   vdelay  adel1, alfo, imsdel
amix    =       adel0+adel1+adel2+adel3+adel4
        out     kenv*amix
        dispfft amix, idur, 1024
        endin
```

Figure 1.55 Orchestra code for *instr 136,* a variable delay line "flanger" instrument.

ments. However, Csound instruments must be designed to work with MIDI. You will need to adapt your traditional Csound instruments before they will work with MIDI devices.

Although not covered in the text of *The Csound Book,* there are a number of chapters on the CD-ROM dedicated to controlling Csound from MIDI keyboards and MIDI files.

Still, without resorting to MIDI, Csound does feature a collection of **Score Statements** and **Score Symbols** (text-based shortcuts) that were created to simplify the process of creating and editing note-lists. Like f-statements, these score commands begin with a specific letter and are sometimes followed by a set of arguments. I employ many score statements in *etude5.sco.*

The first score statement I employ in *etude5.sco* is the **Advance** statement—***a***, shown in figure 1.56. The advance statement allows the *beat-count* of a score to be advanced without generating any sound samples. Here it is used to skip over the first two notes of the score and begin rendering 10 seconds into the piece. The advance statement can be particularly useful when you are working on a long and complex composition and you are interested in fine-tuning something about a sound in the middle or at the end of the piece. Rather than waiting for the entire work to render just to hear the last note, you can advance to the end and only render that section—saving yourself hours of work. The syntax of the advance statement is shown in the comments in figure 1.56.

```
; ADVANCE     NO MEANING    ADVANCE START    ADVANCE SKIP
a             0             0                10

; INS   ST   DUR   AMP   FRQ     ATK   REL   CF1    CF2    BW1   BW2
i 128   1    5     .5    20000   .5    2     8000   200    800   30
i 128   6    5     .5    20000   .25   1     200    12000  10    200

i 128   10   5     .5    20000   .5    2     8000   200    800   30
i 128   14   5     .5    20000   .25   1     200    12000  10    200
i 128   18   3     .5    20000   .15   .1    800    300    300   40
```

Figure 1.56 Score excerpt from *etude5.sco* featuring the **advance** statement.

The second score statement I employ in *etude5.sco* is the **Section** statement—*s*, shown in figure 1.57. The section statement has no arguments. It merely divides a score into sections and allows you to begin counting your start times again from time 0. This is particularly useful if you want to repeat a passage. To do so, you would simply insert an **s** at the end of the first section, copy the section, and paste it after the **s**. Figure 1.57, agacwin from *etude5.sco,* shows exactly this use.

The third score statement I employ in *etude5.sco* is the **Dummy f**-statement—***f 0***, shown in figure 1.58. In Csound you can use the score to load f-tables into memory at any time. This would allow you to replace one waveshape or sample with another during the course of a piece and yet refer to them with the same table number in the orchestra. Likewise, you can also load in a dummy f-table (*f 0*) at any time in a score as a means of extending the length of a particular score section or inserting silence between sections. As illustrated in figure 1.58, I am using an *f 0* statement to insert two seconds of silence between two score sections.

The fourth set of score shortcuts I employ in *etude5.sco* are the **Carry**, **Ramp** and **+** symbols, as shown in figure 1.59. The carry symbol (**.**) copies a p-field value from one note-statement to the next. The ramp symbol (<) linearly interpolates between two p-field values over any number of notes (the number of notes determines the number of points in the interpolation). The **+** symbol only works for *p2,* where it automatically calculates the start time of the current note by adding together the start-time and duration of the previous note (*p2* + *p3*). Thus the current note will be consecutive with the previous one. All three symbols are used in figure 1.59 and the shorthand is translated in figure 1.60.

The final score statement I employ in *etude5.sco* is the **Tempo** statement—***t***, shown in figure 1.61. The Csound *score clock* runs at 60 beats per minute. By default Csound inserts a tempo statement of 60 (60 beats-per-minute or 1-beat-per-second) at the beginning of every score (*t 0 60*). Obviously, this means that when you specify a duration of 1 in *p3* the note-event will last for 1 second. Luckily the t-statement

```
; INS   ST   DUR   AMP   FRQ     ATK   REL   CUT1   CUT2
i 129   0    1.5   3     20000   .1    .1    500    500
i 130   2    1.5   3     20000   .1    .1    500    500
i 131   4    1.5   3     20000   .1    .1    500    500
i 132   6    1.5   3     20000   .1    .1    500    500
i 129   8    1.2   1     20000   .01   .01   5000   40
i 130   11   1.2   1     20000   .01   .01   5000   40
i 131   12   1.2   1     20000   .01   .01   5000   40
i 132   13   1.2   1     20000   .01   .01   5000   40
s
; INS   ST   DUR   AMP   FRQ     ATK   REL   CUT1   CUT2
i 129   0    1.5   3     20000   .1    .1    500    500
i 130   2    1.5   3     20000   .1    .1    500    500
i 131   4    1.5   3     20000   .1    .1    500    500
i 132   6    1.5   3     20000   .1    .1    500    500
i 129   8    1.2   1     20000   .01   .01   5000   40
i 130   11   1.2   1     20000   .01   .01   5000   40
i 131   12   1.2   1     20000   .01   .01   5000   40
i 132   13   1.2   1     20000   .01   .01   5000   40
s
```

Figure 1.57 Cut-and-paste repeated score excerpt from *etude5.sco* featuring the **section** statement.

```
; INS   ST   DUR   AMP   FRQ     ATK   REL   CUT1   CUT2
i 129   0    1.5   3     20000   .1    .1    500    500
i 130   2    1.5   3     20000   .1    .1    500    500
i 131   4    1.5   3     20000   .1    .1    500    500
i 132   6    1.5   3     20000   .1    .1    500    500
i 129   8    1.2   1     20000   .01   .01   5000   40
i 130   11   1.2   1     20000   .01   .01   5000   40
i 131   12   1.2   1     20000   .01   .01   5000   40
i 132   13   1.2   1     20000   .01   .01   5000   40

s
f 0     2    ; DUMMY F 0 STATEMENT - 2 SECONDS OF SILENCE BETWEEN SECTIONS
s

; INS   ST   DUR   AMP   FRQ     ATK   REL   CF1    CF2     BW1   BW2
i 128   0    5     .5    20000   .5    2     8000   200     800   30
i 128   4    5     .5    20000   .25   1     200    12000   10    200
i 128   8    3     .5    20000   .15   .1    800    300     300   40
i 128   10   11    .5    20000   1     1     40     90      10    40
s
```

Figure 1.58 A score excerpt from *etude5.sco* featuring the "dummy" ***f 0*** statement used to insert 2 seconds of silence between two score sections.

```
; INS   ST   DUR   AMPDB   FRQ     FC1    FC2   RESONGAIN
i 134   0    .1    90      8.09    8000   80    1
i .     +    .     <       8.095   <      <     <
i .     .    .     .       8.10    .      .     .
i .     .    .     .       8.105   .      .     .
i .     .    .     .       8.11    .      .     .
i .     .    .     .       8.115   .      .     .
i .     .    .     .       9.00    .      .     .
i .     .    .     .       9.005   .      .     .
i .     .    .     .       9.01    .      .     .
i .     .    .     .       9.015   .      .     .
i .     .    .     80      9.02    9000   60    50
```

Figure 1.59 A score excerpt from *etude5.sco* featuring the **carry** (**.**), **p2 increment**, (**+**) and **ramp** (<) symbols.

```
; INS   ST   DUR   AMPDB   FRQ     FC1    FC2   RESONGAIN
i 134   0    .1    90      8.09    8000   80    1
i 134   .1   .1    89      8.095   8100   78    5
i 134   .2   .1    88      8.10    8200   76    10
i 134   .3   .1    87      8.105   8300   74    15
i 134   .5   .1    86      8.11    8400   72    20
i 134   .5   .1    85      8.115   8500   70    25
i 134   .6   .1    84      9.00    8600   68    30
i 134   .7   .1    83      9.005   8700   66    35
i 134   .8   .1    82      9.01    8800   64    40
i 134   .9   .1    81      9.015   8900   62    45
i 134   1    .1    80      9.02    9000   60    50
```

Figure 1.60 Another view of the *etude5.sco* excerpt shown in figure 1.59 in which the **ramp** (<), **carry** (**.**) and **+** symbols are replaced by the actual numerical values they represent.

lets you change this default value of 60 in both a constant and a variable fashion. Figure 1.61 illustrates both uses.

The statement *t 0 120* will set a constant tempo of 120 beats per minute. Given this setting, the internal beat-clock will run twice as fast and therefore all time values in the score file will be cut in half.

The statement *t 0 120 1 30* is used to set a variable tempo. In this case the tempo is set to 120 at time 0 (twice as fast as indicated in the score) and takes 1 second to gradually move to a new tempo of 30 (twice as slow as indicated in the score). Obviously, using a variable tempo can make your scores less mechanical and more musical.

```
t       0   120           ; FIXED TEMPO STATEMENT: TWICE AS FAST

; INS   ST  DUR  AMPDB  FRQ      FC1     FC2   RESONGAIN
i 134   0   .1   90     8.09     8000    80    1
i .     +   .    <      8.095    <       <     <
i .     .   .    .      8.10     .       .     .
i .     .   .    .      8.105    .       .     .
i .     .   .    .      8.11     .       .     .
i .     .   .    .      8.115    .       .     .
i .     .   .    .      9.00     .       .     .
i .     .   .    .      9.005    .       .     .
i .     .   .    .      9.01     .       .     .
i .     .   .    .      9.015    .       .     .
i .     .   .    80     9.02     9000    60    50
s

t       0   120  1      30  ; VARIABLE TEMPO: TWICE AS FAST TO HALF AS FAST

; INS   ST  DUR  AMPDB  FRQ      FC1     FC2   RESONGAIN
i 134   0   .1   90     8.09     8000    80    1
i .     +   .    <      8.095    <       <     <
i .     .   .    .      8.10     .       .     .
i .     .   .    .      8.105    .       .     .
i .     .   .    .      8.11     .       .     .
i .     .   .    .      8.115    .       .     .
i .     .   .    .      9.00     .       .     .
i .     .   .    .      9.005    .       .     .
i .     .   .    .      9.01     .       .     .
i .     .   .    .      9.015    .       .     .
i .     .   .    80     9.02     9000    60    50
s
```

Figure 1.61 An excerpt from the end of *etude5.sco* in which the **tempo statement** is used in fixed and variable mode.

Working with Csound's text-based score language can be laborious. In fact it has inspired many a student to learn C programming in order to generate their note-lists algorithmically. Real-time and MIDI are both solutions. But, taking advantage of Csound's score shortcuts can make your work a lot easier and your sound gestures, phrases and textures a lot more expressive.

Exercises for Etude 5

- Render the Csound orchestra and score: *etude5.orc* & *etude5.sco.*
- Play and listen to the different sound qualities of the various filters and filter configurations.
- Look up and read about the new opcodes used in *instr 128–136* in the *Csound Reference Manual.*

```
k/ar              rand      k/xamp[, iseed[,isize]]
ar                tone      asig, khp[, iskip]
ar                butterlp  asig, kfreq[, iskip]
ar                butterbp  asig, kfreq, kband[, iskip]
ar                delayr    idlt[, iskip]
ar                comb      asig, krvt, ilpt[, iskip]
ar                vdelay    asig, adel, imaxdel [, iskip]
a1[, a2[, a3, a4]] diskin   ifilcod, kpitch[, iskiptim[, iwraparound[, iformat]]]
```

- In *instr 128* substitute a **loscil** opcode for **rand** opcode and dynamically filter some of your own samples.
- In *instr 128* substitute a **butterbp** for the **reson** and listen to the difference in quality.
- Substitute **butterlp** filters for the **tone** filters in *instr 129–132.* Compare the effectiveness.
- Transform *instr 133* into a resonant highpass filter instrument.
- Make an instrument that combines the serial filter design of *instr 132* with the parallel filter design of *instr 133.*
- Block diagram *instr 134,* a delay line instrument (not covered in the text).
- By adding more **delay** opcodes transform *instr 134* into a *multitap* delay line instrument.
- Modify *instr 135* to make a multiband resonator.
- Add more **combs** and **vdelays** to *instr 135* and create a multitap delay with feedback/multiband-resonantor super-flanger.
- Using the score statements covered in this section, return to etudes 3 and 4. In them, repeat some section, insert some silences, vary the tempo during sections, advance around a bit and ramp through some parameters to better explore the range of possibilities these instruments have to offer.
- In *instr 136,* substitute a **diskin** opcode for the **rand** opcode and flange your samples.
- In *instr 136,* add and explore the dynamic frequency and amplitude modification of the control oscillator.
- Change the waveforms of the control oscillator in *instr 136.* (Try **randh**.)
- Add a resonant-lowpass filter to your modified flanger instrument.
- Go for a walk and listen to your world.

Global Variables

Until now, we have used only local **i**, **k** and **a** variables—those that are associated with the specific instrument. Local variables are great because you could use the same variable name in separate instruments without ever worrying about the *asig* or *amix* data getting corrupted or signals bleeding-through from one instrument to another. In fact, the **instr** and **endin** delimiters truly do isolate the signal processing blocks from one another—even if they have the same exact labels and argument names.

There are times, however, when you would like to be able to communicate across instruments. This would make it possible to pass the signal from a synthesis instrument to a reverb instrument, similar to the way one routes the signals on a mixing console to the effects units, using "aux sends" and "aux returns." In Csound this same operation is achieved using *global* variables. Global variables are variables that are accessible by all instruments. And like local variables, global variables are updated at three basic rates, **gi**, **gk**, and **ga**, where:

gi-rate variables are changed and updated at the note rate.

gk-rate variables are changed and updated at the control rate.

ga-rate variables are changed and updated at the audio rate.

Because global variables belong both to all instruments and to none, they must be *initialized.* A global variable is typically initialized in **instrument 0** and filled from within a local instrument. Where is this mysterious instrument 0? Well, instrument 0 consists of the lines in the orchestra file immediately following the header section and before the declaration of the first *instr.* Thus, in figure 1.62, immediately after the header, in instrument 0, the *gacmb* and *garvb* variables (our 2 global FX buses) are cleared and initialized to 0.

```
sr          =         44100
kr          =         4410
ksmps       =         10
nchnls      =         1

gacmb       init      0
garvb       init      0
```

Figure 1.62 Global variables *gacmb* and *garvb* are initialized in **instrument 0** after the header and before the "first" *instr.*

Sound Design Etude 6: Reverb and Panning

Let's put global variables to use and add some external processing to our instruments. From within *instr 137,* shown in figures 1.63 and 1.64, the dry signal from **loscil** is added (mixed) to the wet signal on a separate reverb and echo bus.

```
asig        loscil    kenv, ifrq, ifun
            out       asig
garvb       =         garvb+(asig*irvbsnd)
gacmb       =         gacmb+(asig*icmbsnd)
```

Note that the dry signal is still sent out directly, using the **out** opcode, just as we have from our first instrument. But in this case that same signal is also globally passed out

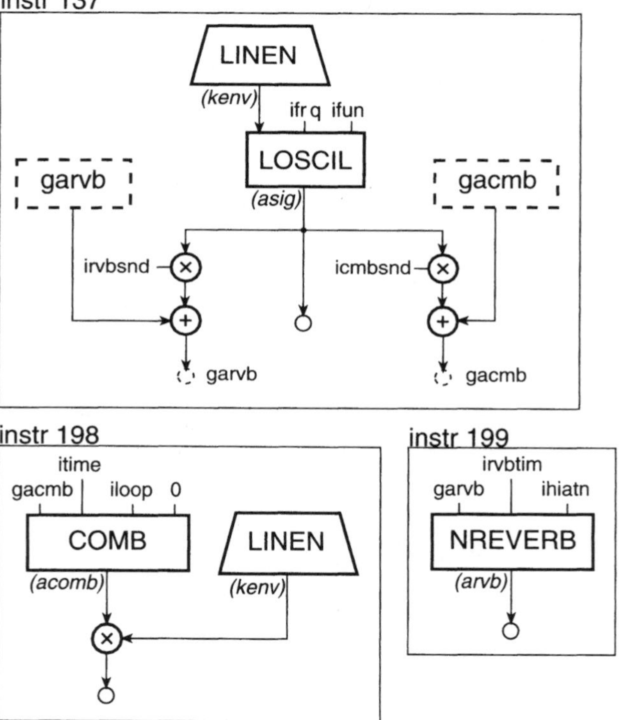

Figure 1.63 Block diagram for *instr 137, 198,* and *199,* a wavetable synthesis instrument (*instr 137*), and two global effects (*instr 198* and *199*).

```
            instr     137           ; GLOBAL COMB/REVERB LOSCIL
idur        =         p3
iamp        =         ampdb(p4)
ifrq        =         cpspch(p5)
ifun        =         p6
iatk        =         p7
irel        =         p8
irvbsnd     =         p9
icmbsnd     =         p10
kenv        linen     iamp, iatk, idur, irel
asig        loscil    kenv, ifrq, ifun
            out       asig
garvb       =         garvb+(asig*irvbsnd)
gacmb       =         gacmb+(asig*icmbsnd)
            endin

            instr     198           ; GLOBAL ECHO
idur        =         p3
itime       =         p4
iloop       =         p5
kenv        linen     1, .01, idur, .01
acomb       comb      gacmb, itime, iloop, 0
            out       acomb*kenv
gacmb       =         0
            endin

            instr     199           ; GLOBAL VERB
idur        =         p3
irvbtim     =         p4
ihiatn      =         p5
arvb        nreverb   garvb, irvbtim, ihiatn
            out       arvb
garvb       =         0
            endin
```

Figure 1.64 Orchestra code for three instruments that work together to add reverb (*instr 199*) and echo (*instr 198*) to a looping oscillator (*instr 137*).

of the instrument and into two others, *instr 198* (echo) and *instr 199* (reverb) as shown in figures 1.63 and 1.64.

It is important to note that in the score file (figure 1.65) all three of these instruments must be turned on. In fact, to avoid transient and artifact noises, global instruments are typically left on for the duration of the section and the global variables are always cleared when the receiving instrument is turned off (*gacmb = 0* and *garvb = 0*).

Our next instrument, *instr 138,* shown in figures 1.66 and 1.67 is based on an earlier FM design, but now the instrument has been enhanced with the ability to pan the signal.

```
; INS   STRT  DUR   RVBTIME         HFROLL
i 199   0     12    4.6             .8

; INS   STRT  DUR   TIME            LOOPT
i 198   0     6     10              .8
i 198   0     6     10              .3
i 198   0     6     10              .5

; INS   STRT  DUR   AMP     FRQ1    SAMPLE  ATK   REL   RVBSND   CMBSND
i 137   0     2.1   70      8.09    5       .01   .01   .3       .6
i 137   1     2.1   70      8.09    5       .01   .01   .5       .6
```

Figure 1.65 Score file for our "global **comb/nreverb loscil**" instrument. The global **nreverb** instrument, *instr 199,* is turned on at the beginning of the score and left on for the duration of the passage. Three copies of our global **comb** instrument *instr 198* are started simultaneously with different looptimes. Finally, two copies of our **loscil** instrument, *instr 137,* start one after another.

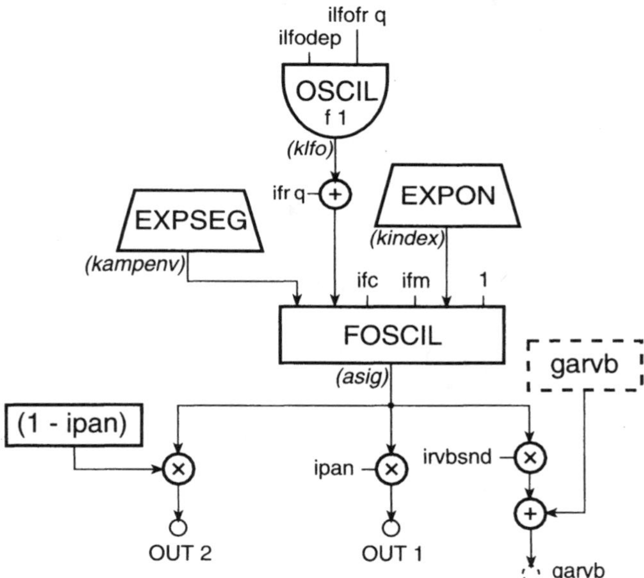

Figure 1.66 Block diagram of *instr 138,* a dynamic FM instrument with panning and global reverb.

```
          instr     138          ; SWEEPING FM WITH VIBRATO & DISCRETE PAN
idur      =         p3
iamp      =         ampdb(p4)
ifrq      =         cpspch(p5)
ifc       =         p6
ifm       =         p7
iatk      =         p8
irel      =         p9
indx1     =         p10
indx2     =         p11
indxtim   =         p12
ilfodep   =         p13
ilfofrq   =         p14
ipan      =         p15
irvbsnd   =         p16
kampenv   expseg    .01, iatk, iamp, idur/9, iamp*.6, idur* (iatk+irel+idur/9),
                    iamp*.7, irel, .01
klfo      oscil     ilfodep, ilfofrq, 1
kindex    expon     indx1, indxtim, indx2
asig      foscil    kampenv, ifrq+klfo, ifc, ifm, kindex, 1
          outs      asig*ipan, asig*(1-ipan)
garvb     =         garvb+(asig*irvbsnd)
          endin
```

Figure 1.67 Orchestra code for *instr 138,* a dynamic FM instrument with vibrato, discrete panning, and global reverb.

You should note that in *instr 138* the panning is realized using a single variable that functions like a panning knob on a traditional mixing console. How is this done? Well, as you know by now, if we multiply a signal by a scalar in a range of 0 to 1 we effectively control the amplitude of the signal between 0 and 100%. So if we simultaneously multiply the signal by the scalar (ipan) and one minus the same scalar (1−ipan), we would have two outputs whose amplitudes would be scaleable between 0 and 100% but would be inversely proportional to each other.

For example, if the scalar is at 1, and that corresponds to 1 times the left output, we would have 100% of our signal from the left and (1 - 1) or 0% signal from the right. If, on the other hand, the amplitude scalar was set to .2, then we would have .2 times left or 20% of our signal coming from the left and 1 - .2 or .8 time the right signal or 80% coming from the right. This algorithm provides a simple means of using a single value to control the left/right strength of a signal and is used in *instr 138* and illustrated in figures 1.66 and 1.67.

The file *etude6.orc* contains four additional *globo-spatial* instruments. All of these instruments are based on those presented in previous etudes. You should recognize the algorithms. But all have been enhanced with panning and global reverb capabilities. You are encouraged to block diagram and study them. Each demonstrates a different panning and reverb approach. You are also encouraged to go back and add global reverb and panning to all of the instruments we have studied so far.

To end the chapter I will present *instr 141,* shown in figures 1.68 and 1.69, which adapts an earlier amplitude modulation design and adds both global reverb and LFO-based panning.

Notice here that the amplitude of the panning LFO is set to .5. This means that this bipolar sinewave has a range of −.5 to +.5. Then, notice that I bias this bipolar signal by adding .5 to it (*kpanlfo* = *kpan* + .5). This makes the signal unipolar. Now the sinewave goes from 0 to 1 with its center point at .5. In *instr 141* the "panning knob" is being turned periodically from right to left (0 to 1) at the frequency of our LFO panning oscillator. Since a biased sinewave is used, the output signal will move from side to side. You surely realize, however, that you can substitute any envelope or oscillator function into this design and thereby move your signal, periodically or aperiodically (1/p3 Hz,) along any path or trajectory.

Moving sounds in space is one of the most exciting aspects of computer-based sound design. The sky is the limit. I hope my ending tutorial instrument is just the beginning of your exploration.

Conclusion

In this introductory chapter I have attempted to introduce the syntax of the Csound language while covering some of the elements of sound design. Given this basic understanding, the subsequent chapters of this text, written by the world's leading educators, sound designers, programmers, and composers, should serve to unlock the secret power of Csound and help you find the riches buried therein. Along the way, I sincerely hope that you not only discover some exquisite new timbres, but that your work with Csound leads to a deep and profound awareness of the true spirit embodied in organized sound . . . and silence.

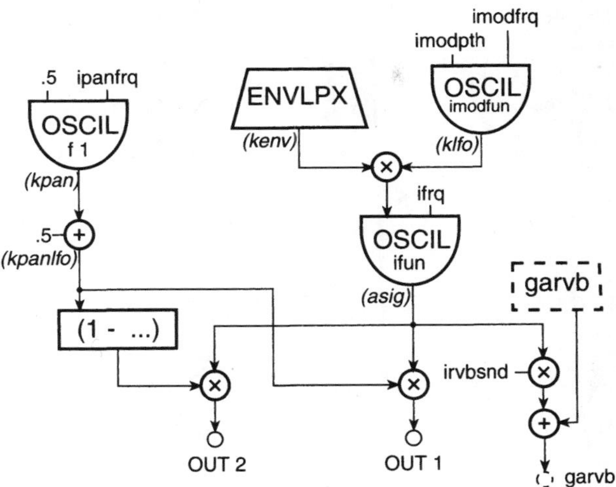

Figure 1.68 Block diagram of *instr 141*, an amplitude modulation instrument with an LFO panner and global reverb.

```
          instr    141       ; AMPLITUDE MODULATION LFO PANNER
idur      =        p3
iamp      =        ampdb(p4)
ifrq      =        cpspch(p5)
ifun      =        p6
iatk      =        p7
irel      =        p8
iatkfun   =        p9
imodpth   =        p10
imodfrq   =        p11
imodfun   =        p12
ipanfrq   =        p13
irvbsnd   =        p14
kenv      envlpx   iamp, iatk, idur, irel, iatkfun, .7, .01
kpan      oscil    .5, ipanfrq, 1
klfo      oscil    imodpth, imodfrq, imodfun
asig      oscil    klfo*kenv, ifrq, ifun
kpanlfo   =        kpan+.5
          outs     asig*kpanlfo, asig*(1-kpanlfo)
garvb     =        garvb+(asig*irvbsnd)
          endin
```

Figure 1.69 Orchestra code for *instr 141*, an Amplitude Modulation instrument with an LFO panner and global reverb.

References

Cage, J. 1976. *Silence.* Middletown, Conn.: Wesleyan University Press.

Chadabe, J. 1997. *Electric Sound: The Past and Promise of Electronic Music.* New York: Prentice-Hall.

De Poli, G., A. Piccialli, and C. Roads. 1991. *Representations of Musical Signals.* Cambridge, Mass.: MIT Press.

De Poli, G., A. Piccialli, S. T. Pope, and C. Roads. 1997. *Musical Signal Processing.* The Netherlands: Swets and Zeitlinger.

Dodge, C., and T. Jerse. 1997. *Computer Music.* 2d rev. New York: Schirmer Books.

Eliot, T. S. 1971. *Four Quartets.* New York: Harcourt Brace & Co.

Mathews, Max V. 1969. *The Technology of Computer Music.* Cambridge, Mass.: MIT Press.

Mathews, Max V., and J. R. Pierce. 1989. *Current Directions in Computer Music Research.* Cambridge, Mass.: MIT Press.

Moore, R. F. 1990. *Elements of Computer Music.* New York: Prentice-Hall.

Pierce, J. R. 1992. *The Science of Musical Sound.* 2d rev. ed. New York: W. H. Freeman.

Pohlmann, Ken C. 1995. *Principles of Digital Audio.* 3d ed. New York: McGraw-Hill.

Roads, C. 1989. *The Music Machine.* Cambridge, Mass.: MIT Press.

Roads, C. 1996. *The Computer Music Tutorial.* Cambridge, Mass.: MIT Press.

Roads, C., and J. Strawn. 1987. *Foundations of Computer Music.* 3d ed. Cambridge, Mass.: MIT Press.

Steiglitz, K. 1996. *A Digital Signal Processing Primer.* Reading, Mass.: Addison-Wesley.

2 Understanding and Using Csound's GEN Routines

Jon Christopher Nelson

Csound uses lookup tables for musical applications as diverse as wavetable synthesis, waveshaping, mapping MIDI note numbers and storing ordered pitch-class sets. These function tables (f-tables) contain everything from periodic waveforms to arbitrary polynomials and randomly generated values. The specific data are created with Csound's f-table generator subroutines, or *GEN* routines. Csound includes a family of GEN routines that write sampled soundfiles to a table, sum sinusoidal waves, draw lines and curves between specified points, create Chebyshev polynomials, calculate window functions, plot individual points in a table and generate random values. This tutorial surveys the Csound f-table generators, interspersing suggestions for efficient and powerful f-table utilization in Csound, including the introduction of a new technique for generating three-dimensional wave terrain synthesis f-tables.

A Csound f-table is an array of floating point values calculated by one of the GEN routines and stored in RAM for use while Csound generates sound. These f-tables are traditionally specified in the Csound score file and are generally restricted in size to lengths of a power of two (2^n) or a power of two plus one ($2^n + 1$). An f-table with a size of 1024 (2^{10}) will contain floating point values in sequential data storage locations with data addresses numbering from 0 to 1023. Tables can be visually displayed as mathematical graphs with data addresses plotted from left to right along the horizontal, or x-axis (abscissa values) and the actual stored data plotted along the vertical, or y-axis (ordinate values) as shown in figure 2.1.

An f-table outputs the data stored at the given address when it receives an input index value. In Csound, f-tables receive isolated indexes as well as streams of index values that scan tables once, periodically or randomly. Although f-tables are defined by score file GEN routines, a variety of orchestra file opcodes create index values and access table data. For example, the **oscil** opcode repeatedly generates index values from 0 to 1023 as it periodically scans a 1024-point f-table, an operation called *wrap-around lookup*. Orchestra file opcodes that include the suffix "***i***" have the

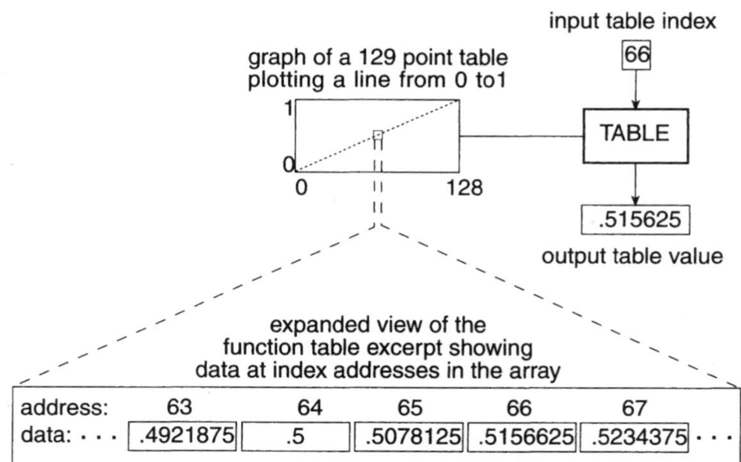

Figure 2.1 A close up of a 129-point function table highlighting the data at addresses 63 through 67.

added capability of linearly interpolating between successive table values. This feature effectively provides an audio smoothing function. For example, periodically scanning a 512-point f-table with a 43 Hz **oscil** opcode at a 44.1 kHz sampling rate reaps approximately two copies of each point in the f-table. In contrast, the **oscili** opcode interpolates between each of these values as shown in figure 2.2. Other interpolating opcodes include **tablei, oscil1i, foscili** and **randi**.

The Extended Guard Point

Although Csound f-table sizes are defined as either 2^n or $2^n + 1$, the space allocation for each f-table array is always $2^n + 1$, providing an *extended guard point* at the end of each table. If the requested table size is 2^n, the extended guard point contains a duplicate of the first value of the f-table. If the requested size is $2^n + 1$, the guard point contains the final value of the requested function. The reason for explicitly defining an extended guard point is that Csound opcodes using a 512-point table send indexes only from 0 to 511 (making the extended guard point seem superfluous). However, interpolating opcodes use the extended guard point value to calculate interpolation values after index 511. As a result, interpolating wrap-around lookup opcodes (**oscili**, **foscili** *and* **phasor-tablei** pairs) should scan 2^n size f-tables. This ensures smooth interpolation between the table end points since the extended guard

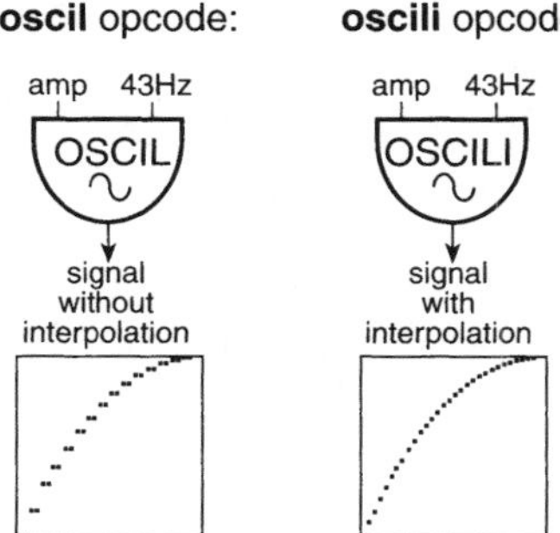

Figure 2.2 A comparison of noninterpolating and interpolating oscillator opcodes.

point will be a copy of the first table value. In contrast, interpolating single scan opcodes (**oscil1i** and **envlpx**) should scan f-tables with a $2^n + 1$ size. For example, the **envlpx** opcode scans a f-table to determine the rise shape of the attack portion of an envelope. If it scans a table with a 2^n size, the extended guard point will contain the first table value. If this attack is slow, the **envlpx** opcode will interpolate between the last table value and the starting table value, creating an amplitude discontinuity that could result in an audible click. Using a table size of $2^n + 1$, however, ensures that the interpolation will create a smooth amplitude envelope transition between the attack and any subsequent pseudo-steady state.

Score F-Statements

A Csound GEN routine is specified by a function, or "f-statement" in the score file. A Csound score may contain hundreds of f-statements, each with many parameters. A prototypical f-statement appears as follows:

```
f    p1    p2    p3    p4    p5 . . .
```

While parameter numbers 5 and higher specify different f-table attributes for different GEN routines, the first four parameters determine the following qualities for all GEN routines:

- *p1* = a unique f-table identification number
- *p2* = f-statement initialization time expressed in score beats
- *p3* = f-table size
- *p4* = GEN routine called to create the f-table

Orchestra file opcodes point to f-tables with arguments containing f-statement identification numbers, or *p1* values. A negative *p1* value in a score file f-statement deletes the f-table sharing the corresponding positive *p1* value at the specified time, in beats, given in *p2*. For example, the f-statement:

```
f   -8     132
```

will delete f-table 8 at beat 132 of the score. This provides a means of managing a computer's limited RAM while performing a score file containing numerous or large f-tables.

Furthermore, a *p1* value of 0 creates a null table that can be used to generate silence at the end of a soundfile. For example, a solitary:

```
f   0      60
```

in a score file creates a soundfile with sixty seconds of silence. This statement can also be used to turn on Csound, enabling the reception of MIDI data for one minute of real-time synthesis.

In addition to specifying the desired f-table GEN subroutine, *p4* values determine whether or not the function will be scaled. A positive *p4* value results in a table that is post-normalized to ordinate values between –1 and 1. Default f-table normalization facilitates more predictable control in applications such as wavetable or nonlinear synthesis. A negative *p4* value inhibits rescaling and should be used for f-table applications requiring raw data, such as storing head-related transfer functions, algorithmic compositional data or MIDI mapping functions.

The GEN Routines

Reading Sampled Sounds into Function Tables with GEN1

Csound enables sound designers to manipulate and transform sampled sounds in a variety of ways. Soundfile filtering, amplitude modulation, waveshaping and panning are all possible using the **soundin** opcode in the orchestra file. Manipulations such as transposition or frequency modulation of soundfiles, however, necessitate writing the soundfile into an f-table. The GEN1 f-statement stores soundfiles in tables and is written as follows:

```
f     #     time     size     1     filecode     skiptime     format
```

The filecode value in *p5* can be an integer or a file name in quotation (double-quote) marks. A *p5* value of 33 reads the soundfile entitled "soundin.33" from the

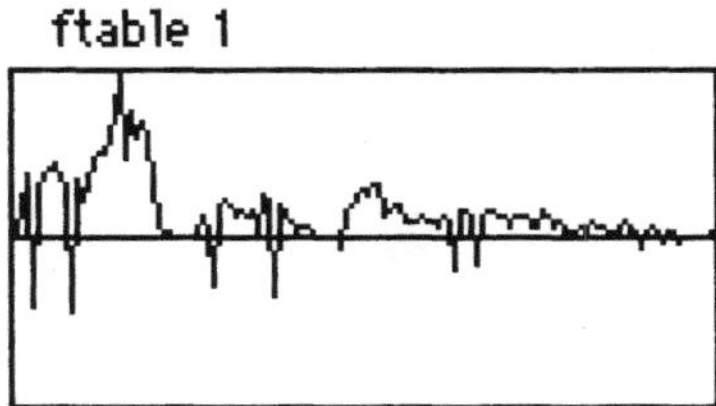

Figure 2.3 The f-table display for the soundfile "great.snd" as read into Csound via GEN1.

SFDIR into the f-table while the *p5* entry "great.snd" loads the soundfile entitled great.snd into the f-table. Csound reads soundfiles from the beginning and reads the sample format from the soundfile *header* unless a skiptime and format are specified in *p6* and *p7.*

GEN1 allows a table size of 0. In this case, the table size is determined by the number of samples in the soundfile. These tables, however, can only be read by the **loscil** opcode. Although **loscil** provides sample playback with transposition and loops, it cannot start at a specified skip time into the table, nor can it read the table backward. These manipulations are possible only if the soundfile is written into a GEN1 table with a 2^n or $2^n + 1$ size. Using these table sizes will probably result in either soundfile truncation or extension with zero values. Any opcode that calls an f-table, however, will be able to read these soundfiles. In figure 2.4 we see a flowchart of a Csound instrument that reads a tabled soundfile using a **line** opcode to provide table lookup values. The accompanying lines of orchestra and score code provide the Csound implementation of this instrument.

In this example, the audio rate line segment *aread* is drawn from a starting sample *iskip* to an ending sample *ilast.* The starting sample is calculated by multiplying the sampling rate with the desired skip time (*p5*). Similarly, the final sample is determined by first multiplying the sampling rate, note duration (*p3*) and a transposition factor (*p6*) and then adding the result to *iskip.* The line segment *aread* provides the index into the raw soundfile data stored in f-table 30, which must have a 2^n size. Multiplying *asnd* with *kenv,* the peak amplitude of which is determined by an amplitude multiplier value (*p4*), imposes an amplitude envelope on this soundfile segment. You might try adding an oscillator to the *aread* value in this example to create an FM instrument.

Normalized soundfiles may be best for some sound playback and processing techniques while raw amplitude data are best for others. Normalized and raw tables containing the same soundfile are generated by using f-statement *p4* values of +1 and

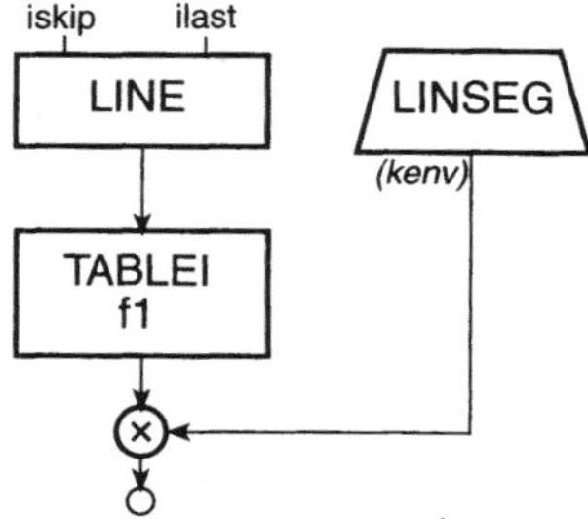

Figure 2.4 Block diagram of *instr 201,* a soundfile reading instrument using a **tablei** opcode

```
        instr    201        ; READING A SOUNDFILE USING TABLEI & GEN1
iskip   =        int(p5*sr)              ; STARTING SAMPLE IN SECONDS
ilast   =        int(sr*p3*p6)+iskip     ; ENDING SAMPLE IN W/ TRANSPOSE
kenv    linseg   0, .05, p4, p3-.05, p4, .02, 0
aread   line     iskip, p3, ilast        ; A-RATE TABLE INDEX
;aread  line     ilast, p3, iskip        ; ILAST TO ISKIP: BACKWARDS!
asnd    tablei   aread, 1                ; SCANS FTABLE 1
asig    =        asnd*kenv               ; IMPOSES ENVELOPE
        out      asig
        endin

f 1 0 262144  1  "speech1.aif"  0 4 0  ; READS AND NORMALIZES
```

Figure 2.5 Orchestra code for *instr 201,* a soundfile reading instrument with accompanying GEN1 call from score file.

−1 respectively. In the example code above, raw sample data are read into f-table 1 and then normalized to allow for amplitude scaling by the **linseg** envelope.

Sinusoidal Wave Generators

Csound also includes function generators that add sets of sinusoidal waves to create composite waveforms. In Csound, single 2π periods of summed sinusoids are written into f-tables by the GEN10, GEN9, GEN19, and GEN11 subroutines. These GEN routines facilitate the creation of sine, cosine, square, sawtooth, triangle, and pulse waveforms, all of which are useful as waveshapes for wavetable synthesis. Periodically cycling through these tables with wrap-around lookup opcodes generates a periodic waveform.

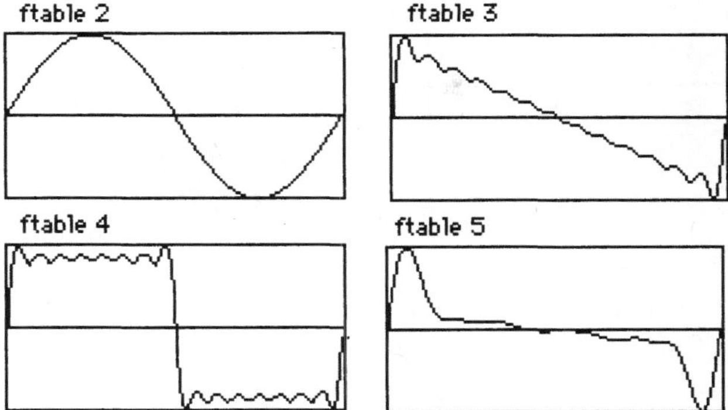

Figure 2.6 F-table display of simple geometric waveshapes—sine, saw, square, and pulse generated using Csound's GEN10 subroutine.

GEN10

GEN10, GEN9, and GEN19 all create composite waveforms by summing sine waves with specified relative strengths. Of these, GEN10 adds harmonic partials that are all in phase. The relative strengths of ascending harmonic partials (1, 2, 3, etc.) are defined in parameter numbers, *p5, p6* and *p7* respectively. Figure 2.7 shows a flowchart for two equivalent oscillators, followed by their accompanying orchestra file and score file code containing a few simple GEN10 waveshapes.

GEN9

Like GEN10, GEN9 creates composite waveforms by adding partials with specified relative strengths. GEN9, however, can create inharmonic partials with unique phase dispositions.

The partial number, strength and phase are defined in groups of three parameters beginning with *p5.* Figure 2.11 shows a few more waveshapes that can be generated with GEN9.

Unlike orchestra opcodes that specify phase as a fraction of a cycle (0–1), f-statements in a score express phase in degrees (0–360). In addition, the partial number need not be an integer. Consequently, specifying partial number .5 in *f 8* (fig. 2.11) generates half of a sine wave, which could be used as an envelope, frequency multiplier, or a table for waveshaping.

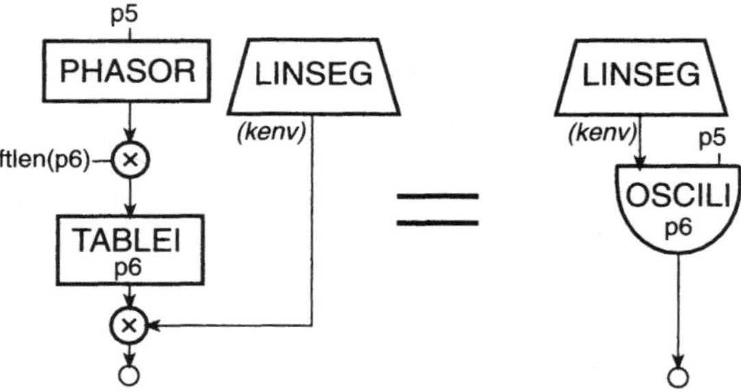

Figure 2.7 Block diagram of *instr 202* and *203,* table-lookup oscillator instruments realized via the **phasor** and **tablei** opcodes and an interpolating table-lookup oscillator.

```
        instr   202             ; TABLE-LOOKUP OSCILLATOR - PHASOR/TABLEI
kenv    linseg  0, .05, p4, p3-.1,    p4*.8, .05, 0
aphase  phasor  p5                    ; PHASES 0-1 P5 TIMES-PER-SECOND
ilength =       ftlen(p6)             ; DETERMINE LENGTH OF F-TABLE
aphase  =       aphase*ilength        ; STEP THROUGH ENTIRE TABLE
asig    tablei  aphase, p6            ; READ TABLE NUMBER FROM P6
        out     asig*kenv             ; IMPOSE ENVELOPE
        endin

        instr   203             ; TABLE-LOOKUP OSCILLATOR - OSCILI
kenv    linseg  0, .05, p4, p3-.1, p4*.8, .05, 0
asig    oscili  kenv, p5, p6
        out     asig
        endin
```

Figure 2.8 Orchestra code for *instr 202* and *instr 203,* table-lookup oscillator instruments using a **phasor/tablei** pair versus an **oscili**.

```
; 8192 POINT SINE
f 2    0  8192    10    1
; SAWTOOTH WAVE - ALL HARMONICS (THROUGH 13TH) AT A STRENGTH OF 1/HARMONIC#
f 3    0  513     10    1 .5 .333 .25 .2 .166 .143 .125 .111 .1 .0909 .0833 .077
; SQUARE WAVE - ODD HARMONICS (THROUGH 17TH) AT A STRENGTH OF 1/HARMONIC#
f 4    0  513     10    1 0 .333 0 .2 0 .143 0 .111 0 .0909 0 .077 0 .0666 0 .0588
; PULSE (TRUMPET?)
f 5    0  513     10    .8 .9 .95 .96 1 .91 .8 .75 .6 .42 .5 .4 .33 .28 .2 .15
```

Figure 2.9 F-table code for simple geometric waveforms as illustrated in figure 2.6.

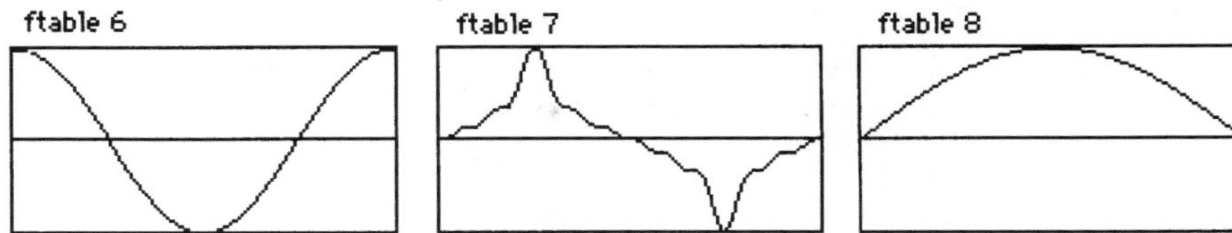

Figure 2.10 F-table displays for three waveforms generated using GEN9—a cosine, a triangle, and a half-sine.

```
; COSINE WAVE (SINE WAVE WITH INITIAL PHASE OF 90 DEGREES):
f 6  0  8192    9  1 1 90
; TRIANGLE WAVE (ODD HARMONICS AT A STRENGTH OF 1/HARMONIC
; NUMBER WITH INVERTED PHASE FOR EVERY OTHER HARMONIC):
f 7  0  513     9  1 1 0 3 .333 180 5 .2 0 7 .143 180 9 .111 0
; HALF OF A SINE:
f 8  0  513     9  .5 1 0
```

Figure 2.11 F-table code for cosine, triangle, and half sine as illustrated in figure 2.10.

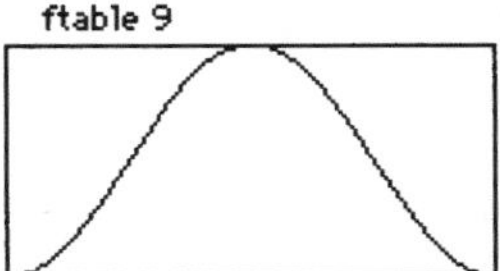

Figure 2.12 Score code and f-table display for a quasi-Gaussian curve generated using GEN19.

GEN19

GEN19 extends GEN9 by adding a DC offset parameter. Beginning with *p5* in the f-statement, the partial number, relative strength, initial phase and DC offset are specified in groups of four parameters. Figure 2.12 shows an f-table display and score code to generate a quasi-Guassian curve that rises from 0 to 1.

```
f 9   0  1024   -19    1 .5 270 .5
```

The DC offset will add .5 to the ordinate values of this sine wave. As a result, these unscaled *(−p4)* values will span from 0 to 1 rather than from −.5 to .5. This provides a good grain envelope for granular synthesis instruments, or this function could serve as an amplitude multiplier that controls both left-right and front-back panning in a four channel orchestra. These same values could also provide table indexes into f-tables containing head-related transfer function data for controlling dynamic filters and reverb times for virtual reality applications.

Inharmonic Partials

Although GEN9 and GEN19 can create inharmonic (noninteger) partials, only partials that are either integers or .5 multiples should be used for wrap-around lookup operations. Other inharmonic partials typically generate nonzero values at the end of the f-table, creating discontinuities and resultant noise. Discontinuities can be diminished by reducing the relative strength of the detuned partial. Moreover, pairing partials with complementary offsets and equal strengths will eliminate discontinuities. For example, partials *x* .75 and *y* .25, where *x* and *y* are positive integers, will exhibit equivalent positive and negative ordinate values at the end of the f-table. Summing these values results in a final table ordinate value of 0 so no discontinuity will exist during wrap-around lookup. Similarly, partials *x* .66 and *y* .33, *x* .2 and *y* .8 and *x* .79 and *y* .21 will also “zero out” at the end of the f-table. Pairs of equal-strength partials with shared offsets and inverse phase relationships also avoid final table discontinuities. For example, partials *x* .9 and *y* .9, where *x* and *y* are unequal positive integers, with shared strengths and respective initial phases of 0 and 180 will add up to 0 at the end of the table. The f-tables in figure 2.14 exhibit sums of 0 at their end points and demonstrate cycle offset and phase inversion cancellation.

Although these inharmonic partial pairing strategies eliminate discontinuities, they will not result in periodic phasing of detuned partials. Periodic phasing can be achieved only by generating a table containing summed high harmonic partials with complex relationships. This results in a f-table with inherent phasing relationships.

While using this type of inharmonic function, a desired fundamental frequency is generated by dividing the desired oscillator rate by the lowest harmonic number present in the function. For example, an f-table containing harmonic partial numbers 21, 22, 25, 27, 31, 33, 34, and 35 should be read with the **oscili** opcode’s *cps* argument set to the desired frequency divided by 21, the lowest partial present. Since this will often result in a low oscillator frequency that scans the table slowly, it is best to use a large table with an interpolating **oscili** opcode.

The phasing relationship in this f-table is still nondynamic. Dynamic phasing is only achieved through mixing multiple oscillators with inharmonic relationships in an orchestra instrument.

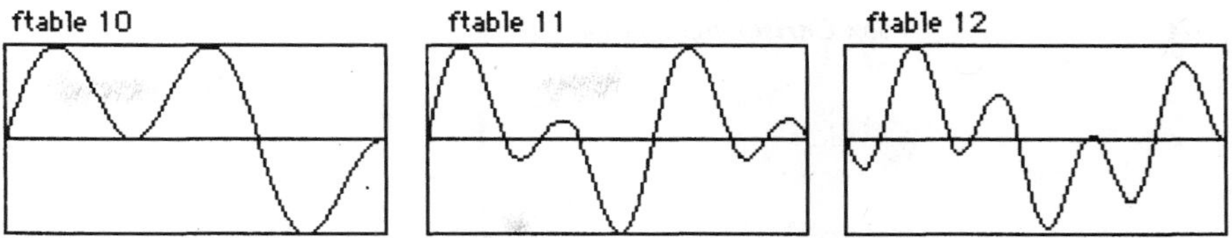

Figure 2.13 F-table display of inharmonic spectra without discontinuities.

```
f 10   0 8192   9 .75    1 0 2.25 1 0     ; CYCLE OFFSET CANCELLATION
f 11   0 8192   9 1.66   1 0 3.33 1 0     ; CYCLE OFFSET CANCELLATION
f 12   0 8192   9 1.25   1 0 4.25 1 180   ; INVERSE PHASE CANCELLATION
```

Figure 2.14 F-table code of inharmonic partial functions without discontinuities.

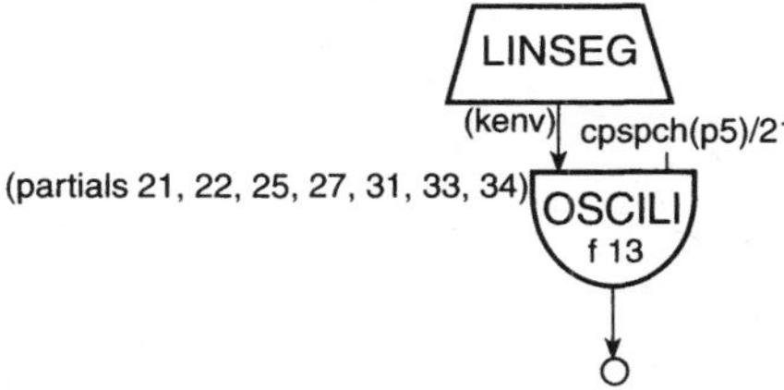

Figure 2.15 Block diagram of *instr 204,* a simple oscillator instrument with "desired" pitch computed as *cpspch(p5)/21 (i.e. the lowest partial).*

```
          instr    204            ; CPSPCH PITCH CONVERTER
ifrq      =        cpspch(p5)
kenv      linseg   0, .05, p4, p3- .1, p4*.8, .05, 0
asig      oscili   kenv, ifrq/21, 13
          out      asig
          endin

f 13  0   8192  9    21 1 0 22 1 0 25 1 0 27 1 0 31 1 0 33 1 0 34 1 0 35 1 0
```

Figure 2.16 Orchestra and f-table code for an oscillator instrument with high order partials illustrated in figure 2.17.

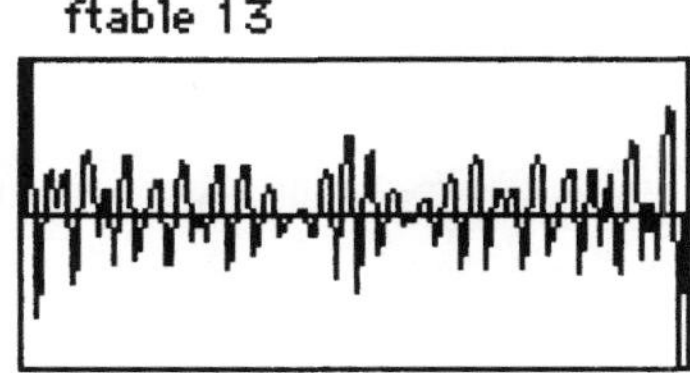

Figure 2.17 F-table display of high-order inharmonic partials as defined by *f 13* in figure 2.16.

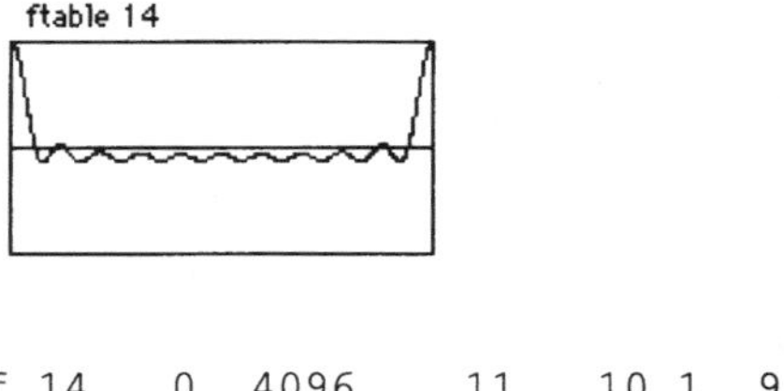


```
f 14   0  4096    11    10 1 .9
```

Figure 2.18 F-table display and score code for a pulse-train generated using GEN11.

GEN11

Unlike GEN10, GEN9, and GEN19, GEN11 adds cosine partials instead of sines. As shown in figure 2.18, this GEN routine is designed to generate pulse-trains with the number of harmonics, the lowest harmonic, and an amplitude coefficient specified in *p5, p6* and *p7* of the f-statement.

Although *f 14* above creates a pulse-train by summing sines, GEN11 generates pulse-trains with fewer parameters. It also calculates the relative amplitudes according to an exponential strength coefficient. GEN11 pulse-trains, however, are nondynamic. For dynamic pulse-trains use the **buzz** and **gbuzz** opcodes.

Drawing Segments

GEN7

Csound also includes four GEN routines that draw lines and curves between specified points. For each of these, the odd-numbered parameters (*p5, p7,* and *p9*) and even-numbered parameters (*p6, p8, p10*), contain ordinate and segment length values respectively. Figure 2.19 illustrates a few waveforms that use GEN7 to draw line segments.

Segment lengths are expressed as table points and values of 0 result in discontinuities. Furthermore, segment lengths generally should add up to the table length. Segment length sums greater than or less than the table length truncate the function or pad the table with zeros respectively.

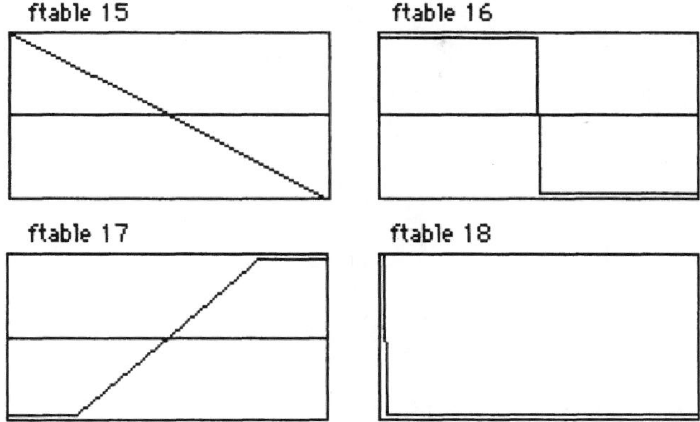

Figure 2.19 F-table display of linear waveforms drawn with GEN7.

```
f 15   0  512    7  1 512 -1                  ; SAWTOOTH
f 16   0  1024   7  1 512 1 0 -1 512 -1       ; SQUARE
f 17   0  512    7  -1 100 -1 312 1 100 1     ; FOR WAVESHAPING
f 18   0  128    7  1 1 1 0 0                 ; A SINGLE IMPULSE
```

Figure 2.20 F-table code for simple waveshapes drawn with GEN7 and shown in figure 2.19.

GEN5

The GEN5 parameters are identical to those of GEN7. Since GEN5 draws exponential segments, however, only nonzero ordinate values are allowed. Figure 2.21 shows a typical example of GEN5 used to draw an exponential envelope function.

GEN8

Although GEN8 creates smooth cubic spline curves, using two equal ordinates separated by a short segment length results in large humps. Figure 2.22 shows a couple of typical GEN8 f-tables.

With a table length of 513, the quasi-Gaussian curve in *f 20* works well for single scan operations.

GEN6

Unlike the other segment-drawing GEN routines, GEN6 requires groupings of three ordinate values separated by intermediary length values to calculate a cubic

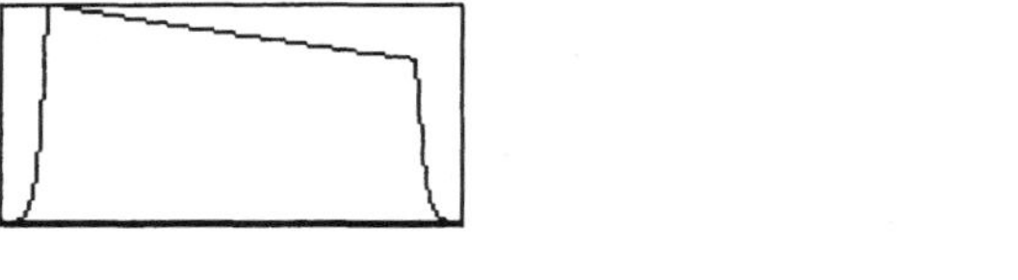


```
f 19    0   1024   5     .001 100 1 824 .75 100 .001
```

Figure 2.21 F-table display and score code of an exponential envelope function drawn with GEN5.

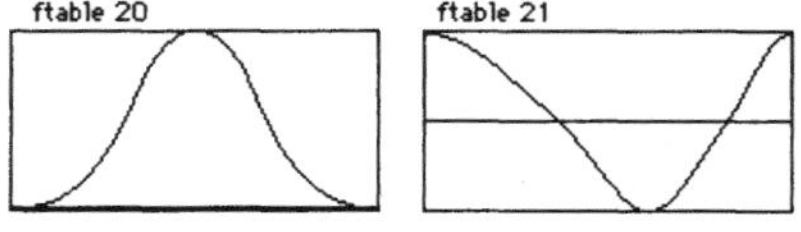


```
; QUASI-GAUSSIAN
f   20   0   513   8     0 150 0.5 50 1 113 1 50 0.5 150 0
; STRETCHED COSINE
f   21   0   2048  8     1 750 0 550 -1 400 0 348 1
```

Figure 2.22 F-table display and score code for two spline curves drawn with GEN8, a quasi-Gaussian, and a stretched cosine.

polynomial function segment. Here, the third ordinate value becomes the first in the next grouping of three. These cubic polynomial segments are relatively smooth if the odd numbered ordinates oscillate between maximum and minimum values while the even ordinates, the points of inflection, maintain somewhat linear relationships between the odd ordinates. Successive maxima or minima odd ordinate values or points of inflection without linear relationships result in segment spikes.

Waveshaping Function Tables

GEN3, GEN13, GEN14, and GEN15 all create polynomial functions that can be used effectively in waveshaping instruments. Of these, GEN3 is the most flexible since it creates a polynomial function over any left (*p5*) and right (*p6*) ordinate value with any number of specified coefficients in *p7* and higher. Figure 2.24 shows a typical example.

GEN13, GEN14, and GEN15, on the other hand, create specific types of functions known as Chebyshev polynomials. Chebyshev polynomials can split a sinusoid into

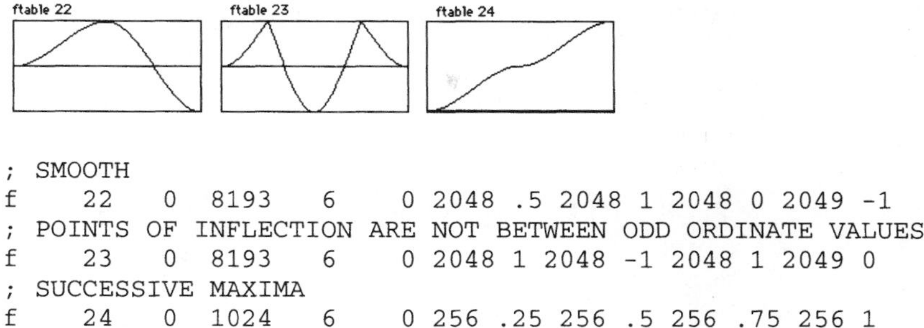


```
; SMOOTH
f    22   0  8193   6     0 2048 .5 2048 1 2048 0 2049 -1
; POINTS OF INFLECTION ARE NOT BETWEEN ODD ORDINATE VALUES
f    23   0  8193   6     0 2048 1 2048 -1 2048 1 2049 0
; SUCCESSIVE MAXIMA
f    24   0  1024   6     0 256 .25 256 .5 256 .75 256 1
```

Figure 2.23 F-table display and score code for 3 cubic polynomial functions.

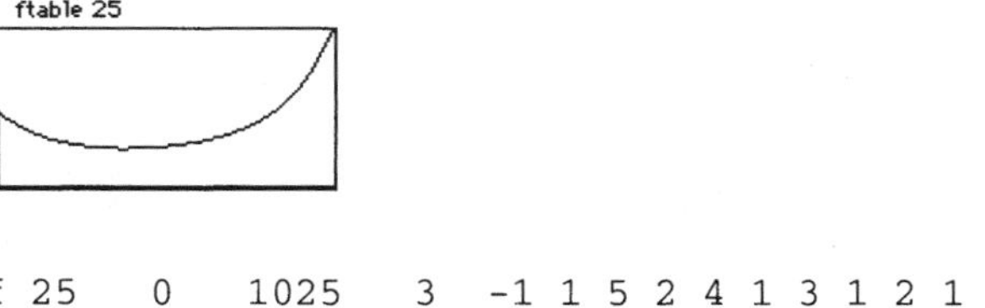


```
f 25   0    1025   3   -1 1 5 2 4 1 3 1 2 1
```

Figure 2.24 F-table display and score code for a polynomial function drawn with GEN3.

harmonic partials in a waveshaping instrument. GEN13 and GEN14 f-statements specify the relative strengths of harmonic partials to generate Chebyshev polynomials of the first and second kind respectively. Specifying the phase of each harmonic with GEN15 generates two f-tables that can be used in a phase-quadrature instrument.

The tables generated with this family of GEN routines have bipolar structures with origins located at the midpoint of the table. Consequently, it is best to use a table length of $2^n + 1$. Waveshaping typically uses a sine wave to provide lookup indexes to one of these tables. If the waveshaping f-table-length equals the waveform resolution (16 bit = 2^{16} = 65536), linear mapping results. A flowchart for a waveshaping instrument can be seen in figure 2.25. The Csound code for the corresponding waveshaping f-table instrument are shown in figure 2.26.

In this example, the index to the table is provided by a 440 Hz sine oscillator with a ramping envelope that reaches a peak amplitude of .49. These sinusoidal amplitude values (y-axis of $f\,2$) provide the lookup indexes (x-axis) into f-table number 26. The *atable* **tablei** opcode sets the table mode at 1, normalizing the table length to x-axis, or abscissa values between 0 and 1. Since the table has a bipolar structure, this **tablei** opcode also has a table offset of .5. This offset value is added to the *aindex* values,

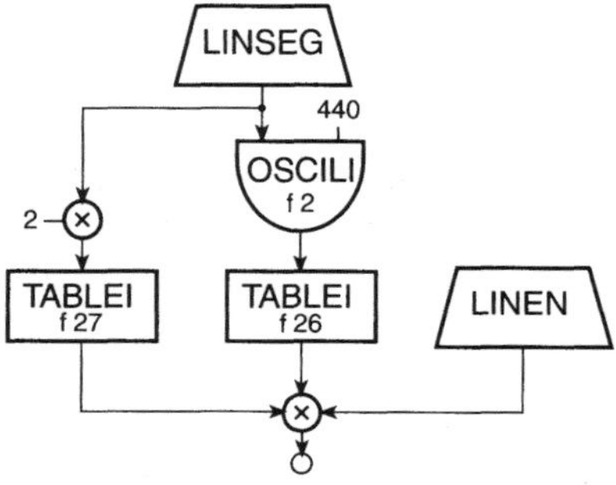

Figure 2.25 Block diagram of *instr 205,* a simple waveshaping instrument with normalization.

```
        instr   205            ; SIMPLE WAVESHAPING
ksweep  linseg  0, p3*.5, .49, p3*.5, 0  ; INDEX SWEEP FUNCTION
aindex  oscili  ksweep, p5, 2            ; SOUND TO WAVESHAPE
atable  tablei  aindex, 26, 1, .5        ; WAVESHAPE AINDEX
knorm   tablei  ksweep*2, 27, 1          ; MAKE NORMALIZATION FUNCTION
kenv    linen   p4, .01, p3, .02         ; AMPLITUDE ENVELOPE
        out     (atable*knorm)*kenv      ; NORMALIZE AND IMPOSE ENVELOPE
        endin

f 26  0  1025   7  -1 256 -1 513 1 256 1 ; WAVESHAPING FUNCTION
f 27  0  513    4  26 1                  ; AMP NORMALIZING FUNCTION
```

Figure 2.26 Orchestra and f-table code for a simple waveshaping instrument, *instr 205.*

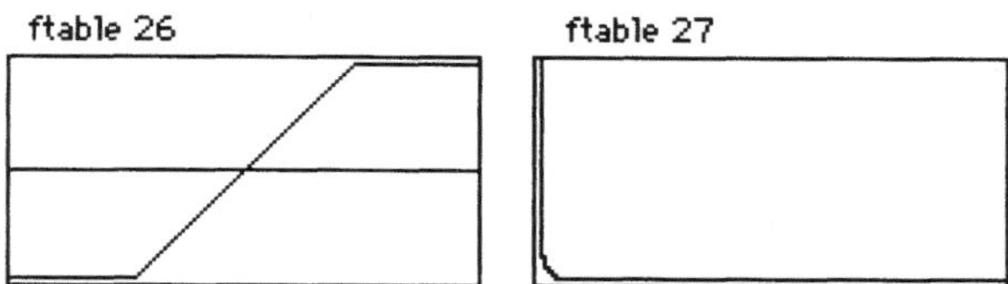

Figure 2.27 F-table displays of a waveshaping function drawn with GEN7 and a normalizing function drawn with GEN4 as defined in figure 2.26.

resulting in table indexes that oscillate around the midpoint of the waveshaping function. When the *ksweep* values that in turn dictate the *aindex* amplitude reach .49, the index values oscillate between .01 and .99, scanning the entire waveshaping function.

Since *f 26* contains a line segment from −1 to +1 over the middle section of the table, the sinusoidal index values generate a sinusoidal wave when the *ksweep* values are below .25. As *ksweep* exceeds .25 throughout the middle section of each note, all *aindex* values less than −.25 and greater than .25 will result in f-table values of −1 and 1 respectively. This nonlinear waveshaping simulates amplifier distortion in which loud input signals are clipped, introducing numerous high partials into the sound. Another possible amplifier distortion model might use GEN9 to create a waveshaping function containing half of a sine wave with an initial phase disposition of 270 degrees.

Waveshaping Amplitude Normalization with GEN4

Clearly, adjusting the range of periodic index values into a waveshaping f-table provides a powerful means of dynamic signal modification, but it also directly alters the amplitude of the sound. For instances in which this causal relationship is undesirable, the waveshaped f-table output must be normalized to exhibit a consistent peak value before imposing an amplitude envelope. The GEN4 subroutine provides the means to accomplish this task by analyzing a waveshaping function and creating a complementary amplitude normalization f-table. Multiplying the outputs of a waveshaping f-table and its complementary GEN4 normalizing f-table generates a waveshaped signal with a consistent peak amplitude value if the sweep function determines the index for both tables. An amplitude envelope can then be imposed on the resultant signal. This technique can be used to create paradoxical sounds in which the nonlinear distortion has no relationship to the amplitude. For example, inversely related sweep and amplitude envelopes can generate a sound that distorts more as the amplitude diminishes.

In *instr 205,* shown in figure 2.27, *f 27* uses GEN4 to analyze *f 26* and create a normalizing function. The GEN4 f-statement specifies the f-table number to analyze in *p5* and defines the table mode in *p6.* Any nonzero value in *p6* will perform the analysis, assuming the waveshaping function has a bipolar structure. This bipolar analysis data must be written into a table that is half the size of the waveshaping f-table. A *p6* value of zero analyzes a function that scans from left to right. In this case, both the waveshaping and normalizing tables must be the same size.

GEN13 and GEN14

Although any GEN routine can create waveshaping functions, Chebyshev polynomials provide more predictable waveshaping results by splitting waves into harmonic partials with specified relative strengths. As the periodic index values increase, the resultant Chebyshev polynomial f-table output generally adds the specified partials in ascending order. GEN14 creates a slightly more gentle curve than GEN13 but the resultant waveshaped signals sound similar. Specifying strengths of more than 20 harmonics in either GEN13 or GEN14 results in large amounts of distortion as the index values approach the table length limits. For both GEN13 and GEN14, the Chebyshev polynomial is drawn over ordinate values that span from $-p5$ to $+p5$ f-statement values while *p6* defines an amplitude scaling factor that is applied to any index into the table. Using a **table** opcode offset argument of .5 and an f-statement *p6* value of .5 provides a simple means of scaling a normalized periodic index. The relative strengths of harmonic partials are defined in *p7* and following. Figure 2.28 defines some typical spectra using GEN13 and GEN14.

Tabling sine waves with amplitudes that move slowly over the entire range of the waveshaping table provides an effective means of exploring the properties of waveshaping functions. After exploring these properties, the amplitude sweeps can be adjusted to highlight the optimum desired dynamic timbres. Wrap-around tables other than sines and GEN1 tables containing sampled sounds can also be waveshaped with interesting results.

Waveshaping Amplitude Normalization with Signification

The basic waveshaping instruments defined in figures 2.26 and 2.28 achieve amplitude normalization through the use of GEN4 f-tables. Unpredictable amplitude fluctuations can also be minimized by inverting the phase of consecutive pairs of harmonics, a procedure called *signification.* In GEN13 and GEN14, harmonic phases are shifted by 180 degrees if a negative harmonic strength is used as in figure 2.30.

Consequently, the f-table will result in a more consistent amplitude output if the harmonic strengths follow the pattern: +, +, −, −, +, +, −, −, etc. Additional waveshaping amplitude normalization models can be found in Roads (Roads 1996) and Le Brun (Le Brun 1979).

```
          instr     206           ; WAVESHAPING WITH NORMALIZATION
iwshpfun  =         p6
inormfun  =         p7
ksweep    linseg    0, p3*.5, .49, p3*.5, 0    ; INDEX SWEEP FUNCTION
aindex    oscili    ksweep, p5, 2              ; SOUND TO WAVESHAPE
atable    tablei    aindex, iwshpfun, 1, .5    ; WAVESHAPE AINDEX
knorm     tablei    ksweep*2, inormfun, 1      ; MAKE NORMALIZATION FUNCTION
kenv      linen     p4, .01, p3, .02           ; AMPLITUDE ENVELOPE
asig      =         (atable*knorm)*kenv        ; NORMALIZE AND IMPOSE ENV
          out       asig
          dispfft   asig, .1, 1024
          endin

; 8192 POINT SINE
f 2     0  8192    10  1
; WAVESHAPING FUNCTION: GEN13 - ODD HARMONICS
f 28    0  4097    13  1 1 1 0 .8 0 .5 0 .2
; AMP NORMALIZING FUNCTION
f 280   0  2049    4   28 1
; WAVESHAPING FUNCTION: GEN14 - SAME HARMONICS
f 29    0  4097    14  1 1 1 0 .8 0 .5 0 .2
; AMP NORMALIZING FUNCTION
f 290   0  2049    4   29 1
; WAVESHAPING FUNCTION: GEN14 - EVEN HARMONICS
f 30    0  4097    14  1 1 0 1 0 .6 0 .4 0 .1
; AMP NORMALIZING FUNCTION
f 300   0  2049    4   30 1
; WAVESHAPING FUNCTION: GEN 13 - OVER 20 HARMONICS
f 31    0  4097    13  1 1 1 .666 .5 .3 0 0 .3 0 .2 .25 .33 0 0 .1 0 .45 .33 .2
                       .1 .1 .15
; AMP NORMALIZING FUNCTION
f 310   0  2049    4   31 1
```

Figure 2.28 Orchestra and f-table code for *instr 206,* a simple waveshaping instrument with normalization that uses Chebyshev polynomials of first (GEN13) and second (GEN14) kind to allow the specification of specific and definable harmonic partials and amplitudes under waveshaping.

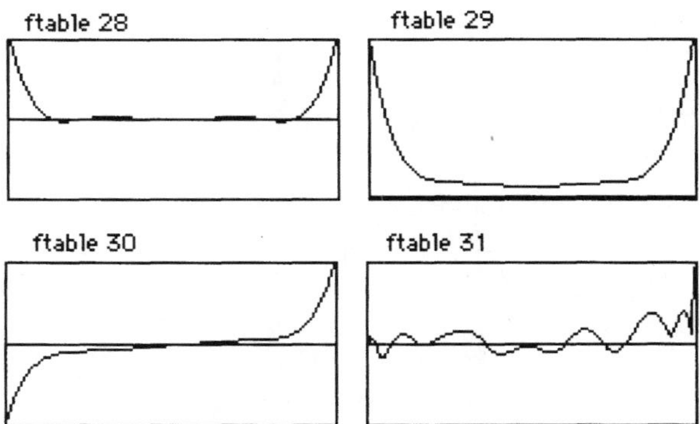

Figure 2.29 Four f-table displays of waveshaping functions—odd harmonics (*f 28*), same harmonics (*f 29*), even harmonics (*f 30*), and over 20 harmonics (*f 31*), using GEN13 and GEN14 as defined by the f-table code in figure 2.28.

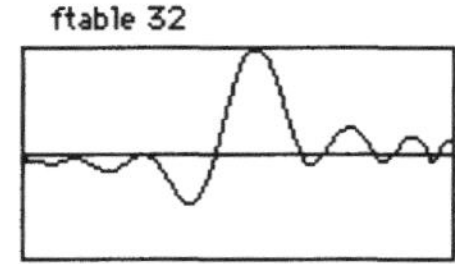


```
; SIGNIFICATION
f 32   0   8193   13   1 1 1 1 -1 -1 1 1 -1 -1 1 1 -1 -1 1 1 -1 -1
```

Figure 2.30 F-table display and code of a waveshaping function generated with GEN13 in which consecutive pairs of harmonics are inverted in phase.

Phase-Quadrature with GEN15

A GEN15 f-statement creates two f-tables with identification numbers *p1* and *p1* + 1. Harmonic partials with phases between 0 and 179 are written into the first table while those with phases between 180 and 359 are written into the second. Using these tables, a *phase-quadrature* instrument generates sounds containing individual harmonics with arbitrarily specified phases. Figure 2.31 shows a flowchart for an amplitude normalized version of Le Brun's phase-quadrature instrument (Le Brun 1979), which is followed by the accompanying Csound code.

This phase quadrature instrument performs waveshaping on sinusoidal waves. As with single table waveshaping instruments, this phase quadrature instrument creates more complex sounds with complex waves or sampled sounds providing the table indexes.

Using GEN12 for Asynchronous Frequency Modulation

Csound's GEN12 subroutine generates the log of a modified Bessel function. This function provides an amplitude scaling factor for the asynchronous FM instrument described by Palamin and Palamin (Palamin and Palamin 1988).

This instrument is an amplitude-modulated FM instrument in which the AM and FM modulating frequencies are synchronized. The lookup into this table is dependent upon the modulation index "I" and a partial strength parameter "r" in Palamin and Palamin's formula I(r−1/r). Parameter *r* values greater than 1 emphasize higher frequencies while values less than 1 emphasize lower frequencies. Parameter *r* values of 1 will not modify the usual FM spectrum. Figure 2.36 is a flowchart for this

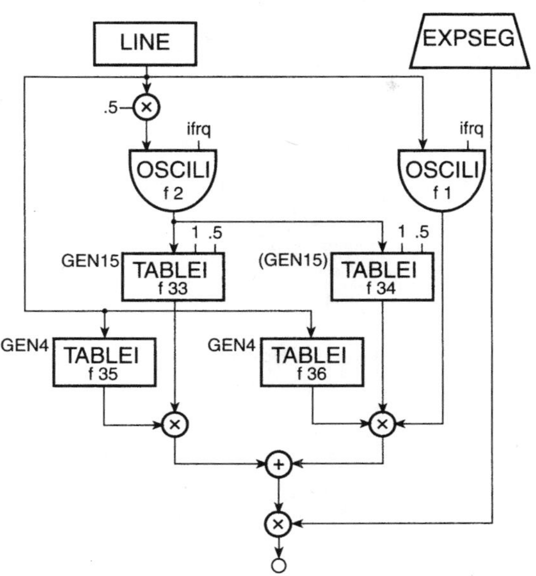

Figure 2.31 Block diagram of *instr 207,* a phase-quadrature waveshaping instrument.

```
        instr   207              ; PHASE-QUADRATURE WAVESHAPING
idur    =       p3
iamp    =       p4
ifrq    =       cpspch(p5)
iswp1   =       p6
iswp2   =       p7
kswp    line    iswp1, idur, iswp2  ; AMPLITUDE SWEEP VALUES
acosi   oscili  kswp*.5, ifrq, 2    ; F 2=COSINE WAVE
asine   oscili  kswp, ifrq, 1       ; F 1=SINE WAVE
atab1   tablei  acosi, 33, 1, .5    ; TABLES ACOSI TO GEN13
atab2   tablei  acosi, 34, 1, .5    ; TABLES ACOSI TO GEN14
knrm1   tablei  kswp, 35, 1         ; NORMALIZING F 35
knrm2   tablei  kswp,. 36, 1        ; NORMALIZING F 36
anrm1   =       atab1*knrm1         ; NORMALIZE GEN13 SIGNAL
anrm2   =       atab2*knrm2*asine   ; NORMALIZE GEN14 SIGNAL
amix    =       anrm1+anrm2         ; MIX GEN13 AND GEN14
kenv    expseg  .001, idur*.1, iamp, idur*.1, iamp*.8, idur*.8, .001
asig    =       amix*kenv
        out     asig
        endin
```

Figure 2.32 Orchestra code for *instr 207,* a phase-quadrature waveshaping instrument with amplitude normalization.

```
; f 33 BELOW GENERATES FUNCTION TABLES 33 AND 34 AS ILLUSTRATED IN FIG 2.34
f 33    0  8193   15    1 1 1 0 1 180 .8 45 .6 270 .5 90 .4 225 .2 135 .1 315

f 35    0  4097   4     33 1        ; AMP NORMALIZATION fn FOR f 33
f 36    0  4097   4     34 1        ; AMP NORMALIZATION fn FOR f 34
; ADDITIONAL TABLE 33/34 PAIRS FOR STUDY (GENERATED BY DEFINING ONLY f 33)
; EVEN HARMONICS WITH NO PHASE SHIFT, ODD HARMONICS WITH PHASE SHIFT
f 33    0  8193   15    1 1 1 0 1 0 1 180 1 180 1 0 1 0 1 180 1 180 1 0 1 0 1 180 1 180
; DIFFERENT HARMONIC STRENGTHS AND PHASES
f 33    0  8193   15    1 1 1 0 1 0 .9 180 .5 270 .75 90 .4 45 .2 225 .1 0
; LOWER HARMONICS NO PHASE SHIFT, UPPER HARMONICS WITH PHASE SHIFT
f 33    0  8193   15    1 1 1 0 1 0 .5 0 .9 0 .3 0 .75 0 .2 180 .6 180 .15 180 .5 180 .1 180
; LOWER HARMONICS WITH PHASE SHIFT, UPPER HARMONICS NO PHASE SHIFT
f 33    0  8193   15    1 1 1 180 1 180 .5 180 .9 180 .3 180 .75 180 .2 0 .6 0 .15 0
                        .5 0 .1 0
```

Figure 2.33 F-table code using GEN15 for phase-quadrature and GEN4 for normalizing functions.

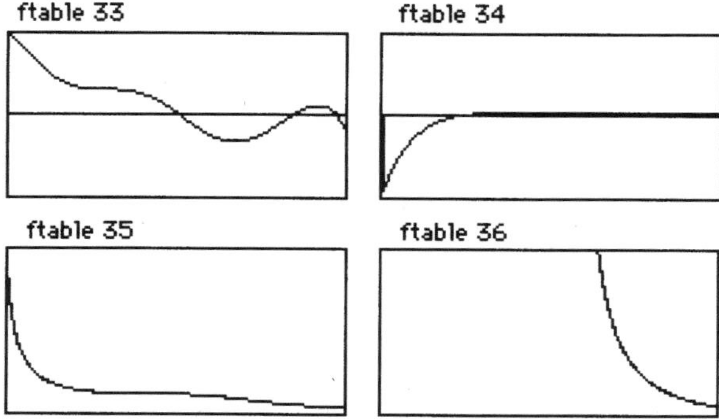

Figure 2.34 F-table displays of a GEN15 phase-quadrature pair (f-tables *f 33* and *f 34*) and their amplitude normalizing function as defined with GEN4 (f-tables *f 35* and *f 36*).

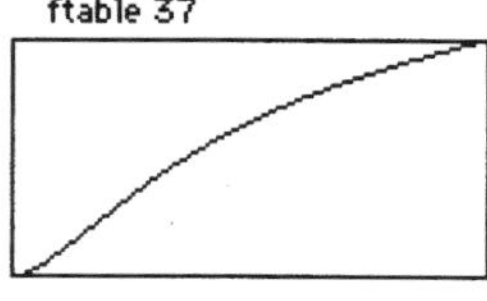


```
f 37  0  1024  -12  40  ; BESSEL FUNCTION-DEFINED FROM 0 TO 40
```

Figure 2.35 F-table display and code of a modified Bessel function produced with GEN12.

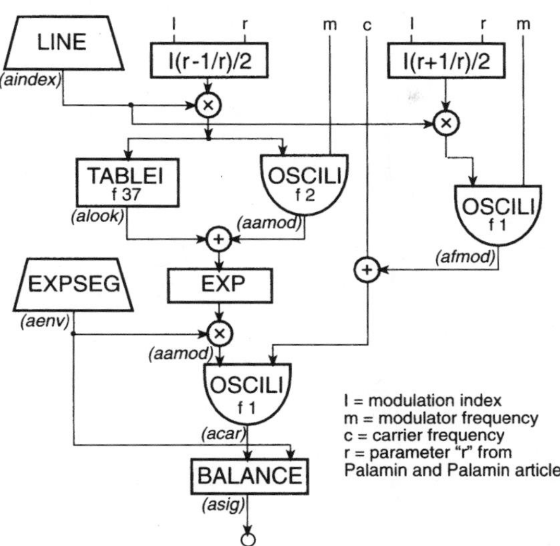

Figure 2.36 Block diagram of *instr 208*, an amplitude modulated FM instrument.

extremely interesting and versatile extension of FM synthesis (Palamin and Palamin 1988) followed by the orchestra code for the Csound implementation in figure 2.37.

GEN2 and GEN17

GEN2 takes parameter values in the f-statement and transfers them directly into a table. For most applications, normalization is undesirable and a value of –2 will be used in *p4* of the f-statement. Although older versions of Csound allowed only 150 parameters in any given f-statement, newer versions either have limits of at least 1024 parameters or they dynamically allocate memory to accommodate parameter number limits dictated solely by the available RAM.

The GEN2 subroutine lends itself well to many algorithmic applications. For example, GEN2 tables containing same-sized weighted pitch-class sets and collections of note durations can be randomly indexed by a k-rate **randh** opcode with an amplitude argument equal to the table length. These random indexes can generate weighted random rhythmic and pitch-class values in a melody generator. GEN2 tables containing ordered data such as a twelve-tone row can be scanned linearly to provide algorithmic compositional parameters. The GEN17 subroutine also writes parameter values directly into a table. GEN17, however, holds these values for a

```
        instr   208         ; AM/FM
idur    =       p3
iamp    =       p4
icarfrq =       p5
imodfrq =       p6
aenv    expseg  .001, idur*.1, iamp, idur*.8, iamp*.75, idur*.1, .001
i1      =       p7*imodfrq               ; p7=MOD. INDEX START
i2      =       p8*imodfrq               ; p8=MOD. INDEX END
adev    line    i1, idur, i2             ; MODULATION FREQUENCY
aindex  line    p7, idur, p8             ; MODULATION INDEX
; R VALUE ENVELOPE: P9-P10 = EXP. PARTIAL STRENGTH PARAMETER START AND END
ar      linseg  1, .1, p9, p3-.2, p10, .1, 1
amp1    =       (aindex*(ar+(1/ar)))/2
afmod   oscili  amp1, imodfrq, 1         ; FM MODULATOR (SINE)
atab    =       (aindex*(ar-1/ar))/2     ; INDEX TO TABLE
alook   tablei  atab, 37                 ; TABLE LOOKUP TO GEN12
aamod   oscili  atab, adev, 2            ; AM MODULATOR (COSINE)
aamod   =       (exp(alook+aamod))*aenv
acar    oscili  aamod, afmod+icarfrq, 1  ; AFM (CARRIER)
asig    balance acar, aenv
        out     asig
        endin
```

Figure 2.37 Orchestra code for *instr 208,* an amplitude-modulated FM instrument as shown in figure 2.37.

number of table points, creating a step function. GEN17 tables are most useful for mapping MIDI note numbers onto register numbers or onto sampled sound f-table numbers. Figure 2.38 shows sample GEN2 and GEN17 tables.

The flowchart in figure 2.39 and the accompanying orchestra code in figure 2.40 provide an example of an instrument that cycles through a twelve-tone row using the row defined in *f 38.*

Window Functions with GEN20

The GEN20 subroutine generates window functions. Such functions can be used as spectrum analysis windows, granular synthesis amplitude envelopes, or in a variety of other applications. The window functions, which are specified with f-statement *p5* values of 1–9, include Hamming, Hanning, Bartlett, Blackman, Blackman-Harris, Gaussian, Kaiser, Rectangle and Sinc. For each of these, the number in *p6* of the f-statement defines the peak window value. Of these, the Kaiser window requires an additional *p7* value between 0 and 1, adjusting the function to approximate a rectangle or a Hamming window. Figure 2.41 shows the f-table display and figure 2.42 defines the corresponding score code for f-statements of each window type.

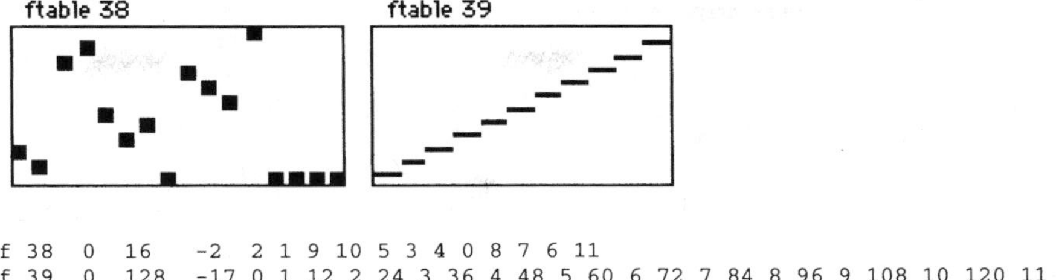


```
f 38   0   16    -2   2 1 9 10 5 3 4 0 8 7 6 11
f 39   0   128   -17  0 1 12 2 24 3 36 4 48 5 60 6 72 7 84 8 96 9 108 10 120 11
```

Figure 2.38 F-table display and score code for non-normalized versions of GEN2 and GEN17, a pitch map, and a MIDI keyboard map.

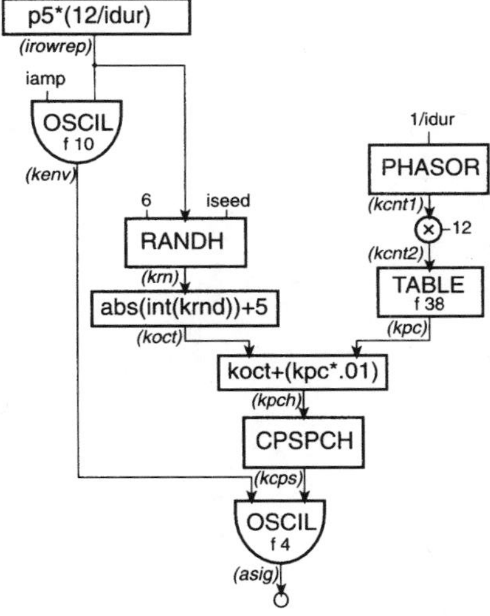

Figure 2.39 Block diagram of *instr 209,* a 12-tone row instrument.

```
          instr   209              ; 12-TONE ROW PLAYER
idur      =       p3
iamp      =       p4
irow      =       12/idur                ; 12 NOTES PER NOTE DURATION
irowrep   =       p5*irow                ; NUMBER OF TIMES TO REPEAT THE ROW
iseed     =       p6                     ; SEED 0-1,SAME SEED = SAME RANDOM SEQ
kenv      oscil   iamp, irowrep, 10      ; f 10 = ENVELOPE FUNCTION
kcnt1     phasor  1/idur                 ; COUNTS 0-1 OVER NOTE DURATION
kcnt2     =       kcnt1*12               ; COUNTS 0-12 OVER NOTE DURATION
kpc       table   kcnt2, 38              ; f 38 = ROW
krn       randh   6, irowrep, iseed      ; DETERMINES RANDOM VALUE
koct      =       (abs(int(krn)))+5      ; CONVERTS TO RANDOM OCTAVE
kpch      =       koct+(kpc*.01)         ; FORMATS PC + RANDOM OCT TO PCH
kcps      =       cpspch(kpch)           ; CONVERTS PCH TO CPS
asig      oscil   kenv, kcps, 4          ; f 4 = SQUARE WAVE
          out     asig
          endin
```

Figure 2.40 Orchestra code for *instr 209,* an instrument that cycles thought table *f 38,* a twelve-tone row defined using GEN2.

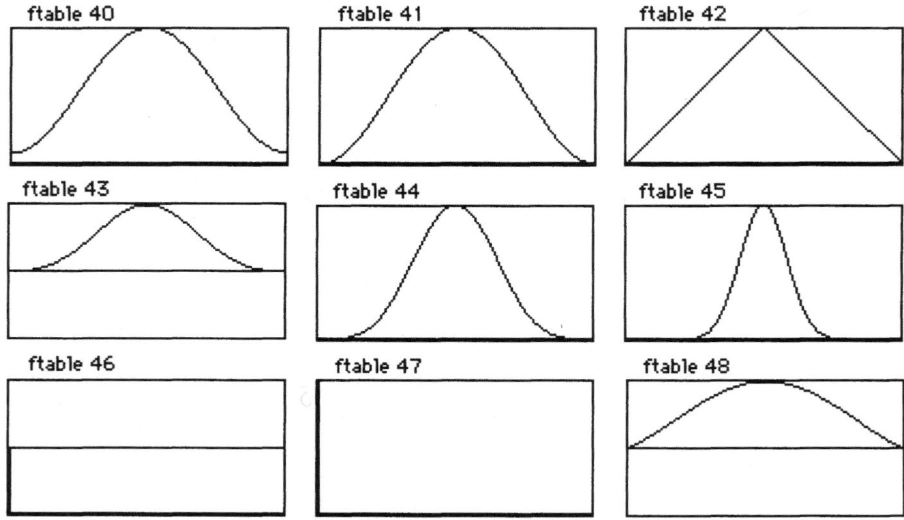

Figure 2.41 F-table displays of standard window functions: Hamming (*f 40*), Hanning (*f 41*), Bartlett (*f 42*), Blackman (*f 43*), Blackman-Harris (*f 44*), Gaussian (*f 45*), Kaiser (*f 46*), Rectangle (*f 47*) and Sinc (*f 48*).

```
f 40   0  513   20   1 1;        Hamming
f 41   0  513   20   2 1;        Hanning
f 42   0  513   20   3 1;        Bartlett
f 43   0  513   20   4 1;        Blackman
f 44   0  513   20   5 1;        Blackman-Harris
f 45   0  513   20   6 1;        Guassian
f 46   0  513   20   7 1.75;     Kaiser
f 47   0  513   20   8 1;        Rectangle
f 48   0  513   20   9 1;        Sinc
```

Figure 2.42 F-table code for generating standard window functions using GEN20 as shown in figure 2.41.

Random Distributions with GEN21

The GEN21 subroutine enables the creation of a variety of f-tables with random distributions. The *p5* values in GEN21 f-statements define different types of random distributions. Values of 1 through 11 in *p5* correspond to Uniform, Linear, Triangular, Exponential, Biexponential, Gaussian, Cauchy, Positive Cauchy, Beta, Weibull and Poisson distributions. As with GEN20, the *p6* values in a GEN21 f-statement define the peak table value. The Beta distribution requires two additional parameters, and the Weibull one additional parameter. A thorough explanation of these random distributions and suggestions for their applications to composition may be found in Dodge and Jerse's *Computer Music* (Dodge and Jerse 1985). Figure 2.43 shows the f-table display and figure 2.44 defines the corresponding score code for f-statements defining each of the GEN21 random distribution types.

Three-Dimensional Tables for Wave Terrain Synthesis

The Csound GEN routines create two-dimensional f-tables for use in the majority of synthesis paradigms. Three-dimensional tables, however, are necessary for wave terrain synthesis. This synthesis technique generates audio waveforms by scanning three-dimensional tables using elliptical orbits through the table terrain. In three-dimensional tables, the axes are plotted as follows:

- *x*-axis plotted left/right
- *y*-axis plotted front/back
- *z*-axis plotted top/bottom

Wave terrain synthesis uses indexes for both the *x* and *y* axes and the resultant *z*-axis values create the actual waveform. This is analogous to tracking the height of a large ball rolling around in a hilly landscape.

By altering the orbit pattern or moving it across the terrain throughout the duration of a note, the waveform can be transformed radically. Moreover, wave terrains that maintain *z*-axis values of 0 around their entire perimeter are of particular interest for wave terrain synthesis. The family of three-dimensional f-tables exhibiting this special property allow index orbits to traverse multiple copies of the table without waveform discontinuities. As an orbit departs one table edge, it can smoothly re-enter at the same point on the opposite table edge. This can be visualized as an elliptical orbit crossing multiple copies of a wave terrain placed next to each other like

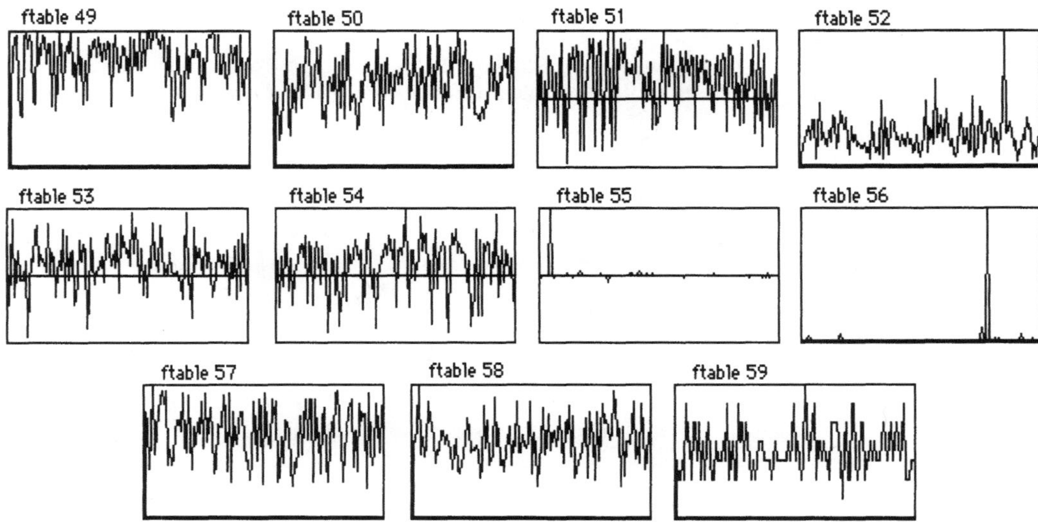

Figure 2.43 F-table displays for random distributions generated using GEN21: Uniform (*f 49*), Linear (*f 50*), Triangular (*f 51*), Exponential (*f 52*), Bi-exponential (*f 53*), Gaussian (*f 54*), Cauchy (*f 55*), Positive Cauchy (*f 56*), Beta (*f 57*), Weibull (*f 58*), Poisson (*f 59*).

```
f 49    0    513    21    1  1           ; Uniform
f 50    0    513    21    2  1           ; Linear
f 51    0    513    21    3  1           ; Triangular
f 52    0    513    21    4  1           ; Exponential
f 53    0    513    21    5  1           ; Biexponential
f 54    0    513    21    6  1           ; Gaussian
f 55    0    513    21    7  1           ; Cauchy
f 56    0    513    21    8  1           ; Positive Cauchy
f 57    0    513    21    9  1  1  2     ; Beta
f 58    0    513    21    10 1  2        ; Weibull
f 59    0    513    21    11 1           ; Poisson
```

Figure 2.44 F-table code for generating various random distributions.

floor tiles. As an orbit amplitude increases to traverse multiple tables, the sonic transformation includes both a timbre change and an ascending pitch.

Although this synthesis model provides an efficient and powerful means of generating dynamic waveforms, wave terrain synthesis remains relatively unexplored. A comprehensive bibliography of the technique includes four articles and a description of the technique in Road's *Computer Music Tutorial* (Bischoff 1978, Borgonovo 1984 and 1986, Mitsuhashi 1982, and Roads 1996).

Although the Csound GEN routines make two-dimensional f-tables, it is possible to create three-dimensional functions by multiplying the outputs of two discretely scanned f-tables representing the *x* and *y* axes. The flowchart in figure 2.45 and the accompanying orchestra code in figure 2.46 provide an example of a wave terrain synthesis instrument. The wave terrain instrument shown in *instr 210* needs to include the following parameters:

- *p4* = amp
- *p5–6* = *xtransverse* init.—final
- *p7–8* = *xoscil* amplitude init.—final
- *p9–10* = *xoscil* frequency init.—final
- *p11* = *xfn*
- *p12–13* = *ytransverse* init.—final
- *p14–15* = *yoscil* amplitude init.—final
- *p16–17* = *yoscil* frequency init.—final
- *p18* = *yfn*
- *p19* = *x*-axis f-table
- *p20* = *y*-axis f-table

In this instrument, the *x* and *y* f-tables must have endpoint values of 0 in order to facilitate the traversal of multiple tables. In addition, the *x* and *y* f-tables should both be post-normalized by using positive *p4* f-statement values. With absolute peak values of 1, the *x* and *y* f-table outputs can be multiplied to generate *z*-axis values. Figure 2.49 shows several three-dimensional terrains that result from multiplying the *x* and *y*-axis f-table data.

The **tablei** opcodes that scan these *x* and *y* tables should also have their *ixmode* argument set to 1, normalizing the indexes to scan the entire table with values from 0 to 1 rather than 0 through the f-table length.

Using a normalized index with fractional values enables wave terrain orbits to easily scan across multiple tables as the *x* and *y* orbit amplitudes exceed values of 1.

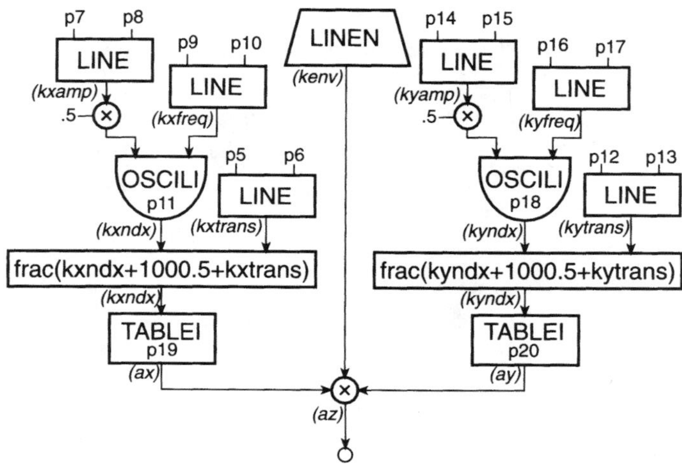

Figure 2.45 Block diagram of *instr 210,* a wave-terrain synthesis instrument for scanning 3D function tables.

```
         instr    210              ; 3D WAVE-TERRAIN
kenv     linen    p4, .02, p3, .02                ; AMP ENVELOPE
                                                  ; X INDEX VALUES:
kxtrans  line     p5, p3, p6                      ; TRANSVERSE X MOVEMENT
kxamp    line     p7, p3, p8                      ; INDEX OSCILLATOR AMP
kxamp    =        kxamp*.5                        ; SCALES XAMP
kxfreq   line     p9, p3, p10                     ; X INDEX OSCIL FREQUENCY
kxndx    oscili   kxamp, kxfreq, p11              ; p11=X INDEX FUNCTION
kxndx    =        frac(kxndx+1000.5+kxtrans)      ; FRACTIONAL VALUES ONLY
                                                  ; Y INDEX VALUES:
kytrans  line     p12, p3, p13                    ; TRANSVERSE Y MOVEMENT
kyamp    line     p14, p3, p15                    ; INDEX OSCILLATOR AMP
kyamp    =        kyamp*.5                        ; SCALES YAMP
kyfreq   line     p16, p3, p17                    ; Y INDEX OSCIL FREQUENCY
kyndx    oscili   kyamp, kyfreq, p18              ; p18=Y INDEX FUNCTION
kyndx    =        frac(kyndx+1000.5+kytrans)      ; FRACTIONAL VALUES ONLY
                                                  ; AUDIO:
ax       tablei   kxndx, p19, 1, 0, 0             ; p19=X FUNCTION
ay       tablei   kyndx, p20, 1, 0, 0             ; p20=Y FUNCTION
az       =        (ax*ay)*kenv                    ; Z-AXIS TERRAIN WAVEFORM
         out      az
         endin
```

Figure 2.46 Orchestral code for *instr 210,* a 3D wave-terrain synthesizer.

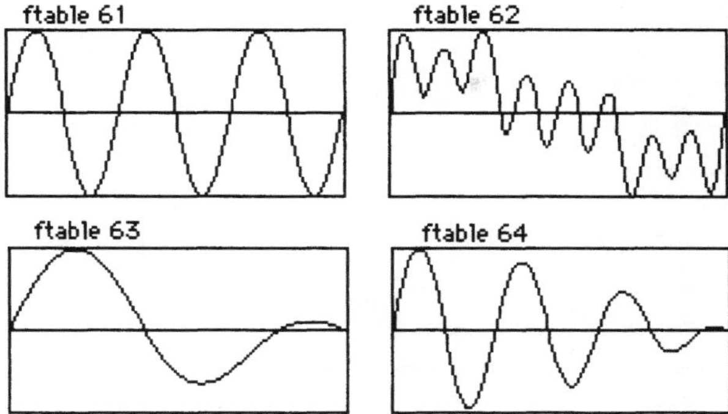

Figure 2.47 F-table displays of x and y coordinates of simple and complex wave-terrains as defined in figure 2.48.

```
f 61    0    8192    10         0 0 1
f 62    0    8192    10         1 .43 0 .25 .33 .11 0 .75
f 63    0    8192    9          1 1 0 1.5 1 0
f 64    0    8192    9          3 1 0 3.5 1 0
```

Figure 2.48 F-table code for generating the x and y-axis coordinates of simple and complex wave-terrains.

This fractional value is derived from the addition of the index function, transverse value and 1000.5, which provides an offset of .5 while avoiding negative values for any index amplitude less than 1000. Altering the frequency or amplitude values for the *x* or *y* oscillators or adding transverse movement in either the *x* or *y* axes will result in sonic transformations. An elliptical orbit is attained in this instrument by using synchronized cosine and sine pairs for the *x* and *y* axis indexes. Other indexes, however, such as triangle, sawtooth, linear, exponential, or other functions will alter the sonic result.

The sonic result of wave terrain synthesis is similar to amplitude modulation. Although the two techniques display similarities, classical AM synthesis uses static waveforms while the moving elliptical *x* and *y* f-table indexes provide greater dynamism in wave terrain synthesis. The wave terrain model provided above can be extended by adding a *w*-axis f-table with a unique index to create a four-dimensional wave terrain f-table. Furthermore, using additional axes with independent indexes creates wave terrains with many dimensions.

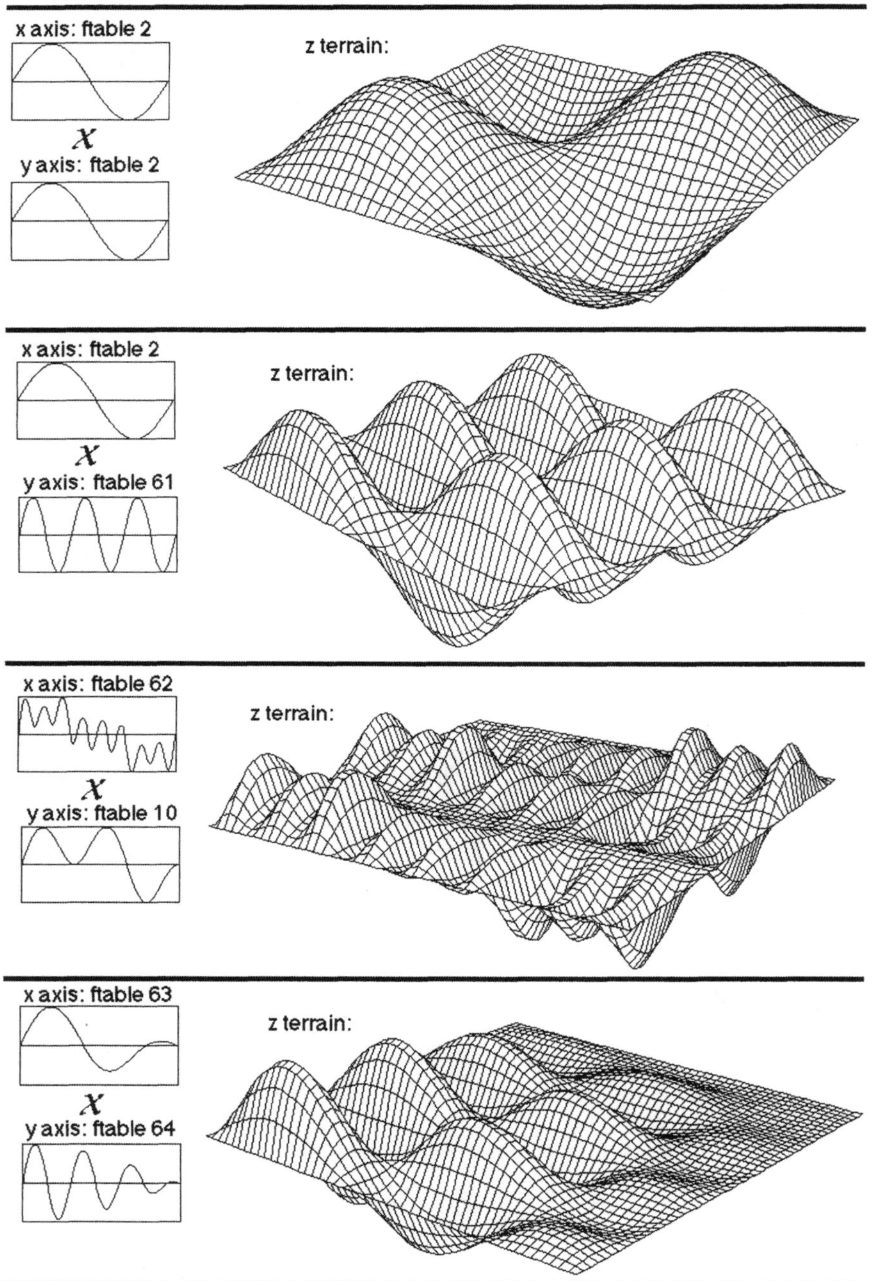

Figure 2.49 Simple and complex wave terrain realized by modulating two f-tables.

Conclusion

The GEN routines in Csound provide an ample assortment of function generators to serve every computer musicians needs. With its diverse set of example f-table instruments, this tutorial serves as a basis for further exploration, study and design. In particular, the model for generating three-dimensional wave terrain synthesis f-tables forges a path for further research in this synthesis technique. Learning to generate and use Csound's wide variety of f-tables provides one of the keys to successfully synthesizing and manipulating sound. Given all the Csound GEN routines, the multitude of possible functions and their musical applications are virtually limitless.

References

Bischoff, J., R. Gold, and J. Horton. 1978. "A microcomputer-based network for live performance." *Computer Music Journal* 2(3): 24–29. Revised and updated version in C. Roads and J. Strawn, eds. 1985. *Foundations of Computer Music.* Cambridge, Mass.: MIT Press.

Borgonovo, A., and G. Haus. 1984. "Musical sound synthesis by means of two-variable functions: experimental criteria and results." In D. Wessel, ed. *Proceedings of the 1984 International Computer Music Conference.* San Francisco: International Computer Music Association, pp. 35–42.

Borgonovo, A., and G. Haus. 1986. "Sound synthesis by means of two-variable functions: experimental criteria and results." *Computer Music Journal* 10(4): 57–71.

Dodge, C., and T. Jerse. 1985. *Computer Music.* New York: Schirmer Books.

LeBrun, M. 1979. "Digital waveshaping synthesis." *Journal of the Audio Engineering Society* 27(4): 250–265.

Mackenzie, J. 1996. "Using strange attractors to model sound." In Clifford Pickover, ed. *Fractal Horizons: The Future Use of Fractals.* New York: St. Martin's Press, pp. 225–247.

Mackenzie, J. 1995. "Chaotic predictive modeling of sound." In *ICMC Proceedings 1995.* San Francisco: International Computer Music Association.

Mitsuhashi, Y. 1982. "Audio signal synthesis by functions of two variables." *Journal of the Audio Engineering Society* 30(10): 701–706.

Palamin, J. P., and P. Palamin. 1988. "A method of generating and controlling musical asymmetric spectra." *Journal of the Audio Engineering Society* 36(9): 671–685.

Roads, C. 1996. *The Computer Music Tutorial.* Cambridge, Mass.: MIT Press.

3 What Happens When You Run Csound

John ffitch

Csound is a reasonably large program. In this chapter, I am not aiming to give a complete description, for which there is no alternative to reading the source code itself. Rather, I plan to give you a general introduction to the various components of the program so that you will understand how they fit together. In addition, I will provide you with sufficient details about the operation of the program so that error and warning messages may be better understood and problems may be both appreciated and avoided.

Running Csound

When running Csound, there are actually three kinds of information that are passed to the program: (1) the various "command-line flags," that set and control detailed aspects of the way Csound works; (2) the orchestra file; and (3) the score file—be it text-based, a MIDI file, real-time MIDI, real-time audio, or any combination of these inputs. For the present, we will not consider MIDI or real-time audio inputs. Rather, we will focus on Csound's traditional text-based score file.

Essentially, the three types of information that the user presents to the Csound program point to the three main functions of the software: (1) general control and house-keeping; (2) orchestra translation; and (3) score translation. You might be asking, "What about the synthesis?" Well, in my three-part division of labor, I will include Csound's rendering or sound synthesis actions as an aspect of part 1 or control.

Argument Decoding

Most implementations of Csound feature some form of graphical user interface (GUI) that allows the user to set program options by selecting from menus, choosing files through dialog boxes and clicking on-screen buttons with a mouse or pointing device. The original interface to Csound, however, was through a text-based "command-line" with options. And in fact, the command-line interface is still accessible from most of today's graphical "front-ends." For the sake of clarity, it is this command-line interface that will be described here.

File Names

Csound requires but two arguments to run: the names of the orchestra and the score files. These can be specified without any additional or special flags. This is because Csound has default settings for all flags. When you run the program, the number of names are checked and an error message would be produced warning if one or both were missing, or if there were more than two file names specified.

Flags

Flags are command-line options. They are introduced with a "-" character. In general, command-line flags control the form of the output, such as the size of the sample (8, 16 or 32bit) or the header format (AIFF, WAVE, Floating Point) as well as specifying the name of the input MIDI file, the name of the listing file used for debugging purposes, and the name of the output file. Other flags control the quantity of messages the system generates, the quality of graphics and a number of other special features. The manual gives a complete list of these flags.

Most flags are checked for validity, so it is possible to get error messages or warnings from the argument decoding. For example, it is wrong to specify both WAVE and AIFF output and any such attempt would give rise to a message. Many graphical user interfaces would not even allow such a selection. With a graphical user interface the checking itself may be done in a different way, but the purpose is the same: to control the detailed behavior of Csound.

Orchestra Compilation

The orchestra file describes the individual instruments in a language for signal processing. In common with all computer languages, this language has to be translated into an internal form that is usable by the control components. This translation takes

```
          instr    301      ; REVERB SEND WITH EXPON AMPLITUDE ENVELOPE
kenv      expon    8000, p3, .01
asig      oscil    kenv, cpspch(p4), 1
          outs1    asig
garvb     =        garvb+(asig*.45)
          endin

          instr    302      ; REVERB SEND WITH GAUSS PITCH ENVELOPE
ifrq      =        cpspch(p4)
k1        gauss    ifrq*2
kenv      linen    1, p3*.8, p3, p3*.1
a1        oscil    8000, ifrq, 2
a2        oscil    5000, ifrq+k1, 2
asig      =        (a1+a2)*kenv
          outs2    asig
garvb     =        garvb+(asig*.2)
          endin

          instr    399      ; SIMPLE REVERB
irvbtime  =        11.6*p4
asig      nreverb  garvb, irvbtime, .4
          outs     asig, asig
garvb     =        0
          endin
```

Figure 3.1 Orchestra code for *instr 301, instr 302* and *instr 399,* a simple stereo orchestra consisting of two instruments and a global reverb. Note that only the reverb instrument generates output to both channels.

place in two parts, as described in the source files *otran.c* and *oload.c,* together with associated files such as *rdorch.c.*

The first stage of any compilation process is the recognition of the words of the language. Csound checks for a number of possible errors. It notices missing labels, variables whose values are used but unassigned, and similar errors. If the orchestra is a particularly big one, or has a large number of variables, Csound will expand from its initial allocations of space for the translation process. This is sometimes accompanied by a short message indicating that expansion has happened. Larger orchestras inevitably take longer to compile and so such a message serves as a warning that you may have to wait a while.

For each opcode there are usually two kinds of associated action, an initialization and an action to be performed at the control or audio rate. The first task the compilation has to achieve is to arrange that each opcode in an instrument be initialized. The second task is to call these opcode-actions with the appropriate arguments for as long as required by the score. The orchestra translation creates structures that facilitate this, but they are only used during the performance. The performance needs to know what to play and when to play and this information is read from the score or MIDI file.

Score Compilation

The score language is just a collection of events, with information about when to play and what to play. As such, the score does not need much alteration or translation. The two main actions needed by the score compiler are: (1) to sort the note events into time-order; and (2) to take account of the number of beats per second plus any accelerations and declarations. The sorting is necessary as Csound allows the notes to be written in any order because it is sometimes more convenient to write one instrument's part in total before writing the other parts. While sorting, the system also takes account of the non-numerical characters in the score language, like the *carry* (.) and the *ramp* (>) characters, expanding them to numeric values. The result

```
i 399    0       42       1

i 301    0.0     0.5      8.05     ; F
i 301    0.5     1.5      8.07     ; G
i 301    2.0     1.0      8.07     ; G
i 301    3.0     0.5      8.07     ; G
i 301    3.5     0.5      8.09     ; A
i 301    4.0     0.5      8.11     ; B
i 301    4.5     1.5      9.00     ; C

i 301    18.0    1.0      8.06     ; F#
i 301    18.0    1.0      8.09     ; A
i 301    19.0    1.0      8.07     ; G
i 301    19.0    1.0      8.04     ; E
i 301    20.0    1.0      8.05     ; F

i 302    1.0     0.5      7.00     ; C
i 302    1.5     0.5      7.02     ; D
i 302    2.0     0.5      7.04     ; E
i 302    2.5     0.5      7.05     ; F
i 302    3.0     2.0      7.05     ; F
i 302    5.0     0.5      7.05     ; F
i 302    5.5     0.5      7.07     ; G

i 302    18.0    1.0      8.00     ; C
i 302    18.0    1.0      8.04     ; E
i 302    19.0    1.0      7.11     ; B
i 302    20.0    1.0      8.00     ; C
i 302    20.0    1.0      7.08     ; G#

t        0 120   10 100   20 120
```

Figure 3.2 Note-list from the score file for the orchestra shown in figure 3.1, a two instrument score in which both parts are listed separately and in which variable tempo is specified.

```
w 0      120   10        100   20          120
i 301    0     0         .5    .2512500    8.05
i 399    0     0         42    22          1
i 301    .5    .25125    1.5   .76875000   8.07
i 302    1     .505      .5    .25625000   7.00
i 302    1.5   .76125    .5    .25874996   7.02
i 301    2     1.02      1     .52499997   8.07
i 302    2     1.02      .5    .26125000   7.04
i 302    2.5   1.28125   .5    .26374995   7.05
i 301    3     1.545     .5    .26625000   8.07
i 302    3     1.545     2     1.0800000   7.05
i 301    3.5   1.81125   .5    .26874995   8.09
i 301    4     2.08      .5    .27125000   8.11
i 301    4.5   2.35125   1.5   .82875030   9.00
i 302    5     2.625     .5    .27625010   7.05
i 302    5.5   2.90125   .5    .27875018   7.07
i 301    18    9.98      1     .51500030   8.06
i 301    18    9.98      1     .51500030   8.09
i 302    18    9.98      1     .51500030   8.00
i 302    18    9.99      1     .51500030   8.04
i 301    19    10.495    1     .50500010   8.07
i 301    19    10.495    1     .50500010   8.04
i 302    19    10.495    1     .50500010   7.11
i 301    20    11        1     .50000000   8.05
i 302    20    11        1     .50000000   8.00
i 302    20    11        1     .50000000   7.08
e
```

Figure 3.3 After compilation, the sorted score file from figure 3.2. Note that the instruments are time and number ordered and that the tempo statement is at the top.

of all this analysis and sorting can be seen in the file *score.srt,* which is produced as a side effect of running Csound. The score in figure 3.2 is shown as written by the user. The score in figure 3.3 is the translated version as it appears in the *score.srt* file.

The sorted and normalized score (reformatted slightly to make it easier to read) is shown in figure 3.3. The most obvious feature of this score is the time-ordering (*p2*) of events. Looking a little closer, you see that there are 6 parameter fields (p-fields) while the original score file only has 4. The additional two fields are the third and fifth, which give the time in seconds of the start time and length of the note. As this score has a nonconstant beat speed, as defined by the **t**-statement, these additional parameters are not such simple values. This form allows Csound to work in seconds, but report the start and end of events in beats, which is easier to relate to the original score. Also, the tempo information in the score's **t**-statement is transformed to the **w**-statement.

Performance

Despite being written in C, Csound is in effect an object-oriented language in its implementation. The instrument definition is, in computer terminology, a *class,* which is used during the performance to create *instances* of the instrument for each "note" that is "played" upon it. Within each of these instances the individual opcodes are also object-like. They are assigned a data area, typically a small amount of memory, which is used to pass arguments between the opcodes. This data area is also reserved for variables associated with that particular instance of the instrument.

Each opcode has two functions associated with it. The first receives the input values and initializes the local variables. Then, for each control period (for each sample at the k-rate) the second function of the opcode is called. A large contributory factor to the speed of Csound is the use of the *control-rate* rather than *audio-rate* for most operations. Since the aim is to render audio signals, the solution is to render all audio rate values in "blocks" of *ksmps* at a time. This allows the domination of the control rate. You can think of the k-rate as the master clock. In fact, audio variables are placed in vectors whose addresses are given in the argument data block.

Thus the main responsibility of the performance system is to schedule the actions required by each note in time order, within each control period and if more than one instrument is active, to perform them in increasing instrument order. When using a score file as input, at each k-rate time, it may be necessary to initialize a number of new notes, deactivate a number of notes and then to call the k-rate functions of all active instruments.

Whenever a new note is to be played, Csound looks to see if there is an instance of the required instrument available, because it was created earlier and is no longer being used. If so, it re-uses this instrument-instance, saving on the overheads of creating the necessary space. If there is no spare created instrument, it makes a new one and outputs the following message:

```
new alloc for instr 301:
```

When a note finishes, the space is retained for a later note on the same instrument. Only at the end of a section are the instruments deallocated. While apparently wasteful, this system saves on the time taken to create new instrument instances and is actually one of the reasons for the speed of Csound. Figure 3.4 shows the typical display from a Csound score and orchestra run.

As you might notice, ends of notes are not always displayed. What the user sees in the display is a report of the score progress as new instruments are allocated, or when new notes are started. This is also because some instruments require internal

```
new alloc for instr 301:
new alloc for instr 399:
B  0.000    ..  0.500  T  0.251  TT  0.251  M:   7997.5   5831.7
B  0.500    ..  1.000  T  0.505  TT  0.505  M:   9882.4   6767.5
new alloc for instr 302:
B  1.000    ..  1.500  T  0.761  TT  0.761  M:   8001.5   15213.6
B  1.500    ..  2.000  T  1.020  TT  1.020  M:   13419.9  18107.3
B  2.000    ..  2.500  T  1.281  TT  1.281  M:   14198.0  25133.5
B  2.500    ..  3.000  T  1.545  TT  1.545  M:   16622.9  25425.0
B  3.000    ..  3.500  T  1.811  TT  1.811  M:   16372.1  16728.2
B  3.500    ..  4.000  T  2.080  TT  2.080  M:   16325.5  16761.4
B  4.000    ..  4.500  T  2.351  TT  2.351  M:   18931.5  20842.4
B  4.500    ..  5.000  T  2.625  TT  2.625  M:   25155.2  22479.2
B  5.000    ..  5.500  T  2.901  TT  2.901  M:   16542.0  22560.7
B  5.500    ..  6.000  T  3.180  TT  3.180  M:   17882.1  25978.8
B  6.000    ..  18.000 T  9.980  TT  9.980  M:   18540.5  18540.5
new alloc for instr 301:
new alloc for instr 302:
B  18.000   ..  19.000 T  10.495 TT  10.495 M:   18262.0  22401.0
B  19.000   ..  20.000 T  11.000 TT  11.000 M:   24652.0  24393.7
B  20.000   ..  21.000 T  11.500 TT  11.500 M:   22107.2  28999.7
B  21.000   ..  42.000 T  22.000 TT  22.000 M:   23660.9  23660.9
```

Figure 3.4 Typical message output during compilation indicating: new instrument allocations (new alloc for *instr 301*); begin time of score events (B 0.000); the duration of the score event (. . 0.500); the current time in this section (T 0.251); the total running time of the piece (TT 0.251) and the maximum amplitude of each channel (M: 7997.5 5831.7).

memory whose size is not known until performance time. In these cases the initialization function itself must allocate the memory. Of course there are internal functions to take care of this, but there may be times when Csound will not run because you have not allocated enough RAM to the application or you do not have enough RAM in your computer.

The other action that could happen at performance-time is the creation of a table. This is rather like playing a note and there are internal functions that create the table. This is described in more detail in a later section.

Messages, Warnings, and Errors

In the process of compiling the Csound orchestra and performing the resulting sounds, the system will most likely produce a number of lines of output. These messages can be divided into three main categories: information, warnings and errors; the last category subdivides into fatal and nonfatal errors.

Information Messages

In common with other computer systems, there are a number of messages that are produced to provide information to the user. Figure 3.5 is an example output from a small Csound rendering.

Every one of the lines in figure 3.5 is an information message. These messages tell us the names and locations of the orchestra and score files (`Csound: Book: ffitch: 303.orc, Csound: Book: ffitch: 303.sco`) and what instrument is defined in it (`instr 303`). It also tells which version of Csound you are using (`MIT Csound: 3.483 (Jul 6 1998)`), where the output was written (`written to Csound:Soundfiles:303.snd (AIFF)`), as well as its size (`87 16384-byte soundblks of shorts`).

Each score event corresponds with a line beginning with the letter B. Each of these lines corresponds with the duration of the event in score-time and real-time, in both the section-time (T) and the overall piece-time (TT). The M information gives the mean amplitude of the score at that event-time. (`B 2.000 .. 3.000 T 3.000 TT 11.000 M: 12426.7`). At the end of each section we are told that instruments are deallocated (`inactive allocs returned to freespace`) and the section peak amp (`end of section 2 sect peak amps: 20606.6`). At the end of the rendering we are reassured from the overall amplitude (`end of score. overall amps: 20606.6`) that the number of samples that were out of range was zero (`overall samples out of range: 0`). Finally, we are told how long it took to compute the file (`**Total Rendering time was: 11.91662 secs`). This information is particularly useful because it is an indication of the system performance. By comparing the time it took to generate the files with the total duration of the file, one can determine if the orchestra and score will run in real-time. For example, in figure 3.5 you can see that the total-time of the score was 16 seconds and the total-rendering-time took only 11.91662 seconds. There are other factors, of course, but given these numbers, this file would probably run in real-time on your system.

There are a number of other information messages that can appear and the command line option *-m* (or the GUI equivalent) can control just how "informative" the system is. It should be noted, however, that if one is attempting to obtain real-time performance, the fewer messages produced, the more time there is for the "performance." Printing, even on a screen, is still slow.

Warning Messages

In computer parlance, a *warning* is a message that suggests that there is a situation of which you should be aware. It might indicate a problem that should be fixed, but

```
orchname: Csound:Book:ffitch:303.orc
scorename: Csound:Book:ffitch:303.sco
sorting score ...
       ... done
orch compiler:
16 lines read
       instr  303
MIT Csound: 3.483 (Jul 6 1998)
(Mills/PPC: 3.4.8a2)
orch now loaded
audio buffered in 8192 sample-frame blocks
writing 16384-byte blks of shorts to Csound:Soundfiles:303.snd (AIFF)
SECTION 1:
ftable 1:
new alloc for instr 303:
B 0.000 .. 2.000 T 2.000 TT 2.000 M: 9373.1
B 2.000 .. 3.000 T 3.000 TT 3.000 M: 12292.8
B 3.000 .. 4.000 T 4.000 TT 4.000 M: 16540.2
end of section 1     sect peak amps: 16540.2
inactive allocs returned to freespace
SECTION 2:
new alloc for instr 303:
B 0.000 .. 4.000 T 4.000 TT 8.000 M: 20606.6
end of section 2     sect peak amps: 20606.6
inactive allocs returned to freespace
SECTION 3:
new alloc for instr 303:
B 0.000 .. 2.000 T 2.000 TT 10.000 M: 9810.3
B 2.000 .. 3.000 T 3.000 TT 11.000 M: 12426.7
B 3.000 .. 4.000 T 4.000 TT 12.000 M: 16152.1
end of section 3     sect peak amps: 16152.1
inactive allocs returned to freespace
SECTION 4:
new alloc for instr 303:
B 0.000 .. 4.000 T 4.000 TT 16.000 M: 19692.0
end of section 4     sect peak amps: 19692.0
end of score.        overall amps: 20606.6
       overall samples out of range: 0
0 errors in performance
87 16384-byte soundblks of shorts written to Csound:Soundfiles:303.snd (AIFF)

**Total Rendering time was: 11.91662 secs
reopened 303.snd for playing
```

Figure 3.5 Complete output of a simple score indicating source directories, Csound version, instrument allocation, event onset times, amplitudes, samples-out-of-range and errors in performance.

if left unaddressed, the results would still be valid and the job would still run. The most common warning message is one pointing out that there have been some samples out of range. Samples out of range means that the requested amplitude was greater than the resolution of the DAC. For instance, if you are writing 16-bit samples, then the maximum value that can be represented is 2^{16} or 32,768. When Csound computes notes, it sums their amplitudes. If two notes sounding at the same time each had an amplitude of 20000, the output amplitude would be 40000 and result in a warning message that there were 102972 samples out of range as in *304.orc.* Typically, if this number is small, indicating that there are only a few samples out of range, you might decide not to do anything about it, even if there were a slight reduction in audio quality and noticeable clicks or crackling. The program is offering advice that a reduction in amplitude might be warranted. Of course, if the number of samples that are too large in magnitude is a significant proportion of the audio output, the resulting audio may be so distorted as to be useless.

Other typical warning messages include remarks that input samples or analysis files have finished before the instrument using them finished playing. Again, this may be what you wanted, or it may indicate a mis-calculation and you would want to increase the size of the input sample or the length of the analysis file.

What you should do with these warnings is to look at them and convince yourself that the situation is what you expected, or is acceptable. If it is neither of these, then it is worth some investigation into the source of the warning. You might then choose to remove the cause of the warning, or perhaps realize that it is acceptable after all. In figure 3.6 the number of samples out of range is reasonably small and so you might choose to live with the added grunge. Alternatively, reducing the amplitude of one of the instruments playing between times 1 and 5.5 in the score might prove the correct action in this case to reduce the noticeable distortion.

Another warning that is frequently seen is the "`pmax = ... note pcnt = ...`" message that appears when there is a mismatch between the number of p-fields provided by a score and the number of p-fields used in an instrument.

For example, figure 3.7 warns us that the first line in the score for *instr 309* provides a value for *p7* even though the instrument only uses up to *p6.* It also warns that *instr 307* requires parameters up to and including *p4,* while the score only provided 3. Other warnings are indicated as well. As with all warnings, you should verify that this is what you wanted or expected and consider correcting the situation.

Error Messages

Error messages indicate that something is definitely wrong and corrections are needed. Most (but not all) errors will lead to the premature stopping of the pro-

```
orchname: Csound:Book:ffitch:304.orc
scorename: Csound:Book:ffitch:304.sco
sorting score ...
       ... done
orch compiler:
19 lines read
       instr  304
       instr  305
MIT Csound: 3.483 (Jul 15 1998)
(Mills/PPC: 3.4.8a3)
orch now loaded
audio buffered in 8192 sample-frame blocks
writing 16384-byte blks of shorts to Csound:Soundfiles:304.snd (AIFF)
SECTION 1:
ftable 1:
new alloc for instr 304:
B 0.000 .. 0.500 T 0.250 TT 0.250 M: 15861.2
new alloc for instr 305:
B 0.500 .. 1.000 T 0.500 TT 0.500 M: 27514.9
new alloc for instr 304:
B 1.000 .. 1.500 T 0.750 TT 0.750 M: 37372.7
        number of samples out of range: 20
new alloc for instr 305:
B 1.500 .. 2.000 T 1.000 TT 1.000 M: 36577.8
        number of samples out of range: 54
new alloc for instr 304:
B 2.000 .. 2.500 T 1.250 TT 1.250 M: 40464.4
        number of samples out of range: 111
new alloc for instr 305:
B 2.500 .. 3.000 T 1.500 TT 1.500 M: 39064.1
        number of samples out of range: 55
new alloc for instr 304:
B 3.000 .. 3.500 T 1.750 TT 1.750 M: 51162.4
        number of samples out of range: 366
new alloc for instr 305:
B 3.500 .. 5.500 T 2.750 TT 2.750 M: 49288.0
        number of samples out of range: 617
B 5.500 .. 7.500 T 3.750 TT 3.750 M: 15807.4
B 7.500 .. 8.000 T 4.000 TT 4.000 M: 8073.8
B 8.000 .. 9.000 T 4.500 TT 4.500 M: 815.1
B 9.000 .. 9.500 T 4.750 TT 4.750 M: 0.0
B 9.500 .. 12.500 T 6.250 TT 6.250 M: 0.0
end of score.          overall amps: 51162.4
        overall samples out of range: 1223
0 errors in performance
34 16384-byte soundblks of shorts written to Csound:Soundfiles:304.snd (AIFF)
```

Figure 3.6 Messages from *304.orc.* Note the error message indicating "samples out of range" in *instr 304* and *instr 305.*

```
orchname: Csound:Book:ffitch:305.orc
scorename: Csound:Book:ffitch:305.sco
sorting score ...
       ... done
orch compiler:
55 lines read
       instr  307
       instr  308
       instr  309
       instr  310
MIT Csound: 3.483 (Jul 15 1998)
(Mills/PPC: 3.4.8a3)
orch now loaded
audio buffered in 8192 sample-frame blocks
writing 32768-byte blks of shorts to Csound:Soundfiles:305.snd (AIFF)
SECTION 1:
ftable 1:
ftable 11:
ftable 51:
ftable 52:
new alloc for instr 308:
B 0.000 .. 1.000 T 1.000 TT 1.000 M: 3686.9 3686.9
new alloc for instr 309:
WARNING: instr 309 pmax = 6, note pcnt = 7
B 1.000 .. 2.000 T 2.000 TT 2.000 M: 7797.4 7423.2
new alloc for instr 307:
WARNING: instr 307 pmax = 4, note pcnt = 3
B 2.000 .. 3.000 T 3.000 TT 3.000 M: 11579.7 13208.2
new alloc for instr 309:
WARNING: instr 309 pmax = 6, note pcnt = 7
B 3.000 .. 4.000 T 4.000 TT 4.000 M: 17053.1 15530.3
new alloc for instr 309:
WARNING: instr 309 pmax = 6, note pcnt = 7
B 4.000 .. 5.000 T 5.000 TT 5.000 M: 16912.9 14230.5
new alloc for instr 310:
new alloc for instr 310:
WARNING: instr 310 pmax = 4, note pcnt = 3
B 5.000 .. 5.100 T 5.100 TT 5.100 M: 20522.9 17494.9
B 5.100 .. 5.200 T 5.200 TT 5.200 M: 16204.1 12399.1
B 5.200 .. 5.300 T 5.300 TT 5.300 M: 16392.6 11418.4
B 5.300 .. 5.400 T 5.400 TT 5.400 M: 20373.0 15302.8
B 5.400 .. 5.500 T 5.500 TT 5.500 M: 20727.0 16972.2
B 5.500 .. 5.600 T 5.600 TT 5.600 M: 15574.4 11174.1
B 5.600 .. 5.700 T 5.700 TT 5.700 M: 23788.3 19189.1
B 5.700 .. 7.000 T 7.000 TT 7.000 M: 16765.4 11694.7
B 7.000 .. 7.100 T 7.100 TT 7.100 M: 27350.8 23295.1
B 7.100 .. 10.000 T 10.000 TT 10.000 M: 16147.2 14967.6
B 10.000 .. 11.000 T 11.000 TT 11.000 M: 12579.9 15027.0
B 11.000 .. 12.000 T 12.000 TT 12.000 M: 10018.8 9908.6
B 12.000 .. 13.000 T 13.000 TT 13.000 M: 5018.3 4896.6
B 13.000 .. 14.000 T 14.000 TT 14.000 M: 30.6 26.2
end of score.        overall amps: 27350.8 23295.1
        overall samples out of range: 0 0
0 errors in performance
76 32768-byte soundblks of shorts written to Csound:Soundfiles:305.snd (AIFF)
```

Figure 3.7 Message from *305.orc* showing warning message indicating both missing and additional p-fields.

gram—the so-called *fatal errors.* Error messages are generally explicit as to the cause of the problem and should give you a good idea of what is required to correct the situation. From the description earlier in this chapter, it is hoped you will have a good idea at what stage of the Csound compilation and performance process the error was detected. Fatal errors include missing or unreadable orchestra files, missing tables for instruments, detected at initialization of notes and thus the incorrect skipping of initialization of an instrument. In the nonfatal cases either a default value is used or an individual note may be deleted. There is a complete and annotated list of Csound messages in the appendix.

Conclusion

In this chapter, an initial glimpse at the internal structure of the Csound program has been given. There is a great deal more to learn if you wish to become a Csound programming expert. Still, I hope that I provided you with sufficient clues to start you off on your investigation. If you decide that you do not want to look any further, I hope that this preliminary view at the underlying structure of the program will help you better understanding the warnings, errors and other messages that Csound presents and assist you as you debug your scores and develop your instruments. Good luck.

Common Messages and their Explanation

An experienced Csound user comes to recognize the familiar informational messages and also is familiar with a number of common error messages. Here is presented a guide to my "favorite" messages and what they might mean. Note that the words in *italics* will be replaced by numbers, strings or characters as indicated.

Also, do remember that:

- **Fatal**—messages of this class cause Csound to stop, as they are irrecoverable.
- **Error**—messages indicate an error, usually of the user getting something wrong in an opcode. They do not cause Csound to stop but the individual note may stop, or other similar patch-up is taken. Errors in the parsing of the orchestra may cause Csound to refuse to run.
- **Warning**—messages are not necessarily errors, but indicate that there may be something wrong. The user should ensure that they are expecting this situation, or correct for later runs.

- **Information** messages are printed by Csound as it runs. These include the names of the orchestra file, number of instruments and so on. They are mainly for reassurance, but they can also indicate small errors.

Message	**Type**
note deleted. I*integer* had *integer* init errors	Information
note deleted. instr *integer*(*integer*) undefined	Information

As a result of previous errors (in the first case initialization errors in some opcode of the instrument and in the second case because the requested instrument does not exist), the note event has been deleted. The required actions are to correct the initialization error, define the instrument, or correct the typing error in the score.

Message	**Type**
audio_in string has *integer* chnls, orch *integer* chnls	Information
audio_in string has sr = *integer*, orch sr = *integer*	Information

While reading an input audio file, there were some inconsistencies noticed, with the orchestra having a different sampling rate or a different number of channels. This could be what was meant, but could indicate a problem.

Message	**Type**
cannot load *string*, or SADIR undefined	Fatal

The system failed to load an analysis file; it could not find it; or the SADIR environment parameter was not set to say where the analysis files are stored.

cannot open *string* for writing	Fatal

The names file could not be written. This could indicate a problem with the host-computer's file-system, or a file being open by another program.

deferred size for GEN1 only	Fatal
deferred size, but filesize unknown	Fatal
deferred size ftable *float* illegal here	Fatal

These three messages refer to the method of deferring the allocation of space for a table until the data are ready. This is only available for tables generated by method 1 and for it to work, the size of the input file must be determinable. An attempt to use a "deferred table" before it is properly filled will also give an error.

`error in score. Illegal opcode` *char* `(ASCII` *integer*`)`	`Error`

In the score file a command was found that was not known. This is usually because an older version of Csound is being used that does not have, for example, the **b** command, or because the score file is corrupted; sometimes this happens when a DOS file is fed to a UNIX system.

`ERROR: line` *integer.* `Unknown label:`	`Error`

In the orchestra, a reference was made to a label that was not defined. This is usually due to a typing error. Correct the label name and re-render. It could also indicate that the text defining the instrument was not complete.

`ERROR: illegal character` *char*`(`*hex*`) in scoreline:`	`Error`

A character was found in the score that was not recognized. Arguments to score events are typically numbers, strings or one of the special ramp and carry indicators. The character that was not recognized is printed, both as a character and in hexadecimal code in case it was unprintable.

`ERROR: too many pfields:`	`Error`

The score attempted to use more that the permitted maximum number of arguments to an instrument or table. This maximum is currently 800 for most systems, but it might be more or less depending on local modifications.

`Ftable does not exist`	`Fatal`

An attempt was made to reference a table that was not defined. This is often a simple user error, in not providing a table that an instrument taken from some other orchestra requires. Of course, it could also be a typing error. Find and correct.

`Ftable` *integer* `now deleted`	`Information`

This message is not so disastrous as it sounds. The score has called for a table to be removed so the memory it occupies can be recycled. It should have been expected.

`FTERROR, ftable` *integer:*	`Information`

This message precedes a number of error messages concerning the creation of f-tables.

`Gen call has illegal x-ordinate values:`	`Fatal`
`Gen call has negative segment size:`	`Fatal`

In GEN17 there are restrictions on the x-values; for instance, they must be in ascending order. In GEN5 and GEN7 segments of the curve must be positive in size.

`GEN01: AIFF file truncated by ftable size`	`Warning`
`GEN01: input file truncated by ftable size`	`Warning`

GEN1 reads in a sound file. If the file is larger that the user-specified table-size then this message occurs. It could be expected or acceptable, or it may indicate a user error in ignoring part of the input sound.

`illegal ftable number`	`Fatal`
`illegal gen number`	`Fatal`
`illegal instr number`	`Error`
`illegal no. of output args`	`Fatal`
`illegal table length`	`Fatal`

There are restrictions on a number of Csound's parameters and arguments; for example, table numbers need to be positive integers. Orchestra/scores that break these rules will be rewarded with one of these messages.

`inconsistent sr, kr, ksmps`	`Fatal`

The variables **sr**, **kr** and **ksmps** must satisfy the equation **kr** * **ksmps** = **sr**. If this constraint is not satisfied, one sees this error message. The corrective action is to change one of the variables, or to omit one so that the default values take over.

`Increasing number of tables from` *integer* `to` *integer*	`Information`

When Csound starts, the number of tables accepted is set to a smallish number (typically 300), but if a table of a larger number is used, then the space grows to accommodate the new table. This message indicates that this expansion has occurred.

`instr` *integer* `had` *integer* `init errors`	`Information`

This message summarizes the errors that occurred in the initialization of the numbered instrument.

`instr` *integer* `pmax =` *integer*, `note pcnt =` *integer*	`Warning`

This warning indicates that the instrument used *pmax* arguments but *pcnt* were provided by the score and that these two values were different. The action is either to fix the score or to fix the orchestra.

`instr` *integer* `redefined`	`Fatal`

Instruments cannot be redefined. This error message usually indicates a problem in merging two orchestras.

`instr` *integer* `seeking MIDI chnl data, no chnl assigned`	`Warning`

An instrument has been scheduled that needs a MIDI channel that has not been assigned. The user needs to review the channels being used and their assignments.

`Insufficient args`	`Fatal`
`Insufficient args and no file header`	`Error`
`Insufficient arguments`	`Fatal`
`Insufficient gen arguments`	`Fatal`

Although these messages seem similar, they arise in a number of different contexts. The first of this group comes from the arguments to an f-table, while the third is from the command-line argument decoding. This shows that is not just sufficient to read the message, but that one also needs to be aware of the stage at which it is generated.

`Integer errors in performance`	Information

At the end of a performance, a count of the number of performance-time errors encountered is printed. This is a summary of the earlier messages.

`Integer integer-byte soundblks of format written to file (WAV)`	Information
`Integer integer-byte soundblks of format written to file (AIFF)`	Information
`Integer integer-byte soundblks of format written to file (IRCAM)`	Information

At the end of a sound rendering, a message like one of these is produced to say how much sound was produced, in what format and to which file it was written.

`Integer syntax errors in orchestra. compilation invalid`	Information

Another summarizing message following errors in the syntax of an orchestra. The earlier messages say what the problems are.

`Memory allocate failure for integer`	Fatal

An internal error occurred when attempting to get some more memory. It is usually the case that the user has made inordinate demands on the system, with large tables, multiple delay lines, or similar excessive uses.

`MIDI channel integer using instr integer`	Information

Just reporting the association between MIDI channels and Csound instruments.

`Missing endin`	Fatal

An instrument has not been properly terminated in the orchestra. You must terminate your instruments with an **endin** statement. This indicates a serious error with the orchestra and Csound cannot continue.

`new alloc for instr integer:`	Information

Each note-event requires a small data-block to maintain the information from one control-period to the next. When a note terminates, the space is not returned to the central pool, but retained for subsequent use by the same instrument, or until the end of a section. When there is no suitable data-block for a new note, this message displays to show simultaneous use of the instrument. It is usually ignorable, but it does show the level of multiple invocation of the instrument and can help when looking for samples-out-of-range.

`no MIDIfile name`	Fatal
`no orchestra name`	Fatal
`no outfilename`	Fatal

In argument decoding, names were missing although they had been indicated. A user error.

`no -s and no soundheader, using sr default` *integer*	Information
`no soundin header, presuming orchestra sr`	Warning

In reading a sound file, there was no indication in the file of the correct sampling rate. Csound takes a default value from the orchestra's **sr** and reports it. This could result in some curious transpositions and you might want to adjust the rates so that they agree with each other.

`null iopadr`	Fatal
`null opadr`	Fatal

Internal errors in preparing an instrument for performance led to some internal structures being empty. Apart from system errors, this can happen with incorrect use of **goto** statements.

`Output arg` *string* `illegal type`	Fatal

The output variable was not of acceptable type for the opcode. Type here refers to **i**-, **k**- or **a**-rate variables, as well as the spectral **w**- type.

`Output name previously used, type` *char* `must be uniquely defined`	Fatal

For d- and w- variables there are additional restrictions that mean they cannot be reused. This message reports a violation of that rule.

`perf-pass statements illegal in header blk`	Fatal

Only a certain number of initialization opcodes can occur outside any instrument, in the header block. An attempt to use a **k**- or **a**- rate opcode in the header will give rise to this message. A common problem is using = rather than **init** in the header.

`Pvanal: frameSize must be 2^r`	Fatal

In the phase vocoder analysis utility, the frameSize parameter must be a power of 2. It is set with the –n option on the command line.

`PVOC ktimpnt truncated to last frame`	Warning
`PVOC timpnt < 0`	Error

The first of these says that the analysis file for use by the phase vocoder opcode was shorter that the input sound, so it was truncated. The second of these is the error produced by an attempt to use a negative time pointer.

Replacing previous ftable *integer*	Information

F-tables can be replaced at any time by alternative ones, by using the second argument that says when the table is required. The message marks a replacement in case it was not intended.

Sample rate overrides: esr = *float*, ekr = *float*, ksmps = *integer*	Information

At least one of the sample rates has been overridden by a command-line switch.

Sfinit: cannot open *string*	Fatal

The named soundfile could not be opened.

`skip time larger than audio data,substituting zero.`	Warning

In the **diskin** opcode, the part of the soundfile skipped is longer that the duration of the sample, so a skip time of zero is used instead.

`Skipping meta event type` *hex*	Information

Csound does not know what to do with the particular MIDI meta event. It is ignored with this message.

`Soundfile write returned bytecount of` *integer,* `not` *integer*	Information

The system had detected that the data written to a sound file were not accepted. The common reason for this is that the file system is full. One should never forget the size of audio files, especially at CD sampling rates and in stereo or more channels.

`Soundin can't find` *string* `in its search paths`	Error
`Soundin cannot open` *string*	Error

These are both failures to read a soundfile, either because it could not be found, or having found it, the opening of the file failed.

`sread: illegally placed string, sect` *integer* `line` *integer*	Error

A string was found in the score where it is not allowed, particularly in the first three arguments of a note-event.

`sread: instr pcount exceeds PMAX`	Error

In the score, an instrument was detected with more arguments than is allowed. The value of PMAX is typically 800.

`sread: requesting more memory`	Information

Just an indication that the score is larger than the space allocated allows, so the space is expanded.

`sread: unexpected char` *char,* `sect` *integer* `line` *integer*	Error

The reported character in the particular section and line is not one that is allowed in a score file. Look at the score and it should be apparent what caused the problem.

`swrite: output, sect` *integer* `line` *integer* `p` *integer* `has illegally terminated` *string*	Error

In writing out the score for sorting into time order, an unterminated string was detected. The section and line are given in the message to assist in finding the problem.

`time advanced` *float* `beats by score request`	Information

A score **a**-statement has advanced time; this message reports that this has happened.

`too many allocs`	Fatal

This rather cryptic message indicates that the program has run out of memory and will stop. One could purchase more memory, reconfigure the machine, or more probably check why the orchestra and score used such a large amount. It could be that a number of large tables are being used.

`too many arguments`	Fatal

The command line that invoked Csound called for more that two files. The first should have been the orchestra; the second should have been the score; so what are the others files? One possible reason is the omission of a command-line flag character "**-**".

`too many arguments to macro`	Error

A macro in either the orchestra or score can only have up to five arguments. This indicates that the orchestra or score needs some simplification.

`twarp: t has non-positive tempo`	Error

All Csound scores are subjected to time warping, which is applying the variations in tempo indicated by a **t**-statement. This cannot work if the tempo is negative or zero. Almost certainly a user error.

`Unknown opcode`	Fatal

The orchestra seemed to want to use an opcode that was not recognized by the parser. This is usually a typing error, or a problem with new versions.

`Unknown sound format` *`integer`*`(0x`*`hex`*`)`	Fatal

Csound can recognize a number of different sound formats (signed and unsigned characters, ulaw bytes, shorts, longs and floats), but the one used is not one of the set. The integer printed in both decimal and hexadecimal is an indication of the format found, which is helpful to a system debugger if this message is unexpected.

Coda

There are of course many more messages than these and each individual composer's style of use tends to generate a personal pattern of errors. So your messages may not be in this set, but there are general lessons to be learnt about the kinds of errors that exist and how they are reported. I hope this enumeration has given you some additional insight into the workings of the program and its sometimes ambiguous utterances.

4 Optimizing Your Csound Instruments

Paris Smaragdis

Even though Csound is a fast and highly optimized synthesis language, inefficiencies in instrument design can force it to be slow. Since modern computer hardware allows us just barely to reach the level of performance of modern synthesizers, it is important that the code be as efficient as possible. It's not too difficult even to double the performance of a Csound orchestra simply by rewriting the code and eliminating clutter. This chapter is about writing efficient instruments and taking full advantage of Csound's power.

How the Orchestra Works

In order to see how we can optimize an orchestra's performance, it is useful to know how it will be rendered by the Csound program. In Csound, the orchestra is executed in a loop-like fashion. Every line of the orchestra that is part of an active instrument is being executed repeatedly so that it continues to generate new samples. In fact, the only parts of the orchestra that are not part of that loop are the **i**-time expressions. It should be evident that if we were to remove even one line from the instrument body, we could save the many executions of this line that would take place while the instrument was "playing."

Optimization

It is important at this point to make the distinction between lines and operations. Even though the line count is a rough indication of efficiency, it is by no means sufficient. A line of code can include from one to tens of operations. Optimizing is

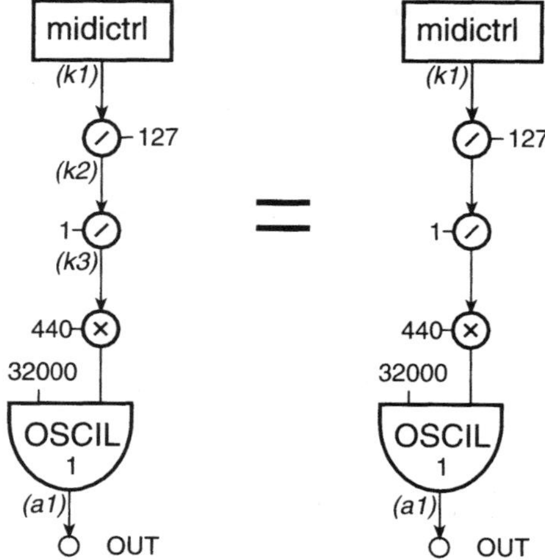

Figure 4.1 Block diagram of *instr 401* and *instr 402* illustrating "in-line" coding.

about reducing that number of operations or replacing them with faster equivalents, not reducing the number of lines. Consider the two instruments shown in figure 4.1 and 4.2.

Even though *instr 402* "looks" faster and more concise, it computes at the same speed as *instr 401.* That is because the number of operations remains the same, despite the fact that there are fewer lines. If we wanted to optimize this instrument we would attempt to reduce the number of operations, as shown in figures 4.3 and 4.4. In this case we have combined the two division operations into one. Taking advantage of algebraic expressions is always an excellent way of removing redundant operations.

In fact, operation reduction, as described above, is one way of optimizing code that applies to most languages. Csound, however, is a high-level language that has a lot of features "under the hood." It is important that we know something about the internals of the code, so that we can optimize with greater success. It is often the case that there are two opcodes that do the same thing, with one being much faster than the other. Substituting the more efficient opcode will of course improve performance. This is knowledge that is not easy to gain. Furthermore, it changes as new versions of Csound and new hardware platforms become available. Tips that incorporate that knowledge will be shown in some of the following sections.

The rest of the chapter will be in the form of a checklist, in no particular order, that contains some standard tips for improving performance.

```
     instr      401        ; SIMPLE (& SLOW) MIDI
k1   midictrl   1                             ; READ A MIDI CONTROLLER
k2   =          k1/127                        ; SCALE IT ...
k3   =          1/k2                          ; INVERT IT ...
a1   oscil      32000, 440*k3, 1              ; AND USE IT
     out        a1
     endin

     instr      402        ; SIMPLE (& SLOW) MIDI
k1   midictrl   1                             ; READ THE MIDI CONTROLLER AGAIN
a1   oscil      32000, 440*1/(k1/127), 1      ; SCALE, INVERT, SQUARE & USE IT
     out        a1                            ; ... IN ONE LINE!
     endin
```

Figure 4.2 Orchestra code, two equally slow MIDI instruments. In *instr 401* **k**-rate expressions are evaluated on individual lines. In *instr 402,* expressions are evaluated in opcode arguments.

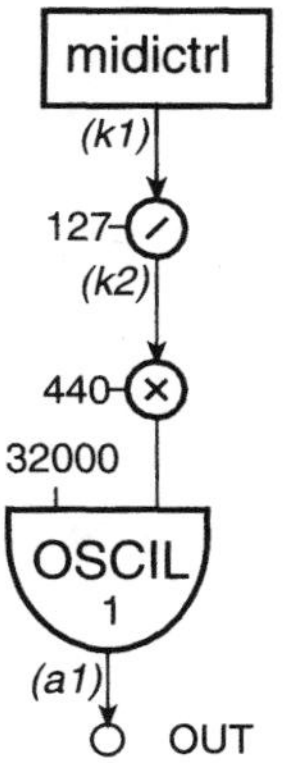

Figure 4.3 Block diagram of *instr 403,* an optimized MIDI instrument.

```
     instr      403        ; SIMPLE OPTIMIZED MIDI
k1   midictrl   1                       ; READ THE CONTROLLER
k2   =          127/k1                  ; FUSE THE TWO DIVISIONS INTO ONE
a1   oscil      32000, 440*k2, 1        ; NOW USE IT
     out        a1
     endin
```

Figure 4.4 Orchestra code for *instr 403,* an optimized MIDI instrument in which the number of computations are reduced by fusing the 2 divisions into 1.

The Optimization Checklist

Optimize the Rates

The easiest way to get better performance with minimal effort is to adjust the sampling and control rates. These two rates offer a performance/quality tradeoff. Even though expert users can select the right combination of rates on the first try, the decision may not be as clear for newer users.

The sampling rate is the most important rate since this is the speed at which the orchestra will operate. If the sampling rate is high then the computer works harder; if it is lower then computation is more relaxed. This would be an easy optimization if there were not any other factor involved. But the sampling rate has to be at least twice as high as the highest audio frequency you wish to generate. If not, then unwanted effects can appear and the sound quality will not be as good.

The high end of our frequency hearing range is around 20000 Hz, which would seem to require that we use a sampling rate of at least 40000. Not all sounds, however, include frequencies as high as that and we can often take advantage of information to improve performance. If you make use of instruments that do not have high-frequency content and you have performance problems, then you can afford to lower the sampling rate.

If you are playing back a cymbal, then you would require almost all the range of audible frequencies in order to have an accurate rendition and the sampling rate would have to be high (such as 40000). But if you are synthesizing an acoustic bass, you can use a much lower sampling rate (22050 or even 11025), since the sound will most likely not contain higher frequencies. Many well known commercial synthesizers use sampling rates lower that the ideal 40000 and still sound great. Do not be tricked into believing that you must use a high sampling rate to get better quality; always let your ears be your guide.

Just to give a feel for how the sampling rate should look: common values start from 8000 and go as high as 48000. Numbers outside that region will either produce low-quality sound or slow performance. Using a sampling rate greater than 48000 is redundant since additional quality would be inaudible. The in-between sampling rates are not always arbitrary numbers. Sound hardware usually handles the following standard sampling rates: 8000, 11025, 22050, 32000 and 44100. Using other values might result in soundfiles that are not playable from mainstream hardware and software.

The control rate has a more subtle effect and a more involved explanation. In order to increase efficiency, Csound can compute more than one sample when an operation is called. It can generate more than one output sample during every iteration and gain in performance. The effect of this is impressive. If the control rate is equal to the sampling rate then we have the worst possible performance. You should never use this setting unless you have a strong reason to do so. If the control rate is set to half the sampling rate performance can improve by 60%. Usual settings have the control rate ranging from one-tenth to one-hundredth of the sampling rate. Such settings will speed up your instrument by more than 400%.

Avoid Interpolating Opcodes

In order to deal with memory constraints on older computers, Csound offers a set of interpolating opcodes (**oscili, foscili, tablei,** etc.). These opcodes perform additional computation so that we can use small f-tables, which usually offer low sound quality, and get the sound quality of large f-tables. In all modern computers, however, there is sufficient memory to render such opcodes useless. By using the original versions of the opcodes, instead of the interpolating versions, the performance improvements can start from to 8% and go up to 30% per oscillator. The only change you need to perform in your code for this optimization is to remove the "**i**" character after **oscili, foscili** and **tablei.**

Use Specialized Opcodes

A common problem is that new users tend to implement certain synthesis techniques by using many simple opcodes. Even though this approach has a strong educational value, it is always inefficient. Csound is a big synthesis language that offers specialized opcodes for a variety of synthesis methods. Before you implement a synthesis method look at the manual and see if an opcode for it exists. Performance gains by using specialized opcodes can range from 20% (for simple FM instruments) to even more than 1000% (for FOF or granular synthesis).

Use the Lowest Variable Rate Possible

Csound opcodes are optimized to work with different rate variables and you always get better performance if you use the lowest rate. Consider for example, the following instrument that implements a simple vibrato, as shown in figures 4.5 and 4.6.

In this example we observed that the vibrato signal was not so fast as to be **a**-rate and we changed it to **k**-rate. Internally, the **oscil** opcode will be more efficient, since it would be using a lower rate variable. Similarly, if you have **k**-rate variables that do not change over time, you can get performance gains by changing them to **i**-rate.

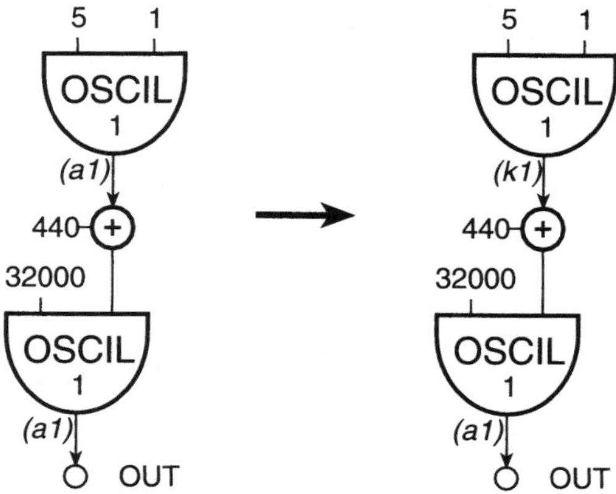

Figure 4.5 Block diagram of *instr 404* and *instr 405*, comparing **a**-rate with **k**-rate vibrato.

```
        instr   404             ; A-RATE VIBRATO
a1      oscil   5, 1, 1                 ; GENERATE THE VIBRATO
a2      oscil   32000, 440+a1, 1        ; USE IT ON AN OSCILLATOR
        out     a2                      ; AND PLAY THE RESULT
        endin

        instr   405             ; K-RATE VIBRATO
k1      oscil   5, 1, 1                 ; GENERATE THE VIBRATO IN K-RATE!
a1      oscil   32000, 440+k1, 1        ; USE IT ON AN OSCILLATOR
        out     a1                      ; AND PLAY THE RESULT
        endin
```

Figure 4.6 Orchestra code for *instr 404,* an inefficient **a**-rate vibrato instrument compared with *instr 405,* and an efficient **k**-rate vibrato instrument.

Eliminate Redundant Operations

Sometimes instruments have many redundant operations. It is common to generate a signal in a certain range and then later to scale it. It is always more efficient to try and generate all signals in the form you want to use them so that they will not have to go through extra processing. For example, consider the instrument in figure 4.7.

Now we have saved one multiplication. Of course you need to be careful when performing this optimization. If *k1* in the above example were used again with a different scaling, then it would not be possible to do this.

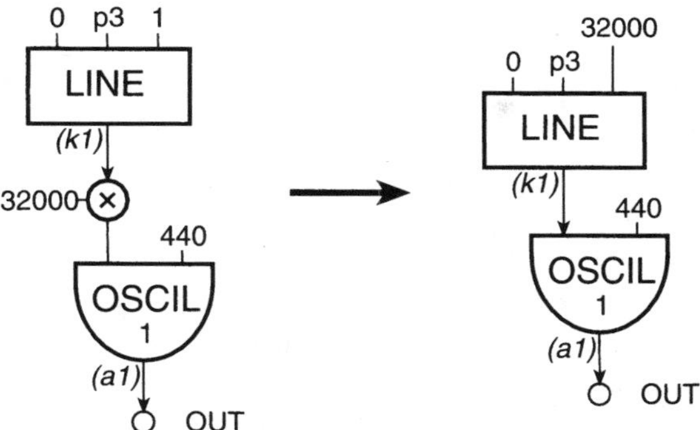

Figure 4.7 Block diagram of *instr 406* and *instr 407*, comparing inefficient and efficient amplitude scaling.

```
    instr  406             ; INEFFICIENT AMPLITUDE SCALING
k1  line   0, p3, 1              ; GENERATE ENVELOPE SCALED BETWEEN 0 AND 1
a1  oscil  32000*k1, 440, 1      ; SCALE IT AND APPLY IT ON AN OSCILLATOR
    out    a1                    ; AND PLAY THE RESULT
    endin

    instr  407             ; EFFICIENT AMPLITUDE SCALING
k1  line   0, p3, 32000          ; GENERATE THE ENVELOPE SCALED THIS TIME
a1  oscil  k1, 440, 1            ; NOW APPLY IT ON THE OSCILLATOR
    out    a1                    ; AND PLAY THE RESULT
    endin
```

Figure 4.8 Orchestra code comparing *instr 406*, an instrument with inefficiently scaled envelope to *instr 407*, an instrument with envelope scaled efficiently by setting the scale directly as an opcode argument.

Precompute Unnecessary Computations

Most synthesis methods offer more control than we want and we often do not take full advantage of an instrument. If we do not make full use the inputs of every opcode, it suggests that we could use something more efficient. Here is a simple example using FM synthesis. If we do not use a varying modulation index and a varying frequency ratio then we are generating a constant waveform, which we can do much faster. In figure 4.9 we show a basic FM instrument in which *f 1* is a sine.

In the instrument shown in figure 4.10, *f 1* is a frequency modulated sine wave. Thus performance improvements can start at 18% and go up very substantially.

```
     instr    408            ; REDUNDANT FM
a1   oscil    32000, 440, 1          ; GENERATE THE MODULATING SIGNAL
a2   oscil    32000, 440+a1, 1       ; GENERATE THE MODULATED CARRIER SIGNAL
     out      a2                     ; AND PLAY THE OUTPUT
     endin
```

Figure 4.9 Orchestra code for *instr 408,* an instrument illustrating redundant oscillator calculation.

```
    instr  409         ; OPTIMIZED STATIC FM
a1  oscil  32000, 440, 1  ; READ FROM A TABLE CONTAINING MODULATED SIGNAL
    out    a1             ; AND PLAY THE OUTPUT
    endin
```

Figure 4.10 Orchestra code for *instr 409,* an optimized static FM instrument that reads a precomputed wavetable.

Use Value Converters Instead of Table Lookups

A standard optimization trick in computer science is to use table lookup instead of function calls. While in most programming languages, table lookup is faster than a function call, in Csound this is not true.

In figure 4.12, *f 2* is a sine wave. The overhead of table lookup is much greater than the direct computation of the sine function. Performance improvement depends on the value converter but it can scale up to twice as fast.

Use Multiplication Instead of Division

It is well known that computers are slower at performing division than multiplication. We can take advantage of that to perform a simple optimization. Expressions that divide a signal can be altered to use multiplication of the inverse as shown in figure 4.13.

Performance improvement is not great, but when used consistently such an alteration can make a significant difference, especially if Csound is run on special purpose hardware such as digital-signal-processing (DSP) boards.

Use Linear Segments Instead of Exponential Segments

If there is no special reason not to do so, you can replace exponential segment opcodes such as **expseg** and **expon** with their linear counterparts **linseg** and **line**. This is a dangerous optimization, since it will change the way the instruments sound; but

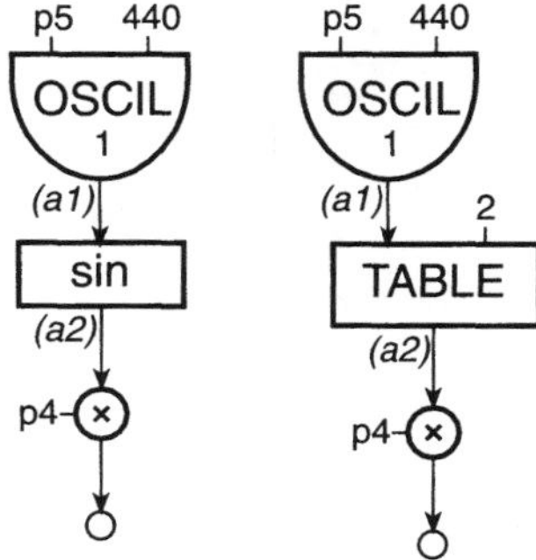

Figure 4.11 Block diagram of *instr 410* and *instr 411,* comparing efficient function calls using Csound's value converters to Csound's more inefficient table look-up.

```
        instr   410            ; USING FUNCTION CALLS
a1      oscil   p5, 440, 1            ; GENERATE A SIGNAL
a2      =       sin(a1)               ; USE A VALUE CONVERTER
        out     a2*p4                 ; AND PLAY THE OUTPUT
        endin

        instr   411            ; USING TABLE-LOOKUP
a1      oscil   p5, 440, 1            ; GENERATE THE SIGNAL
a2      table   a1, 2                 ; USE TABLE LOOKUP TO COMPUTE THE SINE
        out     a2*p4                 ; AND PLAY THE OUTPUT
        endin
```

Figure 4.12 Orchestra code for *instr 410* and *instr 411,* one using Csound's value converters and function calls whereas the other is using inefficient table-lookup.

if sound fidelity has to be sacrificed for performance, this can be one of the first optimizations to take place. Usually the linear opcode is much faster than the exponential version.

Use Fewer Variables

Even though this seems like a memory optimization problem, it also affects performance. Consider the instruments shown in figures 4.15, 4.16, and 4.17. These compare the use of dedicated unique output variables to the reuse of many fewer output variables.

Every time we call *instr 414,* Csound has to allocate space for the five variables called for by this instrument design. Such allocation can be a time-consuming operation, especially in the case of audio variables. Also, since it takes place at an impor-

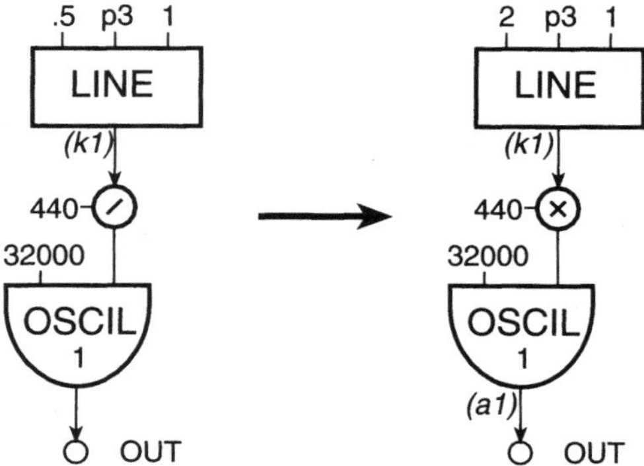

Figure 4.13 Block diagram of *instr 412* and *instr 413,* comparing inefficient division to efficient multiplication.

```
     instr   412            ; USING DIVISION
k1   line    .5, p3, 1                ; GENERATE AN ENVELOPE
a1   oscil   32000, 440/k1, 1         ; APPLY IT ON AN OSCILLATOR
     out     a1                       ; AND PLAY THE RESULT
     endin

     instr   413            ; USING MULTIPLICATION
k1   line    2, p3, 1                 ; GENERATE THE INVERSE OF THE ENVELOPE
a1   oscil   32000, 440*k1, 1         ; APPLY IT WITH MULTIPLICATION ...
     out     a1                       ; ... INSTEAD OF DIVISION
     endin
```

Figure 4.14 Orchestra code for *instr 412* and *413,* comparing inefficient use of division with efficient use of multiplication.

tant point in performance, when other instrument initialization is taking place, it can cause an audible click every time we play a note. A simple way around this is to rewrite the instrument as shown in figure 4.17. This time only one allocation is requested and besides memory savings, we also reduce the risk of clicks. We also help improve data locality, which significantly helps performance on modern computers.

It is important to use this tip judiciously. Constant re-use of a variable can make code hard to decipher and will certainly hinder any future debugging efforts.

Avoid Printing and Disable Messages

A lot of users print debugging statements from their instruments and enable Csound's runtime messages. This is useful when developing an instrument, but printing mes-

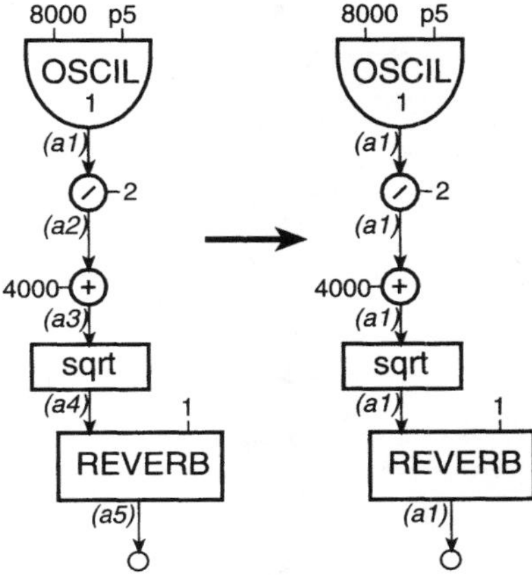

Figure 4.15 Block diagram of *instr 414* and *instr 415,* showing inefficient declaration of unique output variables versus the highly efficient reuse of the same variable.

```
     instr    414         ; USING UNIQUE A-RATE OUTPUT ARGUMENTS
a1   oscil    8000, p5, 1
a2   =        a1/2
a3   =        a2 + 4000
a4   =        sqrt(a3)
a5   reverb   a4, 1
     out      a5
     endin
```

Figure 4.16 Orchestra code for *instr 414* illustrating the use of a unique **a**-rate variable for each output argument.

```
     instr    415          ; REUSES A-RATE OUTPUT ARGUMENTS
a1   oscil    8000, p5, 1
a1   =        a1/2
a1   =        a1 + 4000
a1   =        sqrt(a1)
a1   reverb   a1, 1
     out      a1
     endin
```

Figure 4.17 Orchestra code for *instr 415,* showing the reuse of the same **a**-rate variable for each subsequent output.

sages is one of the most inefficient operations you can ask your computer to perform. If there is no need for printed information, disable the messages using the **–m** 0 flag and remove the print statements from your code. Performance improvements can be extremely high and if you are generating audio in real-time you will also dramatically reduce the danger of audible clicks.

Be Wary of Soundfiles

On all computers, reading and writing to disk is a slow procedure. If you have an instrument that uses the **soundin** opcode you might want to consider rewriting it so that it references the sound from memory using an f-table. This is not always possible owing to memory constraints, but the efficiency gains are big. Also, the soundfile format that you use can make a big difference in performance. If you use a big-endian machine (most UNIX boxes and Macintoshes) it is best to use a big-endian format such as AIFF. For little-endian machines (x86 and DEC Alphas) it is best to use the WAVE format. If a computer has to write to a non-native byte format it will have to go though a conversion routine, which is usually slow. Disk input/output (I/O) can occupy a significant amount of the overall time of the computer's work, so optimizing with respect to this feature is important.

Concluding Remarks

These are some of the most common optimizations used in Csound. Be warned that Csound can behave differently on different architectures and some ways of doing things are not always faster than others. In general, on today's general purpose computers, all of the above tips apply and it is only the performance ratio differences that vary. Also make sure you have a version optimized for your computer. If you have a Power Macintosh do not use the 68K processor version and if you have a Pentium Pro you can get much better performance from a version specifically for this CPU instead of a 486.

Finally, note that, with the exception of the rates and exponential-to-linear sections, the optimizations that were presented do not alter the output of the instrument. Optimization that potentially alters the sound quality is a complicated procedure that requires strong listening and sound design abilities. This is a skill that Csound users develop slowly with experience and one that is hard to teach.

```
        instr   416       ; NEEDING USER OPTIMIZATION
kamp    expseg  .001, .5, 1, p3/3, .8, p3/3, 6, p3/3-.5, .001
kfr     =       440                   ; GENERATE A 3 HARMONIC WAVEFORM
a1      oscili  kamp*5000, kfr, 1
a2      oscili  kamp*5000, kfr*2, 1
a3      oscili  kamp*5000, kfr*3, 1
a4      =       a3*a3                 ; SQUARE THE SIGNAL
a4d     delay1  a4                    ; REMOVE SOME HIGH FREQUENCIES ...
a4dd    delay1  a4d                   ; ... BY FILTERING
a5      =       a4/3+a4d/3+a4dd/3     ; USE THAT AS A MODULATION TO ...
a6      oscil   10000, 440+a5/10, 1   ; ... ANOTHER OSCILLATOR
        out     a6                    ; SEND THE SIGNAL OUT
        endin
```

Figure 4.18 Highly inefficient orchestra as an assignment for user optimization.

To close this chapter, I will present a real-life inefficient instrument in figure 4.18 that you can use to test your optimization knowledge. If you optimize it well enough you should get a significant improvement in the speed of computation. Good luck!

5 Using Csound's Macro Language Extensions

John ffitch

Since version 3.48 of Csound, the system has been enhanced by two macro facilities, one for the score language and one for the orchestra file. Of course, these are similar, but their uses are quite different. A *macro* is a string that gets replaced by some other text, but this simple description does not give any indication of how complex macros can be. Their power is deceptive. These macros can be used to make the writing of scores and orchestras easier and more tuned to an individual's style and taste. In the description here, I present a number of examples showing how macros can be used in Csound, but there will surely be a large number of uses that you will imagine and that will ultimately find a place in your personal world.

Simple Macros in the Score

In the score, macros are textual replacements that are made as the score is being read—even before score sorting. The macro system in Csound is a simple one and uses two special characters to indicate the presence of macros, the characters # and $. To define a macro, one uses the # character, at the start of a line.

```
#define NAME #replacement text#
```

The *NAME* of the macro can be anything made from letters, upper or lower case and digits, though digits may not be used as the first character of the name. The replacement text is any character string (not containing a #) and can extend over more than one line. The exact text used for the replacement is enclosed within two further # characters, which ensures that additional characters are not inadvertently captured and there is complete control over spaces. Remember that the replacing is exact text and takes no account of complete words.

```
#define      ARGS             #1.01 1.99 138#

i 501   0    1      3000     6.00     $ARGS.
i 501   1    1      4500     6.01     $ARGS.
i 501   2    1      5200     6.02     $ARGS.
i 501   3    1      8000     6.03     $ARGS.
```

Figure 5.1 Definition and use of a p-field macro to replace *p4, p5* and *p6* in the score.

```
i 501    0   1     3000    6.00     1.01    1.99    138
i 501    1   1     4500    6.01     1.01    1.99    138
i 501    2   1     5200    6.02     1.01    1.99    138
i 501    3   1     8000    6.03     1.01    1.99    138
```

Figure 5.2 Macro expansion of score in figure 5.1.

```
#define      ARGSA          #1.01 1.99 138#
#define      ARGSB          #2.02 3.99 838#

i 502   0    1      4000     6.01    $ARGSA.
i 502   1    1      5000     6.02    $ARGSB.
i 502   2    1      6000     6.03    $ARGSA.
i 502   3    1      7000     6.04    $ARGSB.
```

Figure 5.3 Definition and use of multiple macros.

To use a macro after it has been defined, the *NAME* must follow a **$** character and must be terminated by a period. If the period is omitted, then the next nonletter or nondigit terminates the name, but this can be ambiguous and so its use is not encouraged. The complete string **$***NAME.* is replaced by the replacement text from the definition. Of course the replacement text can also include macro calls, as long as they are defined by the time of expansion.

If a macro is not required any longer it can be removed with:

#undef *NAME*

A simple example of this could be when a note-event has a set of p-fields that are repeated in all, or nearly all occurrences. We can define a macro for this set of values: 1.01, 1.99 and 138 as shown in figure 5.1. This will get expanded before sorting into the score shown in figure 5.2. This can save typing and is easier to change if, for example, one needed to change one of the parameters. If there were two sets of p-fields one could have a second macro, as there is no real limit on the number of macros one can define.

```
#define    C         #8.00#
#define    Csharp    #8.01#
#define    Dflat     #8.01#
#define    D         #8.02#
#define    Dsharp    #8.03#
#define    Eflat     #8.03#
#define    E         #8.04#
#define    F         #8.05#
#define    ...       ...
```

Figure 5.4 Macros that convert **cpspch** values into actual note names.

```
i 503   0   1   1000   $C.
i 503   1   1   2000   $D.
i 503   2   1   3000   $E.
i 503   3   1   4000   $F.
```

Figure 5.5 A simple note-list employing the **cpspch** macro from figure 5.4.

Another simple use for a macro might be to assist in remembering the relationship between the traditional note names and the decimal notation used in connection with the **cpspch** opcode by defining a set of macros as in figure 5.4.

Clearly this use of the macro facility makes the traditional Csound score easier to read and write. But do note that care is needed with textual macros as they can sometimes do strange things. They take no notice of any meaning and so spaces are significant, which is why the definition has the replacement text surrounded by "#" characters. Used carefully, simply macros are a powerful concept, but they can be abused.

Macros with Arguments

Macros can also be defined with parameters. This can be used in more complex situations, where there are a number of repeats of a string with minor differences. To define a macro with arguments, the syntax is:

```
#define NAME(A#B#C) #replacement text#
```

Within the replacement text the arguments can be substituted by the form **$A**. In fact, the implementation defines the arguments as simple macros. There may be a few arguments, currently up to 5 and their names can be any choice of letters exactly as with macro names.

```
#define       ARG(A)         #2.345 1.03 $A. 234.9#

i 504   0    1      23000    8.00        $ARG(2.0)
i 504   +    4      24000    8.04        $ARG(5.0)
```

Figure 5.6 Definition and use of a macro with an argument.

```
i 504   0   1   3000   8.00   2.345   1.03   2.0    234.9
i 504   +   4   4000   8.04   2.345   1.03   5.0    234.9
```

Figure 5.7 Macro expansion of score in figure 5.6.

```
#define       Flute          #i 505#
#define       Clarinet       #i 506#

$Flute.       0    5    10000    440
$Clarinet.    2    3    11000    220
```

Figure 5.8 Macros that convert instrument numbers to instrument names.

In use, the argument form is a macro and so has the same rules as the other macros. The score with macros and an argument shown in figure 5.6 expands to the notelist shown in figure 5.7. As with the simple macros, these macros can also be undefined with:

#undef NAME

Note that the arguments are not required when undefining a macro.

Another use for macros is when writing a complex score with many instruments, where it is sometimes all too easy to forget to what the various instrument numbers refer. One can use macros to give names to the instrument numbers. An example is shown in figure 5.8.

Multiple File Scores and Repeats

It is sometimes convenient to have the score in more than one file. This use is supported by the **#include** facility, which is part of the macro system. A line containing the text:

#include "*filename*"

```
s                                 ; DEFINE A SECTION...
#include     "section1"
s                                 ; ... AND REPEAT IT
#include     "section1"
```

Figure 5.9 Using the include facility to read a section of score from another file and repeat it.

where the double-quote character, ", causes the text from the named file to be inserted into the score at this point and when input is finished, to revert to the previous input. There is currently a limit of 20 on the depth of included files and macros.

One suggested use of **#include** would be to define a set of macros that are part of the composer's style. Another would be to use **#include** to provide repeated sections.

Repeated Sections

Originally, the way to repeat sections in Csound was to copy and paste the text in the score file. As was previously shown, a newer method would be to employ the **#include** facility. A third alternative would be to use the new **r** directive introduced into the score language in version 3.48.

```
r4     NN
```

The directive above (**r**4 *NN*) starts a repeated section, which lasts until the next **s**, **r** or **e** directive. The section is repeated 4 times in this example. In order that the sections may be more flexible than a simple "copy-and-paste" repetition, the macro *NN* is given the value of 1 for the first time through the section, 2 for the second, 3 for the third and 4 for the fourth. This can be used to change p-field parameters, or indeed ignored. But a macro name must be given even if it is not used. (It should be noted that because of serious problems of interaction with macro expansion, sections must start and end in the same file and not in a macro).

Evaluation of Expressions

In earlier versions of Csound the numbers presented in a score were used as given, but this could be an irksome restriction. There are occasions when some simple arithmetic evaluation would make the construction of the score easier. This need is increased when there are macros. On the accompanying CD-ROM significant score generation techniques are described and for handling real complexity this is the best

```
r3        CNT

i 509     0        [0.3*$CNT.]
i 509     +        [($CNT./3)+0.2]
e
```

Figure 5.10 The repeat directive with expression evaluation in a macro.

```
s
i 509   0       0.3
i 509   0.3     0.533333
s
i 509   0       0.6
i 509   0.6     0.866667
s
i 509   0       0.9
i 509   0.9     1.2
e
```

Figure 5.11 Macro expansion of score in figure 5.10.

approach. However for some simpler cases, the syntax of an arithmetic expression, within square brackets **[ ]**, has been introduced to the score language. Expressions built from the four arithmetic operations **+**, **-**, ***** and **/** are allowed, together with **( )** grouping. The expressions can include numbers and, naturally, macros whose values are numeric or strings that are arithmetic expressions. All calculations are made in floating-point numbers. (Note that unary minus is not yet supported.)

As an example of this syntax use, consider a short section that is to be repeated three times, but with differences in the lengths of notes (see figure 5.10). As the three copies of the section have the macro *$CNT.* set with different values of 1, 2, and 3, this expands to the notelist shown in figure 5.11. The changes from section to section here are fairly major, but the evaluation system could also be used to ensure that repeated sections are subtly different, through the introduction of small changes in amplitude or speed.

One could also use the evaluation mechanism in conjunction with macros to provide alternative ways of describing pitches. If, instead of the macros $C. $Csharp. *etc.*, which we introduced earlier, we used one set of macros for the pitch-class and another for the octave, we could have a system as shown in figure 5.12. Note the use of the + inside the definitions. This allows a score to like the one in figure 5.13. Surely you will be able to think of similar and possibly more readable uses.

```
#define     C          #0.00+#
#define     Csharp     #0.01+#
#define     Dflat      #0.01+#
#define     D          #0.02+#
#define     Dsharp     #0.03+#
#define     Eflat      #0.03+#
#define     E          #0.04+#
#define     F          #0.05+#
#define     ...        ...
#define     oct(N)     #6+$N.#
```

Figure 5.12 Macros that convert cpspch to pitch class and octave.

```
i 510    0    2    5000      [$C.$oct(2)]              $ARGSA.
i 510    2    2    6000      [$Csharp.$oct(2)]         $ARGSB.
i 510    4    2    7000      [$D.$oct(1)]              $ARGSA.
i 510    6    4    8000      [$Eflat.$oct(0)]          $ARGSB.
```

Figure 5.13 Score file employing the pitch class and octave macro from figure 5.12 plus the argument macro from figure 5.3.

Marking and Reusing Note Lists

Another alternative to using either **#include** or repeated sections for reusing parts of a score is provided by the marking and insertion of named sections. The score statement below introduces a marked location in the score.

m `Name`

The mark need not be at the start of a section but it usually will be. Csound will remember this source position and file, then associate it with the given name so it can be used later in an **n** statement. For internal reasons, this statement can only be used in a file and not as part of a macro expansion.

The related **n** statement will include the score from a previously marked location, referred to by name, until the end of the section. The expected use of these two statements is for verse and chorus structure, or a simple *rondo*. The start of the first chorus is marked with the **m** statement. Then subsequent chorus can use the **n** statement. This use is demonstrated in the simple score shown in figure 5.14. Of course, for a chorus as simple as this, a macro might have been simpler to use, but for lengthy repeated loops or grooves, this will prove a useful addition to your repertoire of shortcuts.

```
; 1ST     VERSE
i 511     0          .3    15000        8.00
i 511     +          .     9000         8.02
i 511     +          .     12000        8.04
i 511     +          .     9000         8.00
s
m         Chorus
i 512     0          .3    20000        8.07
i 512     +          .     12000        8.09
i 512     +          .     18000        8.07
i 512     +          .     11000        8.05
s
; 2ND     VERSE
i 511     0          .3    15000        8.04
i 511     +          .     9000         8.00
i 511     +          .     12000        8.02
i 511     +          .     9000         8.00
s
n         Chorus
s
; 3RD     VERSE
i 511     0          .3    15000        8.04
i 511     +          .     9000         8.00
i 511     +          .     12000        8.04
i 511     +          .     9000         8.05
s
n         Chorus
s
; 4TH     VERSE
i 511     0          .3    15000        8.04
i 511     +          .     9000         8.04
i 511     +          .     12000        8.02
i 511     +          .     9000         8.02
s
i 511     0          4     15000        8.00
i 512     .05        4     10000        7.001
```

Figure 5.14 Score that employs the marking and naming statement to conveniently intersperse, reorder, and repeat sections.

Modifying Time

The basic Csound score language has had a facility for varying the rate at which time passes with the **t** "time-warping" statement. Sometimes, however, this is not sufficient for what one really wants. There are two "local" score statements that can be used for organizing components of the score, one that changes the base from which time is counted and another that changes the rate at which time passes for part of a score. The score statements are **b** and **v**.

The **b** score statement sets the internal base-clock, so that all subsequent note-on sets have this new base-time added. The effect is textual and lasts until the end of a section or the next **b** directive.

A typical use for this command would be when you have a phrase or theme that you want to repeat without waiting for all the sound to cease, as in a section end, you could reset the base-time and repeat the actual event list, possibly even with a **#include**.

Using *instr 511* and *512* from an earlier example, one could use the **b** statement to overlap two copies of the motif and form a strict canon. This exact repeat can subsequently be moved to a different starting time by changing the base time-rather than having to modify each event where time is mentioned explicitly.

If the motif is long and complex this is a significant saving in score editing time. Used with the **#include** facility it could make for an interesting use of scores with

```
i 511     0        .5      9500        8.00
i 511     +        .       9000        8.02
i 511     +        .       8000        8.04
i 511     +        .       7000        8.00
i 512     2        .5      6000        8.07
i 512     +        .       7000        8.09
i 512     +        .       8000        8.07
i 512     +        .       9000        8.05
b         1.05
i 511     0        .5      9500        8.00
i 511     +        .       9000        8.02
i 511     +        .       8000        8.04
i 511     +        .       7000        8.00
i 512     2        .5      6000        8.07
i 512     +        .       7000        8.09
i 512     +        .       8000        8.07
i 512     +        .       9000        8.05
```

Figure 5.15 Score that employs the resetting of the base-time to create a canon.

overlapping repeats. But since the expansion takes place prior to the score sorting, the *score.srt* file will have no indication of this operation.

There is one other way in which sounds, associated in the score, can be organized into higher level structures. As you know, the *p2* field is used to set the start time of a "note." It is possible to use the **+** statement as a shorthand way of having the current note's start-time be immediately following the end of the previous event. The following sequence of notes:

```
i 511    0        .5    9500      8.00
i 511    +        .     9000      8.02
i 511    +        .     8000      8.04
i 511    +        .     7000      8.00
```

translates as follows:

```
i 511    0        .5    9500      8.00
i 511    .5       .     9000      8.02
i 511    1        .     8000      8.04
i 511    1.5      .     7000      8.00
```

As you can see, when a **+** statement is placed in *p2,* that note event's start-time is equal to the sum of the previous note's *p2+p3* (the start **+** duration). This wonderful shorthand has one serious limitation, however: it applies only to lists of notes played on the same instrument. To address this limitation, a new version of the **+** statement has been added—**^+**. In its purest form, the **^+** directive will set the start-time of the current note-event equal to the sum of *p2+p3* from the "previous" note-event. The form **^+1** indicates 1 time unit after the *start* of the previous note-event. This (with the **+** directive) provides a way of grouping a small set of events together. Incidentally, the number following a ^ can be negative, so one could arrange to write a motif backward, provided time does not go negative!

The other local-textual operation is to treat all time as passing at a different rate—to allow independent simultaneous tempo control. It is now possible, using the **v** directive, to modify the speed of a number of lines before the global time warping is computed by the **t** directive. A simple use of this would be to generate some phase-shifting of themes, in ways often used in minimal music.

Another suggested use is to have independent time scales for two melodic ideas, but played simultaneously, as employed in many of the works of Charles Ives. As with all these score operations, the real use is for you, the composer, to determine. These operations are not supposed to provide all possible facilities, for which one of the specialized score generation languages is a better approach, but it provides just another small collection of potentially time-saving facilities.

```
i 511   0       .5      9500    8.00
i 511   +       .       9000    8.02
i 511   +       .       8000    8.04
i 511   +       .       7000    8.00
i 512   2       .5      6000    8.07
i 512   +       .       7000    8.09
i 512   +       .       8000    8.07
i 512   +       .       9000    8.05
s
i 511   0       .5      9500    8.00
i 511   +       .       9000    8.02
i 511   ^+.25   .       8000    8.04
i 511   ^+.5    .       7000    8.00
i 512   2       .5      6000    8.07
i 512   ^+-1    .       7000    8.09
i 512   +       .       8000    8.07
i 512   +       .       9000    8.05


w       0       60

f 1     0       0       4096    4096    10      1
f 2     0       0       4096    4096    10      10      0    5    0    1

i 511   0       0       .5      .5      9500    8.00
i 511   .5      .5      .5      .5      9000    8.02
i 511   1       1       .5      .5      8000    8.04
i 511   1.5     1.5     .5      .5      7000    8.00
i 512   2.2     .5      .5      6000    8.07
i 512   2.5     2.5     .5      .5      7000    8.09
i 512   3.3     .5      .5      8000    8.07
i 512   3.5     3.5     .5      .5      9000    8.05
s

w       0       60

i 511   0       0       .55     .55     9500    8.00
i 511   .55     .55     .55     .55     9000    8.02
i 511   .825    .825    .55     .55     8000    8.04
i 512   1.1     1.1     .55     .55     7000    8.09
i 511   1.375   1.375   .55     .55     7000    8.00
i 512   1.65    1.65    .55     .55     8000    8.07
i 512   2.2     2.2     .55     .55     6000    8.07
i 512   2.2     2.2     .55     .55     9000    8.05
```

Figure 5.16 Score that employs the local relative positioning of events followed by the sorted score output found in the *score.srt* file.

```
i 512    0      .3    9000    8.07
i 512    +      .     8000    8.09
i 512    +      .     7000    8.07
i 512    +      .     8000    8.05
i 511    1.2    .3    9000    8.04
i 511    +      .     9000    8.04
i 511    +      .     8000    8.02
i 511    +      .     8000    8.02
b        0
v        1.2
i 512    0      .3    9000    8.07
i 512    +      .     8000    8.09
i 512    +      .     7000    8.07
i 512    +      .     8000    8.05
i 511    1.2    .3    9000    8.04
i 511    +      .     9000    8.04
i 511    +      .     8000    8.02
i 511    +      .     8000    8.02
```

Figure 5.17 Score that employs the local time variation to generate "phase music."

Simple Macros in the Orchestra

The same style of macro facilities are available as part of the orchestra reading. These macros are also textual and are independent of the score macros. The syntax for a simple macro is:

```
#define   NAME   #replacement text#
#undef    NAME
```

This could be used, for example, to provide a standard reverberation scheme as shown in figure 5.18. This will get expanded before compilation into the orchestra shown in figure 5.19.

Unlike the score, however, with its translated *score.srt* file, in the case of the orchestra, one does not see the text of the expansion in a file. Still, orchestra macros can save typing and, in the case for example of a general fx-processing sequence of global instruments, it can lead to a coherent and consistent use.

As in the score, macros in the orchestra can have arguments:

```
#define NAME(A#B#C) #replacement text#
```

We could use this form, for instance, to extend the reverberation system and allow different audio-rate variables to be sent to the reverberation instrument as illustrated in figure 5.20. This expands to the orchestra shown in figure 5.21.

```
#define    REVERB      #garvb    =     garvb+a1
                                 out   a1#

           instr       513             ; MACRO EXAMPLE 1
a1         oscil       p4, p5, p6
           $REVERB.
           endin

           instr       514             ; MACRO EXAMPLE 2
a1         wgpluck2    p8, p4, p5, p6, p7
           $REVERB.
           endin
```

Figure 5.18 Macro used in orchestra to substitute for several lines of code.

```
       instr       513            ; EXPANDED MACRO 1
a1     oscil       p4, p5, p6
ga     =           garvb+a1
       out         a1
       endin

       instr       514            ; EXPANDED MACRO 2
a1     wgpluck2    p8, p4, p5, p6, p7
ga     =           garvb+a1
       out         a1
       endin
```

Figure 5.19 Expansion of reverb macro from figure 5.18 into two different instruments.

```
#define    REVERB(A)       #garvb    =      garvb+$A.
                                     out    $A.#

           instr           515      ; EXPANDED REVERB MACRO 1
a1         oscil           p4, p5, p6
           $REVERB(a1)
           endin

           instr           516      ; EXPANDED REVERB MACRO 2
a2         wgpluck2        p8, p4, p5, p6, p7
           $REVERB(a2)
           endin
```

Figure 5.20 Orchestra macro with unique argument substitutions per instrument.

```
        instr       515          ; EXPANDED REVERB MACRO
a1      oscil       p4, p5, p6
garvb   =           garvb+a1
        out         a1
        endin

        instr       516          ; EXPANDED REVERB MACRO
a2      wgpluck2    p8, p4, p5, p6, p7
garvb   =           garvb+a2
        out         a2
        endin
```

Figure 5.21 Expansion of macros as defined in the orchestra in figure 5.20.

```
#define   CLARINET(I)     #
          instr           $I.
ipanl     =               sqrt(p6)
ipanr     =               sqrt(1-p6)
ka        linen           p4, .01, p3, .1
kv        linseg          0, 0.5, 0, 1, 1, p3-0.5, 1
a1        wgclar          ka, p5, -0.2, 0.15, 0.1, 0.25, 5.735, kv*0.01, 1
          outs            a1*ipanl, a1*ipanr
          $REVERB(a1)
          endin          #
```

Figure 5.22 Defining an entire instrument as a macro.

A rather extreme, but practical, use of macros in the orchestra would be to have each instrument defined as a macro, with the instrument number as a parameter. Figure 5.22 shows what one would write in the file *clarinet.* So now we have a clarinet instrument whose number is a macro argument. If we have similar files for other instruments, an entire orchestra could be constructed from a number of **#include** statements followed by macro calls, as in figure 5.23, to give them specific instrument numbers for the piece—it's just like having your own Csound librarian program. This shows also that the **#include** syntax is allowed in orchestras as well as in scores. It should be noted, however, that there is no evaluation system in the orchestra as it is not needed to the same extent.

Conclusion

The Csound score language is essentially just a list of events. The system allows the user to write the events in any order; there are time-warping controls for tempo; and there are sections for organization. In this chapter we have seen that macros are a

```
#include            "my_orc_header"
#include            "my_orc_macros"
#include            "fx"
#include            "clarinet"
#include            "bassoon"
#include            "guitar"

$CLARINET(517)
$BASSOON(518)
$GUITAR(519)
```

Figure 5.23 Using **#include** and macros to load a "library" of Csound instruments into the orchestra by name and assign their instrument numbers as macro arguments.

useful way in which this simplicity can be extended, in an individual fashion. Clearly, macros and the additional score shortcuts do not take the place of the more general score-writing language described on the CD-ROM, but they can make the task of constructing a score a little easier. In addition, the extensions for repeated and marked sections, together with base-time setting and local variation of time are aimed at facilitating the entry of traditional and popular groove-based structures. These both provide another simple tool for beginners who often complain about the tedium of typing a score.

It was also shown that macros could be used in the orchestra, mainly to customize and personalize the orchestra language a little. Again, there are a number of powerful and intuitive graphical tools for designing Csound instruments, but in many cases, a few macros can simplify the most straightforward and direct way of doing the work and make the code more readable. Finally, using included instrument files, is just another approach that can help you to organize your instrument collection. Over time you will no doubt construct your own library of macros and include them in your scores and orchestras, with the **#include** facility, as a matter of course.

Imitative Synthesis

6 Designing Acoustically Viable Instruments in Csound

Stephen David Beck

Many chapters of this book discuss the fundamental techniques of sound synthesis. It is important to remember that, in the abstract, these methods can create almost any sound imaginable. How do we decide which method or combination of methods will work best? What defines the best method? What makes a synthetic sound interesting and attractive to a listener? Or to a performer?

Acoustic Viability is a principle of synthetic instrument design that recognizes the importance of real instrument acoustics and their impact on timbre and expression. By incorporating this sensibility in your instrument designs, you can create synthetic instruments that are expressive, evocative and compelling. For the performer, whether human or computer, instruments that are acoustically viable are intrinsically more satisfying.

This chapter will discuss the differences between classical and modern acoustic theory and the notion of acoustic viability. There will be examples of building synthetic instruments that are acoustically viable, including transformations across intensity and frequency. The last section will present other options for exploring acoustic viability.

Classical Acoustic Theory

In the late 1800s, Heinrich Helmholtz developed a set of theories and principles that we call the classical acoustic theory. These theories provide a reasonably accurate description of the physics of sound, in particular, musical or instrumental sound. Along with the mathematical theories of Fourier, Helmholtz's ideas about instrumental acoustics remain the basis of most sound synthesis techniques.

According to the classical acoustic theory, instrument sounds are periodic vibrations that travel like waves through air. The number of vibrations per second is the sound's fundamental frequency, which a listener hears as pitch. The timbre of any musical instrument is described by a spectrum of multiple frequencies whose general amplitude varies over time. Component frequencies (partials) within the spectrum have values that are integer multiples of the fundamental frequency. A piano has a spectrum whose partials decrease in relative amplitude. On the other hand, a clarinet has a spectrum where only odd-numbered multiples of the fundamental appear (in decreasing amplitude).

The amplitude envelope, which describes the change of overall amplitude over time, is in three distinct sections: the attack, the steady state, the decay. The attack is the section of time at which the instrument is first heard. The steady state continues for as long as the performer plays the note and the decay is the portion of time when the musician stops playing but the sound continues. A clarinet's amplitude envelope has a modest attack, a well defined sustain and a short decay. A piano's envelope has a sharp attack, no sustain, and a long decay.

According to Helmholtz, it is these differences between harmonic content and between amplitude envelopes that allow us to recognize one instrument sound from another. It is these differences that allow us to recognize the voices of different people.

For the most part, the principles that Helmholtz developed remain an influential and important part of our understanding of acoustics. Both analog and digital synthesizers still use the classical acoustics model as the foundation of their internal design.

The Modern Theory of Acoustics

Like Newton's theories of physics, the classical acoustic model begins to break down when we examine sound on a small scale. When the harmonic content of sound is examined over small time periods, (roughly 40–50 milliseconds), we discover that, contrary to the Helmholtz model, a sound's spectrum changes profoundly over time. During the attack portion of a sound, harmonic content may change rapidly and unpredictably. This phenomenon is called the *initial transient.* During the decay, upper partials tend to disappear before the entire sound fades away. While the sustain portion of the sound is certainly more stable than the attack or decay, it is hardly as static as Helmholtz would suggest.

An examination of the spectra of an instrument playing different notes and different dynamics demonstrates the most important difference between the classical model and our modern understanding of instrumental acoustics. Loud and soft articulations of the same pitch produce substantially different spectra (e.g., a loud note has much more harmonic content than a soft note). In recognizing the timbral changes between the three registers of a clarinet, we can infer that all instruments have such timbral shifts as they move through their performance range. Flute, violin, cello, bassoon, piano, all have profoundly different timbres in their respective registers.

Clearly, the basic premise of classical acoustic theory (a static timbre with an amplitude envelope) is by no means an accurate representation of sound. Nor does the classical model predict the wide variations in timbre owing to dynamics and pitch.

Modern acoustic theory provides us with a more comprehensive understanding of the subtleties of acoustic instrumental timbres. Timbral variations, owing to changes of intensity, are powerful acoustic cues to musical dynamics. And timbral variations owing to changes in frequency are critical components of an instrument's sonic character. Recognizing the importance of these cues is the foundation of Acoustic Viability.

Acoustic Viability: A Design Aesthetic for Synthesis

Perhaps the most attractive part of computer music is the ability to design, create and compose for new sounds and new timbres. But the freedom that comes with the clean slate of synthetic instrument design has its own problems. Namely, where do you start in designing these new sounds? What designs produce interesting sounds? What designs provide composers with instruments capable of the same expressiveness that acoustic instruments have?

Acoustic Viability is a design aesthetic that provides composers with a set of principles to create powerful, expressive and evocative sounds. By recognizing the importance of instrument acoustics and its relationship to expression, synthetic instrument designers can build synthesis processes that respond to changes in loudness, pitch, and articulation that are consistent with our understanding of acoustic instruments.

Although the principle may seem intuitive, its importance cannot be overstated. A common complaint about "standard" synthesis instruments, particularly those that try to emulate orchestral instruments, is that they sound flat, dull, and inexpressive. If a synthetic instrument's timbre responds to variations in pitch and loudness in ways that are consistent with acoustic instruments, then the synthetic instrument will be perceived as being viable in an acoustic space. Its sound becomes acoustically viable. If the virtual space projected beyond the loudspeakers reacts in an acoustically valid manner and the sounds in the space are acoustically viable, then the listener will be convinced the sounds are real, in spite of an intellectual awareness that the sounds are in fact synthesized.

This aesthetic is by no means new. The vast majority of research in sound synthesis has focused on the acoustic properties of musical instruments. The extensive analyses of instrumental sounds by Jean-Claude Risset, et al., demonstrate the principle concern researchers had for the development and extension of synthesis techniques. Analysis/resynthesis techniques (linear-predictive-coding and phase vocoding), the Karplus-Strong plucked-string algorithm, FOF synthesis, granular synthesis and physical modeling are all examples of techniques that were developed or expanded from research using signal analysis methods.

Even Csound and its Music N cousins use the acoustic instrument model in their fundamental design. In Csound "*.orc*" files are the instruments, "*.sco*" files are the scores and the Csound program is the performer that reads the score and plays the instruments. It seems only natural that synthetic instruments should adhere to a few basic acoustic rules.

A Definition of Acoustic Viability

Acoustic Viability can be defined as a collection of design principles that recognize the importance of real-world instrument acoustics and their relationship to musical expression. They include the connection between changes in amplitude, changes in frequency and the impact on spectral content. Equally important are the connections between articulation, frequency and amplitude envelopes.

Musical instruments are mechanical systems that by themselves are at equilibrium. That is, they do not create sound until some form of energy is put into the system. In general terms, all instruments have a method (or methods) for applying mechanical energy to its system. Pianos have keys connected to hammers that strike a set of tuned strings. Violins have strings that are bowed or plucked. Clarinets have a mouthpiece with a single reed that, when blown, creates a vibrating column of air. By changing the amount of energy used to initiate a vibration, the performer can control the overall amplitude of the instrument.

When synthetic instruments are designed with these same considerations, they will provide the composer with sounds that are similarly expressive. The best way to explain these connections is to first examine the physics and mechanics of acoustic instruments and then apply them to synthetic instruments.

Frequency and Timbre

The relationship between the frequency of vibration and timbre is readily apparent in some instruments, but less clear in the abstract. The clarinet, for example, has three distinct registers; three distinct pitch ranges with different timbral characteristics. The *Chalumeau* register is dark and moody, ranging from its lowest note written (E below middle C to F above middle C). The *throat* register is tight and weak, (between F# and A# written above middle C). And the *clarion* register is bright, clear and sometimes piercing, ranging upward from B above middle C to as high as the performer dares.

It is sometimes hard to believe that a single instrument can have such a variety of timbres. But the reality of the clarinet's three registers proves the impact of a resonating body on an instrument's timbre. Resonators, by their nature, tend to amplify certain frequencies louder than others. These resonant zones, or formants, are uniquely related to the size and shape of the instrument and its resonator. It is these properties that give instruments like the flute, the clarinet, the bassoon and the cello such a wide range of timbral possibilities.

Amplitude and Timbre

The relationship between applied energy and timbre is relatively clear. As more energy is put into the instrument, higher modes of vibration are achieved. With that, more partials are present in the frequency spectrum. This is why a note played forte is not just louder in volume than a note played piano, but brighter in timbre as well.

Amplitude, Frequency, and Envelopes

The connection between amplitude, frequency and amplitude envelope is far less obvious. Before an instrument is played, it rests in a state of equilibrium. As with all mechanical systems, there is a certain amount of resistance or inertia that keeps the instrument from vibrating on its own. Performers must overcome that inertia before their instrument will sound properly. The more energy a performer uses, the faster that resistance is overcome and the faster the instrument reaches its "steady-state" vibration.

A piano has strings of different lengths and thickness, ranging from the thick, long low strings to the thin, short high strings. Different fingerings on a wind instrument produce different lengths of air columns—longer columns mean more mass to vibrate. We know from basic physics that large masses have more inertia to overcome, but also have more momentum once they are in motion. Similarly, low notes take longer to sound, but last longer than high notes with the same initial energy. In all instruments, the relative speed of its amplitude envelope is directly related to the pitch (and mass) of a given note—higher pitches are faster than lower pitches.

Translating the Connections to Synthesis

The connections between amplitude, frequency, envelopes and timbre are critical pieces of our ability to identify musical sounds, their dynamics and their pitch. Building synthetic instruments that have these relationships is the foundation of acoustic viability.

The importance of the timbral cues to pitch and dynamics cannot be ignored, especially when designing instruments for real-time performance situations. Performers also depend on these cues for performance feedback. They are trained for years to listen to these subtle cues of timbre from their own instruments. When performers are given an acoustically viable synthetic instrument, the connections between performance technique and timbre become intuitive.

Implementing Acoustic Viability in Csound-Based Synthetic Instruments

Creating acoustically viable instruments in Csound is both a trivial and complex task. Simple ways exist for linking pitch and amplitude parameters, not only to the standard operators but to other opcodes that model acoustic phenomena as well. This section will illustrate some basic techniques for translating changes in pitch and amplitude into changes of timbre and envelope. Sample code will be included to illustrate the examples.

Pitch-Related Transformations

In acoustic instruments, pitch-based timbre shifts are due to the formants of a resonating body. Formants are areas of the frequency spectrum that are naturally amplified by the resonator. These can be modeled with simple **reson** filters that have a low Q value.

Q, the "quality" of a bandpass filter, is defined as the ratio of a **reson**'s center frequency and bandwidth. When Q is on the order of 5 or less, the filter acts as a general boost to that portion of the frequency spectrum. But as Q rises, the filter begins to resonate its center frequency with greater clarity at the exclusion of frequencies outside the stopband.

$$Q = F_{center}/\text{Bandwidth} \tag{6.1}$$

The instrument shown in figure 6.1 attaches two **reson** filters to the end of an **oscil** and **linen** opcode. The filters are at fixed center frequencies. Each has a different Q. The output of the filters is then **balance**d against the prefilter signal to assure reasonable amplitudes.

Low-Q **reson** filters produce a subtle but noticeable spectrum transformation across the instrument's registers. Higher Q values produce more extreme transformations over the frequency spectrum. This can be used to exaggerate the relationship between pitch and timbre. The three instruments in *601.orc* demonstrate the variety of transformations available as each of these **reson** instruments has a more extreme Q value.

Amplitude-Related Transformations

The connection between amplitude and timbre is clear. When higher amounts of energy are put into a vibrating system, higher modes of vibrations are achieved and more partials appear in the spectrum. There are several strategies that can be used to simulate this connection.

Indexing Wavetables to Amplitude

A trivial solution is to index the wavetable in an oscillator according to the oscillator's amplitude. That is, a table maps the amplitude values placed in a *.sco* file to a set of predefined wavetables. The selected wavetable is then placed in the oscillator. This technique is similar to how one maps the appropriate wavetable to pitch in a sampling instrument (using **loscil**).

In the example shown in figure 6.3, the amplitude (in dB) is used as an index for a table that links dB levels to function tables (f-table) indices. The f-tables, defined in the *.sco* file, are waveforms of increasing complexity.

Using Distortion Synthesis Techniques

Frequency Modulation and Amplitude Modulation provide powerful and elegant methods for synthesizing complex waveforms. While instrument builders do not have the specific control of spectral content that is available through wavetable techniques,

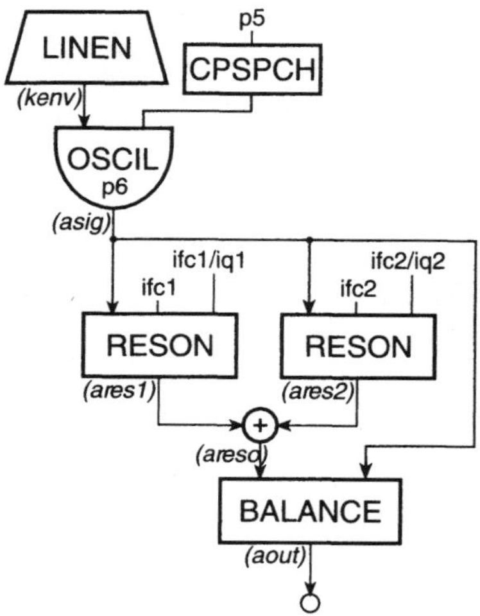

Figure 6.1 Block diagram of *instr 601,* a parallel band-pass filter instrument.

```
        instr    601          ; PARALLEL BANDPASS FILTER
iatt    =        p3*.1                      ; ATTACK IS 10% OF DURATION
idec    =        p3*.1                      ; DECAY IS 10% OF DURATION
ifc1    =        200                        ; Fc OF RESON 1
iq1     =        5                          ; Q OF RESON 1
ifc2    =        550                        ; Fc OF RESON 2
iq2     =        3                          ; Q OF RESON 2
kenv    linen    p4, iatt, p3, idec         ; AMPLITUDE ENVELOPE
asig    oscil    kenv, cpspch(p5), p6       ; OSCILLATOR
ares1   reson    asig, ifc1, ifc1/iq1       ; RESON1 - BANDWIDTH = Fc/Q
ares2   reson    asig, ifc2, ifc2/iq2       ; RESON2 - BANDWIDTH = Fc/Q
areso   =        ares1+ares2                ; ADD FILTERED SIGNALS
aout    balance  areso, asig                ; BALANCE AGAINST ORIGINAL
        out      aout
        endin
```

Figure 6.2 Orchestra code for *instr 601,* a parallel filter instrument with fixed center frequency and bandwidth.

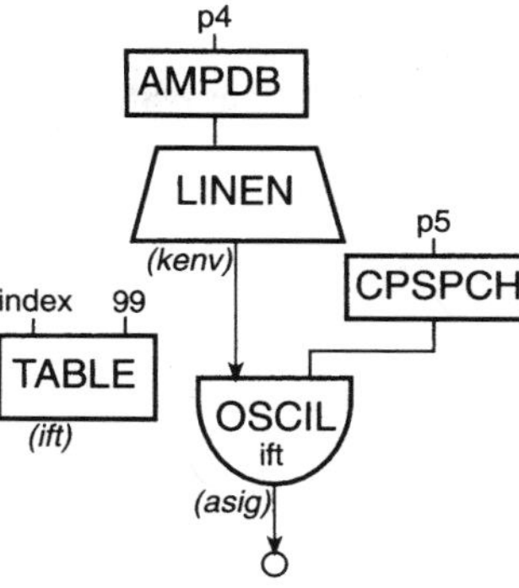

Figure 6.3 Block diagram of *instr 604*, a simple instrument that uses amplitude (p4) to index a table.

```
        instr  604          ; AMPLITUDE CONTROLLED TIMBRE MAPPING
index   =      p4                          ; LOOKUP INDEX FOR FTABLE
ift     table  index, 99                   ; IFT HOLDS FTABLE 99 FOR AMP
kenv    linen  ampdb(p4), p3*.1,p3, p3*.1
asig    oscil  kenv, cpspch(p5), ift       ; OSCIL USES INDEXED VALUE...
        out    asig                        ; ... TO SELECT FTABLE 1-10
        endin
```

Figure 6.4 Orchestra code for *instr 604* in which **oscil** uses indexed values to specify function table.

```
f 1   0 512  10    1 .5 .25                                     ; 3 PARTIALS
f 2   0 512  10    1 .5 .25 .125                                ; 4 PARTIALS
f 3   0 512  10    1 .6 .3 .15 .075                             ; 5 PARTIALS
f 4   0 512  10    1 .7 .35 .165 .0825 .04125                   ; 6 PARTIALS
f 5   0 512  10    1 .8 .5 .3 .2 .1 .05                         ; 7 PARTIALS
f 6   0 512  10    1 .8 .6 .4 .3 .2 .1 .05 .025                 ; 9 PARTIALS
f 7   0 512  10    1 .8 .8 .6 .6 .4 .4 .2 .2 .1 .1              ; 11 PARTIALS
f 8   0 512  10    1 .9 1 .9 .7 .6 .5 .4 .3 .2 .1 .05           ; 12 PARTIALS
f 9   0 512  10    1 .9 1 .9 1 .9 .8 .7 .6 .7 .6 .5 .4          ; 13 PARTIALS
f 10  0 512  10    1 1 1 .9 1 1 .8 1 .6 .7 .6 .5 .4 .3          ; 14 PARTIALS
f 99  0 128  -17   0 1 45 2 60 3 70 4 75 5 80 6 83 7 86 8 89 9 91 10

;ins     st      dur     amp     pch
i 604    0       1       40      8.00
i 604    +       .       55      .
i 604    +       .       65      .
i 604    +       .       72      .
i 604    +       .       77      .
i 604    +       .       81      .
i 604    +       .       84      .
i 604    +       .       88      .
i 604    +       .       90      .
i 604    +       .       91      .
```

Figure 6.5 Score code for *instr 604*, in which *f 99* uses *ampdb(p4)* to index into the non-normalizing version of GEN17 (−17) to return the specific f-table (*f 1–f 10*) used by the **oscil**.

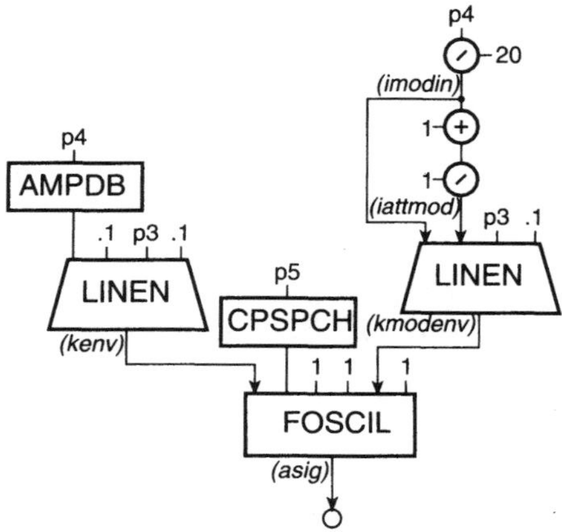

Figure 6.6 Block diagram of *instr 606,* a dynamic FM instrument using the **foscil** opcode.

```
        instr   606    ; FM WITH MODULATION INDEX MAPPED TO AMPLITUDE
imodind =       p4/20                      ; SCALES MOD INDEX TO 0-5
iattmod =       1/(imodind+1)              ; SCALES MOD ATT TO INDEX
kenv    linen   ampdb(p4), .1, p3, .1      ; AMP ENVELOPE
kmodenv linen   imodind, iattmod, p3, .1   ; MOD INDEX ENV
asig    foscil  kenv, cpspch(p5), 1, 1, kmodenv, 1
        out     asig
        endin
```

Figure 6.7 Orchestra code for *instr 606,* a FM instrument with amplitude mapped to attack-time and mod-index.

they do have tools in FM and AM to dynamically alter timbre during the course of a note's duration. This dynamism of timbre is simply not possible using wavetables.

FM and AM provide elegant solutions to the connection between amplitude and spectral content. Scaling amplitude to the modulation index of any FM or AM instrument creates an effective connection between the dynamic of a note and its timbre. If the modulation index is modified by a time-variant envelope, a scaling of the envelope's attack-time further emphasizes the connection and strengthens the aural cue.

The example shown in figure 6.6 ties the amplitude (in dB) to the modulation-index of a **foscil** opcode. The attack time of the index's envelope is also scaled to the amplitude (higher dB = faster attack).

Pitch and Amplitude Transforms on Envelopes

The relationships between pitch, amplitude and envelopes are complex and interrelated. Pitch is a reflection of the amount of mass that must be initiated into a vibrational mode. Low pitches mean higher mass and more inertia to overcome, hence slower attacks in energy-dependent envelopes (i.e., amplitude envelopes, modulation envelopes). But low pitches also mean more momentum within the vibration, which lengthen decays. Higher pitches mean lighter masses, less inertia, faster attacks and shorter decays.

Amplitude is the amount of energy used to overcome the inertial resistance of that mass and sustain vibrational momentum. Low amplitudes mean less energy to overcome the resistance and less energy to sustain the momentum. This results in slower attacks and faster decays. Higher amplitudes mean more energy, inertia is overcome quicker, faster attacks and longer decays.

Devising a computational linkage between pitch and envelopes is relatively straightforward. The same is true for amplitude and envelopes. But creating one that compensates for both is much more complicated. The following example (*instr 607*) modifies an amplitude envelope through a combined multiplier derived from amplitude and pitch values (*p4* & *p5*).

The multiplier is created from lookup-tables that independently correlate amplitude to attack and decay times and pitch to attack and decay times. The amplitude and octave attack values are multiplied together and used to scale the score's attack value. The same for the decay values. The instrument also includes a spectral transform function that returns modulation index scalars from amplitude (a different approach from example *instr 606*).

The scalar values used in the example instrument's f-tables provide realistic transformations between amplitude, frequency and spectral envelopes. For the amplitude-attack lookup-table, an exponential curve returns smaller attack scalars, (meaning shorter attack times), for higher amplitudes. The amplitude-decay table returns exponentially higher scalars, (longer decays), for higher amplitudes. The octave-attack and decay tables both use linear functions that return smaller values, (shorter times), for higher frequencies. Higher amplitudes also return exponentially higher modulation indexes, which result in brighter spectra (more partials).

Real-time Instruments Using MIDI

Using acoustic viability on Csound instruments controlled by MIDI is an essential method of creating an intuitive connection between performance and synthesis.

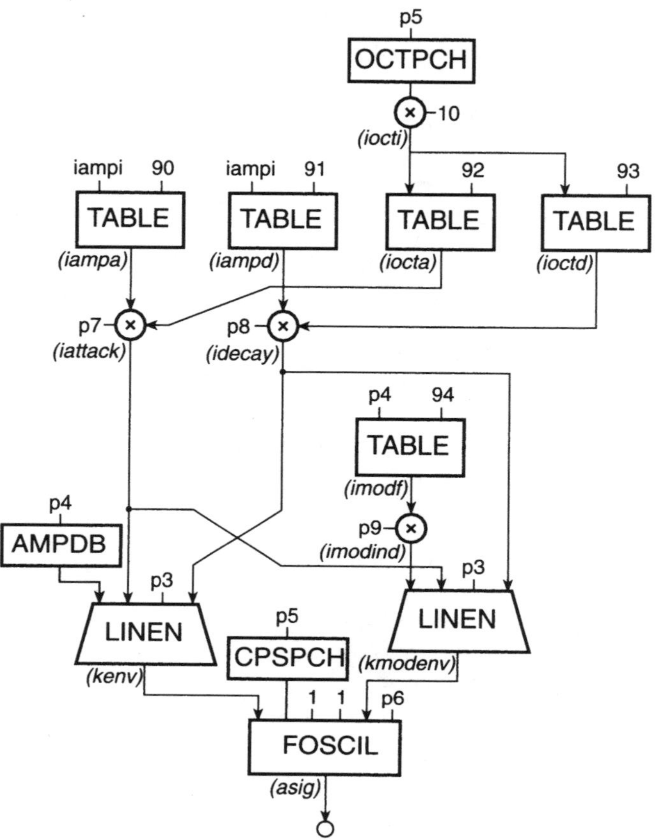

Figure 6.8 Block diagram of *instr 607,* a FM instrument that uses table-lookups to correlate attack, release, and mod-index.

Instead of *p4* score value controlling amplitude, **veloc** would return the velocity of the current MIDI event and **ampmidi** would return the MIDI velocity scaled into an amplitude value. The pitch value read from *p5* would be replaced with **notnum** (raw note number of the current MIDI event) or **cpsmidi** (current note number converted into **cps**).

Other MIDI parameters (aftertouch, channel pressure, pitch bend) can be accessed through Csound and used as additional controllers for synthesis. These values can be easily placed into any of the previous instrument examples.

```
          instr    607         ; FM WITH PITCH & AMPLITUDE MAPPED TO ENVELOPE &
                               ; SPECTRA
iampi     =        p4                            ; AMPLITUDE INDEX (0-96)
iocti     =        octpch(p5)*10                 ; OCTAVE INDEX (0-120)
iampa     table    iampi, 90                     ; f 90 = FN FOR AMP ATK
iampd     table    iampi, 91                     ; f 91 = FN FOR AMP DECAY
iocta     table    iocti, 92                     ; f 92 = FN FOR OCTAVE ATTACK
ioctd     table    iocti, 93                     ; f 93 = FN FOR OCTAVE DECAY
iattack   =        iampa*iocta*p7                ; p7   = ATTACK LENGTH
idecay    =        iampd*ioctd*p8                ; p8   = DECAY LENGTH
; SET TOTAL DURATION TO LENGTH OF NOTE + DECAY VALUE
; IF ATTACK IS LONGER THAN P3, THEN SET TOTAL DURATION TO ATTACK + DECAY
idur      =        (iattack>p3 ? iattack+idecay : p3+idecay)
p3        =        idur
imodf     table    p4, 94                        ; f 94 IS FN FOR MOD SCALAR
imodind   =        imodf*p9                      ; p9 IS MODULATION INDEX
kenv      linen    ampdb(p4), iattack, idur, idecay
kmodenv   linen    imodind, iattack, idur, idecay
asig      foscil   kenv, cpspch(p5), 1, 1, kmodenv, p6
          out      asig
          endin
```

Figure 6.9 Orchestra code for *instr 607,* a FM instrument with pitch and amplitude mapped to envelopes and spectra.

```
f 1   0  128  10  1                                    ; SINE WAVE
                                                       ; AMP ATTACK FACTOR
f 90  0  128  -5  2 60 2 15 1.25 5 .75 5 .6 5 .45 38 .45
                                                       ; AMP DECAY FACTOR
f 91  0  128  -5  .5 60 .5 15 .7 5 1 5 1.2 5 1.75 38 1.75
                                                       ; OCT ATTACK FACTOR
f 92  0  128  -7  2 60 2 15 1.5 5 1 10 1 38 .25
                                                       ; OCT DECAY FACTOR
f 93  0  128  -7  1.5 50 1.5 25 1 15 1 38 .5
                                                       ; MOD INDEX SCALAR
f 94  0  128  -5  .5 60 .5 15 .7 5 1 5 1.5 5 2.25 38 3
```

Figure 6.10 The set of f-tables used to map amplitude and pitch in *instr 607* from figure 6.9.

Completing the Viability Formula

There are other characteristics of acoustic instruments that, when incorporated into a synthetic instrument, help complete the illusion of viability. One of the most obvious is vibrato. A time-variant vibrato function adds substantially to the realism of any synthetic instrument. Other pitch functions, such as the pitch deviation found in initial transients, also help reinforce an instrument's viability.

But the most significant factor in an instrument's acoustic viability is its behavior in space. We identify an instrument's distance from us through the balance between direct and reverberated sound. We locate an instrument's direction through its placement between audio channels. Doppler shifts are critical cues to a moving sound. By dealing with all of the considerations discussed in this section, designers can create comprehensive instruments that are dynamic, expressive, and musical. For real-time synthetic instruments, this complete connection between performance and sound is most important.

Expanding Acoustic Viability in Synthetic Instruments

The goal of acoustic viability is to create synthetic instruments that behave realistically by creating connections of performance and timbre to the synthesis processes. When these principles are applied to synthesis in nonintuitive ways, interesting and sometimes provocative results can occur.

Examples of Unexpected Connections

One direction of expanding the impact of acoustic viability is to create reasonable connections that do not naturally occur. Here are a few suggestions.

In acoustic instruments, vibrato is neither a function of the dynamics nor the pitch of a given note event. The frequency of the vibrato, its depth and the rate at which it appears are all part of a performer's technique and expression. An unexpected connection is created by linking the vibrato depth to the instrument's amplitude. Whether the depth is proportional or inversely proportional to amplitude does not matter. The connection provides an additional mode of expression for an instrument's loudness.

Spatial placement and movement are parameters not available in the acoustic world, but an essential part of the electroacoustic world. Linking a sound object's position in space or motion through space to pitch and amplitude creates a new mode of expression.

Examples of Impossible Transforms

In *instr 607,* transfer-functions, in the form of lookup-tables, are used to translate amplitude and octave information into scaling factors for attack, decay, and modulation-index. The functions were designed to replicate intuitive connections between all the elements. When transfer-functions that represent nonintuitive translations are used, exciting possibilities of impossible (but viable) instruments arise.

For example, inverting the connection between amplitude and envelope rates (using the design in *instr 607*), envelope rates would slow down with higher amplitudes and speed up at lower amplitudes. Such an unlikely scenario would still be acoustically viable in that a specific connection between parameters remains. Surprisingly, the perception of that connection is enough to maintain its expressive quality.

Function Tables as Transforms

One of Csound's major strengths is the flexibility of its f-tables. By using f-tables as transfer-functions, designers are able to carefully sculpt relationships between parameters that are not simply linear or exponential calculations. The functions can be arbitrary breakpoint functions of linear or exponential values, polynomial expressions, spline curves or sets of raw data.

Because these transforms are stored in f-tables, they can be easily changed according to any criteria. And this flexibility leads to new and complex interactions that are infinite in possibility.

Conclusion

The art of sound synthesis has many levels of complexity and subtlety. Finding the right combination of techniques and variables can be a daunting and overwhelming task. Designing sounds simply by trial-and-error is quite often a futile effort. Acoustic viability presents a set of guidelines and strategies for designing synthetic instruments that are psychoacoustically coherent and musically satisfying. For the digital performer, acoustically viable instruments are intuitively responsive. For the composer, these instruments are compelling and musical. And for the listener, the sounds created by these instruments are profoundly real, whether they are recreations of acoustic instruments, or completely new sonic entities. By using acoustic viability, composers can communicate expressive musical ideas using synthetic instruments with the power and emotion of the traditional orchestra.

References

Backus, J. 1969. *The Acoustical Foundations of Music.* New York: W. W. Norton.

Blatter, A. 1980. *Instrumentation/Orchestration.* New York: Longman.

Campbell, M., and C. Greated. 1987. *The Musician's Guide to Acoustics.* New York: Schirmer Books.

De Poli, G., A. Piccialli, and C. Roads. 1991. *Representations of Musical Signals.* Cambridge, Mass.: MIT Press.

Dodge, C., and T. Jerse. 1985. *Computer Music.* New York: Schirmer Books.

Roads, C. 1996. *The Computer Music Tutorial.* Cambridge, Mass.: MIT Press.

Roads, C., and J. Strawn. 1985. *Foundations of Computer Music.* Cambridge, Mass.: MIT Press.

Shatzkin, M. 1993. *Writing For The Orchestra.* Englewood Cliffs, N.J.: Prentice-Hall.

7 Designing Legato Instruments in Csound

Richard W. Dobson

The approach adopted in this chapter is that of an instrumentalist teaching the computer, so to speak, how to sing and articulate a short melody. In the process, both technical (programming-related) and musical (expression and style-related) issues will be explored. As so often in instrumental teaching, the emphasis will be less on the sound *per se* and much more on control, for it is skill in control that enables an artist to sing with expression, however simple the instrument may be. Although the nominal target instrument is the flute, I do not attempt to present more than a token synthesis of its sonic characteristics. The accurate synthesis of any instrument is inevitably complex (and well explored in other chapters of this book) and in the present context it would obfuscate the control-oriented approach presented here. It will be sufficient to provide just enough to draw out specific aspects of expressive control and to demonstrate the general principles involved. Artists with a desire to express through music naturally seek out instruments that offer multiple levels of control. We need to provide these levels; it is a secondary issue whether the instrument we design bears any recognizable relation to anything existing out there.

Legato

In order to develop a model of an instrument capable of true quasi-vocal legato, we need a precise understanding of what legato means, note by note. In terms of common music notation, legato technique is applied to a continuous sequence of notes collected under a slur. Given that a single note can be characterized by attack, sustain and decay stages, a legato phrase is a special case of an extended note, in which the pitch changes during the sustain stage in discrete steps, without breaks, following the notes of the melody. Thus the attack stage of this note is present only for the first pitch and the decay stage only for the last. Such a phrase therefore, comprises at least two notes.

Music notation also defines the *tie,* in which two notes of the same pitch are slurred or tied together. This typically arises for purely notational reasons, for example, when a note at the end of one measure is tied over the bar-line, or a note of irregular duration is required, but can also arise as a compositional device, where the composer wishes to specify some unusual expressive timing that cannot be adequately written for a single note.

It goes almost without saying that a keyboard instrument, such as the piano, is incapable of this form of legato, since it consists of a large set of distinct and mechanically unrelated sound generators (the string and the hammer), whereas vocal legato requires a single mechanism permitting variation of pitch and volume. Keyboard players can only suggest legato by slightly overlapping successive notes. Some degree of legato control was possible on the early monophonic synthesizers and this facility has been carried over to modern polyphonic instruments in the form of MIDI "mono mode." This provides the essential elements of legato control, such as portamento and the takeover of one note by another within a single envelope. A full legato performance is limited, however, by the number of independent continuous control streams made available to the player, such as foot pedals, modulation controls and key pressure. MIDI itself does not directly support vocal legato—these controls have to be encoded as *System-Exclusive* instructions for a particular instrument. This is not really a criticism of MIDI, since it was defined primarily for keyboard instruments and for real-time performance; and whereas human performers routinely read (or think, in the case of an improvisation) several notes ahead, MIDI instruments themselves cannot.

The ability to look ahead is essential for the expressive elements of legato playing—the way one note is played depends on what the next note or notes will be. A player will make a *crescendo* from the first note through several more, to a target note, for example. Such a crescendo may have been marked by the composer; thus both the composer and performer are thinking not in terms of single notes, but in terms of whole phrases or gestures.

The primary technical requirement of a legato instrument is therefore that it achieves continuity of loudness and pitch from note to note. This must be the case even if the instrument we are modeling appears to make instantaneous changes of pitch, as is the case for most wind instruments. We cannot apply truly instantaneous changes of either amplitude or pitch to a waveform without causing an audible glitch. Provision of continuity in turn leads to a consideration of context. Whereas the boundary of a single note consists of the attack and decay stages, the boundary of a slurred note consists of the connection to the previous and following notes. We will need to provide this minimum context to the instrument.

To develop a musically useful instrument we also need to decide precisely *how* we want to change amplitude and pitch from one note to another. Our design must go beyond mere technical continuity to incorporate essential elements of expressive performance. The instrument must be capable of playing a legato phrase of any length, where each note may be at an arbitrary dynamic level and it should be able to give each note an expressive dynamic shape. The most familiar such shape is the swell or *messa di voce.* In the case of the flute, this is usually done by intensifying and relaxing the vibrato. By varying the shape of the swell (making the peak early or late), we can give a note a shape ranging between an accent or diminuendo (early peak) and a crescendo (late peak), which, together with the symmetrical swell itself (and its inverse), form the core expressive resources for most singers and players. If necessary, more elaborate gestures can be constructed from these elements, at the cost of increased complexity in the score. For example, wind-players may use a quick crescendo at the end of a note as a substitute for portamento, which they ordinarily cannot execute. This can be scored using a two-note tie, the second note being given the crescendo shape. Note that in this case, no pitch ramp is required and can be bypassed in the instrument.

The Tie Mechanism: Setting *Hold* from the Score

I have taken as my starting point for a legato instrument in Csound the special *hold* feature of the duration parameter (*p3*) of the standard score. To indicate a held note, the duration parameter must be negative (this is a common programming trick—to use an otherwise impossible or meaningless value to indicate something special). The important point to understand is that, just as in the case of common musical notation, a slur or tie is a relationship between at least two notes. A single note coded as a tie is meaningless. Thus, if a score specifies only a single note with a negative duration, no sound will in fact be generated. A second or final nonheld note must be provided. Through the hold mechanism, this second note will take over the data space of the held note. Thus the amplitude and pitch of the first note will be replaced by that of the second and the net duration may be modified.

The hold feature is illustrated by the following orchestra and score, which also makes use of some of Csound's conditional statements, which here enable the orchestra to have a different behavior for the held and tied notes. For the latter, a simple expressive swell is generated and added to the ongoing initial envelope. By ensuring

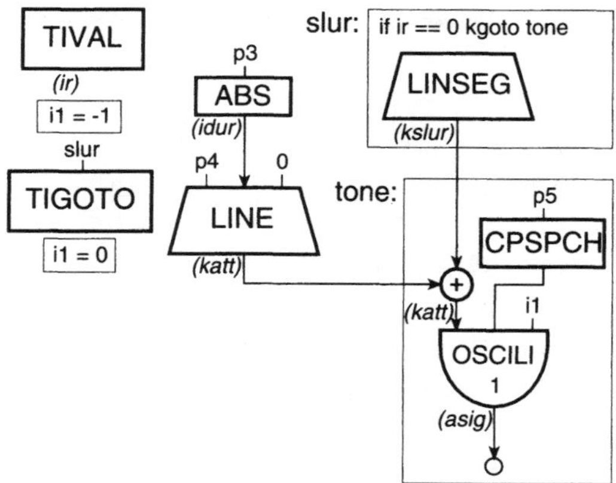

Figure 7.1 Block diagram of *instr 701*, a legato instrument that supports ties.

```
            instr       701         ; A SIMPLE LEGATO INSTRUMENT
idur        =           abs(p3)                    ; NEED POSITIVE DUR FOR ENVELOPE
ir          tival                                  ; FIND OUT IF THIS IS A TIED NOTE
i1          =           -1                         ; SET OSCIL PHASE FOR A TIED NOTE
            tigoto      slur                       ; SKIP REINIT OF ENV ON TIED NOTES
i1          =           0                          ; FIRST NOTE, SO RESET OSCIL PHASE
katt        line        p4, idur, 0                 OVERALL ENVELOPE
slur:
if ir == 0 kgoto tone                              ; NO SWELL IF FIRST NOTE
kslur       linseg      0, idur/2, p4, idur/2, 0   ; SIMPLE SWELL SHAPE
katt        =           katt+kslur                 ; ADD SWELL TO PRIMARY ENVELOPE
tone:
asig        oscili      katt, cpspch(p5), 1, i1    ; REINIT PHASE IF FIRST NOTE
            out         asig
            endin
```

Figure 7.2 Orchestra code for *instr 701*, a legato instrument featuring **tival** and **tigoto** opcodes.

```
f 1     0       1024    10          1 0.95 0.1 0.05 0.01 0.001
; (P4): HELD NOTE SETS INITIAL AMP, TIED NOTE SETS AMP OF SWELL
; INS   ST      DUR     AMP         PCH
i 701   0       -3      20000       8.09    ; HELD NOTE, TAKEN OVER...
i 701   1.5     1.5     5000        9.00    ; BY SECOND, SMALL SWELL
```

Figure 7.3 Score file for *instr 701* featuring the use of a negative *p3* (−3) to enable Csound's "hold" feature.

that the swell starts and ends with zero amplitude, we avoid a glitch at the change-over—so long as we only use two notes.

Initialization

When an instrument is initialized, the internal parameters of each unit generator are reset to their default values and any local memory (e.g., in delay lines and filters) is cleared. Other parameters are then read from the orchestra. In the current context, this means that each time our instrument starts, the phase of the oscillator is reset to default zero. If we need to, we can tell Csound to start the phase at a specific point. For example, setting the initial phase to 0.25 would turn a sinewave (starting at zero amplitude) into a cosine wave (starting at maximum amplitude.)

By setting this optional argument to a negative value, such as -1 (another example of the common programming trick referred to above), we can stop Csound from re-setting the phase, so that for the second note, the oscillator starts from the phase at which the previous note finished. This is not pitch continuity—we need to provide a connecting portamento for that—but without this phase continuity we would almost always get a bad amplitude glitch at the change-over. In fact, whenever we design legato instruments, we will need to prevent reinitialization for any unit generators that retain sample or phase data. This includes all oscillators, filters, delay lines, reverbs, and so on.

In the example above, you will see that the conditional instruction **tigoto** has been used. In Csound, **tigoto** is equivalent to "on a tied note, **igoto** . . ." but it only applies during the initialization stage and is used here to bypass the re-initialization of the primary envelope *katt.* In this case it will simply continue to decay as before (its level and decay rate are remembered, deep within Csound). The interesting result of this is that, even if you set the amplitude of the second note to zero, it will sound with zero expression, continuing the envelope of the first note. Csound does not have a matching inverse test (i.e., "if not a tie, goto . . .") so it has to be coded explicitly as shown, making use of the value obtained from **tival**. Note that all that is needed to turn off the take-over mechanism is to make *p3* positive; in this case two overlapping notes will sound, as usual, each with a complete envelope, but with no swell.

Normally, **tigoto** and **igoto** are used to bypass other initialization statements—to bypass unit generators would result in an opcode not being initialized, in the worst case causing an error. For example, if **igoto** is substituted for **kgoto** in the second test, an error will result, since **linseg** will not have been initialized. In this case however, we are relying firstly on the fact that *katt* has already been initialized by the held note and secondly that its duration (as passed from the score) is enough to support both notes of the slur.

Developing the Model: Setting Context From the Score

The pitch and amplitude ramps need contextual information—parameter fields (p-fields) for the next amplitude and the previous pitch. A special notation is available in the score to do this, without having to enter values explicitly, as illustrated in the four-note phrase shown in figure 7.4.

The notation *pp5* means "the value of the previous *p5*," and refers to the immediately preceding line in the score for the same instrument. Similarly, *np4* looks ahead to the next *p4*. In a tiny score such as this there seems little advantage over entering explicit values, but in more elaborate scores of extended legato passages, where you may be frequently adding or deleting notes, the notation can both clarify what is going on and help reduce errors. Note that **nextamp** for the phrase as a whole must be zero and **prevpch** must match *p5* for the first note of a phrase. I have found these special cases to be useful with extra visual indicators of the score's phrase structure. Note also that the notes are now truly successive (notes do not take over previous notes as in the first example above,) and the start times are defined using the "+" notation to ensure this works (despite the negative *p3* values.) The basic take-over technique of the first example is inadequate for complex multinote phrases with arbitrary amplitude envelopes. The negative *p3* notation, however, is still the most convenient means for ensuring that **tival** is set in the instrument.

Note that the first amplitude segment exists purely for the first note, which must start from zero—for all tied notes, *iamp* and *p4* are the same. These envelopes are incorporated into the complete instrument shown in figure 7.6, which uses conditional statements to deal with the two situations in which the pitch ramp is redundant, the first note and a single-pitch tie, as well as with the special circumstances of the

```
; BASIC P-FIELDS ...                              CONTEXT P-FIELDS
; INS    ST     DUR     AMP      PCH               PREVPCH    NEXTAMP
i 702    0      -1      10000    7.03              7.03       np4
i 702    +      .       4000     8.00              pp5        np4
i 702    .      .       22000    7.06              pp5        np4
; POSITIVE DUR (P3) FOR LAST TIED NOTE
i 702    .      1       4000     7.08              pp5        0
```

Figure 7.4 Score file featuring **pp** and **np** directives to refer to previous and future parameter data.

```
idur    =        abs(p3)
iamp    =        p4                      ; OR ZERO FOR FIRST NOTE
ipch1   =        cpspch(p6)
ipch2   =        cpspch(p5)              ; (0->)p4->p7
amp     linseg   iamp, 0.05, p4, idur-0.1, p4, 0.05, p7
iport   =        0.1                     ; INITIAL 100MSEC PORTAMENTO
kpch    linseg   ipch1, iport, ipch2, idur-iport, ipch2
```

Figure 7.5 Amplitude and pitch envelope segment of orchestra code for *instr 702,* the legato instrument for performing score shown in figure 7.4.

```
           instr   702      ; A MORE ELABORATE LEGATO INSTRUMENT
idur       =       abs(p3)                ; MAIN INIT BLOCK
ipch1      =       cpspch(p6)
ipch2      =       cpspch(p5)
kpch       =       ipch2
iport      =       0.1                    ; 100MSEC PORTAMENTO
iatt       =       0.05                   ; DEFAULT DURS FOR AMPLITUDE RAMPS
idec       =       0.05                   ; ASSUME THIS IS A TIED NOTE:
iamp       =       p4                     ; SO START AT P4 LEVEL...
i1         =       -1                     ; ... AND KEEP PHASE CONTINUITY
ir         tival                          ; CONDITIONAL INIT BLOCK:TIED NOTE?
           tigoto  start
i1         =       0                      ; FIRST NOTE: RESET PHASE
iamp       =       0                      ; AND ZERO IAMP
start:
iadjust    =       iatt+idec
if idur >= iadjust igoto doamp            ; ADJUST RAMP DURATIONS FOR SHORT..
iatt       =       idur/2-0.005           ; ... NOTES, 10MSECS LIMIT
idec       =       iatt                   ; ENSURE NO ZERO-DUR SEGMENTS
iadjust    =       idur-0.01
iport      =       0.005                  ; MAKE AMPLITUDE RAMP...
doamp:                                    ; ... (ARATE FOR CLEANNESS) AND...
ilen       =       idur-iadjust           ; ... SKIP PITCH RAMP GENERATION...
amp        linseg  iamp, iatt, p4, ilen, p4, idec, p7
if ir == 0 || p6 == p5 kgoto slur         ; ...IF FIRST NOTE OR TIE.
; MAKE PITCH RAMP, PORTAMENTO AT START OF NOTE
kpramp     linseg  ipch1, iport, ipch2, idur-iport, ipch2
kpch       =       kpramp
slur:                                     ; MAKE THE NOTE
aamp       =       amp
asig       oscili  aamp, kpch, 1, i1
           out     asig
           endin
```

Figure 7.6 Orchestra code for *instr 702,* a more elaborate legato instrument featuring conditional init block, portamento, and slurring capabilities plus dynamic crescendo and diminuendo.

first note. It also adjusts ramp durations for short notes down to 10 milliseconds (msec.)—grace notes shorter than that are probably errors. Note also the change to the amplitude ramp, in order to preserve the audio quality for the short ramps.

A long 100 msec. portamento has been set so that the effect can be heard clearly. For the flute model, *iport* should be reduced to anything between 10 and 25 msecs. If you want to play with this further, use a new p-field to set a value for *iport.* Similarly, to manage long *crescendi* and *diminuendi,* p-fields for *iatt* and/or *idec* can also be set from the score.

With this instrument the core technical components of legato control have been completed. It can be regarded as a template from which it is possible to develop a variety of instruments and performance styles. You can experiment with the amplitude ramp by changing the times to various combinations of short and long segments, with dynamic changes from note to note (including ties) and with portamento. The one important thing is to ensure that the total of the times in the envelopes adds up to the overall duration (*idur*), otherwise **linseg** will give unwanted results.

Expression Controls

There are two primary components of expression on most melody instruments—dynamic inflection and vibrato. Both are complex and subtle techniques, largely intuitive for most players (even when they think they are thinking about them). Most players understand dynamic inflection from note to note, a smaller number understand it within the note. Among flute-players, the combination of vibrato and inflection within the note is an especially characteristic feature of those trained in the modern French School.

The addition of an expressive swell to the basic instrument is simple, requiring no more than a basic triangular ramp, whose height (amplitude) can be set from the score so that it can vary from note to note. Since it will be added to the main amplitude ramp, the swell can even be negative, down to a limit of $-p4$. By adding a further proportional p-field to the score, we can move the peak-point in time within the note, for *accents* and *crescendi* (when a proportional p-field is simply one between 0 and 1 (exclusively for **linseg**)—in effect, a percentage—then there is no danger of the two halves of the swell not adding up to the exact duration of the note). Note that to avoid any risk of amplitude glitches, the swell ramp must start and end from zero.

Vibrato poses a challenge, both technically and musically. It is important to have as clear an idea as possible of the nature, use and feasibility of vibrato, before commencing synthesis. (Strictly speaking, variation of pitch is vibrato and variation of

```
                                              ; (PUT IN MAIN INIT BLOCK)
irise   =       idur*p9                       ; p9 PROPORTIONAL, 0 < P9 < 1
ifall   =       idur-irise
        ...
slur:                                         ; MAKE THE NOTE
aslur   linseg  0, irise, p8, ifall, 0        ; p8 = AMPLITUDE OF SWELL
aamp    =       amp+aslur
        ...
```

Figure 7.7 Orchestra code excerpt that supports swells.

```
i 703  0 1       10000  8.04  8.04  0    15000  0.5
i 703  + 0.7     10000  9.00  9.00  0    -7000  0.4   ; INVERSE SWELL
i 703  + -0.09   8000   8.11  8.11  np4  5000   0.05
i 703  + -0.09   12000  8.10  pp5   np4  7000
i 703  + 0.09    15000  8.09  pp5   0    9000
i 703  + -1      20000  8.07  8.07  np4  10000  0.6
i 703  + 1       10000  8.06  pp5   0    5000   0.2
```

Figure 7.8 Score file with swells, slurs, and context sensitivity.

volume is tremolo, though in music the latter term is associated primarily with rapid reiteration of notes, such as up and down bowing on a violin. Confusingly, it also applies to the rapid alternation of pitches more than a second apart, which would otherwise be a simple trill). On the flute, vibrato is almost all variation of volume and should, strictly speaking, be called *tremolo,* whereas on the violin it is all pitch variation. Following is a description of the different elements that make up a vibrato.

- *Speed:* between 4–8 Hz, the faster rates are reserved for short notes, or moments. For a wind player this is physically demanding. It is common for the speed to vary not only through a phrase, but also within a note.
- *Depth:* shallow for low to moderate intensity, deep for power. The flute has a poor dynamic range in comparison with other instruments; a progressive deepening of vibrato can be used where a crescendo is marked—the ear hears the peak level of the vibrato as the level of the note. It is usually a bad idea to combine deep vibrato with high speed.
- *Fast notes:* depends on the instrument. On the violin, the fingering and vibrato mechanisms are the same, so that it is not feasible to apply vibrato to fast passage-work, though it can be added to single short notes. On the flute, vibrato and fingering are independent, so it is possible, in principle, to play fast passage-work while adding vibrato.
- *Timing:* on the flute, vibrato will normally start from the start of a note, though delayed vibrato may be used occasionally. Most usually, vibrato will start off slow

and shallow, increasing in both dimensions as the note develops. A player cannot calculate in advance how fast a vibrato must be to fit exactly into a note. Rather, a comfortable and expressive speed is used and a minimal adjustment (speeding up or slowing down) is made toward the end of the note. Vibrato may or may not be inhibited for fast notes.

- *Evenness:* vibrato is as vulnerable to human irregularities as are most other elements of performance. Strictly speaking, therefore, a fully realistic implementation of vibrato must include random variation of both amplitude and frequency. This is avoided in the examples presented here, not only for the sake of simplicity, but also because I found that, when developing this model, even the simplest oscillator-based vibrato can sound acceptably dynamic and nonmechanical, when combined with the simple expression control described here. Excessive use of random modulation can merely lead to the synthesis of bad playing.

To implement all these aspects would involve considerable complexity in both instrument and score. I confine myself here to a relatively simple, fixed implementation that, when combined with the dynamic swell already in place, will nevertheless enable melodic lines of considerable expressiveness to be produced. It is, in any case, easy enough to add further p-fields, for example, to change vibrato speed.

The most important technical issue is how the vibrato is added to the main tone. We already have a swell envelope combined additively, so this would appear to be equally reasonable for vibrato. Indeed, it can be done this way and in most cases it can appear to work reliably, though it will always require amplitudes to be set carefully. The presence of two additive layers, however, will increase the danger, in a legato instrument, of amplitude discontinuities. Instead, recalling that on the flute, dynamic inflections are projected through vibrato, we can *multiply* the expression envelope (which always starts and ends at zero) with the vibrato signal (which must lie within the range 0–1), so that we keep with one safe additive layer. Although this prevents any glitches resulting from phase discontinuities, we nevertheless will need to preserve phase across single-pitch ties. In the orchestra excerpt from *instr 704* shown in figure 7.9, the vibrato is turned off for short notes.

One small detail worth noting here is the phase offset set for the vibrato. Assuming a sinewave shape, this turns it into a cosine, ensuring that vibrato is always applied with the maximum amplitude at the start of the note. It is well worth experimenting with this offset—the differences are audible but subtle and you may feel that this is another control worth managing from the score.

```
idovib  =       1                       ; (MAIN INIT BLOCK)
i2      =       -1                      ; VIBRATO PHASE
        ...
        tigoto  start
i2      =       0.25                    ; VIB STARTS WITH COSINE PHASE
        ...                             ; ADJUST RAMP DURATIONS FOR...
if idur >= iadjust igoto doamp          ; ... short notes, 10msecs limit
idovib  =       0
        ...
slur:                                   ; MAKE THE NOTE
aslur   linseg  0, irise, p8, ifall, 0 ; p8 = AMPLITUDE OF SWELL
if idovib = 0 goto slur1                ; SKIP VIBRATO IF SHORT NOTE
avib    oscili  0.5, 4.5, 2, i2         ; MED SPEED, ASSUME SINE FOR f2!
avib    =       avib+0.5                ; OFFSET SO RANGE = 0...1
aslur   =       aslur*avib              ; APPLY VIBRATO TO SWELL
slur1:
aamp    =       amp+aslur
        ...
```

Figure 7.9 Orchestra code excerpt from *instr 704* with conditional vibrato control.

Completing the Model: Synthesis in Principle

It is useful to consider the general properties of a musical instrument that make it effective for expressive playing. Although players are doubtlessly attracted to their chosen instrument, in the first instance, by its sound, it is not really the sound in itself that makes it expressive. Sounds of, say, a trumpet, a violin, a bassoon, or a flute are different, but they share one vital property: they can be varied in time both timbrally and dynamically. As players develop and mature in their technical skill and musical understanding, this expressive aspect of tone increases in importance, until a point where they will pay many thousands of dollars for an instrument that offers the best controllable range and quality of color. Equally important is the distinctive character of the attack tone. Though it is a common factor within each instrument type, it is also subject to great individual refinement and variation by advanced players. The assertion that all players seek to emulate the human voice can be easily understood anthropomorphically, since the voice exhibits just such characteristics—the attack tone of the instrument corresponds to a vocal consonant and the sustained tone to a vowel. As these naturally change in a vocal utterance, so players strive to achieve similar changes to both elements of their sound.

Even percussion instruments are not devoid of these attributes—though a xylophone may appear to have but one sound, percussionists accumulate a wide variety of beaters with which to elicit a correspondingly wide range of sounds. One well known English player was described once as "talking of brake drums as one might talk of a fine claret." This keenness of aural discrimination and evaluation is no less important to the electroacoustic composer.

For our immediate purposes then, it is less important to achieve a truly accurate timbral synthesis of the flute than to provide *in principle* similar properties—a tone that can be varied timbrally and in which the attack has special identifying characteristics. Flute players are often taught in their early stages that they "must start notes with the tongue." Though this might be true sometimes, advanced players do not tongue simply because they have to, but often because they want to. The sound of a tongued note on the flute is subtle and distinctive and a musical pleasure in its own right, when properly cultivated. It is particularly vivid on the lower-voiced instruments, such as the alto and bass flute, both of which are widely felt to exhibit an especially vocal character.

This "*chiff*" is a complex, semichaotic sound that I have merely approximated here by mixing a shaped noise burst with the main tone, (it could as well be the bow noise for a violin, or the stick noise for a drum). Since my model is based on the sound of a classically trained player, the chiff is discreet—the flute tone found on most synthesizers and samplers is modeled on that of the typical jazz doubler whose first instrument is the saxophone and whose sound consists of as much noise as tone.

I have distinguished two components: a fixed high frequency noise burst and a pitched component that is more evident in the low register. I further distinguish the attack note from tied notes by lengthening the attack ramp itself if the note is long enough to leave room for the chiff. The chiff is therefore highly context-sensitive and requires further conditional statements, in addition to those already provided. These sometimes take the form of a selection from two alternatives depending on another value, for which an especially compact conditional expression is available.

To suggest the thinning of timbre with register, a simple fixed filter is applied to the output tone, to limit the high partials on notes above E, in the second octave. As a final refinement I have also assigned the decay length *idec* from the score, requiring a tenth p-field in the score, in order to set a long diminuendo on a final note.

Note that *instr 705* includes two simple examples of "defensive programming." The first one deals with the case of *p9* being set to zero in the score and the second prevents an overly negative expression amplitude (*p8*) from producing a net negative amplitude. Both are really conveniences—for example, instead of setting some low nonzero value for *p9,* I can write a neat zero and get the effect I want. Similarly, by preventing a net negative amplitude whatever the value of *p8,* I can experiment with *p4* values without having to check *p8* values too.

Although this seems to run counter to the prevailing style amongst Csound programmers, to rely on rigorously correct scores, it does reflect real-life instrumental practice more than some composers may like to admit—there can be a few perform-

```
          instr      705         ; FULL LEGATO INSTRUMENT WITH "CHIFF"
idur      =          abs(p3)                          ; MAIN INIT BLOCK
ipch1     =          cpspch(p6)
ipch2     =          cpspch(p5)
kpch      =          ipch2
iport     =          0.02                             ; TIGHT PITCH
iatt      =          0.02                             ; AND AMPLITUDE RAMPS
idec      =          p10                              ; GET DECAY FROM SCORE
irise     =          idur*p9                          ; SET SWELL PEAK POSITION
                                                      ; ... (IFALL SET LATER)
idovib    =          1                                ; ASSUME WE USE VIBRATO
icut      =          (p5 > 9.01 ? 4000 : 2500)        ; TRIM HIGHEST PARTIALS
                                                      ; ASSUME THIS IS A TIED NOTE
iamp      =          p4                               ; TIED NOTE STARTS AT SCORE AMP
i1        =          -1                               ; PHASE FOR TIED NOTE
i2        =          -1                               ; PHASE FOR VIBRATO
ir        tival      ; TIED NOTE?                     ; CONDITIONAL INIT BLOCK
          tigoto     tie
i1        =          0                                ; FIRST NOTE, RESET PHASE
i2        =          0.25                             ; COSINE PHASE FOR VIBRATO
iamp      =          0                                ; SET START AMP
iatt      =          0.08                             ; STRETCH ATTACK IF FIRST NOTE
tie:
iadjust   =          iatt+idec                        ; LONG NOTE, WE'RE SAFE
if idur >=iadjust igoto doamp                         ; adjust ramp durations for
iatt      =          (idur/2)-0.005                   ; ... SHORT NOTES, 10MSEC LIMIT
idec      =          iatt                             ; CAN'T HAVE ZERO TIMESPAN
iadjust   =          idur-0.01                        ; (ENSURE ILEN != 0 FOR LINSEG)
idovib    =          0                                ; NO VIBRATO ON SHORT NOTES
iport     =          0.005                            ; EVEN TIGHTER PITCH RAMP
doamp:
ilen      =          idur-iadjust                     ; MAKE AMPLITUDE RAMP
amp       linseg     iamp, iatt, p4, ilen, p4, idec, p7
                                                      ; ADD CHIFF ON FIRST NOTE
if ir == 1 goto pitch                                 ; NO CHIFF ON TIED NOTES
ichiff    =          p4/10                            ; MATCH CHIFF TO VOLUME OF NOTE
                                                      ; BALANCE CHIFFS WITH REGISTER
ifac1     =          (p5 > 9.01 ? 3.0 : 1.)           ; (AVOID DIVISION AT AUDIO...
ifac2     =          (p5 > 9.01 ? 0.1 : 0.2)          ; ...RATES)
aramp     linseg     0, 0.005, ichiff, 0.02, ichiff*0.5, 0.05, 0, 0, 0
anoise    rand       aramp
achiff1   reson      anoise, 3000, 500, 1, 1          ; 2 FILTERS FOR FIXED HF CHIFF,
achiff2   reson      anoise, 6000, 1000, 1, 1         ; ... WITH RESCALING
achiff3   reson      anoise,ipch2*2, 20, 0, 1         ; ONE FILTER FOR PITCHED CHIFF,
achiff    =          (achiff1+achiff2)*ifac1+(achiff3*ifac2)
pitch:                                                ; MAKE PITCH RAMP
if ir == 0 || p6 == p5 kgoto expr       ;skip ptchramp gen if 1st note or tie
kpramp    linseg     ipch1, iport, ipch2, idur-iport, ipch2
kpch      =          kpramp
expr:                                                 ; MAKE EXPRESSION ENVELOPE
; p8 SETS PEAK OF EXPRESSION POINT, P9 MOVES IT IF p9==0 (ILLEGAL FOR LINSEG)
irise     =          (p9>0.?irise:iatt)               ; SET MAXIMUM ACCENT SHAPE
ifall     =          idur-irise
; MAKE SURE A NEG p8 DOES NOT TAKE AMP BELOW ZERO
p8        =          ((p8+p4) > 0. ? p8 : -p4)
aslur     linseg     0, irise, p8, ifall, 0           ; MAKE VIBRATO
if idovib == 0 goto play                              ; SKIP VIBRATO IF SHORT NOTE
avib      oscili     0.5, 4.5, 2, 0.25                ; MED SPEED, ASSUME SINE F2
avib      =          avib+0.5
aslur     =          aslur*avib
play:                                                 ; MAKE THE NOTE
aamp      =          amp+aslur
aflute    oscili     aamp, kpch, 1, i1                ; TRIM PARTIALS OF HIGH
asig      butterlp   aflute, icut, 1                  ; ... NOTES, NO REINIT
          out        asig+achiff*0.25                 ; FINAL SCALING OF CHIFF
          endin
```

Figure 7.10 Orchestra code for *instr 705,* full legato instrument with added "chiff" attack noise.

```
f 1    0    1024     10      1 0.95 0.1 0.01 0.01 0.001
f 2    0    1024     10      1        ; VIBRATO
t 0 40 3 40 3 30 ;slow down in bar 2
; BASIC PFIELDS                       CONTEXT....             EXPRESSION.....
;       ST   DUR      AMP     PCH     PFROM   AMPTO  AMP      PEAK   DIM
; BAR 1
i 705   0    -0.75    10000   9.10    9.10    np4    20000    0.5    0.05
i 705   +    -0.125   5000    9.09    pp5     np4    1000     0.5
i 705   +    0.125    5000    9.11    pp5     0      1000
;
i 705   +    -0.75    10000   9.08    9.08    np4    20000    0.8
i 705   +    -0.125   5000    9.07    pp5     np4    1000     0.5
i 705   +    0.125    5000    9.09    pp5     0      1000
;
i 705   +    -0.25    8000    9.06    9.06    np4    10000    0.35
i 705   +    -0.25    7000    9.05    pp5     np4    500      0
i 705   +    -0.25    6000    9.04    pp5     np4    1000     0.4
i 705   +    0.25     4000    9.01    pp5     0      2000     0.7
; BAR 2
i 705   +    -0.75    15000   9.10    9.10    np4    -15000   0.65
i 705   +    -0.125   5000    10.00   pp5     np4    1000     0.5
i 705   +    0.125    5000    9.11    pp5     0      1000     0
; DELAYED VIBRATO ON LAST NOTE AND LONG FINAL DECAY
i 705   +    -0.5     8000    9.10    9.10    np4    0
i 705   +    1.5      8000    9.10    pp5     np4    10000    0.2    0.5
```

Figure 7.11 Score file for first line of Debussy's "Syrinx" to be performed by *instr 705* shown in figure 7.10.

ers who have not, at some time, discreetly rewritten some passage to make it more manageable, or at all playable.

This instrument will play the test score shown in figure 7.8, with the second function table *f 2* added for the vibrato and if the extra p-field for the decay is added. But for those who would like to test the instrument with a piece of real music, I have added in figure 7.11 an interpretation of the first line of Debussy's *Syrinx* for solo flute. The expression is idiosyncratic in places, but it does illustrate all the special facilities described above. The final note is coded as a tie, to enable a delayed vibrato, concluding with a longish *diminuendo.* Note also the difference in timbre for the low D flat, at the end of the first bar.

The remaining unanswered question is, of course, why these values and not others? Some patterns can be explained as pronunciation: accent the first note of a slur and soften the rest (especially for an appoggiatura, for example, as at the end of the first score example above). But as the size of the slur increases other "rules" can take over, such as the need to make a crescendo to the next strong note. Other gestures, such as the inverse swell, are less explainable, except perhaps by reference to those spoken (or sung) at times of particular emotion, or simply by the need for variety. Certainly there is an infinite number of ways of playing even this first line. The published edition conceals the fact that the music was originally composed as incidental music for a play and was written without bar-lines or expression marks. Accordingly, players tend to adopt a particularly free approach to its interpretation. For example, it is almost traditional amongst players schooled in the French style (as taught by Marcel Moyse) to accelerate vigorously through the first bar. Though this may be done purely for expressive reasons, there is no doubt that it also makes the line easier to play in one breath. The values used above correspond to a fairly conservative and literal rendering of the published score and reflect an accordingly restrained style. Some players prioritize tone and their own favorite gestures so much that even pronunciation is sometimes foregone. In short, it is tempting to invent all manner of pseudo-reasons this or that note is played in this or that way. Other players will do some things differently; the reader is encouraged to experiment widely and to listen to a variety of different performances.

Conclusion

It would be an especially valuable exercise to take one recorded performance and attempt to model the expressive nuances as closely as possible. Performers themselves may find such an exercise stimulating and thought-provoking. Composers interested in developing rule-based systems for musical performance should find that this instrument (perhaps with a few extra controls from the score) will realize all but the most complex expressive patterns. For me, the challenge has been to reconcile what I like to think of as an instinctive and spontaneous performance with the ruthless detail required in Csound and the process has indeed been of great value to my own work as a flute teacher and player.

8 Contiguous-Group Wavetable Synthesis of the French Horn in Csound

Andrew Horner and Lydia Ayers

This chapter introduces a wavetable synthesis model for the French horn in Csound. The model is intuitive, since it uses a single spectrum to describe each part of the horn's range. Predefined amplitude envelopes control the desired articulation and ensure that the tone gets brighter with increasing amplitude.

The Horn

The French horn is probably the most mysterious of the brass instruments. Its ethereal sound is due in part to the bell being pointed toward the back wall instead of directly at the audience. The horn has a conical bore wrapped tightly in a circle of valves and tubes. The horn has a much more mellow sound than the trumpet and trombone, more closely related to the tuba, which is also conical. The horn plays prominent roles in orchestras, brass quintets, woodwind quintets and as a solo instrument in hunting calls and fanfares.

The French horn has a much wider range than most people realize (from F2 to F5 on a MIDI scale), though the lower register of the horn is seldom used. The instrument requires considerable skill, since it is easy to miss notes because the upper register uses higher natural harmonics than the other brass instruments.

Previous work on modelling wind instruments has primarily focused on simulating the trumpet (Risset and Mathews 1969; Chowning 1973; Morrill 1977; Moorer, Grey and Strawn 1978; Beauchamp 1982). The horn has not received as much attention, despite its interesting and distinctive character.

This chapter develops a wavetable synthesis model for the horn. An expressive Csound implementation of the model is also given along with a transcription of the opening horn solo in Strauss's *Til Eulenspiegel's Merry Pranks.*

Figure 8.1 Range of the French horn.

The Model

Our wavetable synthesis model uses a spectrum to determine the steady-state response and one amplitude envelope to control the articulation. We use a special case of wavetable synthesis, *contiguous-group wavetable synthesis,* inspired by the idea of group synthesis using disjoint sets of harmonics in each wavetable (Kleczkowski 1989; Eaglestone and Oates 1992; Cheung and Horner 1996). Figure 8.2 is a block diagram of our contiguous-group synthesis instrument. In our model, we allocate the fundamental to group 1, harmonics 2 and 3 to group 2, harmonics 4–7 to group 3 and harmonics 8 and above to group 4. This contiguous grouping is perceptually motivated, roughly corresponding to the division of the frequency range by critical bands (Zwicker and Terhardt 1980).

We find a single representative steady-state spectrum from the original tone and then break it into disjoint groups of harmonics. How do we decide which steady-state spectrum is most representative? One method is picking the brightest spectrum. Another method is picking the least bright spectrum. Unfortunately, either method can select an unrepresentative spectrum if the original tone is unusually bright or dark at times.

A more successful strategy is picking a spectrum with average brightness to ensure that we do not get an extreme solution. Optimization is also possible, although we have found the average brightness solution to be similar and to require much less computation. We can intuitively imagine the amplitude envelopes for these contiguous groups as equalization levels for the different frequency bands. We could use least squares to construct envelopes that would best match the original tone (Cheung and Horner 1996).

This assumes, however, that the original tone has the articulation we want in resynthesis. For wind instruments, articulation seems to vary more owing to musical context than from instrument to instrument. After looking at dozens of sustained tones, we devised the prototype amplitude envelope shown as *ampEnv1* in figure 8.3.

We use this envelope for wavetable 1, which contains the fundamental. For the other groups, we use exponentially-related envelopes. For group 2, we square the

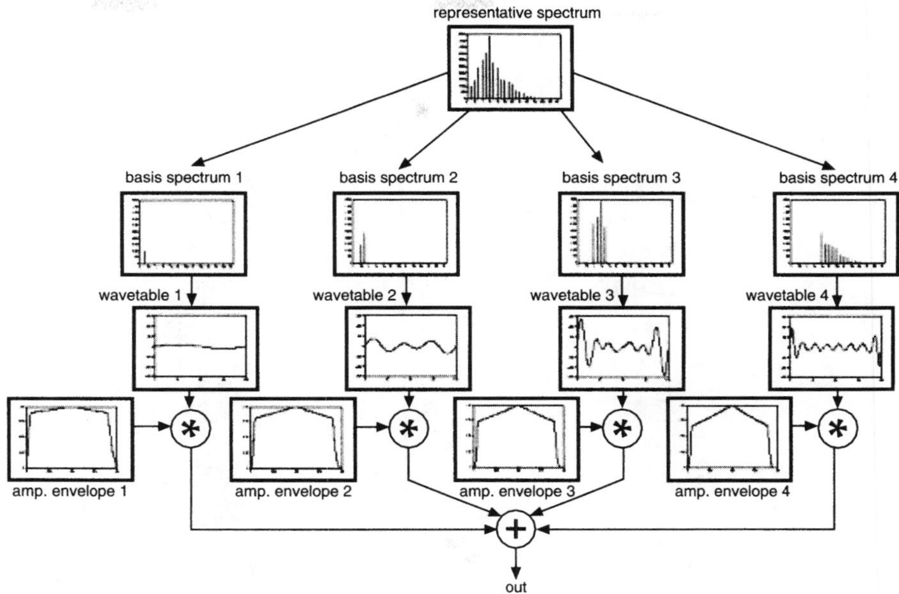

Figure 8.2 Block diagram of the Horner-Ayers contiguous-group synthesis algorithm.

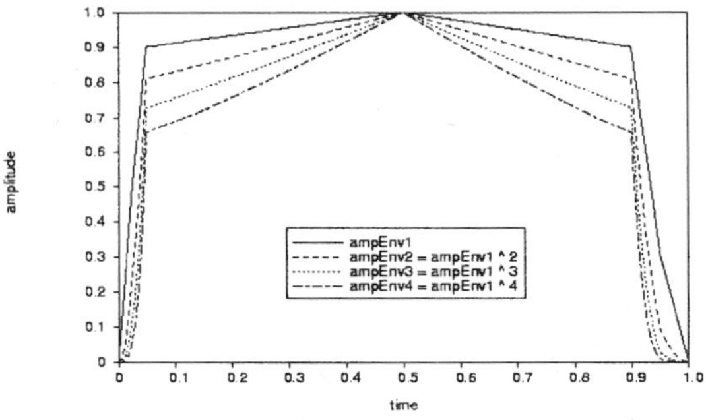

Figure 8.3 Exponentially related amplitude envelope set derived from prototype envelope *ampEnv1*.

prototype amplitude envelope, for group 3 we cube it and for group 4 we raise it to the fourth power.

These relationships ensure that the tone gets brighter as it reaches the peak amplitude value and gradually gets darker during the decay. This approximation certainly loses some spectral nuances, but it guarantees a smooth spectral evolution with the brightness characteristic of acoustic wind instruments. Also, even though the group 1 amplitude envelope contains linear segments, the exponential relationship of the other groups makes the attack and decay exponential.

So far we have only discussed how to match a single tone from an instrument. To represent spectral changes over the instrument's pitch range, we use the same trick as most synthesizers by matching about two pitches from each octave. For unmatched pitches, we simply pick the nearest matched pitch and use its wavetables and amplitude envelopes with the desired fundamental frequency.

The Implementation

To verify the usefulness of our horn design, we created a Csound orchestra of the group synthesis model and derived the following parameters:

- *p4* = overall amplitude scaling factor
- *p5* = pitch in Hz (normal pitch range: F2–F5 (sounding))
- *p6* = percent of vibrato depth, recommended range [0, .5], 0 = no vibrato, 1 = 1% vibrato depth
- *p7* = attack time in seconds, recommended range [.03, .12]
- *p8* = decay time in seconds, recommended range [.04, .25]
- *p9* = overall brightness/filter cutoff factor, 1 being the least bright/lowest filter cutoff frequency (40 Hz) and 9 being brightest/highest filter cutoff frequency (10,240 Hz)

Let us examine the Csound instrument in detail. After the global variables, a few lines of comments describe the parameter fields (p-fields) *p4–p9* and their appropriate values. The lines immediately following move the p-values into i-variables, making reordering of the p-fields easy if desired. The variable *iamp* (*p4*) controls the approximate maximum amplitude the instrument will reach on a sustained note. The variable *ifreq* (*p5*) contains the fundamental frequency. Avoid notes higher than F5, since aliasing can occur as the wavetable's highest harmonics go beyond the Nyquist frequency (half the sampling rate).

```
giseed  =       .5
garev   init    0

        instr   801            ; WAVETABLE FRENCH HORN
iamp    =       p4                              ; OVERALL AMP SCALING FACTOR
ifreq   =       p5                              ; PITCH IN HERTZ
ivibd   =       p6*ifreq/100.0                  ; VIB DEPTH RELATIVE TO FUND.
iatt    =       p7                              ; ATTACK TIME
idec    =       p8                              ; DECAY TIME
isus    =       p3-iatt-idec-.005               ; SUSTAIN TIME
ifcut   tablei  p9, 2                           ; LP FILTER CUTOFF FREQUENCY
kvibd   linseg  .1, .8*p3, 1, .2*p3, .7         ; VIBRATO
kvibd   =       kvibd*ivibd                     ; VIBRATO DEPTH
ivibr1  =       2.5+giseed
giseed  =       frac(giseed*105.947)
ivibr2  =       4.5+giseed
giseed  =       frac(giseed*105.947)
kvrate  linseg  ivibr1, p3, ivibr2              ; TIME-VARYING VIBRATO RATE
kvib    oscil   kvibd, kvrate, 1
kfreq   =       ifreq+kvib
amp1    linseg  0, .001, 0, .5*iatt, .5, .5*iatt, .9, .5*isus, 1,
                .5*isus, .9, .5*idec, .3, .5*idec, 0, 1, 0
amp2    =       amp1*amp1                       ; WAVETABLE ENVELOPES
amp3    =       amp2*amp1
amp4    =       amp3*amp1
irange  tablei  ifreq, 4
iwt1    =       1                               ; WAVETABLE NUMBERS
iwt2    table   (irange*4), 3
iwt3    table   (irange*4)+1, 3
iwt4    table   (irange*4)+2, 3
inorm   table   (irange*4)+3, 3                 ; NORMALIZATION FACTOR
iphase  =       giseed                          ; SAME PHASE FOR ALL TABLES
giseed  =       frac(giseed*105.947)
awt1    oscil   amp1, kfreq, iwt1, iphase       ; WAVETABLE LOOKUP
awt2    oscil   amp2, kfreq, iwt2, iphase
awt3    oscil   amp3, kfreq, iwt3, iphase
awt4    oscil   amp4, kfreq, iwt4, iphase
asig    =       (awt1+awt2+awt3+awt4)*iamp/inorm
afilt   tone    asig, ifcut                     ; LP FILTER...
asig    balance afilt, asig                     ; ... TO CONTROL BRIGHTNESS
garev   =       garev+asig
        out     asig
        endin

        instr   899            ;SIMPLE REVERB
arev    reverb  garev, 1.2                      ; OUTPUT REVERB SIGNAL
        out     .1*arev                         ; SET GAREV TO 0 ...
garev   =       0                               ; ... TO PREVENT FEEDBACK
        endin
```

Figure 8.4 Orchestra code for *instr 801*, an example of continuous-group wavetable synthesis of French Horn.

The variable *ivibd* (*p6*) controls the maximum depth of vibrato relative to the fundamental frequency. A value of 1.0 indicates a 1% vibrato relative to the fundamental frequency (a strong vibrato), while .5 represents a .5% vibrato (a moderate vibrato).

Attack and decay times are stored in *iatt* (*p7*) and *idec* (*p8*), respectively. Attack times for the horn range from about .03 seconds for the higher pitches to .12 seconds for lower pitches. Decay times range from .04 seconds to as much as .25 seconds.

Finally, *ifiltcut* stores a lowpass filter cutoff frequency, determined by *p9* as a brightness index between 1 (least bright) and 9 (most bright), where each increment increases the cutoff frequency by an octave. The brightness factor allows softer dynamics to be played with less brightness.

Next, after enveloping the vibrato depth, the vibrato rate increases from about 3 Hz to about 6 Hz over the duration of the tone. The changing vibrato rate helps the instrument sound more natural, as performers typically use dynamic vibrato rates to push along the phrase. Since we know the note durations in advance in Csound, so we can push the rate appropriately according to the note length (something you cannot do on a real-time synthesizer). Small random perturbations are also added to the vibrato rate.

When we were first designing this instrument, Csound did not have an i-time random number generator, so we used the statement shown in figure 8.5 to quickly generate pseudo-random numbers between zero and one.

Defining *giseed* as a global variable prevents it from being re-initialized on each note. We generated 1,000,000 values using the above formula to check the distribution of the two most significant digits. Figure 8.6 shows that the distribution is basically uniform, indicating that the random number generator is good enough for our purposes. We use *giseed* throughout the instrument design to make each note unique.

After the vibrato code, the amplitude envelopes are defined and the pitch range of the current note is determined. The pitch range determines which wavetables and amplitude normalization factor to use. The **oscil** statements control wavetable lookup. The scaled output of each wavetable is summed into *asig*, which is then normalized to the desired level.

Next, the signal goes into a lowpass filter and is sent to the reverberator in *instr 899*. Since the horn is pointed toward the back when played, the listener rarely hears the direct sound from the instrument. Thus, without reverberation, the instrument sounds unnatural to most people, but quite normal to players used to practicing in small rooms with absorptive walls. We use a 10% reverberation of 1.2 seconds to simulate the sound of a concert hall. Finally, we pass the signal to the output.

```
giseed    =    frac(giseed*105.947)
```

Figure 8.5 Algorithm for generating an i-time pseudo-random number sequence.

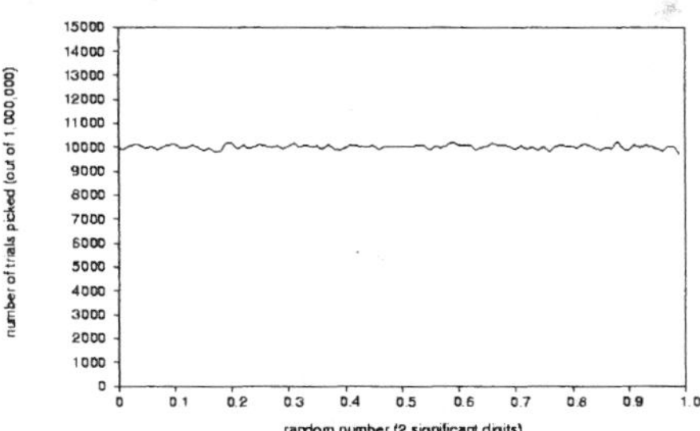

Figure 8.6 Distribution of 1,000,000 values from our pseudo-random number generator.

Figure 8.7 Opening horn solo from Strauss's' *Til Eulenspiegel's Merry Pranks*. The score (for horn in F) sounds a fifth lower than written, except the bass clef notes that sound a fourth higher than written.

The Proof

To verify the usefulness of our horn design, we scored the well-known horn solo from *Til Eulenspiegels' Merry Pranks* by Strauss as an example. The solo is unusual in that it covers the full range of the instrument in a single phrase as shown in figure 8.7.

Conclusion

Our wavetable synthesis model provides an elegant way to represent the horn. Comparing the spectra from each range to see how they differ allows them to be changed, in order to produce horn-like timbres. It is possible to manipulate the few parameters directly.

```
f 1     0   4097   -9    1 1.0 0
f 2     0   16     -2    40 40 80 160 320 640 1280 2560 5120 10240 10240
f 3     0   64     -2    11 12 13 52.476 14 15 16 18.006 17 18 19 11.274 20 21 22
                         6.955 23 24 25 2.260 26 27 10 1.171 28 29 10 1.106 30 10
                         10 1.019
f 4     0   2048   -17   0 0 85 1 114 2 153 3 204 4 272 5 364 6 486 7
f 10    0   5      -9    1 0.0 0
f 11    0   4097   -9    2 6.236 0 3 12.827 0
f 12    0   4097   -9    4 21.591 0 5 11.401 0 6 3.570 0 7 2.833 0
f 13    0   4097   -9    8 3.070 0 9 1.053 0 10 0.773 0 11 1.349 0 12 0.819 0 13
                         0.369 0 14 0.362 0 15 0.165 0 16 0.124 0 18 0.026 0 19
                         0.042 0
f 14    0   4097   -9    2 3.236 0 3 6.827 0
f 15    0   4097   -9    4 5.591 0 5 2.401 0 6 1.870 0 7 0.733 0
f 16    0   4097   -9    8 0.970 0 9 0.553 0 10 0.373 0 11 0.549 0 12 0.319 0 13
                         0.119 0 14 0.092 0 15 0.045 0 16 0.034 0
f 17    0   4097   -9    2 5.019 0 3 4.281 0
f 18    0   4097   -9    4 2.091 0 5 1.001 0 6 0.670 0 7 0.233 0
f 19    0   4097   -9    8 0.200 0 9 0.103 0 10 0.073 0 11 0.089 0 12 0.059 0 13
                         0.029 0
f 20    0   4097   -9    2 4.712 0 3 1.847 0
f 21    0   4097   -9    4 0.591 0 5 0.401 0 6 0.270 0 7 0.113 0
f 22    0   4097   -9    8 0.060 0 9 0.053 0 10 0.023 0
f 23    0   4097   -9    2 1.512 0 3 0.247 0
f 24    0   4097   -9    4 0.121 0 5 0.101 0 6 0.030 0 7 0.053 0
f 25    0   4097   -9    8 0.030 0
f 26    0   4097   -9    2 0.412 0 3 0.087 0
f 27    0   4097   -9    4 0.071 0 5 0.021 0
f 28    0   4097   -9    2 0.309 0 3 0.067 0
f 29    0   4097   -9    4 0.031 0
f 30    0   4097   -9    2 0.161 0 3 0.047 0

t       0   324

;       ST  DUR   AMP     FREQ    VIBR  AT    DEC   BR   PITCH
i 801   1   0.7   6500    261.6   .5    .04   .04   9    ; C4
i 801   2   0.7   8000    348.8   .5    .04   .04   9    ; F4
i 801   3   0.7   7200    392.4   .5    .04   .04   9    ; G4
i 801   4   3.1   6500    418.5   .5    .04   .04   9    ; G#4
i 801   7   .65   8000    436.0   .5    .04   .04   9    ; A4
i 801   8   0.7   6000    261.6   .5    .04   .04   9    ; C4
i 801   9   0.7   7200    348.8   .5    .04   .04   9    ; F4
i 801   10  .7    8000    392.4   .5    .04   .04   9    ; G4
i 801   11  3.1   7500    418.5   .5    .04   .04   9    ; G#4
i 801   14  .65   9000    436.0   .5    .04   .04   9    ; A4
i 801   15  0.7   5500    261.6   .5    .04   .04   9    ; C4
i 801   16  0.7   6500    348.8   .5    .04   .04   9    ; F4
i 801   17  0.7   7500    392.4   .5    .04   .04   9    ; G4
i 801   18  1.7   10000   418.5   .5    .06   .1    9    ; G#4
i 801   20  1.7   10000   436.0   .5    .06   .1    9    ; A4
i 801   22  0.7   6500    470.9   .5    .04   .04   9    ; A#4
i 801   23  0.7   7500    490.5   .5    .04   .04   9    ; B4
i 801   24  0.7   10000   588.6   .5    .04   .04   9    ; D5
i 801   25  0.7   6500    523.2   .5    .04   .04   9    ; C5
i 801   26  0.7   7500    436.0   .5    .04   .04   9    ; A4
i 801   27  0.7   8000    348.8   .5    .04   .04   9    ; F4
i 801   28  0.7   6500    261.6   .5    .04   .04   9    ; C4
i 801   29  0.7   7500    218.0   .5    .04   .04   9    ; A3
i 801   30  3.0   10000   174.4   0     .06   .25   9    ; F3
i 801   33  3.0   5000    130.8   0     .04   .25   9    ; C3
i 801   36  3.1   2000    87.2    0     .04   .25   9    ; F2

i 899   0   46
```

Figure 8.8 Score file for opening horn solo from Strauss's *Til Eulenspiegel's Merry Pranks.*

The exponentially-related envelopes do an effective job of modelling many articulation types. Of course, some types of noisy attacks such as initial "chiffs" do not fit the exponential model. Perhaps future work will identify other relationships between the group amplitudes that will effectively match them.

References

Beauchamp, J. 1982. "Synthesis by spectral amplitude and 'brightness' matching of analyzed musical instrument tones." *Journal of the Audio Engineering Society* 30(6): 396–406.

Cheung, N.-M., and A. Horner. 1996. "Group synthesis with genetic algorithms." *Journal of the Audio Engineering Society* 44(3): 130–147.

Chowning, J. 1973. "The synthesis of complex audio spectra by means of frequency modulation." *Journal of the Audio Engineering Society* 21(7): 526–534.

Eaglestone, B., and S. Oates. 1990. "Analytical tools for group additive synthesis." In *Proceedings of the 1990 International Computer Music Conference.* San Francisco: International Computer Music Association, pp. 66–68.

Kleczkowski, P. 1989. "Group additive synthesis." *Computer Music Journal* 13(1): 12–20.

Moorer, J., J. Grey, and J. Strawn. 1978. "Lexicon of analyzed tones (part 3: the trumpet)." *Computer Music Journal* 2(2): 23–31.

Morrill, D. 1977. "Trumpet algorithms for computer composition." *Computer Music Journal* 1(1):46–52.

Risset, J.-C., and M. Mathews. 1969. "Analysis of instrument tones." *Physics Today* 22(2): 23–30.

Zwicker, E., and E. Terhardt. 1980. "Analytical expressions for critical-band rate and critical bandwidth as a function of frequency." *Journal of the Acoustical Society of America* 68(5): 1523–1525.

9 FM Synthesis and Morphing in Csound: from Percussion to Brass

Brian Evans

Frequency Modulation (FM) is a standard tool in digital synthesis. John Chowning defined its digital implementation in a seminal article published in the early 1970s. (Chowning 1973). His music compositions elegantly illustrate the musical applications of FM.

One of the real powers of FM synthesis is its capability to create dynamic spectra with a minimum of complexity. By interpolating through the small number of parameters used to define an FM instrument, it is possible to change spectra over time. Smooth changes in timbre and in amplitude envelopes are achieved through this parametric interpolation. Control of these parameters makes it possible to "morph" or evolve from one sound into another.

Chowning illustrates this morphing in many of his compositions. A notable example is the tape piece *Sabelithe,* where he transforms a drum into a trumpet using a single FM instrument (Chowning 1988). Chowning, in the above-mentioned article, details the construction of a simulated drum and trumpet using his implementation of an FM instrument. With Csound, these instrument can be recreated from his original *Music V* definitions. We can then explore this early use of instrumental morphing and the application of FM as a musical device.

An FM Review

Imagine a violinist adding a syrupy vibrato to a long, legato note. This is frequency modulation. As the note is played the finger moves ever-so-slightly back and forth on the violin string, maybe five to ten times a second. The pitch is slightly raised and then slightly lowered, up and down, up and down.

Analog electronic music instruments simulate this type of vibrato with a low frequency oscillator (LFO). The voltage output of the LFO adds to the frequency

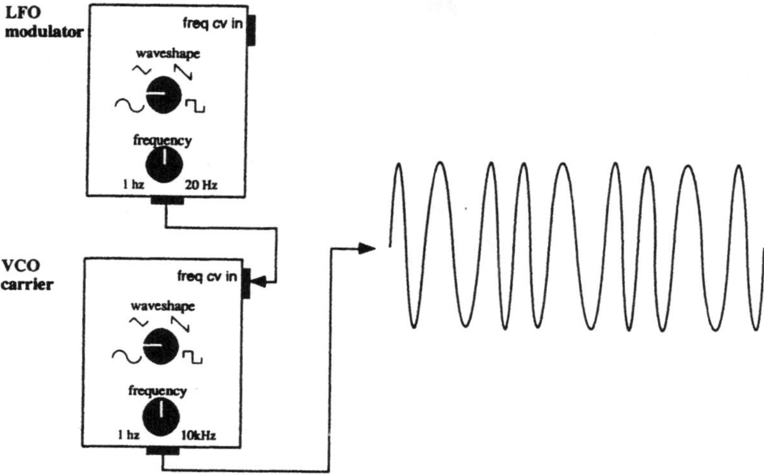

Figure 9.1 An analog synthesis patch that adds an output voltage from an LFO to the voltage controlling the frequency of a VCO. For FM synthesis, the LFO can be replaced with a VCO allowing for modulating frequencies within the audio spectrum (greater that 20 Hz).

voltage of a voltage controlled oscillator (VCO), slightly raising and lowering the frequency of the VCO output as shown in figure 9.1. The modulating oscillator, or *modulator,* defines the vibrato. The oscillator to which the vibrato is applied is the *carrier.*

This simple vibrato patch gets especially interesting when we raise the frequency of the vibrato above 20 Hz (the low-end frequency of human audio perception). When this occurs we no longer hear vibrato, but rather we hear a distortion of the tone being modulated. The defining characteristics of the carrier and modulating waves determine the nature of the distortion. These defining characteristics, or parameters, are few, hence the economy of FM as a synthesis technique.

The primary parameters in FM synthesis are the frequency and amplitude values of the carrier and the modulating oscillators (for the sake of simplicity we will assume the waveshape for each oscillator is a sinewave). The parameters for a basic FM instrument, as seen in figure 9.1 above, can be listed as:

- *c* – frequency of the carrier.
- *m* – frequency of the modulator.
- *amp* – amplitude of the carrier (the amplitude control of the patch).
- *dev* – deviation, the amount of frequency change (in Hz) above and below *c* . . . . . . (the amplitude envelope of the modulator).

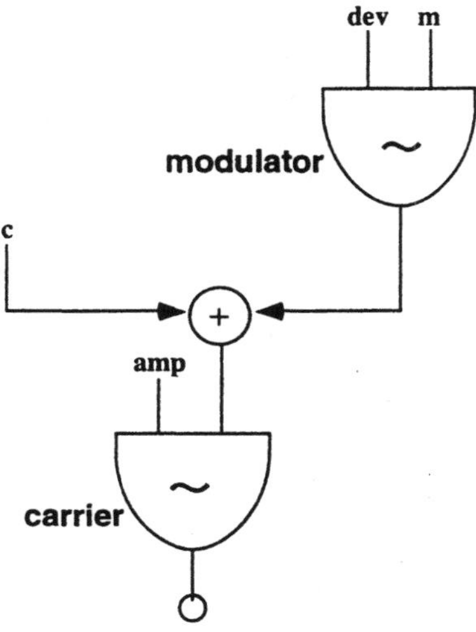

Figure 9.2 This graphic representation of basic FM shows the modulating oscillator output (which would be in Hz) being added to the frequency input of the carrier.

Deviation is the amplitude of the modulating oscillator. Deviation controls the "width" of the modulation. Thinking again of playing a violin, vibrato width relates to how high up and down the neck the finger travels.

A small width or deviation is equivalent to a small amount of finger movement and a narrow vibrato. A larger deviation is equivalent to the finger actually sliding up and down the string creating a vibrato "so wide you could drive a truck through it."

c/m Ratios and FM Index

A spectrum is described in the frequency domain by enumerating the frequencies and amplitudes of the spectrum's sinusoidal components or partials. An FM instrument's spectral components are determined through the relationships between the parameters defining an instance of the instrument.

Complex timbres occur with FM as a result of sidebands sounding above and below the spectral components of the carrier: in the case of the basic FM instrument, the carrier is a sine wave and so has a single sine component. FM sidebands have frequencies that can be calculated as whole number multiples of the modulating frequency. These are added and subtracted to the frequencies of each partial in the carrier spectrum as illustrated in figure 9.3.

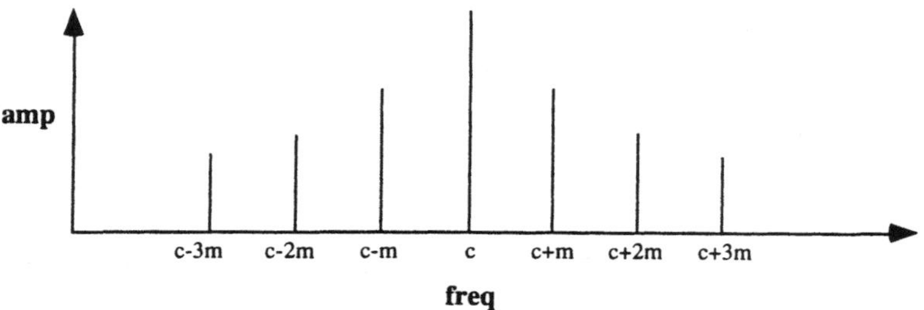

Figure 9.3 The carrier here is a simple sine wave of frequency *c*. FM sidebands are calculated as $c \pm nm$, with $n =$ the counting numbers 1, 2, 3, etc.

The ratio of the carrier frequency to the modulator frequency, commonly called the *c/m ratio* determines the relative frequencies of the partials in the FM spectrum. When *c/m* reduces to a simple rational number such as 1/2 or 3/4 the output spectrum is harmonic. When *c/m* reduces to an irrational number such as $1/\sqrt{2}$ or $2/\sqrt{3}$, partials are in a noninteger relationship and so the spectrum is inharmonic (in practice, complex ratios such as 411/377 or 1/1.617 will create spectra that will sound inharmonic. True irrational numbers can only be approximated digitally anyway).

The ability to create inharmonic spectra so easily is one of the attractions of FM (again, refer to Chowning for the details as to how and why c/m ratios determine the frequencies of the FM spectra components).

The relative amplitudes of the sideband frequencies are dependent on both the deviation and frequency of the modulator, so it is convenient to think of these values together as an *index of modulation.* This modulation index is calculated as the ratio shown in figure 9.4.

With a deviation of zero there will be no modulation and so no sidebands around the carrier. As the deviation increases, however, the amplitudes of the sidebands increase as a function of the index.

The modulation index provides an intuitive measure when thinking about the FM spectra. A higher index value generally indicates more sidebands and more energy in the sidebands. In other words, the higher the index the more complex the spectrum, with the highest sideband of significant amplitude equal to the index+1 (or a frequency of $c+m$ (index+1)). Chowning shows that we can predict the relative amplitudes of the sidebands mathematically (see Chowning 1973 or Dodge 1985).

In summary, an FM spectrum is harmonic when the *c/m* ratio is simple and rational and inharmonic otherwise. A high index indicates a spectrum rich in partials, while a lower index creates a simpler spectrum.

$$\frac{\text{modulation deviation}}{\text{modulation frequency}}$$

Figure 9.4 Formula for computation of FM "modulation index."

FM in Csound

FM is easy to implement in Csound. A basic FM instrument is illustrated in figure 9.5. The instrument is built using two sine wave oscillators with a sine wave defined as *f 1* in the score, using GEN10. The carrier and modulating frequencies are held constant through each note instance. The carrier amplitude is controlled with an ADSR envelope (Attack, Decay, Sustain, Release). The index is also controlled by an ADSR envelope and as the modulation frequency is held constant, the deviation is controlled indirectly by the same envelope (*index=dev/m, dev=index*m*).

This instrument is a Csound version of the FM design that Chowning defined and implemented in *Music V.* The instrument produces dynamic spectra by interpolating between two index values during a note. Following are the parameters defining the ADSR amplitude envelope (times are a percentage of *p3*):

- Starting amp = *p9* Attack time = *p14*
- Peak amp = *p10* Decay time = *p15*
- Sustain amp = *p11* Sustain time = *p16*
- Release amp = *p12* Release time = *p17*
- Ending amp = *p13*

Following are the parameters defining the ADSR frequency deviation envelope (times are a percentage of *p3*):

- Starting amp = *p18* Attack time = *p23*
- Peak amp = *p19* Decay time = *p24*
- Sustain amp = *p20* Sustain time = *p25*
- Release amp = *p21* Release time = *p26*
- End amp = *p22*

The Csound orchestra shown in figure 9.6 is a simple FM instrument, with envelopes controlling the output amplitude and the modulation index. This orchestra uses basic Csound oscillators. However, there are built-in Csound opcodes made specifi-

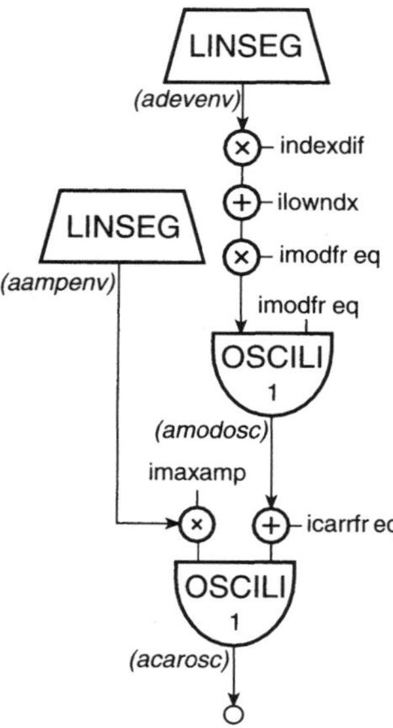

Figure 9.5 Block diagram of *instr 901*. This is a graphic representation of a basic FM instrument implemented in Csound. The ADSR envelopes control both the output amplitude of the instrument and the modulation index (and the deviation indirectly through the index).

```
            instr    901          ; CHOWNING FM
inotedur    =        p3
imaxamp     =        ampdb(p4)
icarrfreq   =        p5
imodfreq    =        p6
ilowndx     =        p7
indxdiff    =        p8-p7
aampenv     linseg   p9, p14*p3, p10, p15*p3, p11, p16*p3, p12, p17*p3, p13
adevenv     linseg   p18, p23*p3, p19, p24*p3, p20, p25*p3, p21, p26*p3, p22
amodosc     oscili   (ilowndx+indxdiff*adevenv)*imodfreq, imodfreq, 1
acarosc     oscili   imaxamp*aampenv, icarrfreq+amodosc, 1
            out      acarosc
            endin
```

Figure 9.6 Orchestra code for *instr 901*, a Chowning FM instrument featuring dynamic spectra. Note that all envelope (**linseg**) times are a percentage of the note duration (*p3*).

```
;          OPCODE    AMP,      FREQ  C,    M,    INDEX,   WAVESHAPE
aFMinst    foscili   20000,    100,  2,    3,    5,       1
```

Figure 9.7 The **foscili** opcode with arguments. A FM synthesizer in a single line of code.

cally to implement Chowning FM. These opcodes, **foscili** and **foscil,** define a unit that is a composite of two oscillators. Parameters for these opcodes include *c/m* ratio values, along with a common frequency value, FM index and output amplitude and a function table (f-table) that defines the waveshape. As the *c/m* ratio values are input in their lowest terms, the effective frequencies of the carrier and modulator are determined by multiplying *c* and *m* by the common frequency value. For example, the line in figure 9.7 defines an FM instrument that will have an output amplitude of 20000 with a carrier frequency of 200 ($freq = 100$, $c = 2$), a modulator frequency of 300 ($m = 3*c$) and an index of 5. The waveshapes for the oscillators in the unit are defined in *f 1,* in the score file. (See the *Csound Reference Manual* for a full description of this opcode).

Chowning's Trumpet

After implementing a basic FM instrument in *Music V* in his article, Chowning lists the parameters for creating a simple brass-like tone:

- *p3* = duration = .6 sec
- *p4* = amplitude = 1000 (scaled amplitude, we will use 88dB)
- *p5* = carrier frequency = 440 Hz
- *p6* = modulator frequency = 440 Hz
- *p7* = low index = 0
- *p8* = high index = 5

The *c/m* ratio here reduces to 1/1, indicating a harmonic spectrum with partial frequencies being multiples of a fundamental at 440 (440, 880, 1320, 1760, etc.). The low index value defines a simple sinusoidal spectrum (index of 0 indicates no modulation and so no sidebands) and the high index (5) will give a more complex spectrum of 6 or so harmonics.

Figure 9.8 shows the amplitude envelope Chowning used in the instrument design. This envelope is also proportionally applied to the index. The amplitude envelope is typical for a brass instrument like a trumpet, with a quick attack, a relatively stable

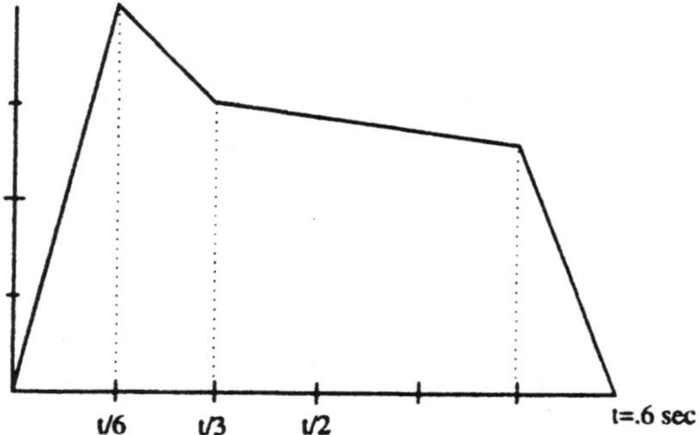

Figure 9.8 This ADSR envelope controls both the output amplitude and the modulation index of Chowning's brasslike FM instrument.

sustain and a quick release. The spectrum will reach maximum complexity at the end of the attack, sustain a complex harmonic spectrum and simplify as it ends. This spectral envelope is also typical of a brass instrument.

Chowning's Drum

Percussion instruments are simple to implement with FM because inharmonic spectra are easily achieved. Chowning illustrates some common percussive sounds using his basic FM instrument. One example is a wood drum instrument with parameters as follows:

- *p3* = duration = .2 sec
- *p4* = amplitude = 1000 (a scaled amplitude, we will use 88 dB)
- *p5* = carrier frequency = 80 Hz
- *p6* = modulator frequency = 55 Hz
- *p7* = low index = 0
- *p8* = high index = 25

Note that the *c/m* ratio is not a simple integer relationship but roughly 1/1.45 and the higher index value is 25, which will create a lot of sideband energy. The index envelope seen in figure 9.9b shows a high index at the start of a note. The high spectral energy dissipates quickly after the index value rapidly decreases. This is a drumlike spectral evolution.

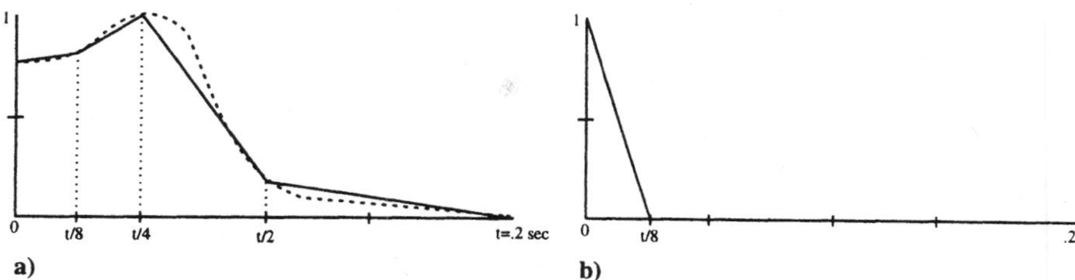

Figure 9.9 a) Chowning uses an exponential envelope (the dotted curve seen here) to control the amplitude of the percussive instrument. We approximate this envelope with a linear ADSR envelope. b) This envelope controls the index of the percussive FM instrument. The index starts with the high value and quickly lowers.

The exponential envelope for amplitude that was specified in Chowning's instrument definition is not possible with a linear ADSR envelope. In the Csound implementation we are using the curved envelope is approximated as shown in figure 9.9a. In general, the percussive envelope has an instantaneous attack, a rapid swell and an equally rapid decay. Different p-values are given to illustrate a variety of percussive sounds.

FM Morphing

Spectral morphing is the idea of evolving from one instrumental timbre to another. Parametric interpolation in FM is one of the earliest examples of morphing and one of the easiest to explore. Chowning used the technique in his first FM composition *Sabelithe,* which dates from 1966 to 1971. Around 4 minutes and 50 seconds into the piece a dramatic moment occurs where a drum slowly morphs into a trumpet.

Using the Csound versions of Chowning's FM instruments we can simulate the instruments he used in *Sabelithe* and explore a similar morph. We can use the parameters we have already defined to create a brass instrument and a drum. All we need to do is create a Csound score that starts with a drum note and ends with a trumpet note. The notes played between the start and end interpolate between the parameters, defining the two different instruments. Using the linear ramping capabilities built into the Csound score language, (the "<"), a simple linear interpolation between the parameters creates a morph from one instrument to the other.

Conclusion

This small exercise shows both the simplicity and power of FM as a musical tool and how John Chowning's ideas, instrument and compositions continue to have potency for musicians looking for rich and ever new sonic worlds to explore.

References

Chowning, J. 1973. "The synthesis of complex audio spectra by means of frequency modulation." *Journal of the Audio Engineering Society* 21(7): 526–534.

Chowning, J. 1988. "Sabelithe." *John Chowning,* WER 2012-50. Mainz, Germany: Wergo.

Dodge, C., and T. Jerse. 1997. *Computer Music: Synthesis, Composition and Performance.* New York: Schirmer.

10 Modeling "Classic" Electronic Keyboards in Csound

Hans Mikelson

A Tone-Wheel Organ with a Rotating Speaker System

This instrument pair simulates the sounds of a tone-wheel organ with a rotating speaker effect like a Hammond B3 organ and a Leslie speaker. The first models the tone-wheel organ and the second models the rotating speaker. The final section discusses some suggestions for further modifications.

Tone-Wheel Organ

The first step toward reproducing this instrument is to consider the internal structure of the tone-wheel organ. The heart of the tone wheel organ is its tone wheel mechanism. This consists of a central shaft with gears coupled to 91 tone wheels. A magnetic pick-up senses the distance to the wheel and generates an electric signal proportional to this distance. Owing to the "flower" shape of the wheels and the filtering effect of the pickups, the signal produced is close to a sine wave. GEN10 can be used to set up a sine table:

```
f 1    0    8192     10      1
```

An organ timbre is created by adding together signals from nine tone wheels. The amount of each harmonic added is controlled by nine drawbars with the following frequencies: Sub-fundamental, sub-third, fundamental, second, third, fourth, fifth, sixth and eighth. The sub-fundamental is one octave below the fundamental. The sub-third is one octave below the third. A separate **oscil** opcode can be used to generate each harmonic. The following Csound code fragment implements this aspect of the sound:

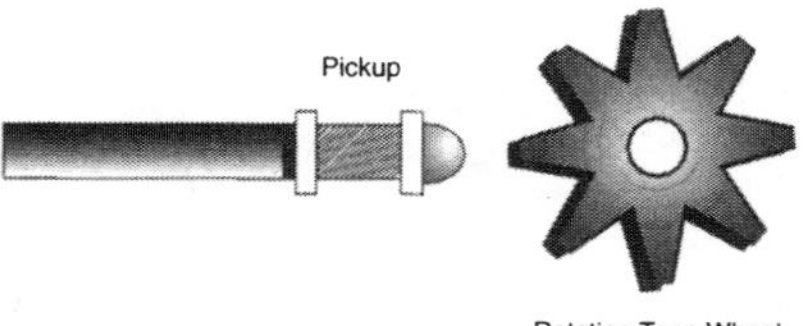

Figure 10.1 Tone-wheel and pickup.

```
asubfund  oscil   p6, .5*ifqc, iwheel1, iphase/(ikey-12)
asub3rd   oscil   p7, 1.4983*ifqc, iwheel2, iphase/(ikey+7)
afund     oscil   p8, ifqc, iwheel3, iphase/ikey
a2nd      oscil   p9, 2*ifqc, iwheel4, iphase/(ikey+12)
a3rd      oscil   p10, 2.9966*ifqc, iwheel4, iphase/(ikey+19)
a4th      oscil   p11, 4*ifqc, iwheel4, iphase/(ikey+24)
a5th      oscil   p12, 5.0397*ifqc, iwheel4, iphase/(ikey+28)
a6th      oscil   p13, 5.9932*ifqc, iwheel4, iphase/(ikey+31)
a8th      oscil   p14, 8*ifqc, iwheel4, iphase/(ikey+36)
```

In this instrument, parameter fields (p-fields) *p6–p14* specify the values of the 9 drawbars. The fundamental frequency is given by *ifqc*. This is multiplied by equally tempered steps to obtain the other eight harmonics.

The twelve lowest tone wheels have only two teeth and, in the Hammond B3 series, had increased odd harmonic content that may be interpreted as having a somewhat rectangular shape. To implement this, f-table 2 (*f 2)* is set up with some odd harmonic content:

```
f 2  0   1024   10 1 0 .2 0 .1 0 .05 0 .02
```

The keyboard key pressed can be calculated from the frequency parameter (*p5*). The key position is used to assign f-table 2 to the lowest twelve frequencies and f-table 1 to the others:

```
iwheel1   init  ((ikey-12) > 12 ? 1 : 2)
iwheel2   init  ((ikey+7) > 12 ? 1 : 2)
iwheel3   init  (ikey > 12 ? 1 : 2)
iwheel4   init  1
```

The phase of the tone wheels depends on the number of “petals” on a wheel and the alignment of the wheels. Some continuous variation in phase, based on the wheel number and the time (*p2*), is desirable. The variable *iphase* is set to *p2* and then divided by the tone-wheel number. In a way, *p2* represents the central shaft of the organ. Finally, the fundamentals are added together into a global variable.

Rotating Speaker Effect

The second aspect of the classic Hammond organ sound is the Leslie rotating speaker. The speaker is powered by a tube amplifier. Structurally, the Leslie speaker system consists of a high-frequency driver pointing up into a plastic horn. The driver remains stationary and the horn rotates, spraying the sound around the room. A low frequency driver directs sound downward into a rotating scoop.

The elements required to model this system were: *distortion,* introduced by the amplifier, *acceleration rates* of the horn and scoop, the *Doppler effects* of the rotating horn and scoop, different *directional effects of different frequencies* and *stereo phase separation,* owing to either microphone placement or separation between the listener's ears.

The first step taken in simulating this system is to add distortion to the sound by passing it through a waveshaping table. GEN8 is used to set up a table such that values close to zero will be reproduced linearly while values further away from zero are compressed. This is done using one of the following tables:

```
f 5  0  8192  8  -.8 336 -.78 800 -.7 5920 .7 800 .78 336 .8
f 6  0  8192  8  -.8 336 -.76 3000 -.7 1520 .7 3000 .76 336 .8
```

As defined here *f* 5 produces a moderate distortion and *f 6* produces increased distortion.

The next aspect to be considered is the acceleration of the horn and the scoop. The slow and fast rates of the high frequency horn are about .8 Hz and 8 Hz, respectively.

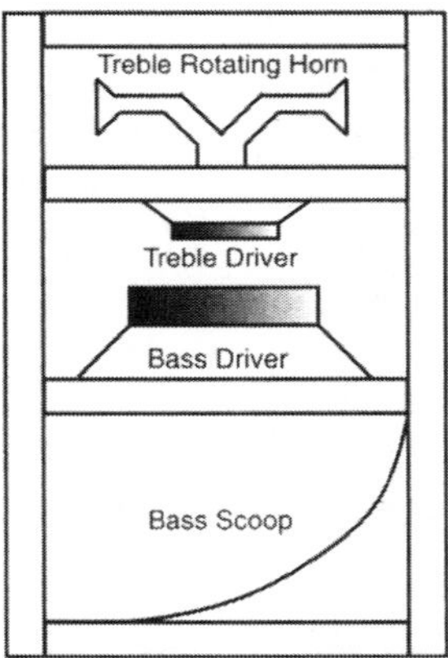

Figure 10.2 Rotating speaker system.

Acceleration of the horn takes about one second. The slow and fast rates of the scoop are about .7 Hz and 7 cycles/sec^2. The acceleration of the bass scoop takes about two seconds. The following envelopes use the **linseg** opcode to set the rotation rates, acceleration rates and hold times. This is set up in a separate instrument, which acts as the foot switch that may be turned on using global variables:

```
gkenv      linseg   gispeedi*.8, 1, gispeedf*.8, .01, gispeedf*.8
gkenvlow   linseg   gispeedi*.7, 2, gispeedf*.7, .01, gispeedf*.7
```

The next step is to produce a Doppler effect that is due to the rotation of the speakers. This is accomplished by setting up a delay line using the **delay** opcode and accessing it with a variable time-delay tap using the **deltapi** opcode. The tap point is controlled by an **oscil** opcode accessing a sine table. Separate taps are used for right and left channels. The magnitude of the oscillation corresponds to the radius of rotation:

```
koscl    oscil    1, kenv, 1, ioff
koscr    oscil    1, kenv, 1, ioff+isep
```

The phase separation between the signals is controlled by the variable *isep*. This can be thought of as the angle of separation between the listener's ears, or the placement of microphones around the speaker. The variable *ioff* is a phase offset that is intended to allow for multiple rotating speakers at different locations in the room. The Doppler effect is repeated for the low frequency section:

```
kdopl      =          .01-koscl*.0002
kdopr      =          .012-koscr*.0002
aleft      deltapi    kdopl
aright     deltapi    kdopr
```

The final aspect to be considered is the presentation of a frequency-dependent stereo image. High frequency sound is more directional than low frequency sound. To simulate this, the frequency is divided into three segments. First, the right and left high frequency components are filtered using the **butterbp** opcode:

```
alfhi      butterbp    aleft, 7000, 6000
arfhi      butterbp    aright, 7000, 6000
```

The center frequency and bandwidth were determined empirically. The high frequency segment is modulated by a narrow pulse, using GEN7 to set up the following table:

```
f 3    0    256    7   0 110 0 18 1 18 0 110 0
```

The middle frequency sound is modulated by a wider pulse and the low frequency is modulated by a sine wave:

```
alfmid    butterbp    aleft, 3000, 2000
arfmid    butterbp    aright, 3000, 2000
```

The pulse table is swept with **oscil** using the same offset and separation as the Doppler tap:

```
kflohi     oscil      1, kenv, 3, ioff
kfrohi     oscil      1, kenv, 3, ioff+isep
kalosc     =          koscllow*.4+1
karosc     =          koscrlow*.4+1
```

Finally, the three filtered and modulated signals for each channel are added together to complete the instrument.

Discussion

My orchestra and score as shown in figure 10.3 can only approximate the rich, warm, gritty character of a real Hammond organ. However, one advantage of using the Csound environment is its flexibility. The shape of the tone wheels can be changed easily. Samples from single tone wheels of actual instruments could be set up in tables. This may improve the simulation. Triangle waves or other waveshapes could be used instead of the sine waves. The instrument could be extended to have any number of additional speakers. Finally, variable delay lines could be set up to simulate the complex echoes produced by the rotating speaker system.

Classic Analog Synthesizers

The following Csound instruments and tables attempt to model a classic analog synthesizer instrument. To produce sound early synthesizers used fairly straightforward periodic waveforms that were then processed through a resonant lowpass filter. This type of filter provided one of the most distinctive elements of the early synthesizer sound. Development of a two-pole resonant lowpass filter and some variations of this filter are discussed. Furthermore, the cascade form of a filter is discussed and a four-pole filter, which uses it, is derived.

```
sr          =         44100
kr          =         2205
ksmps       =         20
nchnls      =         2

            instr     1001          ; GLOBAL INIT: TONE WHEEL/ROTATING SPEAKER
gispeedf    init      p4                               ; INITIALIZE ROTOR SPEED
            endin

            instr     1002          ; THE FOOT SWITCH CONTROLLING ROTOR SPEEDS
gispeedi    init      gispeedf                         ; SAVE OLD SPEED
gispeedf    init      p4                               ; UPDATE NEW SPEED
gkenv       linseg    gispeedi*.8, 1, gispeedf*.8, .01, gispeedf*.8
gkenvlow    linseg    gispeedi*.7, 2, gispeedf*.7, .01, gispeedf*.7
            endin

            instr     1003          ; TONE WHEEL ORGRAN
gaorgan     init      0                                ; GLOBAL SEND TO SPEAKER
iphase      init      p2                               ; CONTINUOUS PHASE CHANGE
ikey        init      12*int(p5)+100*(p5%1)-59         ; KEYBOARD KEY PRESSED.
ifqc        init      cpspch(p5)                       ; CONVERT TO CYCLES/SEC.
iwheel1     init      ((ikey-12) > 12 ? 1 : 2)         ; LOWER 12 TONEWHEELS HAVE
iwheel2     init      ((ikey+7)  > 12 ? 1 : 2)         ; INCREASED ODD HARMONIC
iwheel3     init      (ikey      > 12 ? 1 : 2)         ; CONTENT.
iwheel4     init      1
kenv        linseg    0, .01, p4, p3-.02, p4, .01, 0
asubfund    oscil     p6, .5*ifqc, iwheel1, iphase/(ikey-12)
asub3rd     oscil     p7, 1.4983*ifqc, iwheel2, iphase/(ikey+7)
afund       oscil     p8, ifqc, iwheel3, iphase/ikey
a2nd        oscil     p9, 2*ifqc, iwheel4, iphase/(ikey+12)
a3rd        oscil     p10, 2.9966*ifqc, iwheel4, iphase/(ikey+19)
a4th        oscil     p11, 4*ifqc, iwheel4, iphase/(ikey+24)
a5th        oscil     p12, 5.0397*ifqc, iwheel4, iphase/(ikey+28)
a6th        oscil     p13, 5.9932*ifqc, iwheel4, iphase/(ikey+31)
a8th        oscil     p14, 8*ifqc, iwheel4, iphase/(ikey+36)
gaorgn = gaorgn+kenv*(asubfnd+asub3rd+afnd+a2nd+a3rd+a4th+a5th+a6th+a8th)
            endin

            instr     1004          ; ROTATING SPEAKER
iioff       init      p4
isep        init      p5                  ; PHASE SEPARATION BETWEEN RIGHT AND LEFT
iradius     init      .00025              ; RADIUS OF THE ROTATING HORN.
iradlow     init      .00035              ; RADIUS OF THE ROTATING SCOOP.
ideleng     init      .02                 ; LENGTH OF DELAY LINE.
asig        =         gaorgan                          ; GLOBAL INPUT FROM ORGAN
asig        =         asig/40000          ; DISTORTION EFFECT USING WAVESHAPING.
aclip       tablei    asig, 5, 1, .5      ; A LAZY "S" CURVE, USE TABLE 6 ...
aclip       =         aclip*16000         ; ... FOR INCREASED DISTORTION.
aleslie     delayr    ideleng, 1                       ; PUT "CLIPPED" SIGNAL
            delayw    aclip                            ; INTO A DELAY LINE.
koscl       oscil     1, gkenv, 1, iioff               ; DOPPLER EFFECT IS RESULT
koscr       oscil     1, gkenv, 1, iioff+isep          ; OF DELAYTAPS OSCILLATING
kdopl       =         ideleng/2-koscl*iradius          ; LEFT AND RIGHT ARE
kdopr       =         ideleng/2-koscr*iradius          ; SLIGHT OUT OF PHASE TO
aleft       deltapi   kdopl                            ; SIMULATE SEPARATN BETWN
aright      deltapi   kdopr                            ; EARS OR MICROPHONES
koscllow    oscil     1, gkenvlow, 1, iioff            ; DOPPLER FOR LOW FRQ
koscrlow    oscil     1, gkenvlow, 1, iioff+isep
kdopllow    =         ideleng/2-koscllow*iradlow
kdoprlow    =         ideleng/2-koscrlow*iradlow
aleftlow    deltapi   kdopllow
arightlow   deltapi   kdoprlow
```

Figure 10.3 Orchestra and score code for *instr 1001–1004* a tone-wheel organ (*i1003*) with global rotating speaker (*i1004*).

```
alfhi       butterbp  aleft, 8000, 3000              ; DIVIDE FREQ INTO THREE
arfhi       butterbp  aright, 8000, 3000             ; GROUPS AND MOD EACH WITH
alfmid      butterbp  aleft, 3000, 2000              ; DIFFERENT WIDTH PULSE TO
arfmid      butterbp  aright, 3000, 2000             ; ACCOUNT FOR DIFFERENT
alflow      butterlp  aleftlow, 1000                 ; DISPERSION OF DIFFERENT
arflow      butterlp  arightlow, 1000                ; FREQUENCIES.
kflohi      oscil     1, gkenv, 3, iioff
kfrohi      oscil     1, gkenv, 3, iioff+isep
kflomid     oscil     1, gkenv, 4, iioff
kfromid     oscil     1, gkenv, 4, iioff+isep
; AMPLITUDE EFFECT ON LOWER SPEAKER
kalosc      =         koscllow*.6+1
karosc      =         koscrlow*.6+1
; ADD ALL FREQUENCY RANGES AND OUTPUT THE RESULT
            outs1     alfhi*kflohi+alfmid*kflomid+alflow*kalosc
            outs2     arfhi*kfrohi+arfmid*kfromid+arflow*karosc
gaorgn      =         0
            endin

; SINE
f 1    0   8192 10   1 .02 .01
f 2    0   1024 10   1 0 .2 0 .1 0 .05 0 .02

; ROTATING SPEAKER FILTER ENVELOPES
f 3    0   256  7    .2 110 .4 18 1 18 .4 110 .2
f 4    0   256  7    .4 80 .6 16 1 64 1 16 .6 80 .4

; DISTORTION TABLES
f 5    0   8192 8    -.8 336 -.78 800 -.7 5920 .7 800 .78 336 .8
f 6    0   8192 8    -.8 336 -.76 3000 -.7 1520 .7 3000 .76 336 .8

t 0    200

; INITIALIZES GLOBAL VARIABLES
i 1001 0   1    1

; INS  STA DUR  SPEED
i 1002 0   6    1
i 1002 +   6    10
i 1002 .   12   1
i 1002 .   6    10

; INS  STA DUR  AMP PIT   SUBF SUB3 FUND 2ND 3RD 4TH 5TH 6TH 8TH
i 1003 0   6    200 8.04  8    8    8    8   3   2   1   0   4
i 1003 0   6    .   8.11  .    .    .    .   .   .   .   .   .
i 1003 0   6    .   9.02  .    .    .    .   .   .   .   .   .
i 1003 6   1    .   8.04  .    .    .    .   .   .   .   .   .
i 1003 6   1    .   8.11  .    .    .    .   .   .   .   .   .
i 1003 6   1    .   9.04  .    .    .    .   .   .   .   .   .
i 1003 7   1    .   8.04  .    .    .    .   .   .   .   .   .
i 1003 7   1    .   8.11  .    .    .    .   .   .   .   .   .
i 1003 7   1    .   9.02  .    .    .    .   .   .   .   .   .
i 1003 8   1    .   8.04  .    .    .    .   .   .   .   .   .
i 1003 8   1    .   8.09  .    .    .    .   .   .   .   .   .
i 1003 8   1    .   9.01  .    .    .    .   .   .   .   .   .
i 1003 9   8    .   8.04  .    .    .    .   .   .   .   .   .
i 1003 9   8    .   8.08  .    .    .    .   .   .   .   .   .
i 1003 9   8    .   8.11  .    .    .    .   .   .   .   .   .
i 1003 17  16   200 10.04 8    4    8    3   1   1   0   .   3
i 1003 20  13   200 9.09  8    4    8    3   1   1   0   .   3
i 1003 23  10   200 8.04  8    4    8    3   1   1   0   .   3
i 1003 26  7    200 7.04  8    4    8    3   1   1   0   .   3

; ROTATING SPEAKER
; INS  STA DUR  OFFSET     SEPARATION
i 1004 0   33.2 .5         .1
```

Figure 10.3 continued

```
f 1   0  1024    10   1                           ; SINE
f 2   0  256     7    -1 128 -1 0 1 128 1         ; SQUARE
f 3   0  256     7    1 256 -1                    ; SAWTOOTH
f 4   0  256     7    -1 128 1 128 -1             ; TRIANGLE
```

Figure 10.4 F-tables used to define the basic geometric waveshapes used in "classic" analog synthesizers.

Oscillators

Oscillators from early analog synthesizers generated simple waveforms. Some of the most commonly used are the sine, square, sawtooth and triangle waveforms. These can be set up easily using f-tables, which are then accessed using the **oscil** opcode (see figure 10.4).

Pulse-width modulation is often used in analog synthesis to produce a wider variety of timbres. With pulse-width modulation, a square wave is gradually transformed from a narrow square pulse to a wide square pulse. A sine wave can be used to modulate the pulse-width. The rate of modulation can be set to increase gradually. The following code accomplishes this:

```
ksine      oscil    1.5, ifqc/440, 1
ksquare    oscil    ifqc*ksine, ifqc, 2
axn        oscil    iamp, ifqc+ksquare, itabl1
```

The opcodes **rand** and **buzz** can also be used as sources for modeling an analog synthesizer.

Resonant Lowpass Filter

The key step in reproducing a classic analog sound is the development of a good resonant lowpass filter. A discussion of filter theory will help to illuminate the approach taken in designing this filter (Oppenheim, Willsky, and Young 1983). A general filter can be defined using the differential equation:

$$a_0X + a_1X' + a_2X'' + \ldots = b_0Y + b_1Y' + b_2Y'' + \ldots \qquad (10.1)$$

Where:

- X is the input signal
- Y is the output signal

- X′ is the first derivative of X with respect to time
- X″ is the second derivative of X with respect to time
- Y′ is the first derivative of Y with respect to time
- Y″ is the second derivative of Y with respect to time
- a_i and b_i are coefficients

Those not familiar with calculus can think of the first derivative as being the slope of the function and the second derivative as being the curvature of the function. The number of poles in the filter is determined by the highest order derivative in the equation.

The frequency response of the above equation can be written directly from it, using the following procedure. Replace the undifferentiated terms with a one. Replace the differentiated terms with a frequency raised to the power of the derivative. Construct a ratio with the left half of the equation as the numerator and the right half of the equation as the denominator. For example, the above differential equation would yield the frequency response given in the following equation:

$$H(j\omega) = \frac{a_0 + a_1 j\omega + a_2(j\omega)^2 + \ldots}{b_0 + b_1 j\omega + b_2(j\omega)^2 + \ldots} \tag{10.2}$$

where $j\omega$ represents frequency. A spreadsheet or a math program can be used to observe how this equation responds to changes in the coefficients.

A resonant lowpass filter can be generated by using the filter response function given in the following equation:

$$H(f) = \frac{1}{1 + b_1 j\omega + b_2(j\omega)^2} \tag{10.3}$$

As the frequency approaches zero, b_1 and b_2 vanish as the function approaches one. As the frequency approaches infinity the squared term begins to dominate and this function approaches zero. Resonance is introduced by making b_1 negative and b_2 positive. Carefully adjusting the values of the coefficients results in a peak at the cut off frequency. A typical curve is given in figure 10.5.

The differential equation corresponding to this frequency response is:

$$Y = X + b_1 x + b_2 x \tag{10.4}$$

To be used in Csound, this equation must be converted from the continuous form to a discrete form. One way to do this is to convert the differential equation into a difference equation. The slope Y′ = dY/dt can be approximated by DY/Dt and the curvature Y″ = d²Y/dt² can be approximated by D(DY)/D(Dt). Letting $\Delta t = 1$

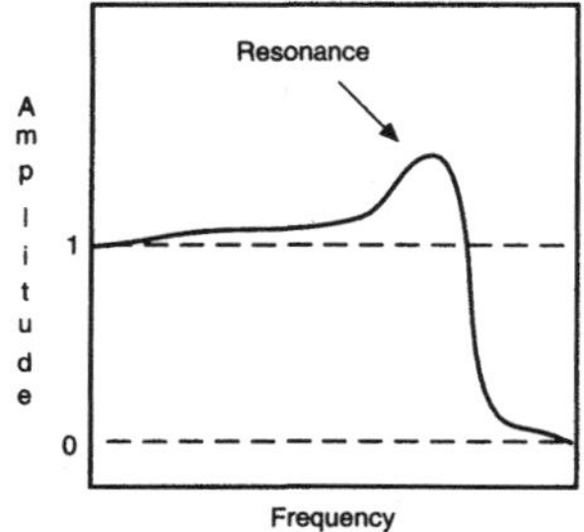

Figure 10.5 Graph of resonant lowpass filter frequency response.

simplifies the algebra involved in solving it. This is valid if the sample rate is constant and the units of time are equal to 1/**sr**. Substituting the difference approximation for the differentials in equation 10.4 and knowing that DY = $Y_n - Y_{n-1}$ yields:

$$Y_n = X_n - b_1(Y_n - Y_{n-1}) - b_2(Y_n - 2Y_{n-1} + Y_{n-2}) \tag{10.5}$$

This can be solved for Y_n to obtain:

$$Y_n = \frac{X_n + (b_1 + 2b_2)Y_{n-1} - b_2 Y_{n-2}}{1 + b_1 + b_2} \tag{10.6}$$

A Csound implementation follows:

```
aynm1    init    0
aynm2    init    0
ayn      =       ((kb1+2*kb2)*aynm1-kb2*aynm2+axn)/(1+kb1+kb2)
aynm2    =       aynm1
aynm1    =       ayn
```

Unfortunately, the difference equation only approximates the differential equation. Numerical methods could be used to solve the equation to any degree of precision, but this would be computationally expensive. The more common approach is to adjust the coefficients to give a similar response. For the difference equation:

$$b_0 Y_n + b_1 Y_{n-1} + b_2 Y_{n-2} + \cdots = a_0 X_n + a_1 X_{n-1} + a_2 X_{n-2} + \cdots \tag{10.7}$$

the frequency response is:

$$H(j\omega) = \frac{a_0 + a_1 e^{j\omega} + a_2 e^{2j\omega} + \ldots}{b_0 + b_1 e^{j\omega} + b_2 e^{2j\omega} + \ldots} \tag{10.8}$$

Note that:

$$e^{j\omega} = \cos(\omega) + j\sin(\omega) \tag{10.9}$$

The following relationships were determined empirically to produce fairly independent response of frequency and resonance throughout a useful range of these parameters:

$$b_1 = \frac{100}{Q\sqrt{\omega_{co}}} - 1 \tag{10.10}$$

$$b_2 = \frac{1000}{\omega_{co}} \tag{10.11}$$

Where Q is resonance and ω_{co} is cut-off frequency. This can be written in Csound as:

```
kb1     =     100/irez/sqrt(kfco)-1
kb2     =     1000/kfco
```

This completes the basic two-pole filter. Some modifications of the filter will be considered next. The Roland *TB–303* is a much sought after synthesizer owing to its unique sound. This is in part due to the unusual character of its filter. It has been suggested that one of the aspects of this filter that make it unique is the circuitry that prevents the filter from going into self-oscillation. When resonance is increased, the filter distorts instead of self-oscillating. This type of behavior can be simulated in Csound by doing the following: isolate the resonating portion of the signal and pass it through a distortion table. Add the distorted signal to an original lowpass-filtered signal:

```
atemp     tone      axn, kfco
aclip1    =         (ayn-atemp)/100000
aclip     tablei    aclip1, 7, 1, .5
aout      =         aclip*20000+atemp
```

This produces an interesting sound with some of the character of the TB–303. Extension of the above techniques to higher order filters presents some problems. As the order of the equations increases, the coefficients become extremely sensitive to small changes and round-off errors. One form of higher-order filters that does not have this defect is called the *cascade form.* The Csound code shown in figure 10.6 implements the cascade form to obtain a four-pole filter.

This technique can be extended to obtain higher order filters. Figure 10.7 shows the orchestra and score code for one of the instruments from *1002.orc* that models an analog synthesizer with a resonant lowpass filter:

```
ayn1     =   ((ka1+2*ka2)*ayn1m1-ka2*ayn1m2+axn)/(1+ka1+ka2)
ayn1m2   =   ayn1m1
ayn1m1   =   ayn1
ayn      =   ((kb1+2*kb2)*ayn2m1-kb2*ayn2m2+ayn1)/(1+kb1+kb2)
ayn2m2   =   ayn2m1
ayn2m1   =   ayn
```

Figure 10.6 Orchestra code excerpt for the simulation of a 4-pole filter by cascading two 2-pole filters.

```
sr          =           44100
kr          =           44100
ksmps       =           1
nchnls      =           1

            instr       1007            ; TB-303 EMULATOR
idur        =           p3
iamp        =           p4
ifqc        =           cpspch(p5)
irez        =           p7
itabl1      =           p8
kaenv       linseg      0, .01, 1, p3-.02, 1, .01, 0             ; AMPENV
kfco        linseg      p6, .5*p3, .2*p6, .5*p3, .1*p6           ; FRQSWEEP
ka1         =           100/irez/sqrt(kfco)-1           ; ATTEMPTS TO SEPARATE...
ka2         =           1000/kfco                       ; ...FREQ. FROM RES.
aynm1       init        0                               ; INITIALIZE YN-1 TO ZERO
aynm2       init        0                               ; INITIALIZE YN-2 TO ZERO
axn         oscil       iamp, ifqc, itabl1              ; OSC
; REPLACE THE DIFFERENTIAL EQUATION WITH A DIFFERENCE EQUATION.
ayn         =           ((ka1+2*ka2)*aynm1-ka2*aynm2+axn)/(1+ka1+ka2)
atemp       tone        axn, kfco
aclip1      =           (ayn-atemp)/100000
aclip       tablei      aclip1, 7, 1, .5
aout        =           aclip*20000+atemp
aynm2       =           aynm1
aynm1       =           ayn
            out         kaenv*aout                      ; AMP ENVELOPE AND OUTPUT
            endin

f   1     0      1024    10      1                              ; SINE
f   2     0      256     7       -1 128 -1 0 1 128 1            ; SQUARE
f   3     0      256     7       1 256 -1                       ; SAW
f   4     0      256     7       -1 128 1 128 -1                ; TRI
f   5     0      256     7       1 64 1 0 -1 192 -1             ; PULSE
f   6     0      8192    7       0 2048 0 0 -1 2048 -1 0 1 2048 1 0 0 2048 0
f   7     0      1024    8       -.8 42 -.78 400 -.7 140 .7 400 .78 42 .8
r   4     NN
t   0     400
; DISTORTION FILTER INSTRUMENT TB-303
;   INS    STA    DUR    AMP     PITCH    FC     Q      TAB
i   1007   0      1      5000    6.07     5      50     3
i   1007   +      .      <       6.07     <      .      3
i   1007   .      .      <       6.05     <      .      3
i   1007   .      .      <       6.02     <      .      3
i   1007   .      .      <       6.07     <      .      3
i   1007   .      .      <       6.02     <      .      3
i   1007   .      .      <       6.10     <      .      3
i   1007   .      .      8000    6.06     100    20     3
s
```

Figure 10.7 Orchestra and score code excerpt from *1002.orc* featuring *instr 1007,* a Roland *TB-303* emulation instrument with a distorted resonant lowpass filter.

Conclusion

The filters presented in this chapter provide a useful basis for future work in simulating analog synthesizers. Some further things to try would be to modify the distortion table in the distortion filter to unusual shapes. Development of more complex waveforms, such as a oscillator-sync or a sample-and-hold waveform would also be interesting. Waveforms with sharp edges stimulate the resonance aspect of the filter and may result in more interesting timbres. Also highpass and bandpass filters could be developed using the methodology described in this section.

References

Baker, B. *Hammond Leslie FAQ.* http://wcbi.com/organs/hammond/faq/

Henricksen, C. 1981. "Unearthing the mysteries of the leslie cabinet." *Recording Engineer/Producer Magazine,* http://wcbi.com/organs/hammond/faq/mystery/mystery.html

Oppenheim, A., A. Willsky, and I. Young. 1983. *Signals and Systems.* Englewood Cliffs, N.J.: Prentice-Hall.

Rossing, Thomas D. 1982. *The Science of Sound.* Reading, Mass.: Addison-Wesley.

Algorithmic Synthesis

11 A Survey of Classic Synthesis Techniques in Csound

Rajmil Fischman

The development of digital synthesis and processing owes a great deal to the "classic" techniques employed in the early years of electroacoustic music. These involved processes that in most cases were based on the capabilities of analog devices. Even today, when the flexibility offered by digital systems allows tighter control of spectral characteristics and application of sophisticated mathematical models, the theoretical principles underpinning the "classic" processes still offer a powerful set of tools for the achievement of complex morphologies, which is greatly enhanced by the versatility of the new technology.

"Classic" techniques may be categorized according to the principles involved in their realization, as shown in figure 11.1.

Frequency-domain techniques are based on the assumption that any signal can be considered to be the sum of sines or cosines—each with its own amplitude, frequency and phase—according to theoretical principles developed by Fourier (1768–1830). Mathematically, this may be expressed as follows:

$$s(t) = \sum_{i=0} A_i \sin(2\pi f_i t + \varphi_i) \qquad (11.1)$$

where A_i, f_i and φ_i are, respectively, the amplitude, frequency and phase of the *ith* sinewave.

On the other hand, *granular synthesis* is a *time-domain technique* based on the construction of signals from the combination of short sounds, called *grains.*

Linear techniques are processes that do not distort the input and, as a consequence, do not create new frequencies that were not already contained in the input before it was processed. Linear procedures process signals in three possible ways: *delay* of samples, *scaling* (which is equivalent to multiplying a sample by a constant) and *addition* or *subtraction* of scaled samples (which may or may not have been delayed).

Nonlinear techniques consist of the controlled distortion of a signal, which results in the creation of frequencies not found before it was processed. This can be achieved

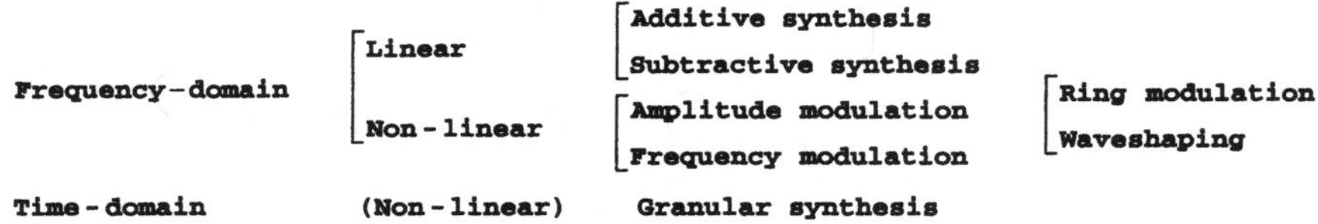

Figure 11.1 Classic synthesis techniques classified according to their principles of realization.

in various ways. For example, it is possible to use a signal in order to modify the amplitude of another (amplitude modulation) by multiplying the former by the latter. Alternatively, a signal may be used to modify the frequency of another (frequency modulation).

We will now proceed to examine the various techniques in more detail.

Additive Synthesis

Additive processes consist of synthesis by means of a direct implementation of equation 11.1. Sinewaves of various frequencies and amplitudes are added together (mixed) in order to produce complex sounds. This is illustrated in *1101.orc* and *1101.sco*. The former consists of the instrument shown in figures 11.2 and 11.3.

Instr 1101 contains a simple oscillator that may produce a single sinewave or a combination of components, depending on the type of waveform defined by the f-table *(p6)*. The maximum amplitude, determined by *p4,* is fed to an envelope generator *(kenv)*, which controls the amplitude of the oscillator. The frequency of the oscillator is given by *p5*. The attack is 0.1 seconds and the decay is 0.2 seconds.

The score produces the following sounds. First, the individual components of a bassoon-like sound, based on data presented by Backus (1977, p 116), are played separately. These are then superimposed in ascending frequency order. At this point it is possible to appreciate how the overall timbre changes as components are added. Finally, they are all mixed together in order to produce the synthetic "bassoon," which is used in a short musical passage from *The Sorcerer's Apprentice* by Dukas.

The individual components are generated by *f 1* using GEN10:

```
f 1    0  8192 10    1
```

The waveform in the "bassoon" passage of the final section of this example is generated with *f* 2, which uses GEN10 to produce a waveform resulting from combining eight components, each with its own relative amplitude:

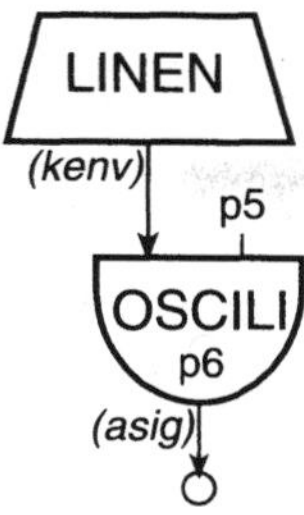

Figure 11.2 Block diagram of *instr 1101,* a simple oscillator instrument with an amplitude envelope.

```
        instr   1101              ; SIMPLE OSCILLATOR
kenv    linen   p4, 0.1, p3, 0.2           ; ENVELOPE
asig    oscili  kenv, p5, p6               ; OSCILLATOR
        out     asig                       ; OUTPUT
        endin
```

Figure 11.3 Orchestra code for *instr 1101,* a simple oscillator instrument.

```
f 2   0  8192   10   .24 .64 .88 .76 .06 .5 .24 .08
```

In its simplest form, additive synthesis may be used to produce a *static spectrum.* This is a combination of sines and cosines in which the amplitude and frequency of each component remain unchanged throughout the duration of the sound. Within these constraints, timbral identity is determined by the particular set of relative amplitudes, frequencies and—to a lesser extent—phases of the components. For example, consider the sounds in figure 11.4. Close inspection of sounds 1 and 2 reveals that their frequency components have relative ratios 1, 2, 3, 4, 5, 6, and 7, namely:

```
200    =   2 x 100        and   220    =    2 x 110
300    =   3 x 100              330    =    3 x 110
400    =   4 x 100              440    =    4 x 110
etc.                            etc.
```

The same happens to the corresponding amplitudes, which have relative ratios 1, 1.5, 2, 2.5, 2, 1.5, 1. Therefore, we expect these sounds to have the same timbre (and different pitch), in spite of the fact that they do not have any common frequency components. On the other hand, the frequency ratios in sound 3 are 1, 3, 5, 7, 9, 11, 13 and the relative amplitudes are 7, 6, 5, 4, 3, 2, 1. These are not the same as sound 2; thus in spite of having some common frequencies with the latter, sound 3 has a different timbre. Sounds 1, 2 and 3 are realized in *1102.orc* and *1102.sco.* The orchestra uses *instr 1102,* which is similar to *instr 1101,* except for the fact that *p6* and *p7*

Sound 1		Sound 2		Sound 3	
Amp.	Freq.(Hz)	Amp.	Freq.(Hz)	Amp.	Freq.(Hz)
500	100	1000	110	3500	110
750	200	1500	220	3000	330
1000	300	2000	330	2500	550
1250	400	2500	440	2000	770
1000	500	2000	550	1500	990
750	600	1500	660	1000	1210
500	700	1000	770	500	1430

Figure 11.4 The static spectra of three additive synthesis sounds.

indicate the attack and decay and *p8* indicates the function table. The score file *1102.sco* implements the spectrum of sounds 1, 2, and 3 from figure 11.4 using the function tables shown in figure 11.7.

Frequency ratios may also determine whether a signal has pitch. If *f* is the lowest frequency component of a sound, its spectrum is said to be *harmonic* when all other components are integer multiples of *f.* In this case, the sound will normally have a definite pitch determined by *f,* which is called the *fundamental.* The components are then said to be *harmonics:* the first harmonic is *f,* the fundamental; the second harmonic is *2f,* the third *3f* and so on. When the relative frequencies of the components are not integer multiples of *f,* the spectrum is *inharmonic* and it is more difficult to recognize pitch. Increasing deviation from harmonic ratios causes sounds to become less pitched. The files *1103.orc* and *1103.sco* demonstrate this: the first event is a sound with a 280 Hz fundamental and six additional harmonics with relative amplitudes 1, 0.68, 0.79, 0.67, 0.59, 0.82, and 0.34. This is followed by an inharmonic sound in which the lowest component is also $f = 280$ Hz but the other six are not integer multiples of *f* but rather *1.35f, 1.78f, 2.13f, 2.55f, 3.23f,* and *3.47f.* Although the relative amplitudes of the components are kept, the second sound does not resemble the first and has no definite pitch because its spectrum is inharmonic.

In order to implement a sound with seven components, *instr 1103* uses seven oscillators that are subsequently mixed and multiplied by the overall envelope *(kenv).*

The relative amplitudes of the components are given in *p6, p8, p10, p12, p14, p16,* and *p18.* The frequencies of the oscillators are obtained by multiplying the reference frequency *f* (given by *p5*) by the component ratios specified in *p7, p9, p11, p13, p15, p17,* and *p19.* For example, if $f = 280$ Hz and the second component has a relative amplitude of 1 and a frequency ratio of 1.35, the values of *p5, p8,* and *p9* will be 280, 1 and 1.35, respectively. The oscillator producing this component will be:

```
a1      oscil    p8, p5*p9, 1                  ; 1ST COMPONENT
```

And the components are mixed using the following statement:

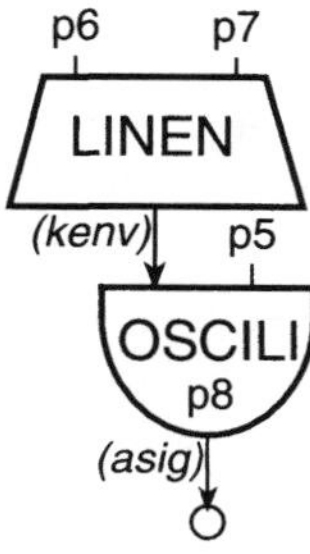

Figure 11.5 Block diagram of *instr 1102,* a variable waveform oscillator instrument.

```
        instr    1102        ; SIMPLE OSCILLATOR WITH AMPLITUDE ENVELOPE
kenv    linen    p4, p6, p3, p7           ; ENVELOPE
asig    oscili   kenv, p5, p8             ; OSCILLATOR
        out      asig                     ; OUTPUT
        endin
```

Figure 11.6 Orchestra code for *instr 1102,* a variable waveform single oscillator instrument with variable attack and release amplitude envelope.

```
f 1  0   8192  10  500 750 1000 1250 1000 750 500
f 2  0   8192  10  1000 1500 2000 2500 2000 1500 1000
f 3  0   8192  10  3500 0 3000 0 2500 0 2000 0 1500 0 1000 0 500
```

Figure 11.7 Harmonically complex f-tables for use in *instr 1102.*

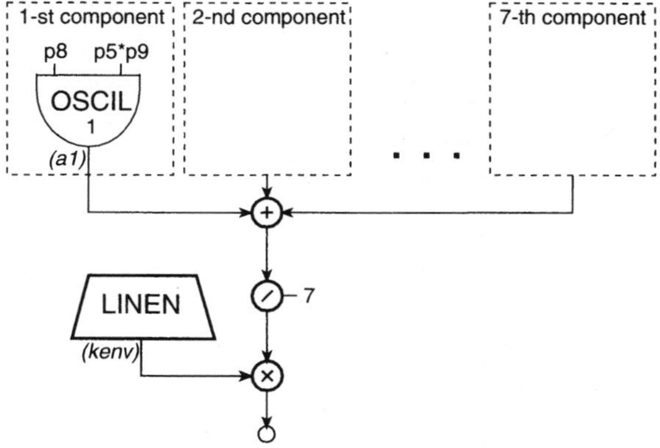

Figure 11.8 Block diagram of *instr 1103,* a seven partial additive synthesis instrument with common amplitude envelope.

```
out     kenv*(a1+a2+a3+a4+a5+a6+a7)/7          ; MIX AND OUTPUT
```

So far, the discussion has focused on static spectra. Most sounds in nature, however, have *dynamic spectra,* whereby the amplitude and frequency of each component change throughout the duration of a sound. This means that A_i, f_i and ϕ_i in equation 11.1 are time-dependent.

Using additive synthesis in order to achieve dynamic spectrum may become a laborious task given the amount of data involved. Convincing results may sometimes require the use of a large number of components, each of which requires independent amplitude, frequency and phase control. In *1104.orc* and *1104.sco* I present an example of dynamic spectrum synthesis realized with an instrument that employs six oscillators, each with variable amplitude and frequency. In addition, the output is spatialized. The amplitude and frequency of each component vary by a percentage specified respectively in *p8* and *p9.* These are translated into fractions using the following statements:

```
imaxaf    =    p8/100.00     ; MAXIMUM AMPLITUDE FLUCTUATION
imaxff    =    p9/100.00     ; MAXIMUM FREQUENCY FLUCTUATION
```

The implementation of each component takes account of these fluctuations by including time-varying controllers for amplitude and frequency. For example, the first component is implemented using the set of statements shown in figure 11.10.

Amplitude fluctuation is controlled by *kampfl* according to a function table given by *iafunc1.* The maximum value of *kampfl* is *imaxafl,* which is calculated as a fraction of *iramp1,* the relative amplitude of the component specified in the score. Therefore, adding *kampfl* to *iramp1* in the **oscili** statement means that the actual relative amplitude will fluctuate around *iramp1* depending on the shape of *iafunc1.* A similar procedure uses *kfreqfl* and *ifreqfl* to control the frequency of the component.

Components are mixed using the following statements:

```
iampsum = iramp1+iramp2+iramp3+iramp4+iramp5+iramp6 ; MAX AMPLITUDE
asig    = kenv*(a1+a2+a3+a4+a5+a6)/(iampsum)        ; BALANCED MIX
```

In order to spatialize the output, the number of channels is set to 2 in the header (*nchnls*= 2), an **outs** statement is used instead of **out**, and *asig* is multiplied by time-varying scaling factors *kpleft* and *kpright* before it is sent to the left and right channels:

```
outs    kpleft*asig, kpright*asig        ; OUTPUT
```

kpleft and *kpright* are calculated according to the following algorithm: if *kpan* is the instantaneous position along the line joining the speakers, *kpan* $= -1$ and *kpan* $=$ 1 represent respectively the positions of the left and right speakers. Values between

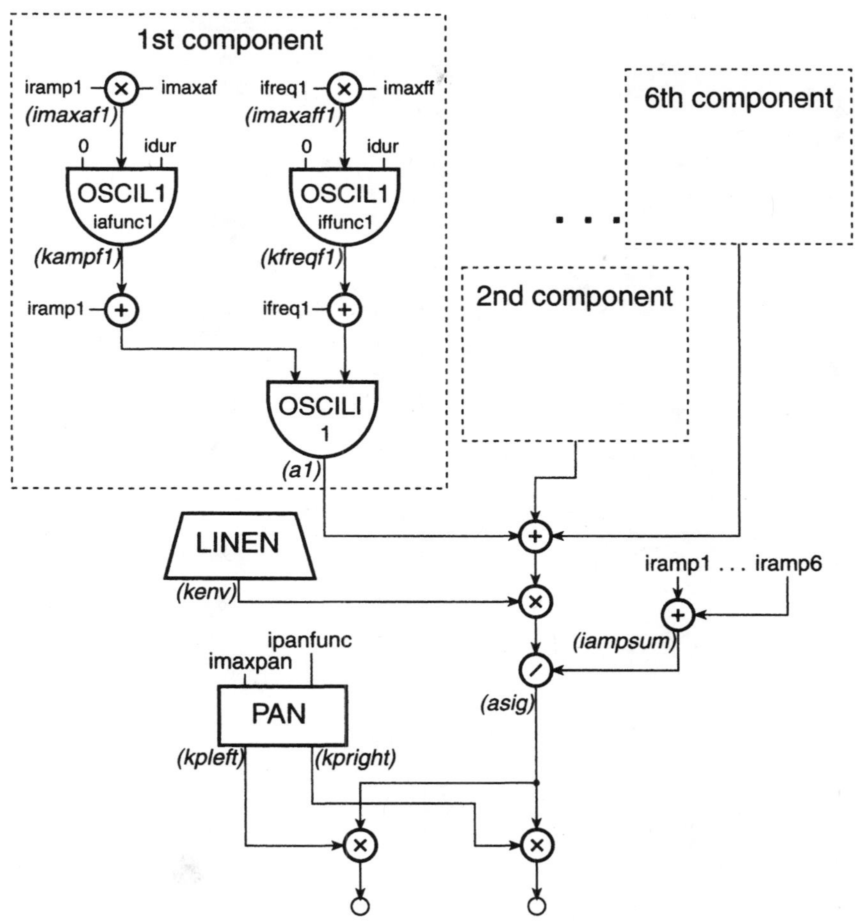

Figure 11.9 Block diagram of a six component additive synthesis instrument with variable amplitude and frequency of each partial, plus a group envelope and panning.

```
iramp1    =       p10                               ; RELATIVE AMPLITUDE
imaxaf1   =       iramp1*imaxaf                     ; MAXIMUM AMP FLUCTUATION
iafunc1   =       p12                               ; AMPLITUDE FLUCTUATION FN
ifreq1    =       p11*ifreq                         ; FREQUENCY
imaxff1   =       ifreq1*imaxff                     ; MAXIMUM FREQ FLUCTUATION
iffunc1   =       p13                               ; FREQUENCY FLUCTUATION FN
kampf1    oscil1  0,imaxaf1,idur,iafunc1            ; AMPLITUDE CONTROL
kfreqf1   oscil1  0,imaxff1,idur,iffunc1            ; FREQUENCY CONTROL
a1        oscili  iramp1+kampf1, ifreq1+kfreqf1, 1  ; OSCILLATOR
```

Figure 11.10 Orchestra code for the first component of additive instrument shown in figure 11.9.

-1 and 1 represent positions between the speakers (*kpan* $= 0$ is the center). Values below -1 represent positions beyond the left speaker.

If the source is between the speakers then:

$$kpleft = \frac{\sqrt{2}}{2}\frac{(1 - kpan)}{\sqrt{1 + kpan^2}} \quad ; \quad kpright = \frac{\sqrt{2}}{2}\frac{(1 + kpan)}{\sqrt{1 + kpan^2}} \quad (-1 \leq kpan \leq 1) \tag{11.2}$$

If the source is beyond the left speaker:

$$kpleft = \frac{\sqrt{2}}{\sqrt{1 + kpan^2}} \; ; \; kpright = 0 \quad (kpan < -1) \tag{11.3}$$

If the source is beyond the right speaker:

$$kpleft = 0 \; ; \; kpright = \frac{\sqrt{2}}{\sqrt{1 + kpan^2}} \quad (kpan > 1) \tag{11.4}$$

The spatial trajectory of the output is generated by the statement:

```
kpan  oscil1  0, imaxpan, idur, ipanfunc   ; PANNING TRAJECTORY
```

where *imaxpan* is 2 and *ipanfunc* (*p34*) is the function table determining the shape of the trajectory. Since there are different formulas for the position of the source, the instrument must check the value of *kpan* and decide which formula to apply using **if** . . . **kgoto** statements.

Summary

Additive synthesis may be used to create dynamic spectra. Each component requires the following parameters:

1. Amplitude envelope.
2. Time-varying frequency.

Subtractive Synthesis

This is the counterpart of additive procedures. While the latter constructs spectra using single sinewaves in order to implement the equation, subtractive synthesis uses

```
if kpan < -1 kgoto beyondl                           ; CHK PAN BEYOND LEFT SPKR
      if kpan >1 kgoto beyondr                       ; CHCK PAN BEYOND RIGHT SPKR
ktemp     =           sqrt(1+kpan*kpan)              ; PAN BETWEEN SPEAKERS
kpleft    =           isr2b2*(1-kpan)/ktemp
kpright   =           isr2b2*(1+kpan)/ktemp
          kgoto       donepan
beyondl:                                             ; PAN BEYOND LEFT SPEAKER
kpleft    =           isr2/(1+kpan*kpan)
kpright   =           0
          kgoto       donepan
beyondr:                                             ; PAN BEYOND RIGHT SPEAKER
kpleft    =           0
kpright   =           isr2/(1+kpan*kpan)
donepan:
```

Figure 11.11 Orchestra code excerpt for panning algorithm supporting both an equal-power pan and a wide-stereo effect.

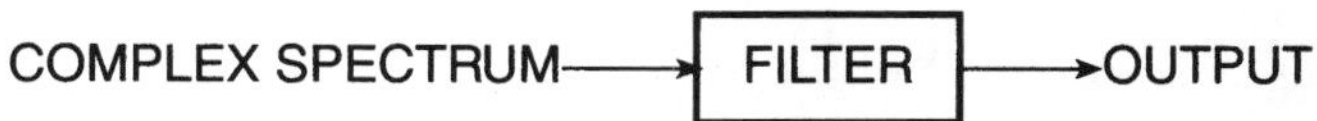

Figure 11.12 Block diagram of a basic subtractive synthesis system.

complex spectra as inputs that are shaped by enhancing or attenuating the component sinewaves, as illustrated in figure 11.12. Mathematically, this means that the values of A_i in equation 11.1 are modified.

The output depends on the choice of sources and the behavior of the filters. In addition, some type of amplification may be required after filtering as a result of power loss owing to the attenuation of components.

The main consideration regarding choice of sources is their spectral content. If we intend to process frequencies in a certain region of the spectrum, it is important to ensure that these frequencies exist in the source; otherwise there will be nothing to filter. For this reason, *noise* and *trains of pulses* are frequently used, since they offer a uniform spread of components throughout the auditory range.

Ideal *white noise* is probably the richest available source. For practical purposes, it is possible to consider it as a signal that contains all frequencies evenly distributed throughout the auditory range. White noise is normally obtained using a generator that produces a random number every sample. The aural result is rather like a hiss.

An ideal *train* or *sequence* of *pulses* consists of a signal containing an infinite number of harmonics, all of which have the same relative amplitude. In practice, approximations of a pulse sequence may be obtained by combining as many harmonics as possible up to the upper threshold of the auditory range. It is also important to consider the limitations imposed by the sampling rate **sr** (according to the sampling theorem, the highest frequency sampled with **sr** must be less than **sr**/2). The file

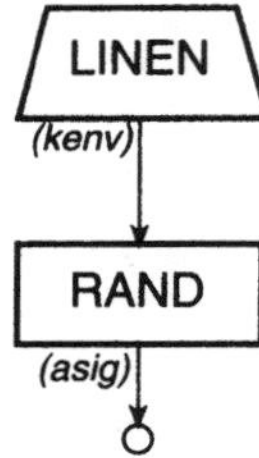

Figure 11.13 Block diagram of *instr 1105,* a white noise generator.

```
        instr     1105        ; ENVELOPE-CONTROLLED WHITE NOISE
kenv    linen     p4, p6, p3, p7          ; ENVELOPE
asig    rand      kenv                    ; NOISE SOURCE
        out       asig                    ; OUTPUT
        endin
```

Figure 11.14 Orchestra code for *instr 1105,* an envelope controlled white noise instrument.

1105.orc consists of instruments that produce white noise and trains of pulses. For *instr 1105* a **rand** generator is used to produce white noise as shown in figure 11.13.

For *instr 1106* a **buzz** is used to produce a train of pulses with as many harmonics as possible given the sampling rate (**sr**). If the frequency of the fundamental is *p5,* then the frequency of the *n*th harmonic is *n* times *p5.* This frequency must be less than *sr/2;* therefore, the maximum number of harmonics, *iinh,* must be equal or less than *sr/2/p5.* Since the number of harmonics must be an integer, the operator **int** is used in order to calculate *iinh.* Figure 11.15 shows a block diagram of *instr 1106.* The file *1105.sco* produces white noise (*instr 1105*) followed by a train-of-pulses (a pulse-train *instr 1106)* with a fundamental of 75 Hz.

Filters are characterized by their response, which represents the frequency regions they attenuate and enhance. Figure 11.17 shows the four ideal types of filters used in subtractive synthesis. These are classified as follows:

1. Filters that only pass frequencies above a *cut-off* value f_c, or highpass.
2. Filters that only pass frequencies below f_c, or lowpass.
3. Filters that only pass components with frequencies inside a band above and below a *center frequency* f_c, or bandpass. The size in Hz of the bandpass is the *bandwidth* (bw).
4. Filters that only pass components with frequencies outside a band above and below a *center frequency* f_c, or bandreject.

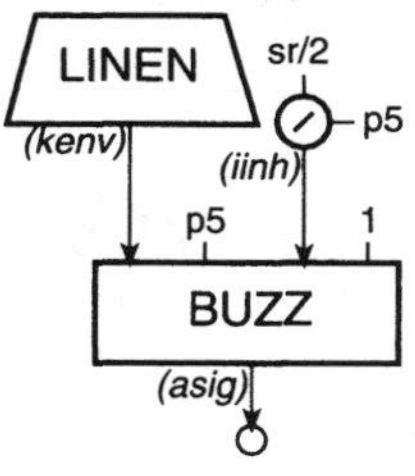

Figure 11.15 Block diagram of *instr 1106,* a buzz (pulse train) instrument with an amplitude envelope.

```
      instr    1106            ; PULSE TRAIN WITH AMPLITUDE ENVELOPE
iinh  =        int(sr/2/p5)           ; MAXIMUM NUMBER OF HARMONICS
kenv  linen    p4, p6, p3, p7         ; ENVELOPE
asig  buzz     kenv, p5, iinh, 1      ; OSCILLATOR
      out      asig                   ; OUTPUT
      endin
```

Figure 11.16 Orchestra code for *instr 1106,* a **buzz** instrument with controls for the number of harmonics in the pulse-train.

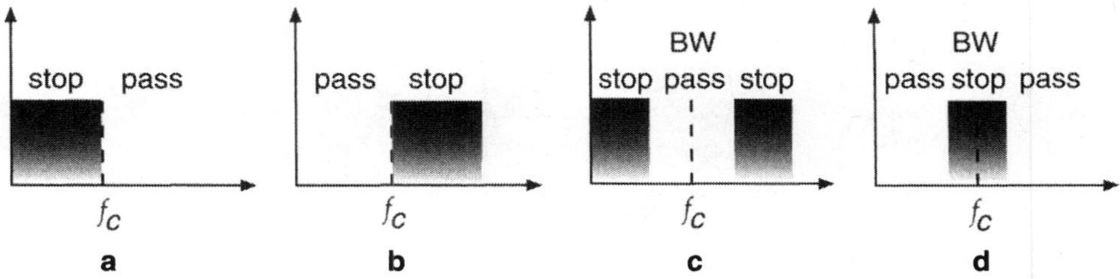

Figure 11.17 Ideal filter types: (a) Highpass, (b) Lowpass, (c) Bandpass, and (d) Bandreject.

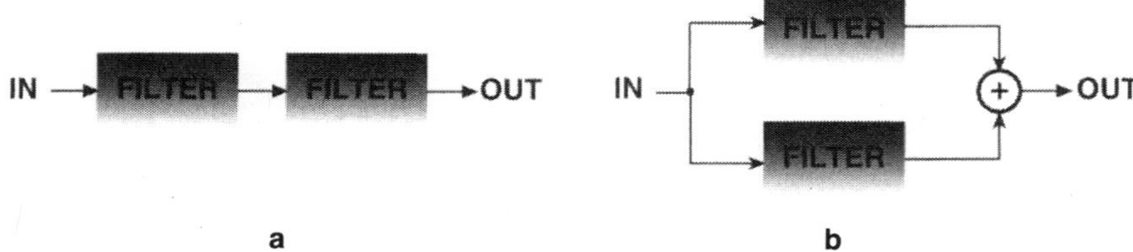

Figure 11.18 Filter connections: (a) Cascade, and (b) Parallel.

The four filter types shown in figure 11.17 represent ideal filters. In practice, the transition between pass and stop regions is not as sharp as in the figure. Its slope is known as the *roll-off* and is measured in decibels per octave, which is the change in attenuation when the frequency is doubled. The fact that there is a slope means that the cut-off frequency must be re-defined as the value at which the attenuation is –3 dB, which is equivalent to a drop in amplitude by a factor of about 0.71.

In order to achieve sharper responses, filters may be *cascaded* by using the output of one filter as the input of another. Filters may also be connected in *parallel,* with two or more filters sharing the same input and having their outputs mixed into one signal; thus achieving complex response curves. Cascade and parallel connections are shown in figure 11.18.

We have seen above that in order to achieve a dynamic spectrum it is necessary to vary the amplitudes and frequencies of components in time. Linear filters cannot alter the frequencies of the components of a source; however, they can change their amplitudes. This may be done by varying the cut-off frequency in low and highpass filters and by varying the center frequency and bandwidth in bandpass and bandreject filters.

As an example, the files *1107.orc* and *1107.sco* produce sounds resembling vowel articulation by modeling the mechanism driving the vocal chords: a rich pulse (maximum possible harmonics) is passed through five parallel bandpass filters.

The center frequencies and bandwidths of the filters fluctuate randomly in the vicinity of values corresponding to the filtering processes in human speech. The rate at which the random numbers are generated is varied between a minimum *(irfmin)* and a maximum *(p9)*, according to the control variable *krfl:*

```
irfmin  =        p8                  ; MINIMUM RANDOM RATE
itfl    =        p9-p8               ; MAXIMUM FLUCTUATION
irfunc  =        2                   ; FLUCTUATION FUNCTION
        ...
        ...
```

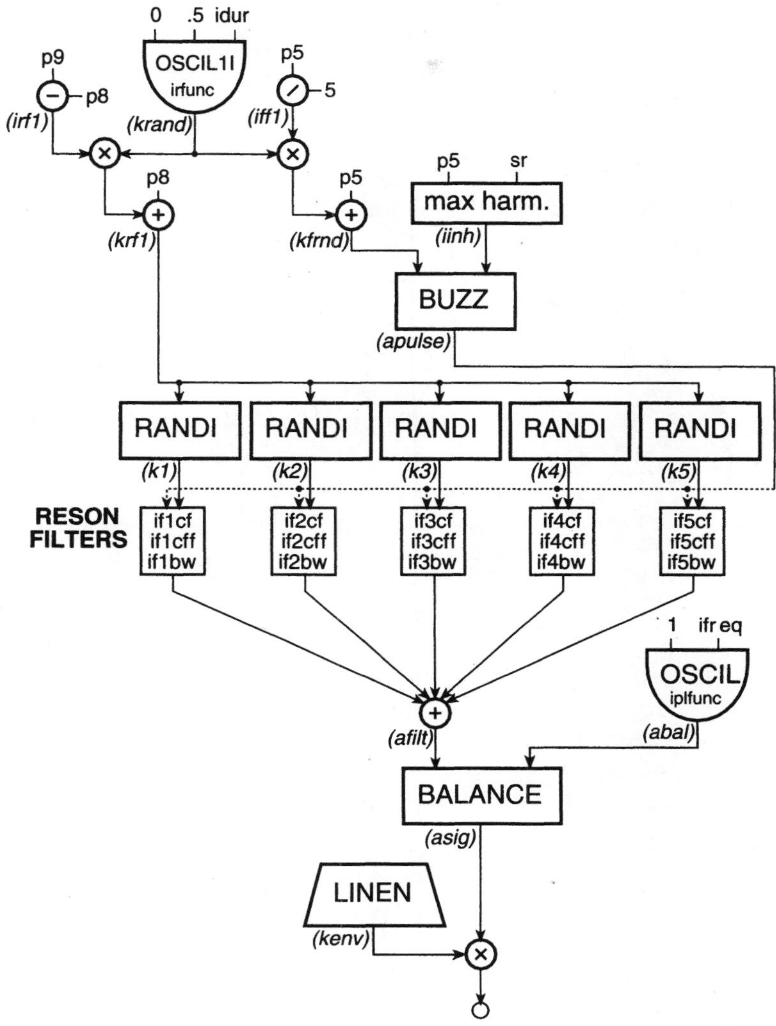

Figure 11.19 Block diagram of *instr 1107,* a parallel, pseudo-random, formant-filter instrument.

```
ifreq       =       p5                          ; FREQUENCY OF FUNDAMENTAL
iffl        =       p5/5                        ; MAXIMUM FREQUENCY FLUCTUATION
iinh        =       int(sr/2/(p5+iffl))         ; MAXIMUM NUMBER OF HARMONICS
iplfunc     =       1                           ; FUNCTION TABLE FOR BUZZ (SINE)
            ...
            ...
kfrnd       =       ifreq+iffl*krand            ; FREQUENCY FLUCTUATION
apulse      buzz    1, kfrnd, iinh, iplfunc     ; PULSE GENERATOR
```

Figure 11.20 Orchestra code excerpt from *instr 1107,* a pulse-train generator with fluctuating frequency.

```
krand    oscil1i  0, .5, idur, irfunc   ; OSCIL BETWEEN -.5 AND .5
krand    =        krand+.5              ; CORRECT BETWEEN 0 AND 1
krfl     =        irfmin+irfl*krand     ; RATE OF RANDOM GENERATORS
```

Each filter uses a **randi** generator in order to produce center frequency and bandwidth fluctuations. For example, the first formant is controlled by *k1,* which is multiplied by the maximum center frequency fluctuation, *if1cff* and added to a minimum center frequency *if1cf.* The bandwidth is controlled similarly:

```
k1        randi    1, krfl, .12                       ; RANDOM GENERATOR
          ...
          ...                                         ; FIRST FORMANT
afilt1    reson    apulse, if1cf+k1*if1cff, if1bw*(1+k1), 0
```

The input to the formant filter is *apulse,* a train of pulses generated using **buzz.** Its fundamental frequency is made to fluctuate by up to 1/5 of its value. This process is controlled by *krand,* which is scaled by *iffl*—the maximum frequency fluctuation and added to *ifreq*—the minimum frequency value, to produce *kfrnd,* the frequency input to the pulse generator shown in figure 11.20.

Finally, the filtered pulses are mixed, balanced with a sinewave and sent to the output:

```
afilt    =        afilt1+afilt2+afilt3+afilt4+afilt5  ; MIX FILTR OUT
abal     oscil    1, ifreq, iplfunc                   ; SINEWAVE CONTROL SIG
asig     balance  afilt, abal                         ; OUTPUT BALANCE
         out      kenv*asig
```

Summary

There are three important factors that must be considered in order to obtain dynamic spectra using subtractive procedures:

1. Choice of source (may be time-varying). White noise or a pulse-train are commonly used.
2. Time-varying filters.
3. Output balance.

Ring Modulation

This nonlinear technique consists of the use of a signal, the *modulator,* to modify the amplitude of another signal, the *carrier.* Each sample of the modulator multiplies a corresponding sample of the carrier, distorting the latter and creating new spectral components.

The simplest case of amplitude modulation is that of a sinewave that multiplies another sinewave. If the frequencies of the carrier and modulator are, respectively, f_m and f_c, the output is:

$$s(t) = \sin(2\pi f_m t)\sin(2\pi f_c t) \tag{11.5}$$

But, from the trigonometric identity for the product of two sines, we have:

$$s(t) = \frac{1}{2}\left[\cos(2\pi[f_c + f_m]t) - \cos(2\pi[f_c - f_m]t)\right] \tag{11.6}$$

The equation above represents a spectrum containing two components with frequencies f_c+f_m and f_c-f_m. These are called *sidebands,* because they appear on both sides of the carrier, as shown in figure 11.21.

The modulation process requires caution. In the first place, it is important to ensure that f_c+f_m does not exceed half of the *sampling rate* (**sr/**2) in order to comply with the sampling theorem, avoiding *aliasing,* which causes frequencies over **sr/**2 to reflect, appearing to be lower, thus assuming a different spectral "identity." Second, if f_c and f_m are close, their difference may be below the auditory range; this occurs when f_c-f_m

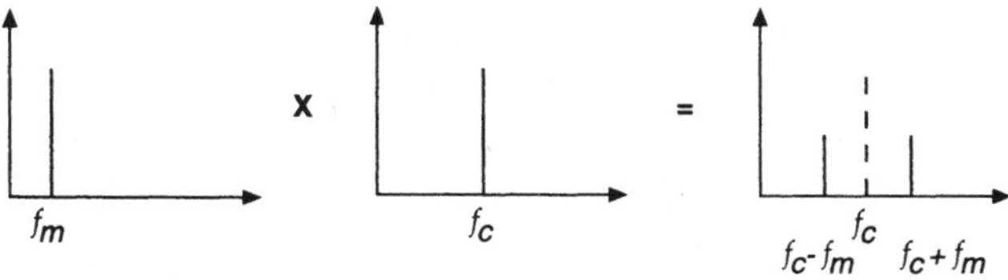

Figure 11.21 Spectrum of simple amplitude modulation.

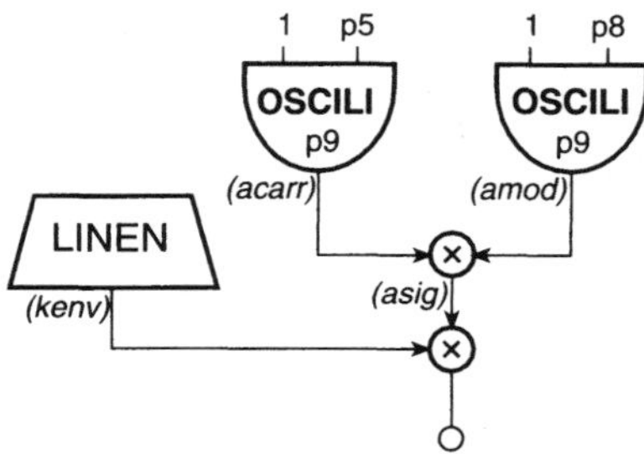

Figure 11.22 Block diagram of *instr 1109,* an amplitude modulation instrument with amplitude envelope.

```
        instr    1109          ; SIMPLE AMPLITUDE MODULATION
kenv    linen    p4, p6, p3, p7                    ; ENVELOPE
acarr   oscili   1, p5, p9                         ; CARRIER
amod    oscili   1, p8, p9                         ; MODULATOR
asig    =        acarr*amod                        ; MODULATION
        out      kenv*asig                         ; OUTPUT
        endin
```

Figure 11.23 Orchestra code for *instr 1109,* the amplitude modulation instrument shown in figure 11.22.

is below about 20 Hz. If f_c is larger than f_m, the difference will be a negative number. But from the identity:

$$\cos(-a) = \cos(a) \tag{11.7}$$

We can infer that only the absolute value of the difference is important and that the sign can be ignored. In other words, a negative frequency reflects as a positive one.

A simple implementation of an amplitude modulator consists of two oscillators, a carrier and a modulator, which have their outputs multiplied, as shown in figure 11.22.

The effects of modulation using sinewaves are shown in *1109.orc* and *1109.sco.* The orchestra consists of two instruments: *instr 1108* is identical to *instr 1101* and is used to produce separate pairs of sinewaves. Whereas *instr 1109* is used to carry out the amplitude modulation by multiplying the sinewaves. The score produces pairs followed by their product, in the order shown in figure 11.24.

It is worth noticing that the 10 Hz modulator of the first pair is inaudible; however, its effect on the 400 Hz carrier results in two distinct sidebands in the auditory range. Furthermore, the third pair produces a difference sideband of 15 Hz. Therefore, only the 785 Hz component is perceived.

Sinewave pair		Modulated output	
Carrier (Hz)	Modulator (Hz)	f_c+f_m	f_c-f_m
400	10	410	390
400	170	570	230
400	385	785	15

Figure 11.24 Table of amplitude modulated input signals and output results.

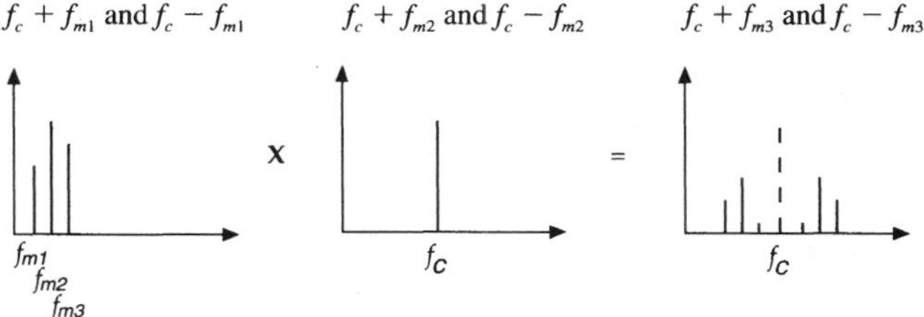

Figure 11.25 Modulator with 3 components.

The process above can be extended to signals with several components. For example, the modulator may consist of three frequencies, f_{m1}, f_{m2} and f_{m3}. Each of these can be considered individually when the modulator is applied to a carrier f_c, as illustrated in figure 11.25. Therefore, the output consists of the following pairs:

$f_c + f_{m1}$ and $f_c - f_{m1}$ $\quad$ $f_c + f_{m2}$ and $f_c - f_{m2}$ $\quad$ $f_c + f_{m3}$ and $f_c - f_{m3}$

The file *1110.orc* consists of *instr 1110,* a modified version of *instr 1109* that allows use of different function tables for both carrier and modulator (the function for the carrier is given in *p9* and that for the modulator in *p10*). The file *1110.sco* includes two ring-modulation processes. In the first, a 110 Hz signal with 5 harmonics modulates a 440 Hz carrier. In the second, the same carrier (440 Hz) is modulated with a 134 Hz signal. When synthesized, it is immediately apparent that the first sound is pitched while the second is not. This can be explained by inspection of the output frequencies. The components of the first modulator are 110, 220, 330, 440, and 550 Hz. In the second case, they are 134, 268, 402, 536, and 670 Hz; therefore the components of the respective outputs can be calculated as shown in figure 11.26.

The output of the first sound has the following components; 0 (not heard), 110, 220, 330, 550, 660, 770, 880, and 990 Hz, which produce a harmonic series having a definite pitch. On the other hand, the second output is composed of 38, 96, 172, 230, 306, 574, 708, 842, 976, and 1110 Hz, which produce an inharmonic spectrum.

Carrier: 440 Hz - Modulator: 110 Hz	
440+110 = 550	440-110 = 330
440+220 = 660	440-220 = 220
440+330 = 770	440-330 = 110
440+440 = 880	440-440 = 0
440+550 = 990	440-550 = -110

Carrier: 440 Hz - Modulator: 134 Hz	
440+134 = 574	440-134 = 306
440+268 = 708	440-268 = 172
440+402 = 842	440-402 = 38
440+536 = 976	440-536 = -96
440+670 = 1110	440-670 = -230

Figure 11.26 Tables evaluating result of amplitude modulating a complex source, consisting of five harmonics, with a 110 Hz sine wave and a 134 Hz sine wave.

The example above shows that it is possible to predict harmonicity when the frequencies of carrier and modulator components are known. This may, however, be a laborious task when using complex modulators. Obviously, if the modulator is an inharmonic signal, the output will also be inharmonic. If the modulator is harmonic, it is enough to check the result of dividing the carrier by the modulator, called the *carrier to modulator ratio,* or the *c/m* ratio. If *c/m* is an integer, then the carrier is a multiple of the modulator and subtracting or adding the later to f_c will create another multiple. Therefore, all the frequencies will be multiples of f_m, which will effectively become the fundamental. Similarly, if *c/m* is of the form 1/n, where n is an integer, the modulator is a multiple of the carrier and, as a consequence, the output frequencies will also be multiples of f_c. When *c/m* deviates from an n/1 or 1/n ratio, the output frequencies become more and more inharmonic. Small deviations (e.g., 1.001) will still produce pitched sounds because the output components will be close to actual harmonic values. In fact, these small deviations produce beating, which may add some liveliness. The effect of the carrier to modulator ratio is shown in *1110a.orc* and *1110a.sco.* The orchestra consists of *instr 1110* (described above) and the score contains the following:

1. 300 Hz sine carrier, 8 harmonic modulator with 300 Hz fundamental (c/m=1).
2. 300 Hz sine carrier, 8 harmonic modulator with 297.03 Hz fundamental (c/m=1.01).
3. 300 Hz sine carrier, 8 harmonic modulator, 212.13 Hz fundamental (c/m=1.4142~$\sqrt{2}$).

Ring modulation can also be used to produce dynamic spectrum. The morphology of the resulting sound can be controlled through the following parameters:

1. Duration.
2. Overall amplitude.
3. Frequency of the carrier.

4. Carrier to modulator ratio, which also determines the modulator frequency from the frequency of the carrier.
5. Fraction of the carrier that is actually modulated (a small percentage will produce less noticeable distortion).

The file *1111.orc* contains an instrument that implements time-varying: amplitude, carrier-frequency, carrier-to-modulator ratio, and modulation-fraction using control variables *kamp, kcar, kcmr,* and *kmp.*

The functions given by *p7, p8, p9,* and *p10* are fed to control oscillators. The output of the first one, *kamp,* determines the envelope, with a peak value of *p4.* The second controls the carrier frequency, which can be as high as *p5.* The third, *kcmr,* controls the carrier-to-modulator ratio, which can reach a maximum of *p6.* The frequency of the modulator is the product of the carrier-frequency and the carrier-to-modulator ratio.

In order to modulate only part of the carrier, *kmp* multiplies the modulated carrier *acarr*amod,* producing *aoutm* and *1-kmp* multiplies the unmodulated carrier, *acarr,* producing *aoutnm.* Modulated and unmodultated signals are then mixed and enveloped to produce *aout.*

The file *1111.sco* consists of a short musical excerpt that demonstrates some of the possible sonorities obtainable with *instr 1111.* It takes advantage of the fact that all the control variables use **oscil1,** which means that the same function may produce a sharp attack in a short sound, becoming smeared as the sound becomes longer. This is exactly what happens during the first five beats in the score. Furthermore, the maximum carrier-to-modulator ratio may be altered in the score to produce different timbral shades. This is the case with the fast percussive sounds between beat 5.5 and beat 12.

Summary

The following parameters may be controlled in order to produce diverse sonorities using ring-modulation:

1. Duration.
2. Overall amplitude.
3. Frequency of the carrier.
4. Carrier-to-modulator ratio.
5. Fraction of the carrier that is actually modulated.

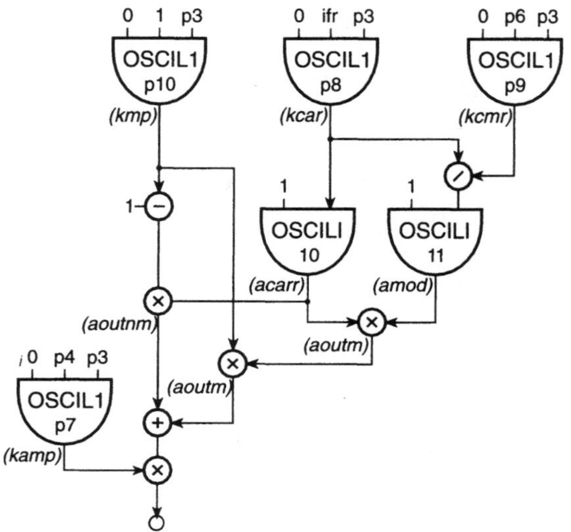

Figure 11.27 Block diagram of *instr 1111*, a dynamic Ring-modulation instrument.

```
         instr    1111       ; RING MODULATION
ifr      =        cpspch(p5)
                                                 ; ENVELOPES
kamp     oscil1   0, p4, p3, p7                  ; AMPLITUDE
kcar     oscil1   0, ifr, p3, p8                 ; CARRIER FREQ
kcmr     oscil1   0, p6, p3, p9                  ; C/M
kmp      oscil1   0, 1, p3, p10                  ; MODULATION FRACTION
                                                 ; MODULATION
acarr    oscili   1, kcar, 10                    ; CARRIER
amod     oscili   1, kcar/kcmr, 11               ; MODULATOR
aoutm    =        acarr*amod*kmp                 ; MODULATED SIGNAL
aoutnm   =        acarr*(1-kmp)                  ; UNMODULATED SIGNAL
                                                 ; MIX AND OUTPUT
         out      kamp*(aoutm+aoutnm)
         endin
```

Figure 11.28 Orchestra code for *instr 1111*, a dynamic Ring-modulation instrument with time varying: amplitude, carrier frequency, modulating frequency, and modulation ratio.

Waveshaping

Another way of producing distortion consists of the creation of a dependency between the amplification applied to a sample and its actual value. For instance, samples with absolute values, (with 16 bits, a sample may assume values between $-2^{16} = -32{,}768$ and $2^{16}-1 = 32{,}767$), under 20,000 may be multiplied by a factor of 1 whereas samples over 20,000 may be multiplied by 0.5; producing compression of the louder parts of a signal, as shown in figure 11.29.

This type of dependency effectively maps the set of possible values of the input onto a set of output values by means of a *transfer function.* The general waveshaping process is illustrated in figure 11.30.

Waveshaping may produce various degrees of distortion depending on the chosen transfer function. If the latter approximates a linear device, the effect will not be as pronounced as with more extreme functions. Furthermore, the input may be a fairly simple signal; even sinewaves may be used effectively in order to produce reasonably complex spectra as shown in figure 11.33.

A transfer function may be implemented in Csound using the **table** opcode, where the value of a sample is used as the index of the function table as shown in the block diagram and instrument in figures 11.31 and 11.32.

The waveshaping table in *instr 1112* processes the signal *ain.* Since the latter can be positive or negative, the upper half of the table processes the positive samples and the lower half the negative ones. Therefore the offset needs to point to the middle of the table. Since the samples are numbered from 0 to the size of the table minus 1, the value of the offset should be half of the table-size minus 1. The table is given by *p9* and its size is *ftlen(p9).*

The files *1112.orc* and *1112.sco* make use of *instr 1112* in order to demonstrate the difference between near-linear and heavy nonlinear processing: a sinewave processed by a linear device is heard first, followed by two waveshaped versions of itself using functions *f 3* and *f 4.* The function implementing the linear device is:

```
f 2  0  8192     7  -1 8192 1
```

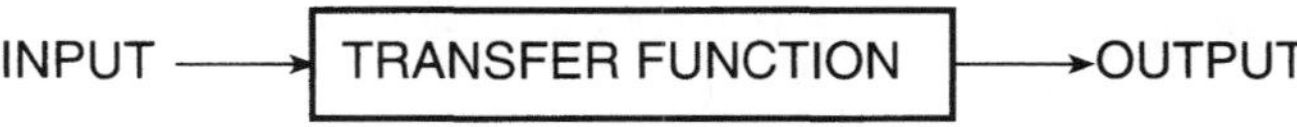

Figure 11.29 The waveshaping process.

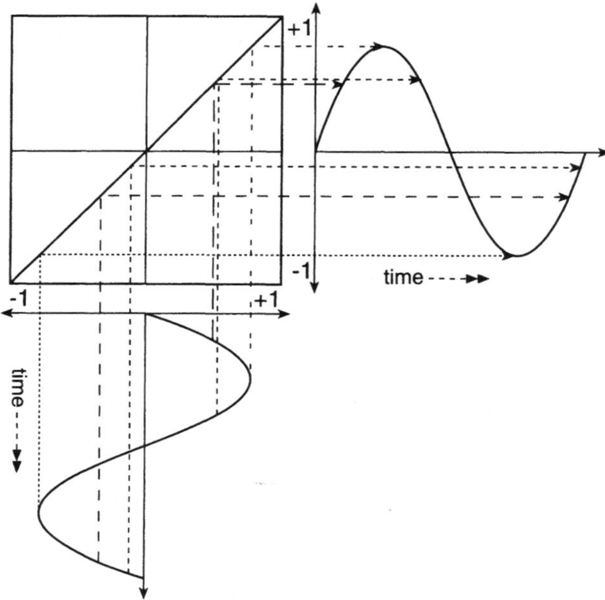

Figure 11.30 Waveshaping a sinusoidal waveform with a linear transfer function. The input is below and the output is to the right.

The near linear and heavy distortion functions are respectively:

```
f 3  0 8192   9 0.5 1 270
f 4  0 8192   7 -1 2048 -1 0 0.3 2048 0 -0.5 2048 0 0 0.8 2048 0.8
```

In general, it is desirable and useful to be able to predict the frequency content of the output in order to control the result of a waveshaping process. It is wise to avoid transfer functions that contain leaps—such as that defined by *f 4,* since these may produce frequencies above half the sampling rate. Instead, smooth functions that involve relatively simple procedures when evaluating the spectral content of the output should be used. A family of functions that fits this requirement is the set of polynomials, since, when using a sine for input, the frequency of the highest component produced will be equal to the frequency of the input multiplied by the degree of the polynomial (i.e., the value of its highest power). This may be illustrated by means of an example:

$$4x^3 - x \tag{11.8}$$

If the polynomial of the third degree is used as a transfer function that is fed a sinusoidal input of frequency *f*, we should expect the highest frequency in the output

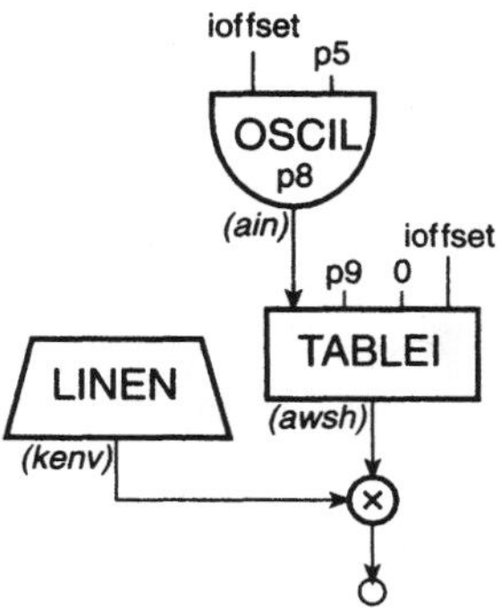

Figure 11.31 Block diagram of *instr 1112,* a simple waveshaping instrument.

```
            instr     1112       ; SIMPLE WAVESHAPING
ioffset     =         ftlen(p9)/2-1               ; OFFSET
kenv        linen     p4, p6, p3, p7              ; ENVELOPE
ain         oscil     ioffset, p5, p8             ; INPUT
awsh        tablei    ain, p9, 0, ioffset         ; WAVESHAPING VALUE
            out       kenv*awsh                   ; OUTPUT
            endin
```

Figure 11.32 Orchestra code for *instr 1112,* a simple waveshaping instrument.

to be 3*f.* Replacing a sinewave of frequency *f,* using the trigonometric identity for the sine of three times an angle and performing some algebraic manipulation, we obtain:

$$s(t) = 2\sin(2\pi ft) - \sin(2\pi[3f]t) \tag{11.9}$$

As expected, the highest frequency, *3f,* appears in the second term. A further refinement is provided by a family of polynomials that produce a specific harmonic of a sinewave, known as *Chebyshev* polynomials. The first four Chebyshev polynomials of the first kind are shown in figure 11.35.

It is easy to check that these produce the desired harmonics by replacing sin(*2pft*) instead of *x* in any of the polynomials above. And with the aid of Chebyshev polynomials, it is possible to achieve any combination of harmonics, each with a specified relative amplitude. For instance, if the combination shown in figure 11.36 is required the transfer function will be:

$$y(x) = 0.8T_1(x) + T_3(x) + 0.67T_7(x) + 0.5T_8(x) \tag{11.10}$$

So far, the input has consisted of sinusoids with an amplitude of 1. If the former is multiplied by an amplitude factor *K*, normalized between 0 and 1, the relative ampli-

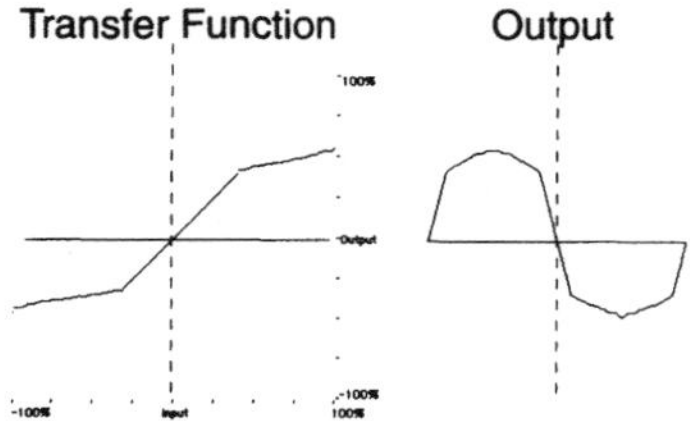

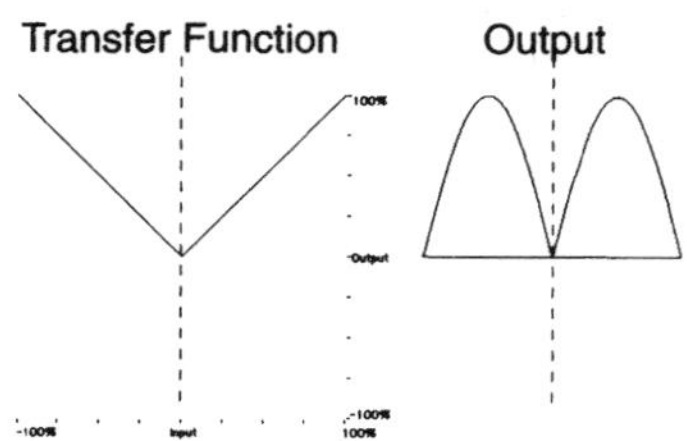

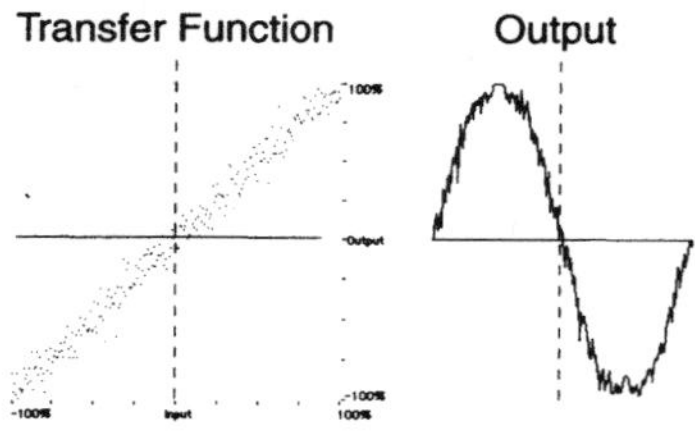

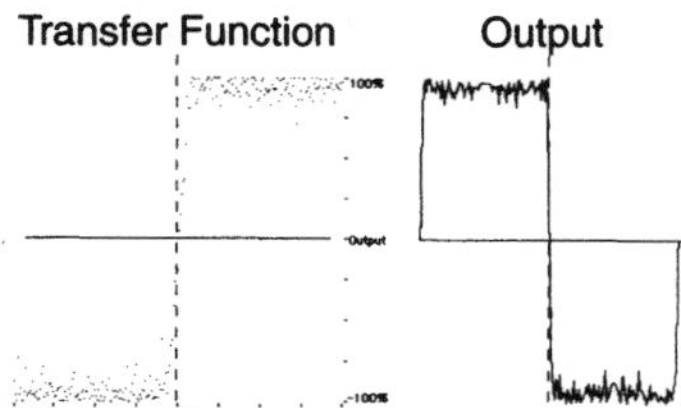

Figure 11.33 A set of transfer functions and their outputs. The input is a sinewave as shown in figure 11.30.

```
f 3  0   8192    9  0.5 1 270
f 4  0   8192    7  -1 2048 -1 0 0.3 2048 0 -0.5 2048 0 0 0.8 2048 0.8
```

Figure 11.34 Transfer functions for waveshaping.

$T_0(x) = 1$	the output is a 0 Hz frequency (DC component).
$T_1(x) = x$	the output is equal to the input sinewave.
$T_2(x) = 2x^2-1$	the output is the second harmonic of the input.
$T_3(x) = 4x^3-3x$	the output is the third harmonic of the input.

Figure 11.35 The first four Chebyshev polynomials of the first kind.

Harmonic	**Relative amplitude**
fundamental	0.8
3	1
7	0.67
8	0.5

Figure 11.36 Table of user specified harmonic number and relative amplitudes.

tude of the harmonics will be affected. Feeding this type of input to the waveshaper in our equation by using the identity for the sine of 3 times an angle and rearranging terms, will result in the following output:

$$s(t) = [3K^3 - K]2\sin(2\pi ft) - K^3\sin(2\pi[3f]t) \tag{11.11}$$

Different values of K will produce different relative amplitudes of the fundamental f and the third harmonic $3f$. For example, if $K = 0.1$, the amplitude of the third harmonic is 0.001 and that of the fundamental is 0.097, a ratio of 1/97. When $K = 1$, the amplitude of the third harmonic is 1 and that of the fundamental is 2.9, however, a ratio of about 1/3. Therefore, changing the value of K makes the third harmonic more prominent.

In general, varying the value of K influences the presence of higher harmonics and with it, the amount of distortion applied to a signal. For this reason, K is called the *distortion index.* This suggests a relatively simple way of obtaining dynamic spectra that consist of varying the amplitude of the input by means of an envelope before it is passed through a waveshaper. In other words, K may become a function of time.

Finally, it is important to realize that the role of the distortion index has a shortcoming: in order to use the full range of a waveshaper, the input envelope must cover a wide dynamic range. This could result in loud passages next to quiet ones that may require post-processing amplification.

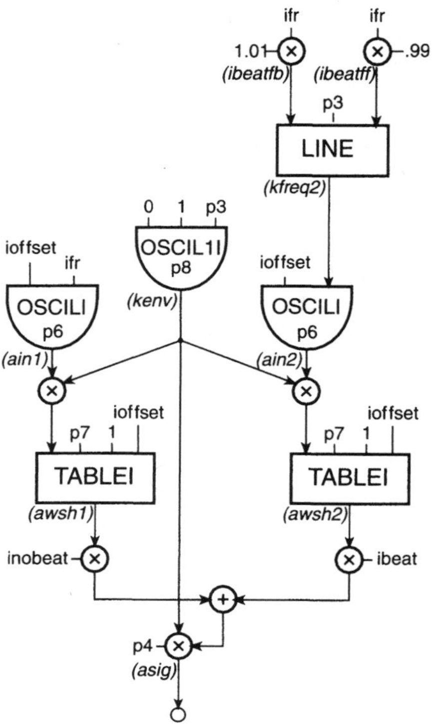

Figure 11.37 Block diagram of *instr 1113,* a dynamic waveshaping instrument.

The relationship between the amplitude of a signal and its harmonic content makes waveshaping suitable for synthesis of brass-like instruments, which are a class characterized in part by the prominence of high components when the overall amplitude increases. The files *1113.orc* and *1113.sco* produce a short brass-like fanfare using the instrument shown in figures 11.37 and 11.38.

In our example *instr 1113* is composed of two waveshapers: the first one processes a sinewave of constant frequency *f* and the second processes a sinewave that varies its frequency throughout the duration of each note from *1.01f* to *0.99f.* The outputs of these waveshapers are mixed in a relative proportion of 0.8:0.2 (*inobeat:ibeat*), producing a variable beating pattern that further enhances the waveshaping process. The reader may notice that *ioffset* is 0.5 and not half of the table size minus one. This is because the **table** statements are used in normalized mode (the waveshaped signal varies between −0.5 and +0.5).

```
         instr    1113        ; DUAL WAVESHAPING
ifr      =        cpspch(p5)                    ; PITCH TO FREQ
ioffset  =        .5                            ; OFFSET
ibeatfb  =        1.01*ifr                      ; BEGIN VALUE OF BEATING FREQ
ibeatff  =        0.99*ifr                      ; FINAL VALUE OF BEATING FREQ
inobeat  =        0.8                           ; PROPORTN NON-BEATING OSCIL
ibeat    =        0.2                           ; PROPORTN BEATING OSCIL
kenv     oscil1i  0, 1, p3, p8                  ; ENVELOPE (DISTORTION INDEX)
kfreq2   line     ibeatfb, p3, ibeatff          ; FREQUENCY CHANGE
ain1     oscili   ioffset, ifr, p6              ; FIRST OSCILLATOR
awsh1    tablei   kenv*ain1, p7, 1, ioffset     ; WAVESHAPING 1ST OSCIL
ain2     oscili   ioffset, kfreq2, p6           ; SECOND OSCILLATOR
awsh2    tablei   kenv*ain2, p7, 1, ioffset     ; WAVESHAPING 2ND OSCIL
asig     =        kenv*p4*(inobeat*awsh1+ibeat*awsh2)
         out      asig
         endin
```

Figure 11.38 Orchestra code for *instr 1113,* a dual waveshaping instrument.

Summary

The following issues should be considered when implementing a waveshaping process:

1. The waveshaper function determines the amount of distortion as a function of amplitude. Chebyshev functions may be used with sinewaves in order to produce various combinations of harmonics. It is also possible to interpolate between two or more waveshaping functions by cross-fading the outputs.
2. The distortion index is essentially the envelope of the sound. It determines which region of the waveshaper is used at a given moment.

Frequency Modulation

The application of frequency modulation (FM) to musical synthesis was initially proposed by John Chowning (1973). He showed that the use of a *modulator* in order to modify the frequency of a *carrier,* may be controlled to produce varied dynamic spectra with relatively little computational overheads. In its simplest form, both the carrier and the modulator are sinewaves; however, unlike ring modulation, sinewave FM generates enough spectral complexity to allow the synthesis of reasonably rich and varied timbres. The mathematical expression for a signal of frequency f_m that modulates a carrier of frequency f_c is:

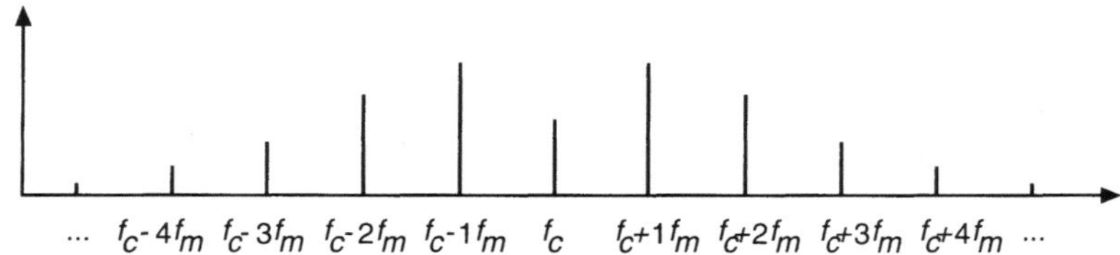

Figure 11.39 Spectrum of frequency modulation process.

$$s(t) = \sin\left(2\pi f_c t + I\sin(2\pi f_m t)\right) \qquad (11.12)$$

Where *I*, called the *modulation index,* controls the degree of distortion applied to the carrier. Its function can be compared with that of the distortion index in waveshaping and will be discussed below.

Equation 11.12 may be manipulated by expressing the sine functions as a power series that, after a rather lengthy process, results in the following expression

$$s(t) = \sum_{n=0} J_n(I)\left[\sin(2\pi[f_c + nf_m]t) + \sin(2\pi[f_c - nf_m]t)\right] \qquad (11.13)$$

The equation above describes a spectrum with sidebands at frequencies $f_c \pm f_m$, $f_c \pm 2f_m$, $f_c \pm 3f_m$, etc. above and below the carrier f_c, as shown in figure 11.39.

The amplitude of each pair of components is determined by the coefficients J_1, J_2, J_3, etc., which are functions of the index *I*. The actual mathematical dependency of J_n on *I* is given by a family of curves known as *Bessel functions.* (Mathematical expressions and a graphic representation of Bessel functions can be found in various calculus textbooks. Graphic plots are also shown in Chowning [1973]). In practice, the influence of *I* may be evaluated by means of a simple rule of thumb: the total number of audible sidebands is *2(I)* (*I* sidebands above and *I* sidebands below the carrier). Therefore, the total number of components, including the carrier, is *2(I)+1.* This is illustrated in *1114.orc* and *1114.sco.* The orchestra uses a **foscili** opcode to implement FM, where *p5*p6* is the frequency of the carrier, *p5*p7* is the frequency of the modulator, *p8* is the index and *p9* is the function table that generates the carrier and the modulator—a sinewave in this case.

The score includes five examples of a 212 Hz modulator applied to a 100 Hz carrier, with respective index values of 0, 1, 2, 3 and 4. The first sound (I=0) contains the carrier alone, the second includes the first pair of sidebands, the third extends the spectrum to the next pair and so on. When *1114.sco* is synthesized, it is possible to hear how the top frequency component becomes higher as more sidebands become audible. In short, the index determines how many components will be audible.

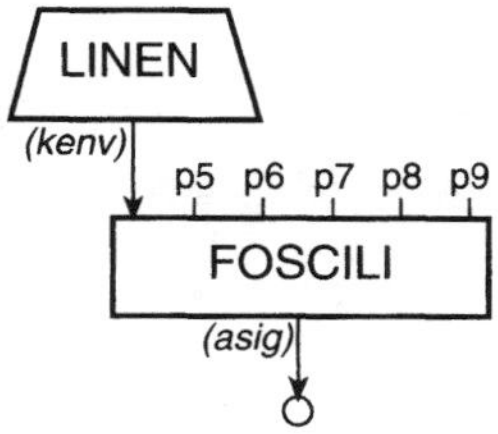

Figure 11.40 Block diagram of *instr 1114,* a simple static FM instrument.

```
        instr       1114        ; SIMPLE STATIC FM
kenv    linen       p4, .1, p3, .1              ; ENV (ATTACK = DECAY = .1 SEC)
asig    foscili     kenv, p5, p6, p7, p8, p9  ; FM OSCILLATOR
        out         asig                        ; OUTPUT
        endin
```

Figure 11.41 Orchestra code for *instr 1114,* a simple static FM instrument.

We saw above that ring modulation may generate negative frequencies. This also happens in Frequency Modulation (FM). In this case, formula 11.13 only contains sines (as opposed to cosines in ring modulation); therefore, from the trigonometric identity:

$$\sin(-a) = -\sin(a) \qquad (11.14)$$

we can infer that negative components reflect with a change of sign. This is equivalent to a phase shift of π, or half a cycle.

The *carrier to modulator ratio* is also an important FM parameter and has a similar effect on the output to that of the ring modulation *c/m.* If *c/m* is not a rational number, the spectrum will be inharmonic, but if the *c/m* can be represented as a ratio of integers

$$\frac{f_c}{f_m} = \frac{N_c}{N_m} \qquad (11.15)$$

then the fundamental will be $f = f_c/N_c = f_m/N_m$ and the spectrum will be harmonic. Also, f_c and f_m will be respectively the N_cth and N_mth harmonics. If the fundamental f is below the auditory range, however, the sound will not be perceived as having definite pitch, as demonstrated in *1114a.orc* and *1114a.sco,* which use *instr 1114* to produce the three sounds shown in figure 11.42. Furthermore, because the harmonic content depends on the difference between the carrier and multiples of the oscillator frequency, we can conclude that if $N_m = 1$, the spectrum will contain all the harmonics. If N_m is even, every second harmonic will be missing and the spectrum will

```
c=80Hz  c/m=1               I=2  Fundamental=80Hz
c=80Hz  c/m=13/19           I=2  Fundamental=80/13=6.154Hz  Lacks clear pitch
c=80Hz  c/m=1.4142~√2       I=2                             Sound is inharmonic
```

Figure 11.42 Table of tutorial parameter values and description of their sound.

```
f+2f       = 3f        f-2f       = -f
f+2x(2f)   = 5f        f-2x(2f)   = -3f
f+3x(2f)   = 7f        f-3x(2f)   = -5f
f+4x(2f)   = 9f        f-4x(2f)   = -7f
etc.
```

Figure 11.43 Table of odd partials resulting from a c/m ration of 1:2.

contain *f*, 3*f*, 5*f*, etc. For example, if $c/m = 1/2$, then $N_m = 2$, $f_c = f$ and $f_m = 2f$; therefore, the spectrum will only contain odd harmonics, which are the result of adding *f* to a multiple of 2*f*, as shown in figure 11.43. Similarly, if $N_m=3$, every third harmonic will be missing.

Dynamic FM spectra may be obtained by making *I* and *c/m* functions of time. In fact, a time-varying index alone provides enough versatility to produce a variety of sounds, as illustrated in *1115.orc* and *1115.sco* in which *instr 1115* controls the envelope and the index using the variables *kenv* and *kidx*. The score file *1115.sco* produces a passage that includes various types of sounds based on settings for bells, woodwind, brass and membranophones, proposed by Chowning (1973), in which *c/m* is fixed for each type and only the index changes between a maximum and a minimum value (*p8* and *p9,* respectively). The modulation-index, *I*, is driven by an oscillator with different generating functions given in the score, according to the desired type of sound. The overall amplitude envelope also plays an important role in modeling these sounds. For example, the sudden attack resulting from hitting the body of a bell and the subsequent slow decay into a pitched sound may be modeled using an exponential amplitude envelope that lasts a few seconds, an inharmonic carrier-to-modulator ratio and a modulation-index that initially favors high partials (*kidx*=6) and decays slowly to zero, gradually making the carrier more prominent (*kidx*=1.2). The amplitude and index envelopes are modeled with the following function tables:

```
f 11  0   512  5 1 512 .0001  ; BELL AMPLITUDE
f 12  0   512  5 1 512 .2     ; BELL INDEX
```

The instrument statement below produces a 4 second bell using an inharmonic carrier to modulator ratio of 1/1.215 and a maximum index of 6.

```
; INS  ST DUR AMP   PTCH C M     MAXI MINI OSCFN AMPFN NDXFN
i 1115 0  4   10000 8.01 1 1.215 6    0    1     11    12
```

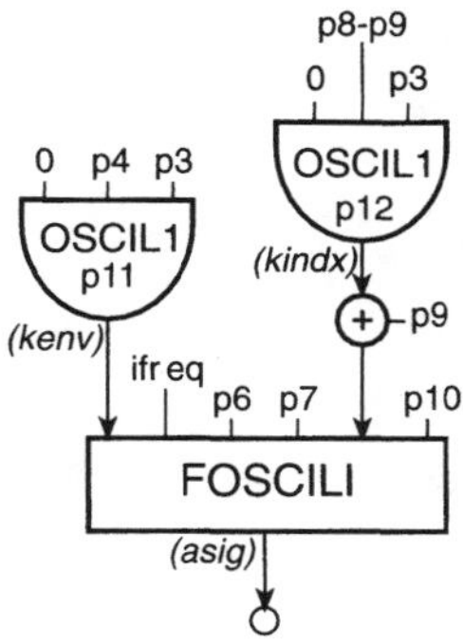

Figure 11.44 Block diagram of *instr 1115,* a dynamic FM instrument.

```
        instr    1115           ; FM WITH AMPLITUDE AND SPECTRAL ENVELOPES
ifreq   =        cpspch(p5)                              ; PITCH TO FREQUENCY
kenv    oscil1   0, p4, p3, p11                          ; AMPLITUDE ENVELOPE
kindx   oscil1   0, p8-p9, p3, p12                       ; TIME-VARYING INDEX
asig    foscili  kenv, ifreq, p6, p7, p9+kindx, p10      ; FM OSCILLATOR
        out      asig                                    ; OUTPUT
        endin
```

Figure 11.45 Orchestra code for *instr 1115,* a dynamic FM instrument with amplitude and spectral envelopes.

Summary

There are two important parameters that determine the spectral characteristics of sounds produced by frequency modulation.

1. The carrier to modulator ratio determines the location of frequency components.
2. The index determines which components will be prominent.

Granular Synthesis

Granular synthesis theory was first developed by Gabor (1947), who argued that signals can be conceived as the combination of short sonic grains. A particular grain may be indistinguishable from another grain; however, combinations of large numbers of these sonic units may yield different morphologies, depending on the internal constitution of the grains and on the particular way in which the combination is structured.

According to psychoacoustic theory, human perception becomes ineffective in recognizing pitch and amplitude when sonic events become too short: the threshold has been estimated to be in the region of 50 milliseconds (Whitfield 1978). Therefore, typical durations of grains usually fall between 10 to 60 milliseconds.

A grain usually consists of a waveform with an envelope, as shown in figure 11.46. In principle, the former could be any signal—ranging from pure sinewaves to recorded samples of complex sounds. The envelope can have various shapes—for example, it could be a Gaussian curve, a triangle, a trapezoid, half-a-sine, etc. When grains are combined, the shape of the waveform and envelope are influential factors that determine the timbre of the overall sonic result. As a rule of thumb, complex waveforms will lead to sounds with larger noise content. Also, envelopes with edges (such as triangles and trapezoids) will produce rougher signals. Furthermore, depending on the sampling rate, if the duration of a grain is short, the attack and/or decay of a trapezoid may become vertical, causing clicks. On the other hand, smooth envelopes such as half-sines may be effective in preventing clicks at shorter durations.

Because grains are short, it is necessary to manipulate these in large numbers to obtain any significant results; sometimes, the numbers may reach up to 1000 grains per second of sound. Therefore, it is useful to adopt high level organizational strategies that take care of the manipulation of the various parameters associated with grain characteristics and with their combination.

Throughout the history of electronic synthesis, there have been various approaches and, even now, new strategies are being developed. In the early sixties, Xenakis (1971) proposed organization of grains according to a synchronous process: time may be divided into frames that are then played in succession at a constant rate, similar to movie frames that produce continuous movement. Each frame consists of two axes—one of which measures frequency and the other amplitude—and contains a particular set of grains, each with its own amplitude-frequency values. Therefore, when the frames are "played," a particular succession of grains with varying frequency and density is obtained.

Another strategy, perhaps the most popular to date, consists of the creation of asynchronous "clouds," described in depth by Roads (1985, 1991). The main idea behind a cloud of grains is that the tendencies of the various parameters that influence the resulting musical sound may be controlled by means of a process that is partly random and partly deterministic. For example, the frequency of the grain waveform may be generated by a random device that produces values falling between a lower and upper limit determined by the composer. These limits may change in time, producing dynamic spectra.

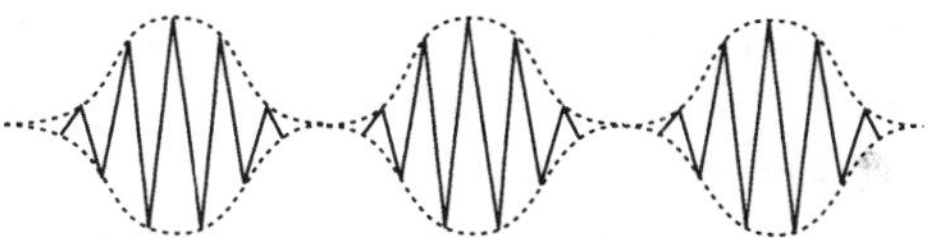

Figure 11.46 Grains with triangular waveforms and Gaussian envelopes.

The following list describes the most typical parameters:

- *Grain duration:* typically between 5 and 50 milliseconds. Values above this range may lose the "anonymity" of grains and may be used effectively in order to create a transition between granular textures and gestural material. Grain duration may also produce ring modulation effects (Roads 1991, pp. 157–161).
- *Grain waveform type:* which may vary from a pure sinewave to complex spectral types. In fact, the waveform of the grains may be made to change by interpolating gradually between two extreme cases. Another method of creating time-varying waveforms consists of using a frequency modulation unit with varying carrier to modulator ratio and FM index.
- *Grain envelope:* typical envelopes include bell-shaped Gaussians, raised sinusoidals and trapezoids (attack-sustain-decay).
- *Cloud density:* which is the number of grains per time unit. Since the cloud is asynchronous (grains do not occur at regular intervals): on the one hand, some grains may overlap and, on the other hand, lapses of silence may occur. It these lapses are short, they will not be perceived as such but will rather as fluctuations in amplitude, affecting the timbre of the output.
- *Cloud amplitude envelope:* which controls the overall amplitude of the cloud. Furthermore, the relative amplitude of each grain may be made to fluctuate between minimum and maximum values.
- *Cloud frequency band:* the grain waveform frequency at any given moment may be constrained to a spectral band determined by two time-varying functions; one for the higher limit and one for the lower limit.
- *Cloud spatial movement:* which may be controlled according to the number of outputs available.
- *Cloud width or grain spatial scatter:* the localization of the cloud at any moment may vary from confinement to a point in space to wide spatial spread, according to the degree of scattering of the grains in relation to the path along which the cloud moves.

The files *1116.orc* and *1116.sco* produce a 20 second cloud created by using an instrument that implements the parameters described above. The overall envelope of the cloud is produced using an **oscil1** statement with duration *idur* (*p3*) amplitude *imaxamp* (*p4*) and function *iampfunc* (*p5*)

```
kenv    oscil1  0, imaxamp, idur, iampfunc  ; OVERALL ENVELOPE
```

The lower limit of the frequency band varies between a minimum *ilfbmin* and a maximum *ilfbmax,* given respectively by *p11* and *p12.* The difference of these values, *ilfbdiff,* is fed to an **oscil1** statement driven by the function *ilbffunc* (*p3*). The output of the oscillator is then added to *lbfmin* in order to obtain the time-varying lower limit *klbf.*

```
ilfbmin  =      p11                             ; MINIMUM FREQ OF LIMIT
ilfbmax  =      p12                             ; MAXIMUM FREQ OF LIMIT
ilfbdiff =      ilfbmax-ilfbmin                 ; DIFFERENCE
ilbffunc =      p13                             ; LOWER LIMIT FUNCTION
klfb     oscil1 0, ilfbdiff, idur, ilbffunc     ; LOWER LIMIT FLUCTUATION
klfb     =      ilfbmin+klfb                    ; LOWER LIMIT
```

A similar procedure is applied in order to produce the upper limit of the frequency band (*kufb*), the carrier-to-modulator ratio (*kcmr*), the index (*kidx*) and the width of the cloud (*kgscat*).

Spatialization of the cloud is implemented using the same algorithm employed in the dynamic additive synthesis instrument described previously in this chapter. The only difference consists of the addition of grain scatter to the overall panning.

```
kpan     =        kpan+kgscat          ; ADD GRAIN SCATTER
```

The grains are produced by applying a periodic envelope to an otherwise continuous sound. The rate at which the grains are produced is the same as the frequency of the envelope generator; therefore, if the duration of the grain is *kgdur,* the rate at which the envelope for that grain is generated is *kgrate* = 1 /*kgdur.* The code used to control the grain duration is listed below:

```
imingd   =      p6/1000.0                   ; MINIMUM GRAIN DURATION
imaxgd   =      p7/1000.0                   ; MAXIMUM GRAIN DURATION
igddiff  =      imaxgd-imingd               ; DIFFERENCE
igdfunc  =      p8                          ; GRAIN DURATION FUNC TABLE
kgdur    oscil1 0, igddiff, idur, igdfunc   ; GRAIN DURATION FLUCTUATION
kgdur    =      imingd+kgdur                ; GRAIN DURATION
kgrate   =      1.0/kgdur                   ; GRAIN RATE
```

Since *p6* and *p7* give the minimum and maximum grain duration in milliseconds, it is necessary to divide these by 1000 in order to obtain *imingd* and *imaxgd* in seconds. The maximum fluctuation in grain duration is *igddiff,* which is used as amplitude for an oscillator driven by the grain duration function *igdfunc* (*p8*). Therefore, *kgdur* is the result of adding the output of the oscillator to the minimum duration *imingd.* Finally, *kgrate* is calculated.

The grain envelope uses *kgrate* as its frequency and *igefunc* (*p10*) as the generating function table.

```
igefunc    =        p10                     ; GRAIN ENVELOPE FUNC TABLE
kgenvf     =        kgrate                  ; GRAIN ENVELOPE FREQUENCY
kgenv      oscili   1.0, kgenvf, igefunc    ; ENVELOPE
```

Also, *kgrate* is used to generate the relative amplitude and waveform frequency of the grain. This is done by using a **randh** statement that produces values between specified maxima and minima. The relative amplitude consists of a scaling factor that may assume values between *hmaxfc* (=0.5) and 1.

```
ihmaxfc   =       0.25                    ; HALF OF MAXIMUM AMPLITUDE DEV
kgafact   randh   ihmaxfc, kgfreq, iseed/3  ; -IHMAXFC<RAND NUMBER<+IHMAXFC
kgafact   =       1.00-(ihmaxfc+kgafact)    ; 2<MAXFC<SCALING FACTOR<1.00
```

The waveform frequency assumes a random value between the low and high limits of the cloud's frequency band *(klfb and kufb*).

```
kgband =      kufb-klfb                  ; CURRENT FREQUENCY BAND
kgfreq randh kgband/2, kgrate, iseed ; GENERATE FREQUENCY
kgfreq =      klfb+kgfreq+kgband/2       ; FREQUENCY
```

A grain is generated using a **foscili** opcode that uses the cloud's instantaneous carrier-to-modulator ratio and index *(kcmr and kidx).*

```
igfunc    =         p9                                      ; GRN. WAVE FN
agrain    foscili   kgenv, kgfreq, 1, kcmr, kidx, igfunc    ; FM GENERATOR
```

In order to avoid mechanical repetition and achieve grain overlap, a random variable delay is applied to each generated grain. The maximum possible delay value is equal to the grain duration *(kgdur*). The actual delay is produced using a **randi** generator.

```
kgdel  randi     kgdur/2, kgrate, iseed/2 ; RANDOM SAMPLE DELAY
kgdel  =         kgdel+kgdur/2            ; MAKE IT POSITIVE
adump  delayr    imaxgd                   ; DELAY LINE
adelgr deltapi   kgdel
       delayw    kgafact*agrain
```

After the grain is delayed, an additional delay line applies Doppler shift to the moving grain according to its spatial position *kpan.* This assumes a speaker distance of 10 meters.

```
ihspeakd =       5.0                               ; HALFSPKRSDISTNCE(M)
isndsp   =       331.45                            ; SOUNDSPEEDINAIR(M/SEC)
impandel =       (imaxpan+imaxscat)*ihspeakd/isndsp ; MAX PAN DELAY
kpdel    =       kpan*ihspeakd/isndsp              ; FIND PAN DELAY
adump    delayr  impandel                          ; SET MAX DOPPLERDELAY
agdop    deltapi abs(kpdel)                        ; TAPDELAY VIA PANVAL
         delayw  adelgr                            ; DELAY SIGNAL
```

The output of the Doppler processor is then multiplied by *kpleft* and *kpright* to create the left and right channels.

```
asig     =       kenv*agdop
         outs    kpleft*asig, kpright*asig
```

The cloud generated by *1116.sco* has an amplitude envelope that is half of a sinewave. The grain duration varies between 10 and 30 milliseconds: initially, grains assume the longer duration, which becomes shorter toward the middle section and then increases up to about 24 msec., shortening slightly toward the end to 21 msec. The frequency band is initially narrow, around 2500 Hz, widening and narrowing as the sound progresses, with a lower boundary that varies between a minimum of 1000 Hz and a maximum of 2500 Hz and an upper boundary that varies between 2500 and 4670 Hz. The carrier-to-modulator ratio assumes an initial value of 1 and progresses for 1.25 seconds toward 4, its maximum value; it then hovers between a minimum of 1.48 and a maximum of 2.911. The FM index changes between 1 and 8, reaching the maximum (producing higher frequency components) after 12.5 seconds. Also *f 9* controls the spatial movement in the stereo field, including Doppler shift and *f 10* controls the scattering of grains by means of a sinusoid with its second harmonic. This means that maximum scatter happens at about 2.5 and 17.5 seconds—which correspond respectively to 1/8th and 7/8ths of a cycle—and minimum scatter happens in the vicinity of 10 seconds (half a cycle).

Summary

The following parameters are typically used to control the characteristics of a cloud of grains:

1. Grain duration.
2. Grain waveform type (which may be varied using different techniques such as FM synthesis).
3. Grain envelope.

4. Cloud density.
5. Cloud amplitude.
6. Envelope.
7. Cloud frequency band.
8. Cloud spatial movement.
9. Cloud width (grain spatial scattering).

Conclusion

This chapter surveyed "classic" synthesis techniques that derive from the capabilities of devices available in the early stages of electroacoustic music development. These may be classified into frequency-domain and time-domain techniques. Frequency-domain techniques can be linear—including additive and subtractive synthesis, or nonlinear, including ring-modulation, waveshaping and frequency-modulation. The most popular time-domain "classic" technique is granular synthesis.

Although the above techniques are called classic, they are by no means a thing of the past. In fact some of these are only beginning to fulfill their true potential since the advent of computer systems with fast processing speeds, which have given a new lease of life and extended the possibilities they offer, particularly in the generation of dynamic complex spectra. Subtractive and additive principles have developed into sophisticated mechanisms such as linear predictive coding (**LPC**) and phase vocoding. The combination of subtractive and granular synthesis has led to the development of formant-wave-function synthesis (**FOF**) and wavelet analysis and synthesis. Furthermore, given that different techniques are conductive to the synthesis of different classes of sounds, combinations of "classic" procedures are effectively used to achieve sonorities that would be extremely difficult—if not impossible—to realize by means of a single technique.

Therefore, truly understanding "classic" techniques is essential in order to comprehend the possibilities offered by new technology and use this to achieve new and interesting timbral resources—particularly given the many interesting and complex hybrid combinations.

Finally, the reader should realize that composition is not only about sounds on their own; new sonorities are also the result of context. Thus, far from being concerned only with the internal properties of sonic structures, electroacoustic composition is more than ever dependent on the way sounds are combined with each other, on how they interact and on the way they can be used to shape our perception of time.

References

Backus, J. 1977. *The Acoustical Foundations of Music.* New York: W. W. Norton & Co.

Chowning, J. 1985. "The synthesis of complex audio spectra by means of frequency modulation." *Journal of the Audio Engineering Society* 21: 526–534. Reprinted in C. Roads and J. Strawn, eds. *Foundations of Computer Music.* Cambridge, Mass.: MIT Press, pp. 6–29.

Dodge, C., and T. Jerse. 1985. *Computer Music, Synthesis Composition and Performance.* New York: Schirmer Books, Macmillan.

Fischman, R. 1991. *Musical applications of digital synthesis and processing techniques. realization using csound and the phase vocoder.* Keele: unpublished.

Gabor, D. 1947. "Acoustical quanta and the theory of hearing." *Nature.* 159 (4044): 591–594.

Roads, C. 1985. "Granular synthesis of sound." In C. Roads and J. Strawn, eds. 1985. *Foundations of Computer Music.* Cambridge, Mass.: MIT Press, pp.145–159.

Roads, C. 1991. "Asynchronous granular synthesis." In G. De Poli, A. Piccialli, and C. Roads, eds. *Representation of Musical Signals.* Cambridge, Mass.: MIT Press, pp. 143–186.

Vercoe, B. 1993. *Csound.* Software and manual. Cambridge, Mass.: MIT Press.

Whitfield, J. 1978. "The neural code." In E. Carterette and M. Friedman, eds. 1978. *Handbook of Perception.* Vol. 4, *Hearing.* Orlando: Academic.

Williams, C. S. 1986. *Designing Digital Filters.* Englewood Cliffs, N.J.: Prentice-Hall.

Wishart, T. 1985. *On Sonic Art.* York: Imagineering Press.

Xenakis, I. 1971. *Formalized Music.* Bloomington: Indiana University Press.

12 FM Synthesis in Csound

Russell Pinkston

FM, or frequency modulation, has been for decades one of the most widely used digital synthesis techniques. It was first gainfully employed in radio, of course, and also implemented on some of the earliest voltage controlled synthesizers. It was not common as a tool for timbre generation until the mid–1970s, however, following the publication of John Chowning's seminal article, "The Synthesis of Complex Audio Spectra by Means of Frequency Modulation" (Chowning 1973). Subsequently, the Yamaha Corporation used it in their popular DX7 synthesizers and the synthesis technique quickly attained "celebrity status."

In a nutshell, FM consists of using one audio wave (the modulator) to continuously vary (modulate) the frequency of another audio wave (the carrier). The amount of change induced in the carrier frequency is sometimes referred to as the "peak deviation" and it is proportional to the amplitude of the modulator. When the frequency of the carrier is in the audio range (between 20 and 20 kHz), but the frequency of the modulator is in the subaudio range (< 20 Hz), our ears are able to track the continual deviation in the carrier frequency. The result is a common musical effect, called *vibrato*. If the frequency of the modulator is in the audio range, however, we can no longer track the deviation induced in the carrier. Instead of hearing the carrier's frequency change, we perceive a change in its timbre, which is due to the generation of "sidebands"—new frequency components that appear on either *side* of the carrier frequency (both above and below), at intervals of the modulating frequency. The number of sidebands generated is directly proportional to the amplitude of the modulator. This phenomenon makes FM a useful and efficient technique for the synthesis of complex spectra. The theory of FM synthesis is complicated and since it has been explained in great detail elsewhere, I will not attempt to do more than summarize the most important aspects here.

In his now famous article, John Chowning gives the following formula for FM, using simple sine waves for both carrier and modulator:

$$y_t = A\sin(\omega_c t + I\sin(\omega_m t)) \quad (12.1)$$

where:

- A is the amplitude of the carrier
- w_c is the frequency of the carrier in radians/second
- I is the Index of Modulation
- w_m is the frequency of the modulator in radians/second

In Chowning's formula, the amplitude of the modulator is specified using the variable I, which stands for the "Index of Modulation." Chowning states that the Index of Modulation is approximately equal to the number of "significant" sidebands generated and he defines it as the peak deviation in the carrier frequency divided by the frequency of the modulator, that is,

$$I = \frac{D}{M} \quad (12.2)$$

where:

- I = Index of Modulation
- D = Peak deviation of the carrier frequency in Hertz
- M = Frequency of the Modulator

In simple FM, the nature of the spectrum generated (i.e., the position of the sidebands) is determined by the relationship of the carrier frequency (f_c) to the modulator frequency (f_m), while the richness of the spectrum (the number of sidebands present) is proportional to the amplitude of the modulator. Consequently, one can easily obtain a wide variety of rich and time-varying spectra, simply by controlling the relationship of carrier and modulator frequencies precisely and gating the modulator.

Whenever the relationship between the carrier and modulator frequencies can be expressed as a ratio of integers (1:1, 2:1, 3:2, 5:4, etc.), the sidebands belong to a harmonic series and there tends to be a clear sense of fundamental pitch. When the relationship cannot be reduced to a ratio of integers, the spectrum will be inharmonic and sound either clangorous (metallic) or noisy, especially with high indices of modulation.

A Simple Frequency Modulation Instrument

The Csound instrument in figure 12.1 implements Chowning's FM formula in a relatively simple and straightforward manner.

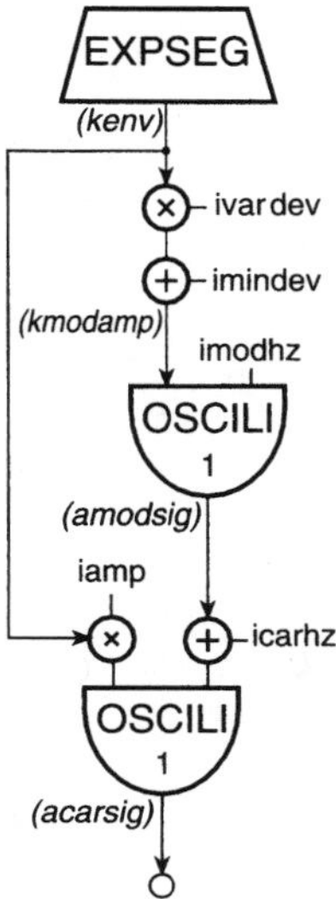

Figure 12.1 Block diagram of *instr 1201,* a simple Chowning FM instrument.

```
         instr    1201       ; SIMPLE CHOWNING FM
isine    =        1                                 ; F 1 HAS SINE TABLE
iamp     =        p4                                ; PEAK AMP OF CARRIER
icarhz   =        p5                                ; CARRIER FREQUENCY
imodhz   =        p6                                ; MODULATOR FREQUENCY
index    =        p7                                ; MAX INDEX OF MODULATION
index1   =        p8                                ; MINIMUM INDEX
irise    =        p9                                ; RISE TIME
idecay   =        p10                               ; DECAY TIME
isteady  =        p3-irise-idecay                   ; STEADY STATE TIME
imaxdev  =        index*imodhz                      ; D = I * M
imindev  =        index1*imodhz                     ; MINIMUM DEVIATION
ivardev  =        imaxdev-imindev                   ; VARIABLE DEVIATION
kenv     expseg   .001, irise, 1, isteady, 1, idecay, .001
kmodamp  =        imindev+ivardev*kenv              ; AMPLITUDE OF MODULATOR
amodsig  oscili   kmodamp, imodhz, isine            ; GATED MODULATOR
acarsig  oscili   iamp*kenv, icarhz+amodsig, isine
         out      acarsig
         endin
```

Figure 12.2 Orchestra code for *instr 1201,* a simple Chowning FM instrument with modulator and carrier sharing the same **expseg** envelope generator.

```
f 1      0    2048  10     1                                              ; SINE
;        ST   DUR   AMP    CARHZ  MODHZ  NDX   NDX1  RISE   DECAY
i 1201   0    .6    20000  440    440    5     0     .1     .2           ; BRASS
i 1201   1    .6    20000  900    300    2     0     .1     .2           ; WOODWIND
i 1201   2    .6    20000  500    100    1.5   0     .1     .2           ; BASSOON
i 1201   3    .6    20000  900    600    4     2     .1     .2           ; CLARINET
i 1201   4    15    20000  200    280    10    0     .001   14.99        ; BELL
```

Figure 12.3 Score file for *instr 1201,* using Chowning's recommended settings for imitating acoustic instruments—Brass, Woodwind, Bassoon, Clarinet, and Bell.

Figure 12.3 shows a sample score for *instr 1201* in which a variety of acoustic instrument timbres are imitated.

Clearly, *instr 1201* is a straightforward implementation of simple FM, similar to the one provided in the Chowning article, and the score contains the parameters used in Chowning's own example sounds. The instrument, however, is so limited as to be almost useless in actual practice. For one thing, there is no separate envelope provided for the modulator, a highly desirable improvement. But most important, it would be awkward to have to specify the exact frequencies of carrier and modulator in Hertz for every note. Since it is the *relationship* between the carrier and modulator frequencies that governs the nature of the spectrum, it would far more convenient to specify a single basic pitch for each note and have Csound compute the actual carrier and modulator frequencies based on the desired *ratio.* Indeed, Csound provides an opcode called **foscil** that does this automatically.

```
ar foscil  xamp, kcps, kcarfac, kmodfac, kindex, ifn[, iphase]
```

The parameters of **foscil** are similar to those of **oscil**, including parameters for amplitude (*xamp*), fundamental frequency (*kcps*), the number of the table containing a stored function (*ifn*) and the optional initial phase (*iphase*). In addition, there are parameters for carrier and modulator factors (*kcarfac* and *kmodfac*) that are multiplied by the *kcps* parameter to produce the actual carrier and modulator frequencies and a modulation index variable (*kindex*), which is multiplied by the modulator frequency to produce the peak deviation in the carrier, according to the formula ($D = I * M$). There is also an interpolating version called **foscili**, analogous to **oscili**. Using **foscili**, *instr 1202,* an improvement of *instr 1201,* can be written as shown in figures 12.4–12.6.

Phase Modulation

Although classic FM synthesis as described in Chowning's article is a powerful technique that has been used in countless pieces of computer music, it has some draw-

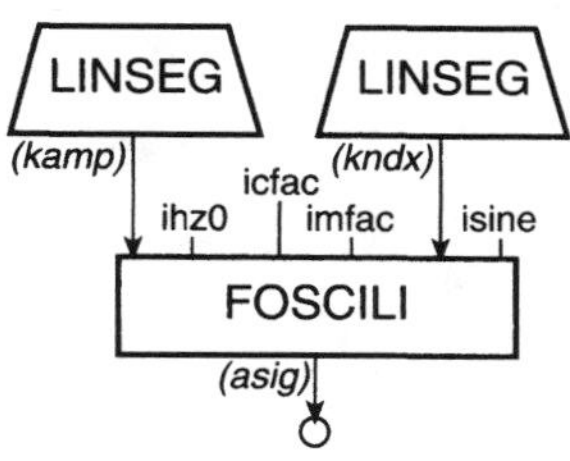

Figure 12.4 Block diagram of *instr 1202,* an improved Chowning FM instrument using Csound's **foscili** opcode.

```
      instr   1202          ; BETTER SIMPLE FM
isine =       1                  ; F 1 HAS A SINE WAVE - BEST FOR SIMPLE FM
iamp  =       p4                 ; PEAK AMP OF CARRIER
ihz0  =       cpspch(p5)+p18     ; BASIC PITCH + DETUNE
icfac =       p6                 ; CARRIER FACTOR
imfac =       p7                 ; MODULATOR FACTOR
index =       p8                 ; MAXIMUM INDEX VALUE
ieva  =       p9                 ; ATTACK TIME OF MAIN ENVELOPE
ievd  =       p10                ; DECAY TIME OF MAIN ENVELOPE
iamp2 =       p11*iamp           ; MAIN AMP SUSTAIN LEVEL
ievr  =       p12                ; RELEASE TIME OF MAIN ENVELOPE
ievss =       p3-ieva-ievd-ievr  ; ENV STEADY STATE
indx1 =       p13*index          ; INITIAL/FINAL INDEX
idxa  =       p14                ; ATTACK TIME OF INDEX
idxd  =       p15                ; DECAY TIME OF INDEX
indx2 =       p16*index          ; SUSTAINED INDEX
idxr  =       p17                ; RELEASE TIME OF INDEX
idxss =       p3-idxa-idxd-idxr  ; INDEX STEADY STATE
kndx  linseg  indx1, idxa, index, idxd, indx2, idxss, indx2, idxr, indx1
kamp  linseg  0, ieva, iamp, ievd, iamp2, ievss, iamp2, ievr, 0
asig  foscili kamp, ihz0, icfac, imfac, kndx, isine
      out     asig
      endin
```

Figure 12.5 Orchestra code for *instr 1202,* an improved FM instrument with independent carrier and modulator envelopes.

backs. These drawbacks are associated with the fact that a conventional digital oscillator is, in effect, an integrator. It produces an output sample from its current phase location (position in the wavetable), then increments the phase by a value proportional to the current frequency input and finally stores the result until the next output is required. Consequently, its current phase is always equal to the sum of all previous increments. When we change the frequency of an oscillator by adding the constantly changing output of another oscillator to it, we may introduce unwanted side-effects, such as DC bias and carrier "drift," which may linger indefinitely. These side-effects don't tend to become apparent until one tries to implement more complex modulation

```
f 1      0       2048  10     1     ; SIMPLE SINE WAVE
;        ST      DUR   AMP    PCH   CFAC  MFAC  INDEX  RISE   DEC
i 1202   0       1     20000  8.09  1     1     5      .05    .01
;        AFACT   REL   XFAC1  XRIS  XDEC  XFAC2 XREL   DETUNE
         1       .2    0      .1    .5    .25   .25    0
i 1202   2       .     .      .     3     1     2      .      .
         .       .     .      .     .01   1     .25
i 1202   4       .     .      6.09  5     1     1.5

i 1202   6       .     .      8.09  3     2     4      .      .
         .       .     .5     .     .     1
; THREE NOTES SLIGHTLY DETUNED AND SLIGHTLY STAGGERED ENTRANCES
i 1202   8       6     10000  6.00  1     1.4   10     3      1.9
         .7      1     0      3     1.9   .25   1
i 1202   8.005   .     .      .     .     .     .      .      .
         .       .     .      .     .     .     .      1
i 1202   8.012   .     .      .     .     .     .      .      .
         .       .     .      .     .     .     .      -1
```

Figure 12.6 Score file for an improved Chowning FM instrument, *instr 1202*, with parametric control of virtually all parameters including detuning of carrier and independent envelopes for modulation-index and carrier amplitude.

schemes, such as stacked modulators, or feedback, both of which are common in so-called FM synthesizers, such as the Yamaha DX7.

Consider the case of feedback, for example, which would seem to be impossible with classic FM: if an oscillator is frequency modulating itself and the sum of its basic (carrier) frequency and the current deviation ever equals zero (which will occur if the modulation index is ever greater than or equal to 1), the oscillator will stop incrementing and never start again. In fact, the Yamaha DX7 is only able to use feedback because it *doesn't* really implement classic frequency modulation, but a closely related technique known as "Phase Modulation."

In Phase Modulation, the instantaneous phase of the carrier oscillator is altered by the modulator, not its frequency. The spectrum produced is virtually identical to FM, but without the undesirable side-effects. In fact, the formula from Chowning's article given above is actually the one for phase modulation, rather than frequency modulation, so we can implement it more or less verbatim. In that formula, the amplitude of the modulator (Index of Modulation) is assumed to be a value in radians, as opposed to Hertz (cycles per second). Hence, we needn't concern ourselves with Chowning's $I = D/M$ equation, as we must with classic FM; we simply plug in the desired index directly, as the amplitude of the modulator.

To implement Phase Modulation (PM) in Csound, we must use a **tablei** opcode for the carrier, instead of **oscili**, since we need to access the internal phase directly. The **tablei** opcode will reference a single cycle of a sine wave for its stored function, just like **oscili** and it must be used in conjunction with a **phasor** opcode, which converts an input frequency argument into a moving "phase" value. (Note that the output of **phasor** is *not* a value in degrees or radians, as might be expected, given its name. Instead it moves from 0 to 1 repeatedly, once per cycle and hence is appropriate for use as a normalized index for **table** opcodes, which may have functions of arbitrary length. This implies, however, that we must divide the desired "Index of Modulation" (amplitude of the modulator) by 2π, to convert it from radians to a normalized **table** index, as well) (see figures 12.7 and 12.8).

As you can see, *instr 1203* is virtually identical to *instr 1202,* except that the **foscil** opcode is replaced by an **oscili**, **tablei**, and a **phasor**, implementing Phase Modulation instead of Frequency Modulation. In fact, we can use the same score data from figure 12.6 and compare the sound of the two instruments. Note that the FM and PM instruments sound virtually identical using the same score, which is to be expected in simple modulation involving one carrier and one modulator. The advantages of Phase Modulation, however, become apparent in more complex algorithms.

A Phase Modulation Instrument with a Double Modulator Stack

In *instr 1204* we implement a simple case of complex modulation—a "stack" algorithm: a single carrier being modulated by a modulator, which is itself being modulated by a second modulator. Following the example of the Yamaha DX7, each oscillator (either an **oscili**, or a **phasor/tablei** combination) is provided with an envelope generator (here, an **envlpx**). The pair is referred to as an "operator" (figures 12.9–12.10).

The algorithm in *instr 1204* is one that would produce distinctly different sounding results if implemented using FM, instead of phase modulation. In fact, it would be a useful and enlightening exercise to try doing the same thing with 3 **oscili** opcodes and classic frequency modulation. The sound of the FM version is not necessarily bad, but it is strikingly different, especially with high indices of modulation.

Although *instr 1204* contains a more complex algorithm than *instr 1203,* in other respects, it is actually a bit simpler, by using **envlpx** opcodes instead of multistage **linseg** opcodes and dispensing with the detune option. This is only to keep the example from getting too long, for as we begin making more complex algorithms with multiple operators, the number of score parameters required starts to mushroom. But most commercial synthesizers use complex envelopes and have a multitude of performance parameters (the Yamaha DX7 has more than 200), so it is important to find a practical method to include them in our Csound instruments without turning

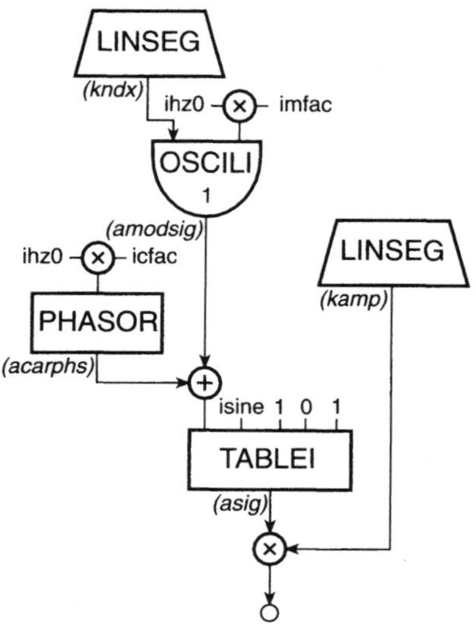

Figure 12.7 Block diagram of *instr 1203,* a phase-modulation instrument.

```
         instr   1203        ; SIMPLE PHASE MODULATION (PM)
isine    =       1                           ; F 1 HAS A SINE WAVE
iamp     =       p4                          ; PEAK AMP OF CARRIER
ihz0     =       cpspch(p5)+p18              ; THEORETICAL FUNDAMENTAL+DETUNE
icfac    =       p6                          ; CARRIER FACTOR
imfac    =       p7                          ; MODULATOR FACTOR
i2pi     =       6.2832                      ; 2 PI RADIANS PER CYCLE
indx     =       p8/i2pi                     ; MAXIMUM INDEX VALUE/2PI
ieva     =       p9                          ; ATTACK TIME OF MAIN ENVELOPE
ievd     =       p10                         ; DECAY TIME OF MAIN ENVELOPE
iamp2    =       p11*iamp                    ; MAIN AMP SUSTAIN LEVEL
ievr     =       p12                         ; RELEASE TIME OF MAIN ENVELOPE
ievss    =       p3-ieva-ievd-ievr           ; ENV STEADY STATE
indx1    =       p13*indx                    ; INITIAL/FINAL INDEX
idxa     =       p14                         ; ATTACK TIME OF INDEX
idxd     =       p15                         ; DECAY TIME OF INDEX
indx2    =       p16*indx                    ; SUSTAINED INDEX
idxr     =       p17                         ; RELEASE TIME OF INDEX
idxss    =       p3-idxa-idxd-idxr           ; INDEX STEADY STATE
kndx     linseg  indx1, idxa, indx, idxd, indx2, idxss, indx2, idxr, indx1
kamp     linseg  0, ieva, iamp, ievd, iamp2, ievss, iamp2, ievr, 0
amodsig  oscili  kndx, ihz0*imfac, isine     ; THE MODULATOR
acarphs  phasor  ihz0*icfac                  ; MOVING PHASE AT CARRIER FRQ
; PHASE MODULATION OF CARRIER TAKES PLACE HERE:
asig     tablei  acarphs+amodsig, isine, 1, 0, 1
         out     asig*kamp                   ; NOTE: NORMALIZED INDEX...
         endin                               ; ...AND WRAP FLAG ARE ON
```

Figure 12.8 Orchestra code for *instr 1203,* a phase-modulation instrument with similar parameters and design to *instr 1202.*

```
         instr    1204          ; PHASE MODULATION WITH MODULATOR STACK
; COMMON PARAMETERS:
isinefn  =        1
irisefn  =        2                       ; EXPONENTIAL RISE
iparmfn  =        p6                      ; NUMBER OF PARAMETER f-table
idur     =        p3
iamp     =        p4
icps     =        cpspch(p5)              ; THEORETICAL FUNDAMENTAL
irise    table    0, iparmfn              ; MAIN ENVLP RISE TIME
idec     table    1, iparmfn              ; MAIN ENVLP DECAY TIME
icarfac  table    2, iparmfn              ; CARRIER RATIO
im1fac   table    3, iparmfn              ; MODULATOR 1 RATIO
index1   table    4, iparmfn              ; MODULATOR 1 INDEX
im1rise  table    5, iparmfn              ; MODULATOR 1 RISE
im1dur   table    6, iparmfn              ; MODULATOR 1 DUR
im1dec   table    7, iparmfn              ; MODULATOR 1 DECAY
im2fac   table    8, iparmfn              ; MODULATOR 2 RATIO
index2   table    9, iparmfn              ; MODULATOR 2 INDEX
im2rise  table    10, iparmfn             ; MODULATOR 2 RISE
im2dur   table    11, iparmfn             ; MODULATOR 2 DUR
im2dec   table    12, iparmfn             ; MODULATOR 2 DECAY
i2pi     =        6.2832                  ; USED TO COMPUTE PK DEVS
; PARAMETERS FOR INDIVIDUAL OPERATORS:
im1hz    =        icps*im1fac             ; COMPUTE MOD 1 FREQUENCY
im2hz    =        icps*im2fac             ; COMPUTE MOD 2 FREQUENCY
icarhz   =        icps*icarfac            ; COMPUTE CARRIER FREQUENCY
im1dev   =        index1/i2pi             ; CONVERT FROM RADIANS TO...
im2dev   =        index2/i2pi             ; ...NORMALIZED INDICES FOR
TABLE
; USE DEFAULT OF P3 FOR MOD1 AND MOD2 ENVELOPE DURATIONS:
im1dur   =        (im1dur == 0 ? p3 : im1dur)
im2dur   =        (im2dur == 0 ? p3 : im2dur)
; COMPLEX MODULATION WITH STACKED MODULATORS
kmod1    envlpx   im1dev, im1rise, im1dur, im1dec, irisefn, 1, .01, 0
amod1    oscili   kmod1, im1hz, isinefn
aphs2    phasor   im2hz
aphs2    =        aphs2+amod1             ; MODULATE THE PHASE OF MOD2
amod2    tablei   aphs2, isinefn, 1, 0, 1
kmod2    envlpx   im2dev, im2rise, im2dur, im2dec, irisefn, 1, .01, 0
amod2    =        amod2*kmod2
acarphs  phasor   icarhz
acarphs  =        acarphs+amod2
acarsig  tablei   acarphs, isinefn, 1, 0, 1
kenv     envlpx   iamp, irise, idur, idec, irisefn, 1, .01, 0
asig     =        acarsig * kenv
         out      asig
         endin
```

Figure 12.9 Orchestra code for *instr 1204,* a phase-modulation instrument with stacked modulators.

```
f 1    0      2048   10     1                   ; SINE
f 2    0      513    5      .001   513    1     ; EXPONENTIAL RISE

; PARAMETER DATA:           RISE   DECAY  CARFAC M1FAC INDEX1 M1RIS M1DUR
f 3    0      16     -2     .25    .5     1      1     5      .5    0
;      M1DEC  M2FAC  INDEX2 M2RIS  M2DUR  M2DEC
       1      1      3      1      0      1

; IN   ST     DUR    AMP    PCH    PARMS
i 1204 0      2      20000  7.07   3
i 1204 +      .      .      8.07
i 1204 +      .      .      9.07
i 1204 +      .      .      6.07
```

Figure 12.10 Score file for phase *instr 1204*, phase-modulation with stacked modulators in which some parameter data is passed to the instrument via an f-table (*f 3*) that employs a non-normalized GEN2 (−*2*) subroutine.

score preparation into a nightmare. One approach is to use f-tables, instead of p-fields, to store parameter data. This is the method used in *instr 1204*.

Parameters are placed in a function table using GEN2, which is used for direct data entry. (Note that the GEN number (*p4* of the f-statement) must be negative, so that the function will not be automatically rescaled). Placing parameters that do not change from note to note in a function table, instead of in the p-fields of i-statements, makes entering individual note data much easier. Moreover, this is similar to the approach taken in most commercial digital synthesizers, reflecting the basic philosophy of MIDI, itself. All that is necessary to trigger a new note on a MIDI synthesizer is to send a MIDI NOTEON message, which contains a channel, pitch (note number) and velocity. Almost all the other parameters required for the synthesizer to play that note on the currently active synthesis patch are stored internally in tables. Those fixed parameters are only changed via a MIDI PROGRAM CHANGE message, which may switch synthesis algorithms or load a new set of parameter data.

Yamaha DX7 Emulation

The final instrument in this chapter is an example of how to emulate a commercial digital synthesizer using Csound. It is a model of the original Yamaha DX7, with the addition of a stereo output and pan position, but minus a few other bells and whistles, such as EG Bias, and Aftertouch. It includes a crude vibrato, but it doesn't attempt to implement the full Yamaha LFO mechanism. It does implement 6-operator FM, however, with the Yamaha-style envelope generators, velocity sensitivity, and rate scaling. Moreover, it generates notes whose final decay begins *after p3* has elapsed, which is analogous to the way MIDI synthesizers operate.

Ideally, an instrument that emulates an existing synthesizer should sound exactly the same as the original, given the same input parameters. In practice, this is difficult to achieve. For example, Yamaha uses an arbitrary scale of 0–99 for many parameters of the DX7, such as the rates and levels of the envelope generators, which are then mapped internally to real values. These internal mappings are usually not documented by the manufacturer. Consequently, a large part of designing an emulation instrument involves guesswork and trial and error, searching for appropriate values. For this reason, it is a good idea to use external tables for all such parameters, rather than entering values directly into the code. That way, it is easy to experiment with different mappings in the score, without having to continually change the instrument. In the case of the DX7, there was actually a fair amount of documentation available. The principal sources, other than the Yamaha DX7 manual, were the book *FM Theory and Applications* by John Chowning and David Bristow and "Appendix C" of the manual for the original Opcode DX/TX Editor, "Inside DX/TX Envelopes," which provided accurate information about the rates and levels of the DX7 envelope generators, as well as tables for fixed frequency values, rate scaling, etc.

For reasons of space, it is not possible to provide a line-by-line explanation of this instrument. A few features and idiosyncrasies should be pointed out, however. For one thing, the instrument is actually less complicated and more efficient than it seems. Most of the orchestra code is executed at i-time and is devoted to converting the input parameter data from Yamaha's arbitrary scales to real values that can actually be used. Also, since there are six operators with identical parameters, each of which must be converted and processed, there is a lot of redundant code. Iterative processing is usually done via arrays and program loops, but there is no built-in mechanism within Csound for that sort of thing. Hence, a crude loop structure was implemented manually using **if . . . goto** statements, which reduced the size of the instrument considerably. (Yes, this is a classic example of a "kludge.") This sort of programming is generally not to be recommended in Csound. A far better approach would be to write a stand-alone utility that would convert Yamaha parameter values to Csound values and put them into the appropriate f-tables in the score. Then the instrument would be far simpler, although we would still have to copy and label more than a hundred parameters.

Note the use of **ihold** and **turnoff** in this example. The **ihold** statement at the beginning of the instrument turns it on indefinitely, which is similar to the DX7 receiving a MIDI NOTEON message. Then *p3* of the score is used as the length of time the synthesizer key is pressed—the time between the NOTEON and the NOTEOFF as it were—and is labeled "idur" in the instrument. As soon as *idur* seconds have elapsed, a **timout** statement begins skipping the normal envelope generators and branches instead to the final decay section. From that time on, we wait

```
          instr     1205          ; DX7 EMULATOR - ALGORITHM 16
          ihold                             ; TURN ON NOTE INDEFINITELY
isine     =         1                       ; f-table 1 IS A SINE WAVE
idur      =         p3                      ; DUR BEFORE FINAL DECAY
ibase     =         cpspch(p4)              ; p4 IS KEYBOARD PITCH
iroct     =         octpch(p4)
irbase    =         octpch(4.09)            ; BASE OF RATE SCL TABLE
irrange   =         octpch(13.06)-irbase
iveloc    =         p5                      ; 0 <= p5 <= 127
ileft     =         sqrt(p6)                ; p6 IS LEFT CHANNEL FACTOR
iright    =         sqrt(1-p6)
idelay    =         p7                      ; VIB DELAY
ivibwth   =         p8                      ; MAX VIBRATO WIDTH
ilfohz    =         p9                      ; LFO RATE
iop1fn    =         p10                     ; PARAM TABLES FOR 6 OPERATORS
iop2fn    =         p11
iop3fn    =         p12
iop4fn    =         p13
iop5fn    =         p14
iop6fn    =         p15
iampfn    =         p16                     ; AMP/LEVEL MAP FUNCTION
ipkamp    =         p17                     ; FINAL AMPLITUDE SCALING
irsfn     =         p18                     ; RATE SCALING FUNCTION
idevfn    =         p19                     ; LEVEL/PKDEV MAP FUNC
irisefn   =         p20                     ; EG RISE RATE FN
idecfn    =         p21                     ; EG DECAY RATE FN
ivsfn     =         p22                     ; VEL SENSITIVITY FN
ivelfn    =         p23                     ; VEL/AMP FAC MAP FN
iveloc    table     iveloc,ivelfn           ; MAP THIS NOTE'S VELOC
ifeedfn   =         p24
ifeed     table     p25,ifeedfn             ; 0 <= p25 <= 7 (FEEDBK)
ifeed     =         ifeed/(2 * 3.14159)     ; CONVERT RADS TO TABLE INDEX
idetfac   =         4                       ; MAX DETUNING DIVISOR
imap128   =         127/99                  ; MAPPING CONSTANT 99->127
irscl     table     (iroct-irbase)/irrange*127,irsfn
irscl     =         irscl*6
iop       =         1                       ; START LOOP WITH OP1
iopfn     =         iop1fn

loop:
                                            ; READ OPERATOR PARAMETERS
ilvl      table     0,iopfn                 ; OPERATOR OUTPUT LEVEL
ivel      table     1,iopfn                 ; VELOCITY SENSITIVITY
iegr1     table     2,iopfn                 ; EG RATE 1
iegr2     table     3,iopfn                 ; EG RATE 2
iegr3     table     4,iopfn                 ; EG RATE 3
iegr4     table     5,iopfn                 ; EG RATE 4
iegl1     table     6,iopfn                 ; EG LEVEL 1
iegl2     table     7,iopfn                 ; EG LEVEL 2
iegl3     table     8,iopfn                 ; EG LEVEL 3
iegl4     table     9,iopfn                 ; EG LEVEL 4
iams      table     10,iopfn                ; AMPLITUDE MOD SENSITIVITY
imode     table     11,iopfn                ; OPERATOR MODE (FIXED OR RATIO)
ifreq     table     12,iopfn                ; OPERATOR RATIO OR FREQUENCY
idet      table     13,iopfn                ; DETUNE
irss      table     14,iopfn                ; RATE SCALING SENSITIVITY
```

Figure 12.11 Orchestra code for *instr 1205,* an emulation of the Yamaha DX-7 Synthesizer: algorithm 16, featuring a 6-operator loop and the use of ihold and **iturnoff** for sustain.

```
                                              ; INITIALIZE OPERATOR
ihz       =        (imode > 0 ? ifreq : ibase * ifreq) + idet/idetfac
iamp      =        ilvl/99                    ; RESCALE TO 0 -> 1
ivfac     table    ivel,ivsfn                 ; VEL SENSITIVITY CURVE
                                              ; SCALE EG LEVELS TO OP OUTPUT
LVL
iegl1     =        iamp*iegl1
iegl2     =        iamp*iegl2
iegl3     =        iamp*iegl3
iegl4     =        iamp*iegl4
                                              ; FACTOR IN VELOCITY
iegl1     =        iegl1*(1-ivfac)+iegl1*ivfac*iveloc
iegl2     =        iegl2*(1-ivfac)+iegl2*ivfac*iveloc
iegl3     =        iegl3*(1-ivfac)+iegl3*ivfac*iveloc
iegl4     =        iegl4*(1-ivfac)+iegl4*ivfac*iveloc

irs       =        irscl*irss                 ; APPLY RATE SCALING
iegr1     =        (iegr1+irs > 99 ? 99 : iegr1+irs)
iegr2     =        (iegr2+irs > 99 ? 99 : iegr2+irs)
iegr3     =        (iegr3+irs > 99 ? 99 : iegr3+irs)
iegr4     =        (iegr4+irs > 99 ? 99 : iegr4+irs)

                                              ; RISETIMES DIFF FROM DECAYS
irfn      =        (iegl1 > iegl4 ? irisefn : idecfn)
iegd1     table    iegr1,irfn                 ; CONVERT RATE->DUR
ipct1     table    iegl4,irfn+1               ; PCT FN IS NEXT ONE
ipct2     table    iegl1,irfn+1
iegd1     =        abs(iegd1*ipct1-iegd1*ipct2)
iegd1     =        (iegd1 == 0 ? .001 : iegd1)

irfn      =        (iegl2 > iegl1 ? irisefn : idecfn)
iegd2     table    iegr2,irfn
ipct1     table    iegl1,irfn+1
ipct2     table    iegl2,irfn+1
iegd2     =        abs(iegd2*ipct1-iegd2*ipct2)
iegd2     =        (iegd2 == 0 ? .001 : iegd2)

irfn      =        (iegl3 > iegl2 ? irisefn : idecfn)
iegd3     table    iegr3,irfn
ipct1     table    iegl2,irfn+1
ipct2     table    iegl3,irfn+1
iegd3     =        abs(iegd3*ipct1-iegd3*ipct2)
iegd3     =        (iegd3 == 0 ? .001 : iegd3)

iegd4     table    iegr4,idecfn
          if       (iegl3 <= iegl4) igoto continue
ipct1     table    iegl3,irfn+1
ipct2     table    iegl4,irfn+1
iegd4     =        abs(iegd4*ipct1-iegd4*ipct2)
iegd4     =        (iegd4 == 0 ? .001 : iegd4)
continue:
      if (iop > 1) igoto op2
op1:
i1egd1    =        iegd1
i1egd2    =        iegd2
i1egd3    =        iegd3
i1egd4    =        iegd4
i1egl1    =        iegl1
i1egl2    =        iegl2
```

Figure 12.11 continued

```
i1egl3     =       iegl3
i1egl4     =       iegl4
i1ams      =       iams
i1hz       =       ihz
iop        =       iop + 1
iopfn      =       iop2fn
           igoto   loop

op2:       if      (iop > 2) igoto op3
i2egd1     =       iegd1
i2egd2     =       iegd2
i2egd3     =       iegd3
i2egd4     =       iegd4
i2egl1     =       iegl1
i2egl2     =       iegl2
i2egl3     =       iegl3
i2egl4     =       iegl4
i2ams      =       iams
i2hz       =       ihz
iop        =       iop + 1
iopfn      =       iop3fn
           igoto   loop

op3:       if      (iop > 3) igoto op4
i3egd1     =       iegd1
i3egd2     =       iegd2
i3egd3     =       iegd3
i3egd4     =       iegd4
i3egl1     =       iegl1
i3egl2     =       iegl2
i3egl3     =       iegl3
i3egl4     =       iegl4
i3ams      =       iams
i3hz       =       ihz
iop        =       iop + 1
iopfn      =       iop4fn
           igoto   loop

op4:       if      (iop > 4) igoto op5
i4egd1     =       iegd1
i4egd2     =       iegd2
i4egd3     =       iegd3
i4egd4     =       iegd4
i4egl1     =       iegl1
i4egl2     =       iegl2
i4egl3     =       iegl3
i4egl4     =       iegl4
i4ams      =       iams
i4hz       =       ihz
iop        =       iop + 1
iopfn      =       iop5fn
           igoto   loop

op5:       if      (iop > 5) igoto op6
i5egd1     =       iegd1
i5egd2     =       iegd2
i5egd3     =       iegd3
i5egd4     =       iegd4
i5egl1     =       iegl1
i5egl2     =       iegl2
i5egl3     =       iegl3
```

Figure 12.11 continued

```
i5egl4      =         iegl4
i5ams       =         iams
i5hz        =         ihz
iop         =         iop + 1
iopfn       =         iop6fn
            igoto     loop

op6:
i6egd1      =         iegd1
i6egd2      =         iegd2
i6egd3      =         iegd3
i6egd4      =         iegd4
i6egl1      =         iegl1
i6egl2      =         iegl2
i6egl3      =         iegl3
i6egl4      =         iegl4
i6ams       =         iams
i6hz        =         ihz

                                                    ; SIMPLE LFO
kvary       expseg    .001,idelay,1,1,1
klfo        oscili    kvary,kvary*ilfohz,isine      ; LFO
kvib        =         1+klfo*ivibwth

            timout    idur,999,final                ; SKIP DURING FINAL DECAY
k1sus       linseg    i1egl4,i1egd1,i1egl1,i1egd2,i1egl2,i1egd3,i1egl3,1,i1egl3
k2sus       linseg    i2egl4,i2egd1,i2egl1,i2egd2,i2egl2,i2egd3,i2egl3,1,i2egl3
k3sus       linseg    i3egl4,i3egd1,i3egl1,i3egd2,i3egl2,i3egd3,i3egl3,1,i3egl3
k4sus       linseg    i4egl4,i4egd1,i4egl1,i4egd2,i4egl2,i4egd3,i4egl3,1,i4egl3
k5sus       linseg    i5egl4,i5egd1,i5egl1,i5egd2,i5egl2,i5egd3,i5egl3,1,i5egl3
k6sus       linseg    i6egl4,i6egd1,i6egl1,i6egd2,i6egl2,i6egd3,i6egl3,1,i6egl3
k1phs       =         k1sus
k2phs       =         k2sus
k3phs       =         k3sus
k4phs       =         k4sus
k5phs       =         k5sus
k6phs       =         k6sus
            kgoto     output                        ; SKIP OUT FROM HERE DURING IDUR
final:                                              ; GO HERE AFTER IDUR ELAPSED
k1fin       linseg    1,i1egd4,0,1,0
k1phs       =         i1egl4+(k1sus-i1egl4)*k1fin
k2fin       linseg    1,i2egd4,0,1,0
k2phs       =         i2egl4+(k2sus-i2egl4)*k2fin
k3fin       linseg    1,i3egd4,0,1,0
k3phs       =         i3egl4+(k3sus-i3egl4)*k3fin
k4fin       linseg    1,i4egd4,0,1,0
k4phs       =         i4egl4+(k4sus-i4egl4)*k4fin
k5fin       linseg    1,i5egd4,0,1,0
k5phs       =         i5egl4+(k5sus-i5egl4)*k5fin
k6fin       linseg    1,i6egd4,0,1,0
k6phs       =         i6egl4+(k6sus-i6egl4)*k6fin

; ALGORITHM-SPECIFIC CODE: THIS IS ALGORITHM 16

            if        k1fin > 0 kgoto output        ; TEST CARRIER ENVELOPE
            turnoff                                 ; WHEN CARRIER OSCIL(S) DONE...
                                                    ; ... TURN OFF.
output:                                             ; ENVELOPE OUTPUT SCALING
k1gate      tablei    k1phs,iampfn                  ; USE AMPFN FOR ANY CARRIER
k2gate      tablei    k2phs,idevfn                  ; USE DEVFN FOR ANY MODULATOR
```

Figure 12.11 continued

```
k3gate    tablei    k3phs,idevfn
k4gate    tablei    k4phs,idevfn
k5gate    tablei    k5phs,idevfn
k6gate    tablei    k6phs,idevfn

a6sig     init      0                         ; INITIALIZE FOR FEEDBACK
a6phs     phasor    i6hz*kvib
a6sig     tablei    a6phs+a6sig*ifeed,isine,1,0,1
a6sig     =         a6sig*k6gate

a5phs     phasor    i5hz*kvib
a5sig     tablei    a5phs+a6sig,isine,1,0,1
a5sig     =         a5sig*k5gate

a4sig     oscili    k4gate,i4hz*kvib,isine

a3phs     phasor    i3hz*kvib
a3sig     tablei    a3phs+a4sig,isine,1,0,1
a3sig     =         a3sig*k3gate

a2sig     oscili    k2gate,i2hz*kvib,isine

a1phs     phasor    i1hz*kvib
a1sig     tablei    a1phs+a2sig+a3sig+a5sig, isine, 1, 0, 1
a1sig     =         a1sig*k1gate
                                              ; FINAL AMP SCALING AND PANNING:
          outs      a1sig*ipkamp*ileft, a1sig*ipkamp*iright
          endin
```

Figure 12.11 continued

until the envelope of the carrier operator has reached zero before issuing the **turnoff** statement. Depending on which DX7 algorithm is being implemented, there may be more than one operator serving as a carrier, in which case it would be necessary to test them all. Note that an alternate method of extending the duration of a note beyond *p3* of the score is to use an opcode such as **linenr**.

The implementation of the envelope generators in this instrument is somewhat complicated. Yamaha envelopes consist of four levels, or breakpoints and four *rates* (not durations). The same 0–99 scale is used for both rates and levels, which must be mapped to usable values. As it happens, the rate mapping for rise segments is quite different than the one for decay segments. Moreover, the rates must be converted into durations, as required by Csound envelope generators. Finally, although Yamaha's diagrams of its envelope generators show the segments as linear, they really are not. Consequently, for the sake of simplicity, I used **linseg** opcodes for the timing of segments, then **table** opcodes to map the linear amplitudes onto the Yamaha operator output levels. The amplitude scaling data were provided in the Chowning/Bristow book. Note that a different table must be used for any operator that will serve as a modulator. The only difference between the two tables is that one has been divided by 2π, so it is properly scaled for use as a normalized **table** index.

```
; TEST SCORE FOR YAMAHA DX7: ALGORITHM 16 ORCHESTRA
; (IMITATES THE "PLUK16.1" VOICE...SORT OF)

f 1   0     512      10     1
; OPERATOR OUTPUT LEVEL TO AMP SCALE FUNCTION  (DATA FROM CHOWNING/BRISTOW)
f 2   0     128      7      0       10     .003     10    .013
      10    .031     10     .079    10     .188     10    .446
      5     .690     5      1.068   5      1.639    5     2.512
      5     3.894    5      6.029   5      9.263    4     13.119
      29    13.119
; RATE SCALING FUNCTION
f 3   0     128      7      0       128    1
; EG RATE RISE FUNCTION FOR LVL CHANGE BETWEEN 0 AND 99 (DATA FROM OPCODE)
f 4   0     128      -7     38      5      22.8     5     12       5
      7.5   5        4.8    5       2.7    5        1.8   5        1.3
      8     .737     3      .615    3      .505     3     .409     3
      .321  6        .080   6       .055   2        .032  3        .024
      3     .018     3      .014    3      .011     3     .008     3
      .008  3        .007   3       .005   3        .003  32       .003
; EG RATE RISE PERCENTAGE FUNCTION
f 5   0     128      -7     .00001  31     .00001   4     .02      5
      .06   10       .14    10      .24    10       .35   10       .50
      10    .70      5      .86     4      1.0      29    1.0
; EG RATE DECAY FUNCTION FOR LVL CHANGE BETWEEN 0 AND 99
f 6   0     128      -7     318     4      181      5     115      5
      63    5        39.7   5       20     5        11.2  5        7
      8     5.66     3      3.98    6      1.99     3     1.34     3
      .99   3        .71    5       .41    3        .15   3        .081
      3     .068     3      .047    3      .037     3     .025     3
      .02   3        .013   3       .008   36       .008
; EG RATE DECAY PERCENTAGE FUNCTION
f 7   0     128      -7     .00001  10     .25      10    .35      10
      .43   10       .52    10      .59    10       .70   10       .77
      10    .84      10     .92     9      1.0      29    1.0
; EG LEVEL TO PEAK DEVIATION MAPPING FUNCTION (INDEX IN RADIANS/2PI)
f 8   0     128      -7     0       10     .000477  10    .002
      10    .00493   10     .01257  10     .02992   10    .07098
      5     .10981   5      .16997  5      .260855  5     .39979
      5     .61974   5      .95954  5      1.47425  4     2.08795
      29    2.08795
; VELOCITY TO AMP FACTOR MAPPING FUNCTION (ROUGH GUESS)
f 9      0      129       9              .25        1        0
; VELOCITY SENSITIVITY SCALING FUNCTION (SEEMS LINEAR)
f 10     0      8         -7             0          8        1
; FEEDBACK SCALING FUNCTION (SEEMS LINEAR)
f 11     0      8         -7             0          8        7
; OPERATOR 1 PARAMS:                     OUTLVL     KEYVEL   EGR1 EGR4 EGR2    EGR3
f 12     0       32       -2             99         1        99   38   33      14
;                                                            EGL1 EGL4 EGL2    EGL3
                                                             99   0    80      0
;                                                            AMS  DET  FIXED?  FREQ
                                                             0    0    1       1
;                                                            RSS
                                                             2
; OPERATOR 2 PARAMETERS
f 13     0       32       -2             67         6        75   19   45      36
                                                             99   0    87      0
                                                             0    -2   0       11.22
                                                             2
; OPERATOR 3 PARAMETERS
f 14     0       32       -2             99         7        99   46   30      34
                                                             99   0    80      0
                                                             0    0    0       .5
                                                             0
```

Figure 12.12 Score file for *instr 1205,* in which function tables as well as note statement p-fields are used to pass parameter data.

```
; OPERATOR 4 PARAMETERS
f 15    0     32      -2           78      7     90   82   67    21
                                                 99   0    85    0
                                                 0    0    0     7
                                                 0

; OPERATOR 5 PARAMETERS
f 16    0     32      -2           99      4     99   8    64    0
                                                 85   0    48    0
                                                 0    0    0     3
                                                 0

; OPERATOR 6 PARAMETERS
f 17    0     32      -2           99      1     99   82   75    0
                                                 99   0    87    0
                                                 0    0    1     2570
                                                 0

; YAMAHA DX7 ALGORITHM 16
; p2 = START       p3 = DUR     p4=PCH        p5=VEL
; p6 = PANFAC      p7=VIBDEL    p8=VIBWTH     p9=LFOHZ
; p10 = OP1FN      p11=OP2FN    p12=OP3FN     p13=OP4FN
; p14 = OP5FN      p15=OP6FN    p16=AMPFN     p17=PKAMP
; p18 = RSFN       p19=DEVFN    p20=ERISFN    p21=EDECFN
; p22 = VSFN       p23=VELFN    p24=FEEDFN    p25=FEEDBK

i 1205    0       .49     6.00    107     0      0      0      0
          12      13      14      15      16     17     2      20000
          3       8       4       6       10     9      11     7
i 1205    1.00    .54     6.07    107     1
i 1205    2.00    .16     6.08    85      .1
i 1205    2.49    .20     7.03    100     .9
i 1205    3.01    .20     7.04    84      .2
i 1205    3.50    .18     7.11    100     .8
i 1205    4.01    .15     8.00    85      .3
i 1205    4.24    .13     8.07    79      .7
i 1205    4.50    .07     8.08    82      .4
i 1205    4.72    .09     9.03    100     .6
; DELAYED VIBRATO ON LAST NOTE
i 1205    4.98    .16     9.00    110     .5     1      .05    7
f 0       9                               ; ALLOW FOR THE FINAL DECAY
```

Figure 12.12 continued

Finally, note that other 6-operator FM algorithms may be implemented quite easily with this same basic instrument. In fact, all 32 original DX7 algorithms have now been implemented based on this instrument and they are available on the CD-ROM. But other combinations of 6 operators are also possible. The only code that needs to be modified is below the comment line "Algorithm-specific code." The operators must be rearranged, feedback implemented on the correct operator and the trick is to remember to change the envelope output scaling functions appropriately, using *iampfn* for any carrier, but *idevfn* for any modulator. Also, note that **oscili** opcodes can be employed for any operator that isn't being modulated. Thus, in this example, which implements DX7 algorithm 16, operator 2 and operator 4 use **oscili** opcodes, but the remaining operators must use the **phasor/tablei** pairs.

References

Chowning, J. 1973. "The synthesis of complex audio spectra by means of frequency modulation." *Journal of the Audio Engineering Society* 21(7).

Chowning, J., and D. Bristow. 1985. *FM Theory and Applications—By Musicians for Musicians.* Tokyo: Yamaha Music Foundation.

Opcode Systems: *DX/TX Editor/Librarian Manual.* Appendix, pp. 108–114. Palo Alto, Calif.: Opcode Systems, 1986.

Schottstaedt, W. 1977. "The simulation of natural instrument tones using frequency modulation with a complex modulating wave." *Computer Music Journal* 1(4): 46–50.

13 Granular Synthesis in Csound

Allan S. C. Lee

There are two granular synthesis unit generators in Csound. The first is called **grain**, which was written by Paris Smaragdis and the other one is called **granule**, which was developed by me.

The **grain** unit generator uses a function table as the source of a single stream of grains with grain density controlled by the parameter *xdens*. A second f-table is used for generating the envelope. Each grain starts at a random position within the source f-table and sustains for a duration specified by *kgdur*.

The **granule** opcode embodies a high level approach and was developed to provide an easy way for composing music with granular synthesized sound. Multiple voices and random offset of parameters are built into the generator. Wide sound-field effects with multiple outputs can be produced by assigning an opcode statement to each individual channel and setting a different random number seed for each statement. In this chapter, background information on granular synthesis with a focus on the implementation of the **granule** opcode and step-by-step working examples will be presented.

Background Information

As described in the paper *Introduction to Granular Synthesis* (Roads 1988), the theory of granular synthesis was initially suggested by Dennis Gabor in his paper *Acoustical Quanta and the Theory of Hearing* (Gabor 1947). In Gabor's theory, any sound can be described by sonic grains. This suggestion was mathematically verified by Bastiaans (1985).

Since 1971, composers such as Lippe (1993), Roads (1978) and Truax (1988) have been using many different techniques to synthesize sounds using grains. These techniques range from dedicated software to custom built digital-signal-processing (DSP) hardware. In the *Computer Music Tutorial* (Roads 1996), Roads outlines existing granular synthesis methods in five categories: Fourier and wavelet grids, pitch-synchronous overlapping streams, quasi-synchronous streams, asynchronous clouds, and time-granulated or sampled-sound streams with overlapped quasi-synchronous or asynchronous playback.

Both the **grain** and **granule** opcodes fall into the last category listed above. The opcodes read in a small chunk of sound data (normally from 1 millisecond to 100 milliseconds) from a source f-table and apply an envelope to it, then generate streams of grains. In the case of the **grain** opcode, it reads a random portion of the source sound data to produce sonic grains. The result is that the original sampled sound is granulated and rearranged randomly with a grain density controlled by the parameter *xdens*. In the case of the opcode **granule**, it reads a small part of the source data linearly in the time domain, with or without random offset in the starting position, to generate multiple streams of grains.

Implementation of the GRANULE Opcode

Granular synthesis using Csound can be achieved by using conditional statements or a combination of existing unit generators, but this is complicated and would require a large orchestra and score file to generate a short output.

To simplify and streamline the process, the unit generator **granule** was developed as a high-level composition tool. A Csound f-table is used as the source, hence, unlimited types of sounds, ranging from a simple FM timbre to a sampled sound, can be used as the source for the grains. Also, since this is a regular Csound unit generator, it can be fully integrated into normal Csound compositions and sound designs.

Granular synthesis can be classified as a form of additive synthesis. A high number of grains are added together to produce output, as illustrated in figure 13.1.

A "grain" is a signal with an amplitude envelope, which can be of any shape. For computation efficiency, linear attack and decay are used. An optional f-table for generating grains with different envelope shapes is also implemented. Linear time-scaling and pitch-shifting of the original sample is also supported. In the *Csound Reference Manual* we see that the **granule** opcode is defined as follows:

```
ar granule xamp, ivoice, iratio, imode, ithd, ifn, ipshift,
           igskip, igskip_os, ilength, kgap, igap_os, kgsize,
           igsize_os iatt, idec[, iseed[,ipitch1[, ipitch2[,
           ipitch3[, ipitch4[, ifnenv]]]]]]
```

These 22 parameters give full control of the characteristics of the synthesis. And although there are 22, most of these parameters are i-rate and thus the synthesis is not as complicated as it appears to be. Their general function is illustrated in figure 13.2.

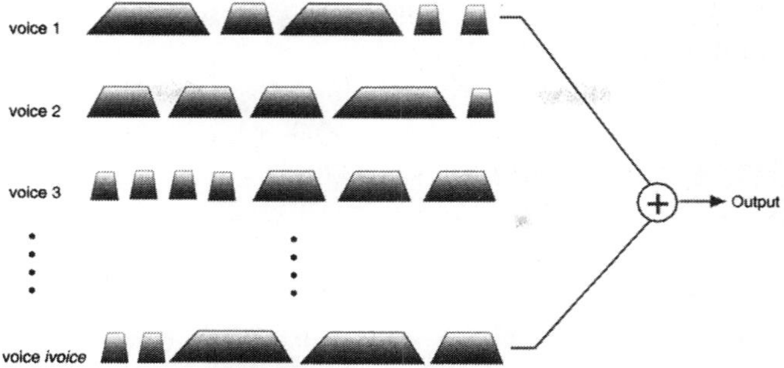

Figure 13.1 Granular synthesis illustrated as an additive synthesis of gated streams of voices.

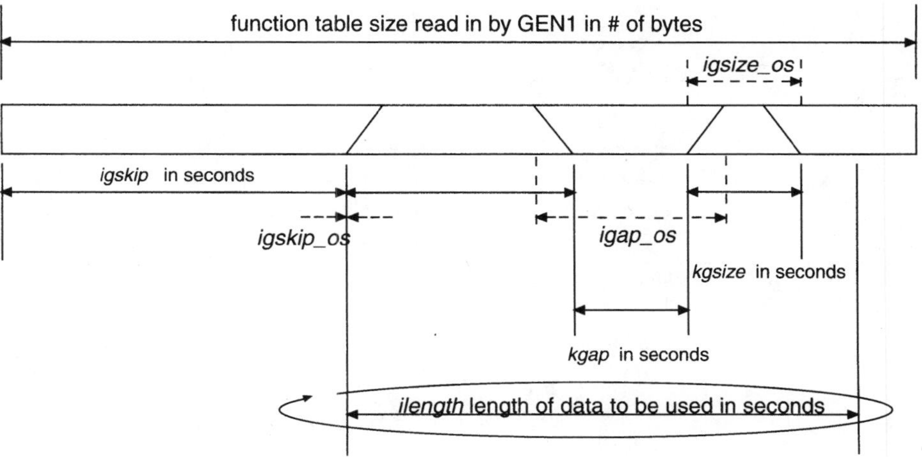

Figure 13.2 An illustration of how the parameters of the **granule** opcode operate.

The parameter *xamp,* which is similar to most of the other Csound unit generators, controls the overall output amplitude.

The parameter *ivoice* defines the number of voices or streams to be generated. The greater the value of *ivoice,* the higher the grain density that will be produced, hence the richer the sound. It takes longer, however, to generate the output. (My suggestion is to use *ivoice* with a value around 10 to experiment with the sound and to use a higher value for production).

The parameter, *iratio,* defines the speed of the sampling pointer moving along the f-table, relative to the audio rate defined in **sr**. For example, a value of 0.1 would stretch (expand) an original one-second sample by a factor of ten, producing ten seconds of output, whereas, a value of 10 would compress the same one-second sample by a factor of ten producing 0.1 second of output.

The parameter *imode* controls the direction of the sampling pointer; a value of +1 causes the pointer to acquire data from the source function table in the normal direction (forward), a value of −1 makes the pointer acquire data from the source f-table in reverse direction, a value of 0 will cause the pointer to acquire data forward and backward randomly for each grain.

The parameter *ithd* defines the threshold value. Samples in the f-table below this value will be skipped. The thresholding process is simply to compare the value of each sample with the value *ithd* and to skip the sample if the value is less. It is a simple design for skipping silent space within a sound sample, but it will cause some distortion.

The parameter *ifn* is the f-table number of the source sound sample opened by an f-statement in the score file.

The parameter *ipshift* is the pitch shift control. When *ipshift* is set to 0, the pitch will be set randomly up and down an octave for each grain. When *ipshift* is set to 1, 2, 3, or 4, as many as four different pitch shifts can be set for the number of voices defined in *ivoice.* When *ipshift* is set to equal 4, the value of *ivoice* needs to be set equal to 4 or greater. The optional parameters *ipitch1, ipitch2, ipitch3,* and *ipitch4* are used to quantify the pitch shifts. Time scaling techniques, with linear-interpolation between data points, are used to produce the pitch shift relative to the original pitch. A value of 1 will generate the original pitch, a value of 2 will be one octave up and a value of 0.5 will be one octave down.

The next three parameters *igskip, igskip_os* and *ilength* are designed for easy control of the precise location within the function being used as a source. As you know, the GEN1 subroutine creates f-table in sizes of powers of two. This means that there might be some zeroes or other unwanted data at the end of the f-table. The value of *igskip* defines the starting point within the function table and *ilength* defines the length of data to be used. Both parameters are measured in seconds. The sampling pointer of the unit generator moves from the starting point defined by *igskip* and runs to the end of *ilength* before looping back to the starting point. The parameter *igskip_os* provides a random offset of the sampling pointer in seconds; a value of 0 implies no offset.

The two parameters, *kgap,* gap size in seconds, and *igap_os,* the random offset in % of *kgap,* define the gap or delay between grains within each voice stream. The value of *kgap* can either be time-varying and generated by Csound functions or be set to a constant value. When the value of *igap_os* is set to 0, no offset will be produced.

The two parameters, *kgsize,* grain size in seconds, and *igsize_os,* the random offset in % of *kgsize,* define the size of each grain. As above, the value of *kgsize* can either be generated by Csound functions or set to a constant value. If no random offset is desired, set *igsize_os* to 0%.

The two parameters, *iatt* and *idec,* define the attack and decay of the grain envelope in % of grain size.

The parameter, *iseed,* is optional; it is the seed for the random number generator, the default value being 0. 5. In a multichannel design, using different values for each output would generate a different random sequence for each channel, producing a wide sound-field effect.

The final optional parameter, *ifnenv,* defines the shape of the grain envelope. The default value is 0 and linear attack (*iatt*) and decay (*idec*) are used as described in figure 13.3. A positive value will be interpreted as an f-table number and the data stored in it will be used to generate the attack curve of the envelope. The decay curve will be a mirrored image of the attack curve. If a full envelope image is stored in this f-table, then *iatt* must equal 100% and *idec* 0% in order to generate a full envelope for each grain, as illustrated in figure 13.4.

Working Examples

A series of working examples are defined and described below to demonstrate the characteristics of the **granule** unit generator. The following is the listing of three orchestra files: the first one, *1301.orc* is for a single channel output, the second one, *1302.orc* is for two channels and the third one, *1304.orc,* is for four channels. The **linseg** statement is used to generate a simple overall envelope of 5% attack and decay, in order to eliminate "clicks" at the beginning and the end. All the parameters are passed in from the score file. In the two channel version, two **granule** opcodes are called. They share all the parameters, except *iseed* (*p20*)—for which an arbitrary value of 0.17 is added to give a different seed for each opcode. These different seeds will generate different random offsets for all the offset parameters, providing a slight

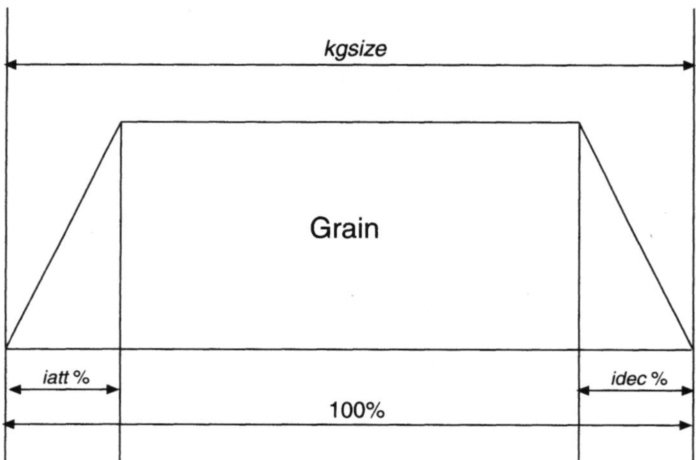

Figure 13.3 Linear grain envelope as defined by the *iatt* and *idel* parameters when *ifnenv* is set to 0.

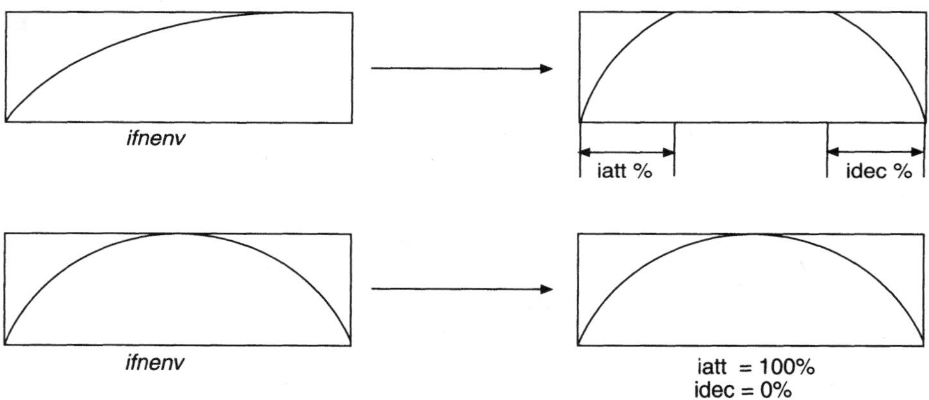

Figure 13.4 Symmetrical grain envelopes from function tables as specified by the *ifnenv* parameter.

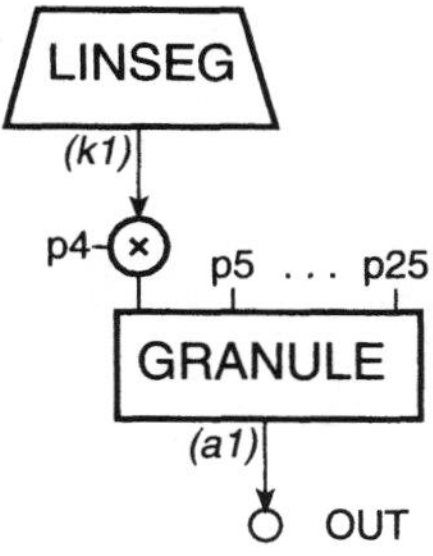

Figure 13.5 Block diagram of *instr 1301,* A simple granular synthesizer.

```
    instr    1301          ; SIMPLE GRANULAR WITH GRANULE OPCODE
k1  linseg   0, 0.05*p3, 1, 0.9*p3, 1, 0.05*p3, 0
a1  granule  p4*k1, p5, p6, p7, p8, p9, p10, p11, p12, p13, p14, p15, p16,
             p17, p18, p19, p20, p21, p22, p23, p24, p25
    out      a1
    endin
```

Figure 13.6 Orchestra code for *instr 1301,* A simple granular synthesizer with **linseg** amplitude envelope.

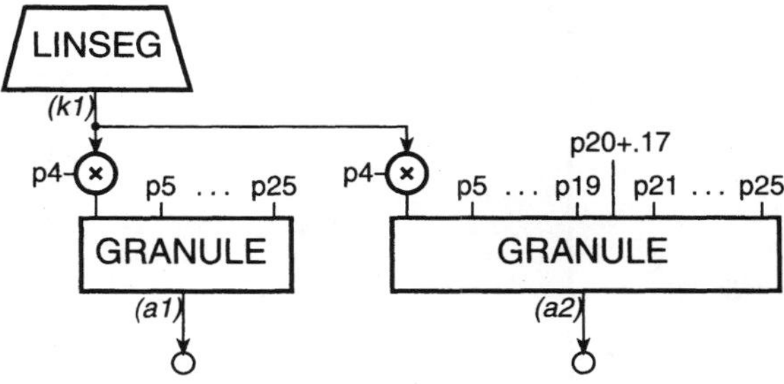

Figure 13.7 Block diagram of *instr 1302,* A stereo granular synthesizer.

```
    instr    1302        ; STEREO GRANULAR WITH COMMON AMPLITUDE ENVELOPE
k1  linseg   0, 0.05*p3, 1, 0.9*p3, 1, 0.05*p3, 0
a1  granule  p4*k1, p5, p6, p7, p8, p9, p10, p11, p12, p13, p14, p15, p16,
             p17, p18, p19, p20, p21, p22, p23, p24, p25
a2  granule  p4*k1, p5, p6, p7, p8, p9, p10, p11, p12, p13, p14, p15, p16,
             p17, p18, p19, p20+0.17, p21, p22, p23, p24, p25
    outs     a1, a2
    endin
```

Figure 13.8 Orchestra code for *instr 1302,* a stereo granular synthesizer with a common amplitude envelope.

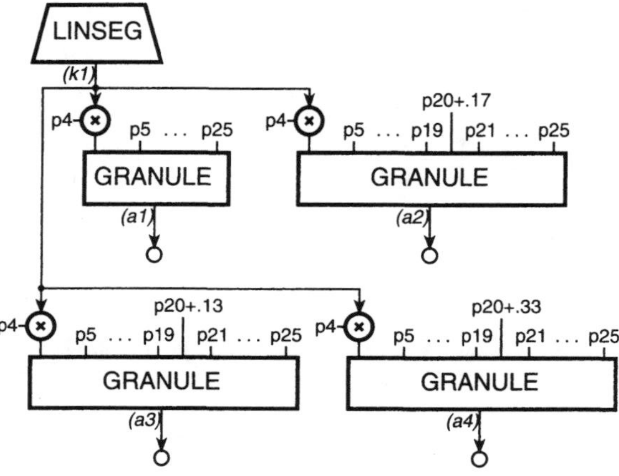

Figure 13.9 Block diagram of *instr 1304,* a quad granular synthesizer.

```
    instr    1304         ; QUAD GRANULAR
k1  linseg   0, 0.05*p3, 1, 0.9*p3, 1, 0.05*p3, 0
a1  granule  p4*k1, p5, p6, p7, p8, p9, p10, p11, p12, p13, p14, p15, p16,
             p17, p18, p19, p20, p21, p22, p23, p24, p25
a2  granule  p4*k1, p5, p6, p7, p8, p9, p10, p11, p12, p13, p14, p15, p16,
             p17, p18, p19, p20+0.17, p21, p22, p23, p24, p25
a3  granule  p4*k1, p5, p6, p7, p8, p9, p10, p11, p12, p13, p14, p15, p16,
             p17, p18, p19, p20+0.13, p21, p22, p23, p24, p25
a4  granule  p4*k1, p5, p6, p7, p8, p9, p10, p11, p12, p13, p14, p15, p16,
             p17, p18, p19, p20+0.33, p21, p22, p23, p24, p25
    outq     a1, a2, a3, a4
    endin
```

Figure 13.10 Orchestra code for *instr 1304,* A quad granular synthesizer with a common amplitude envelope.

delay between all the grains; this is sufficient to generate a wide stereo sound field. Obviously, in the case of the four-channel output, four **granule** opcodes are used and each is given a different values for *iseed.*

The first set of examples use a simple 220 Hz sine tone as the source. The orchestra and score files *sine220.orc* and *sine220.sco,* used to generate 10 seconds of a 220 Hz sine tone, are shown in figure 13.11. The output of this orchestra and score should be generated as an AIFF file that is named *sine220.aif* and placed in the samples directory, **SADIR**, for use in the first set of granular synthesis examples.

The three notes from *1301.sco* shown in figure 13.12 are used to generate three distinctly different granular textures.

Obviously, a single-channel output can be generated by using the *1301.sco* with *1301.orc;* a stereo output can be generated from running *1301.sco* with *1302.orc;*

```
        instr     1303          ; 220 HZ SINE TONE
a1      oscil     20000, 220, 1, 0
        out       a1
        endin

f 1       0  524288   10   1
i 1303    0  10
```

Figure 13.11 Orchestra and score for generating a 220 Hz sine tone with 524288 points of resolution.

```
; SOURCE FILE IS A 220 HZ SINE WAVE
f 1      0  524288  1       "sine220.aif"    0 4 0
; GRAIN SIZE IS SET TO 5 MS, GAP SET TO 100 MS
i 1301   0  10        3500  12 1 1 0 1 4 0 0 10 0.1 30 .005 30 20 20 0.39 1 1.42
                            0.29 4 0
; GRAIN SIZE SET TO 50 MS, GAP SET TO 100 MS
i 1301   12 10        3500  12 1 1 0 1 4 0 0 10 0.1 30 .05 30 20 20 0.39 1 1.42
                            0.29 4 0
; GRAIN SIZE SET TO 50 MS, GAP SET TO 10 MS
i 1301   24 10        3500  12 1 1 0 1 4 0 0 10 0.01 30 .05 30 20 20 0.39 1 1.42
                            0.29 4 0
```

Figure 13.12 The first score file for *instr 1301,* each of the three notes has a different grain size and gap size.

and quad output by running *1301.sco* with *1304.orc.* (It should be noted, however, that your hardware may not support quad playback.)

In the first ten second "note" from *1301.sco,* the grain size is set to equal 5 milliseconds, the gap is set to equal 100 milliseconds and four different pitches are used. Since the grain size is quite small, the sound is "grainy" and the pitches are not noticeable. In the second 10 second "note" from *1301.sco,* the grain size is increased to 50 milliseconds. In this case, the different pitches are quite noticeable owing to the greater grain size, but the result still sounds discontinuous because of the relatively large gap. Finally, in the third ten second "note" from *1301.sco* the gap is reduced to 10 milliseconds. The result is a smoother and richer granular sound.

The second set of examples use a sampled environmental sound as the source. Four seconds of a mono soundfile, *seashore.aif,* sampled at 44.1 kHz, is used to play the two notes from *1302.sco* shown in figure 13.13.

Most of the parameters are the same as the first set of examples. Grain size is set to 50 ms and the gap is set to 10 ms. But since the length of the source sound file, *seashore.aif,* is 4 seconds, *ilength* is set to equal 4. Notice that in the first note, the soundfile is repeated twice, since there are only 4 seconds of sound in the source and the note duration is 8 seconds. In contrast, the second note, which has a duration of

```
f 1     0    524288    1        "seashore.aif" 0 4 0
; GRAIN SIZE IS SET TO 50 MS, GAP IS SET TO 10 MS
i 1301  0    8         7000   12    1  1 0 1 4 0 0 4 0.01 30 .05 30 20 20
                                     0.39 1 1.42 0.29 4 0
; GRAIN SIZE IS SET TO 50 MS, GAP IS SET TO 10 MS
i 1301  10   16        7000   12   .25 1 0 1 4 0 0 4 0.01 30 .05 30 20 20
                                     0.39 1 1.42 0.29 4 0
```

Figure 13.13 Score file *1302.sco* that granulates and time-scales a sound file.

```
f 1     0        524288      1          "female.aif" 0 4 0
; GRAIN SIZE IS SET TO 50 MS, GAP IS SET TO 10 MS
i 1301  0    10   6000   12      1 1 0 1 4 0 0 6 0.01 30 .05 30 20 20 0.39 1
                             1.42 0.29 4 0
; GRAIN SIZE IS SET TO 50 MS, GAP IS SET TO 10 MS
i 1301  12   10   6000   12    .25 1 0 1 4 0 0 6 0.01 30 .05 30 20 20 0.39 1
                             1.42 0.29 4 0
; GRAIN SIZE IS SET TO 50 MS, GAP IS SET TO 10 MS
i 1301  24   10   3000   48    .25 1 0 1 4 0 0 6 0.01 30 .05 30 20 20 0.39 1
                             1.42 0.29 4 0
```

Figure 13.14 The file *1305.sco* for use with either *1301, 1302, or 1304.orc* to granulize a sample of a female singing voice.

16 seconds, does not repeat the soundfile at all, since *iratio* is set to *0.25.* Imagine that the rate at which the source sound samples are read is one-quarter of the audio rate, hence for eight seconds of output, it only needs four seconds of source samples. This is one of the typical applications of granular synthesis, to "stretch" or extend a sound in the time domain; it brings out the inner details of the sound by slowing down the tempo.

In the set of examples in figure 13.14, six seconds of a mono sound file, *female.aif,* sampled at 44.1 kHz is used. It is the sound of a woman singing.

In *1305.sco,* you will notice that most of the parameters are the same in the three "notes," except *ivoice, iratio* and *xamp.* The value of *ivoice* is set to equal 12 in the first two "notes," then it is set to 48 in the third. The higher value of *ivoice* in the third "note" produces a smoother sound, but as mentioned earlier, will take much longer to render. Also, notice that *xamp* in the third "note" is set lower to stop the output from getting out of range. The *iratio* in the first note is set to 1 and then to 0.25 in the second and third "notes," hence the tempo of these notes is slowed down.

Finally we switch to Csound **grain** opcode for a comparative example. In the *Csound Reference Manual,* the arguments are given as follows:

```
ar    grain   xamp, xpitch, xdens, kampoff, kpitchoff, kgdur,
              igfn, iwfn, imgdur[, igrnd]
```

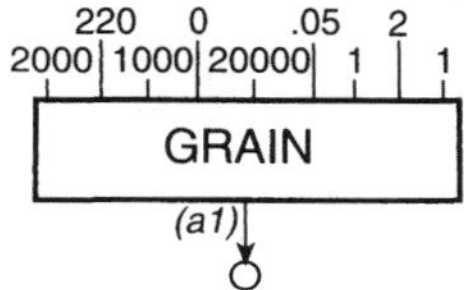

Figure 13.15 Block diagram of *instr 1306*, a simple granular synthesizer using the **grain** opcode.

```
        instr     1306          ; SIMPLE GRANULAR WITH GRAIN OPCODE
a1      grain     2000, 220, 1000, 0, 20000, .05, 1, 2, 1
        out       a1
        endin

f 1         0      8192     10    1
f 2         0      1025     20    2    1

i 1306      0      10
```

Figure 13.16 Orchestra and score for *instr 1306*, a simple granular synthesizer using the **grain** opcode with a Hanning window envelope (*f 2*) and a sinewave as the source (*f 1*).

The example above uses a single cycle of a sine function as the source and a Hanning window as the envelope, to produce 10 seconds of granular sound. The grain density, *xdens* is set to equal 1000 grains per second. The parameters *xpitch* and *kpitchoff* are set to 220 Hz and 20,000 Hz respectively, producing a wide range of frequencies at the output. The grain size (grain duration) *kgdur* is set to 50 milliseconds. The result is a beautifully dispersed granular texture—a "new-millennium sample-and-hold" sound.

Conclusion

As demonstrated in the various examples above, both granular synthesis opcodes are simple to use and understand, in principle; and both are capable of generating rich and colorful textures. The results, however, depend on the type and nature of the source samples. In using granular synthesis for composition, much effort should be spent in choosing the source and then fine tuning the parameters to produce the desired sound.

References

Bastiaans, M. 1985. "On the sliding-window representation of signals." IEEE *Transactions on Acoustics, Speech and Signal Processing* ASSP 33(4): 868–873.

Gabor, D. 1947. "Acoustical quanta and the theory of hearing." *Nature* 159(1044): 591–594.

Lippe, C. 1993. "A musical application of real time granular sampling using the IRCAM signal processing workstation." *Proceedings of the 1993 International Computer Music Conference.*

Roads, C. 1978. "Automated granular synthesis of sound." *Computer Music Journal* 2(2): 61–62.

Roads, C. 1998. "Introduction to granular synthesis." *Computer Music Journal* 12(2): 11–13.

Roads, C. 1996 . "Multiple wavetable, wave terrain, granular and subtractive synthesis." *Computer Music Tutorial.* Cambridge, Mass.: MIT Press.

Truax, B. 1998. "Real time granular synthesis with a digital signal processor." *Computer Music Journal* 12(2): 14–26.

14 FOF and FOG Synthesis in Csound

Michael Clarke

The **fof** (*Fonction d'Onde Formantique*) synthesis unit-generator is based on the synthesis method originally developed by Xavier Rodet for the CHANT program at IRCAM. It produces a series of partials, shaped into a formant region, that can be used in building up a vocal or instrumental simulation. Since the unit-generator works in the time domain, generating a sequence of excitations or grains, it can also be used for granular synthesis, as well as for interpolation between timbral and granular synthesis. Whereas the grains in FOF synthesis are normally based on a stored sine-wave, FOG (*FOF Granular*) synthesis (Eckel, Iturbide, and Becker 1995; Clarke 1996a, b) is designed specifically for use with waveforms derived from soundfiles. Generating grains with many of the particular characteristics of FOF synthesis, the **fog** control parameters are designed to facilitate the transformation of prerecorded sounds. In Csound, **fog** can be used both as a form of time-stretching and as pitch-shifting and to generate more radical granular transformations of the original material.

FOF Synthesis: A Theoretical Overview

Detailed descriptions of the theory of FOF synthesis can be found elsewhere (Rodet 1984; Rodet, Potard, and Barrière 1984). A brief description of the underlying theory is given here as it may be helpful in understanding how the unit-generator works.

It is important to realize that, although FOF synthesis is often used to generate a carefully shaped spectrum and the names of many of its parameters refer to the frequency domain (e.g., fundamental frequency, formant frequency, bandwidth), it in fact operates in the time domain, producing a sequence of excitations (grains comprising enveloped sine-waves.) The resulting spectral contour is shaped, perhaps surprisingly, by adjustments to the time domain. In normal usage, FOF produces a periodic sequence of excitations (though often modified by vibrato). The frequency at which these excitations are generated is heard as the fundamental frequency of the formant region. The output of the unit-generator is a set of overtones of this fundamental, whose relative amplitudes are shaped by a spectral envelope (figure 14.1).

It is the shape of the local envelope, that is, the amplitude envelope used for each excitation, that determines the contour of the formant envelope in the frequency-domain. In brief, the shorter the grain envelope, the broader the spectral envelope of the formant region. Conversely, lengthening the grain envelope narrows the formant region. Different aspects of the local envelope shape (its rise time and decay rate) alter the shape of the formant region in precise ways, permitting detailed control over the synthesized timbre.

Most natural timbres comprise several formant regions. In imitating these timbres, it is therefore necessary to sum the output of several **fof** opcodes, each representing a single formant region.

The FOF Unit-Generator: The Arguments

This section considers each argument in turn and examines its basic function. More complex examples of FOF synthesis are described in my chapter *From Research to Programming to Composition,* on the accompanying CD-ROM. The arguments of the **fof** unit-generator are (figure 14.2):

```
ar fof xamp, xfund, xform, koct, kband, kris, kdur, kdec,
       iolaps, ifna, ifnb, itotdur [, iphs[, ifmode]]
```

A single formant region can be produced by the orchestra and score shown in figure 14.3. Starting from this model, changes will be made to each of the input parameters in turn to illustrate their basic operation.

- *xamp* = amplitude

The constant amplitude of the initial instrument may be modified to take an envelope, like a simple **linseg** function:

```
a2   linseg            0, p3*.3, 20000, p3*.4, 15000, p3*.3, 0
a1   fof               a2, ....(as before)...
```

FOF synthesis is built from a series of often-overlapping excitations or grains that are summed. Factors such as the envelope shape of the grains and the number of grains occurring simultaneously (dependent on the grain lengths and the fundamental frequency) can therefore effect the overall amplitude. This is not normalized and so care is needed to avoid samples out of range.

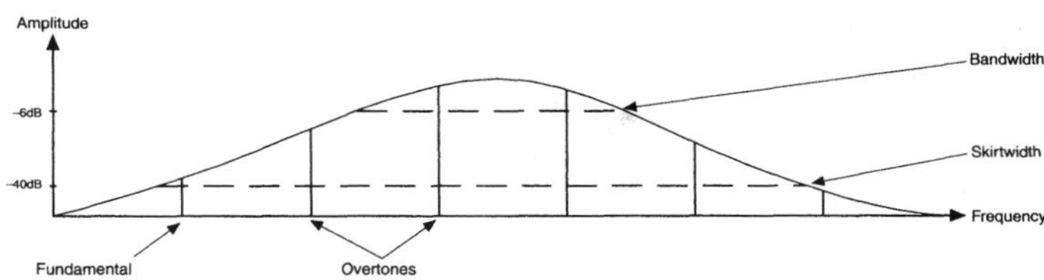

Figure 14.1 A spectral envelope.

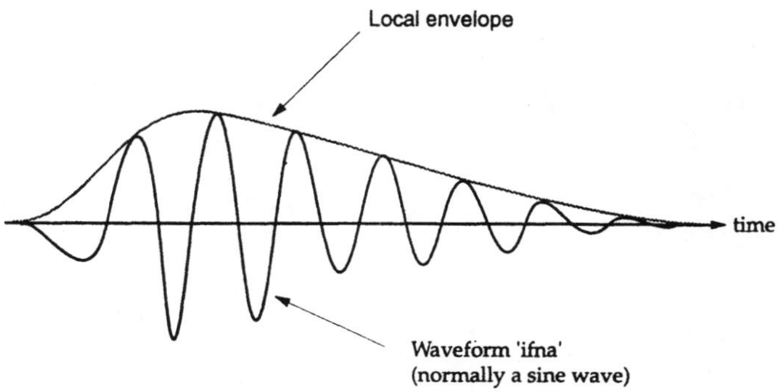

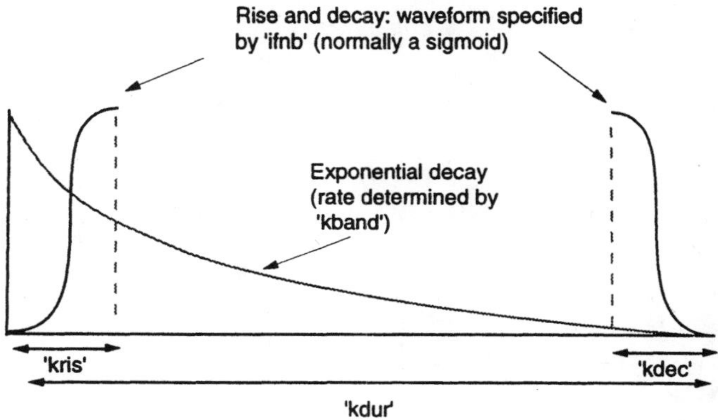

Figure 14.2 Time domain parameters for **fof**, which control its spectral envelope, the function which is sampled (*fna*), the rise and decay waveform (*fub*), the exponential decay time (*ktand*), and the rise (*krise*), decay (*kdec*), and duration (*kdur*).

```
    instr  1401         ; SINGLE FORMANT FOF
a1  fof    15000, 200, 650, 0, 40, .003, .02, .007, 5, 1, 2, p3
    out    a1
    endin

f 1        0   4096   10    1
f 2        0   1024   19    .5 .5 270 .5

i 1401     0   3
```

Figure 14.3 Orchestra file for *instr 1401,* an FOF synthesizer producing a single formant.

- *xfund* = fundamental frequency

The fundamental frequency of the formant region is controlled by this parameter. It may for example be modulated by an oscillator to produce a vibrato, as in this exaggerated example:

```
a2  oscil     20, 5, 1
a1  fof       15000, 200+a2, ...(as before)...
```

This parameter can also be used to move between timbral synthesis and granular textures. Since FOF synthesis produces a rapid succession of (normally) overlapping excitations or grains. The argument *xfund* controls the speed at which new excitations are formed. If the fundamental is low these excitations are perceived as separate grains. In such cases the fundamental is no longer a pitch but a pulse speed. If the parameter is also varied randomly (perhaps using the **rand** unit-generator) so that a regular pulse is no longer audible, *xfund* becomes the density of grain distribution. The possibility of moving between pitch and pulse and between timbre and granular texture is one of the most interesting aspects of **fof**. The following provides a simple demonstration. The transformation from pulse to pitch will be most easily heard if the note duration is lengthened to about 10 seconds:

```
a2  expseg    5, p3*.8, 200, p3*.2, 150
a1  fof       15000, a2, .....(as before)...
```

- *koct* = octaviation coefficient

Skipping a parameter for now, *octaviation* provides a rather unusual means of controlling the fundamental. This parameter is normally set to 0. For each unit increase in *koct* (1, 2, 3 etc.) the fundamental will drop by one octave. This change of pitch is not achieved by a glissando in the normal sense. Rather, alternate excitations are gradually reduced in intensity as the parameter moves from one unit to the next (e.g., 0 to 1,) until only half the number of excitations remain (figure 14.4).

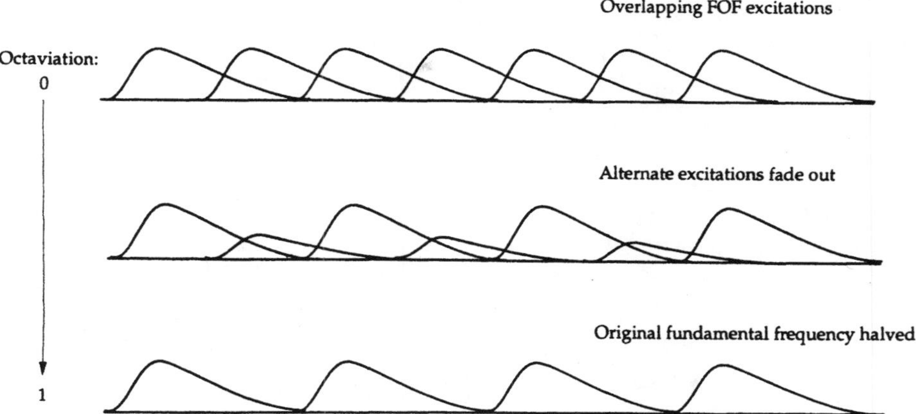

Figure 14.4 Octaviation.

```
k1   linseg     0, p3*.1, 0, p3*.8, 6, p3*.1, 6
a1   fof        15000, 200, 650, k1, ...(as before)...
```

The **linseg** and **fof** code shown above produce a drop of six octaves; if the note is sufficiently long, it should be possible to hear the alternate excitations fading out toward the end of the example.

- *xform* = formant frequency
- *ifmode* = formant mode (0 = striated, non–0 = smooth)

The spectral output of an **fof** unit-generator resembles that of an impulse generator, filtered by a bandpass filter. It is a set of partials above a fundamental (*xfund*) with a spectral peak at the formant frequency (*xform*). Motion of the formant can be implemented in two ways. If *ifmode* = 0, data sent to *xform* has effect only at the start of a new excitation. That is, each new excitation gets the current value of this parameter at the time of creation and holds it until the excitation ends. Successive overlapping excitations can have different formant frequencies, creating a richly varied sound. This is the mode of the original CHANT program. If *ifmode* is nonzero, the frequency of each excitation varies continuously with *xform.* This allows glissandi of the formant frequency. To demonstrate these differences, a low fundamental is used so that the granules can be heard separately. The formant frequency is audible, not as the center frequency of a "band," but as a pitch in its own right. Compare the following, in which only *ifmode* is changed:

```
a2    line   400, p3, 800
a1    fof    10000, 2, a2, 0, 0, .003, .5, .1, 3, 1, 2, p3, 0, 0
a2    line   400, p3, 800
a1    fof    10000, 2, a2, 0, 0, .003, .5, .1, 3, 1, 2, p3, 0, 1
```

In the first case, the formant frequency moves by step at the start of each excitation, whereas in the second it changes smoothly. A more subtle difference is perceived with higher fundamental frequencies (note that the later **fof** parameters were changed in this example to lengthen the excitations so that their pitch could be heard more easily).

The *xform* argument also permits frequency modulation of the formant frequency. Applying FM to an already complex sound can lead to strange results, but here is a simple example:

```
acar     line  400, p3, 800
index    =     2.0
imodfr   =     400
idev     =     index*imodfr
amodsig oscil idev, imodfr, 1
a1       fof   15000, 5, acar+amodsig, 0, 1, .003, .5, .1, 3, 1, 2, p3, 0, 1
```

- *kband* = formant bandwidth
- *kris, kdur, kdec* = risetime, duration and decaytime (in seconds) of the excitation envelope

These parameters control the shape and length of the **fof** granules. They are shaped in three segments: a rise, a middle decay and a terminating decay. For low fundamentals these are perceived as an amplitude envelope, but with higher fundamentals (above 30 Hz) the granules merge together and these parameters affect the timbre of the sound. Note that these four parameters influence a new granule only at the time of its initialization and are fixed for its duration; later changes will affect only subsequent granules. The first example uses a low fundamental frequency:

```
k1     line    .003, p3, .1
a1     fof     15000, 2, 300, 0, 0, k1, .5, .1, 2, 1, 2, p3
```

Run this with a note length of 10 seconds. Notice how the attack of the envelope of the granules lengthens. The shape of this attack is determined by the shape of *ifnb* (here a sigmoid).

Next is an example of *kband* changing over time:

```
k1     linseg  0, p3, 10
a1     fof     15000, 2, 300, 0, k1, .003, .5, .1, 2, 1, 2, p3
```

Following its rise, an excitation has a built-in exponential decay and *kband* determines its rate. The larger the *kband,* the steeper the decay; zero means no decay. In the above example the successive granules had increasingly fast decays.

The next example demonstrates the operation of *kdec.* Because an exponential decay never reaches zero, a terminating decay is necessary to prevent discontinuity in the signal. The argument *kdur* determines the overall duration (in seconds from the start of the excitation) and *kdec* sets the length of the terminating decay. This decay therefore starts at the time determined by *kdur - kdec.* In this example, the terminating decay starts early in the first granules and then becomes progressively later and shorter. Note that *kband* is set to zero so that only the terminating decay is evident.

```
k1   linseg    .8, p3, .003
a1   fof       15000, 1, 300, 0, 0, .003, .9, k1, 2, 1, 2, p3
```

In the next example the start time of the termination remains constant, but its length gets shorter, as does the grain itself:

```
k1   expon   .3, p3, .003
a1   fof     15000, 2, 300, 0, 0, .003, .01+k1, k1, 2, 1, 2, p3
```

It may be surprising to find that for higher fundamentals, the local envelope determines the spectral shape of the sound. Electronic and computer music, however, have often shown that parameters of music once considered to be independent (for example pitch, timbre and rhythm) are in fact different aspects of the same phenomenon. The inverse relationship of time and frequency also has a parallel in the uncertainty principle of modern physics. In general, the longer the local envelope segment, the narrower the band of partials around that frequency. The argument *kband* determines the bandwidth of the formant region at −6dB and *kris* controls the skirtwidth at −40dB. Increasing *kband* increases the local envelope's exponential decay rate, thus shortening it and increasing the −6dB spectral region. Increasing *kris* (the envelope attack time) inversely makes the −40dB spectral region smaller.

The next example changes first the bandwidth and then the skirtwidth. The difference should be apparent:

```
k1   linseg   100, p3/4, 0, p3/4, 100, p3/2, 100          ; KBAND
k2   linseg   .003, p3/2, .003,p3/4, .01, p3/4, .003      ; KRIS
a1   fof      15000, 100, 440, 0, k1, k2, .02, .007, 3, 1, 2, p3
```

In the first half of the note, *kris* remains constant while *kband* broadens then narrows again. In the second half, *kband* is fixed while *kris* lengthens (narrowing the spectrum), then shortens again.

Note that *kdur* and *kdec* do not shape the spectrum significantly. They simply tidy up the decay so as to prevent unwanted discontinuities that would distort the sound. For vocal imitations, these parameters are typically set at .017 and .007 and left unchanged. With high ("soprano") fundamentals it is possible to shorten these values and save computation time (reducing overlaps).

- *iolaps* = number of overlap spaces

Granules are created at the rate of the fundamental frequency and new granules are often created before earlier ones have finished, resulting in overlaps. The number of overlaps at any one time is given by *xfund* * *kdur.* For a typical "bass" note the calculation might be 200 * .018 = 3.6 and for a "soprano" note 660 * .015 = 9. 9. The **fof** opcode needs at least this number (rounded up) of spaces in which to operate. The number can be over-estimated at no computation cost and at only a small space cost. If there are insufficient overlap spaces during operation, the note will terminate.

- *ifna, ifnb* = stored function tables

These two parameters identify two function tables. Normally, *ifna,* which defines the waveform on which the granules are based, is a sine wave. Normally, *ifnb* is the waveform used for the rise and final decay of the local envelope, typically a sigmoid. Definitions for both of these functions can be found as *"f 1"* and *"f 2",* respectively.

- *itotdur* = total duration within which all granules in a note must be completed

So that incomplete granules are not cut off at the end of a note, the **fof** opcode will not create new granules if they will not be completed by the specified time. Normally given the value of *p3* (the note length), this parameter can be changed for special effects; **fof** will output zero after time *itotdur.*

- *iphs* = initial phase (optional, defaulting to 0)

Specifies the initial phase of the fundamental, which is normally zero, but giving different **fof** generators different initial phases can be helpful in avoiding "zeros" in the spectrum.

Vocal Imitation

In doing a vocal imitation, all the **fof** opcodes share a common fundamental frequency, modified by a complex vibrato which is modeled on the CHANT program.

Each **fof** has its own settings to determine the shape of its formant region. A list of formant data for different vowels can be found in the appendix and in the *Csound Reference Manual.* The output of all the **fof** generators is summed.

Transformations based on this vocal model can be found among the examples for the CD-ROM chapter *From Research to Programming to Composition.*

FOG Synthesis: An Introduction

FOG synthesis is essentially similar to FOF synthesis, but the unit-generator and its control parameters are adapted for use in granulating soundfiles. Many of the **fog** input parameters have a direct parallel with those of FOF synthesis but the names reflect their orientation toward granular synthesis. The granulation of soundfiles has been explored by a number of people, including Barry Truax (1994). Using the **fof** algorithm as the basis for granulation has certain characteristic features, in particular the shape of the local envelope and the precise timing of grains (Clarke 1996a). FOG synthesis permits time-stretching and pitch shifting of the original sounds, although with side effects (which can often be interesting compositionally), as well as the creation of new textures through the random variation of certain parameters.

The FOG Unit-Generator: The Arguments

The arguments of the **fog** unit generator are:

```
ar fog xamp, xdens, xptch, xspd, koct, kband, kris, kdur,
       kdec, iolaps, ifna, ifnb, itotdur [, iphs[, ifmode]]
```

The orchestra and score shown in figures 14.5 and 14.6. will be used as the basis for a number of variations, which will demonstrate the basic functioning of the **fog** unit-generator. Initially, those parameters which are significantly different from FOF synthesis will be described and demonstrated.

- *ifna* = stored function table

As in FOF synthesis, *ifna* is a stored f-table, but here this table normally contains data from a soundfile. In the score above, note that the f-table reads data from the file “basmrmba.aif.” This file, a bass marimba phrase, can be found on the accompanying CD-ROM and should be used for running these examples.

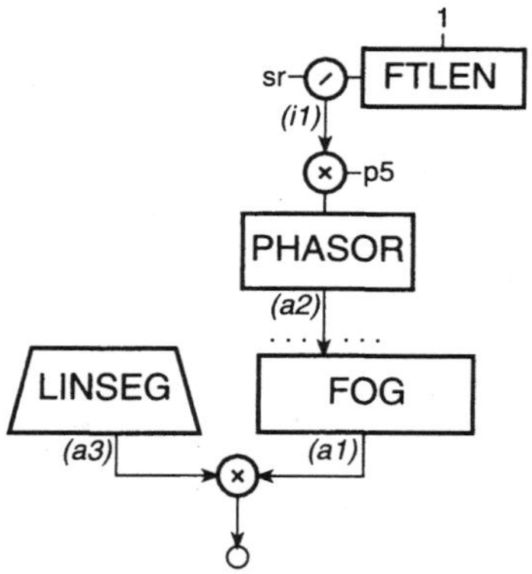

Figure 14.5 Block diagram of *instr 1414*, a basic FOG synthesizer.

```
    instr   1414          ; BASIC FOG
a3  linseg  0, p3*.01, 1, p3*.9, 1, p3*.09, 0
i1  =       sr/ftlen(1)   ; SPEED FACTOR (RELATIVE TO SR & TABLE LENGTH)
a2  phasor  i1*p5         ; PHASE INPUT FOR SPEED
a1  fog     15000, 100, p4, a2, 0, 0, .01, .02, .01, 2, 1, 2, p3, 0, 1
    out     a1*a3
    endin

f 1     0       131072   1    "basmrmba.aif"    0 4 1
f 2     0       1024     19   .5 .5 270 .5

;       START   DUR           XPTCH             XSPD
i 1414  0       3.2           1                 1
```

Figure 14.6 Orchestra and score code for *instr 1414*.

- *xspd* = speed

The *xspd* argument does not have a direct parallel in FOF synthesis. It determines the rate at which successive grains progress through the stored f-table (*ifna*). In FOF synthesis, the sine wave which forms the basis of the excitations/grains is always reset to zero phase (i.e., the start of the f-table) at the start of each grain. In FOG synthesis, successive grains may begin to read from different places in the function table. Thus *xspd* controls the rate of progression by means of an index moving between 0 and 1. To recreate the speed of the original soundfile, account must be taken both of the sample rate (**sr**) and the length of the f-table. Hence, in the instrument above, the line:

```
i1      =       sr/ftlen(1)
```

```
        instr   1415            ; DYNAMIC SPEED CHANGE OF FOG PLAYBACK
a3      linseg  1, p3*.2, 1, p3*.4, 2, p3*.05, -1, p3*.35, -1          ; SPEED CHANGE
i1      =       sr/ftlen(1)     ; SPEED FACTOR (RELATIVE TO SR AND TABLE LENGTH)
a2      phasor  i1*a3           ; PHASE INPUT FOR SPEED
a1      fog     15000, 100, 1, a2, 0, 0, .01, .02, .01, 2, 1, 2, p3, 0, 1
        out     a1
        endin

f 1         0           131072    1     "basmrmba.aif"0 4 1
f 2         0           1024      19    .5 .5 270 .5

;           START       DUR
i 1415      0           20
```

Figure 14.7 Orchestra and score code for dynamic speed change of FOG playback.

This is then modified by *p5*, which enables the speed of playback to be varied in the score. A value of 1, as in the example above, recreates the original speed of the soundfile. Lower values for *p5* decrease the speed; higher values increase it. A negative value will reverse the direction of playback. (Try running the example above with different values for *p5* in the note statement of the score). The example shown in figure 14.7 demonstrates the possibility of dynamically changing the speed.

- *xptch* = pitch factor

The argument *xptch* results in a change of pitch. Whereas *xspd* determines the start point for each successive grain reading from the f-table, *xptch* determines the speed at which each grain progresses from this starting point. It does not therefore change the general rate of progression through the f-table, but does change the perceived pitch. A value of 1 results in the original pitch. In terms of the internal workings of the unit-generator, there is a close parallel between the *xptch* parameter in FOG synthesis and the *xform* parameter in FOF synthesis.

- *xdens* = grain density

The argument *xdens* determines the rate at which new grains are generated and is directly parallel to *xfund* in FOF synthesis. In the orchestra shown in figure 14.9, the number of grains falls rapidly, resulting in the disintegration of the original sound recording.

- *kband, kris, kdur, kdec* = grain envelope shape

The arguments *kband, kris, kdur* and *kdec* all function as in FOF synthesis, controlling the local envelope (the amplitude envelope of each grain). The original example of FOG synthesis shown in figure 14.6 outputs the original sound unaltered. This is in part because *xptch* (*p4*) and *xspd* (*p5*) are both set to 1. It also depends on

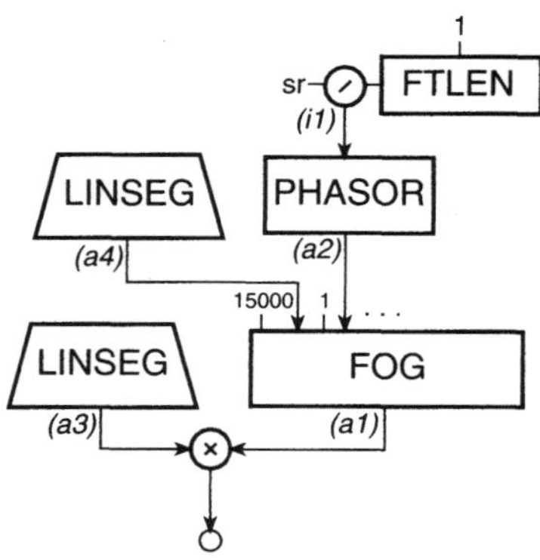

Figure 14.8 Block diagram of *instr 1416,* a FOG instrument that "disintegrates" a sample.

```
        instr       1416            ; SAMPLE-BASED FOG THAT 'DISINTEGRATES'
a4      linseg      100, p3*.7, 5, p3*.3, 5
a3      linseg      0, p3*.01, 1, p3*.9, 1, p3*.09, 0      ; SIMPLE ENVELOPE
i1      =           sr/ftlen(1)     ; SPEED FACTOR (RELATIVE TO SR AND TABLE LENGTH)
a2      phasor      i1              ; PHASE INPUT FOR SPEED
a1      fog         15000, a4, 1, a2, 0, 0, .01, .02, .01, 2, 1, 2, p3, 0, 1
        out         a1*a3
        endin

f 1       0          131072    1      "basmrmba.aif"    0 4 1
f 2       0          1024      19     .5 .5 270 .5

;         START      DUR
i 1416    0          9
```

Figure 14.9 Orchestra and score code for *instr 1416,* as illustrated in figure 14.8.

the successive grains overlapping, so that the sound is continuous and the local envelopes of the grains overlap, adding up to unity at all times: in effect they cancel each other out. For this to work, careful coordination is needed of the parameters *kris, kdur* and *kdec,* together with *xdens. kris* and *kdec* are both set to .01 (10 milliseconds): they are symmetrical, and if the decay of one excitation can be made to overlap precisely with the rise of the next, they will cancel each other out. In this case this is done by setting *kdur* (the duration of the envelope) to .02 and *kdens* to 100. A density of 100 means that new grains will be created 100 times per second, that is, a new grain will start .01 seconds after the last. Therefore, successive grains will overlap by .001 seconds, the first .001 seconds of the new grain (corresponding to its rise time) overlapping with the last .001 seconds of the previous grain (corresponding to its decay time). The local envelope rise and decay therefore crossfade symmetrically,

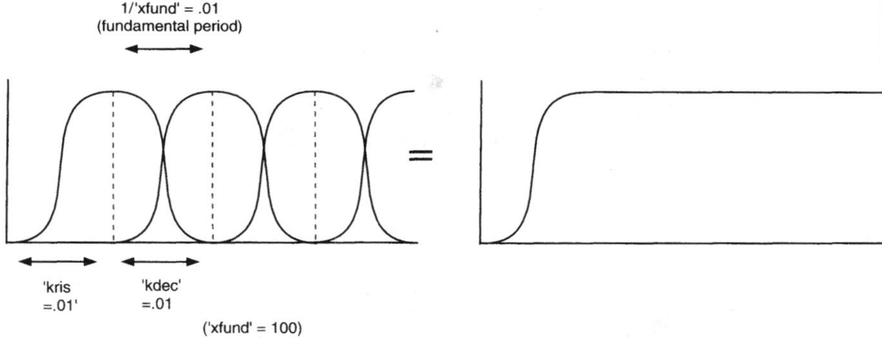

Figure 14.10 Overlapping grains to produce a continuos sound.

canceling each other out and leaving the original signal unchanged. *kband* is set to 0, so that there is no exponential decay to disrupt the symmetry of the local envelope (figure 14.10).

In general, the following conditions must be met for cancellation of envelopes to work as demonstrated above:

- *kband* = 0
- *kris* = *kdec*
- *kdens* = 1/(*kdur* - *kdec*)
- *ifnb* = stored function table

The argument *ifnb* specifies the stored f-table used for the local envelope rise and decay (as with FOF). It is read forward for the rise and backwards for the decay. In the above examples it has been a sigmoid, as usual, but other shapes, for example a linear envelope, may be used. The smoothness and continuity of the sigmoid, however, help in reducing the side-effects of the processing. (A symmetrical shape is also important for the envelope cancellation described above.)

- *xamp* = amplitude

Finally, *xamp* adjusts the amplitude of the output and functions as in **fof**. It is dependent upon the number of overlaps and their envelopes.

Granular Use of FOG

In granular synthesis, random distribution of various parameters is often used to create a rich and complex texture. The modular structure of Csound enables the composer to devise many different instruments, in which one or more parameters are randomly or statistically distributed. It is perhaps in such situations that the full potential of FOG synthesis for the composer becomes evident. Examples of such uses can be found in some of the Csound orchestras and scores accompanying the CD-ROM chapter *From Research to Programming to Composition.*

References

Clarke, J. M. 1996a. "Composing at the intersection of time and frequency." *Organised Sound* 2: 107–117. Cambridge, England: Cambridge University Press.

Clarke, J. M. 1996b. "TIM(br)E." *Proceedings of the International Computer Music Conference.* Hong Kong: International Computer Music Association.

Dodge, C., and T. Jerse. 1985. *Computer Music.* New York: Schirmer.

Eckel, G., M. R. Iturbide, and B. Becker. 1995. "The development of GiST, a granular synthesis toolkit based on an extension of the FOF generator." *Proceedings of the International Computer Music Conference.* Banff, Canada: International Computer Music Association, pp. 296–302.

Rodet, X. 1984. "Time-domain formant-wave-function synthesis." *Computer Music Journal* 3: 9–14.

Rodet, X., Y. Potard, and J.-B. Barrière. 1984. "The CHANT project: From the synthesis of the singing voice to synthesis in general." *Computer Music Journal* 3: 15–31.

Truax, B. 1994. "Discovering inner complexity: time-shifting and transposition with a real time granulation technique." *Computer Music Journal* 2: 38–48.

15 Processing Samples with Csound's FOF Opcode

Per Byrne Villez

This tutorial presents a practical introduction to the powerful **fof** synthesizer implemented in Csound. It is a practical tour of the unit generator, focusing on some of its most powerful aspects. As with granular synthesis, FOF synthesis allows the sound designer to blur the perception of the listener by changing sound streams from continuous to discrete events and vice versa. In this primer, I have strayed from the pure synthesis aspects of **fof** and incorporated digitized samples. It would be helpful to be familiar with the **fof** syntax, but as long as the reader can compile Csound orchestras and scores he or she will be able to work through the material provided.

To begin with, the examples are kept simple, gradually gaining in complexity and power. By the end of the primer, the user should be acquainted with many versatile FOF techniques. The examples generally aim to synthesize traditional acoustic instruments. They will demonstrate that, by using digitized sound as the input to a **fof** generator, little effort is required to infuse life into an otherwise dull sample loop. This is not exactly technically challenging, but seems to be a problem for most manufacturers of commercial samplers and sample-based synthesizers.

Csound's **fof** opcode, when used with samples, can be used to create realistic acoustic structures with great economy of processing time. With more effort, truly complex textures can be created. This is important for students and experimenters alike, as it allows the speedy compilation of complex timbres with the minimum of coding and memory. Generally, my source samples are mono and only 1 or 2 cycles in duration.

FOF Syntax

The Csound Reference Manual presents the **fof** opcode as follows:

```
ar fof xamp, xfund, xform, koct, kband, kris, kdur, kdec,
       iolaps, ifna, ifnb, itotdur [, iphs[, ifmode]]
```

```
        instr    1501            ; SIMPLE FOF
a1      fof      15000, 440, 800, 0, 80, .003, .02, .007, 50, 1, 2, p3, 0, 0
        out      a1
        endin

f 1       0     4096    10    1
f 2       0     1024    19    .5 .5 270 .5

i 1501    0     10
```

Figure 15.1 Orchestra and score code for *instr 1501,* a simple FOF synthesizer.

The basic orchestra and score shown in figure 15.1 will help describe the syntax of a basic **fof** synthesizer in Csound.

An outline of the **fof** opcode's arguments and a brief description follows:

- *ar*—Output type (audio or a-rate)
- fof—*ugen* call
- *xamp*—Overall amplitude (constant or k-rate)
- *xfnd*—Fundamental frequency of **fof** oscillator or **fof** pulse train (constant or k-rate)
- *xform*—Formant frequency (constant or k-rate)
- *koct*—Octaviation, fundamental octave deviation (A coefficient of zero is the initial octave. A value of 2 is 2 octaves down. 3.7 is an octave and a fifth down (constant or k-rate).
- *kband*—Bandwidth of the formant in Hz (constant or k-rate)
- *kris*—Attack of **fof** grain envelope (constant or k-rate)
- *kdur*—Duration of grain envelope (constant or k-rate)
- *kdec*—Decay of grain envelope (constant or k-rate)
- *iolaps*—Grain overlaps (This is calculated by *xfund*kdur.* This should be rounded up and the effects of any k-rates on the fundamental such as vibrato or jitter must be considered.)
- *ifna*—Function-table (f-table) for formants specified in the score
- *ifnb*—Function-table for grain envelope (*kris, kdur, kdec*), also specified in the score
- *idur*—Duration (If the score specifies a note of 10 seconds and *idur* specifies a value of 7, the **fof** generator will cutoff at 7 seconds. This is useful when allowing a reverb tail to decay without any direct sound.)
- *[iphs]*—Initial phase of the **fof** generator

- *[ifmode]*—Formant mode (A value of 0 causes the *xform* parameter to be altered only on each new **fof** grain, causing the formant frequency to make jumps. A setting of 1 causes this frequency to be altered smoothly without interruption, making possible formant-frequency pitch-bends inside the grain.)

SOUNDIN

Below is the score layout for the **fof** examples presented in this chapter. We will use GEN1 for the sine waves and sample imports and GEN19 for the **fof** grain envelopes.

```
; F#     TIME SIZE  1    FILENAME        SKIPTIME FORMAT CHANNEL
f 1      0    32768 1    "tambura.aif"   0        0      0
f 19     0    1024  19   .5              .5       270    .5
; p1     p2   p3    p4
i 1502   0    5     155
```

Where:

- *f #*—a label to identify the f-table number
- *time*—the action time of the f-table in beats
- *size*—the number of sample frames in the table (This will be discussed in more detail further on in the tutorial. The number of samples and the base pitch of the digitized sound are related.)
- *1*—the f-table has been post normalized, –1 means prenormalized or skip the normalization process
- *filename*—the name of the sample file to be input (Make sure that the filename is surrounded by double quotes.)
- *skiptime*—where you want the sample to start playing from, in milliseconds (The skiptime is important when trying to get a clean cycle of the sample into the **fof** granule; bad settings can lead to unwanted harmonics at high **fof** fundamentals and clicks at lower pitches. Experiment with altering this parameter to achieve the cleanest result. It can be used to create movement within a sound by having two channels out of phase with each other, or alternatively to break up a speech sample or such into separate regions, without having to go outside of Csound.)
- *format*—a value of 0 means "take the sample file format information from the header" of the sample
- *channel*—the channel number to read into the table

Our score parameters are as follows:

- *p1*—instrument number: *instr 1502*
- *p2*—instrument start time in seconds: *0*
- *p3*—instrument duration in seconds: *5*
- *p4*—FOF fundamental pitch in Hertz: *155*

Tambura Example

The first processing example is constructed using a short sample from an East Indian instrument called the tambura. The tambura is a 4-stringed drone instrument in the bass register used in Indian classical music (figure 15.2).

The wave is not particularly simple in its spectral content, but demonstrates how a short snippet of sound can be looped effectively and smoothly. There is an important relationship between the number of samples in the table and the original sampling rate of the digitized sound. In the above example, the user will have noticed that the number of samples is 32768. This is because the original sampling rate of the sample Tambura.aif is 22050 Hz at 16 bits. For a sampling rate of 44100 Hz that number would be doubled to 65536:

```
f 1     0     32768     1     "tambura.aif"      0 0 0
```

This relationship maintains the original pitch of the sample. If the above example is compiled, the reader will not fail to notice that, even though the resulting timbre has a smooth loop, it has little or no sonic interest whatsoever; it is completely lifeless. There are various ways in which we could animate the tambura. To realize this, we modify the formant frequency parameter, *xform:*

```
a1   fof    5000, p4, 1, 0, 0, .003, .02, .005, 20, 1, 19, p3, 0, 1
```

```
        instr      1502         ; FOF THAT PROCESSES A TAMBURA SAMPLE
a1      fof        5000, p4, 1, 0, 0, .003, .02, .005, 20, 1, 19, p3, 0, 1
        out        a1
        endin

f 1      0     32768     1     "tambura.aif"       0 0 0
f 19     0     1024      19    .5 .5 270 .5

i 1502   0     8         155
```

Figure 15.2 Orchestra and score code for *instr 1502,* an instrument that does FOF processing of a Tambura sample.

Figure 15.3 Formant frequency.

Altering the formant pitch by using the formant frequency parameter in the orchestra, instead of using the number of samples in the score has the advantage of allowing the parameter to be treated as a variable instead of a constant and consequently, allowing the production of frequency domain effects such as frequency modulation (FM), chorusing, delay and flanging. It works in the following way.

A quantity of 1 will produce the sample's base pitch and 1 cycle of the sample per grain. Notice I did not say *fit,* the latter would depend on the **fof** grain envelope parameters. Setting the value to 2 would produce an octave above the base pitch and therefore 2 cycles of the sample per grain. This logic of pitch unity applies upward and not downward (e.g., 0.5) and it does not necessarily have to be a natural integer. It could be a floating point number with a fractional part.

By using **linseg** or **expseg** envelopes, we can gradually change the formant frequency. Doing this modifies the resonant qualities of the timbre against the fundamental, thus animating the sound:

```
ktwist   linseg  1, p3*.7, 1.2, p3*.2, 1.1, p3*.1, 1
```

This produces a formant frequency gradation from 1 to 1.2, to 1.1, to 1, whereas before we had the static value of 1:

```
a1  fof  5000, ifq, 1, 0, 0, .003, .02, .005, 20, 1, 19, idur, 0 , 1
```

Now we substitute *ktwist* for *1* and we get:

```
a1  fof  5000, ifq, ktwist, 0, 0, .003, .02, .005, 20, 1, 19, idur, 0, 1
```

The finalized version of the Tambura processing instrument can be found in *1503.orc* and *1503.sco.* It develops the techniques shown above and creates a realistic acoustic model of the Tambura including a typical musical pattern.

Far more dramatic results can be obtained by changing the range of *ktwist* as in *1504.orc* and *1504.sco,* which takes the waveform from an analog synthesizer (*analog.aif*) and modulates the formant pitch with a fairly steep frequency envelope, multiplying the base formant with a range from 36 to 1. The effect is similar to a resonating lowpass filter with a tight Q (resonance) and could be used as a quick way to produce classic analog textures. Using this process, however, has the effect of decreasing the amplitude as the formant frequency rises. Some form of compensation is needed and the next example does just this. If the reader does decide to go for higher multiples of the formant frequency, he or she must make sure that the sampling rate can handle the resulting aliasing generated by such a process.

Juice Bottle Example

We have seen that dramatic modulation effects can be produced by changing the formant frequency. Not all samples respond in this way, however. The recording of a blown plastic juice bottle was patched into the following Csound instrument:

```
f 1     0    65536    1     "bottle.aif"    0 0 0
f 2     0    65536    1     "bottle.aif"    .01 0 0
```

Note that *f 2* is the same as *f 1,* except for the *skiptime,* which starts 0.01 seconds later. Because *f 1* is used in the left channel and *f 2* in the right channel, we have just created a phase difference between them. This changes the timbral characteristics of the overall sound, thinning it out as such. It is as if we had applied subtle equalization to the overall timbre as can be heard in *1505.orc* and *1505.sco.*

Again, because the main objective was to recreate the acoustics of the original instrument, a classic FOF synthesis technique is employed.

Jitter

Jitter is useful for recreating the random fluctuations of pitch found in human singing and acoustic instrument playing. It can be safely said that there are not many performers who can keep a truly steady pitch on a sustained note. In fact, this is one element that makes music more "human." To imitate this, the **randi** random signal generator is employed to modulate the **fof** fundamental:

```
k50         randi         .01, 1/.05, .8135
k60         randi         .01, 1/.111, .3111
k70         randi         .01, 1/1.219, .6711
kjitter     =             (k50+k60+k70)*p4
```

The displacement and rate of change are just enough to promote the desired effect and even though it is not truly a random modulation, it is sufficient for the purpose of experimentation. The random signal generator is useful for a variety of textures. It can be used to dismantle any sense of fundamental (3 to 30 Hz with displacements of a quartertone upward) as shown in the files *1506.orc* and *1506.sco.* It can also create the breathy noises (rates and displacements of 200 Hz and .4 of an octave respectively) found in the files *1507.orc* and *1507.sco* and as we shall see later, it can be used to create huge sonic washes.

Envelope *kblow* is used to control the overall pitch of the fundamental. It begins at 1 Hz so that the attack portion of the blown bottle can be distinguished from the sustained part of the sound. It then proceeds to the actual fundamental specified in the score.

```
kblow   linseg    1, p3*.02, 1, p3*.02, ifq, p3*.96, ifq
```

The arguments *kdur* and *kdec* control the amplitude characteristics of the **fof** granule. They allow the initial attack of breath on the bottle to be heard. Subsequently these synchronize with *kblow*, halving the envelope duration from 1 second to 0.5.

```
kdur    linseg    1, p3*.02, 1, p3*.02, .5, p3*.96, .5
kdec    linseg    1, p3*.02, 1, p3*.02, .5, p3*.96, .5
```

Overlaps

There is a special relationship between the fundamental, *kdur and overlaps.* Setting these incorrectly can lead to longer processing times, or much worse, the computer crashing outright. Overlaps are worked out with the following arithmetic:

*overlaps = fundamental * kdur*

The example in question requires 123.47 Hz, times the maximum *kdur,* 1. This totals 124 overlaps. Still, it is not that simple, we have not yet taken into account the effects of *kjitter* on the fundamental. This has been summed with *kblow* to form *kf0:*

```
kf0     =         kblow+kjitter
```

Therefore it is safer to be generous and allocate 150 overlaps:

```
a1   fof   kenv, kf0, ktwist, 0, 0, .003, kdur, kdec, 150, 1, 19, p3, 0 , 1
a2   fof   kenv, kf0, ktwist2, 0, 0, .003, kdur, kdec, 150, 2, 19, p3, 0, 1
```

A Room in a Box

Subtle artificial room ambiance is an effect that demands a lot of Csound coding. The sweeping effects produced in the *tambura* (*1503.orc)* and *analog* (*1504.orc)* examples worked well because they contained rich upper harmonics. The effect on smoother timbres is far more subtle. "Air" is produced around the instrument, similar to the result of a good microphone technique or the use of an ambient program from an expensive digital reverberator. This is the result of phase differences set in the score's f-tables, together with the motions of *ktwist* and *ktwist2* gradually deviating the original formant pitch. The gradually changing formant pitches and the amount of wavetable within each **fof** grain create this spatial blurring. Consequently, the sound becomes thinner and more open, receding into the distance.

Choir Example

The sample in the following example uses the English word *or* spoken by a seven year old boy. Besides the clash of the sample's fundamental and the **fof** fundamental, the resulting timbre is fairly simple as in *1508.orc* and *1508.sco.* Now compile the files *1509.orc* and *1509.sco.* The multiple voice effect is the result of the jitter technique used previously, but in a new dimension. We saw how artificial imperfections could be reproduced in a digital timbre by the use of artificial randomness. It is this lack of dirt that makes so much computer animation look like, well, computer animation. The files *1509.orc* and *1509.sco* use a faster modulation frequency. Before, we were modulating the fundamental at approximately 20 Hz with a fairly small pitch deviation. Now we are using rates of between 110 and 122 Hz with a displacement of .03 of an octave:

```
k50        rand       .03, 110, .8135
k60        randi      .03, 122, .5111
k70        randi      .03, 104, .6711
kjitter    =          (k50+k60+k70)*p4
```

The resulting sound is a swarming choir cluster from only two modulated **fof** oscillators. The extra movement is produced by gliding the fundamental between the ranges of 49 Hz and 53 Hz, using two further envelopes:

```
kfund1     linseg  50, p3*.5, 49, p3*.5, 50
kfund2     linseg  51, p3*.5, 53, p3*.5, 51
```

For a further example of *choralization*, compare the previous instrument with the files *1504.orc* and *1504.sco.* They are the same, except that the latter uses the analog wave presented earlier. Clearly, this is a richer variation of the analog sweep presented earlier.

Octaviation

The next example uses the same sample as employed in the previous instrument. As in the files that processed the bottle sample, the fundamental has been kept at 1 Hz for part of the sound duration, it then glides up toward the fundamental *ifq*, perceived in the score at 149 Hz:

```
kfund  linseg   1, p3*.04, 1, p3*.3, ifq, p3*.66, ifq
```

Now, compare the above with the following example, *1511.orc* and *1511*.sco. It sounds similar to the files *1510.orc* and *1510.sco,* yet it uses a different parameter altogether. It is called *octaviation* and is one of the most powerful **fof** devices. Basic octaviation gradually removes or introduces every other granule in the **fof** "pulse-train," or fundamental.

```
koct linseg 7, p3*.04, 7, p3*.3, 0, p3*.66, 0
a1   fof    kenv, kf0, kforms, koct, 0, .003, kdur, kdec, 150, 1, 19, p3, 0, 1
```

The line starting *koct* substitutes the line starting with *kfund.* The parameter represents how many octaves to deviate from the original octave, 0. In this case it starts 7 octaves down at 1.1640625 Hz, the nearest to the previous example's 1 Hz and moves to the 0th octave at 149 Hz. The multiple voices are due to long **fof** grains overlapping each other. This is caused by opening the **fof** grain's amplitude envelopes to 1 second (usually only 20 ms). This is long enough to smear new grains over existing ones.

Octaviation as Disintegration

The most-well known **fof** *octaviation* "trick" allows the sound stream to "evaporate" in front of the listener. The following example, *1512.orc* and *1512.sco* does just this. Here, the singing voice evaporates into drops of water. This file is different from the others, in that, not only is it more complex but it also takes the pure synthesis approach to **fof**.

I started by analyzing recordings of a singing style originating in Tuva, Siberia and Mongolia, which is similar to some Buddhist chants. At a workshop I attended some years ago, I was told by a Mongolian singer that the technique originated from Mongolian shepherds, who copied the sound of the wind whistling and howling

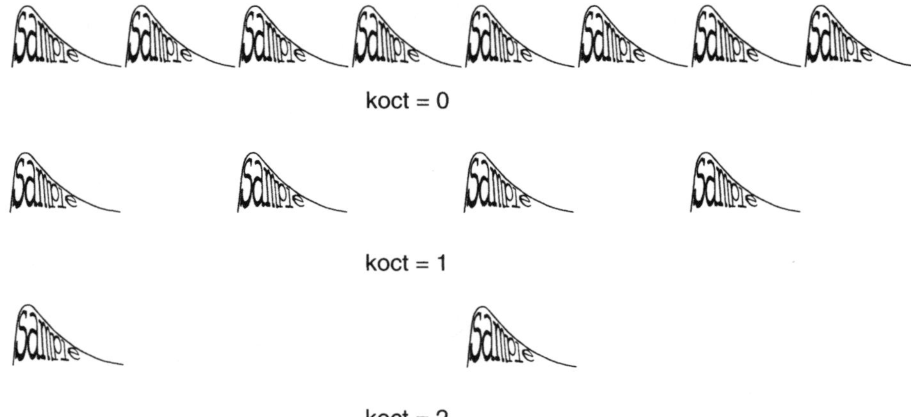

Figure 15.4 Octaviation.

between the mountain crevices. The singing style is called *sygyt* or *khoomei*. Melodies are sung by reinforcing resonances within the singers nasal cavities. The effect can be best described as a mid-range vocal drone with a piercing melody "whistled" on top.

Five different **fof** oscillators are used to create the necessary formants. This is the usual number employed for good vowel imitation. Two of the formants are controlled by formant amplitude and pitch-shifting envelopes:

Formant level envelopes in (-dB's * –1)

```
kflvl    linseg   7.8, p3*.05, 7.8, p3*.05, 12.4, p3*.2, 12.4,
                  p3*.05, 7.8, p3*.05, 7.8, p3*.1, 12.4, p3*.4,
                  12.4
kflvl2   linseg   21.9, p3*.05, 21.9, p3*.05, 16.9, p3*.2, 16.9,
                  p3*.05, 21.9, p3*.05, 21.9, p3*.1, 16.9,
                  p3*.4, 16.9
```

Singing formants envelopes (Hz)

```
ksing1   linseg   953, p3*.05, 953, p3*.05, 1252, p3*.2, 1252,
                  p3*.05, 953, p3*.05, 953, p3*.1, 1252, p3*.4,
                  1252
ksing2   linseg   2552, p3*.05, 2552, p3*.05, 2495, p3*.2, 2495,
                  p3*.05, 2552, p3*.05, 2552, p3*.1, 2495,
                  p3*.4, 249
```

The *octaviation* is carried out by a further envelope to take the fundamental down in octave steps, from the frequency 108 Hz (0) to 0.4218 Hz (8).

```
koct     linseg  0, (p3-3)*.5, 0, (p3-3)*.2, 6, (p3-3)*.3, 8
```

As the fundamentals of each **fof** begin to *octaviate,* they are desynchronized by individual envelopes, which create disparate sound streams, just like individual drops of water. This is done by multiplying the fundamental by a constantly changing variable, in the case of *a1,* from 1 to 1.1.

```
kd1       linseg    1, p3*.3, 1, p3*.7, 1.1
kfreq1    =         kfq*kd1
a1        fof       kamp1, kfreq1, 317, koct, 80, .003, .02,
                    .007, 50, 1, 2, ip3, 0, 1
```

Normalization

One important feature of this exercise is to normalize the output levels. Details like this are important when working with complex instruments. Often, the user cannot predict what the overall effect of summing individual oscillator levels might be. The numerical complexity in effecting this is great. Yet there is an elegant way to get around it and in our example it is implemented in the following way:

- Csound's maximum output is 32000. We use this number as a constant *kconst*=32000.
- Change all minus signs to positive. The 5 formant levels in our example are 12, *kflvl, kflvl2,* 26.9 and 45.1 (as we saw earlier, *kfvl* and *kfvl2* are envelopes that gradually change levels).
- Divide 1 over the sum of all the available levels and assign to this result a *klabel:*

```
knorm    =       1/(12+kflvl+kflvl2+26.9+45.1)
```

- Individually multiply each level by *kconst* (32000) and multiply this result by *knorm:*

```
kamp1    =       (kconst*12)*knorm
```

Include this arithmetic in your instruments and your soundfiles will always be at their maximum level, without distortion.

Finally, to add a sparkle to this drama we add some reverb, by using *nreverb.* Complexity can be added to the signal by using two separate summed reverbs.

Route *a6* through two different reverb settings.

```
ar1   nreverb   a6, 10, 0          ; REVERB GENERATOR 1
ar10  nreverb   a6, 7, 1           ; REVERB GENERATOR 2
```

Add these together and output *a6* with a degree of the reverb:

```
ar100   =       ar1+ar
        out     a6+(ar100*.03)
```

To allow the reverberation tail to decay after the **fof** generator, 3 seconds have been subtracted from its *idur,* to force it to close 3 seconds earlier than specified by *p2* in the score. This is simply done by subtracting the tail length required, in seconds, from the appropriate parameter.

```
koct  linseg  0, (p3-3)*.5, 0, (p3-3)*.2, 6, (p3-3)*.3, 8
ip3   =       p3-3
a1    fof     kamp1, kfreq1, 317, koct, 80, .003, .02, .007, 50,
              1, 2, ip3, 0, 1
```

Finally, a third of the treated signal *ar* (100*.03) is added to the **fof** signal *a6.*

Summary

Further possibilities can be explored using the techniques described in this chapter; re-harmonization, re-melodification, sample amplitude control, FM, striated changes to the formant frequency by changing *ifmode.* Furthermore, the recently implemented **fof2** opcode allows further control over elements like the phase of the sample. This should permit time randomization and stretching. From the simplicity of the first example to the relative complexity of the latter, the reader will be more aware of the possibilities presented in using samples inside **fof** grains. I hope I have encouraged users to experiment further in this direction.

References

Jaffe, D. A. 1995. "Ten criteria for evaluating synthesis techniques." *Computer Music Journal* 19(1): 76–78.

Rodet, X. 1984. "Time-domain formant-wave-function synthesis." *Computer Music Journal* 8(3): 8–14.

Rodet, X., Y. Potard, and Jean-Baptiste Barrière. "The CHANT project: from the synthesis of the voice to synthesis in general." *Computer Music Journal* 8(3): 15–31.

Mathematical Models

16 A Look at Random Numbers, Noise, and Chaos with Csound

John ffitch

Random numbers are useful compositional and sound design aids. In this chapter we consider the various random number generators available in Csound and with a minimal amount of mathematics, we consider the ways in which they could be used in a sonic design context.

When a mathematician uses the term *random* it has a precise meaning—that it is not possible to predict the value before it is obtained. In fact, there are ways of testing a series of values to see if they are truly random. This is not necessarily the definition used by other people. The Oxford English Dictionary considers randomness to be more concerned with lack of purpose, but captures the same essence. The critical feature is that while a random event may not be predictable as a single action, there are things that can be said about a sufficient number of such random events.

The major idea in considering a random value is that of a "distribution." If we continue to obtain random numbers by some mechanism, we can count the number of times we get a number on the ranges of 0 to 10, 10 to 20 and so forth. It is sometimes useful to see this process as placing the numbers in buckets labeled with each range. If we plot a graph, where for each bucket we draw a bar proportional in height to the number of times we got a number in that bucket, we will begin to see a *distribution.* Such a graph is called a *histogram.* To get the true mathematical model, we have to shrink the range for each bucket and increase the number of values we take.

An alternative way of thinking about this is that there is a large collection of potential values that we are just sampling (called technically the population) and the distribution is just a way of saying how many numbers of each value there are in this collection; what we are doing is to take samples from this collection. Many uses of statistics are concerned with estimating what the distribution is from a sample; common examples are opinion polls and market research. A distribution has to be normalized, as in the description above we have talked about taking larger and larger numbers of sample values. The normalization is used to make the area under the curve equal to 1 and so the area bounded by the curve and two particular values of x is the probability that a value chosen at random from the population will fall between these two values of x.

We can see now that there are a large number of methods of obtaining random values, depending on the shape of the distribution graph. Of course, to make use of this discussion there has to be a way in which we can obtain random numbers. Strictly speaking, within a deterministic computer this is impossible. Lottery systems, for example, use noncomputational processes and we have to rely on an approximation called pseudo-random numbers. This is considered later in the chapter.

There are many uses of such statistics in music; a common one being the analysis of the chorales of J.S.Bach in order to determine what progressions of notes are characteristic of that composer. Then a score generation technique could be based on these distributions of the next note, using a Markov chain algorithm. Within the Csound context we are more interested in the use of random values drawn from a known distribution. These are considered in this chapter.

A large number of people have attempted to create musical scores by deciding on the next note by some random process. In general, this leads to tunes that are aimless and have no direction. However it need not be like this. With careful choices of the underlying distribution and subtle use of the values, it is possible to generate interesting and meaningful music. Seminal here is Iannis Xenakis, who has frequently used stochastic processes (random numbers) in his music (Xenakis 1992).

Uniform Distribution

The simplest distribution is the uniform distribution, when every value in a range is equally likely. The graph of the distribution is just a rectangle (figure 16.1).

1/(xmax-xmin)

In Csound there are two ways in which one can use this distribution. The simplest version is the opcode **rand**. In its audio format it generates values at audio rate with the value *xmin* being the negation of *xmax* and range being a specified amplitude.

```
ar   rand  1000
```

The **rand** opcode above would generate "white noise;" that is, noise with all frequencies equally likely, with an energy of $1000/\sqrt{2}$. Such noise is a rich source for filtering in subtractive synthesis. For example, *instr 1601* takes white noise and filters it to a band of frequencies centered on 333 Hz.

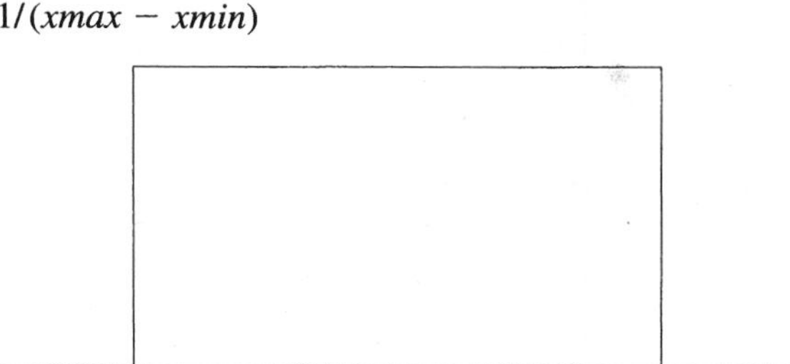

Figure 16.1 Uniform distribution.

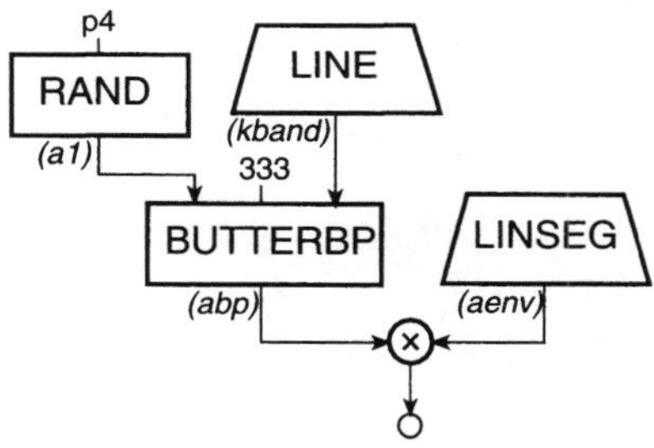

Figure 16.2 Block diagram of *instr 1601,* a subtractive synthesizer using white noise as input.

```
        instr      1601    ; FILTERED NOISE WITH "DECLICKING" ENVELOPE
kband   line       p5, p3, p6
aenv    linseg     0, p3*.01, 1, p3*.8, .6, p3*.1, 0
a1      rand       p4
abp     butterbp   a1, 333, kband
        out        abp*aenv
        endin
```

Figure 16.3 Orchestra code for *instr 1601,* filtered noise with a "declicking" envelope.

In order to create a clean start and stop, it is useful to add a "de-clicking" envelope, which removes any sudden amplitude jumps. Random sequences may start and stop at any amplitude value, which will lead to clicking if not considered carefully.

This could be used, for example, to generate 7 seconds of white noise, which adds an increasingly wide frequency band.

```
i 1601  0  7   30000     0       666
```

There is of course a k-rate version of this opcode and other versions of the uniformly distributed random number generator that generate random numbers at a slower rate than the sampling rate, with interpolation (**randi**) or holding of values (**randh**).

Normal Distribution

The distribution associated with a particular random process can be any curve for which the area below it is 1 and so there are a large number of possible types of random numbers. In fact, there is one particular shape of a distribution that occurs frequently. It is called the *normal distribution,* the *bell curve,* and sometimes the *Gaussian distribution.* This particular shape appears in a large number of physical situations; we will consider just one.

If one tosses a single coin, then there are only two outcomes, it lands heads or tails, ignoring the extremely unlikely case of staying on its edge. With an unbiased coin there is an equal chance of a head or a tail. Now toss the coin twice; there are four possibilities, which we can summarize as HH, HT, TH, and TT. If we award a score of $+1$ to a head and a -1 to a tail, we can expect the most likely score to be zero, but $+2$ and -2 are possible. If we toss the coin four times we would still get zero as the most likely value, but there is a chance of other values. This distribution is called the *binomial distribution* and is a discrete function, depending on the number of times we toss the coin. If we continue this tossing of the coin and remember the average score, we would expect the answer to be zero, or very close, but many other values can happen. As the number of coin tosses tends to infinity, this process converges to the normal distribution. The curve can be described mathematically as $exp(-x^2)/sqrt(2\pi)$ and looks as shown in figure 16.4, where the tails of the distribution get arbitrarily close to zero as $|x|$ gets large. The division by sqrt(2π) is needed to ensure that the total area under the curve is 1, as required for a distribution that gives probabilities. In fact, there is a family of these bell curves based on the spread of the curve. We cannot describe this by where the curve reaches zero, since it never does. Instead the spread of the curve must be described by such things as the value

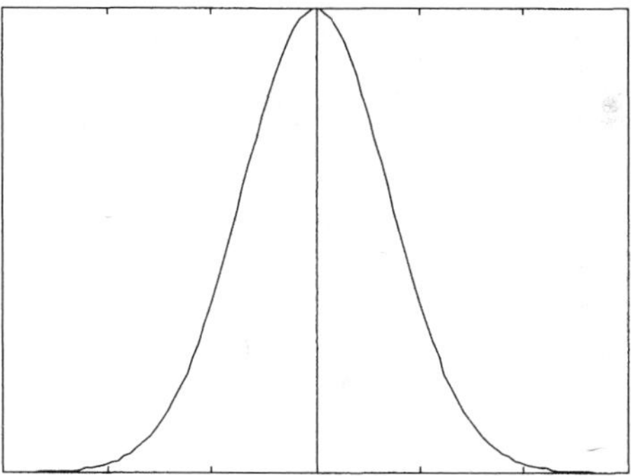

Figure 16.4 Gaussian distribution.

of x, for which half the area lies in the range −x to *x*. The commonest descriptions of the spread of the normal distribution, or indeed any distribution, are called the *variance,* calculated as the sum of the squares of the distance from the average value as:

$$\int^2 (x - mean) f(x) dx \qquad (16.1)$$

As this value is the product of two distances it represents an area; for many uses a distance is preferred as a measure of the spread of the curve and so the *standard deviation* which is the square root of the variance is defined, usually represented by σ. The standard deviation is dimensionally a distance and so is a direct way of talking about the spread of the curve. For practical purposes all the area under the curve is within 3 standard deviations of the symmetry point.

This Gaussian distribution is extremely useful when we want values that concentrate on a special value, with increasingly less chance of being a long way away. A simple application would be in a flexible chorusing effect. In *instr 1602* a single pure tone is generated at 333 Hz and then thickened by the addition of a second sine wave on each channel at a frequency displaced by a random value drawn from the Gaussian distribution. On each control period the additional frequency is adjusted. As we are using the opcode **gauss** the values are zero on average and are much more likely to be small than large. The parameter to the **gauss** opcode is a measure of the spread of the bell-curve, the practical maximum value it can give.

In this case the additional pitch could be in the range of 300 to 366 Hz, but most likely will be closer to 333 Hz. The inspiration for this idea is the typical chorusing effect, but instead of using fixed frequencies, each voice is attempting to sing the correct pitch and is missing and then adjusting. The stereo effects on headphones can be quite striking.

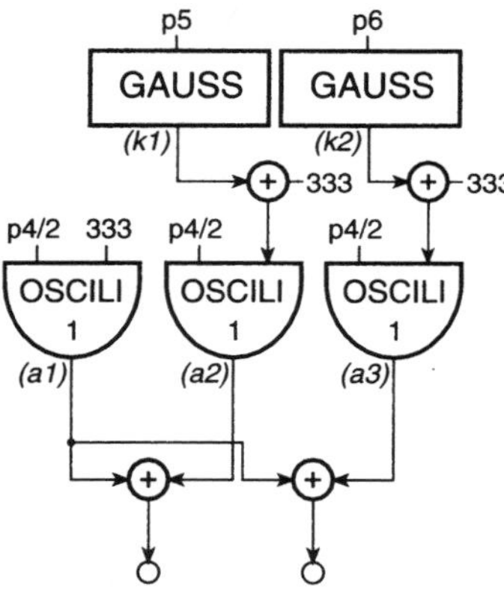

Figure 16.5 Block diagram of *instr 1602,* a chorusing instrument with Gaussian "blur."

```
     instr   1602     ; ADDITIVE WITH "GAUSSIAN" FREQUENCY DEVIATION
k1   gauss   p5
k2   gauss   p6
a1   oscili  p4/2, 333, 1
a2   oscili  p4/2, 333+k1, 1
a3   oscili  p4/2, 333+k2, 1
     outs    a1+a2, a1+a3
     endin

f 1        0  8192   10       1

i 1602     0  2      10000    33    33
i 1602     +  .      15000    33    33
i 1602     +  .      20000    33    33
```

Figure 16.6 Orchestra and score code for *instr 1602,* an additive instrument with chorusing featuring Gaussian deviation of center frequency around 333 Hz.

This particular distribution for random variables appears in almost all cases that involve averaging and so is a good model of errors. For that reason this is also sometimes called the *error curve.* It describes, for example, the horizontal distance from the center that arrows fall when shot at a target, that is, the horizontal error in the shot; the breadth of the distribution is a measure of how good the archer is. Many teachers see this distribution, or a similar one, in examination marks.

It is important to realize that probability is concerned with what we *expect* to happen before the event, not what has happened. Just because we see a value far away from the average, in a Gaussian distribution, we should not think something has gone wrong with the process or model. Until we have attempted a large number of tests, or had a large number of parallel universes, we will not see the true distribution. This concept is captured by the *Law of Large Numbers,* which informally says that the more tests we run the better the approximation we will see to the underlying distribution. This does affect the manner in which Csound calculates the binomial distribution. In fact, the Csound algorithm uses the rectangular distribution and averaging. This will be discussed in more detail below. It is necessary to realize, however, that the calculations are only approximate. In particular, although all values between $-\infty$ and $+\infty$ are theoretically possible in a true Gaussian distribution, the Csound algorithm cannot generate a random value outside the range specified by the k-rate argument.

The Exponential and Poisson Distributions

Both the distributions described in the first section above are symmetric, that is, values above and below the average are equally likely. Not all distributions are like this. We will consider the Poisson process, which is a model of how long one has to wait for something to happen. In a Poisson process, each incident is independent of previous incidents.

Consider some event that has a fixed chance of happening in the next minute, such as catching a fish, or one's bus arriving. If we assume that the probability is independent of which minute it is (that is, we are ignoring rush hours in the bus example) then we could ask how long do we have to wait, or the probability that a bus will arrive in a fixed period.

A simple example can be seen by returning to the coin tossing. We decide to toss the coin until it shows a heads and we will do this a number of times. Each attempt is called a *trial.* We know that the chance for each toss is 1 in 2 (50%) but long runs of tails are possible. Clearly in about half the times we try, we expect to get the head on the first toss. If we get the required result, we finish the trial. If it is a tail, however, we toss again and in half of the second throws we expect a head, which is a quarter of all trials. We can draw a picture of this distribution in the same way that we did for the normal distribution. It will fall away from an initial peak. This is called the *exponential distribution.* If we do the same process, but we are considering a continuous process, such as catching the fish, a similar shape will occur, but it will depend, in detail, on the skill of the fisherman, which translates into the chance of catching a fish in the next minute.

The mathematical form of this curve is $a*exp(-ax)$. We are only concerned with positive x. The parameter a is an encoding of the chance (or fisherman's skill). The average time we have to wait is $1/a$.

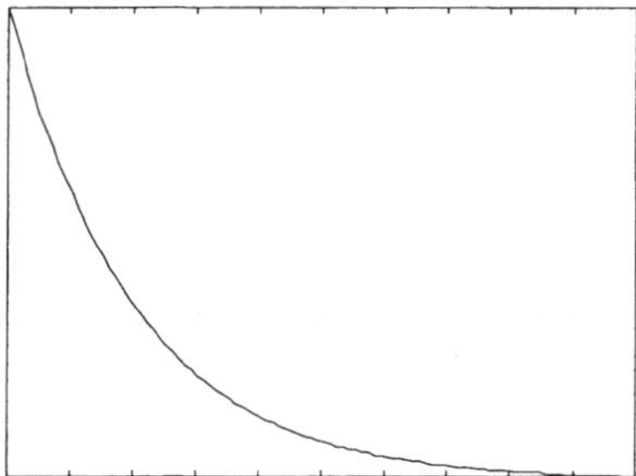

Figure 16.7 Exponential distribution.

The other related question is to ask how long we have to wait for a certain number of events to occur, each one of which is independent of the others and equally likely. This is slightly different from the earlier distributions in that it is a discrete one—it only makes sense for the integer values. This model is described by the Poisson distribution, in which the chance of getting the number n is given by the equation $exp(\lambda)*(\lambda^n)/n$. The average value of this distribution is lambda and the shape is somewhat like that shown in figure 16.8.

If we consider a fisherman who catches fish at a random rate of a, then the number of fish we would expect him to catch in a time t is given by the Poisson distribution with $\lambda = at$.

Musical applications of these ideas are numerous, from modeling small fluctuations within a single note of an instrument to large scale uses of score generation. Both distributions are available in a Csound orchestra.

```
kexp      exprand      krange
aexp      exprand      krange
kpoi      poisson      klambda
apoi      poisson      klambda
```

In the case of the Poisson distribution the k-rate parameter is the same as the parameter λ in the above. For the exponential distribution the *krange* parameter is actually $6.9078/a$, as we could only expect 1 value in 1000 to be above this value (and indeed the Csound implementation cannot get values above it).

A useful metaphor that can guide the use of random values within a score is that of the way in which a crowd behaves. Xenakis describes how in a political demonstration each individual person behaves in an individual way, but is influenced by higher level forces. For example, if one person starts to chant a slogan, there is a chance that it will be picked up by others. Each event of a song starting will either

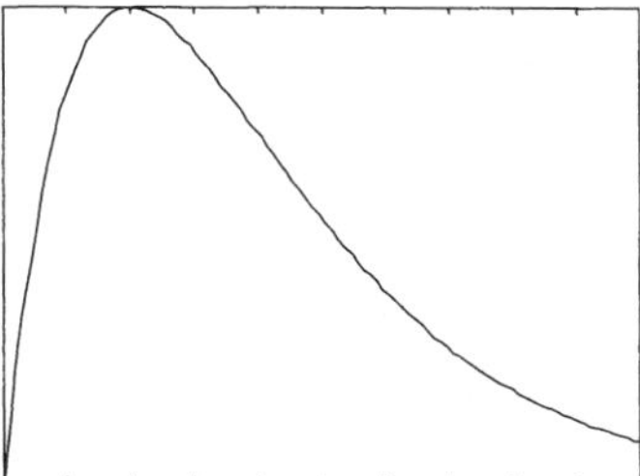

Figure 16.8 The Poisson distribution.

die out if insufficient people join in, or will grow until it becomes the collective action of the crowd. The crowd moves as individuals, but with an average motion toward the goal. We can use this metaphor to control musical movement to a climax and to control when individual voices join in a new idea.

Xenakis takes this process to great lengths, postulating stochastic processes to generate all aspects of the music, pitch, timbre, speed, amplitude and note density. A stochastic process is one in which all transitions are governed by random values drawn from suitable distributions.

Csound provides all the distributions mentioned in this chapter so far, as well as triangular distributions, Cauchy distributions, Weibull distributions, and the Beta distribution. The shapes of these distributions are shown in figures 16.9 and 16.10. The detailed reasons why these distributions are studied are beyond this introductory text. The triangle is clearly useful when one wants values concentrated on a central value with a finite spread of values and can be used as roles similar to the Gaussian distribution, as can the Cauchy distribution, which has more values away from the peak than does the Gaussian curve.

The Weibull distribution, $t*x^{(t-1)}*exp(-(x/s)^t)/s^t$, is quite variable in shape depending on the parameter t. For $t = 1$ this is the same as the exponential distribution. For values of t between 0 and 1 it has a concentration of probability toward zero. As t gets larger, a hump appears looking like a distorted bell curve. The hump gets more pronounced for larger t. Clearly the Weibull distribution could be used to make smooth transitions between exponential and Gaussian distributions. The parameter s just scales the horizontal spread (figure 16.11).

The final distribution that is available within Csound is the Beta distribution. The interesting cases are when the two parameters, a and b, are both less than 1, then the distribution has its large values at the ends of the graph and is small in the middle. It gives a distribution where one end or the other is the most likely value but the transition is smooth. The parameters control the relative likelihood of the end points. The

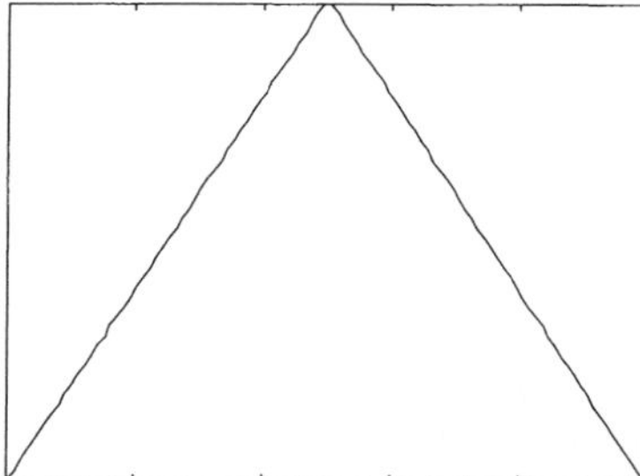

Figure 16.9 Triangular distribution.

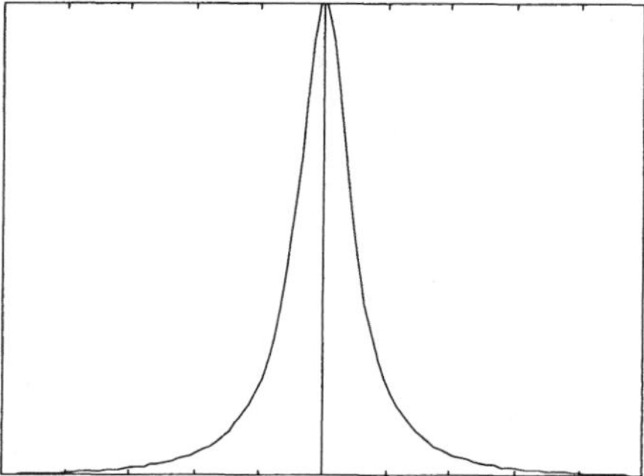

Figure 16.10 Cauchy distribution.

parameter a controls likelihood at zero and b at 1. The smaller the parameter the more concentration there is on the related end point (figure 16.12).

Pseudo-Random Numbers and their Calculation

A sequence of numbers is said to be random if the knowledge of the sequence so far gives no clue as to the next number in the sequence. Unfortunately when we are using computers we can only create a sequence of numbers by an algorithm or program and that is a deterministic process. The next number can be found from this program and so the sequence cannot be truly random.

The simple solution to this conundrum is the pseudo-random number sequence. This is a deterministic sequence, but if one does not inspect the algorithm and only looks at the output, it is extremely difficult to see the pattern. There is indeed a

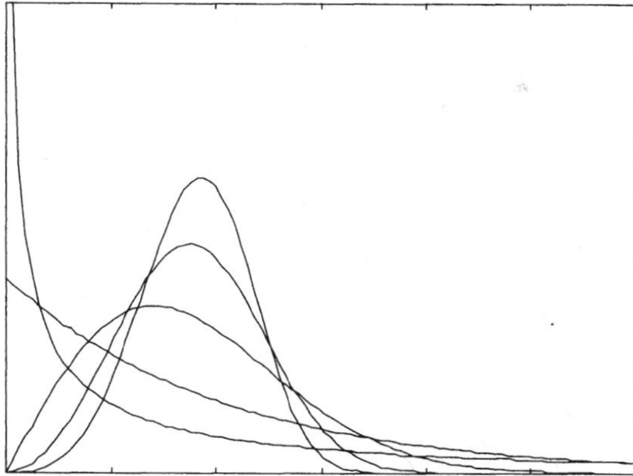

Figure 16.11 Weibull.

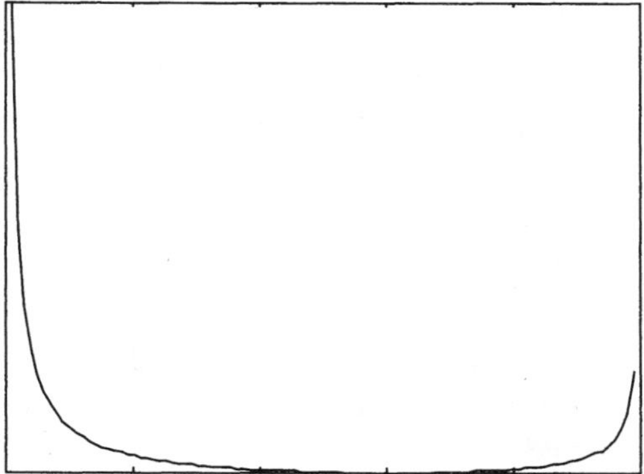

Figure 16.12 Beta distribution (a=0.2, b=0.4).

large body of mathematical literature in suggesting methods for generating pseudo-random numbers, but most rely on a simple recurrence relation, with well chosen parameters. Do not be misled into thinking that arbitrary programs will do instead; there are serious mathematical problems here.

For example, in ANSI Standard C there is a suggested sequence for 32 bit C:

$$x_{n+1} = 1103515245\ x_n + 12345 \tag{16.2}$$

and only the top 16 bits are used. This is usually provided in C so programs can be ported that require random numbers, but in fact it is not a particularly good sequence. There is a better sequence:

$$Xn = (X_{n-24} + X_{n-55}) \bmod 2^{31} \qquad (16.3)$$

with particular initial 55 starting values, but that is not universally available. It seems to have a long cycle before it repeats.

As there is a need for Csound-written pieces to be reproducible, it uses a 16-bit pseudo-random number generator:

$$X_n = 15625\ X_{n-1} + 1 \bmod 2^{16} \qquad (16.4)$$

Again this is not particularly good, in the sense that the sequence fails some of the tests for randomness, but it has been used for many years and composers rely on it.

Whatever sequence is used, they all need at least one initial value, called a *seed.* This can be set to a particular value to create a particular sequence, or a starting value in a long cycle and so allow the recreation of a work even though there is a random element. In Csound this seed can be reset by the opcode **seed**, which affects the sequence of all random variables, except **rand**, **randi** and **randh**. These last three opcodes reset the sequence with an optional argument.

In a pseudo-random sequence there is a way of determining the next value, but it is not very obvious. In a true random sequence, as Max Mathews so eloquently puts it, "only God knows the next number."

Csound's Algorithms for Distributions

The pseudo-random sequence generated by the formula of the previous section give an approximation to a rectangular distribution. In order to create pseudo-random values for other distributions some new techniques are necessary.

As the Gaussian distribution is describable by an averaging process from a uniform distribution, it is possible to derive an algorithm for this distribution by averaging. Csound averages 12 uniform random values, which is an acceptable approximation. The other distributions use similar scaling and averaging algorithms. For example, an exponential distribution can be constructed from the uniform distribution by taking the logarithm of the random variable and there are methods of constructing triangular and other distributions by other simple techniques. The study of random sequences and their construction is one of concern to statisticians and for further information on random variables it is best to consult the literature there.

Adding Noise

One of the problems of synthetic instruments is that they are too "clean" and "sterile" sounding and as such, they lack the impact of physical instruments. Of course one's personal aesthetic may desire such a sound, but for many listeners, the purity of the sound can be a distraction. One solution to this problem is to inject some elements of noise into the instrument. This can be done in a wide variety of ways. Not only do we have the range of different distributions available to us but we can use randomness at various stages of the instrument.

As a simple example of this let us consider a basic frequency modulation bell sound as shown in figures 16.13 and 16.14. There are a number of places where some degree of randomness can be inserted. These range from adding a small random element to the amplitude *aenv,* to randomizing the frequency *amod* and so forth back through the instrument. It is worth experimenting with the different places, as well as different distributions and ranges. This opens a whole field of potential sounds.

In addition, the bell can be given greater impact by adding an initial burst of noise to simulate the action of the physical clanger. This needs to be short. In *instr 1604* as shown in figures 16.15 and 16.16 simple white noise is added and filtered to be related to the bell's frequency. Similarly, when creating wind sounds, some noise to mimic the sound of the breath escaping can add greatly to the creation of a "nonclinical" sound.

Colored Noise

In a similar way to random values coming in different varieties, noise can also be classified. It is usual to assign colors to the more interesting noises. We have already seen that *white noise,* which is where the power density is constant over some finite frequency range, can be generated by random values from a rectangular distribution, as typified by the **rand** opcode. Noise in which the power density decreases 3 dB per octave with increasing frequency (density proportional to 1/f) over a finite frequency range is commonly called *pink noise.* The significant property of this kind of noise is that each octave contains the same amount of *power.*

At the other end of possibilities there is *blue noise,* where the power density increases similarly with frequency with a density proportional to *f.* This kind of noise is said to be good for dithering.

These colors are clearly derived from analogy with the spectrum of color. The other frequently encountered colored noise is *brown noise,* which is in reality not

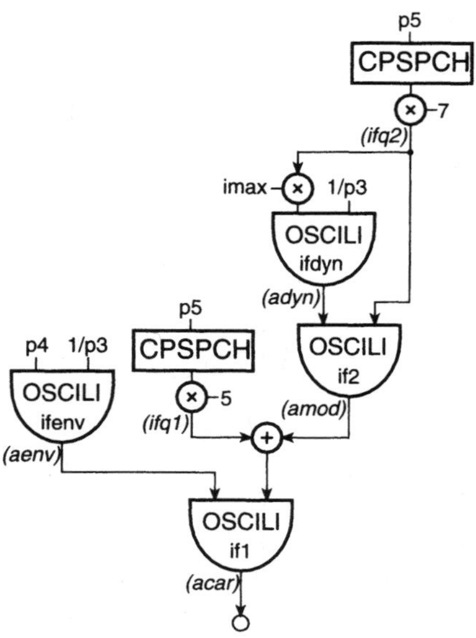

Figure 16.13 Block diagram *instr 1603,* a basic FM instrument.

```
        instr   1603     ; BASIC FM "BELL"
ifenv   =       2                          ; BELL SETTINGS: AMP AND INDEX...
ifdyn   =       3                          ; ...ENVELOPES ARE EXPONENTIAL
ifq1    =       cpspch(p5)*5               ; DECREASING, N1:N2 IS 5:7
if1     =       1                          ; DURATION = 15 SEC
ifq2    =       cpspch(p5)*7
if2     =       1
imax    =       10
aenv    oscili  p4, 1/p3, ifenv            ; ENVELOPE
adyn    oscili  ifq2*imax, 1/p3, ifdyn     ; DYNAMIC
amod    oscili  adyn, ifq2, if2            ; MODULATOR
acar    oscili  aenv, ifq1+amod, if1       ; CARRIER
        out     acar
        endin
```

Figure 16.14 Orchestra code for *instr 1603,* a basic FM "bell" instrument.

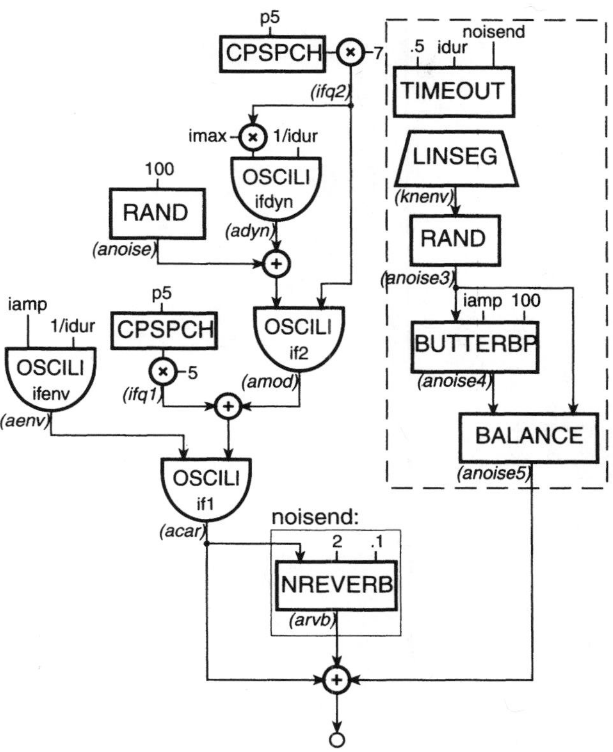

Figure 16.15 Block diagram of *instr 1604,* enhanced FM bell instrument with random variation of various parameters.

related to the color but to Brownian motion (originally the way in which a molecule moves in a fluid and the process responsible for the milk spreading throughout a cup of coffee without stirring). In Brownian noise the power density is proportional to $1/f^2$; this is also the noise of a random walk.

There are claims in the literature that all good music has the distribution of frequencies within the piece like pink noise. While this result is not universally accepted, it could be an interesting area to explore. Unfortunately, calculating pink noise is not particularly easy; if you wish to explore this area, then refer to a standard text on statistics. On the other hand, brown noise can be calculated from white noise, by adding the random values together and using each partial sum as a value.

The algorithm shown in figure 16.17, due to Moore (and following Gardner 1978), will generate a set of 2^n numbers with an approximately pink distribution of frequency.

```
          instr     1604   ; ENHANCED FM "BELL" WITH NOISE BURSTS
idur      =         p3
iamp      =         p4
ifenv     =         2              ; BELL SETTINGS:
ifdyn     =         3              ; AMP AND INDEX ENV ARE EXPONENTIAL
ifq1      =         cpsoct(p5)*5   ; DECREASING, N1:N2 IS 5:7, IMAX=10
if1       =         1              ; DURATION = 15 SEC
ifq2      =         cpsoct(p5)*7
if2       =         1
imax      =         10
aenv      oscili    iamp, 1/idur, ifenv         ; ENVELOPE
adyn      oscili    ifq2*imax, 1/idur, ifdyn    ; DYNAMIC
anoise    rand      100
amod      oscili    adyn+anoise, ifq2, if2      ; MODULATOR
acar      oscili    aenv, ifq1+amod, if1        ; CARRIER
          timout    0.1, idur, noisend
knenv     linseg    iamp, 0.05, iamp, 0.05, 0
anoise3   rand      knenv
anoise4   butterbp  anoise3, iamp, 100
anoise5   balance   anoise4, anoise3
noisend:
arvb      nreverb   acar, 2, .1
amix      =         acar+anoise5+arvb
          out       amix
          endin
```

Figure 16.16 Orchestra code for *instr 1604,* an enhanced FM bell instrument mixed with a filtered noise burst to simulate striker.

```
void pink_seq(int N)
{
        float *r = (float*)malloc(N*sizeof(float));
        int len = 1<<N;   float range = 2.0/(float)N;
        int lastn = len-1;
        int n;
        for (n=0; n<len; n++) {
        float R = 0.0;
        int i;
        for (i=0; i<N; i++) {
        int iup = 1<<i;
        if ((iup & n) != (iup & lastn))
        r[i] = ((float)rand()/(float) RAND_MAX - 0.5) * range;
        R += r[i];
        printf("%f\n", R);
        lastn = n;
        }
}
```

Figure 16.17 Algorithm in C for the generation of "pink" noise.

```
x =                                                    (16.7)
(1/1048576)e⁴ a⁹ cos(9ct)
-(65/1048576)e⁴ a⁹ cos(7ct)
+(335/262144)e⁴ a⁹ cos(5ct)
-(7797/1048576)e⁴ a⁹ cos(3ct)
-(1/32768)e³ a⁷ cos(7ct)
+(43/32768)e³ a⁷ cos(5ct)
-(417/32768)e³ a⁷ cos(3ct)
+(1/1024)e² a⁵ cos(5ct)
-(21/1024)e⁵ a⁵ cos(3ct)
-(1/32)e a³ cos(3ct)
+a cos(ct))
```

Figure 16.18 Periodic solution of equation 16.6.

The Onset of Chaos

There is a class of mathematical processes that are related to randomness, despite being generated by deterministic equations. As a simple example of these processes we consider briefly Duffing's equation:

$$x'' + x = e * x^3 \quad (16.5)$$

where e is a small constant.

If the constant is zero then the solution of this equation is a straightforward cosine function of frequency 1 and so is related to a pure tone. For small e this is a perturbation of the harmonic sound, in fact of a slightly different fundamental frequency and the solution can be expressed in the form of additive synthesis as an overtone series. The new frequency is:

$$c = 1 - (3/8)ea^2 - (15/256)e^2a^4 - (123/8192)e^3a^6 - (921/262144)e^4a^8 + \quad (16.6)$$

and the periodic solution to the equation is as shown in figure 16.18.

Alternatively, the solution can be approximated by numerical integration with small steps as shown in figure 16.19. Also, the k-rate and a-rate need to be the same for smooth integration.

The same equation can be used to generate score events that show a repetitive structure. A more interesting equation for this purpose is van der Pol's equation:

$$y'' + ey'(1 - y) + y = 0 \quad (16.8)$$

```
        instr     1605     ; CUBIC OSCILLATOR USING THE DUFFING EQUATION
ax      init      1                            ; DUFFINGS SYSTEM OR...
ay      init      0                            ; ... CUBIC OSCILLATOR
ke      init      p6                           ; AX = Y
ka      init      p7                           ; AY = EX^3-AX
kh      init      p5
kampenv linseg    0, .01, p4, p3-.02, p4, .01, 0
axnew   =         ay
ay      =         ay+kh*(ke*ax*ax*ax-ka*ax)
ax      =         axnew
        outs      kampenv*ax, kampenv*ay
        endin

t       0      400

i 1605  0      10    30000    .01     .1    100
i 1605  +      10    30000    .01     .3    100
i 1605  +      10    30000    .01     .6    100
```

Figure 16.19 Orchestra and score code for *instr 1605,* a cubic oscillator instrument via the Duffing equation.

which shows cyclical behavior and from any starting values the solution evolves to a circular evolution. For small e this transition is small, but for larger values it is more abrupt.

Equations of this type, circular motion with nonlinear terms, are an interesting area to investigate either musically or mathematically. But to quote Richard Strauss, "beyond this point is chaos."

References

Gardner, M. 1978. "White and brown music, fractal curves and 1/f fluctuations." *Scientific American* 238 (4): 16–31.

Moore, F. R. 1990. *Elements of Computer Music.* Englewood Cliffs, N.J.: Prentice-Hall.

Xenakis, I. 1992. *Formalized Music.* Rev. ed. New York: Pendragon Press.

17 Constrained Random Event Generation and Retriggering in Csound

Russell Pinkston

One of the most idiomatic uses of the traditional analog synthesizer was to create a patch that generated a single event from a "trigger" and then to create a series of such events automatically by using something like a voltage-controlled timer or pulse generator, to produce the triggers at a controlled rate. Consequently, a complex series of events could be initiated by the push of a button, or a single step in an analog sequencer and then treated as a single entity—a phrase, or a gesture. The gestures, in turn, could be processed and transformed in various ways and combined with other gestures to produce rich and complex contrapuntal textures. This capability encouraged composers to work at a higher level than the individual note and the music produced tended to be more rhythmically free, timbrally varied and generally less keyboard-oriented than some of the music produced using MIDI systems.

Csound provides a mechanism for generating multiple notes or events from a single i-statement in the score. It involves reinitializing portions of an instrument design during performance using the following Csound opcodes:

```
reinit      start_label
rigoto      target_label
rireturn
```

When a statement in Csound is reinitialized, it undergoes exactly the same processing that takes place at the beginning of a note triggered by an i-statement in the score, but it happens in the middle of a performance. As soon as a **reinit** statement is encountered, normal k-rate execution is temporarily suspended and a reinitialization pass begins at the statement following the *start_label.* All i-time expressions are recalculated, envelope generators and oscillators reset, filter and delay line buffers cleared, etc., until an **endin** or **rireturn** statement is reached. The *start_label* may be anywhere in the instrument, but must be above the **rireturn**, if one is used.

Obviously, **reinit** must be contained in a portion of the instrument code that is only conditionally executed, so that an instrument is not forced to reinitialize itself

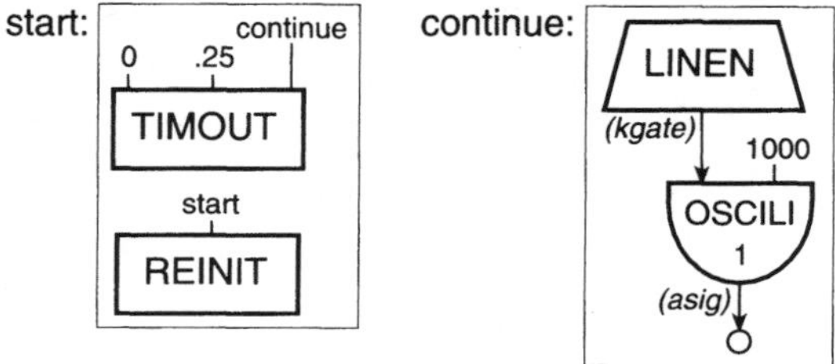

Figure 17.1 Block diagram of *instr 1701,* periodic reinitialization via the **timout** and **reinit** opcodes.

```
          instr    1701          ; PERIODIC RE-INITIALIZATION
start:    timout   0, .25, continue   ; BRANCH TO CONTINUE FOR .25SECS, THEN...
          reinit   start              ; REINIT ALL, BEGINNING WITH THE TIMOUT
continue:
kgate     linen    p4, .02, .25, .1   ; MAKE A .25-SECOND LINEAR ENVELOPE
asig      oscili   kgate, 1000, 1     ; MAKE A 1 KHZ BEEP TONE, USING F 1
          out      asig
          endin                       ; REINIT WILL END HERE, IF NO RIRETURN
```

Figure 17.2 Orchestra code for *instr 1701,* a periodic reinitialization instrument that beeps 4 times per second.

on every k-period. The opcode most often used for this purpose is **timout**, which forces a branch to the *target_label* beginning at time *istart,* for *idur* seconds.

```
timout      istart, idur, target_label
```

Figures 17.1 and 17.2 illustrate a simple example showing periodic reinitialization. The example will generate a series of .25 second tones ("beeps"), from a single i-statement in the score, 4 per second, for as long as the instrument is playing. The **timout** causes program execution to skip over the **reinit** statement, starting immediately (*istart* = 0) for exactly .25 seconds (*idur* = .25), which is just enough time for the **linen** to complete its .25 second envelope. After that, however, branching stops and the **reinit** is executed, which results in a temporary suspension of normal k-rate processing.

A *reinitialization pass* begins at the **timout** statement, which has the label **start:** and proceeds through the entire instrument until the **endin** statement is encountered. Consequently, the **timout** opcode is reset, along with all the remaining opcodes in the instrument block (since no **rireturn** statement is used in this example). When reinitialization is complete, k-rate processing resumes, the **timout** causes the **reinit** statement to be skipped for another .25 seconds, **linen** generates a new envelope and

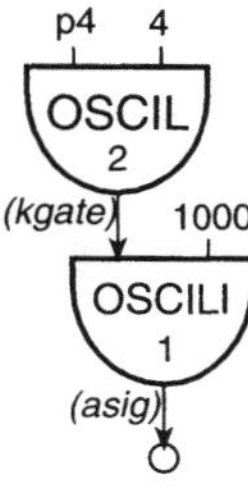

Figure 17.3 Block diagram of *instr 1702,* reinitialization via amplitude modulation with a low frequency oscillator.

```
        instr    1702      ; AMPLITUDE MODULATION WITH LFO
iamp    =        p4
ifn1    =        1
ifn2    =        2                  ; ifn 2 HAS LINEAR ENVELOPE SHAPE
kgate   oscil    p4, 4, 2           ; ENVELOPE OSCIL HAS FREQ OF 4 HZ
asig    oscili   kgate, 1000, 1     ; MAKE A 1 KHZ BEEP TONE, USING IFN 1
        out      asig
        endin
```

Figure 17.4 Orchestra code for *instr 1702,* amplitude modulation with LFO.

a new beep is produced. The process will continue until the i-statement's duration has expired and the instrument is turned off. Note that we could have placed a **rireturn** immediately after the **linen** statement, since only the envelope generator actually requires reinitialization here.

Of course, the identical effect could be obtained without the **timout/reinit** mechanism, by simply using an **oscil** with an appropriate function to generate the envelope, instead of the **linen** and giving it a frequency argument of 4 Hz (see figures 17.3 and 17.4).

As you can see, *instr 1702* also generates a repeating beep, since the *kgate* **oscil** references a function containing the shape of a complete linear envelope, which will be repeated 4 times per second. In fact, for this trivial case, it would be both simpler and more efficient than using **timout** and **reinit**. But there are circumstances in which the reinitialization method of generating repeating events is preferable. Consider the design variation shown in figures 17.5 and 17.6.

There are several important differences in *instr 1703:* an overall phrase-dynamic (*crescendo-diminuendo)* is applied to the beeping, but more significantly, the rate of beeping changes gradually from 10 Hz to 1 Hz over the course of the note (as *kdur* moves from .1 to 1), while the duration of the beep is fixed (.1 second). This is an

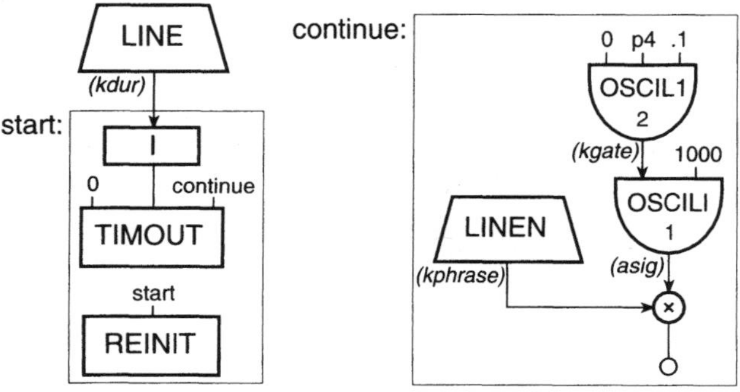

Figure 17.5 Block diagram of *instr 1703,* a reinit instrument with a "phrase" envelope.

```
          instr    1703          ; REINIT WITH PHRASE-ENVELOPE
kphrase   linen    1, p3*.5, p3, p3*.5    ; GRADUAL RISE&FALL IN AMP OVER p3
kdur      line     .1, p3, 1              ; KDUR CHANGES FROM .1 TO 1 OVER p3
start:    timout   0, i(kdur), continue   ; BRANCH TO CONTINUE FOR KDUR SECS,
          reinit   start                  ; THEN REINIT ALL, BEGINNING WITH
continue:                                 ; ... THE TIMOUT
kgate     oscil1   0, p4, .1, 2           ; f 2 HAS ENVSHAPE; DUR FIXED AT .1
asig      oscili   kgate, 1000, 1         ; MAKE A 1 KHZ BEEP TONE, USING f1
          out      asig*kphrase           ; APPLY THE OVERALL PHRASE DYNAMIC
          endin                           ; REINITIALIZATION STOPS HERE
```

Figure 17.6 Orchestra code for *instr 1703,* reinit instrument with phrase-envelope illustrated in figure 17.5.

instance in which using **timout** and **reinit** is the only way to achieve the desired result, because using an **oscil** to gate the signal (as we did in *instr 1702*) would result in an envelope whose shape and duration would be tied to the frequency of repetitions—as the rate is slowed down, the envelopes would be longer and have more gradual rise and decay shapes. Here, since we will reinitialize it for every beep, an **oscil1** can be used to generate the beep envelopes, whose duration and shape will be independent of the rate of repetitions.

Notes: Phrase Envelope Instrument—*instr 1703*

- A **linseg**, **expseg** or **envlpx** opcode could also be used here to generate a fixed length envelope shorter than *kdur,* but not **linen**, because it continues to decay (and go negative) if executed longer than its duration parameter. The **oscil1** opcode is probably the most flexible and easiest Csound opcode to use for this purpose.

```
f 1      0        8192     10       1
; LINEAR ENVELOPE FUNCTION
f 2      0        512      7        0    41    1    266    1    205    0
; INS    START    DUR      AMP
i 1703   0        4        10000
```

Figure 17.7 Score code for *instr 1703.*

- The statements that generate *kphrase* and *kdur* are above the *start:* label and hence are not reinitialized along with the **timout** and **oscil1**. Consequently, they produce values that change smoothly and gradually over the course of the entire note.
- It should be noted that the **timout** opcode's *idur* argument, which must be an i-time expression, is obtained by using the *karg* function, which forces an i-time result from the current value of the *kdur* variable.

A More Complex Example: Making Popcorn

Now that the basic reinitialization mechanism has been demonstrated, let us try a more complicated example, one that incorporates some random elements. Let us say we wanted to imitate the sound of popcorn popping. First, there is only an occasional pop, then a few more at random intervals, then progressively more and more until the popping is virtually constant, then progressively fewer and fewer pops occur until, eventually, all silent and "it's time for the butter." Each pop has approximately the same sound—same duration and amplitude and more or less the same timbre. In the example instrument shown in figure 17.8, the "pops" are simply bandpass filtered white noise with a short (.075 second) exponential envelope. The key difference between this example and the previous ones is that the **timout/reinit** pair uses a constrained random gap-time (time interval between pops), whose limits vary over the course of the note.

An **expseg** is used to produce an exponential decay from *p6* (the longest gap time) to *p5* (the shortest gap time) over the first half of the note (*p3/2*), followed by an exponential rise back to *p6* over the second half of the note. The actual gap time *(igap)* between any two pops is a random value between .035 and .035+*kvary* seconds. As *kvary* moves from *p6* to *p5* and back, the average gap time diminishes and then increases again. The result is that pops occur infrequently at first, then gradually become more frequent, then less frequent again, but always somewhat unpredictably.

Thirty seconds of popcorn can be made using the orchestra and score shown in figure 17.9.

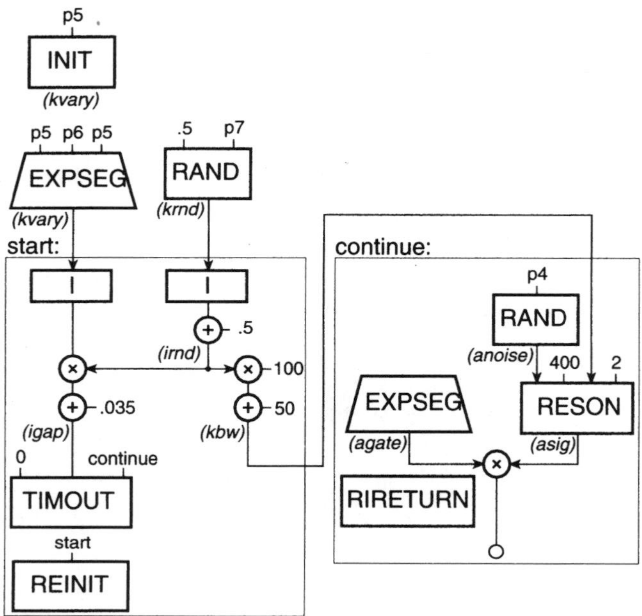

Figure 17.8 Block diagram of *instr 1704,* a reinit design with random elements simulating popping popcorn.

```
          instr     1704          ; A "POPCORN" SIMULATOR
kvary     expseg    p5, p3/2, p6, p3/2, p5    ; VARY GAP DURS BETWEEN p5 AND p6
krnd      rand      .5, p7                    ; p7 IS RANDOM SEED
kvary     init      p5                        ; BEGIN WITH MAXIMUM POSSIBLE GAP
start:                                        ; START OF REINIT BLOCK
irnd      =         .5+i(krnd)                ; OFFSET IRND TO BETWEEN 0 AND 1
igap      =         .035+irnd*i(kvary)        ; BETWEEN .035 AND .035+KVARY SECS
kbw       =         50+100*irnd               ; SMALL RANDOM VAR IN FILTER BW
          timout    0, igap, continue         ; SKIP REINIT FOR IGAP SECONDS
          reinit    start
continue:                                     ; POPCORN ENVELOPE
agate     expseg    .0001, .005, 1, .07, .0001
          rireturn                            ; END REINITIALIZING HERE
anoise    rand      p4                        ; WHITE NOISE FOR POPS
asig      reson     anoise, 400, kbw, 2       ; BANDPASS FILTERING
          out       asig*agate                ; APPLY ENVELOPE
          endin

; INS     START     DUR     AMP      MAXVARY     MINVARY     RANDSEED
i 1704    0         30      18000    5           .035        .12345
```

Figure 17.9 Orchestra and score code for *instr 1704,* a "popcorn" simulator as illustrated in figure 17.8.

Notes: Popcorn Instrument—*instr 1704*

- The **expseg** and **rand** opcodes that are producing *kvary* and *krnd,* respectively must be outside the reinit block.
- The assignment statement that produces *kbw* must be contained in the reinit block, because even though *kbw* only gets updated at k-time, Csound will precalculate the expression (50+100+*irnd*) at i-time, since it contains only constants and i-type variables. In other words, if this expression were placed outside the reinit block (directly in the **reson** opcode's *kbw* field, for example), it would not change during performance, even though the *irnd* variable was being changed owing to reinitialization.
- A **rireturn** is used immediately following the **expseg** producing the envelopes, because nothing else needs reinitialization.
- The bandwidth of the **reson** filter (*kbw*) is given a slight random variation, to make the individual pops sound a little different.

A Three-Part Gesture Instrument

The next example combines elements of everything covered so far (figure 17.10). A single i-statement produces a complete musical phrase, or "gesture," which has three distinct parts (figure 17.11). Part 1 consists of two oscillators tuned an octave apart that are randomly gated together, amplitude modulated with a low-frequency oscillator (LFO), and made to swell gradually. Part 2 is actually a variation of the popcorn instrument, which generates a random sequence of tuned percussive sounds, the last of which is forced to match the pitch of the final part of the gesture. Part 3 begins with the last pop of part 2 and consists of a single oscillator that pans back and forth rapidly from left to right, with the panning rate slowing as the sound decays. The duration of the entire gesture is controlled by *p3* of the i-statement, of course, but the portion of *p3* allocated to the individual parts of the gesture is determined by factors in *p9* and *p10.* An **oscil1i** is used to apply an overall panning curve, which is stored in a function table (f-table) in the score.

Notes: Three-Part Gesture Instrument—*instr 1705*

- In this instrument, **timout** is used for an additional purpose: it controls the timing and duration of each part of the gesture, by causing execution to skip over a block

```
          instr    1705      ; 3 PART "GESTURE" INSTRUMENT
iamp1     =        p4                             ; INITIALIZATION BLOCK:
iamp2     =        p4*1.5                         ; FINE AMP ADJUSTMENTS
iamp3     =        p4*.5
idur1     =        p3*p9                          ; PORTION OF p3 FOR PT 1
idur2     =        p3*p10                         ; PORTION OF p3 FOR PT 2
idur3     =        p3-idur2-idur1                 ; THE REST TO PART 3
icps1a    =        cpspch(p5)
icps1b    =        icps1a*2
icps3     =        cpspch(p6)
iwave1    =        1                              ; OSC WAVESHAPE FOR PT 1
iwave3    =        2                              ; OSC WAVESHAPE FOR PT 3
ihamm     =        3                              ; HAMMING FUNC FOR LFO
ipanfn    =        p14                            ; PAN CONTROL FUNC (0-1)
iseed1    =        p7
iseed2    =        p8
imindur   =        p11                            ; MIN NOTE LEN FOR PART2
imaxnum   =        p12                            ; MAX GAP FACTOR (>= 1)
ioctrng   =        p13                            ; RANDOM PITCH RANGE
itime     =        0                              ; TIME COUNTER FOR PT 2
ilast     =        0                              ; LAST NOTE FLAG FOR PT 2
kpan      oscil1i  0, 1, p3, ipanfn               ; OVERALL PAN CONTROL FOR...
kleft     =        sqrt(kpan)                     ; ... PHRASE
kright    =        sqrt(1-kpan)
part1:                                            ; CRESCENDO TO PART 2
          timout   idur1, p3, part2               ; WAIT IDUR1 SECONDS
kenv1     expseg   1, idur1, iamp1, 1, iamp1
klfo1     oscil    1, 7, ihamm
kgate     randi    .5, 5                          ; OUTPUT BETWEEN +/- .5
kgate     =        .5+kgate                       ; OFFSET TO BETWEEN 0 - 1
asiga     oscili   kgate, icps1a, iwave1
asigb     oscili   1-kgate, icps1b, iwave1
asig1     =        (asiga+asigb)*kenv1*klfo1
          outs     asig1*kleft, asig1*kright
          kgoto    end
part2:             ; RANDOM SERIES OF POPS
          timout   idur2, p3, part3               ; WAIT FOR IDUR2 SECONDS
krndur    rand     .5, iseed1                     ; OUTPUT BETWEEN +/- .5
krndhz    rand     .5, iseed2                     ; COMPUTE NEXT DURATION
reset:                                            ; BETWEEN 0 AND IMAXNUM
irndur    =        (.5+i(krndur))*imaxnum         ; MAKE DUR = IMINDUR*N ...
idur      =        imindur+imindur*int(irndur+.5)
if (itime+idur<idur2) igoto choose                ; ... UNTIL LAST NOTE, CHOOSE
ilast     =        1                              ; LAST NOTE - SET FLAG
idur      =        idur2-itime                    ; TRIM DURATION TO FIT
ipitch    =        octpch(p6)                     ; USE PART 3 PITCH, SO...
          igoto    continue                       ; SKIP RANDOM SELECTION
choose:                                           ; SELECT A RANDOM PITCH
irndoct   =        i(krndhz)*ioctrng              ; BETWEEN +/- IOCTRNG/2
ipitch    =        octpch(p5)+irndoct             ; AROUND PITCH OF PART 1
continue:
itime     =        itime+idur                     ; KEEP TRACK OF TIME
icf       =        cpsoct(ipitch)/2               ; FILTER SETTINGS
ibwmin    =        icf/20
ibwvar    =        icf*4
```

Figure 17.10 Orchestra code for *instr 1705,* a three-part gesture instrument.

```
kenv2    expseg    .01, .005, 1, idur-.005, .001
         timout    0, idur, skip              ; SKIP FOR IDUR SECONDS
         reinit    reset                      ; THEN REINIT FROM RESET
skip:
anoise    rand      iamp2
apitch    oscili    iamp2/2, cpsoct(ipitch+kenv2*.25), iwave1
afilt1    butterbp  anoise+apitch, icf, ibwmin+kenv2*ibwvar
afilt2    butterbp  afilt1, icf, ibwmin+kenv2*ibwvar
          rireturn                            ; END REINIT PASS HERE
asig2     =         afilt2*kenv2              ; APPLY AMP ENVELOPE
          outs      asig2*kleft, asig2*kright
          if        (ilast!=1) kgoto end      ; GOTO END TIL LAST NOTE
part3:                                        ; DIMINUENDO AND RITARD.
kenv3     line      1, idur3, 0               ; LINEAR DECAY FOR AMP
klfohz    expon     20, idur3, 1              ; EXP DECAY FOR LFO RATE
klfo3     oscil     1, klfohz, ihamm          ; HAMMING WINDOW FOR LFO
asig3     oscili    kenv3*iamp3, icps3, iwave3
          outs      asig3*kleft*klfo3, asig3*kright*(1-klfo3)
end:
          endin
```

Figure 17.10 continued

```
; OSCIL WAVE SHAPE FOR PART 1
f 1      0      8192      10   1
; OSCIL WAVE SHAPE FOR PART 2
f 2      0      8192      10   1      0      .25    0      .125
; HAMMING WINDOW FUNCTION FOR LFO GATING
f 3      0      8192      20   1
; FIXED CENTER PANNING FUNCTION (.5 CONSTANT)
f 4      0      3         -7   .5     3      .5
; PAN LEFT TO RIGHT
f 5      0      129       7    1      129    0
; PAN RIGHT TO LEFT
f 6      0      129       7    0      129    1
; PAN CENTER TO LEFT TO RIGHT TO CENTER
f 7      0      129       7    .5     32     1      64     0      33     .5

; INS    ST DUR AMP     PCH1  PCH3   SEEDS       DUR FACS     MIN   MAX   OCT   PAN
;                                    PT1   PT2   PT1   PT2    DUR   N     RNG   FN
i 1705   0  10  32000   9.00  8.11   .4    .3    .4    .035   .04   4     1     4
i 1705   4  10  30000   9.08  7.09   .2    .1    .4    .05    .05   5     2     7
i 1705   8  10  26000   7.06  9.01   .8    .7    .4    .1     .06   7     3     6
i 1705   9  9   .       8.09  8.03   .6    .51   .3    .2     .06   4     3     5
```

Figure 17.11 Score code for *instr 1705,* a three part gesture instrument.

of statements once they have completed their particular task. Hence the first **timout**, which is at the beginning of the code labeled *part 1:* waits for *idur1* seconds and then branches to the statement labeled *part 2:* for the remainder of the note *(p3)*. At the bottom of the code for part 1 is the statement **kgoto** *end,* which keeps the code for parts 2 and 3 from being executed as long as part 1 is playing. Similarly, the timout at the beginning of part 2 waits for *idur2* seconds and then branches to part 3 for the remainder of the note.

- Since the last "pop" of part 2 is supposed to coincide with the beginning of part 3 of the gesture, it is necessary to execute the code for both part 2 and part 3 simultaneously for a brief period of time. This is accomplished with the use of a "flag," *ilast,* which is initialized to 0, but set to 1 when the last pop starts. The final statement of the part 2 code section is **if** (*ilast* != 1) **kgoto** *end,* which means that part 3 will be skipped as long as the flag is 0, but as soon as it is set to 1, the final part of the gesture commences.
- A simple method is used to determine when the final note of part 2 is about to be played. The variable *itime* is initialized to 0 at the beginning of the gesture. During part 2, each time a new pop is generated, a new *idur* value is computed and added to *itime.* As long as *itime+idur* is less than the total duration of part 2, *idur2,* we have not reached the last note, so we can go choose a new random pitch and proceed as usual. But when *itime+idur* does equal or exceed *idur2,* we do not take the conditional branch **igoto** *choose,* but instead drop through, set our *ilast* flag equal to 1, trim *idur* to equal exactly the remainder of *idur2,* select the pitch of part 3 for our final pop and then branch around the customary random pitch calculation. Note that all the branches must be **igoto** statements so that they are executed during the reinitialization passes.
- The rhythm of the percussive sounds in part 2 is randomized, but constrained to adhere to a grid based on the smallest allowed durational value, *imindur.* This is accomplished by generating a random number between +/− .5, adding .5 to it and then multiplying by *imaxnum,* which must be some number greater than 1. The result is a random number between 0 and *imaxnum,* which is stored in *irndur.* Using the **int** function to take the integer part of that, multiplying the result by *imindur* and then adding it to *imindur,* yields a random duration that is equal to *imindur* plus N times *imindur,* where N is an integer between 0 and *imaxnum.* Consequently, the pops in part 2 will occur at random intervals, but they will always fall somewhere on the rhythmic grid.
- The pitches in part 2 are also randomly derived, but constrained to fall within a designated band *(ioctrng)* centered around the pitch of part 1. A new random pitch

is selected for each new pop except for the last one, which is set to the pitch of part 3.

Constrained Random Music Instrument

The final example (figure 17.12) actually generates a short algorithmic composition from a score containing just four i-statements (figure 17.13). The pitches, durations and pan position of all notes are selected randomly, but with significant constraints. The only pitch classes allowed for the two primary voices are those contained in a C minor 7 chord (C, Eb, G, Bb) and the only durations allowed are .25 and .125—quarter notes and 8th notes, if 1 second represents a whole note. The amplitude of a note is related to its duration—the longer, the louder—which tends to make the music sound syncopated, although not metrical. The net result is strongly rhythmic music in C minor, which does not sound particularly random.

Notes: Algorithmic Music Machine—*instr 1706*

- The three **rand** opcodes are above the **reinit** block so that they continue to produce a steady stream of random numbers at the k-rate, over the course of *p3*. Whenever the code that follows is reinitialized, the statements that use *kdurloc, kpchloc* and *kpan* grab whatever their current values happen to be via the Csound **i**(*kvalue*) function. Each **rand** must have a different *iseed* value, or the "random" sequences produced by the three opcodes would be identical. Similarly, each i-statement should pass a different set of seed values and table numbers, or the music produced will be exactly the same each time.
- The values of *kdurloc* and *kpchloc* are not used directly, but are first offset by .5 (to place them in the range 0–1) and then used as normalized indices into tables containing a limited set of acceptable values. Consequently, although the choices for pitch and duration are made randomly, the possible results are carefully controlled.
- The tables may be of various sizes (subject to Csound's power of 2 rule) and are filled with the acceptable choices for pitch and duration in the desired proportions. For example, pitch function 3 (*f* 6 in the example score) has eight locations and contains four 7.03s, two 7.05s, one 6.10, and one field that is blank (zero). Consequently, although short-term results may vary over time, about 50% of the ran-

```
         instr    1706     ; ALGORITHMIC MUSIC GENERATOR
ipkamp   =        p4                          ; INITIALIZATION BLOCK:
idurfn   =        p5                          ; THE POSSIBLE DURATIONS
ipchfn   =        p6                          ; THE POSSIBLE PITCHES
iampfn   =        p7                          ; AMP SCALING FUNCTION
iprise   =        p8                          ; PHRASE ENV RISE TIME
ipdec    =        p9                          ; PHRASE ENV DECAY TIME
inrise   =        p10                         ; INDIVIDUAL NOTE AMP RISE
indec    =        p11                         ; INDIVIDUAL NOTE AMP DECAY
iseed1   =        p12                         ; FOR DURATION RAND OPCODE
iseed2   =        p13                         ; FOR PITCH RAND OPCODE
iseed3   =        p14                         ; FOR PANNING RAND OPCODE
ipkdur   =        .2501                       ; MAX EXPECTED DUR
                                              ; THE PHRASE ENVELOPE:
kphrase  expseg   .001, iprise, 1, p3-iprise-ipdec, 1, ipdec, .001
kdurloc  rand     .5, iseed1                  ; GET RANDOM TABLE INDICES
kpchloc  rand     .5, iseed2                  ; BETWEEN -.5 AND +.5
kpan     rand     .5, iseed3
noteinit:                                     ; START REINIT BLOCK
idurloc  =        .5+i(kdurloc)               ; MAKE POSITIVE I-TIME VAR
idur     table    idurloc, idurfn, 1          ; SELECT FROM DUR TABLE
iamp     table    idur/ipkdur, iampfn, 1      ; RELATE AMP TO DUR
iamp     =        .25+.75*iamp                ; AMP RANGE FROM .25 TO 1
ipchloc  =        .5+i(kpchloc)               ; MAKE A POSITIVE I-VAR
ipch     table    ipchloc, ipchfn, 1          ; SELECT FROM PCH TABLE
icps     =        (ipch==0?0:cpspch(ipch))    ; ALLOW FOR 0S (RESTS)
ilfac    =        i(kpan)+.5                  ; MAKE POSITIVE
ileft    =        sqrt(ilfac)                 ; "FILL THE HOLE...
iright   =        sqrt(1-ilfac)               ; ...BETWEEN THE SPEAKERS"
if (icps == 0) goto rest                      ; A TABLE VAL OF 0 = A REST
irise    =        inrise*idur                 ; COMPUTE NOTE RISE TIME
idecay   =        indec*idur                  ; COMPUTE NOTE DECAY TIME
isust    =        idur-irise-idecay           ; SUSTAIN PORTION
knote    expseg   .001, irise, 1, isust, 1, idecay, .001
asig     pluck    knote*iamp*ipkamp, icps, icps, 0, 1, 0, 0
asig     =        asig*kphrase                ; APPLY THE PHRASE ENVELOPE
         outs     asig*ileft, asig*iright     ; APPLY THE PANNING
rest:    timout   0, idur, exit               ; TIMOUT CAN BE ANYWHERE
         reinit   noteinit                    ; IN THE REINIT BLOCK
exit:    endin                                ; WHICH ENDS HERE
```

Figure 17.12 Orchestra code for *instr 1706,* an algorithmic music generator.

domly selected pitches will be 7.03, 25% will be 7.05, 12.5% will be 6.10 and 12.5% will be 0s, which produce rests.

- When a rest is to be generated, all the statements involved with producing sound (the *knote* expseg, pluck, etc.) are skipped, so no samples are generated or output. The **timout** statement is still executed, however, in order to obtain the correct duration of silence.
- When a zero value is obtained from the duration table, it is effectively ignored, since a **timout** with *idur* = 0 results in the succeeding **reinit** statement being

```
; PITCH FUNCTION 1 - A C MINOR 7 CHORD WITH OCTAVE DOUBLINGS
f 1     0       8       -2      6.00    6.07    7.00    7.07
                                8.00    8.03    8.07    8.10
; AMP FACTOR FUNCTION (QUARTER SINE WAVE)
f 2     0       129     9       .25     1       0
; DURATION FUNCTION 1 - JUST QUARTERS OR 8THS
f 3     0       2       -2      .25     .125
; DURATION FUNCTION 2 - MOSTLY 8THS, SOME QUARTERS AND 16THS
f 4     0       8       -2      .25     .25     .125    .125    .125
                                .125    .0625   .0625
; PITCH FUNCTION 2 - LOTS OF FS WITH SOME QUARTER AND 8TH-TONE DETUNINGS
; SOME RESTS, TOO.
f 5     0       32      -2      9.05    9.05    9.05    9.05    9.05
        10.05   10.05   10.05   8.05    8.05    9.055   9.055   10.055
        9.045   9.      .045    8.055   8.055   10.055  10.055  9.0525
        9.0525  9.0525  9.0475  9.0475  9.0475
; PITCH FUNCTION 3 - LOW EBS AND FBS, AN OCCASIONAL BB OR REST
f 6     0       8       -2      7.03    7.03    7.03    7.03    7.05
                                7.05    6.10
; DUR FUNCTION 3 - ONLY 3 CHOICES: TWO THIRDS 16THS, ONE THIRD 8TH NOTES
f 7     0       4       -2      .0625   .0625   .125
; GENERATE A SHORT COMPOSITION USING TABLES FOR PITCHES AND DURATIONS

; TWO PRIMARY VOICES FOR THE BASIC RHYTHM TRACK
; INS   ST      DUR     PKAMP   DURFN   PCHFN   AMPFN   RISE    DECAY
i 1706  0       40      16000   3       1       2       .001    3
;       NOTE ENVLP FACS RANDOM SEED VALUES
;       RISE    DECAY   DUR     PCH     PAN
        .001    .1      .030251 .071983 .022186
; INS   ST      DUR     PKAMP   DURFN   PCHFN   AMPFN   RISE    DECAY
i 1706  2       38      16000   3       1       2       .001    3
;       NOTE ENVLP FACS RANDOM SEED VALUES
;       RISE    DECAY   DUR     PCH     PAN
        .001    .1      .070703 .012719 .081447
; SOLO VOICE WITH SOME QUARTER-TONES AND SHORTER DURATIONS AFTER 12 BEATS
; INS   ST      DUR     PKAMP   DURFN   PCHFN   AMPFN   RISE    DECAY
i 1706  12      12      20000   4       5       2       2       3
;       NOTE ENVLP FACS RANDOM SEED VALUES
;       RISE    DECAY   DUR     PCH     PAN
        .001    .1      .010149 .100153 .012345
; SECOND, FASTER SOLO WITH LOWER PITCHES AT 25.125 BEATS
; INS   ST      DUR     PKAMP   DURFN   PCHFN   AMPFN   RISE    DECAY
i 1706  25.125  10      16000   7       6       2       2       3
;       NOTE ENVLP FACS RANDOM SEED VALUES
;       RISE    DECAY   DUR     PCH     PAN
        .001    .1      .030251 .071983 .022186
```

Figure 17.13 Score code for *instr 1706,* an algorithmic music machine. Note that tables are used to "constrain" the random pitch, duration, and amplitudes.

executed immediately, causing an additional reinitialization pass and another fetch from the duration table.

- The amplitude of a note is determined by dividing its duration by the longest possible duration and using the result to reference a scaling function. The scaling function used in this example is the first quarter of a sine wave, so the longest durations will have the maximum amplitude, notes half the maximum duration will be about .7 of the maximum amplitude (–3dB ca), etc. Note that *ipkdur* in the instrument is set to .2501—just slightly more than the longest duration stored in the table (.25), so that the ratio of *idur/ipkdur* will never quite reach 1.

Conclusion

Using Csound instruments such as the Constrained Random Music Instrument (*instr 1706*) is probably not the best way to generate compositions algorithmically. Although the Csound orchestra has some of the functionality of higher level languages, it cannot compete with a general purpose programming language such as C or LISP when it comes to implementing sophisticated custom algorithms. Indeed, the basic architecture of all the Music N style languages, of which Csound is a direct descendent, reflects the underlying assumption that the purpose of the orchestra is to generate and process sounds that are triggered by individual notes in the score. The format of the score, in turn, was deliberately kept simple and the task of generating and processing was kept separate from the task of performing it.

For the most part, this division of labor makes perfect sense, especially with respect to algorithmic composition. It would be far easier to write a stand-alone program in C to generate a score from a complex algorithm than to try to implement the same thing in orchestra code. Moreover, Csound provides the Cscore utility to make the task of working with score data relatively straightforward. There are instances, however, in which complex instruments such as the ones that have been described in this chapter are both useful and convenient. The only serious limitation concerning the generation of multiple notes within an instrument, using a retriggering mechanism such as **timout/reinit**, is that such notes cannot overlap. Consequently, techniques such as granular synthesis, which produce numerous overlapping "grains" of sound, or the algorithmic generation of polyphonic compositions cannot readily be implemented within a single instrument. On the other hand, using multiple instances of instruments that generate individual monophonic voices can sometimes achieve the desired results.

18 Using Global Csound Instruments for Meta-Parameter Control

Martin Dupras

The implementation of sound algorithms in Csound can be greatly simplified by the use of global variables and meta-level control signals. We will see that such flexibility can help achieve time independence of control parameters. It also makes possible the sharing of control information across instruments, as well as the use of feedback within an instrument.

Control Instruments

Many algorithms can be easily implemented in a single instrument. Complex algorithms may require, however, that they be split into two or more instruments. Such algorithms may rely on information that happens before or after the note boundaries. Others may require control parameters that evolve over the duration of several notes.

Suppose we want to play a sequence of "slurred" notes. One way to do this is to use the "*pp*" statement in the score to pass the last ending pitch to the instrument (see figures 18.1 and 18.2).

There is a caveat to this approach. Each note may start with an undesirable click because when a new note is invoked, the oscillator is reset and its internal **phasor** jumps back to the beginning of the table, thus creating a discontinuity in the signal. One way to solve this problem is to split the instrument into a control instrument and a sound-generating instrument (see figures 18.3 and 18.4). The control instrument will receive the note-ons and note-offs as well as the pitch, compute portamento for the slurring effect and send the instantaneous frequency to the second instrument. Since the latter will play continuously for the duration of the score, **oscil** will not be reset and there will be no click.

Sound-generating instruments can receive control signals from more than one instrument. This allows for considerable flexibility, because many asynchronous sequences of events can control various aspects of the algorithms.

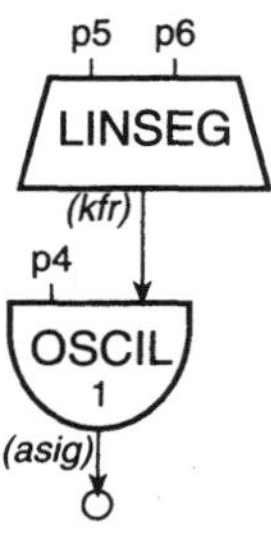

Figure 18.1 Block diagram of *instr 1801,* a simple oscillator instrument with portamento.

```
        instr     1801             ; SIMPLE PORTAMENTO
kfr     linseg    p5, p3*.1, p6, p3*.9, p6    ; p5 = FREQ OF LAST NOTE
asig    oscil     p4, kfr, 1                  ; p6 = FREQ FOR THIS NOTE
        out       asig
        endin

f 1          0      8193      10        1

i 1801       0      0.4       10000     440       440
i 1801       +      .         .         pp6       660
i 1801       +      .         .         pp6       550
```

Figure 18.2 Orchestra and Score code for *instr 1801,* featuring "pp" directive to relate current pitches to previous ones.

For example, we can implement a low-frequency oscillator (LFO) in a second control instrument and use it to modulate the frequency of the oscillator (see figures 18.5 and 18.6).

Because the LFO is implemented in a separate instrument, its output is available to other instruments. This is analogous to what happens in an analog synthesizer. In this manner we can model a simple analog patch synthesizer with three independent oscillators, an LFO and an ADSR (attack-decay-sustain-release) generator (see figure 18.7).

A significant advantage to this approach is that simultaneous notes can be played and share the same control signal. Thus, a control signal such as an LFO can be applied equally to each note of a chord (see figure 18.8).

Note that care must be taken to ensure that the global variables are initialized before being used. The order of instruments is also important, because Csound computes instruments in ascending order and therefore, it makes sense to ensure that the control signals are computed before the sound-generating instruments in which they are used.

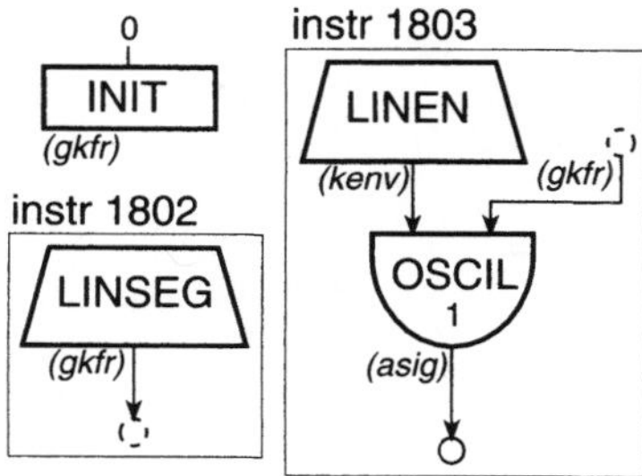

Figure 18.3 Block diagram of *instr 1802* and *1803,* global frequency control.

```
gkfr    init    0                                    ; INIT FREQUENCY

        instr   1802          ; CONTROLS 1803 FREQUENCY
gkfr    linseg  p5, p3*.1, p6, p3*.9, p6
        endin

        instr   1803          ; SIMPLE OSCIL
kenv    linen   p4, .01, p3, .01
asig    oscil   kenv, gkfr, 1
        out     asig
        endin

f 1       0       8193      10        1

i 1802    0       0.4       0         440       440
i 1802    +       .         .         pp6       660
i 1802    +       .         .         pp6       550

i 1803    0       1.2       10000
```

Figure 18.4 Orchestra and score code for *instr 1802* and *1803,* a global frequency control pair. Note *instr 1802* has no “local” output.

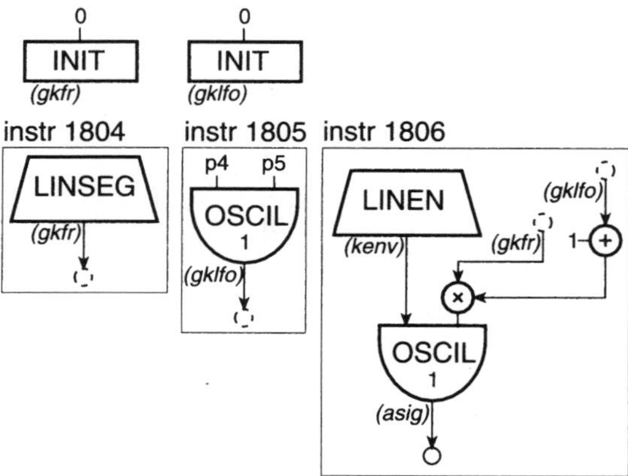

Figure 18.5 Block diagram of *instr 1804, 1805,* and *1806,* a set featuring separate global frequency and global LFO control instruments.

```
gkfr     init     0                                 ; INITIAL FREQUENCY
gklfo    init     0                                 ; INITIAL LFO VALUE

         instr    1804           ; CONTROLS 1806 FREQUENCY
gkfr     linseg   p5, p3*.1, p6, p3*.9, p6
         endin

         instr    1805           ; SIMPLE OSCIL
gklfo    oscil    p4, p5, 1
         endin

         instr    1806           ; SIMPLE OSCIL
kenv     linen    p4, .01, p3, .01
asig     oscil    kenv, gkfr*(1+gklfo), 1
         out      asig
         endin

f 1      0        8193     10       1

i 1804   0        0.4      0        440      440
i 1804   +        .        .        pp6      660
i 1804   +        .        .        pp6      550
i 1805   0        1.2      0.14     4.5
i 1806   0        1.2      10000
```

Figure 18.6 Orchestra and score code for *instr 1804, 1805,* and *1806,* a global LFO and Portamento set.

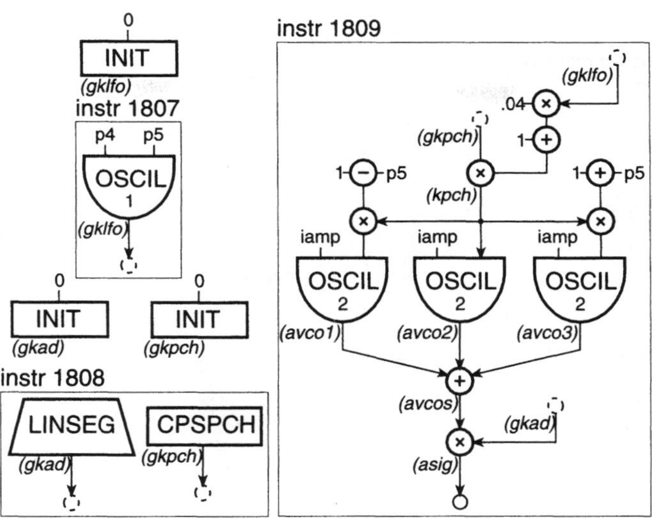

Figure 18.7 Block diagram of *instr 1807,1808,* and *1809,* an analog synthesizer model with three oscillators (*instr 1809*), a global LFO (*instr 1807*) and pitch control (*instr 1808*).

```
gklfo    init      0
gkpch    init      0
gkad     init      0

         instr     1807          ; GLOBAL LFO
gklfo    oscil     p4, p5, 1
         endin

         instr     1808          ; GLOBAL ADSR
gkad     linseg    0, p3*p4, 1, p3*p5, p6, p3*p7, 0
gkpch    =         cpspch(p8)
         endin

         instr     1809          ; SIMPLE VCO
iamp     =         p4*0.333
kpch     =         gkpch*(1+0.04*gklfo)
avco1    oscil     iamp, kpch*(1-p5), 2        ; p4=%DETUNE
avco2    oscil     iamp, kpch, 2
avco3    oscil     iamp, kpch*(1+p5), 2
avcos    =         avco1+avco2+avco3
asig     =         gkad*avcos
         out       asig
         endin

f 1     0    8193    10       1
f 2     0    2       2        1       -1

i 1807  0    1.8     0.26     4.30
i 1808  0    0.6     0.05     0.12    0.43    0.32    8.00
i 1808  +    0.6     0.08     0.12    0.30    0.45    8.02
i 1808  +    0.6     0.08     0.12    0.30    0.45    8.05
i 1809  0    1.8     20000    0.02
```

Figure 18.8 Orchestra and score code for *instr 1807, 1808,* and *1809,* an analog synthesizer model with global controls.

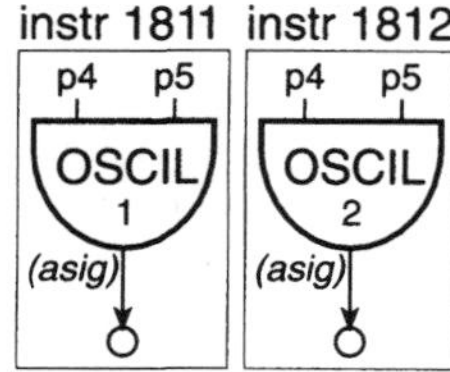

Figure 18.9 Block diagram of *instr 1811* and *1812,* two simple fixed-frequency oscillator instruments.

```
        instr   1811        ; FIXED-FREQUENCY OSCIL FOR SPECTRAL FUSION 1
asig    oscil   p4, p5, 1
        out     asig
        endin

        instr   1812        ; FIXED-FREQUENCY OSCIL FOR SPECTRAL FUSION 2
asig    oscil   p4, p5, 2
        out     asig
        endin

f 1     0        8193     10      1
f 2     0        2        10      1

i 1811  0        5      12000    240
i 1812  0        5      10000    367
```

Figure 18.10 Orchestra and score code for *instr 1811* and *1812* illustrating mixing via note statements.

Spectral Fusion

The use of global control instruments is especially useful to create "spectral fusion." This technique relies on auditory perception to create the illusion that two spectra belong to the same source, by modulating their spectra simultaneously.

When two notes of different timbres are played together, they tend to be perceived as distinct tones (see figures 18.9 and 18.10). If a single, common vibrato is applied to the two sounds, however, they tend to fuse. The vibrato creates the illusion of a single spectrum (see figures 18.11 and 18.12).

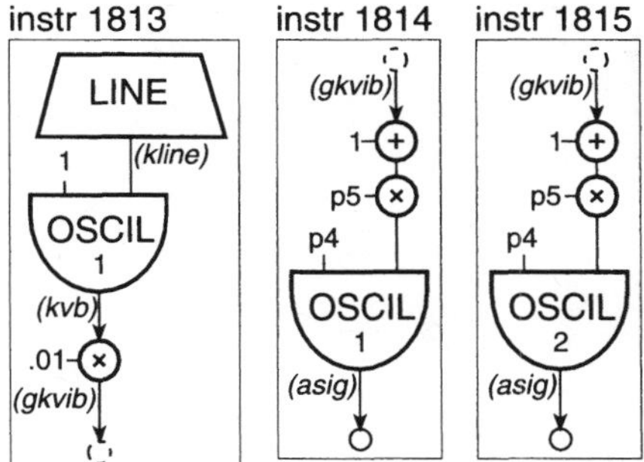

Figure 18.11 Block diagram of *instr 1813, 1814,* and *1815,* illustrating a common global vibrato applied to a pair of simple static oscillator instruments to promote spectral fusion.

```
gkvib   init   0

        instr 1813          ; GLOBAL VIBRATO
kline   line   p5, p3, p6         ; FROM P5 TO P6 IN P3
kvb     oscil  1, kline, 1
gkvib   =      kvb*0.01           ; CHANGE RANGE
        endin

        instr 1814          ; FIXED-FREQUENCY OSCIL FOR SPECTRAL FUSION 3
asig    oscil  p4, p5*(1+gkvib), 1
        out    asig
        endin

        instr 1815          ; FIXED-FREQUENCY OSCIL FOR SPECTRAL FUSION 4
asig    oscil  p4, p5*(1+gkvib), 2
        out    asig
        endin
```

Figure 18.12 Orchestra code for *instr 1813, 1814,* and *1815,* which realize spectral fusion through a common global vibrato.

Time-Varying Stochastic Generators

In some cases, such as some granular-synthesis techniques, control signals are useful to impose a direction to a stream of events. Because the control signal can evolve over the duration of the score, each instance of an instrument triggered by a note event from the score can access the instantaneous values of the control signal, thus effectively "mapping" the direction onto the sound event.

In the next example we will use a meta-control instrument to generate complex random values that will be used in a sound-producing instrument. First, let us design

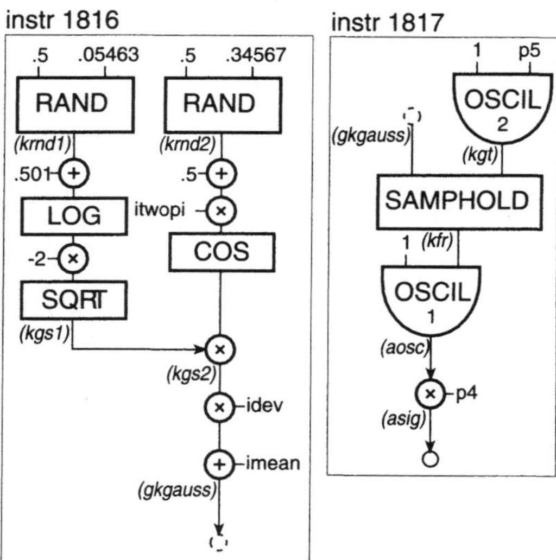

Figure 18.13 Block diagram of *instr 1816* and *1817,* a time-varying stochastic generator pair.

the control instrument using the **rand** opcode. But since **rand** produces a uniform distribution of numbers, how can we generate a more complex distribution, such as a normal (Gaussian) curve?

One method, as shown in figures 18.13 and 18.14, consists of assigning the output of a complex mathematical expression to a k-rate variable. But this yields an extremely slow instrument, because the result of the expression has to be computed on every k-rate pass. Additionally, the mathematical expression may not be particularly intuitive.

A more effective method consists in loading a table with a set of values statistically distributed according to the expected distribution. If we index that table with a uniformly distributed random generator, **rand**, the output is close to the expected result (see figures 18.15 and 18.16). Instead of computing a complex expression many times, it then only has to be computed once when the table is created. The computation time for creating the table is extremely small compared to calculating the expression in the instrument.

Furthermore, we can load a table with virtually any distribution and achieve the same relative computation cost. There is however a trade-off in accuracy, because by filling the table with our distribution we explicitly calculate a finite amount of values (equal to the size of the table), whereas the direct use of a mathematical expression in the instrument yields the precise result of the expression for the current parameters.

```
gkgauss  init     0

         instr    1816   ; TIME-VARYING STOCHASTIC GENERATOR 1
itwopi   =        6.283185
imean    =        250                       ; MEAN FREQ
idev     =        50                        ; STD DEVIATION
krnd1    rand     0.5, .05463
krnd2    rand     0.5, .34567
kgs1     =        sqrt(-2.0*log(0.501+krnd1))
kgs2     =        kgs1*cos(itwopi*(0.5+krnd2))
kgauss   =        kgs2*idev+imean
gkgauss  =        kgauss
         endin

         instr    1817   ; TIME-VARYING STOCHASTIC GENERATOR 2
kgt      oscil    1, p5, 2
kfr      samphold gkgauss, kgt
aosc     oscil    1, kfr, 1
asig     =        aosc*p4
         out      asig
         endin

f 1      0         8193       10          1
f 2      0         513        2           1

i 1816   0         20
i 1817   0         20         2000        1.14
i 1817   0         20         2000        0.75
i 1817   0         20         2000        2.14
i 1817   0         20         2000        3.47
```

Figure 18.14 Orchestra and score code for *instr 1816* and *1817,* a stochastic instrument pair illustrated in figure 18.13.

Probability Masks

Another type of useful stochastic generator is a probability mask. Whereas a uniform distribution yields random numbers between fixed values (say between –1 and 1), the probability mask allows numbers to be picked uniformly between two instantaneous values. This is achieved by rescaling the output of a random number generator (**rand**, for example) to the range bound by the time-varying values. If we want a simple linear evolution of these parameters, we can use a design similar to the one shown in figure 18.17.

If we want to use more complex curves, we can use **linseg**, **expseg**, etc. instead of **line**. As curves increase in complexity, however, this becomes harder to manage. One

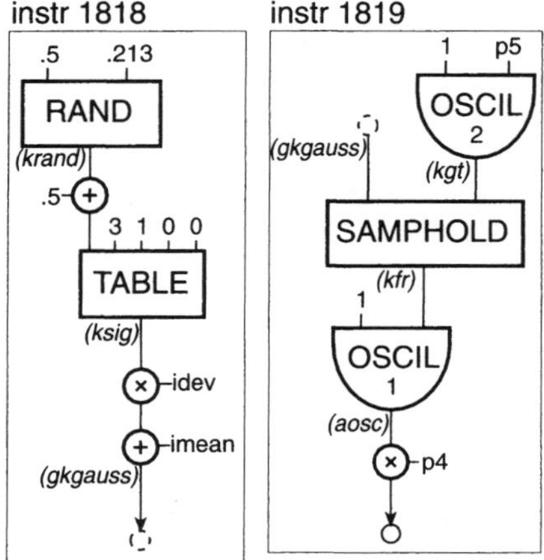

Figure 18.15 Block diagram of *instr 1818* and *1819,* an efficient and intuitive time-varying stochastic generator pair.

```
gkgauss init      0

        instr     1818  ; EFFICIENT TIME-VARYING STOCHASTIC GENERATOR 1
imean   =         250
idev    =         50
krand   rand      0.5, 0.213
ksig    table     0.5+krand, 3, 1, 0, 0
gkgauss =         ksig*idev+imean
        endin

        instr     1819  ; EFFICIENT TIME-VARYING STOCHASTIC GENERATOR 2
kgt     oscil     1, p5, 2
kfr     samphold  gkgauss, kgt
aosc    oscil     1, kfr, 1
        out       aosc*p4
        endin

f 1      0      8193      10       1
f 2      0      513       2        1
f 3      0      1024      21       6              ; NORMAL CURVE

i 1818   0      20        0
i 1819   0      20        2000     1.14
i 1819   0      20        2000     0.75
i 1819   0      20        2000     2.14
i 1819   0      20        2000     3.47
```

Figure 18.16 Orchestra and score code for the table-constrained stochastic generator instrument pair illustrated in figure 18.15.

```
iminst    =      0                      ; STARTING MIN VALUE
iminnd    =      0.5                    ; ENDING MIN VALUE
imaxst    =      0.6                    ; STARTING MAX VALUE
imaxnd    =      0.9                    ; ENDING MAX VALUE
kmin      line   iminst, p3, iminnd
kmax      line   imaxst, p3, imaxnd
krnd1     rand   0.5                    ; FROM -.5, TO .5
krnd2     =      krnd1+0.5              ; BIAS FROM 0 TO 1
krng      =      kmax-kmin
kmsk      =      krnd2*krng+kmin
```

Figure 18.17 Orchestra code for a probability mask, this is an example of a linear evolution between two instantaneous values.

solution is to store the evolution of the minima and maxima for the whole duration of the score in a table. This makes it easy to alter the curves without modifying the instrument. These curves can be generated in programs other than Csound (in a mathematics package, for instance) if the GEN routines are not sufficient. In most cases however, GEN routines should be more than adequate.

Context-Sensitive Instruments

We can use the techniques we have seen so far to make instruments "listen" to each other. This is especially useful since most commercial synthesizers or synthesis methods do not have the kind of flexibility that Csound affords for implementing such methods.

Our first example will consist of an FM instrument playing a series of notes of varying amplitudes (see figures 18.18 and 18.19).

A second instrument will also play an independent series of notes, but its amplitude will be controlled by the first instrument, so that when the latter plays loud, the second one will play softly and vice-versa (see figures 18.20 and 18.21).

To broadcast the loudness of the *instr 1821* to *instr 1822* we only need to add a global variable inside the first instrument. This variable will send the power value of the signal generated by the first instrument (see figure 18.20).

We can then use that global variable inside *instr 1822* to control the amplitude of each note as an inverse function of *gkpwr.*

It is possible to send information from within *instr 1822* back to *instr 1821.* To illustrate this idea, we will create *instr 1824* and have it receive a signal from *instr 1823;* ring modulate it with a sine wave whose frequency will be passed from the score to

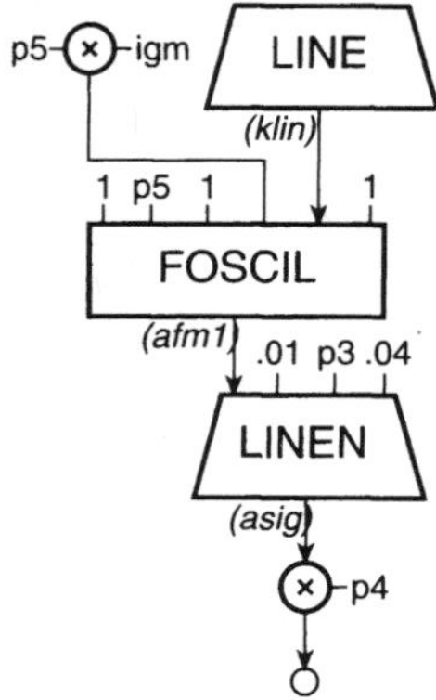

Figure 18.18 Block diagram of *instr 1820,* a simple FM instrument with pitch and amplitude envelopes.

```
          instr     1820          ; SIMPLE FM
igm       =         1.618
klin      line      3, p3, 0
afm1      foscil    1, p5, 1, p5*igm, klin, 1
asig      linen     afm1, 0.01, p3, 0.04
          out       asig*p4
          endin

f 1       0          8193          10          1
i 1820    0          3             20000       125
```

Figure 18.19 Orchestra and score code for *instr 1820,* a simple FM instrument.

instr 1824 and send the ring-modulated signal back to *instr 1823.* In effect, we will have created auxiliary inputs and outputs in *instr 1823* to send and receive the signal to be processed by *instr 1824* (see figures 18.22 and 18.23).

Feedback Instruments

In some cases, we may want to create a "feedback loop" by sending the output of an instrument back to itself. Some applications of feedback include physical modeling and nonlinear systems.

As with any feedback system, great care must be taken to ensure that the value being fed back does not grow infinitely. Additionally, because we need to use global

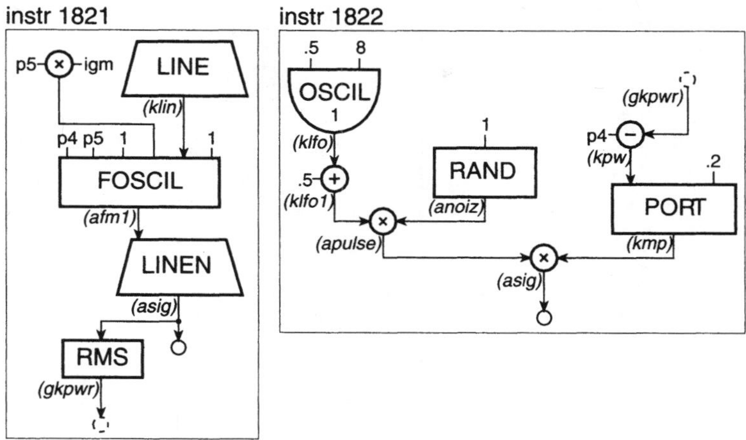

Figure 18.20 Block diagram of *instr 1821* and *1822*, context sensitive instrument that use a global **rms** opcode to control relative amplitude of each note.

```
        instr   1821        ; CONTEXT SENSITIVE GLOBAL RMS
igm     =       1.618
imp     =       p4
kln     line    3, p3, 0
afm1    foscil  imp, p5, 1, p5*igm, kln, 1
asig    linen   afm1, 0.01*p3, p3, 0.6*p3
        out     asig
gkpwr   rms     asig
        endin

        instr   1822        ; PULSED NOISE
klfo    oscil   0.5, 8, 1
klfo1   =       klfo+0.5             ; RESCALE [0-1]
anoiz   rand    1
apulse  =       anoiz*klfo1
kpw     =       p4-gkpwr             ; POWER CURVE
kmp     port    kpw, 0.2             ; SMOOTH CURVE
asig    =       apulse*kmp
        out     asig
        endin

f 1     0       8193    10      1

i 1821  0       3       20000   125
i 1822  0       1       20000   50
i 1822  +       .       20000   75
i 1822  +       .       20000   250
```

Figure 18.21 Orchestra and score code for *instr 1821* and *1822,* a context sensitive instrument pair.

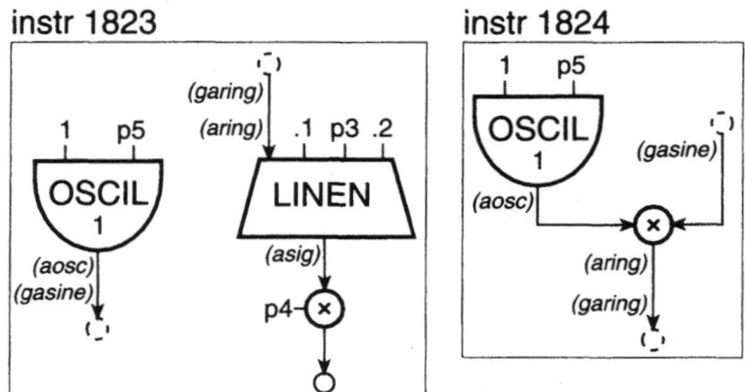

Figure 18.22 Block diagram of *instr 1823* and *1824*, featuring intercommunication from one to another and then back to the first.

```
garing   init     0
gasine   init     0

         instr    1823          ; PASSES DATA TO 1824
aosc     oscil    1, p5, 1
gasine   =        aosc                                ; SEND
aring    =        garing                              ; RETURN
asig     linen    aring, 0.1, p3, 0.2
         out      asig*p4
         endin

         instr    1824          ; PASSES DATA TO 1823
aosc     oscil    1, p5, 1
aring    =        aosc*gasine
garing   =        aring
         endin

f 1      0        8193          10            1

i 1823   0        4             20000         200
i 1823   +        .             20000         300
i 1824   0        2             0             50
i 1824   +        .             .             75
i 1824   +        .             .             150
i 1824   +        .             .             800
```

Figure 18.23 Orchestra and score code for *instr 1823* and *1824* that pass data back and forth between each other.

```
gafb        init        0                           ; INITIAL VALUE

            instr       1825          ; GLOBAL FEEDBACK
kline       line        0, p3, 1
aosc        oscil       1, p5*(1+kline*gafb), 1
asig        linen       aosc, 0.07, p3, 0.075
            out         asig*p4
gafb        =           asig
            endin

f 1         0           8193          10            1

i 1825      0           3             20000         400
i 1825      +           .             .             75
i 1825      +           .             .             135
```

Figure 18.24 Orchestra and score code for *instr 1825,* a global feedback instrument.

variables within the instrument, we must make sure the global value is initialized before being used in the instrument. This must be done before the instrument, if the feedback is to be sustained across notes. If the feedback is to be constrained within the note then the global variable must be assigned a value at init time to ensure that the value will not be reset at every k-rate or a-rate pass.

By default, if we simply use a global variable, the signal will be delayed by one sample. Thus, the actual delay time in seconds depends on the sample rate. This must be taken into account when creating the instrument. Also, it is best to design, test and execute the instrument at the same sample rate, since changing it will modify the behavior of the algorithm.

Now, let us create an instrument where the oscillator modulates its own frequency (see figure 18.24). First of all, we have to make sure that the value to be fed back is in a usable range. Thus, we will set the amplitude of the oscillator to 1 and multiply it later at the output. The frequency of the **oscil** will be the multiplication of *p5* (the "base frequency" of the oscillation) by the feedback signal and a time-varying re-scaling value, changing from 0 to 1 over the course of the note.

Feedback systems are, in general, nonlinear because they rely on previous states of the system. This makes feedback instruments hard to predict and control. Therefore, much experimentation is needed in order to obtain satisfying results.

Conclusion

The techniques we have seen are only a few possibilities afforded by the use of control instruments and meta-parameters. I hope that the examples will trigger ideas and improve the elaboration of future algorithms in simpler and more powerful ways.

References

Knuth, D. E. 1981. *The Art of Computer Programming.* 2d ed. Reading, Mass.: Addison-Wesley.

19 Mathematical Modeling with Csound: From Waveguides to Chaos

Hans Mikelson

Modeling Acoustic Instruments Using Digital Waveguides

Digital waveguide modeling has become one of the most active areas of research in sound synthesis in recent years. It is based on the solution of the wave equation, a differential equation that describes the behavior of a wave in a medium:

$$U_{tt} = c^2[U_{xx} + U_{yy} + U_{zz} + \ldots] \quad (19.1)$$

Where:

- U is the wave function
- c is the speed of propagation of the wave in the medium
- U_{ii} is the second derivative of the wave function with respect to i

Boundary values and initial conditions are usually specified as well (Lomen and Mark 1988; Gerald 1980). Plucked string instruments and many wind instruments can be approximated by the one-dimensional wave equation. For wind instruments, breath pressure is usually given as an input to the system. A drum membrane can be approximated by the two dimensional wave equation. Solving the wave equation mathematically is often difficult and solving the wave equation numerically is computationally intensive.

Digital waveguides provide a computationally efficient method of expressing the wave equation (Smith 1992). For a general one-dimensional case, a bi-directional delay line is used to simulate samples of a traveling wave and its reflection. A more complex system may have a bi-directional delay line for each separately vibrating section.

A Waveguide Bass

This instrument is derived from the Karplus-Strong algorithm, one of the most easily implemented waveguide models (Karplus and Strong 1983). It is accomplished as follows: fill a delay line with random numbers, take the average of the current output and the previous output and add this average to the input of the delay line. This simple procedure produces sounds remarkably like a plucked string (see figures 19.1 and 19.2).

The initial noise in the delay line is representative of a string in a high energy state. The average is a type of digital filter. It represents damping, which occurs at the ends of the string. This simple delay line, filter and feedback sequence is typical of waveguide instruments.

At low frequencies the initial noise begins to dominate the sound in the Karplus-Strong algorithm. To eliminate this problem and more closely simulate a plucked string's initial state, a filtered triangle waveform was selected as an initial state of the delay line.

```
iplk    =       1/ifqc*p6
kenvstr linseg 0, ipluck/4, -p4/2, ipluck/2, p4/2, ipluck/4, 0, p3-ipluck,0
aenvstr =       kenvstr
ainput  tone    aenvstr, 200
```

The duration of the initial pulse, parameter *p6,* can give the effect of different plucking styles.

Filters and initial conditions can introduce an offset from zero. When these are fed back into the system they can rapidly produce off-scale values. To solve this problem, a special type of filter called a *DC blocker* is introduced.

```
ablkin    init   0
ablkout   init   0
ablkout   =      afeedbk-ablkin+.99*ablkout
ablkin    =      afeedbk
ablock    =      ablkout
```

The sum of the input and the DC-blocked feedback is fed into a delay line of length 1/frequency. This instrument is slightly flat owing to the delays introduced by the filters. Subtracting about 15 samples brings it into tune.

```
adline    delay   ablock+ainput, 1/ifqc-15/sr
afiltr    tone    adline, 400
```

Some resonances are generated and scaled to simulate the resonance of an acoustic bass body:

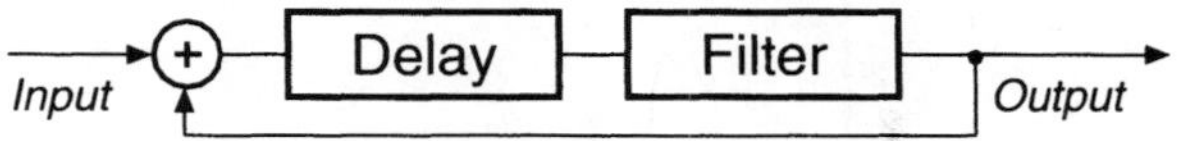

Figure 19.1 A block diagram of the Karplus-Strong Plucked-string algorithm.

```
          instr   1901          ; WAVEGUIDE PLUCKED BASS
ifqc      =       cpspch(p5)
ipluck    =       1/ifqc*p6
kcount    init    0
adline    init    0
ablock2   init    0
ablock3   init    0
afiltr    init    0
afeedbk   init    0
; OUTPUT ENVELOPE
koutenv   linseg  0, .01, 1, p3-.11, 1, .1, 0
kfltenv   linseg  0, 1.5, 1, 1.5, 0
; THIS ENVELOPE LOADS THE STRING WITH A TRIANGLE WAVE
kenvstr   linseg  0,ipluck/4,-p4/2,ipluck/2,p4/2,ipluck/4,0,p3-ipluck,0
aenvstr   =       kenvstr
ainput    tone    aenvstr, 200
; DC BLOCKER
ablock2   =       afeedbk-ablock3+.99*ablock2
ablock3   =       afeedbk
ablock    =       ablock2
; DELAY LINE WITH FILTERED FEEDBACK
adline    delay   ablock+ainput, 1/ifqc-15/sr
afiltr    tone    adline, 400
; RESONANCE OF THE BODY
abody1    reson   afiltr, 110, 40
abody1    =       abody1/5000
abody2    reson   afiltr, 70, 20
abody2    =       abody2/50000
afeedbk   =       afiltr
aout      =       afeedbk
          out     50*koutenv*(aout+kfltenv*(abody1+abody2))
          endin
```

Figure 19.2 Orchestra code for *instr 1901,* a waveguide plucked-bass.

```
abody1    reson     afeedbk, 110, 40
abody1    =         abody1/5000
abody2    reson     afeedbk, 70, 20
abody2    =         abody2/50000
```

These are modified by an envelope to produce a swell shortly after the initial pluck. This is added to the output from the delay line, scaled again and used as the output from the instrument:

```
out     50*koutenv*(afeedbk+kfltenv*(abody1+abody2))
```

This instrument could be enhanced by introducing a bridge delay line for transmitting the string vibrations to the body, or modifying the string-filter for fingered and open strings. Perhaps a system of waveguides could be set up to simulate the acoustic bass body.

A Slide-Flute

The next instrument considered is a slide-flute derived from Perry Cook's instrument (Cook 1995). The input to this system is a flow of air. Noise is added to simulate a breath sound.

The feedback section of this instrument consists of two delay lines. One delay line models the embouchure for the air-jet and the other models the flute bore. Optimally, the embouchure delay is equal to one-half of the length of the flute bore:

```
atemp1    delayr     1/ifqc/2
ax        deltapi    afqc/2
          delayw     asum2
```

The interaction between the embouchure and the flute bore is modeled by a cubic equation, x-x^3:

```
ax       delay      asum2, 1/ifqc/2; EMBOUCHURE DELAY
apoly    =          ax-ax*ax*ax     ; CUBIC EQUATION
```

The end of the flute bore reflects low frequencies. This is modeled with a lowpass filter at the beginning of the bore delay line. The bore delay is then fed back into the system in two places, before the embouchure delay, where it is added to the flow and before the filter, where it is added to the output from the cubic equation.

The pitch is changed by changing the length of the bore delay line:

```
afqc     =        1/ifqc-asum1/20000-9/sr+ifqc/12000000
```

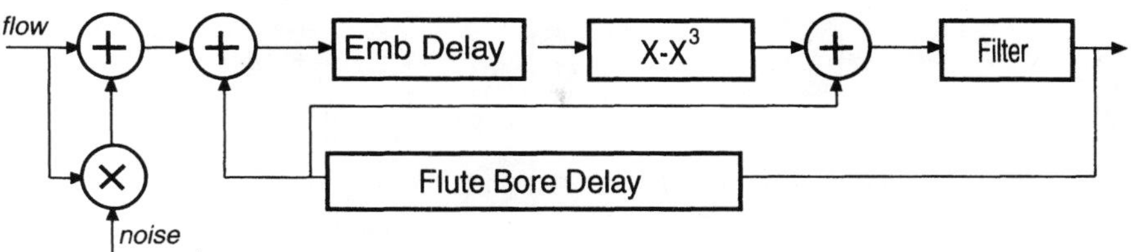

Figure 19.3 A block diagram of Perry Cook's slide-flute.

```
            instr     1902        ; WAVEGUIDE SLIDE-FLUTE
aflute1     init      0
ifqc        =         cpspch(p5)
ipress      =         p6
ibreath     =         p7
ifeedbk1    =         p8
ifeedbk2    =         p9
;FLOW SETUP
kenv1       linseg    0, .06, 1.1*ipress, .2, ipress, p3-.16, ipress, .02, 0
kenv2       linseg    0, .01, 1, p3-.02, 1, .01, 0
kenvibr     linseg    0, .5, 0, .5, 1, p3-1, 1    ; VIBRATO ENVELOPE
; THE VALUES MUST BE APPROXIMATELY -1 TO 1 OR THE CUBIC WILL BLOW UP
aflow1      rand      kenv1
kvibr       oscil     kenvibr*.1, 5, 3
; IBREATH CAN BE USED TO ADJUST THE NOISE LEVEL
asum1       =         ibreath*aflow1+kenv1+kvibr
asum2       =         asum1+aflute1*ifeedbk1
afqc        =         1/ifqc-asum1/20000-9/sr+ifqc/12000000
; EMBOUCHURE DELAY SHOULD BE 1/2 THE BORE DELAY
;ax         delay     asum2, (1/ifqc-10/sr)/2
atemp1      delayr    1/ifqc/2
ax          deltapi   afqc/2                      ; - asum1/ifqc/10 + 1/1000
            delayw    asum2
apoly       =         ax-ax*ax*ax
asum3       =         apoly+aflute1*ifeedbk2
avalue      tone      asum3, 2000
; BORE: THE BORE LENGTH DETERMINES PITCH. SHORTER IS HIGHER PITCH.
atemp2      delayr    1/ifqc
aflute1     deltapi   afqc
            delayw    avalue
            out       avalue*p4*kenv2
            endin
```

Figure 19.4 Orchestra code for *instr 1902,* a waveguide slide-flute.

In order to be able to tune precisely, an interpolating variable delay tap was used to implement the bore delay. The **delayr**, **delayw** and **deltapi** opcodes were used for this.

```
atemp2     delayr    1/ifqc
aflute1    deltapi   afqc
delayw     avalue
```

In a real flute, pitch varies slightly based on breath pressure. Vibrato can be introduced in this way. To implement this in the waveguide model, the delay tap length includes a term based on the pressure.

```
atemp      delayr    1/ifqc
aflute1    deltapi   1/ifqc-12/sr+asum1/20000
           delayw    avalue
```

One modification of this instrument could be to make the embouchure delay length a function of pressure, to allow for overblowing techniques. This can be tricky, because overblowing occurs at a lower pressure for low frequencies. Re-tuning the flute would also be required.

A Waveguide Clarinet

The next instrument considered is a waveguide clarinet derived from an instrument by Perry Cook (Cook 1995). In this instrument a bi-directional delay line is used. A bi-directional delay line consists of two delay lines of the same length, whose outputs feed each others' inputs. Breath pressure is fed into the system at the input of the forward delay line and at the output of the reflection delay line.

Another feature used in this instrument is a feedback table. Rather than having constant feedback, feedback is set up in a table, referenced by the pressure difference between the input pressure and the reflected wave.

```
asum2      =         -apressm-.95*arefilt-kemboff
areedtab   tablei    asum2/4+.34, p9, 1, .5
amult1     =         asum2*areedtab
```

The table can be modified to account for variations in reed stiffness and embouchure. The bell at the end of a clarinet functions as a filter, low frequencies are reflected back into the bore and high frequencies are allowed to pass out of the bore. This is implemented as a pair of filters. The output from the lowpass filter feeds the reflection delay line and the output from the highpass filter is scaled and used as the output of the instrument.

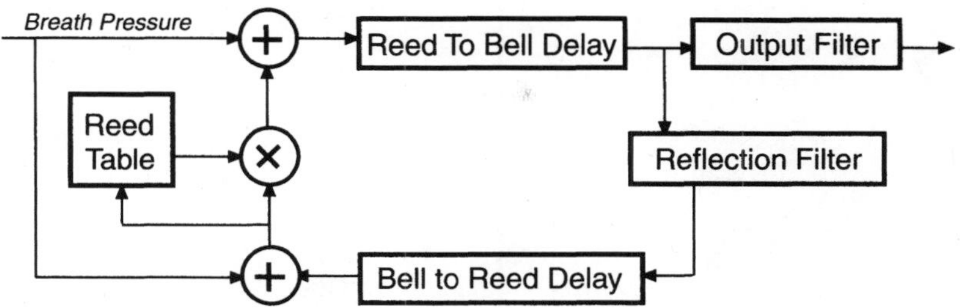

Figure 19.5 A block diagram of a waveguide clarinet.

```
            instr    1903        ; WAVEGUIDE CLARINET
areedbell   init     0
ifqc        =        cpspch(p5)
ifco        =        p7
ibore       =        1/ifqc-15/sr
; ENVELOPE FROM PERRY COOK'S CLARINET
kenv1       linseg   0, .005, .55 + .3*p6, p3 - .015, .55 + .3*p6, .01, 0
kenvibr     linseg   0, .1, 0, .9, 1, p3-1, 1          ; VIBRATO ENVELOPE
; SUPPOSEDLY HAS SOMETHING TO DO WITH REED STIFFNESS
kemboff     =        p8
; BREATH PRESSURE
avibr       oscil    kenvibr*.1, 5, 3
apressm     =        kenv1+avibr
; REFLECTION FILTER FROM THE BELL IS LOWPASS
arefilt     tone     areedbell, ifco
; THE DELAY FROM BELL TO REED
abellreed   delay    arefilt, ibore
; BACK PRESSURE AND REED TABLE LOOK-UP
asum2       =        -apressm-.95*arefilt-kemboff
areedtab    tablei   asum2/4+.34, p9, 1, .5
amult1      =        asum2*areedtab
; FORWARD PRESSURE
asum1       =        apressm+amult1
areedbell   delay    asum1, ibore
aofilt      atone    areedbell, ifco
            out      aofilt*p4
            endin
```

Figure 19.6 Orchestra code for *instr 1903,* a waveguide clarinet.

A Waveguide Drum

This instrument is an attempt to extend the waveguide model to two dimensions. There are two parts to this instrument defined as separate Csound instruments: the drum and the drum stick. The drum can be thought of as a square membrane with waves traveling from each of the four corners to each of the other three corners.

These waves are represented as bi-directional delay lines in the following code:

```
alineab     delay      anodea+gadrum+afiltr, ilength/ifqc
alineba     delay      anodeb+gadrum+afiltr, ilength/ifqc
alinebc     delay      anodeb+gadrum+afiltr, iwidth/ifqc
alinecb     delay      anodec+gadrum+afiltr, iwidth/ifqc
alinecd     delay      anodec+gadrum+afiltr, ilength/ifqc
alinedc     delay      anoded+gadrum+afiltr, ilength/ifqc
alinead     delay      anodea+gadrum+afiltr, iwidth/ifqc
alineda     delay      anoded+gadrum+afiltr, iwidth/ifqc
alineac     delay      anodea+gadrum+afiltr, idiagnl/ifqc*irt2
alineca     delay      anodec+gadrum+afiltr, idiagnl/ifqc*irt2
alinebd     delay      anodeb+gadrum+afiltr, idiagnl/ifqc*irt2
alinedb     delay      anoded+gadrum+afiltr, idiagnl/ifqc*irt2
```

The membrane can be left on for accumulation of successive impulses and can be turned off to simulate muting. The output from the drum is fed into a delay line, meant to simulate the drum body.

```
atube       delay      anodea, itube/ifqc
afiltr      tone       atube, 1000
afiltr      =          afiltr/ifdbck2
```

The second part of this instrument simulates the drum stick striking the drum. This sends an impulse into the drum membrane. The pitch determines the duration of the impulse and along with the filter can be thought of as specifying the type of drum stick.

This drum can be adjusted to produce a wide variety of percussion sounds. Sounds similar to a bongo, conga, wood blocks, struck glass bottles, bells and others can be produced.

A pitch dependence on amplitude could be introduced to simulate the drum head tightening during an impact. One drawback of this instrument is the large number of delay lines, requiring extensive computation. It is possible to simplify this system substantially. Another problem with this instrument is that the timbre tends to change with pitch. This presents a problem for reproducing marimba-like tones.

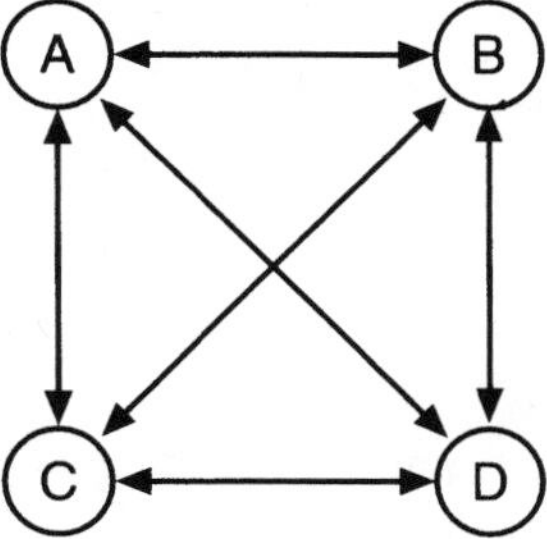

Figure 19.7 A simplified diagram of a waveguide square drum. Each double-arrowhead line represents a bi-directional delay line.

```
            instr   1904        ; DRUM STICK
gadrum      init    0
;FREQUENCY
ifqc        =       cpspch(p5)
; INITIALIZE THE DELAY LINE WITH NOISE
ashape      linseg  0,1/ifqc/8,-1/2,1/ifqc/4,1/2,1/ifqc/8,0,p3-1/ifqc,0
gadrum      tone    ashape, p6
            endin

            instr   1905        ; SQUARE DRUM
irt2        init    sqrt(2)
itube       init    p7
ifdbck1     init    p8
ifdbck2     init    p9
anodea      init    0
anodeb      init    0
anodec      init    0
anoded      init    0
afiltr      init    0
ablocka2    init    0
ablocka3    init    0
ablockb2    init    0
ablockb3    init    0
ablockc2    init    0
ablockc3    init    0
ablockd2    init    0
ablockd3    init    0
; FREQUENCY
ifqc        =       cpspch(p5)
ipfilt      =       p6
; AMPLITUDE ENVELOPE
kampenv     linseg  0, .01, p4, p3-.02, p4, .01, 0
; DELAY LINES
```

Figure 19.8 Orchestra code for *instr 1904* and *1905,* a drumstick and a waveguide drum.

```
alineab    delay   anodea+gadrum+afiltr, 1/ifqc
alineba    delay   anodeb+gadrum+afiltr, 1/ifqc
alinebc    delay   anodeb+gadrum+afiltr, 1/ifqc
alinecb    delay   anodec+gadrum+afiltr, 1/ifqc
alinecd    delay   anodec+gadrum+afiltr, 1/ifqc
alinedc    delay   anoded+gadrum+afiltr, 1/ifqc
alinead    delay   anodea+gadrum+afiltr, 1/ifqc
alineda    delay   anoded+gadrum+afiltr, 1/ifqc
alineac    delay   anodea+gadrum+afiltr, 1/ifqc*irt2
alineca    delay   anodec+gadrum+afiltr, 1/ifqc*irt2
alinebd    delay   anodeb+gadrum+afiltr, 1/ifqc*irt2
alinedb    delay   anoded+gadrum+afiltr, 1/ifqc*irt2
; FILTER THE DELAYED SIGNAL AND FEEDBACK INTO THE DELAY
; IMPLEMENTS DC BLOCKING
ablocka1   =       -(alineba+alineca+alineda)/ifdbck1
ablocka2   =       ablocka1-ablocka3+ablocka2*.99
ablocka3   =       ablocka1
anodea     =       ablocka2
; NODE B
ablockb1   =       -(alineba+alineca+alineda)/ifdbck1
ablockb2   =       ablockb1-ablockb3+ablockb2*.99
ablockb3   =       ablockb1
anodeb     =       ablockb2
; NODE C
ablockc1   =       -(alineba+alineca+alineda)/ifdbck1
ablockc2   =       ablockc1-ablockc3+ablockc2*.99
ablockc3   =       ablockc1
anodec     =       ablockc2
; NODE D
ablockd1   =       -(alineba+alineca+alineda)/ifdbck1
ablockd2   =       ablockd1-ablockd3+ablockd2*.99
ablockd3   =       ablockd1
anoded     =       ablockd2
; BODY RESONANCE
atube      delay   anodea, itube/ifqc
afiltr     tone    atube, 1000
afiltr     =       afiltr/ifdbck2
; SCALE AND OUTPUT
           out     anodea*kampenv*1000
           endin
```

Figure 19.8 continued

Summary

Waveguide instruments have introduced a new opportunity for expression in electronic musical instruments. Since they are based on physical systems, their response to playing dynamics is similar to the response of an acoustic instrument. Programming a waveguide instrument can be tedious. They are difficult to get to start oscillating and once they do start oscillating, they tend to blow up easily. They are also difficult to tune over a wide range of pitches. Creating waveguide instruments is in some ways similar to creating acoustic instruments. They both require careful crafting and meticulous adjustments to produce quality sound.

Chaos and Complex Systems

This set of instruments is based on systems of differential equations. These systems can exhibit a variety of behaviors ranging from increasing without bound to approaching a constant value. Some of these systems, called *strange attractors,* exhibit chaotic behavior. They follow a path that is repetitive yet nonrepeating. These systems can be used to produce unusual and bizarre timbres because of their complex nature.

The Lorenz Attractor

The Lorenz Attractor, discovered by Edward Lorenz, is one of the first chaotic systems to be discovered (Pickover 1991). It describes the motion of convection currents in a gas or liquid. It is defined by the following set of equations:

$$\begin{aligned} dx/dt &= \sigma(y - x) \\ dy/dt &= -y - xz + rx \\ dz/dt &= xy - bz \end{aligned} \tag{19.2}$$

Where σ is the ratio of the fluid viscosity of a substance to its thermal conductivity, r is the difference in temperature between the top and the bottom of the system and b is the width to height ratio of the box used.

These equations can be approximated as follows:

```
            instr       1908          ; LORENZ ATTRACTOR
ax          init        p5
ay          init        p6
az          init        p7
as          init        p8
ar          init        p9
ab          init        p10
ah          init        p11
ipanl       init        p12
ipanr       init        1-ipanl
kampenv     linseg      0, .01, p4, p3-.02, p4, .01, 0
axnew       =           ax+ah*as*(ay-ax)
aynew       =           ay+ah*(-ax*az+ar*ax-ay)
aznew       =           az+ah*(ax*ay-ab*az)
ax          =           axnew
ay          =           aynew
az          =           aznew
            outs        ax*kampenv*ipanl, ay*kampenv*ipanr
            endin
```

Figure 19.9 Orchestra code for *instr 1908*, a Lorenz Attractor instrument.

```
adx     =       as*(ay-ax)                  ; COMPUTE DX
ady     =       -ax*az+ar*ax-ay             ; DY
adz     =       ax*ay-ab*az                 ; AND DZ
ax      =       ax+ah*adx                   ; UPDATE X
ay      =       ay+ah*ady                   ; Y
az      =       az+ah*adz                   ; AND Z
        outs    ax*kampenv, ay*kampenv      ; SCALE AND OUTPUT
```

The variable *h* represents the time step and can be used to modify the frequency of the system. Smaller values of *h* result in a more accurate approximation of the system. As the value of *h* is increased, the approximation becomes less and less accurate until the system becomes unstable, when *h* is somewhat larger than *.1*. The *x* and *y* coordinates are scaled and given as the output for the instrument. Initial values of the coordinates and coefficients are provided in the score.

```
;       START  DUR  AMP  X   Y   Z   S   R   B      H
i 1908  0      8    600  .6  .6  .6  10  28  2.667  .01
```

The values listed are the historic values of the coefficients. This system will produce drastically different results with different initial values of the coordinates and different coefficients (see figure 19.9).

```
          instr    1909         ; ROSSLER'S ATTRACTOR
ax        init     0
ay        init     0
az        init     0
ih        init     p5
aa        init     .375
ib        init     p6
ic        init     p7
ipanl     init     p8
ipanr     init     1-ipanl
kampenv   linseg   0, .01, p4, p3-.02, p4, .01, 0  ; AMPLITUDE ENVELOPE
aa        oscil    1/7, .5, 1
aa        =        aa+.3
axnew     =        ax+ih*(-ay-az)
aynew     =        ay+ih*(ax+aa*ay)
aznew     =        az+ih*(ib+ax*az-ic*az)
ax        =        axnew
ay        =        aynew
az        =        aznew
          outs     kampenv*ax*ipanl, kampenv*ay*ipanr
          endin
```

Figure 19.10 Orchestra code for *instr 1909,* Rossler's Attractor instrument.

The Rossler Attractor

The Rossler Attractor (Gleick 1987) is a chaotic system defined by the following equations:

$$\begin{aligned} dx/dt &= -y - z \\ dy/dt &= x + Ay \\ dz/dt &= B + xz - Cz \end{aligned} \tag{19.3}$$

This can be implemented using the methods described for implementing the Lorenz attractor (see figure 19.10).

Planet Orbiting in a Binary Star System

This instrument is based on simulating the orbit of a planet in a binary star system (Dewdney 1988). The planet is initialized to some location and the stars are given positions and masses. For each sample, the position, velocity, and acceleration of the planet is calculated based on the laws of gravity and momentum.

$$F = \frac{m_1 m_2 G}{r^2} \tag{19.4}$$

$$F = ma \tag{19.5}$$

Using these equations together produces a formula for acceleration:

$$a = \frac{m_{star} G}{r^2} \tag{19.6}$$

To simplify the equation, the mass is expressed in units such that the gravitational constant equals one. For a three-dimensional system, each dimensional component of acceleration may be calculated separately, by multiplying the acceleration by the difference, for each dimension divided by the radius, as follows:

$$\begin{aligned} a_x &= \frac{m_{star}}{r^2}\frac{\Delta x}{r} \\ a_y &= \frac{m_{star}}{r^2}\frac{\Delta y}{r} \\ a_z &= \frac{m_{star}}{r^2}\frac{\Delta z}{r} \end{aligned} \tag{19.7}$$

The acceleration due to each star is calculated separately and summed to obtain an overall acceleration. Once the total acceleration has been determined the velocity may be incremented:

$$\begin{aligned} v_x &= v_x + a_x \\ v_y &= v_y + a_y \\ v_z &= v_z + a_z \end{aligned} \tag{19.8}$$

The position is similarly incremented:

$$\begin{aligned} x &= x + v_x \\ y &= y + v_y \\ z &= z + v_z \end{aligned} \tag{19.9}$$

The instrument shown in figure 19.11, *instr 1910,* implements a planet orbiting in a binary star system as described above. Note that the one is added to the radius squared, to stabilize the system by avoiding division by zero during a close approach between a planet and a star. If computation of an actual star system is desired, the gravitational constant should be included. The one added to the radius-squared term should also be omitted.

```
            instr   1910    ; PLANET ORBITING IN BINARY STAR SYSTEM
kampenv     linseg  0, .01, p4, p3-.02, p4, .01, 0
; PLANET POSITION (X, Y, Z) & VELOCITY (VX, VY, VZ)
kx          init    0
ky          init    .1
kz          init    0
kvx         init    .5
kvy         init    .6
kvz         init    -.1
ih          init    p5
ipanl       init    p9
ipanr       init    1-ipanl
; STAR 1 MASS & X, Y, Z
imass1      init    p6
is1x        init    0
is1y        init    0
is1z        init    p8
; STAR 2 MASS & X, Y, Z
imass2      init    p7
is2x        init    0
is2y        init    0
is2z        init    -p8
; CALCULATE DISTANCE TO STAR 1
kdx         =       is1x-kx
kdy         =       is1y-ky
kdz         =       is1z-kz
ksqradius   =       kdx*kdx+kdy*kdy+kdz*kdz+1
kradius     =       sqrt(ksqradius)
; DETERMINE ACCELERATION DUE TO STAR 1 (AX, AY, AZ)
kax         =       imass1/ksqradius*kdx/kradius
kay         =       imass1/ksqradius*kdy/kradius
kaz         =       imass1/ksqradius*kdz/kradius
; CALCULATE DISTANCE TO STAR 2
kdx         =       is2x-kx
kdy         =       is2y-ky
kdz         =       is2z-kz
ksqradius   =       kdx*kdx+kdy*kdy+kdz*kdz+1
kradius     =       sqrt(ksqradius)
; DETERMINE ACCELERATION DUE TO STAR 2 (AX, AY, AZ)
kax         =       kax+imass2/ksqradius*kdx/kradius
kay         =       kay+imass2/ksqradius*kdy/kradius
kaz         =       kaz+imass2/ksqradius*kdz/kradius
; UPDATE THE VELOCITY
kvx         =       kvx+ih*kax
kvy         =       kvy+ih*kay
kvz         =       kvz+ih*kaz
; UPDATE THE POSITION
kx          =       kx+ih*kvx
ky          =       ky+ih*kvy
kz          =       kz+ih*kvz
aoutx       =       kx*kampenv*ipanl
aouty       =       ky*kampenv*ipanr
            outs    aoutx, aouty
            endin
```

Figure 19.11 Orchestra code for *instr 1910,* a planet orbiting in a binary star system.

One modification could be to add more stars to the system. It is difficult to find a system that remains stable over a long period of time. Eventually, a close encounter with a star accelerates the planet to escape velocity from the system.

Summary

There seems to be a great deal of room for exploration in this area. You will find that many different dynamical systems are useful as tone generators. These systems also work well at low frequencies for modulating pitch, amplitude and panning. At low amplitudes they can be used to introduce subtle complex modulations to otherwise sterile sounds.

References

Cook, P. 1995 . "Integration of physical modeling for synthesis and animation." *International Computer Music Conference.* Banff.

Cook, P. 1995. "A meta-wind-instrument physical model and a meta-controller for real time performance control." *International Computer Music Conference.* Banff.

Dewdney, A. 1988. *The Armchair Universe.* New York: W. H. Freeman and Co.

Gleick, J. 1987. *Chaos.* New York: Viking Penguin.

Gerald, C. 1980. *Applied Numerical Analysis.* 2d ed. Reading, Mass.: Addison-Wesley.

Karplus, K., and A. Strong. 1983. "Digital synthesis of plucked-string and drum timbres." *Computer Music Journal* 7(4).

Lomen, D., and J. Mark. 1988. *Differential Equations.* Englewood Cliffs, N.J.: Prentice-Hall.

Pickover, C. 1991. *Computers and the Imagination.* New York: St. Martin's Press.

Smith, J. O. III. 1992. "Physical modeling using digital waveguides." *Computer Music Journal* 16(4): 74–91.

Signal Processing

Understanding Signal Processing through Csound

20 An Introduction to Signal Processing with Csound

Erik Spjut

Signal processing has become a vital part of a modern engineer's vocabulary. From earthquake retrofitting to direct-from-satellite TV broadcasts to chemical-process control, a knowledge of signal processing and dynamic systems has become essential to an engineer's education. Learning signal processing, however, is often a dull exercise in performing integrations, summations, and complex arithmetic. Csound has a number of features that make it valuable as an adjunct to the traditional course work. First, it was designed from the ground up to follow the principles of digital signal processing, although this fact is probably hidden from the casual user. Second, hearing a swept filter or an aliased sine wave brings the signal processing concepts home in an immediate and visceral way.

This chapter introduces the student of signal processing to the powerful examples available in Csound. It also introduce the concepts of signal processing to the Csound practitioner in the hope that you will better understand why Csound does what it does and also be better able to make Csound do what you want.

Because all of the topics are interrelated, occasional use or mention is made of later topics in the derivation of earlier topics. The order of presentation keeps forward references to a minimum.

Even though Csound is powerful, it will not do every sort of calculation that you might desire. Often you need to do some sort of symbolic or numeric calculation to figure out what values to use in Csound. These sorts of calculations are best done using a program like *Mathematica, Maple, MathCAD,* or *Matlab.* I have given some examples of these sorts of calculations using *Mathematica* to assist the interested reader. Just as you do not really need to know how to do long divisions in order to use a calculator, you do not really need to know calculus to use *Mathematica* to integrate.

Mathematical Conventions

Variables

A *variable* is a symbol for a quantity or thing that can change or vary. Common variables in algebra are x and y. Some of the variables used in this chapter are t (usually stands for time), T (a time interval or period), f (frequency of a continuous signal) and F (frequency of a discrete signal).

Functions

A *function* is the way one variable depends on (or relates to) another variable, for example, in the equation

$$y = 3x + 5 \tag{20.1}$$

the variable y is a function of the variable x. The function says "take whatever value x has currently, multiply it by three and add five to that result." That final result is the current value of y. Often, when one variable such as y is a function of another variable, such as t or n, but we do not know (or care) exactly what the function is, we write $y(t)$ or $y[n]$. When speaking, we read $y(t)$ as "*y-of-t*" and $y[n]$ as "*y-of-n*". Three of the most common functions in signal processing are the *sine* of x (written as $\sin x$), the *cosine* of x (written as $\cos x$) and the *exponential* of x (written as e^x or $\exp x$). A function where $y(-t) = y(t)$ (like $y(t)=t^2$) is called an *even* function. A function where $y(-t) = -y(t)$ (like $y(t)=t$) is called an *odd* function. Many functions are neither even nor odd.

Independent and Dependent Variables

If a variable is not a function of another variable it is called an *independent variable,* because it can vary in any way it pleases. If a variable *is* a function of another variable, it is called a *dependent variable,* because its value depends on the value of some other variable. In signal processing, in addition to being either independent or dependent, our variables are often *complex.*

Complex Numbers

A *complex number* is a mathematical shorthand for combining two independent numbers into one symbol. If the two independent numbers in our complex number are a and b, mathematicians would write the complex number as $a + ib$ and engineers would write it as $a + jb$. For historical reasons, a is called the *real part*, b is called the *imaginary part*, and i or j is called the *imaginary unit*. It is defined by $j^2 = -1$. Engineers use j as the imaginary unit instead of i, because i is reserved for current. *Mathematica* uses "I" for the imaginary unit.

Complex Addition and Subtraction

If we have two complex numbers $a + jb$ and $c + jd$, we can define the relationships for addition as the sum of the real parts and the sum of the imaginary parts:

$$(a + jb) + (c + jd) = (a + c) + j(b + d) \tag{20.2}$$

and subtraction as the difference of the real parts and the difference of the imaginary parts:

$$(a + jb) - (c + jd) = (a - c) + j(b - d) \tag{20.3}$$

Polar Form

If we think of a complex number as a point on a Cartesian coordinate system (a rectangular graph) we can define the distance from the origin to the complex number as the *magnitude* or absolute value of the complex number:

$$|a + jb| = \sqrt{a^2 + b^2} \tag{20.4}$$

Complex Numbers in Both Cartesian and Polar Form

We can think of the angle between the positive x-axis and the line segment from the origin to the complex number as the *angle* (also known as the *phase angle*, or the *phase* or the *argument*) of the complex number:

$$\angle(a + jb) = \arctan\frac{b}{a} \tag{20.5}$$

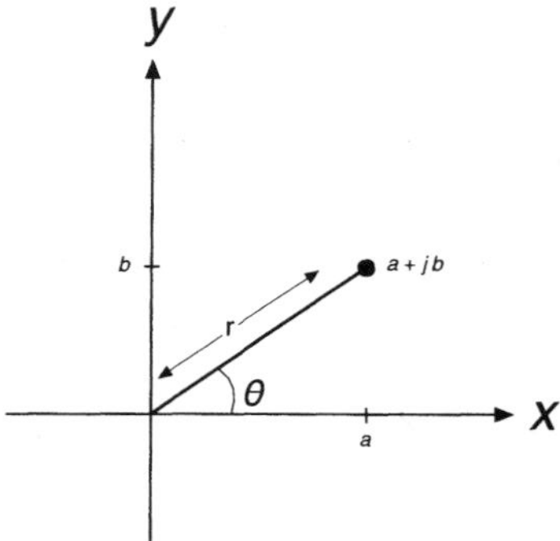

Figure 20.1 A complex number in both Cartesian and Polar form.

The function *arctan* is the arctangent. It means "the-angle-whose-tangent-is".

A complex number expressed as a magnitude and an angle is in polar form. For signal processing it is usually most convenient to write the magnitude as r and the angle as θ, so that our complex number becomes $re^{j\theta}$, where $r^2 = a^2 + b^2$ and $\tan\theta = b/a$ (see figure 20.1).

Complex Multiplication and Division

With two complex numbers, $r_1e^{j\theta_1}$ and $r_2e^{j\theta_2}$, in polar form, multiplication is the product of the magnitudes and the sum of the angles:

$$(r_1e^{j\theta_1})(r_2e^{j\theta_2}) = (r_1r_2)e^{j(\theta_1+\theta_2)} \tag{20.6}$$

Division is the ratio of the magnitudes and the difference of the angles:

$$\frac{r_1e^{j\theta_1}}{r_2e^{j\theta_2}} = \left(\frac{r_1}{r_2}\right)e^{j(\theta_1-\theta_2)} \tag{20.7}$$

There are formulas for multiplication and division using a and b instead of r and θ, but they usually make calculations much harder.

Complex Variables

By analogy with complex numbers, the *complex variable* z contains two normal (real) variables x and y:

$$z = x + jy \tag{20.8}$$

Again we call x the real part and y the imaginary part. We can (and usually do) express complex variables in polar form:

$$z = re^{j\theta} \tag{20.9}$$

Where $r = \sqrt{x^2 + y^2}$ and $\theta = \arctan y/x$, but r and θ are now variables instead of numbers.

Complex Functions

A *complex function* or a function of a complex variable is made up of two normal functions, again a real part and an imaginary part. As an example, let us look at the function e^z, since it is used so frequently in signal processing (we got ahead of ourselves and already used part of it in our definition of polar form).

$$e^z = e^{x+jy} = e^x e^{jy} = e^x(\cos y + j\sin y) = e^x \cos y + je^x \sin y \tag{20.10}$$

The real part of e^z is the product of the exponential of x and the cosine of y, $e^x \cos y$ and the imaginary part is the product of the exponential of x and the sine of y, $e^x \sin y$. In terms of polar form, the magnitude of e^z is e^x and the angle is y.

(It may be worth noting that *Mathematica* treats almost all variables and functions as being complex. For example, *Mathematica* will evaluate Exp[I Pi/2] or Exp[3 + 2 I] as readily as Sin[Pi/2].)

Summation

The symbol:

$$\sum_{n=0}^{27} f(n) \tag{20.11}$$

is a summation symbol. It means to take the *index variable* (the variable on the bottom, usually n), let it take on all integer values from the starting index (the number on the bottom) to the ending index (the number on the top), substitute the integer into the main expression and add up the values of all of the substitutions.

For example,

$$\sum_{n=3}^{7} n^2 = 3^2 + 4^2 + 5^2 + 6^2 + 7^2 = 9 + 16 + 25 + 36 + 49 = 135 \tag{20.12}$$

Integration and Differentiation

The symbol:

$$\int \tag{20.13}$$

is the integration symbol. Mathematicians usually define an integral in terms of limits and infinitesimal. It is usually adequate to think of an integral as the area between a real function and the x-axis. A large part of a calculus class is devoted to learning how to evaluate integrals of functions.

Mathematica can integrate a large number of functions symbolically (meaning the result is a function) and almost any function numerically (meaning the result is a number). For example, the integral of the sine of x, which is written:

$$\int \sin x \tag{20.14}$$

is evaluated symbolically in *Mathematica* as *Integrate[Sin[x],x]* and the integral of the cosine of x from 0 to π, which is written:

$$\int_0^{\pi} \cos x \tag{20.15}$$

is evaluated numerically in *Mathematica* as *Integrate[Cos[x],{x,0,Pi}]*.

The symbol:

$$\frac{dy}{dx} \tag{20.16}$$

is the derivative of the function y with respect to the variable x. Mathematicians again define derivatives in terms of limits and infinitesimal. It is usually adequate to think of a derivative as the slope of a function. A small part of a calculus class is devoted to learning how to take derivatives of functions.

Mathematica will evaluate the derivative of almost any function. For example, the derivative of the cosine of x with respect to x, which is written:

$$\frac{d \cos x}{dx} \tag{20.17}$$

is evaluated in *Mathematica* by *D[Cos[x],x]*.

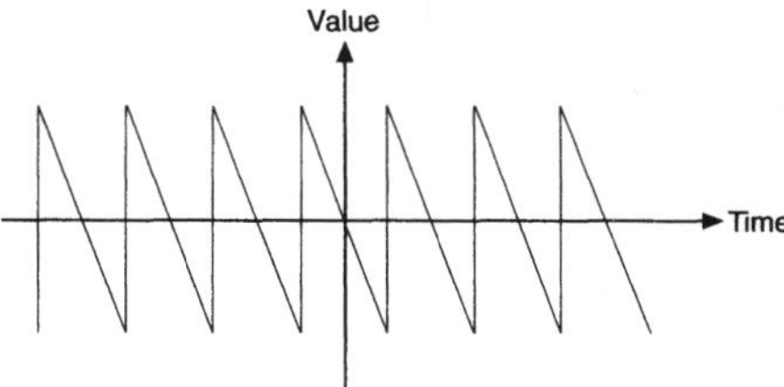

Figure 20.2 A continuous-time signal.

Signals

A *signal* is a function of one or more independent variables. The purpose or use of a signal is to convey information. Examples of common signals are the voltage coming out of an audio amplifier, the Dow-Jones industrial average, the outside temperature, the display on a computer screen, and the output from a radio transmitter. Csound is structured for processing signals of a single independent variable, so we will restrict ourselves to signals that are a function of only one independent variable, that being either time or sample number.

Continuous Signals

Signals are divided into two classes, *continuous-time* and *discrete-time*. Continuous-time signals have a value at any instant of time. Most physical phenomena, such as temperature, sound, or a person's weight are continuous-time signals (see figure 20.2). Two continuous-time signals that are important in signal processing are $\sin(2\pi f_0 t)$ and $\cos(2\pi f_0 t)$. Engineers often use the Euler formula as a shorthand notation for representing these two signals at the same time:

$$e^{j2\pi f_0 t} = \cos(2\pi f_0 t) + j\sin(2\pi f_0 t) \tag{20.18}$$

where $j = \sqrt{-1}$. One can get back to sines and cosines with:

$$\cos(2\pi f_0 t) = \frac{e^{j2\pi f_0 t} + e^{-j2\pi f_0 t}}{2} \tag{20.19}$$

and:

$$\sin(2\pi f_0 t) = \frac{e^{j2\pi f_0 t} - e^{-j2\pi f_0 t}}{2j} \tag{20.20}$$

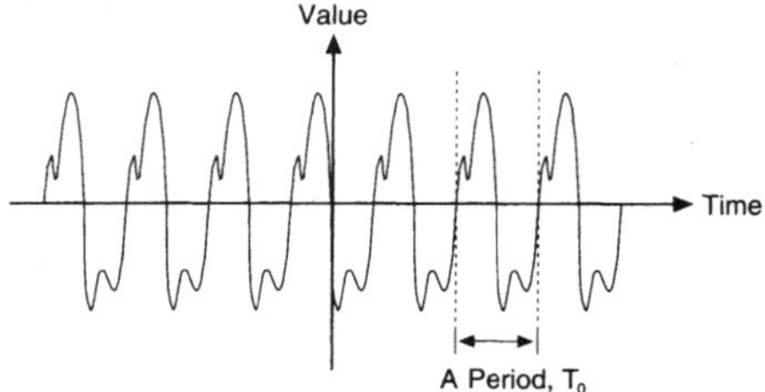

Figure 20.3 A periodic signal.

Periodic Signals

The signals sin $(2\pi f_0 t)$, cos $(2\pi f_0 t)$ and $e^{j2\pi f_0 t}$ are all *periodic* signals (see figure 20.3), meaning that for some value T, the signal $x(t) = x(t + T)$. If f_0 in sin $(2\pi f_0 t)$, cos $(2\pi f_0 t)$, or $e^{j2\pi f_0 t}$ is not equal to 0, then the smallest positive value of T for which $x(t) = x(t + T)$ is called the *fundamental period,* T_0 . $T_0 = 1/|f_0|$. For an arbitrary periodic signal (where $x(t) = x(t + T_0)$), f_0 is called the *fundamental frequency.*

In the abstract world of signals, a periodic signal like sin $(2\pi f_0 t)$ started before the dawn of time and goes on past the end of the universe. Those of us who are not deities do not have the patience to listen to such signals. Our signals must have a start and an end. For us mere mortals, a reasonably long section of sin $(2\pi f_0 t)$ can be generated by the instrument shown in figures 20.4 and 20.5.

Csound has some special facilities for generating periodic signals, but we need to wait for a little more background before we fully understand how they work. Let us listen to the examples first and then learn how they work.

For a periodic function, $x(t) = x(t + T)$, we do not really have to let time go from the start to the end. We can just let time run from 0 to T and then start over. If we have a new variable, say t', defined as $t' = t/T$, then we can generate $x(t)$ by letting t' run from 0 to 1 and then start over at 0.

Discrete Signals

The other class of signals, *discrete-time signals,* only have values at fixed instants of time. For example, the closing value of the Dow Jones industrial average is a discrete-time signal that only has a value determined at the closing bell (4 p.m. Eastern Time in the United States). In between the closing bells, the closing value is undefined. In other words, it makes no sense to talk about the closing-bell value at noon. Discrete-time signals are often represented graphically as "lollipop diagrams," where

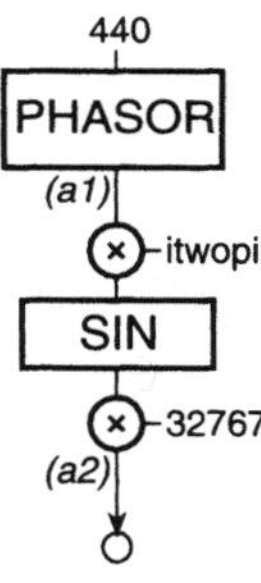

Figure 20.4 Block diagram of *instr 2001,* a 440 Hz sinusoidal oscillator at full amplitude synthesized mathematically by solving for *sin(x).*

```
        instr   2001      ; 440 HZ SINE WAVE AT FULL AMPLITUDE
itwopi  =       2*3.141592653589793238
a1      phasor  440
a2      =       32767*sin(itwopi*a1)
        out     a2
        endin

i 2001  0       5
```

Figure 20.5 Orchestra and score code for *instr 2001,* a sine wave synthesizer as shown in figure 20.4.

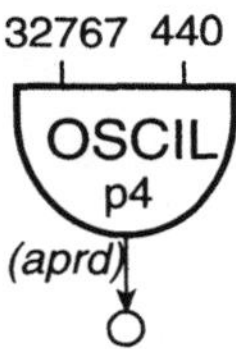

Figure 20.6 Block diagram of *instr 2002,* a simple Csound oscillator instrument.

```
        instr     2002        ; SIMPLE 440 HZ OSCILLATOR
aprd    oscil     32767, 440, p4
        out       aprd
        endin

; ONE PERIOD OF A SINE WAVE
f 1     0   8192  10  1
; ONE PERIOD OF AN APPROXIMATE SAWTOOTH WAVE
f 2     0   8192  10  1 0.5 0.333 0.25 0.2 0.1667 0.1429 0.125 0.111 0.1
; ONE PERIOD OF AN APPROXIMATE SQUARE WAVE
f 3     0   8192  10  1 0 0.333 0 0.2 0 0.1429 0 0.111 0
; ONE PERIOD OF AN APPROXIMATE TRIANGLE WAVE
f 4     0   8192  10  1 0 -0.111 0 0.04 0 -0.0204 0 0.0123 0 -0.0083 0 0.0059

i 2002  0   5   1
i 2002  6   5   2
i 2002  12  5   3
i 2002  18  5   4
```

Figure 20.7 Score code for *instr 2002* with function for sine, saw, square, and triangle called consecutively by each note.

the height of the lollipop stick corresponds to the value of the signal at that time. The lollipop itself is meant to remind you that the function only has values at discrete points (see figure 20.8).

Because a discrete-time signal only has a value at discrete times, we can number these discrete times, for example, t_0, t_1, t_2, . . . *The values of the discrete-time signal,* x, can then be represented as either $x(t_0)$, $x(t_1)$, $x(t_2)$, . . . , or $x[0]$, $x[1]$, $x[2]$, . . . , where $x[n] = x(t_n)$ and n is called the *index variable.*

The natural representation of a signal in a computer is as a discrete-time signal. A computer has individual memory or storage locations, so the values of a discrete-time signal can be stored in successive memory locations. Csound has a lot of built-in facilities for generating and storing discrete-time signals.

The GEN routines (in the *.sco* file) all create discrete-time signals that are stored in a section of memory called a *table.* You use an *index* into a table to find a particular stored value of the function. You can store a complete discrete-time signal in the computer using a GEN routine and then generate the signal by indexing the table with the integers from 0 to *table-length* − 1. Since tables can be of different lengths, it is sometimes easier to say you want a value halfway through the table or three-quarters of the way through the table, instead of at index 4095. The Csound opcode **table** lets you access a table either way. The line:

```
a1      table      73, 1, 0
```

will assign *a1* the value at index 73 in function table (f-table) 1.

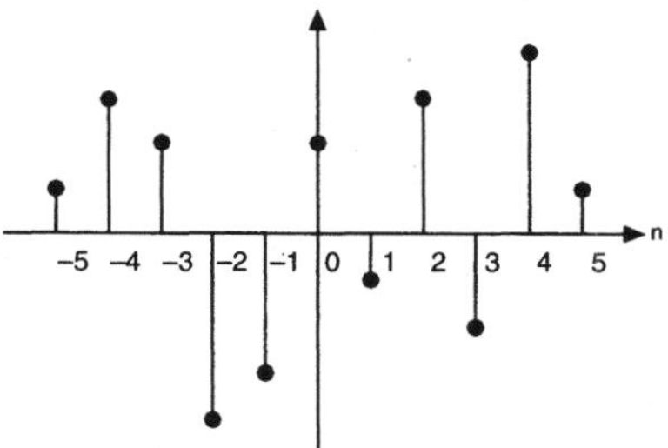

Figure 20.8 A discrete-time signal.

The line:

```
a2        table        0.25, 2, 1
```

will assign *a2* the value one-quarter of the way through f-table 2.

One advantage of **table** is that you do not have to access the values in order. If you access the **table** in reverse order, you will obtain the function going in reverse. You can access the **table** in any sort of order and create a different signal for each order of access.

In order to access the entire **table** you need some way to generate all of the integers from 0 to the *table-length* − 1, at a fixed rate. The Csound opcode **phasor** generates normalized indices (that run from 0 to 1) at a rate you specify. You can either multiply the output of **phasor** by the **table** length, or set it to use normalized indices. The **phasor** opcode generates indices that run from 0 to 1. Then it resets back to 0 and repeats, behaving just like we wanted our variable t' to behave (see figure 20.5).

There are two ways to change the frequency of a waveform stored in a table. You can change the length of time between samples, or you can change the number of samples skipped between times. Csound uses the latter approach. For example, if you keep the sampling rate the same, but only use every other sample, you double the frequency. If you use every third sample, you triple the frequency. That is essentially how **phasor** works. It uses the specified frequency to determine the size of jump it will take in a **table**.

We can create a discrete-time periodic signal by using the output of **phasor** to index a **table** containing one period of our periodic signal. In fact, the Csound opcode **oscil** combines a **phasor** with a **table** (see figures 20.6 and 20.7). To summarize, you can generate a discrete-time periodic signal in Csound by filling a **table** with one period of a function and then using either a **phasor-table** pair or an **oscil** (compare figures 20.4 and 20.5 with figures 20.6 and 20.7).

A natural question then arises: How can one convert a discrete-time signal such as the output from Csound into a continuous signal, such as a sound? Or how can one convert a continuous-time signal such as a sound into a discrete-time signal, such as an *.aif* file? Under a specific criterion, known as the *sampling theorem,* these tasks can be accomplished exactly, without the loss or addition of any information. But before we discuss the sampling theorem, we have a few additional topics to cover.

Fourier Series

It was discovered long ago that any reasonable periodic signal (one that has a maximum value less than infinity and a finite number of wiggles or jumps in a period) can be represented as a weighted sum of integrally-related (meaning that the frequencies are related by integers) sines and cosines or complex exponentials. This weighted sum is known as a *Fourier series* and the weightings are known as the *Fourier coefficients.* Mathematically, the periodic signal $x(t)$ is given by the sum:

$$x(t) = \sum_{k=-\infty}^{+\infty} a_k e^{2\pi jkf_0 t} \quad (20.22)$$

where the summation is the Fourier series and the a_k are the Fourier coefficients. If the periodic function is an even function, the complex exponentials can be rewritten as cosines:

$$x(t) = \sum_{k=0}^{\infty} a_k \cos 2\pi k f_0 t \quad (20.22)$$

If the periodic function is an odd function, the complex exponentials can be rewritten as sines:

$$x(t) = \sum_{k=1}^{\infty} a_k \sin 2\pi k f_0 t \quad (20.23)$$

The a_k can be calculated by evaluating the integral of the product of the function and the appropriate complex exponential over one period and dividing by the period. Mathematically:

$$a_k = \frac{1}{T_0} \int_{T_0} x(t) e^{-j2\pi k f_0 t} dt \quad (20.24)$$

A set of sines, cosines or complex exponentials, where the frequencies are related by $f_k = kf_0$, where $k = 0, \pm 1, \pm 2, \pm 3, \ldots$ are said to be *harmonically related* and the individual terms are called the *harmonics* or *partials.* The terms where $k = \pm 1$ are called the *fundamental harmonic* or *fundamental.* The terms where $k = \pm 2$ are called the *second harmonic* or *second partial.* The terms where $k = \pm 3$ are called the *third harmonic* or *third partial* and so forth. Much of the tone quality or timbre of a musical note is governed by the number and relative strengths of the harmonics in the note. As an interesting side-note: the a_k can be thought of as a discrete-time signal.

The Csound function generators, GEN9, GEN10 and GEN19 are designed to create a table with one period of a periodic function from the Fourier coefficients. They differ in the amount of detail you have to specify about each harmonic. As an example, a sawtooth wave (which is an odd function) has the following Fourier series:

$$x(t) = \frac{2}{\pi}\sum_{k=1}^{\infty}\frac{1}{k}\sin\left(\frac{2\pi k}{T_0}t\right) \tag{20.25}$$

and the Fourier coefficients are given by:

$$a_k = \frac{2}{\pi}\frac{1}{k} \tag{20.26}$$

Since the GEN routines automatically rescale the functions, we can ignore the $2/\pi$ and just use $1/k$ as the Fourier coefficients. The first ten coefficients are 1, 1/2, 1/3, 1/4, 1/5, 1/6, 1/7, 1/8, 1/9 and 1/10. The more terms we include, the closer we get to a sawtooth wave. In Csound we would include the following line in the score file to create a table with one period of an approximate sawtooth wave (see figure 20.9).

```
f 2  0  16384  10   1 0.5 0.3333 0.25 0.2 0.1667 0.1429 0.125 0.1111 0.1
```

Two other common periodic signals are the square wave (see figure 20.10):

$$x(t) = \frac{4}{\pi}\sum_{k=1}^{\infty}\frac{1}{k}\sin\left(\frac{2\pi k}{T_0}t\right), \quad a_k = \begin{cases}\frac{4}{\pi}, \frac{1}{k}, & \text{for } k \text{ odd}\\ 0, & \text{for } k \text{ even}\end{cases} \tag{20.27}$$

```
f 1  0  16384  10  1 0 0.3333 0 0.2 0 0.1429 0 0.1111 0
```

. . . and the triangle wave (see figure 20.11):

$$x(t) = \frac{8}{\pi^2}\sum_{k=1}^{\infty}\frac{(-1)^{(n-1)/2}}{k^2}\sin\left(\frac{2\pi k}{T_0}t\right), \quad a_k = \begin{cases}\frac{8}{\pi^2}\frac{(-1)^{(n-1)/2}}{k^2}, & \text{for } k \text{ odd}\\ 0, & \text{for } k \text{ even}\end{cases} \tag{20.28}$$

```
f 3  0  16384  10  1 0 -0.1111 0 0.04 0 -0.0204 0 0.0123 0 -0.0083 0 0.0059
```

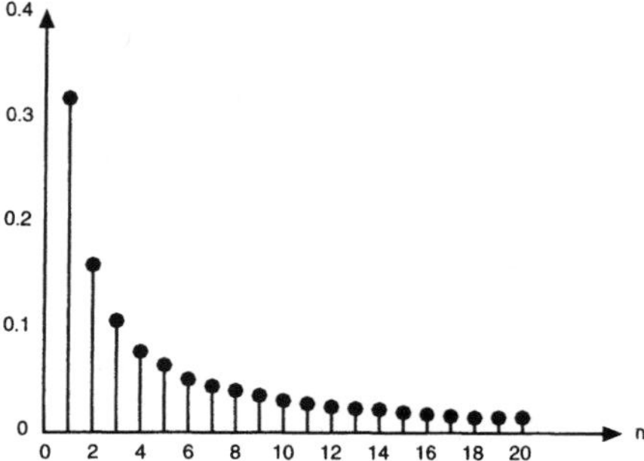

Figure 20.9 Sawtooth Fourier coefficients.

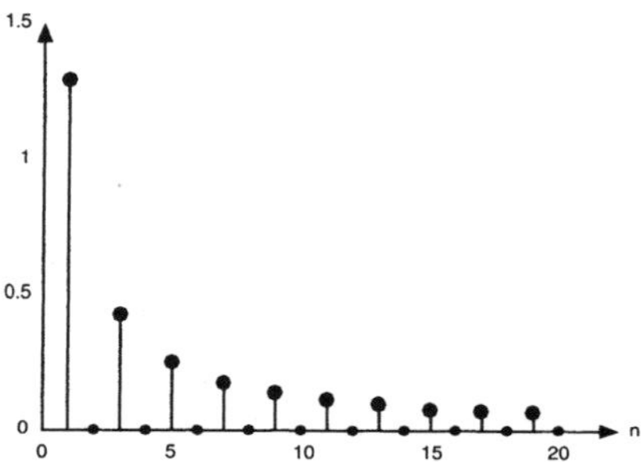

Figure 20.10 Square wave Fourier coefficients.

If your calculus is not really sharp, you can use a program such as *Mathematica* to calculate the Fourier coefficients for you. You still have to come up with an expression for one period of the periodic function. But *Mathematica* will then calculate the Fourier series and the Fourier coefficients.

For example, one period of a sawtooth wave is described by $y = -(2x + 1)$. The following *Mathematica* commands will give you the first ten terms of the Fourier series and also give you the first ten coefficients.

```
<<Calculus 'Fourier Transform'
y=-(2x-1)
FourierTrigSeries[y,{x,0,1},10]
Table[Pi/2 FourierSinSeriesCoefficient[y,{x,0,1},n],{n,1,10}]
```

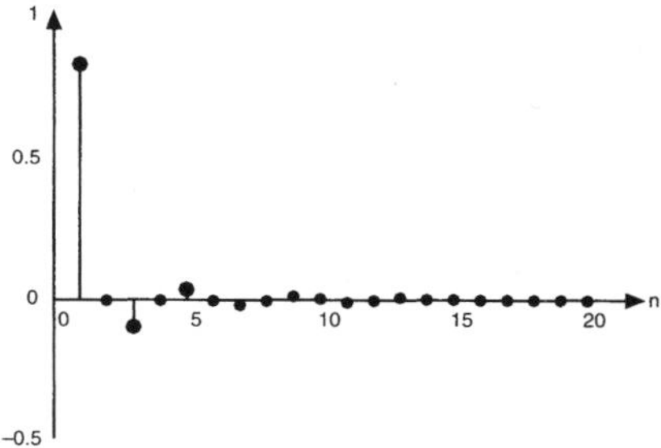

Figure 20.11 Triangle wave Fourier coefficients.

The Fourier Transform

Not all signals are periodic. It turns out that even aperiodic continuous-time signals can be constructed from the sum of sines and cosines or complex exponentials. We need the weighted sum of sines and cosines or complex exponentials at all possible frequencies, however, instead of at just harmonically-related frequencies. The mathematical way to sum lots of little bits right next to each other is to integrate. Instead of the discrete a_k we had for the Fourier series, we now have a continuous function of frequency, so the continuous-time signal $x(t)$ can be constructed from the weighted sum of all frequencies with the weighting function being $X(f)$, that is:

$$x(t) = \int_{-\infty}^{\infty} X(f)e^{j2\pi ft}df \tag{20.29}$$

We can evaluate $X(f)$ from $x(t)$ with the formula:

$$X(f) = \int_{-\infty}^{\infty} x(t)e^{-j2\pi ft}dt \tag{20.30}$$

The equation for calculating $X(f)$ is called the *Fourier Transform.* The equation for reconstructing $x(t)$ from $X(f)$ is called the *Inverse Fourier Transform.* The importance for us in these transforms is that we now have two ways of looking at a continuous-time signal. We can look at it as a function of time (*time domain*), or as a function of frequency (*frequency domain*). Since humans hear the pitches of notes as a function of frequency and not as functions of time, the frequency domain is often a valuable place to examine musical signals.

Plotted below is the function (see figures 20.12, 20.13, and 20.14):

$$y = \begin{Bmatrix} 0 & ,t < 0 \\ e^{-t} & ,t \geq 0 \end{Bmatrix} \tag{20.31}$$

and its Fourier transform. The plots were generated with *Mathematica* from the following instructions:

```
<<Calculus'FourierTransform'
foft=UnitStep[t]Exp[-t]
fofw=FourierTransform[foft,t,w]
foff=fofw/.w->2 Pi f
Plot[foft,{t,-5,5}]
Plot[Abs[foff],{f,-5,5}]
Plot[Arg[foff],{f,-5,5}]
```

For discrete-time or sampled signals, the discrete-time Fourier transform is calculated as:

$$X(F) = \sum_{n=-\infty}^{\infty} x[n]e^{-2\pi jnF} \tag{20.32}$$

where the frequency F is given as a fraction of the sampling frequency. $X(F)$ is a continuous periodic function with a period of 1. The inverse transform is:

$$x[n] = \int_{1\ \text{cycle}} X(F)e^{2\pi jnF}dF \tag{20.33}$$

The integration is performed over any range of F with a length of 1, for example, 0 to 1 or $-1/2$ to 1/2. We will make use of both of these formulas in the section on filters.

Because the Fourier transform can consist of complex numbers, it is customary to plot functions in the frequency domain as a plot of magnitude (or absolute value) versus frequency and phase (or phase angle or argument) versus frequency. Csound has a built-in function for plotting the magnitude of a Fourier transform but not the phase. The opcode **dispfft** and the analysis program **pvanal** use the *Fast Fourier Transform* (FFT), which is an efficient method for calculating a sampled version of the discrete-time Fourier transform.

The Impulse

An aperiodic signal with a special place in signal processing is the *impulse*, $\delta(t)$. A continuous-time impulse is a strange limiting case of taking a signal, like a rectangular pulse and making it narrower and narrower, while increasing the height in such a

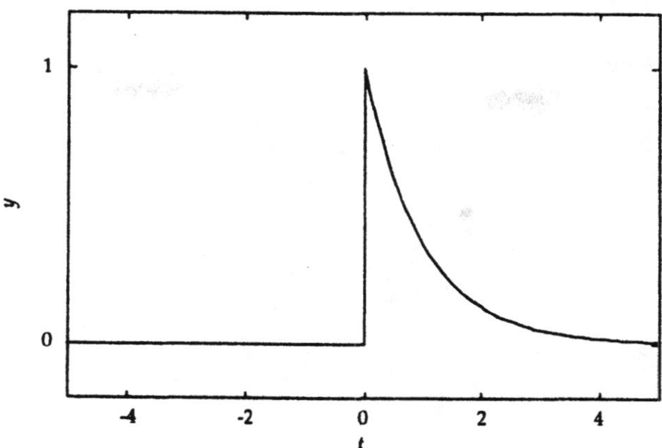

Figure 20.12 The function of time.

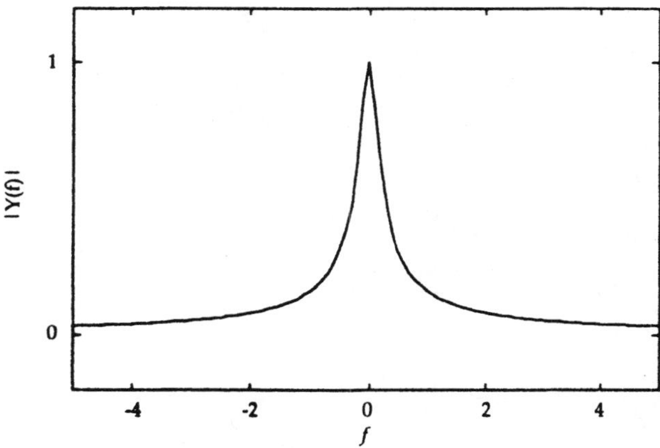

Figure 20.13 The magnitude of its Fourier transform.

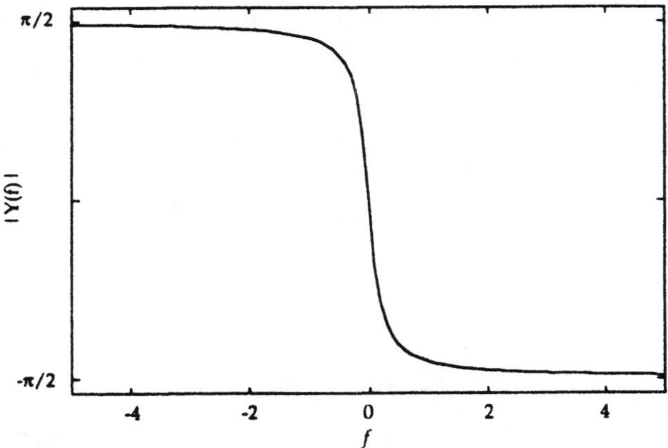

Figure 20.14 The phase of its Fourier transform.

way that the area remains constant. The true impulse (like the ideal fashion model) is infinitely tall and infinitely thin but has an area of 1. The discrete-time impulse, $\delta[n]$, is much simpler. It is a single sample of value 1 surrounded by zeros (see figure 20.15).

The impulse has several properties that make it useful. The first is its sampling property. You can find the value of a function at a given time t_0 or index n_0, with the following formulas: the integral (or sum) of the product of the impulse and a function is the value of the function at the impulse's time, that is:

$$\int_{-\infty}^{\infty} x(t)\delta(t - t_0)dt = x(t_0) \tag{20.34}$$

or

$$\sum_{n=-\infty}^{\infty} x[n]\delta[n - n_0] = x[n_0] \tag{20.35}$$

This property is most useful in designing FIR filters (described below). The second property is the impulse's frequency content. The Fourier transform of the impulse is a constant, that is:

$$\Delta(f) = \int_{-\infty}^{\infty} \delta(t)e^{-j2\pi ft}dt = e^{-j2\pi f(0)} = 1 \tag{20.36}$$

or

$$\Delta(F) = \sum_{n=-\infty}^{\infty} \delta[n]e^{-2\pi jFn} = e^{-2\pi jF(0)} = 1 \tag{20.37}$$

In other words, an impulse contains all possible frequencies in equal strength (see figure 20.16). That property makes it ideal for testing filters and evaluating their performance.

You cannot really hear an impulse. But you can hear the impulse response of your computer and sound system (I will explain what an impulse response is a little later). The following Csound code will generate an impulse to let you hear the impulse response of your computer and sound system (see figures 20.17 and 20.18).

Often one does not want an impulse with all possible frequencies, but rather a periodic or pitched signal with all of the harmonics at equal strength. A train of impulses will have the desired characteristics. Unfortunately, in a sampled system, the period of a pulse-train must be an integer multiple of the sampling period, which greatly limits the frequencies that can be used. Csound provides a way around this limitation. The opcode **buzz** is designed to provide a signal with equal-strength harmonics for any desired frequency. The Csound instrument shown in figures 20.19 and 20.20 will give you a **buzz**.

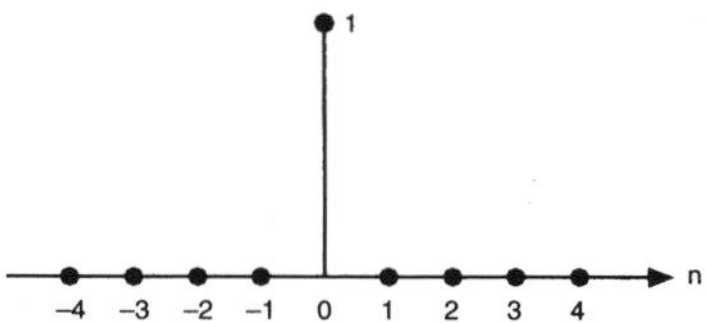

Figure 20.15 The discrete-time impulse.

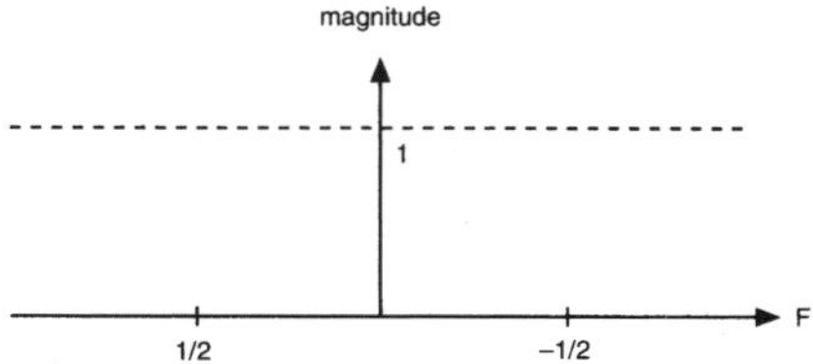

Figure 20.16 The Fourier transform of the discrete-time impulse.

As the frequency sweeps from 10 Hz to 640 Hz you should hear the transition from individual clicks to a buzzing sound. The transitions (the "gear shifts") are heard because one has to specify the number of harmonics in **buzz**; the maximum number allowed without aliasing (explained below) decreases with increasing frequency.

Often a signal will have one or more frequency ranges where there is no information, which means that $X(f) = 0$. Such a signal is called *band-limited,* meaning the information content is limited to certain frequency ranges or bands (see figure 20.21).

The Sampling Theorem and Aliasing

With this background we are ready to tackle converting continuous signals to discrete signals and back. The *Sampling Theorem* states that a band-limited continuous signal with $X(f) = 0$ for $|f| > f_M$ is uniquely determined by its samples, if the sampling frequency is at least twice the band-limited frequency, $f_s > 2f_M$, where the sampling frequency is the reciprocal of the sampling period $f_s = 1/T_s$. The original signal, $x(t)$, can be reconstructed from its samples by generating an impulse-train whose amplitudes equal the sample values and passing the impulse-train through an ideal lowpass filter with a gain of T_s and a cutoff frequency greater than f_M and less than $f_s - f_M$.

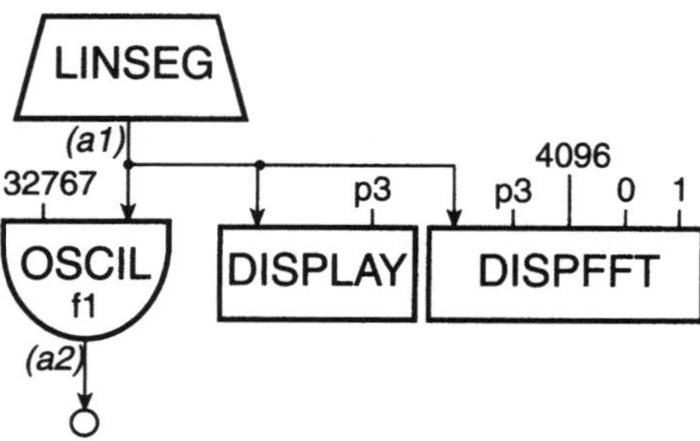

Figure 20.17 Block diagram of *instr 2003,* an instrument that generates an impulse and displays it in both the time and frequency domains to let you hear and measure the impulse response of your system.

```
kr      =        44100                 ; AVOID PROBLEMS

        instr    2003          ; SINGLE IMPULSE
idur1   =        7/sr                  ; READ THE TABLE ONCE
idur2   =        1/sr
ifreq   =        sr/8                  ; READ THE TABLE AT 1 POINT PER SAMPLE
a1      linseg   ifreq, idur1, ifreq, idur2, 0, 1, 0
a2      oscil    32767, a1, 1          ; SCALE THE AMPLITUDE SO YOU CAN HEAR IT
        out      a2
        display  a1, p3                ; DISPLAY THE IMPULSE RESPONSE
        dispfft  a1, p3, 4096, 0, 1    ; DISPLAY THE FREQUENCY RESPONSE
        endin

; CREATE A TABLE WITH AN IMPULSE IN THE SECOND POSITION
f 1     0    8     2    0 1 0 0 0 0 0 0 0
; PLAY THE IMPULSE AND WAIT A WHILE
i 2003     0     0.2
```

Figure 20.18 Orchestra and score code for *instr 2003,* which generates a single impulse and displays the impulse and frequency response.

The details of converting from a continuous signal to a discrete signal and back again are usually handled by the analog-to-digital (ADC) and digital-to-analog (DAC) converters in your computer or sound card. Most ADC's have filters on them to remove any frequency content higher than one-half the sample rate. Consequently, when recording a signal into a computer, one does not normally have to worry about making sure that the signal is band-limited.

When generating or processing a signal inside the computer, however, one has to be careful not to generate any frequency content above one-half the sample rate. Csound has *absolutely* no built-in protection against this. In fact, there is no general way to protect against this.

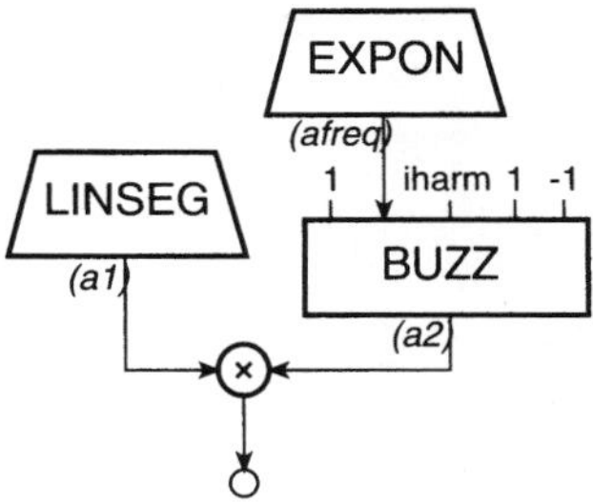

Figure 20.19 Block diagram of *instr 2004,* an instrument that generates a pitched "impulse train" using Csound's **buzz** opcode.

```
        instr   2004        ; PITCHED PULSE TRAIN
iharm   =       int(44100/(p4>p5 ? p4:p5)/2)-1     ; MAX HARM W/O ALIAS
a1      linseg  0, 0.05, 30000, p3-0.1, 30000, 0.05, 0, 1, 0
afreq   expon   p4, p3, p5
a2      buzz    1, afreq, iharm, 1, -1
        out     a1*a2
        endin

f 1       0    16384    10    1

i 2004    0     6    10     20
i 2004    6     6    20     40
i 2004    12    6    40     80
i 2004    18    6    80     160
i 2004    24    6    160    320
i 2004    30    6    320    640
```

Figure 20.20 Orchestra and score code for *instr 2004,* an instrument that generates a sweeping train of impulses with all the harmonics at equal strength.

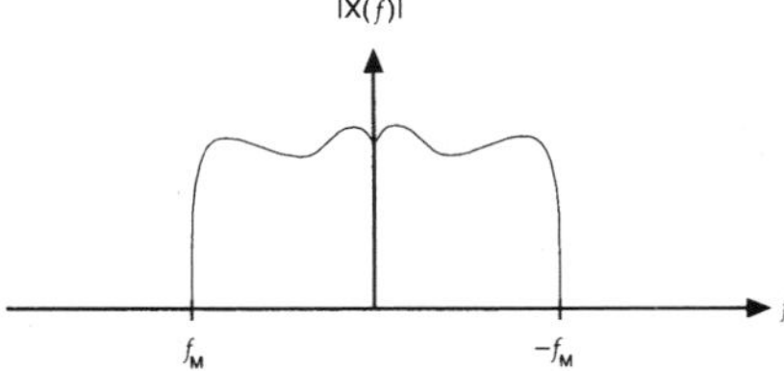

Figure 20.21 A band-limited signal.

If you generate a frequency above one-half of the sampling rate and attempt to play it, the actual frequency you hear will depend upon just how high above one-half the sampling rate the frequency is. For frequencies between $1/2f_s$ and f_s, the frequency you will hear is $f_s - f$. For frequencies between f_s and $3/2f_s$, the frequency you will hear is $f - f_s$. The pattern repeats.

This reappearance of a high frequency as a much lower frequency is called *aliasing* (i.e., the high frequency appears as its low-frequency alias). The Csound code in figures 20.22 and 20.23 illustrates aliasing.

The result sweeps the waveform from 20 Hz to 176,400 Hz, which is four times the sample rate. Humans cannot hear sounds at 176,400 Hz, but you will hear the alias of 176,400 Hz quite clearly. For the sine wave you should be able to hear the pitch sweep up and down four times. For the others, you will hear the partials sweep up and down repeatedly before the fundamental starts to sweep back down. For the **buzz** wave, all of the harmonics are the same strength so you will hear an audio mess.

Aliasing is neither a good nor a bad thing. However, if you are not expecting it, aliasing may generate "noise" (my definition of "noise" is any sound that you do not want to hear). It is best not to depend on aliasing in a Csound instrument, because changing the sampling rate will dramatically change the sound. Another way to think about aliasing is that the discrete-time frequency, $F = f/f_s$, only has a useful range from $-1/2$ to $1/2$. Any frequency generated outside this range will be aliased back into this range (see figure 20.24). The most common causes of aliasing in Csound are sampling a table too rapidly or having too high a modulation index in a modulating scheme such as FM (discussed below).

Systems

A *system* is anything that takes an input signal and transforms it into an output signal. Systems are normally classified as either *linear* or *nonlinear* and *time-invariant* or *time-varying*. A time-invariant system is one in which a given input causes a given output no matter when the input occurs. For example, consider a doorbell as a system with a push on the button as the input and the ringing sound as the output. No matter when you push the button, the bell will ring; the system is time-invariant. If you consider the system to be the doorbell, the residents, and the front door taken together, this new system is time-varying, that is, the response that you get to a push on the doorbell depends on the time of day. Mathematically a system is time-invariant if the input $x(t - t_0)$ gives rise to the output $y(t - t_0)$.

A linear system is one in which the output is directly proportional to the input. Most doorbells are not linear because pushing the button twice as hard does not

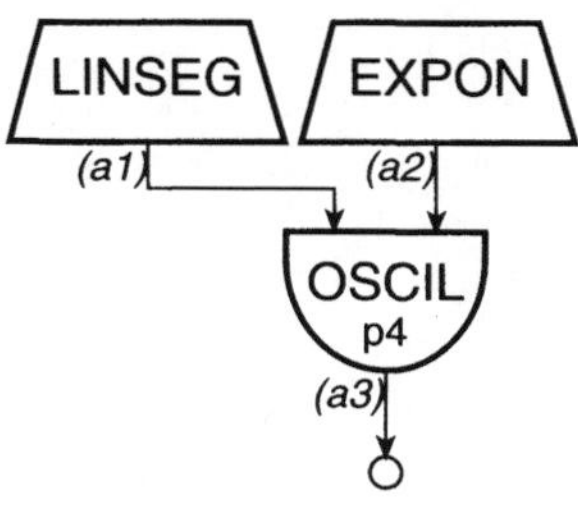

Figure 20.22 Block diagram of *instr 2005,* an instrument designed to illustrate the sounds and concepts of aliasing.

```
          instr       2005         ; ALIASING
a1        linseg      0, 0.01, 20000, p3-0.01, 20000, 0.01, 0, 1, 0
a2        expon       20, p3, 176400
a3        oscil       a1, a2, p4
          out         a3
          endin

; SINE
f 1  0    8192    10    1
; SQUARE
f 2  0    8192    10    1000 0 333 0 200 0 143 0 111 0 91 0 77 0 67 0 59 0 53 0
; SAWTOOTH
f 3  0    8192    10    1000 500 333 250 200 167 143 125 111 100 91 83 77 71 67
                        63 59 56 53 50
; IMPULSE-LIKE
f 4  0    8192    10    1 1 1 1 1 1 1 1 1 1 1 1 1 1 1 1 1 1 1 1

i 2005    0       20      1
i 2005    21      20      2
i 2005    42      20      3
i 2005    63      20      4
```

Figure 20.23 Orchestra and score code for *instr 2005,* an instrument whose frequency moves from 20 Hz to 176,400 Hz—4x the sample rate.

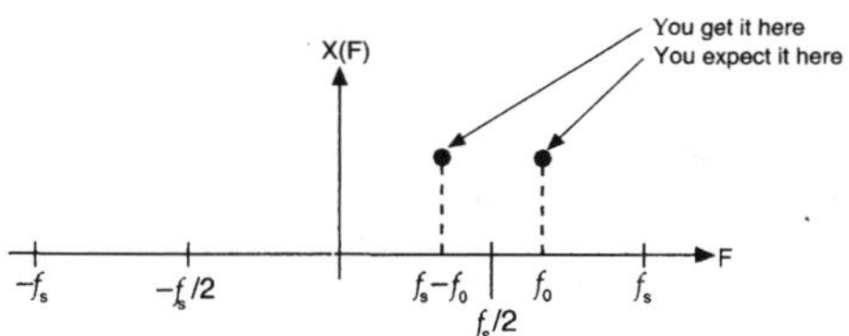

Figure 20.24 Aliasing.

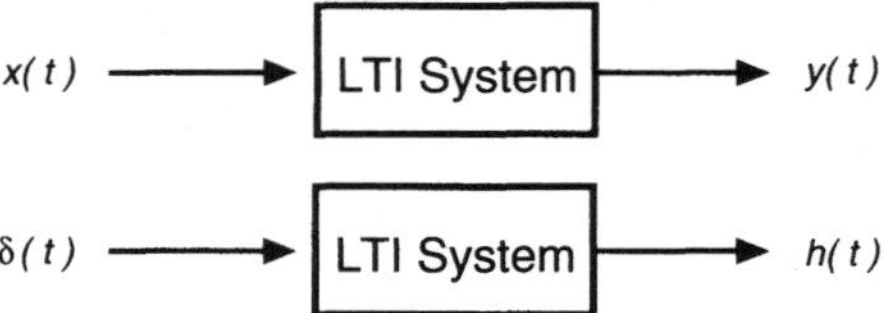

Figure 20.25 Block diagram of linear time-invariant systems in the time and frequency domains.

cause the bell to ring twice as loud. A properly functioning grocery clerk is a linear system because they will charge you twice as much for two boxes of corn flakes and they will charge you the sum of three times the price of one box of corn flakes and twice the price of one doughnut if you buy three boxes of corn flakes and two doughnuts.

Mathematically, a linear system has the following properties: if $x_1(t)$ and $x_2(t)$ are inputs to a system; a and b are constants and $y_1(t)$ is the system response to $x_1(t)$ and y_2(t) is the system response to $x_2(t)$, then the system is linear if the response to $ax_1(t) + bx_2(t)$ is $ay_1(t) + by_2(t)$.

From a design and analysis standpoint, linear time-invariant systems are the most useful because you can predict their behavior from limited information. Most of the rest of this chapter will be concerned with linear time-invariant (LTI) systems.

Impulse Response and Convolution

If you input an impulse into an LTI system you will get an output signal called the *impulse response,* $h(t)$, for continuous systems and $h[n]$ for discrete systems (see figure 20.25). It has been proven that you can get the response to any input signal, $x(t)$, from the impulse response by *convolution* of $x(t)$ with $h(t)$. The symbol for convolution is usually the asterisk—"*." For continuous signals:

$$y(t) = x(t) * h(t) = \int_{-\infty}^{\infty} x(\tau)h(t - \tau)d\tau \qquad (20.38)$$

For discrete signals:

$$y[n] = x[n] * h[n] = \sum_{k=-\infty}^{\infty} x[k]h[n - k] \qquad (20.39)$$

For discrete systems with short impulse responses, the convolution sum is fairly easy to program and runs quite quickly. For long impulse responses, however, such as reverberation in a cathedral, the speed and memory requirements for convolution become quite overwhelming. Most people do not have the mathematical background to perform the convolution integral for continuous signals and we have found that even among those who do, relatively few enjoy performing the integration. It would be nice if there were an easier way. A special property of sines, cosines and complex exponentials provides such a way.

Frequency Response and Convolution

Sines, cosines and complex exponentials are *eigenfunctions* of LTI systems, which means that the output from a complex exponential input is a complex exponential with exactly the same frequency. The output is multiplied, however, by a (possibly complex) constant. In other words, for an input of $e^{j2\pi ft}$ you get an output of $H(f)e^{j2\pi ft}$, where $H(f)$ is a constant that depends on f but not on t. Since we learned above that any reasonable signal can be constructed from a weighted sum (or integral) of complex exponentials, we can find the response of an LTI system as:

$$y(t) = \int_{-\infty}^{\infty} H(f)X(f)e^{j2\pi ft}df \quad \text{or} \quad Y(f) = H(f)X(f) \qquad (20.40)$$

For discrete-time systems the result is $Y(F) = H(F)X(F)$. You may have guessed by now that $H(f)$ is the Fourier transform of the impulse response, $h(t)$. $H(f)$ is the *transfer function* or *frequency-response function* of the system. In other words, multiplication in the frequency domain corresponds to convolution in the time domain. The procedure is to take the Fourier transform of the input signal and the impulse response, multiply the two transforms and take the inverse transform of the result to get the output signal.

The Csound orchestra and score shown in figures 20.26 and 20.27 can be used to find the impulse response and the frequency response of an LTI Csound opcode or section of code.

The opcode **convolve** and its analysis utility companion, **cvanal,** implement frequency-domain convolution. The **cvanal** utility takes the Fast Fourier Transform of a soundfile, creating a frequency-response function (the soundfile is assumed to be the impulse response of some system or filter). The **convolve** opcode takes the frequency-response function, multiplies it by the Fourier Transform of the input signal and takes the Inverse Fourier Transform.

The Csound code shown in figures 20.28, 20.29 and 20.30 is designed to do a comparison. Note: because Csound's analysis files are machine specific (you cannot

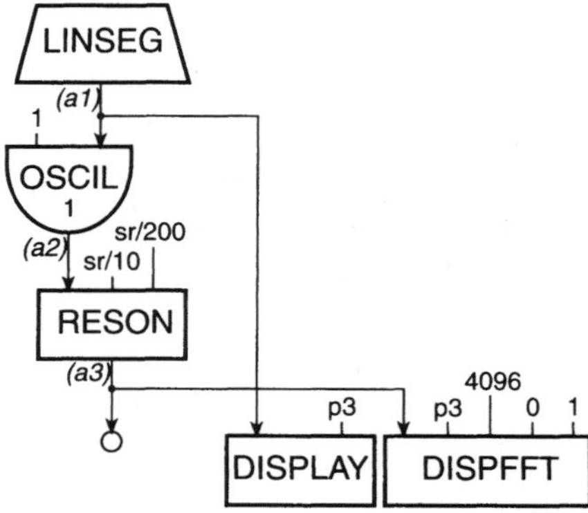

Figure 20.26 Block diagram of *instr 2006,* an instrument designed to find the impulse and frequency response of a linear time-invariant opcode (**reson**).

```
        instr    2006          ; IMPULSE RESPONSE OF RESON FILTER
idur1   =        7/sr                  ; READ THE TABLE ONCE
idur2   =        1/sr
ifreq   =        sr/8                  ; READ THE TABLE AT 1 POINT PER SAMPLE
a1      linseg   ifreq, idur1, ifreq, idur2, 0, 1, 0
a2      oscil    1, a1, 1
a3      reson    a2, sr/10, sr/200     ; THE SYSTEM UNDER TEST
        out      a3
        display  a1, p3                ; DISPLAY THE IMPULSE RESPONSE
        dispfft  a3, p3, 4096, 0, 1    ; DISPLAY THE FREQUENCY RESPONSE
        endin
; CREATE A TABLE WITH AN IMPULSE IN THE SECOND POSITION
f 1     0       8     2     0 1 0 0 0 0 0 0

i 2006  0       0.185759637                   ; CREATE 2^14 (8192) SAMPLES
```

Figure 20.27 Orchestra and score code for *instr 2006,* an instrument that generates an impulse response of a **reson** filter.

use PC analysis files on a Mac or vice versa) the impulse responses on the accompanying CD-ROM must be preanalyzed by the Csound **cvanal** utility before they can be used for convolution.

Csound has some other facilities for performing frequency-domain convolution but they will not be discussed here. The interested reader is directed to **pvoc** and **pvanal**, as well as to the **spectral data types**.

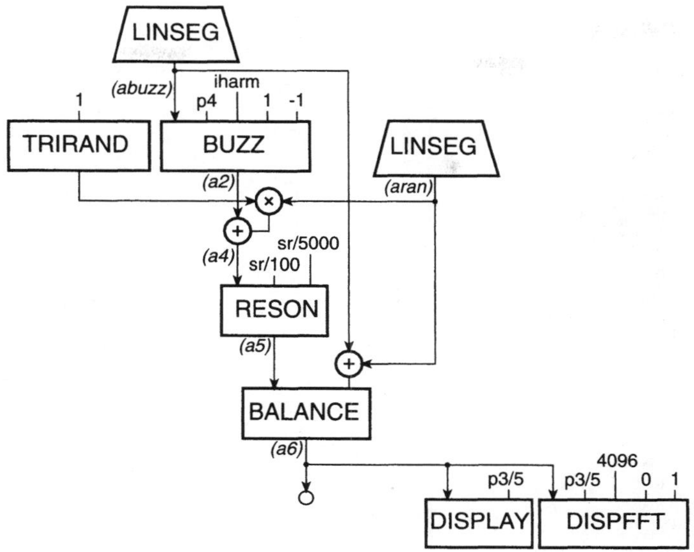

Figure 20.28 Block diagram of *instr 2007,* an instrument designed to do a comparison test and measure the impulse and direct implementation frequency response of an LTI opcode and the convolution method as shown in figure 20.29.

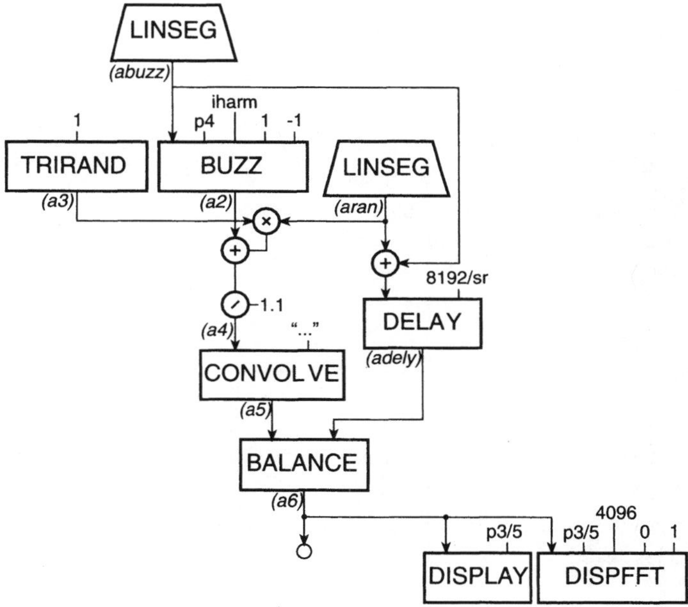

Figure 20.29 Block diagram of *instr 2008,* an instrument designed to compare the impulse and frequency response of the convolution opcode with the direct method shown in figure 20.28.

```
        instr    2007        ; DIRECT IMPLEMENTATION OF CONVOLUTION
iharm   =        int(44100/(p4)/2)-1        ; AVOID PROBLEMS WITH DELAYS
abuzz   linseg   0,0.45*p3,0,0.1*p3,10000,0.44*p3,10000,0.01*p3,0,1,0
aran    linseg   0, 0.01*p3, 10000, 0.44*p3, 10000, 0.1*p3, 0, 1, 0
a2      buzz     abuzz, p4, iharm, 1, -1
a3      trirand  1
a4      =        a2+a3*aran
a5      reson    a4, sr/100, sr/5000        ; SAME AS TEST IMPULSE
a6      balance  a5, abuzz+aran
        out      a6
        display  a6, p3/5                   ; DISPLAY IMPULSE RESPONSE
        dispfft  a6, p3/5, 4096, 0, 1       ; DISPLAY FREQUENCY RESPONSE
        endin

        instr    2008        ; CONVOLUTION USING CONVOLVE OPCODE
iharm   =        int(44100/(p4)/2)-1
abuzz   linseg   0,0.45*p3,0,0.1*p3,10000,0.44*p3,10000,0.01*p3,0,1,0
aran    linseg   0, 0.01*p3, 10000, 0.44*p3, 10000, 0.1*p3, 0, 1, 0
ahalt   linseg   0, 8192/44100, 0, 0.001, 1, p3, 1
a2      buzz     abuzz, p4, iharm, 1, -1
a3      trirand  1
a4      =        (a2+a3*aran)/1.1
a5      convolve a4, "reson_100_5000.con"   ; USE CVANAL TO MAKE
adely   delay    abuzz+aran, 8192/sr
a6      balance  a5, adely
        out      a6
        display  a6, p3/5                   ; DISPLAY IMPULSE RESPONSE
        dispfft  a6, p3/5, 4096, 0, 1       ; DISPLAY FREQUENCY RESPONSE
        endin

f 1     0      16384    10    1             ; SINE TABLE

i 2007 0      6        110.25
i 2008 6      6        110.25
```

Figure 20.30 Orchestra code for *instr 2007* and *2008*, a direct implementation of an instrument that generates an impulse and measures the time and frequency responses (*2007*) and a convolution instrument for comparison (*2008*).

Difference Equations

For continuous-time signals and systems, the behavior of the systems is often based on linear constant-coefficient *differential* equations. For discrete-time signals and systems, systems are often described by constant coefficient *difference* equations. The general form of a constant-coefficient difference equation is:

$$\sum_{k=0}^{N} a_k y[n-k] = \sum_{k=0}^{M} b_k x[n-k] \tag{20.41}$$

If one assumes that the system is initially at rest, one can calculate the frequency response and the impulse response from the difference equation in the following way:

The discrete-time Fourier Transform of the difference equation is:

$$\sum_{k=0}^{N} a_k e^{-2\pi jkF} Y(F) = \sum_{k=0}^{M} b_k e^{-2\pi jkF} X(F) \tag{20.42}$$

which can be rearranged to:

$$H(F) = \frac{Y(F)}{X(F)} = \frac{\sum_{k=0}^{M} b_k e^{-2\pi jkF}}{\sum_{k=0}^{N} a_k e^{-2\pi jkF}} \tag{20.43}$$

The impulse response is then found from the inverse Fourier transform of $H(F)$.

Block Diagrams

Difference equations are often represented by *block diagrams* in the form illustrated in figure 20.31. A circle with a plus sign is a summation operator. The box with the D in it is a delay operator. It corresponds to shifting the index from n to $n-1$. The coefficient by the arrow corresponds to multiplication by the coefficient. Thus we can rewrite equation 20.41 as a block diagram (see figure 20.32). The coefficients by the arrows correspond to multiplication by the coefficients in the previous equation.

FIR and IIR Systems

If all of the a_k are zero, except for a_0, then the output only depends on the present and past inputs and not on the past outputs. The impulse response of such a system returns to zero after the impulse has passed through the Mth input. Such a system is said to have a *finite impulse response,* because the impulse response has a finite duration and the system is known as an *FIR* system. If any of the a_k are not zero, then, in general, the impulse response never truly returns to zero, although it may get very small. These systems have feedback because the present value of the output depends on all of the previous ones. Such a system is said to have an *infinite impulse response* and is known as an *IIR* or *recursive* system (because of the feedback).

Stable Systems

A system is said to be *stable* if a finite or bounded input produces a finite or bounded output. One can determine the stability of a system by examining the roots of the

x[n] —b→ y[x] means $y[n] = bx[n]$

x[n] —[D]→ y[x] means $y[n] = x[n-1]$

x[n] —(+)→ y[x] means $y[n] = x[n] + w[n]$
w[n]

Figure 20.31 Typical figures and form of block diagrams used to represent difference equations.

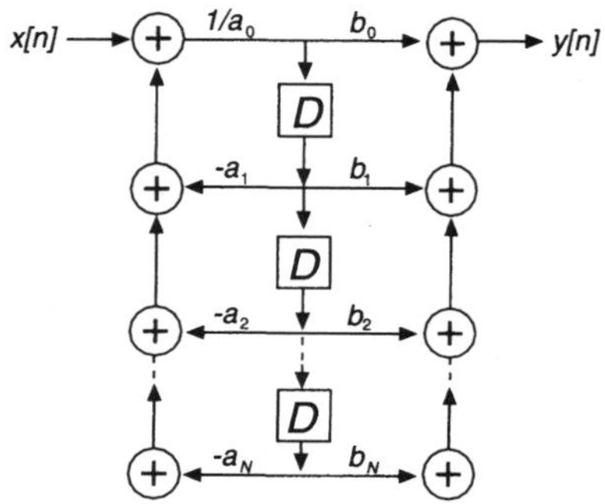

Figure 20.32 The block diagram of equation 20.41.

equation obtained, by replacing the factors of $e^{-2\pi jF}$ with z^{-1}, for example, $e^{-2\pi jkF} \rightarrow z^{-k}$, setting the denominator of the transfer function to zero and solving for z. If the magnitudes or absolute values of all of the roots are less than 1, the system is stable. If the magnitude of any of the roots is greater than 1 the system is unstable. As an example, take the system with the transfer function:

$$H(F) = \frac{1}{1 + e^{-2\pi jF} + 2e^{-4\pi jF}} \tag{20.44}$$

First, replace the factors of $e^{-2\pi jF}$ with z^{-1}.

$$H(z) = \frac{1}{1 + z^{-1} + 2z^{-2}} \tag{20.45}$$

Then, set the denominator equal to zero.

$$1 + z^{-1} + 2z^{-2} = 0 \tag{20.46}$$

Solve the equation for z.

$$z = -\frac{1}{2} + j\frac{\sqrt{7}}{2}, -\frac{1}{2} - j\frac{\sqrt{7}}{2} \quad (20.47)$$

Check the magnitudes.

$$|z| = \sqrt{2}, \sqrt{2} \quad (20.48)$$

Since at least one (in this case both) of the roots has a magnitude greater than 1, the system is unstable.

The transfer function of an FIR system has no denominator and so it is always stable. In Csound, an unstable system usually shows up as having infinity (INF) appear as the magnitude of the largest sample.

Filters

A *filter* is a system with a specified or predetermined frequency response. The usual purposes of a filter are either to remove undesired frequencies or emphasize desired ones. The four classic types of filters are *lowpass, highpass, bandpass* and *bandreject* or *notch* (see figure 20.33). For musical purposes one usually includes parametric equalization filters, shelving filters, comb filters and allpass filters. Filters can be divided up into FIR or IIR filters. For a given response, IIR filters require fewer elements or operations but cause nonlinear phase shifts. FIR filters require many more elements but can be specified with linear phase shifts.

Csound has several built-in filters. The **tone**, **atone**, **reson** and **areson** opcodes are all IIR filters. The **butterlp**, **butterhp**, **butterbp** and **butterbr** are second-order IIR filters. Both sets implement the four classic filter types. The **lpread/lpreson** (**lpfreson**) opcodes implement high-order (up to 40 or 50) IIR filters from predefined tables of filter coefficients. The **comb** and **alpass** opcodes implement comb and allpass filters. The impulse and frequency responses for **tone** are shown in figures 20.34 and 20.35. As shown above, the impulse responses can be used with **convolve** to compare direct implementation with convolution (see figure 20.30). At the end of the chapter (see figure 20.50) I have included impulse and frequency response plots of a number of Csound's built-in filters.

Generating Filters from Scratch

Csound also provides some tools for generating filters from scratch. Discrete-time filters are usually constructed from difference equations as discussed above. The

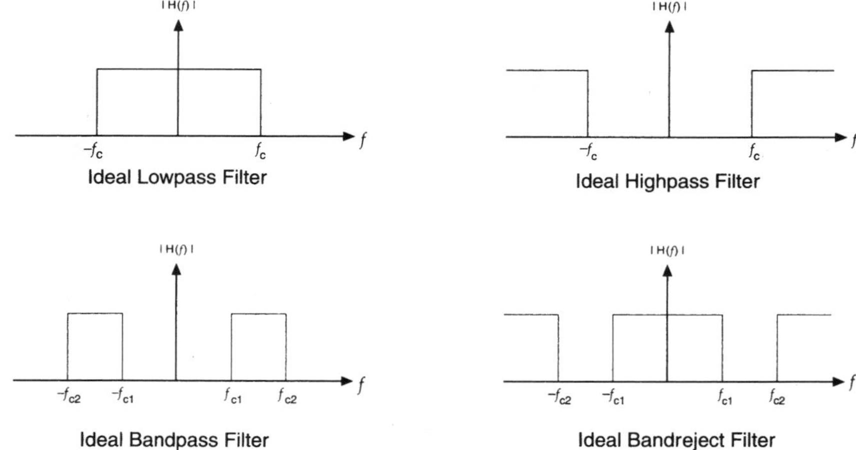

Figure 20.33 Ideal versions of the four "classic" filters.

most difficult task in constructing a filter, however, is determining the coefficients in the difference equation. The task is similar to fitting a polynomial to an arbitrary function. Csound has no built-in facilities for calculating the coefficients. You have to do that yourself. (I will give you some hints on how, after we finish discussing how to implement a filter in Csound). Once the coefficients are calculated, however, Csound does provide facilities for implementing the filter.

The **delay1** opcode in Csound is the same as the *D* operator in the block diagrams shown in figures 20.31 and 20.32 and is useful for creating FIR filters. Filters longer than about 20 delays are unwieldy and are better implemented with **convolve**. The following example demonstrates implementing an FIR filter from scratch.

FIR Example

The difference equation:

$$y[n] = \frac{1}{4}x[n] + \frac{1}{2}x[n-1] + \frac{1}{4}x[n-2] \qquad (20.49)$$

is an FIR system and has the frequency response:

$$H(F) = e^{-2\pi jF}\left(\frac{1}{4}e^{2\pi jF} + \frac{1}{2} + \frac{1}{4}e^{-2\pi jF}\right) = e^{-2\pi jF}\left(\frac{1}{2}\cos 2\pi F + \frac{1}{2}\right) \qquad (20.50)$$

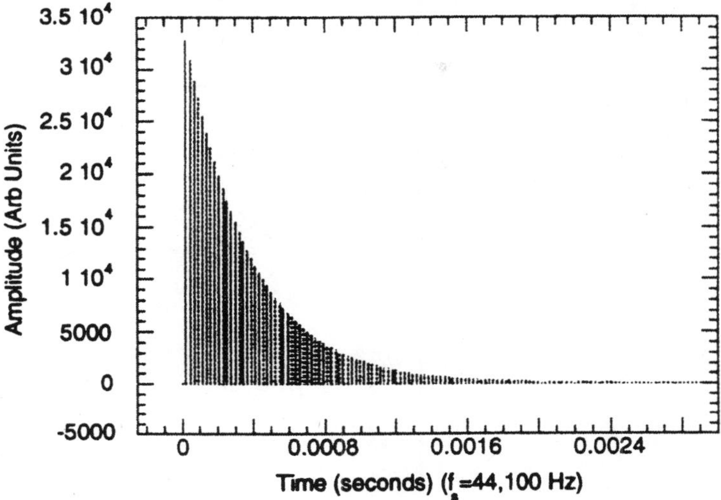

Figure 20.34 Impulse response for **tone** (khp=f_s/100). An impulse response plots the amplitude (or intensity) of the output from a filter when the input is an impulse. In this case, the output decays exponentially with time.

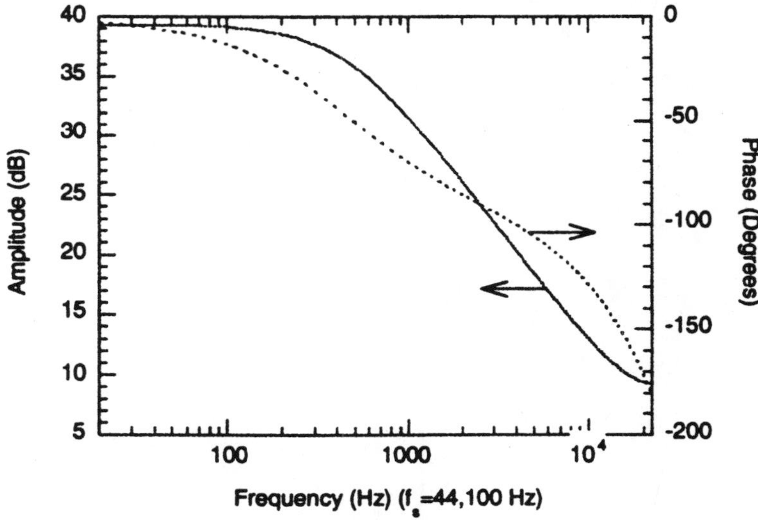

Figure 20.35 Frequency response for **tone** (khp=f_s/100). A frequency response plot shows how a given system or filter amplifies or attenuates a signal as you change its frequency. It also shows how the signal's phase would change as you change its frequency. In this case, the gain is constant up to about 441 Hz. Above 441 Hz the gain drops with frequency. The phase shift is almost 0° at low frequency and drops to −180° at 1/2 of the sampling rate.

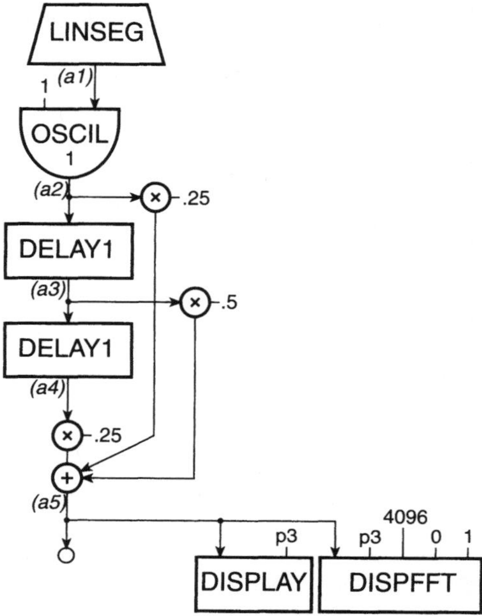

Figure 20.36 Block diagram of *instr 2009*, an instrument that implements and tests the FIR filter defined in equation 20.49.

which is basically a linear-phase lowpass filter. A Csound instrument to implement and test this filter is shown in figures 20.36 and 20.37.

IIR Example

The difference equation:

$$y[n] + \frac{1}{2}y[n - 1] + \frac{1}{2}y[n - 2] = x[n] \tag{20.51}$$

can be rewritten as:

$$y[n] = x[n] - \frac{1}{2}y[n - 1] - \frac{1}{2}y[n - 2] \tag{20.52}$$

an IIR system that has the frequency response:

```
kr   =          44100                         ; AVOID ASSORTED PROBLEMS
     instr      2009        ; FIR FILTER EXAMPLE
a1   linseg     sr/8, 7/sr, sr/8, 1/sr, 0, 1, 0
a2   oscil 1, a1, 1                           ; GENERATE AN IMPULSE
a3   delay1     a2                            ; FILTER DELAY 1
a4   delay1     a3                            ; FILTER DELAY 2
a5   =          0.25*a2+0.5*a3+0.25*a4        ; SUMMATION
     out        a5
     display    a5, p3                        ; DISPLAY IMPULSE RESPONSE
     dispfft    a5, p3, 4096, 0, 1            ; DISPLAY FREQUENCY RESPONSE
     endin
; CREATE A TABLE WITH AN IMPULSE IN THE SECOND POSITION
f 1     0   8     2     0 1 0 0 0 0 0 0

i 2009  0   0.185759637  ; CREATE 2^14 (8192) SAMPLES (A NICE FFT #)
```

Figure 20.37 Orchestra and score code for *instr 2009*, a simple lowpass design implemented by delaying, scaling, and summing the input signal with the scaled delayed copies of the original.

$$H(F) = \frac{1}{1 + \frac{1}{2}e^{-2\pi jF} + \frac{1}{2}e^{-4\pi jF}} \tag{20.53}$$

sort of a bandpass-highpass response. A Csound instrument to implement and test this filter is shown in figure 20.38.

Always check an IIR filter that is built from scratch for stability. It is easy to make an unstable IIR filter. When using filters in musical applications, it is common to change filter parameters such as the cutoff frequency or the bandwidth during a note. Strictly speaking, if you change the parameters with time, the filter is no longer time-invariant and the analysis techniques we have discussed no longer apply. If the changes are slow compared with the fundamental frequency of the note, however, approximating the filter as an LTI system is usually adequate.

Filter Design

Designing an IIR filter to meet specified performance characteristics is a little beyond what we can do in one chapter. The interested reader is directed to the references and the CD-ROM. Designing an FIR filter can also be quite involved. However there is one relatively straightforward method that uses the techniques we have discussed up to this point.

The first step is to plot or sketch the magnitude of the desired frequency response as mentioned under the heading The Fourier Transform above. The discrete-time

```
          instr     2010          ; IIR FILTER EXAMPLE
a1        linseg    sr/8, 7/sr, sr/8, 1/sr, 0, 1, 0
a2        oscil     1, a1, 1                   ; GENERATE IMPULSE
aprev1    init      0                          ; INIT Y(N-1) TO 0
aprev2    init      0                          ; INIT Y(N-2) TO 0
ainput    =         a2
; y(n) = a0x(n)-b1y(n-1)-b2y(n-2)
aoutput   =         1*ainput-0.5*aprev1-0.5*aprev2
aprev2    =         aprev1
aprev1    =         aoutput
          out       aoutput
          display   aoutput, p3                ; DISPLAY IMPULSE RESPONSE
          dispfft   aoutput, p3, 4096, 0, 1    ; FREQUENCY RESPONSE
          endin

; CREATE A TABLE WITH AN IMPULSE IN THE SECOND POSITION
f 1   0    8      2  0 1 0 0 0 0 0 0

i 2010     0  0.185759637         ; CREATE 2^14 (8192) SAMPLES
```

Figure 20.38 Orchestra and score code for *instr 2010,* an IIR bandpass filter based on equation 20.52.

frequency response must be a periodic function, so we have to sketch or plot one full period of the function. A plot of one period of an ideal lowpass filter with a cutoff frequency of 1/8 (Remember the useful range of F is from 0 to 1/2) is given in figure 20.39.

The next step is to decide how many points to include in the filter. It should be an odd number. The larger the number, the better the filter, but the more work you will have to do. Next, for calculation purposes, you need to find the index range. For example, for a 5-point filter, the index range is from -2 to 2. For a 15-point filter the index range is from -7 to 7. Call the ending index N.

With the index range in hand you need to calculate the Inverse Fourier Transform for the points in the index range. The result will be a set of raw filter coefficients, $a[n]$. Because our filter uses only a finite number of points we will have to smooth the coefficients. We will do this using a *window.* Every DSP specialist has his or her own favorite window. We will use the *Hamming* window:

$$w[n] = 0.54 + 0.46\cos\frac{\pi n}{N} \qquad (20.54)$$

where n is the coefficient index and N is the ending index. The final filter coefficients, $b[n]$, are found by multiplying the raw coefficients by the window coefficients:

$$b[n] = a[n] \cdot w[n] \qquad (20.55)$$

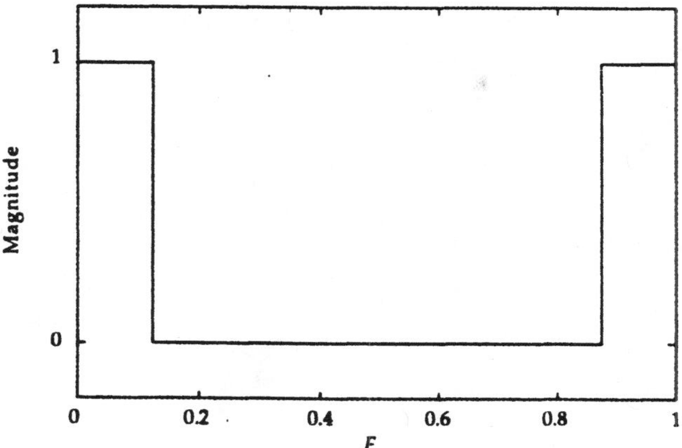

Figure 20.39 Plot of one period of an ideal lowpass filter with a cutoff frequency of 1/8.

For short filters, the coefficients can be used as explained above. For longer filters, the coefficients should be put into a soundfile as sound samples (using something other than Csound), then **cvanal** should be used to convert the response to a frequency response and **convolve** should be used to implement the filter.

It is usually wise to check how close the actual filter came to the desired filter. You do so by taking the Fourier Transform of the filter coefficients with the equation above. The summation only runs from $-N$ to N instead of $-\infty$ to ∞, however. The results for a 41-point filter ($N=20$) are shown in figure 20.40.

Mathematica can handle most of the calculation work for you. The following *Mathematica* commands will calculate and plot the results for a 41-point filter with a cutoff frequency of 1/8.

```
<<Calculus'FourierTransform'
XofF=1-UnitStep[F-1/8]+UnitStep[F-7/8]
Plot[XofF,{F,0,1},AxesLabel->{F,mag}]
xofn=Integrate[XofF Exp[2 Pi I F n],{F,0,1}
Nmax=20
RawFilter=Table[Limit[xofn,n->z],{z,-Nmax,Nmax}]
Window=Table[0.54+0.46Cos[n Pi/Nmax],{n,-Nmax,Nmax}]
Filter=Window RawFilter
ListPlot[RawFilter,Prolog->PointSize[0.02],PlotRange->All]
ListPlot[Filter,Prolog->PointSize[0.02],PlotRange->All]
InverseTable=Table[Exp[-2 Pi I n F],{n,-Nmax,Nmax}]
NewXofF=Apply[Plus,(Filter InverseTable)]
Plot[Abs[NewXofF],{F,0,1},AxesLabel->{F,mag}]
```

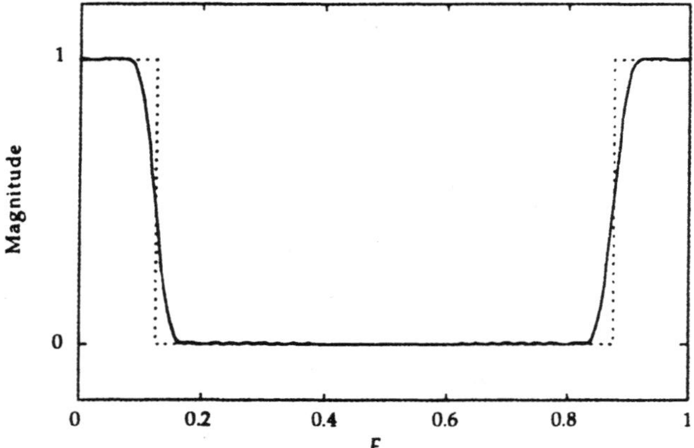

Figure 20.40 The plot for a 41-point filter with a cutoff frequency of 1/8 as calculated by *Mathematica* using the commands above.

The only reason for the <<Calculus'FourierTransform' line is for the UnitStep function. *Nmax* can be changed to create larger or smaller filters.

You have probably guessed by now that the impulse response of an FIR filter contains the filter coefficients in sequence. In other words, the filter coefficient $b[n]$ equals the impulse response, $h[n]$. This idea is the guiding principle behind **convolve**. Since any soundfile *could* be the impulse response of *some* filter we can assume that it is and use the soundfile as an FIR filter. The result of using the opening bars of Beethoven's "Ninth Symphony" to filter "Wild Thing" will probably not be what you would expect, but it can be done.

Modulation

Modulation is the use of one signal to change the properties of another signal. Modulation is not a time-invariant process, but the methods we have developed to this point can provide a surprising amount of insight into modulation.

Frequency Modulation

A very common form of modulation in digital music production is *frequency modulation,* or FM. A thorough understanding of FM is well beyond the scope of this chapter, but a brief example will be given. In modulation, one signal is normally called the *carrier signal,* $c(t)$ and the other is called the *modulating signal,* $x_m(t)$. In FM the modulating signal changes the frequency of the carrier. For example:

$$y_{FM}(t) = A\sin[2\pi f_0 t + I_M x_M(t)] \tag{20.56}$$

where $c(t) = A\sin(2\pi f_0 t)$ and I_M is the modulation index. For communications systems, $x_m(t)$ is usually band-limited, f_0 is usually much higher than any frequency component in $x_m(t)$ and I_M is fairly small. For musical applications, f_0 is usually comparable to the frequency components in $x_m(t)$ and I_M is rather large. One less common use for FM is to create alien voices for science-fiction movies. The example in figures 20.41 and 20.42 demonstrates modulating a sine wave with a spoken voice. The sound file *Hamlet.aif* is on the accompanying CD-ROM but any recording of a spoken voice may be used.

A thorough exploration of FM requires Bessel functions and other unpleasantries that we will forego at this point.

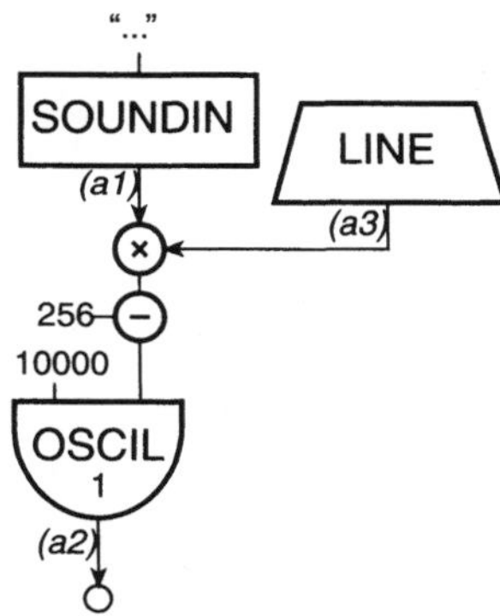

Figure 20.41 Block diagram of *instr 2011,* an instrument that frequency modulates a sine wave with a male speaking voice.

```
        instr    2011          ; FM SCI-FI VOICE EXAMPLE
a1      soundin  "Hamlet.aif"
a3      line     0, p3, 0.4                ; MODULATION INDEX
a2      oscil    10000, 256-a3*a1, 1       ; MODULATE
        out      a2
        endin

f 1     0     4096    10    1              ; SINE TABLE
i 2011  0     22
```

Figure 20.42 Orchestra and score code for *instr 2011,* a FM instrument with a sinusoidal carrier and a **soundin** modulator.

Amplitude Modulation

A less common form of modulation in music production, though still valuable and much more amenable to analysis, is *amplitude modulation* or *AM*. In AM the carrier is multiplied by the modulating signal.

$$y_{AM}(t) = x_M(t)c(t) \tag{20.57}$$

There is usually a symmetry between operations in the frequency domain and operations in the time domain. Since convolution in the time domain corresponds to multiplication in the frequency domain, it should come as no surprise that multiplication in the time domain corresponds to convolution in the frequency domain. The Fourier transform of $c(t) = A\cos(2\pi f_0 t)$ is two impulses, one at f_0 and the other at $-f_0$. If $x_m(t)$ is band-limited, then the convolution of $C(f)$ with $X_M(f)$ generates two copies of $X_M(f)$, one centered at f_0 and the other at $-f_0$. Figure 20.45 illustrates the concept.

Implementing AM in Csound is surprisingly straightforward. One simply multiplies two audio-rate variables together. Figures 20.43–20.44 illustrate creating sci-fi voices using AM. The resultant voice is much more intelligible than the FM version. The sound file *Hamlet.aif* is on the accompanying CD-ROM, but any recording of a spoken voice may be used.

Voice Scrambler-Descrambler

One final example makes use of most of the concepts we have covered in this chapter. A common use for DSP is a voice scrambler for the telephone. Most telephones are band-limited. This example uses a band limit of 8 kHz. If one amplitude modulates an 8 kHz carrier with a band-limited voice and then filters out all frequencies above 8 kHz and below –8 kHz, one ends up with a perfectly reversed voice spectrum. It is hard to understand someone speaking upside down (see figure 20.49). The Csound example shown in figures 20.46 and 20.47 performs the modulation and filtering. (The soundfile *Sharp_8kHz_Lowpass.aif* must be processed with **cvanal** to generate *Sharp_8kHz_Lowpass.con* before the code can be run.)

To recover the original voice, one can modulate the new signal with an 8 kHz carrier and then filter out all frequencies above 8 kHz and below –8 kHz. This process reverses the spectrum once again, restoring it to its original state. One needs only to change the name of the input file and use the *2013.orc* file to perform the descrambling as shown in *instr 2014* (figure 20.48).

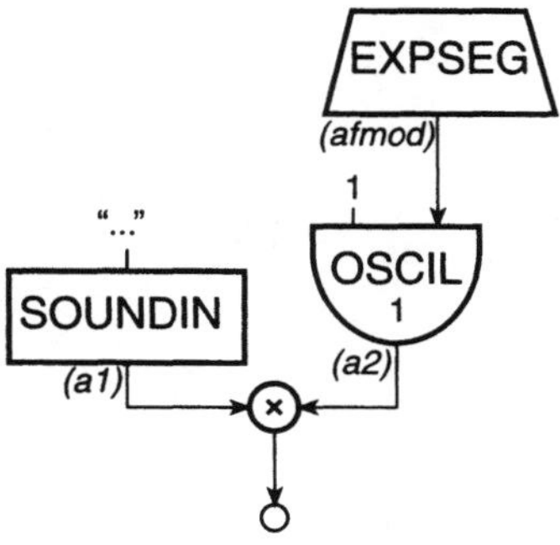

Figure 20.43 Block diagram of *instr 2012,* an instrument that amplitude modulates a soundfile of a male speaking voice with a sine wave.

```
        instr     2012          ; AM SCI-FI VOICE EXAMPLE
afmod   expseg    8000, p3, 40          ; VARY CARRIER FREQUENCY
a1      soundin   "Hamlet.aif"
a2      oscil     1, afmod, 1           ; GENERATE CARRIER
        out       a1*a2                 ; MODULATE
        endin

f 1     0     4096     10   1           ; SINE TABLE
i 2012  0     22
```

Figure 20.44 Orchestra and score code for *instr 2012,* an AM instrument with a **soundin** modulator.

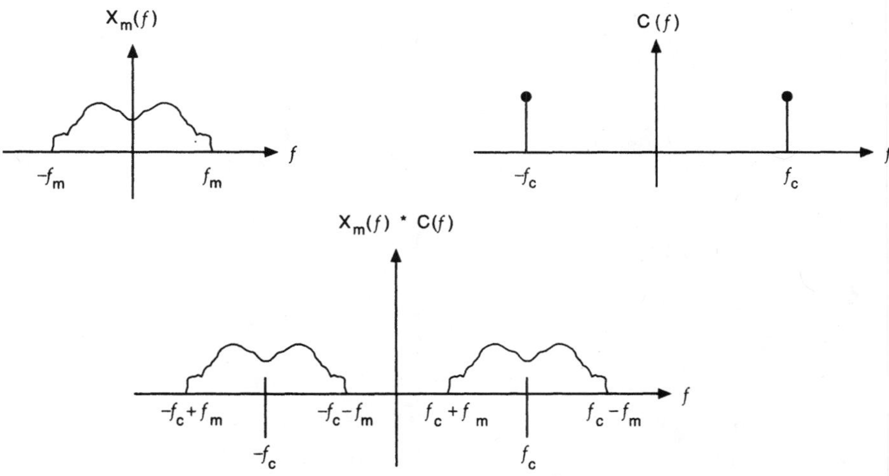

Figure 20.45 Amplitude modulation.

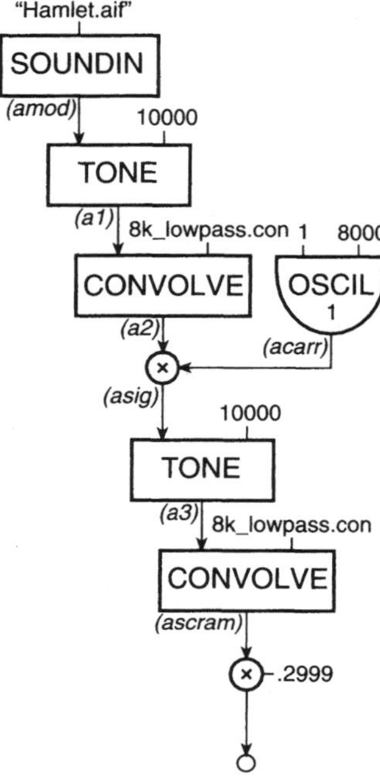

Figure 20.46 Block diagram of *instr 2013,* an instrument that reverses the spectrum of a **soundin** and thus creates a voice scrambler/descrambler.

The difference is that the scrambling orchestra band-limits the input signal to 8 kHz before scrambling. Because the scrambled signal is already band-limited to 8 kHz, the prefiltering is not necessary for descrambling.

This example works well in Csound at the common sampling rate of 44.1 kHz but will not run properly at 22 kHz, because the modulation creates sound at frequencies up to 16 kHz before the lowpass filtering. At the lower sampling rate the portion of the scrambled spectrum from 11 to 16 kHz aliases back into the range of 11 to 6 kHz, so the lowpass filter cannot remove it. The voice would be well scrambled but impossible to unscramble.

Conclusion

This chapter has only scratched the surface of signal processing and Csound. I hope I have convinced you, however, that Csound is a valuable, if not an optimal, tool for

```
        instr    2013       ; PHONE VOICE SCRAMBLER
acarr   oscil    1, 8000, 1                        ; GEN CARRIER
amod    soundin  "Hamlet.aif"                      ; THE FILE TO SCRAMBLE.
a1      tone     amod, 10000                       ; GENTLE PREFILTER
a2      convolve a1, "Sharp_8kHz_Lowpass.con"      ; SHARP PREFILTER
asig    =        a2*acarr                          ; MODULATE
a3      tone     asig, 10000                       ; GENTLE FILTER
ascram  convolve a3, "Sharp_8kHz_Lowpass.con"      ; SHARP FILTER
        out      ascram*0.2999
        endin

f 1     0   16384   10    1                        ; SINE TABLE

i 2013  0   24
```

Figure 20.47 Orchestra and source code for *instr 2013,* which scrambles a **soundin** using the convolve opcode.

```
        instr    2014      ; PHONE VOICE DESCRAMBLER
acarr   oscil    1, 8000, 1                           ; GEN CARRIER
amod    soundin  "VoiceScrambler.aif"                 ; FILE TO DESCRAMBLE
asig    =        amod*acarr                           ; MODULATE
a3      tone     asig, 10000                          ; GENTLE FILTER
adescr  convolve a3, "Sharp_8kHz_Lowpass.con"         ; SHARP FILTER
        out      adescr*0.7246
        endin

f 1     0   16384   10    1                           ; SINE TABLE

i 2014  0   24
```

Figure 20.48 Orchestra and source code for *instr 2014,* which descrambles a previously scrambled.

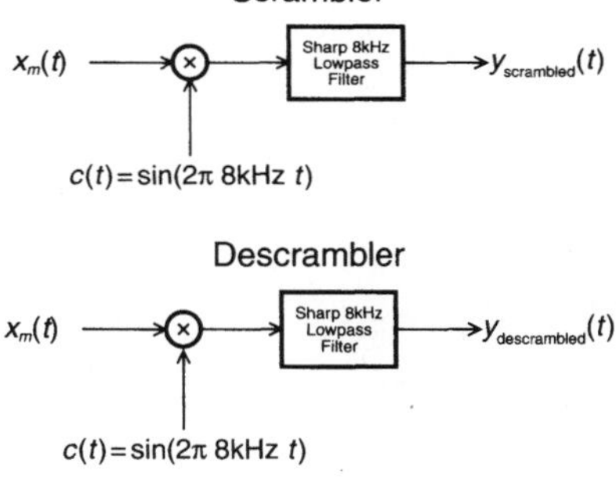

Figure 20.49 Block diagram of voice scrambler/descrambler.

exploring the concepts of digital signal processing and that signal-processing methods and techniques are valuable for understanding what Csound does and why.

References

Chamberlin, H. 1980. *Musical Applications of Microprocessors.* Rochelle Park, N.J.: Hayden.

Hamming, R. W. 1983. *Digital Filters.* Englewood Cliffs, N.J.: Prentice-Hall.

Oppenheim, A. V., A. S. Willsky, and I. T. Young. 1983. *Signals and Systems.* Englewood Cliffs, N.J.: Prentice-Hall.

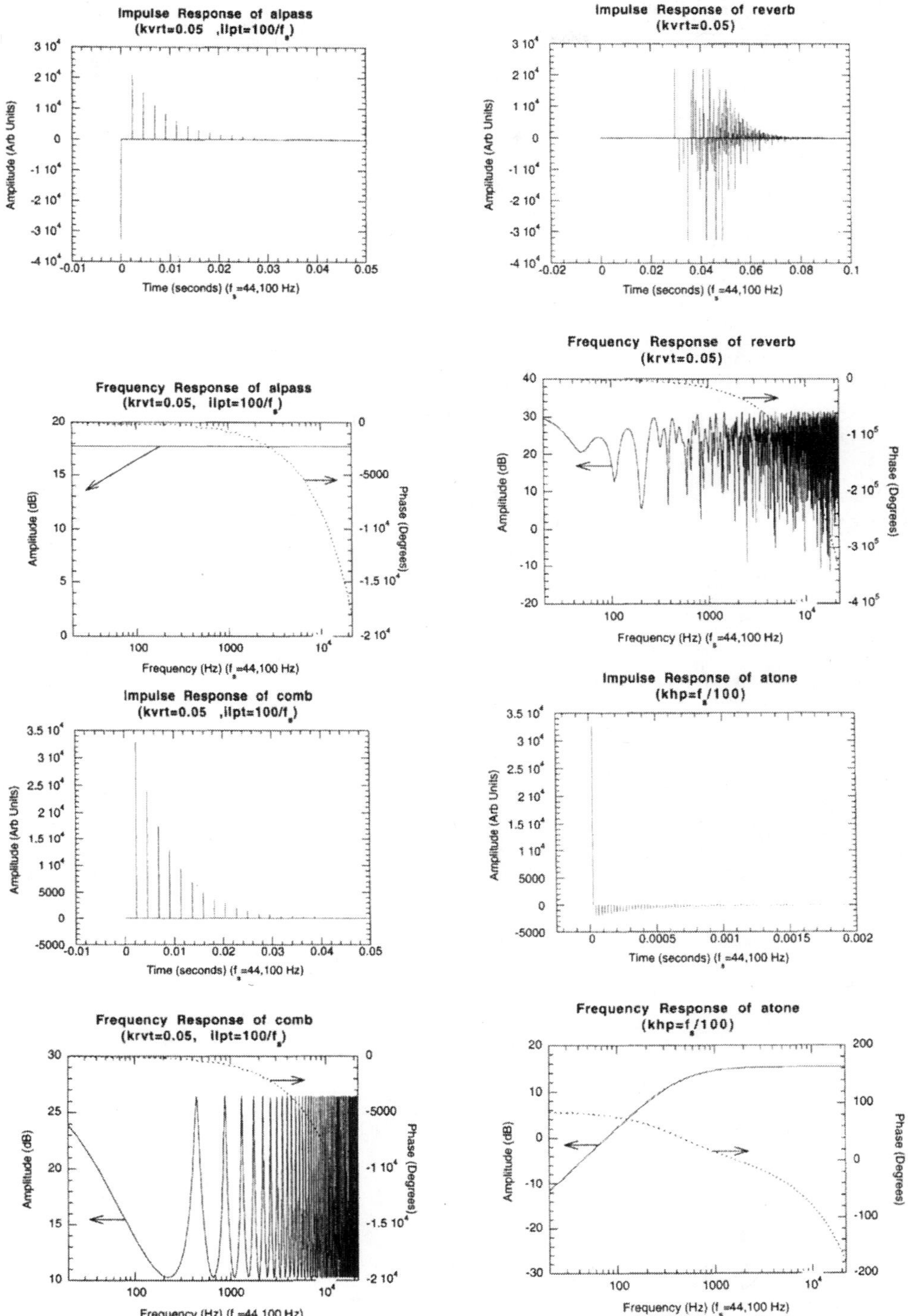

Figure 20.50 Impulse and frequency response graphs.

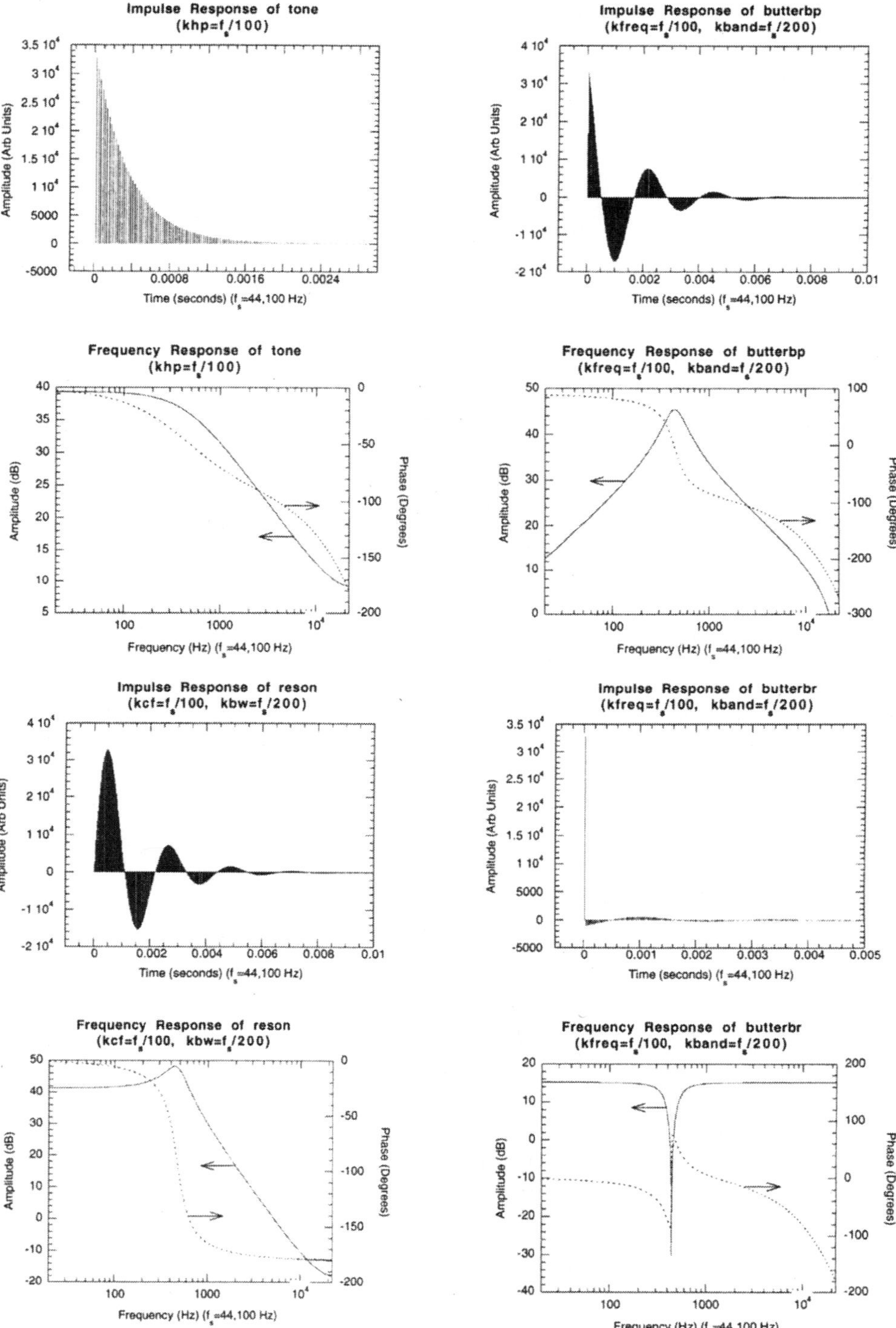

Figure 20.50 continued

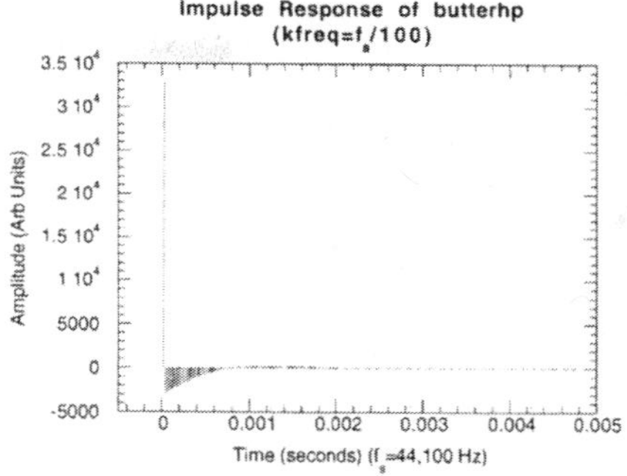

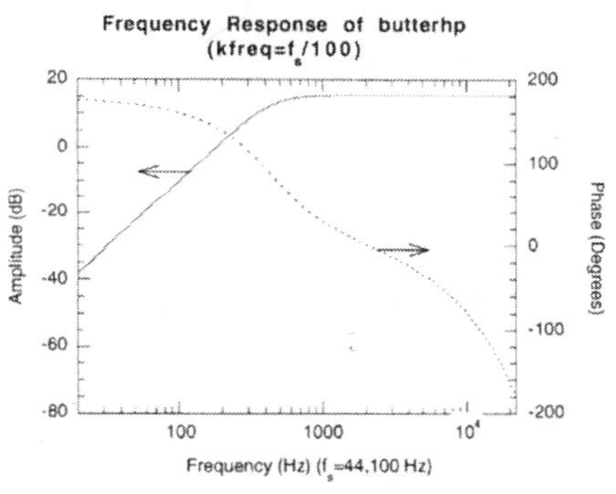

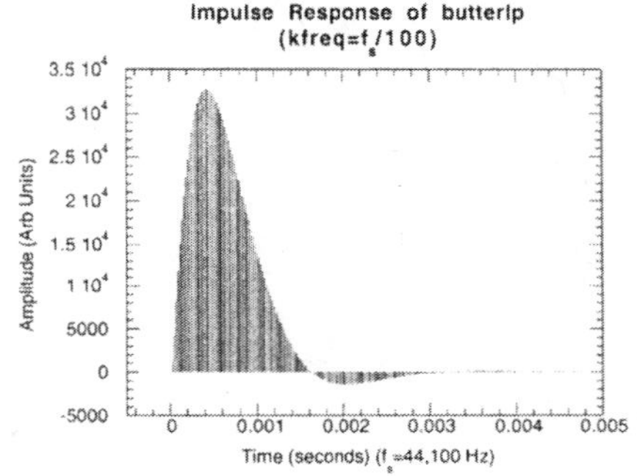

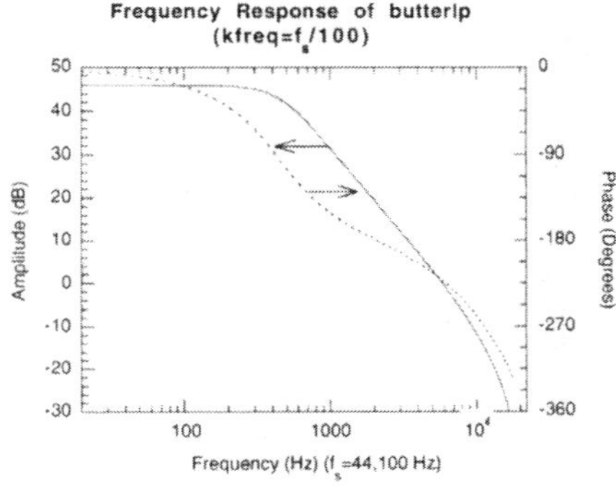

Figure 20.50 continued

21 Understanding Csound's Spectral Data Types

Barry Vercoe

Most of the signals in Csound are discrete-time sequences of floating-point values, varying at a fixed audio rate or control rate, or at some nonperiodic rate determined by score events, MIDI events and control sensing. They can often replace each other as inputs to compound generators, so that an audio oscillator can take an amplitude that is variously an i-time constant, a control signal, or an audio signal. Also, a Csound instrument normally progresses from event constants to control signals to audio signals and we spend most of our sound-design time making this progression real.

Spectral data types are different. Although they represent audio and control signals and likewise vary at some fixed rate over time, they cannot be plugged into normal signal slots, nor can normal signals substitute for them. They create a separate network of data communication, often with several simultaneously different refresh rates, and generally maintain an orderly world of their own. Moreover, the entrance and exit to this world is the reverse of the above: we begin with audio signals and end with control signals. The goal of this chapter then is to make this progression seem just as real.

The reason for this reverse is signal analysis, sensing and detection. Csound utilities such as **lpanal** and **pvanal** do analyze signals, producing output that can lead to effective reconstruction under time or frequency modifications, but there is little real *sensing* or *detection* in these processes and certainly none that squarely represents what you and I would sense in a sound either acoustically or musically. While **lpanal** and **pvanal** exploit the elegance of all-pole filters and Fast Fourier Transforms (with linearly spaced filter bins of equal bandwidth), the human cochlea has evolved hair-cell collectors that are exponentially spaced with proportional bandwidths. Both systems have had their reasons. The problem with mathematically elegant analysis, however, is that it appeals mostly to computers (and some people). What the rest of us really need for computer-assisted music performance are sound analysis and sensing mechanisms that work just like our own.

The Csound spectral data types are based on perceptually relevant methods of analysis and feature detection. From the initial massaging of audio input data to the gradual mounting of evidence favoring a certain pitch, pulse or tempo, the methods and opcodes I have devised are inspired by what we currently know about how humans "get" a musical signal. As a result, the opcodes enable one to build models of human auditory perception and detection within a running Csound instrument. This gives the resulting pitch and rhythm detectors both relevance and strength. In describing the nature and use of these opcodes below I will occasionally allude to their physiological and perceptual roots. For a more detailed account, however, see my chapter "Computational auditory pathways to music understanding" in (Vercoe 1997).

Opcodes

A feature-detecting sequence that uses spectral data types is formed from a small set of opcodes that can be grouped as shown in figure 21.1.

The connecting data object *wsig* contains not only spectral magnitudes, but also a battery of other information that makes it self-defining. In a chain of processing opcodes, each will modify its input spectral data, but the output object will retain the self-defining parts to pass on to the next opcode. This opcode will in turn "know" things, such as which spectrum opcode is periodically refreshing the first link in the chain, the time of last refresh, how often refreshes occur, how many spectral points there are per octave, whether they are magnitude or dB, the frequency range, etc. All of this means that an ending operator like **specdisp** or **specptrk** can tell from its

```
ENTERING:                  wsig          spectrum   xsig,      ...

PROCESSING AND VIEWING:    wsig          specaddm   wsig       ...
                           wsig          specdiff   wsigin
                           wsig          specscal   wsigin,    ...
                           wsig          spechist   wsigin
                           wsig          specfilt   wsigin,    ...
                                         specdisp   wsig,      ...

LEAVING:                   koct, kamp    specptrk   wsigin,    ...
                           ksum          specsum    wsig,      ...
```

Figure 21.1 Csound's spectral data type opcodes.

input how often it must do work and how detailed this must be. It can also opt to ignore some changes and work at a slower pace.

The originating spectral analysis of audio is done by:

```
wsig   spectrum  xsig, iprd, iocts, ifrqs, iq[, ihann, idbout,
                 idisprd, idsinrs]
```

The analysis is done every *iprd* by a set of exponentially spaced Fourier matchings, wherein a windowed segment of the audio signal is multiplied by sinusoids with specific frequencies. The process is first performed for the top octave, for *ifrqs* different frequencies exponentially spaced. The window size is determined by *iq,* the ratio of Fourier center frequency to bandwidth. For efficiency, the data are not actually windowed at all, but the sinusoids are and these can be viewed by making *idsines* nonzero. Next, the audio data are downsampled and the process repeated for the next octave and so on, for as many octaves as requested. To fill the window of the lowest bin in the lowest octave, the downsampled data must be kept around for some time. The stored down-samples (dynamically changing) can be periodically displayed by giving *idisprd* a nonzero value.

Keeping downsampled audio to fill a slow-moving low-frequency window brings us to a problem we will encounter later. Both the Hanning and Hamming-shaped windows are symmetric (bell-shaped sinusoidal) and designed to focus analytic attention on their temporal center. To make the centers of all frequency-analysis windows coincide at the exact same time-point, the higher frequency windows are delayed until the low frequency window is complete. This introduces an input-output time delay across the **spectrum** opcode. The amount of delay depends on both the window size (indirectly *iq*) and the number of octaves (*iocts*). While this delaying strategy might at first seem unnecessarily fussy, the coincident windows turn out to make a big difference for some spectral operations like **specptrk**, as we will see shortly.

Once we have reliable spectral data, the other opcodes can then proceed with their work. The unit **specaddm** does a weighted add of two incoming *wsigs,* while **specdiff** calculates the difference between consecutive frames of a single varying spectrum. This latter can be seen as a delta analyzer, operating independently on each "channel" of the spectrum to produce a differential spectrum as output. In fact, it reports only the positive differences to produce a positive difference spectrum and is thus useful as an energy onset detector. The units **spechist** and **specfilt** are similar to each other, the first accumulating the values in each frequency channel to provide a running histogram of spectral distribution, while the second injects each new value into a first-order lowpass filter attached to each channel. We will see this used in one of the examples below.

The units **specptrk** and **specsum** have only control signal output and provide a way back into standard Csound instrument processing. The first is a pitch detector, which reports the frequency and amplitude as control signals.

```
koct, kamp  specptrk  wsig, kvar, ilo, ihi, istrt, idbthresh,
                      inptls, irolloff [, iodd, iconfs,
                      interp, ifprd, iwtflg]
```

The detection method involves matching the spectral data of *wsig* with a template of harmonic partials (optionally odd, with some roll-off per octave). Matching is done by cross-correlation to produce an internal spectrum of candidate pitches over a limited pitch range (*ilo* to *ihi*). The internal spectrum is then scanned for the strongest candidate, which, if confirmed over *iconfs* consecutive *wsigs,* is declared the winner. The output is then modified accordingly.

The combination of suitably scaled **spectrum** and **specptrk** units creates a robust pitch detector, capable of extracting the most prominent component of a mixed source signal (e.g., a sitar against a background drone). We can observe some of this at work: we can display the original spectrum via a **specdisp** and we can display the cross-correlation spectrum of the present unit by giving *ifprd* a nonzero value. When an incoming signal has almost no energy at the fundamental (e.g., a high bassoon-like nasal sound), this tracker will still report the human-perceived fundamental pitch. And whereas traditional pitch detectors have difficulty with fast-moving tones like octave scoops, this tracker will stay with the signal, largely because we have time-aligned all the windows of octave down-samples (as described above). Lastly, the pitch resolution of any tone is not restricted to the frequency bins-per-octave of the originating spectrum, but employs parabolic interpolation to obtain much higher resolution.

With an understanding of the above we are now in a position to consider some applications.

A Beat Tracker and Tempo Follower

Energy assessment in the human auditory system is a complex affair. It is not measured immediately but is integrated over time, and we cannot gauge the full intensity of a single impact for about 300 milliseconds. If another impact should occur within that period, the integration of the first is incomplete and the second impact becomes the beneficiary of the remainder (Povel and Okkerman 1981). Consequently, when a stream of impacts arrives grouped in pairs, the first of each pair will seem *softer* than the second, even when both have the same physical intensity. This leads us to the perception of a "lilting" rhythm, and the same phenomenon is at the base of all human rhythmic perception.

A machine will not see it that way. An instrumentation-quality intensity detector will report something much closer to the truth. And if it is digital, even its own integration time (in the low nanoseconds) will be thwarted by the sample-and-hold process.

So how do we get a computer to hear rhythms the way we do? We could program a set of rules that would reinterpret the intensity patterns along human perceptual lines; for a complex score, this could be time consuming. Or we could model the above energy integration in the data gathering itself. This latter is the strategy implemented in Csound's spectral data processing, and an instrument that would track audible beats and follow a changing tempo in human-like fashion would look as shown in figure 21.2.

Every .01 seconds we form a new spectrum, 8 octaves, 12 frequencies per octave, with a bandwidth Q of 8. We use a *Hamming* window, request magnitudes in dB and skip the display of downsampled data. We next apply *Fletcher-Munson* scaling, using stored function tables *f 3* and *f 4,* to simulate the frequency-favoring effect of the auditory canal.

For the inner ear, calculation of a positive difference spectrum is relevant for the following reason: when the human cochlea receives a sudden increase in energy at a hair cell, the neural firing rates on its attached auditory nerve fibers register a sudden increase, then a rapid adaptation to more normal behavior. By contrast, when it receives a sudden decrease in energy, the hair cell almost ignores the event. Clearly our hearing has evolved to be highly sensitive to new onsets (life-threatening?) and almost oblivious to endings, and our music reflects this with event-oriented structures flavored with percussive sounds. We give our machine a similar predilection on each frequency channel with **specdiff**.

The energy integration phenomenon, however, is not visible on the auditory nerve fibers. Apparently this must be happening at a later stage of processing and we can measure it only by psychoacoustic experiment (Povel and Okkerman 1981). It is not yet clear how this actually works. We simply presume in the above model to inject the positive difference data directly into integrating filters (**specfilt**), whose time constants are frequency dependent and are conveyed via stored f-table *f 5.* Finally, we sum the energy sensation across all frequency bins to produce a running composite, in *ksum4.* This is a simple sum, purposely disregarding the effects of simultaneous masking on loudness perception (Zwicker and Scharf 1965), since our real goal is to compare the energies across time.

To the extent that *ksum4* adequately represents the fluctuation in our own sensations, we can now perform pulse and tempo estimation on a single channel of k-rate

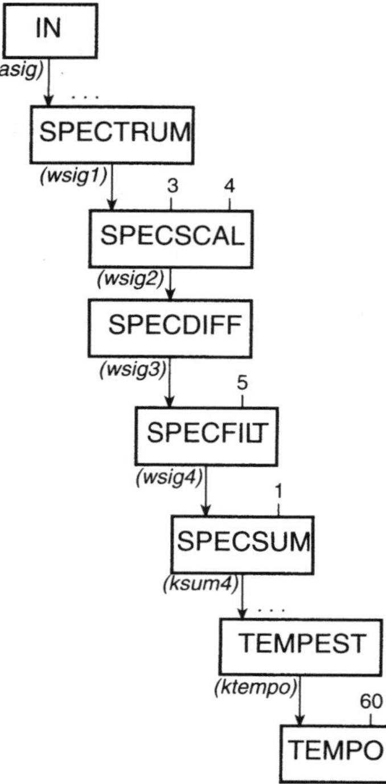

Figure 21.2 Block diagram of *instr 2101*, a beat tracker and tempo follower.

```
        instr     2101      ; BEAT TRACKER, TEMPO FOLLOWER
asig    in                                ; GET MICROPHONE INPUT
                                          ; FORM A SPECTRAL DATA TYPE
wsig1   spectrum  asig, .01, 8, 12, 8, 0, 1, 0
wsig2   specscal  wsig1, 3, 4             ; FLETCHER-MUNSON SCALING
wsig3   specdiff  wsig2                   ; POSITIVE DIFFERENCE SPECTRUM
wsig4   specfilt  wsig3, 5                ; INJECT INTO INTEGRATING FILTERS
ksum4   specsum   wsig4, 1
                                          ; GET TEMPO...
ktempo  tempest   ksum4, .01, .1, 3, 1, 30, .005, 90, 2, .04, 1
        tempo     ktempo, 60              ; ... AND CONTROL THE PERFORMANCE
        endin
```

Figure 21.3 Orchestra code for *instr 2101*, an instrument for taking microphone input and controlling the tempo of the performance based on beat tracking.

data. The **tempest** unit does not traffic in spectral data types, so it will not be described here beyond what is already covered in the Csound manual and further in (Vercoe 1997). It does however afford some good graphic display of the short-term (echoic) memory modeling from which the beat structure and tempo are derived, along with its development of rhythmic expectations that are an essential part of human beat and tempo tracking, and the reader is advised to try running the unit with the input values given above so as to observe them.

The final **tempo** opcode takes us beyond analysis and observation. Although it does nothing for the beat-tracking instrument itself, the **tempo** opcode takes the machine-estimated running *ktempo* and passes it to the Csound scheduler, which controls the timing of every new event. Therefor if the above instrument is inserted into another working orchestra and score, and the command-line flag **-t 60** is invoked, you can control that orchestra's performance by simply tapping into the microphone. A live demonstration of this was intially given at the 1990 ICMC (Vercoe and Ellis 1990), when Dan Ellis controlled the tempo of a Bach performance by tapping arbitrary drum rhythms on a table near a microphone.

A Pitch Tracker and Harmonizer

Since the same human ear that detects rhythms is also responsible for sensations of pitch, we can build a model of this new phenomenon using many of the same initial principles. The two paths of course eventually diverge, and we will be forced to consider some of the special needs of pitch acuity as we get deeper into the search. Given a good sense of pitch, it is not hard to build automatic harmonizers and pitch-to-MIDI converters. We will look briefly at both of these before forming some conclusions.

The two examples we will use, however, employ opcodes that are not part of the normal Csound distribution. These are from my Extended Csound, a version I have developed that can run complex instruments in real-time using the Analog Devices 21060 floating-point DSP accelerator (Vercoe 1996). In that system, some number of DSPs (1–6) on a plug-in audio card can dynamically share the computational load of a large Csound orchestra, which often contains new opcodes that extend both its repertoire and its real-time performance capacity. Although my personal exploration into these real-time complexities is currently dependent on such accelerators, I fully expect the experience gained will eventually migrate to more generally accessible platforms. The interested reader will also find additional presaging examples of Extended Csound on the CD-ROM that accompanies this volume.

A Csound instrument that can pitch-track an incoming audio signal and turn that into a five-part harmony would look as shown in figures 21.4 and 21.5.

First, we take one channel from our stereo microphone and give it some simple equalization (EQ) to heighten the voice partials. Our spectral analysis is similar to the above, with the following new considerations: we will form a new spectrum only every .02 seconds, since percussive rhythm is not the likely input. We request 6 octaves of downsampling, 24 frequencies per octave, with a bandwidth Q of 12. We also request a *Hanning* window and root magnitude spectral data.

The choice of 24 frequency bins of Q 12 merits some discussion. Both are weighted toward pitch-tracking rather than intensity measurement as was the case above, yet they still fall short of an ideal model of the ear. The human cochlea has about 400 hair-cell detectors per octave in this frequency region. On the other hand those detectors are broad-band, with a Q of 4 (1/3 octave). Broad-band implies fast energy collection, where things like binaural sensing of direction depend on accurate measurement of interaural time differences. This is not our goal here, and we opt for slower, more narrowly focused filters, one quarter-tone apart. The parabolic interpolation in **specptrk** will do the rest.

We are now sending **specptrk** some favorable data. The range restriction of 6.5 to 8.9 (in decimal octaves) is sufficient to cover my voice range even on a good day and we give it an initial hint of 7.5. So that it will not try to pitch-track just microphone noise, we set a minimum threshold of 10 dB, below which it will output zeroes for both pitch and amplitude. Since I may decide to sing some strange vocal sounds (e.g., with missing fundamentals), we ask for an internal template of 7 harmonic partials, with a rolloff of .7 per octave. We request just 3 confirmations of any octave leap (proportionally less for smaller intervals) and ask that the pitch and amplitude outputs be k-rate interpolated between consecutive analyses. Finally, we ask it to display the running cross-correlation spectrum so that we can observe the various pitch candidates in dynamic competition.

There was a price to pay for all this, it may be recalled. So that the tracker would stay locked onto fast-moving voice "scoops," we carefully delayed all channels of analysis until the low-frequency window was full and the other windows could be centrally aligned. The amount of delay incurred by **spectrum** is reported on the user console at i-time. For a sampling rate of 16K, a Q of 12 and 6 octaves of downsampling, that value is 66 milliseconds. Having now emerged from the spectral data type world with a running pitch value, we now delay the audio signal by this amount so that the audio and its pitch estimate are synchronized.

We are now ready for the harmonizer. The **harmon4** unit is not part of regular Csound, but an addition that exists in Extended Csound (Vercoe 1996). It is similar to Csound's **harmon** unit, but depends on other processing modules (such as

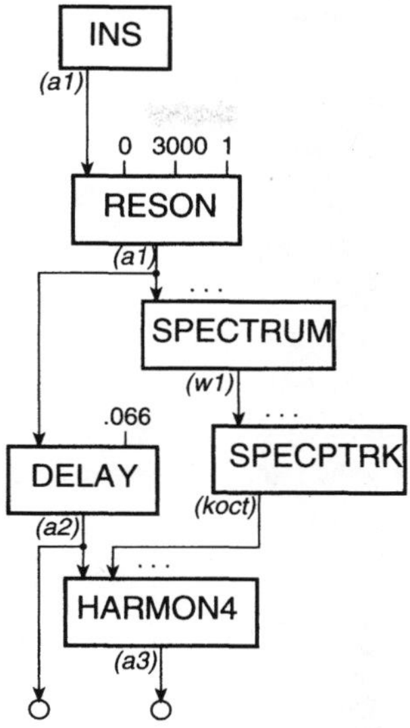

Figure 21.4 Block diagram of *instr 2102,* a pitch tracker and harmonizer.

```
             instr      2102      ; PITCH TRACKING HARMONIZER
a1, a0       ins                                 ; GET MICROPHONE INPUT
a1           reson      a1, 0, 3000, 1           ; AND APPLY SOME EQ
w1           spectrum   a1, .02, 6, 24, 12, 1, 3  ; FORM A SPECTRAL DATA TYPE
                                                 ; FIND THE PITCH
koct, kamp   specptrk   w1, 1, 6.5, 8.9, 7.5, 10, 7, .7, 0, 3, 1, .1
a2           delay      a1, .066                 ; TIME ALIGN PITCH AND AUDIO
                                                 ; ADD 4 NEW PARTS
a3           harmon4    a2, koct, 1.25, .75, 1.5, 1.875, 0, 6.5
             outs       a2, a3                   ; AND SEND ALL 5 TO OUTPUT
             endin
```

Figure 21.5 Orchestra code for *instr 2102,* a pitch tracking harmonizer instrument shown in figure 21.4.

specptrk) to provide a reliable pitch estimate. Like **harmon**, **harmon4** will pitch-shift the original audio stream while preserving the vocal formants and vowel quality. Also, like **harmon**, the pitch-shifts can be specified either as frequency ratios (with the source) or as specific cps values. Its main advantage is better sound quality and the ability to generate up to four vocal transpositions at once.

If you have an Extended Csound accelerator card you can run the **harmon4** instrument as shown above. The four transpositions are given as ratios from the source: .75, 1.25, 1.5 and 1.875, outlining a major triad in 6–4 position with an added major seventh at the top. This is basically the instrument that I demonstrated live at the 1996 International Computer Music Conference (Vercoe 1996), and the voice transposing quality is quite good. If you have only the standard Csound distribution, you should replace the **harmon4** line with the following:

```
a3        harmon    a2, cpsoct(koct), .2, 1.25, .75, 0, 110, .1
```

The transposed voice quality will not be as good, and there are only two added voices instead of four, but the example will serve to demonstrate the effect.

One can imagine many variants of the above. A simple one is to replace the fixed-ratio harmonies with independently derived pitches, as from an external MIDI keyboard, or from some algorithm cognizant, say, of the "changes" in a jazz standard. Another is to replace **harmon4** with a different generator, either a Csound looping sample oscillator reading a different sound (a voice-controlled trombone is fun), or a pitch-to-MIDI converter that would let you take your voice control outside the system to another device:

```
midiout       kamp, koct, iampsens, ibendrng, ichan
```

The possibilities for experimentation and development here are quite unbounded and the reader is encouraged to develop his or her own instruments or opcodes that would take advantage of the feature detection that spectral data types provide.

Conclusion

Csound's spectral data types, based on perceptual methods of gathering and storing auditory relevant data, provide a fresh look at how to enable computer instruments to extract musically important information from audio signals. They offer a new future of computer-assisted ensemble performance connected by sound, not merely by electrical signals. While we do not yet have a full understanding of how humans do the feature extraction that informs both their own performance and their listening, we have shown that imbedding what we do know within a computer instrument can give it an ensemble relevance that normally only live performers achieve. This is why listening to a live performance is still so exciting and this is where computer music eventually must go.

References

Povel, D., and H. Okkerman. 1981. "Accents in equitonal sequences." *Perception and Psychophysics* 30: 565–572.

Vercoe, B. 1996. "Extended Csound." *Proceedings of the International Computer Music Conference*, pp. 141–142.

Vercoe, B. 1997. "Computational Auditory Pathways to Music Understanding." In Deliege, I. and J. Sloboda (eds). *Perception and Cognition of Music* (pp. 307–326). East Sussex: Psychology Press.

Vercoe, B., and D. Ellis. 1990. "Real time Csound: software synthesis with sensing and control." *Proceedings of the International Computer Music Conference,* pp. 209–211.

Zwicker, E., and B, Scharf. 1965. "A model of loudness summation." *Psychological Review 72:* 3–26.

Delay, Chorus, Reverberation, and 3D Audio

22

Using Csound to Understand Delay Lines and Their Applications

Russell Pinkston

A delay line is a simple mechanism that records an input signal, stores it temporarily and then plays it back again. In its most trivial application, it can be used to produce simple "slapback echo" effects. But in truth, a simple delay line is the basis for a wide variety of synthesis and signal processing algorithms, some of which are highly sophisticated. Examples include reverberation, phasing, flanging, chorus, pitch-shifting and harmonization, not to mention all types of digital filtering. Delay lines are also central to some of the most advanced synthesis techniques, such as physical modeling. Indeed, it can be argued that the delay line is the single most important basic function in audio signal processing.

To understand how a digital delay line works, let us look at something comparable in the analog studio. An effect called *tape echo* can be created by simultaneously monitoring both the record and playback heads of a standard reel-to-reel tape deck while recording. We hear a sound as it is being recorded on tape, then a short time later as it is played back. The delay time is a function of the tape speed and the physical distance between the record and playback heads on the tape recorder. Since we can't change the distance between the heads, the only way we can affect the delay time is by changing the speed of the tape: the slower the tape goes by the heads, the longer the delay before we hear the echo and vice versa. If we don't want to waste a lot of good tape, we can use a short tape loop. In theory, it just needs to be longer than the distance between the record and playback heads, but in practice, of course, it has to be long enough to fit over the tape transport mechanism.

A digital delay line is, in effect, a model of a classic analog tape recorder with a tape loop. Instead of recording the analog waveform on a moving strip of magnetic tape, however, the digital waveform is stored sample-by-sample in memory, in what is referred to as a "circular buffer." The buffer isn't actually circular, of course, but it functions like the loop of tape in our analog delay system, which is recorded over and over again as it continually circles through the transport mechanism and passes by the record and playback heads. In a circular buffer, however, the memory doesn't move—the "heads" do.

Essentially, we record (write data) into a buffer starting at the beginning and continuing until the end of the buffer is reached, after which we "circle back" and start recording at the beginning again, erasing what was stored there previously. Meanwhile, we keep playing back (reading data) some distance behind where we are recording. Both the record and playback points keep moving in the same direction, continually "chasing" one another and "wrapping around" when they reach the end of the buffer.

As in the analog tape echo system, the length of the delay in a digital system is a function of the distance (i.e., the number of samples) between the record and playback points and the speed at which we are recording (the sample rate). But unlike our analog model, in a digital delay system the distance between the record and playback points is not necessarily fixed. It can vary anywhere from a single sample to the full length of the buffer. Moreover, in some delay lines, the distance can be varied dynamically, with interesting results. Finally, there can be multiple output (playback) points in a single delay line, referred to as "taps," each of which may be moving independently in relation to the input (record) point.

Csound provides the following basic digital delay lines:

```
ar      delay1    asig[, iskip]
ar      delay     asig, idlt[, iskip]
ar      vdelay    asig, adlt, imaxdlt[, iskip]
```

The first of these opcodes, **delay1**, is a fixed, one sample, delay that is intended for use in constructing FIR filters. The other two opcodes, however, are standard delay lines with a single output tap that allows the delay time to be specified in seconds: **delay** has a fixed delay time *idlt,* while **vdelay** has a variable delay time *adlt,* which can range from 1/sr seconds (1 sample period) to *imaxdlt* seconds.

Figures 22.1 and 22.2 show an example of a simple instrument that generates a stereo slapback echo from a plucked string sound using the Csound **delay** opcode.

In order to demonstrate the basic idea as clearly as possible this instrument was deliberately kept simple. It works fine and produces the expected results. The design, however, has a number of problems or "inelegancies" that may not be immediately apparent. The first problem is that we have tied our "sound" to a particular "effect." We might not always want echoes on our plucked string and we might want to use our echo unit on some other sounds.

Aside from limiting our creative options, however, this approach makes our lives much more difficult in terms of the score, because the instrument will always need to execute long enough to produce not only the **pluck**, but also both *echoes.* Conse-

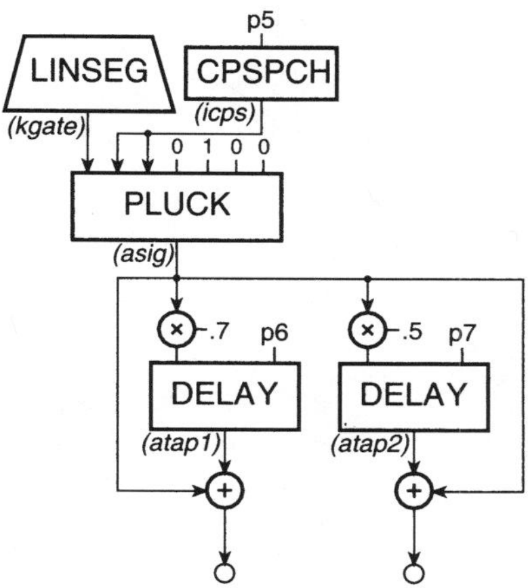

Figure 22.1 Block diagram of *instr 2201,* a stereo slap-back echo instrument.

```
        instr   2201            ; PLUCK WITH ECHOES
kgate   linseg  p4, .1, 0, 1, 0                        ; .1 SEC GATE
icps    =       cpspch(p5)                             ; p4=AMP, p5=PITCH
asig    pluck   kgate, icps, icps, 0, 1, 0, 0          ; p6 & p7 = DELAY IN SEC
atap1   delay   asig*.7, p6                            ; MAKE TWO SLAPBACK ECHOES,
atap2   delay   asig*.5, p7                            ; ... EACH ONE SOFTER
        outs    asig+atap1, asig+atap2                 ; ADD STEREO ECHOES
        endin

; NOTE: P3 MUST BE LONG ENOUGH TO INCLUDE BOTH ECHOES
; INS   ST        DUR       AMP       PCH          ECHO1     ECHO2
i 2201  0         .5        20000     7.00         .3        .4
i 2201  1         .         .         7.07
i 2201  1.5       .         .         8.04
i 2201  2         .         .         8.10
```

Figure 22.2 Orchestra and score code for *instr 2201,* stereo slap-back echo of a plucked string.

quently, the *p3* duration setting of the note statements will not correspond to the musical note durations, as usual and things might get pretty complicated if we used a variable tempo statement, because the delay times are in seconds, not beats.

Also, we are wasting memory, because each **delay** opcode allocates its own internal buffer at initialization time (*i-time*). The size of each buffer is determined by the delay time in seconds, specified in the score as *p6* and *p7,* respectively. Hence, with a sample rate of 44100, the buffer of the first **delay** opcode would be .3 * 44100 = 13230 samples long and the second .4 * 44100 = 17640 samples long. Admittedly, that isn't very much memory these days. But what if we want to play a big chord, or a long passage of very fast notes, whose echoes would overlap? Every time Csound

```
        instr   2202          ; DRY PLUCK
gasend  init    0                                 ; INIT GLOBAL "SEND"
kgate   linseg  p4, .1, 0, 1, 0                   ; .1 SECOND RAMP
icps    =       cpspch(p5)                        ; p5 IN PCH
asig    pluck   kgate, icps, icps, 0, 1, 0, 0     ; SIMPLE PLUCK
        outs    asig, asig                        ; STRAIGHT OUT
gasend  =       gasend+asig                       ; ADD TO GLOBAL VAR
        endin

        instr   2203          ; GLOBAL EFFECT
atap1   delay   gasend*p4, p6                     ; USE GLOBAL VAR FOR INPUTS
atap2   delay   gasend*p5, p7
        outs    atap1, atap2                      ; STEREO ECHOES
gasend  =       0                                 ; CLEAR GLOBAL VAR
        endin

; PLAY A SHORT 2-PART HARMONY; NOTE DURS = PLUCK DURS
; INS   ST      DUR     AMP     PCH
i 2202  0       .1      15000   7.00
i 2202  0       .       .       7.04
i 2202  1       .       .       7.07
i 2202  1       .       .       8.05
i 2202  1.5     .       .       8.04
i 2202  1.5     .       .       8.00
i 2202  2       .       .       8.10
i 2202  2       .       .       9.02
; GLOBAL DELAY INSTR IS ON FOR ENTIRE PASSAGE + LONGEST ECHO
; INS   ST      DUR     FAC1    FAC2    ECHO1   ECHO2
i 2203  0       2.5     .7      .5      .3      .4
```

Figure 22.3 Orchestra and score code for *instr 2202* and *2203,* a combination of a dry plucked string instrument (*2202*) with a "global" effect instrument (*2203*).

needs to allocate a new instance of our instrument to make a note, it will also need to allocate a new pair of delay buffers. The approach shown in figure 22.3 is both more flexible and more efficient, even though it may look a bit more complicated.

Global Stereo Echo Notes

This example plays the same melody as before, with a simple harmony added. This requires that the note amplitudes in the score be reduced somewhat, to avoid samples out of range. Instrument 2202 is basically the same as instrument 2201, but without the delay lines (see figure 22.3). It now just produces a "dry" (un-echoed) pluck, which is sent directly to both output channels via **outs**. It also adds its signal into the variable *gasend,* however, which functions like an "effects send" on a traditional mixing console. The *ga* prefix indicates that it is a *global* audio-rate variable—accessible anywhere in the orchestra.

The **delay** opcodes are now placed in a separate, *higher numbered* instrument (*2203*) that receives input from the global variable *gasend.* Only one instance of this instrument is required. It serves as an effects unit that may be used by the whole orchestra and hence must be turned on for the entire duration of the passage it is processing, plus the longest delay time.

The *gasend* variable is initialized in *instr 2202* and must be cleared after it is used by *instr 2203.* Otherwise, the samples being added by all copies of *instr 2202* would simply accumulate indefinitely. The basic concept is that we are "mixing" the outputs of multiple instruments together and "sending" them to a single "effects unit." Hence, the sending instruments *add* to the global variable, while the receiving instrument uses the sum for input and then zeros the global variable.

Using Csound Global Variables

Csound executes the instruments in the orchestra in ascending order. Consequently, an instrument that is receiving input from a global variable should have a higher instrument number than any instruments that are producing output for that variable. Otherwise the input received by the processing instrument will be delayed one k-period.

If multiple instruments (or copies of a single instrument) are using the same global variable for output, they must add (mix) into the variable (i.e., with an assignment statement such as *gavar* = *gavar* + *avar*) so as to preserve the current contents. Note that in order to avoid a syntax error from such a statement when the orchestra is compiled, the global variable must already have been defined previously, either in the same instrument or in an another instrument somewhere higher in the orchestra. Typically, the first instrument that will use the global variable for output will contain a statement such as *gavar* **init** *0.*

One approach to using multiple global variables as effects sends is to put all of them in a single instrument at the top of the orchestra and make sure that that instrument is turned on (playing) for the entire score. The function of such an instrument is to first define all the global variables before any other instruments attempt to reference them and then to zero them on every sample, either *before any* or *after all* other instruments have used them. Consequently, it must have either the lowest or the highest instrument number in the orchestra. The advantage of this method is that none of the other instruments using these variables have to worry about defining and/or clearing them, which keeps the orchestra code cleaner and helps to avoid syntax errors.

Using Variable Delay Lines

The most common use for a variable delay line is to produce a temporary pitch change in an audio signal. It is common knowledge that if a sound is recorded at one speed and played back at a different speed, it produces a proportional change in pitch and an inversely proportional change in duration. Similarly, in a digital delay line, if the record and playback points keep moving through the circular buffer at the same rate, we hear a fixed delay time without any change in pitch. If they move at different speeds, however, both the delay time and the perceived pitch of the output will vary.

In the Csound delay opcodes, the record point always moves at the same speed (the sample rate), but the speed of the playback point can vary. If the playback point is moving more rapidly than the record point, the delay time will gradually shorten and the pitch will be raised. Conversely, if the playback point is moving more slowly than the record point, the delay time will gradually lengthen and the pitch will be lowered. Obviously, if two points are moving at different constant speeds around a circle, one point will eventually overtake the other, so a pitch change in any one direction can only be temporary. Hence, a common practice with a variable delay line is to apply a low frequency oscillator (LFO) to the delay time parameter, which causes a periodic fluctuation in the delay time and, indirectly, the pitch. As the delay time increases, the playback point is moving more slowly than the record point and the pitch drops; as the delay time increases, the playback point is moving more rapidly than the record point and the pitch rises.

The waveshape used for the LFO is typically a sine, which results in a smooth "vibrato" effect. The greater the amplitude of the LFO (amount of change in the delay), the greater the depth of the vibrato. The delay time is never allowed to reach zero or exceed the buffer length, so the record and playback points will never actually meet, but the distance between them (and hence, the speed of the playback pointer) is continually changing (see figures 22.4 and 22.5).

Delay-line Vibrato Notes

Once again, this example is deliberately kept simple, in order to demonstrate both the basic technique and the gross effect. A single instrument contains both the sound generator and the effect, which is not ideal, as has been discussed. Moreover, this is not clearly the best way to generate a vibrato in a synthesized wave, but the variable delay method will work with any input signal, including recorded sounds. To get a perceptible vibrato with a single delay line, the maximum delay time has to be moderately long and the amount of variation (LFO amplitude) fairly large.

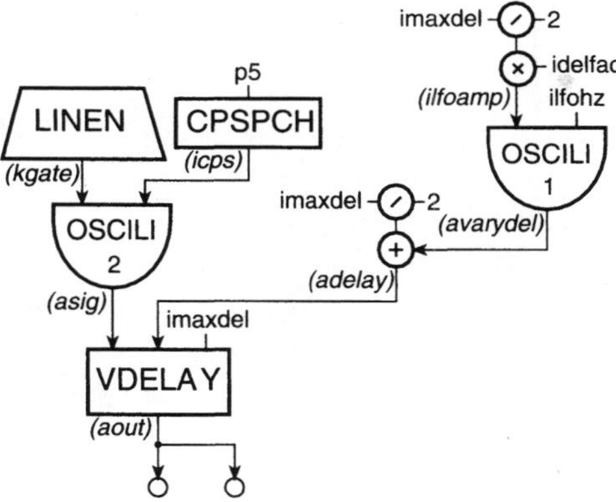

Figure 22.4 Block diagram of *instr 2204,* a variable delay vibrato instrument.

```
            instr    2204          ; VDELAY VIBRATO
icps        =        cpspch(p5)                     ; BASIC PITCH
ilfohz      =        p6                             ; LFO RATE IN CPS
idelfac     =        p7                             ; BETWEEN 0 & .999
imaxdel     =        p8                             ; MAX DELAY IN SECS
ilfoamp     =        idelfac*imaxdel/2              ; LFO FN IS +/- 1
kgate       linen    p4, .1, p3, .2                 ; BASIC NOTE ENVLP
avarydel    oscili   ilfoamp, ilfohz, 1             ; FN1 IS LFO WAVE
asig        oscili   kgate, icps, 2                 ; FN2 IS OSC WAVE
adelay      =        imaxdel/2+avarydel             ; OFFSET TO .5 MAX
aout        vdelay   asig, adelay, imaxdel          ; VARYING DELAY
            outs     aout, aout
            endin

; LFO WAVE IS A SINE
f 1       0    512  10       1
; OSCIL WAVE
f 2       0    512  10       1       .5       .3             .2          .1
; LFO DEPTH FACTOR IS .9, GRADUALLY INCREASE MAX DELAY TIME
; INS     ST   DUR  AMP      PCH     LFOHZ    DEPTH          MAXDLT
i 2204    0    3    10000    8.00    5        .9             1
i 2204    +    .    .        .       .        .              2
i 2204    +    .    .        .       .        .              3
i 2204    +    .    .        .       .        .              4
```

Figure 22.5 Orchestra and score code for *instr 2204,* a variable delay-line vibrato instrument.

Flanging

The same basic algorithm used in the previous instrument can also be used to create a well-known effect called *flanging*. The term derives from the practice of playing the same recording from two tape decks simultaneously and alternately applying pressure to the flange of one or the other machines supply reels. This causes a slight, temporary slowing of the tape speed of the affected machine, which slightly lowers the pitch of the recording. When the detuned signal from that deck is combined with that of the other deck, the result is a distinctive "wooshing" sound that sweeps up and down throughout the frequency spectrum, caused by frequency cancellations and reinforcements between the two signals.

The effect can be simulated digitally by combining the original sound with a copy sent through a delay line with a varying delay time. The delay time must be short (on the order of a few milliseconds) and vary at a relatively slow rate of speed and the delayed signal must be combined with the original in order to create the flange effect. The effect can be accentuated by incorporating a feedback loop into the delay line, but it is a wise precaution to use a **balance** opcode to make sure that the feedback stays in control. In the following example, we will use a single delay line that has two variable taps, each of which is controlled by a separate LFO. The output of one tap is sent to the left speaker, the other to the right.

The following Csound delay opcodes must be used if multiple taps from the same delay buffer are needed:

```
ar      delayr     idlt[, iskip]
ar      deltap     kdlt
ar      deltapi    xdlt
        delayw     asig
```

These are the most flexible Csound delay opcodes, but they are a bit more complicated to use. The **delayr** and **delayw** opcodes must be used together in order to establish the delay line and write a signal into it. The **delayr** opcode, which allocates a delay buffer *idlt* seconds long, must come first. After the **delayr**, any number of **deltap** or **deltapi** opcodes may be used, followed by the **delayw** opcode, which actually writes data into the buffer. The **deltapi** opcode is simply the interpolating version of **deltap**. It is slightly less efficient, but it produces a significantly better sound when the delay time is varying. Figure 22.6 shows a global stereo flanger effect instrument and figure 22.7 shows the corresponding Csound code.

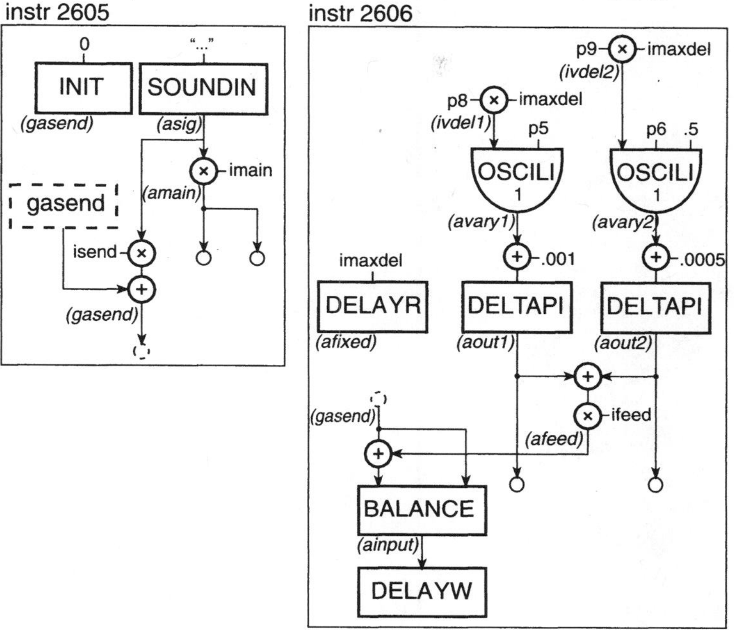

Figure 22.6 Block diagram of *instr 2205* and *2206,* a soundin instrument (*2205*) with a global output to a stereo flanger instrument (*2206*).

Flanging Notes

In this example (see figure 22.7), *instr 2205* uses basically the same method as *instr 2202* to send its signal to the effects instrument: it initializes the global variable *gasend* to zero at i-time, then mixes a portion of the signal from the **soundin** opcode into *gasend* on every sample. The only addition is the variables *imain* and *isend,* which are used to control the proportion of the signal sent directly to the outputs and/or to the effects unit, respectively. Once again, the effects instrument (*instr 2206*) must zero the global variable (*gasend*) after it has been used as an input.

In *instr 2206,* a single delay circuit is established by the **delayr/delayw** pair, which allocates a buffer large enough for a delay of *imaxdel* seconds. The output of **delayr** (*afixed*) is not used, but a result variable is required nonetheless.

The **deltapi** opcodes are used to provide two variable taps, whose delay times are controlled by two **oscili** opcodes. The **oscili** opcodes both use Hamming window

```
sr        =         44100
kr        =         44100                          ; SR SHOULD EQUAL KR WHEN
ksmps     =         1                              ; ... USING AUDIO FEEDBACK.
nchnls    =         2

          instr     2205          ; SOUNDIN 1
imain     =         p4                             ; MAIN AMP FACTOR
isend     =         p5                             ; SEND AMP FACTOR
gasend    init      0
asig      soundin   "speech1.aif"                  ; THE SOURCE SOUND
amain     =         asig*imain                     ; ATTEN MAIN SIG
          outs      amain, amain
gasend    =         gasend+asig*isend              ; ADD TO EFFECTS SEND
          endin

          instr     2206          ; STEREO FLANGER
ifeed     =         p4                             ; FEEDBACK FACTOR
ilfohz1   =         p5                             ; 1ST LFO SPEED
ilfohz2   =         p6                             ; 2ND LFO SPEED
imaxdel   =         p7                             ; MAX DELAY TIME
ivdel1    =         p8*imaxdel                     ; TAP1 VARY AMOUNT
ivdel2    =         p9*imaxdel                     ; TAP2 VARY AMOUNT
avary1    oscili    ivdel1, ilfohz1, 1             ; HAMMING WINDOW FN
avary2    oscili    ivdel2, ilfohz2, 1, .5         ; START OUT OF PHASE
afixed    delayr    imaxdel                        ; IMAXDEL SEC BUFFER
aout1     deltapi   .001+avary1                    ; TWO VARYING TAPS
aout2     deltapi   .0005+avary2                   ; STAGGER A LITTLE
afeed     =         (aout1+aout2)*ifeed            ; FEEDBACK BOTH
ainput    balance   gasend+afeed, gasend           ; BALANCE WITH ORIG
          delayw    ainput                         ; DELAY W/FEEDBK
          outs      aout1, aout2                   ; SPLIT OUTPUTS
gasend    =         0                              ; ZERO SEND VAR
          endin

; LFO WAVE IS A HAMMING WINDOW FUNCTION
f 1       0    512  20        1
; SOUND PRODUCING INSTRUMENT
; INS     ST   DUR  MAIN      SEND
i 2205    0    8    .4        .8
; FLANGE EFFECT UNIT
; INS     ST   DUR  FEEDBK    LFOHZ1    LFOHZ2    MAXDEL    DEPTH1    DEPTH2
i 2206    0    8    .9        .2        .7        .005      .8        .9
```

Figure 22.7 Orchestra and score code for *instr 2205* and *2206*, a dry soundin instrument (*2205*) with global sends to a stereo flanger instrument (*2206*).

functions, whose values range from 0–1. They have different frequencies and amplitudes (peak delay times), producing two completely independent variable delay taps. The "depth" of the flange produced by each **deltapi** is determined by the values of *p8* and *p9* from the score, which must have values between 0–1, since they will be multiplied by *imaxdel* to determine the actual peak delay time for each tap, which cannot be longer than the size of the buffer.

The outputs of the **deltapi** opcodes are first sent to separate output channels (which produces a simulated stereo effect from a mono input signal), then summed and fed back into the delay line. The feedback accentuates the flange effect, but it must be controlled carefully. The variable *ifeed* attenuates the summed signal before it is added back into the delay input, which provides one means of limiting gain. It is wise, however, to use a **balance** opcode as well, which ensures that the feedback will not become uncontrolled.

Whenever audio feedback (or "recursion") is used in Csound, *ksmps* must always be smaller than the feedback interval. In this example, **kr** is set equal to **sr**, so a feedback interval as small as a single sample can be implemented.

The maximum delay time in this example is short (.005 seconds) and the taps set to .8 and .9 of *imaxdel,* yielding peak delays of .004 and .0045, respectively. These short delay times result in slight detunings, which are appropriate for flanging. Longer delay times cause proportionally larger amounts of pitch shift, which can also be an interesting effect. If the pitch shifting becomes too great, however, it results in an audible vibrato and the distinctive sound of flanging is lost.

The minimum delay time for the Csound **deltapi** opcode is one k-period. Here, the opcodes are given minimum delay values of .001 and .0005, respectively. The times are staggered slightly to avoid the resonant peak that would occur when both times are initially the same and then summed and fed back into the delay network.

Continuous Pitch Shifting

In both of the previous examples, the delay times were varied periodically, with the result that the playback point was sometimes moving faster than the record point and sometimes moving slower, but the points were never allowed to meet. This produced a "vibrato" effect, with the pitch sometimes higher and sometimes lower and constantly fluctuating. To produce a continuous pitch shift using a delay line, the playback point must consistently move at a different rate from the record point, which will eventually result in the two points meeting somewhere as they move around the circular buffer. When that happens, the delay instantly changes from the maximum to the minimum, or *vice-versa,* which causes an audible click or pop.

To solve this problem, we can use two delay taps one-half of a buffer-length apart and crossfade back and forth between them, so that we are never listening to a tap at the moment when it meets and crosses the record point. This is the basic method used by some commercial pitch shifters.

The amount of pitch shift produced by a variable delay line depends on the rate at which the delay time is changing. The more rapid the rate of change, the greater the interval of shift. If the delay time is shortening, the pitch will be shifted up; if it is lengthening, the pitch will be shifted down. The exact amount of shift is determined by the ratio of the speed of the playback point to that of the record point. The Csound **deltapi** opcode, however, does not allow us to specify the speed of the playback point directly; we can only affect it indirectly by changing the delay time dynamically. This is a bit awkward and counter-intuitive, so a brief explanation may be useful.

For a moment let us think of the delay buffer as a short wavetable. If the table contains *D* seconds of sound, then it should take exactly *D* seconds to play back that sound if we don't plan to change the pitch. If the table were being used as the stored function for a Csound **oscil** opcode, which assumes its function contains one cycle of a fundamental, we would need to use a frequency input of $1/D$ cycles per second (Hz) in order to play back the sound exactly once in *D* seconds and reproduce the original pitch.

To shift up by an octave, we would simply double the frequency to $2/D$ Hz; to shift down an octave, we would halve the basic frequency ($.5/D$ Hz). In fact, we could get any relative pitch we wanted by simply taking the ratio of the desired frequency to the original frequency and multiplying it by $1/D$, where *D* is the original duration of the sound. So, we can define a simple formula for pitch shifting a recorded sound by "resampling" with an **oscil:**

$$oscil\_cps = \frac{newhz}{oldhz} * \frac{1}{D} \qquad (22.1)$$

In effect, gradually changing the delay time of a **deltap** opcode from the maximum delay time to zero is the same thing as moving the playback point all the way through (completing one cycle of) a wavetable, relative to the record point. So we can think about the rate of change in delay time (and the resulting pitch shift) in terms of cycles per second, just as we did with **oscil**—each time we sweep the delay time from the maximum to zero (or *vice versa*), we are completing a single "cycle."

But in a delay line, of course, the playback point is already moving at a rate of $1/D$th of the buffer per second, even when there is no pitch shift and the delay time is constant. Consequently, anything we do to alter the pitch by dynamically changing the delay time is simply being added to that basic rate. So we can use almost the same formula for pitch shifting with **deltap** that we used with **oscil**; but we need to subtract out the rate at which the playback point is already moving for untransposed playback, which is $1/D$, hence:

$$xdlt = \left(\frac{newhz}{oldhz} * \frac{1}{D}\right) - \frac{1}{D} \quad (22.2)$$

or

$$xdlt = (newhz/oldhz - 1)/D \quad (22.3)$$

Consequently, if $newhz = oldhz$, then $(newhz/oldhz - 1)/D$ is zero, which produces no pitch shift. If $newhz/oldhz = 2$, then *xdlt* is $1/D$, which when added internally to the **deltap** basic rate ($1/D$), results in a playback speed of $2/D$, producing an octave pitch shift up. Similarly, if $newhz/oldhz = .5$, then *xdlt* equals $-.5/duration$, which when added internally to the basic rate, results in a playback speed of $+.5/duration$, which causes an octave drop in pitch.

Figure 22.8 shows a simple example of a continuous pitch shifter that allows the user to specify the amount of shift in semitones.

Pitch-Shift Notes

The ratio for pitch shifting is calculated by converting the number of semitones specified in *p6* to a fraction of an octave (*insemis*/12), then adding the fraction to an arbitrary base octave (8 = middle C) and comparing the CPS frequency of the resulting pitch to the frequency of the base octave (see figure 22.8).

Two **phasor** opcodes are used to control the delay times and gating functions of the two **deltapi** opcodes. They are given the same input frequency, *-irate,* but one of the **phasor** opcodes has an initial phase of *.5*. This results in the two delay taps being kept precisely 1/2 buffer length apart and the two **tablei** opcodes used for gating being similarly offset by 1/2 the length of the triangle window function they both reference. The delay times are changing gradually and continually, as are the gate signals, *agate1* and *agate2*. Whenever the delay time of a particular **deltapi** opcode approaches the wraparound, between *0* and *idelay* seconds, its gate function is approaching zero; when it approaches the midpoint—*idelay*/2, its gate function is approaching 1. The outputs of the two taps are summed, so that we are always listening to both of them, but we never hear the click of the wraparound.

The frequency argument to the **phasor** opcodes is negated, which causes their outputs to ramp down from 1 to 0 (shortening the delay times and raising the pitch) when *irate* is positive, but ramp up from 0 to 1 (lengthening the delay times and lowering the pitch) when *irate* is negative.

```
         instr    2207        ; PITCH SHIFTER
igain    =        p4                      ; OVERALL GAIN
idelay   =        p5                      ; N SECONDS DELAY
insemis  =        p6                      ; N SEMITONES TO SHIFT
ifract   =        insemis/12              ; FRACTION OF AN OCTAVE
ibasehz  =        cpsoct(8)               ; USE MIDDLE C AS BASIS
inewhz   =        cpsoct(8+ifract)        ; REL FREQ OF NEW PITCH
iratio   =        inewhz/ibasehz          ; RATIO NEW HZ TO OLD
irate    =        (iratio-1)/idelay       ; SUBTRACT 1/1 SPEED
kenv     linen    igain, .01, p3, .05     ; OVERALL ENV CONTROL
ainput   soundin  p7                      ; P7 IS SOUNDIN.NNN
actl1    phasor   -irate                  ; MOVING PHASE 1-0
agate1   tablei   actl1, 1, 1, 0, 1       ; WINDOW FUNC =TRIANGLE
actl2    phasor   -irate, .5              ; PHASE OFFSET OF .5
agate2   tablei   actl2, 1, 1, 0, 1       ; TRIANGLE WINDOW FUNC
afixed   delayr   idelay                  ; ALLOC DELAY LINE
asig1    deltapi  actl1*idelay            ; 2 VARIABLE TAPS
asig2    deltapi  actl2*idelay            ; OFFSET 1/2 BUFFER LEN
         delayw   ainput
asig1    =        asig1*agate1            ; GATE TAP OUTPUTS
asig2    =        asig2*agate2            ; SEPARATELY
asum     =        asig1+asig2             ; AND SUM
         out      asum*kenv               ; OVERALL ENVELOPE
         endin

f 1      0    513   20     3      ; TRIANGLE WINDOW FN
; PLAY PITCH SHIFTED CHORD FROM SOUNDIN.890 - A SINGLE CELLO SAMPLE
; INS    ST   DUR   GAIN    MAXDEL      NSEMITONES    SOUNDIN#
i 2207   0    2      .45     .1         -12           890
i 2207   .    .      .       .          -5
i 2207   .    .      .       .          4
i 2207   .    .      .       .          12
```

Figure 22.8 Orchestra and score code for *instr 2207,* a continuous pitch-shift instrument.

This pitch shifting algorithm will work regardless of the length of the delay *(p5).* The longer the delay line, however, the more of an audible delay there is in the output. On the other hand, the shorter the delay line, the more rapid the gating between the two taps, which can cause audible aliasing with large transposition values and/or short delay times. The gating length of the delay for this example was chosen to be *.1 seconds,* which is a reasonable compromise.

This example does not use a separate "effects" unit that receives input from a global variable, which is generally to be preferred, because the score plays a four-note chord from a single **soundin** file and a separate delay network is required for each transposed pitch in the chord.

Harmonizer Instrument

The final example is an extension of the previous instrument, with the addition of an LFO and a feedback loop, which produces the distinctive interval cycling that is the hallmark of commercial harmonizers. In the example shown in figure 22.9, the harmonizer is placed in an effects instrument and it receives input from the global variable *gasend.*

Harmonizer Notes

The addition on an LFO requires that the rate variable be changed from *irate* to *krate.* Note that if the LFO frequency (*ilfohz1*) is zero, the **oscili** opcode is skipped altogether during performance (see figure 22.9).

The outputs of the two **deltapi** opcodes are fed back into the **delayw** opcode, but the only limits are the *igain* and *ifeed* variables, so it is possible for uncontrolled feedback to occur, which will result in samples out of range and clipping. A **balance** opcode could be employed, but its use would prevent the distinctive interval cycling that continues after notes in commercial harmonizers.

With longer delay times, larger intervals and significant feedback, the interval cycling effect is most pronounced. With shorter delay times, smaller intervals, feedback and LFO, the harmonizer can serve as a flanger.

If feedback is employed with short delays, it may be necessary to make *kr = sr,* as was done in the stereo flanger instrument (*instr 2206*).

Conclusion

In this chapter we have explained some of the basic concepts associated with digital delay lines and demonstrated several of the most common applications for them. We have only scratched the surface of this subject, however from what has been presented, one can clearly see that digital delay lines are exceedingly flexible and powerful functions, capable of an enormous variety of subtle and complex effects and the reader is strongly encouraged to experiment further with them. A particularly useful exercise is to study a typical commercial multieffects box and try to implement some of the effects in Csound. Most of these devices include documentation on the various algorithms and with manual in hand, a good ear and a little patience, it is often not difficult to emulate them using the standard Csound opcodes.

```
        instr    2208           ; SOUNDIN 2
gasend  init     0                              ; INIT THE GLOBAL VAR
idry    =        p4                             ; AMT OF SIGNAL TO OUT
iwet    =        p5                             ; AMT OF SIGNAL TO EFFECT
ainput  soundin  p6
        out      ainput*idry
gasend  =        gasend+ainput*iwet
        endin

        instr    2209           ; HARMONIZER WITH FEEDBACK
igain   =        p4                             ; OVERALL GAIN
idelay  =        p5                             ; N SECONDS DELAY
insemis =        p6                             ; N SEMITONES TO SHIFT
ifeed   =        p7                             ; FEEDBACK FACTOR
ilfohz  =        p8                             ; LFO FREQ
ifract  =        insemis/12                     ; FRACTION OF AN OCT
ibasehz =        cpsoct(8)                      ; MIDDLE C AS BASIS
inewhz  =        cpsoct(8+ifract)               ; DESIRED REL PITCH
iratio  =        inewhz/ibasehz                 ; RATIO NEW HZ TO OLD
irate   =        (iratio-1)/idelay              ; SUBTRACT 1/1 SPEED
krate   init     irate                          ; COPY TO KVAR
        if       (ilfohz==0) goto continue
krate   oscili   irate, ilfohz, 2               ; LFO SINE FN
continue:
kenv    linen    igain, .01, p3, .05            ; OVERALL ENV CONTROL
actl1   phasor   -irate                         ; MOVING PHASE 1-0
agate1  tablei   actl1, 1, 1, 0, 1              ; TRIANGLE WINDOW FUNC
actl2   phasor   -irate, .5                     ; PHASE OFFSET OF .5
agate2  tablei   actl2, 1, 1, 0, 1              ; TRIANGLE WINDOW FUNC
ajunk   delayr   idelay                         ; ALLOC DELAY LINE
asig1   deltapi  actl1*idelay                   ; 2 VARIABLE TAPS
asig2   deltapi  actl2*idelay                   ; OFFSET 1/2 BUFF LEN
asig1   =        asig1*agate1                   ; GATE TAP OUTPUTS
asig2   =        asig2*agate2                   ; SEPARATELY
asum    =        asig1+asig2                    ; AND SUM
ainput  =        gasend+asum*ifeed
        delayw   ainput
        out      asum*kenv                      ; OVERALL ENVELOPE
gasend  =        0                              ; ZERO GLOBAL VARIABLE
        endin

f 1     0     513  20     3                     ; TRIANGLE WINDOW FN
f 2     0     513  10     1                     ; SINE FN
; PLAY SOUNDIN.890 - A SINGLE CELLO SAMPLE
; INS       ST    DUR   DRY     WET    SOUNDIN#
i 2208      0     2     0       1      890
; ARPEGGIO: HARMONIZE UP 5 SEMITONES WITH FEEDBACK
; INS       ST    DUR   GAIN    DELAY NSEMIS       IFEED       LFOHZ
i 2209      0     4     .45     .33   5            .9          0
; PLAY SOUNDIN.891 - A SINGLE TIMPANI STROKE
; INS       ST    DUR   DRY     WET    SOUNDIN#
i 2208      4     2     0       1      891
; GLISS: HARMONIZE DOWN .1 SEMITONES WITH MAX FEEDBACK
; INS       ST    DUR   GAIN    DELAY NSEMIS       IFEED       LFOHZ
i 2209      4     4     .4      .0123 -.1          .99         0
; PLAY SOUNDIN.892 - A SINGLE BASS SAMPLE
; INS       ST    DUR   DRY     WET    SOUNDIN#
i 2208      8     4     .5      .8     892
; FLANGE: +/- .2 SEMITONES WITH FEEDBACK AND SLOW LFO
; INS       ST    DUR   GAIN    DELAY NSEMIS       IFEED       LFOHZ
i 2209      8     4.5   .75     .05   -.2          .7          .5
```

Figure 22.9 Orchestra and score code for *instr 2208* and *2209,* a soundin instrument (2208) with sends to a global harmonizer instrument (2209) with internal LFO and feedback.

23 An Introduction to Reverberation Design with Csound

Eric Lyon

This chapter introduces the creative design of Csound reverberators. Before proceeding to orchestra design, we will introduce some basic concepts of reverberation. A full treatment of the subject is beyond the scope of the chapter. Fortunately, there are several excellent texts providing more in-depth technical and mathematical information on the subject, such as Moorer (1979) and Begault (1994).

Reverberation is the result of sound propagation in an environment with reflective surfaces. When you strike a bass drum or stroke a violin, sound propagates in all directions from the vibrating surfaces of the instrument in the elastic "*medium*" known as air. The sound wave continues traveling outward at the speed of sound until it encounters a not-so-elastic medium such as a wall or a person. At this point, part of the energy of the wave is absorbed and part is reflected back. As illustrated in figure 23.1, the reflected wave continues to propagate until it hits another reflective surface.

Thus there is a gradual buildup of complexity as more and more reflections pile onto each other. At the same time there is a gradual loss of amplitude as the reflections dissipate their energy through friction and repeated collisions with surfaces. When the source sound stops, the reverberation will continue for a certain amount of time before dying away. The amount of time for the energy to die down below audibility is known as the "reverberation time," as seen in figure 23.2.

Reverberation provides the listener with information about both the environment and the sound source. The ratio between the direct signal and the reverberated signal indicates the distance of the source. The amount of time between early reflections indicates the size of a space. In a larger space, it takes longer for a sound to reach a wall and therefore the time interval between the reflections is longer. If the space is large enough, the first few reflections will be heard distinctly and perceived as echoes. When the reflections become close together, we perceive a "wash" of sound rather than distinct echoes. If the source is in motion, Doppler shift results. Familiar

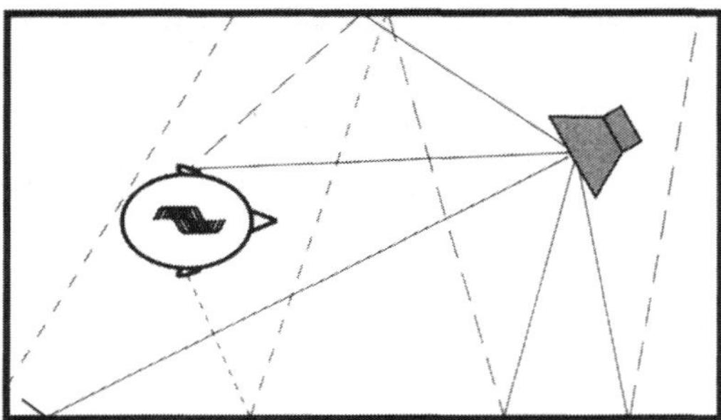

Figure 23.1 Propagation of sound in an enclosed space.

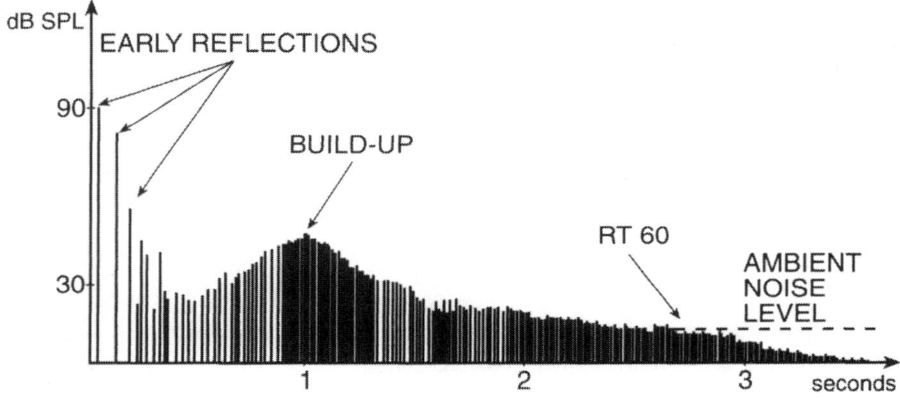

Figure 23.2 Temporal progress of reverberation.

as the change of perceived pitch of a train siren as the train approaches (higher pitch) and then recedes (lower pitch).

Stereo hearing allows us to estimate direction of the sound because of interaural time delay (ITD), the time interval between the sound entering one ear and entering the other. It turns out that we make even more precise localization measurements by perceiving the filtering effect on sound due to angle of incidence on the head, shoulders and, especially, the pinnae (outer ears).

Since reverberation conveys much information about acoustic spaces, there have been a number of "room simulation" approaches to reverberation design. Although we will not pursue that approach here, we should note that rooms have striking frequency impact on sound. Waveforms that "fit" the distance between opposing walls (or floor/ceiling) will be reinforced and result in so-called standing waves with different degrees of loudness at different locations in the room. A good way to experience the effects of room response is to generate a slow scale of sine waves over the audio frequency range with a resolution of a 1/4 tone. You may be surprised at the range of amplitude variation you hear. A striking demonstration of the filtering effects of rooms is heard in the composition "I Am Sitting in a Room" by Alvin Lucier, in which a recording of spoken voice is played into the room from one tape recorder and recorded to a second deck, repeatedly, so that the filtering effects of the room are increasingly reinforced. After a few generations, the voice gradually becomes unintelligible and is replaced by a remarkable variety of room resonances (Lucier 1990).

Reverberator Design Examples: Enhancements to Csound's Reverb Opcode

With this background information, we begin our experiments with Csound. In our first orchestra (see figures 23.3 and 23.4), we will use the Csound "house" reverberator. We will drive the reverberator with a short, enveloped burst of band-limited white noise. Although not the most attractive sound in the world, it is quite useful for testing reverberators since digital white noise contains all frequencies up to the Nyquist Frequency (one half of the sampling rate) and the sharp attack will reveal the transient response. If white noise sounds good in your reverberator, most other sounds will too.

We will separate the noise generator from the reverberator and write the noise into a global variable. The advantage of this strategy is that any signal can be mixed into the *ga*-variable. Think of it as an "effects-send" buss. Next, we modify this orchestra slightly so that we may control the ratio of wet to dry signal (see figure 23.5).

You may have noticed that despite our description of reverberation as a carrier of spatial information, our orchestras have been monophonic. We will simulate the stereo diffusion of reflections with the Csound delay unit (see figure 23.6). We will scatter the signal and route it to two reverberation units. Note that we must set the control rate equal to the sample rate. This is necessary for variable delay times to be represented internally with sample-level precision. There is nothing special about these delay times, however, as they were generated at random by a computer program.

Now we are definitely hearing a stereo field. We will use one more trick to further enrich the stereo field. We will run the output of each reverb channel through a slowly time-varying delay line, simulating Doppler shift (see figure 23.7).

At this point I recommend playing the reverb orchestras we've designed using sampled sounds. Simply replace the noise generation orchestra with soundfile reading orchestra shown in figure 23.8 and adjust the durations in the score file.

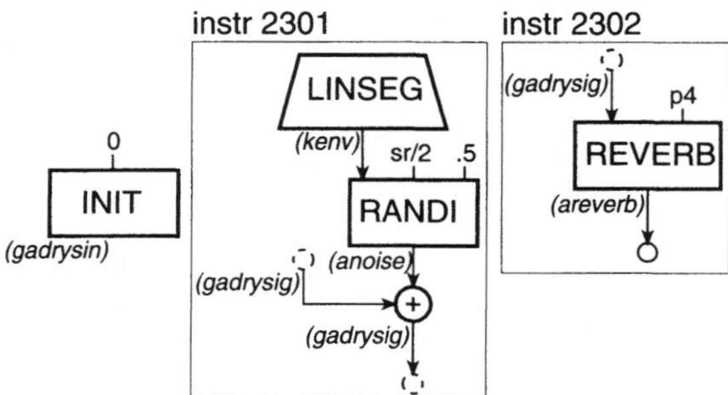

Figure 23.3 Block diagram of *instr 2301* and *2302,* an instrument that produces a gated burst of white noise (*2301*) and sends it to a global reverb instrument (*2302*).

```
gadrysig  init    0                              ; INITIALIZE GLOBAL VARIABLE

          instr   2301            ; NOISE BURST
kenv      linseg  9000, .1, 1000, p3-.1, 0 ; ENVELOPE
anoise    randi   kenv, sr/2, .5            ; CREATE NOISE BURST
gadrysig  =       gadrysig+anoise           ; ADD BURST TO GLOBAL VAR
          endin

          instr   2302            ; REVERB UNIT
irevtime  =       p4
areverb   reverb  gadrysig, irevtime        ; REVERBERATE SIGNAL
          out     areverb                   ; OUTPUT SIGNAL
gadrysig  =       0                         ; ZERO OUT GLOBAL VARIABLE
          endin

; INS     ST      DUR
i 2301    0       .15
; INS     ST      DUR          REVERB_TIME
i 2302    0       5.3          5
```

Figure 23.4 Orchestra and score code for *instr 2301* and *2302* as shown in figure 23.3.

We will make one final modification to the Csound reverb before designing some reverberators from scratch. You may have noticed that the house reverb sounds a bit "harsh." Harshness is often the perceptual result of too much high frequency energy. We will put a lowpass filter at the end of the signal chain to roll off the high end (see figure 23.9). Csound currently offers two lowpass filter opcodes: **tone** and **butterlp**. The Butterworth filters give a sharper cutoff, which is often desirable. In this case however, the more gradual rolloff of **tone** works better to simulate the gradually increased attenuation of high frequencies in sound propagation. The Butterworth filters, by contrast, are more useful for isolating spectral bands.

```
                instr         2303          ; NOISE BURST WET/DRY
iwetamt         =             p4
idryamt         =             1-p4
kenv            linseg        19000, .1, 1000, p3-.1, 0
anoise          randi         kenv, sr/2, .5
gadrysig        =             gadrysig + anoise*iwetamt
                out           anoise*idryamt
                endin

                instr         2304          ; REVERB WET/DRY
irevtime        =             p4
areverb         reverb        gadrysig, irevtime
                out           areverb+gadrysig
gadrysig        =             0
                endin

; INS           ST        DUR       REVERB_AMT
i 2303          0         .2        0
i 2303          2         .2        .1
i 2303          4         .2        .25
i 2303          6         .2        .5
; INS           ST        DUR       RT60
i 2304          0         1.5       1.3
i 2304          2         1.5       1.3
i 2304          4         1.5       1.3
i 2304          6         1.5       1.3
```

Figure 23.5 Orchestra and score code for *instr 2303* and *2304,* a gated noise instrument (*2303*) with variable control over the mix between the direct signal and the amount of signal sent to the global reverb instrument (*2304*).

```
                instr     2305                  ; STEREO DIFFUSION OF ECHOES
irevtime        =         p4
adelayline      delayr    0.2
amtap1          deltap    0.0430
amtap2          deltap    0.0320
amtap3          deltap    0.1458
amtap4          deltap    0.1423
amtap5          deltap    0.0103
amtap6          deltap    0.0239
amtap7          deltap    0.0446
amtap8          deltap    0.1035
amtap9          deltap    0.1067
amtap10         deltap    0.0087
amtap11         deltap    0.0837
amtap12         deltap    0.1676
                delayw    gadrysig
adiffleft       =         amtap1+amtap2+amtap3+amtap4+amtap5+amtap6
adiffright      =         amtap7+amtap8+amtap9+amtap10+amtap11+amtap12
arevleft        reverb    adiffleft, irevtime
arevright       reverb    adiffright, irevtime
                outs      arevleft/6, arevright/6
gadrysig        =         0
                endin
```

Figure 23.6 Orchestra code for *instr 2305,* an instrument that simulates a stereo diffusion of echoes with a band of **deltap** opcodes inserted between a **delayr** and **delayw** pair.

```
              instr       2306          ; DOPPLER SHIFT
irevtime      =           p4
adelayline    delayr      0.2
amtap1        deltap      0.0430
amtap2        deltap      0.0320
amtap3        deltap      0.1458
amtap4        deltap      0.1423
amtap5        deltap      0.0103
amtap6        deltap      0.0239
amtap7        deltap      0.0446
amtap8        deltap      0.1035
amtap9        deltap      0.1067
amtap10       deltap      0.0087
amtap11       deltap      0.0837
amtap12       deltap      0.1676
              delayw      gadrysig
adiffleft     =           amtap1+amtap2+amtap3+amtap4+amtap5+amtap6
adiffright    =           amtap7+amtap8+amtap9+amtap10+amtap11+amtap12
arevleft      reverb      adiffleft, irevtime
arevright     reverb      adiffright, irevtime
alfo1         oscili      .02, .342, 1
alfo2         oscili      .02, .337, 1, .33
alfo1         =           alfo1+0.025
alfo2         =           alfo2+0.025
achn1dll      delayr      .05
amvleft       deltapi     alfo1
              delayw      arevleft
achn2dll      delayr      .05
amvright      deltapi     alfo2
              delayw      arevright
              outs        amvleft/6, amvright/6
gadrysig      =           0
              endin
```

Figure 23.7 Orchestra code for *instr 2306,* a stereo global reverb with time varying delay on each channel to simulate Doppler shift.

```
            instr      2307          ; SCALEABLE GLOBAL SEND LEVELS
idryamt     =          1-p4
iwetamt     =          p4
asndfile    soundin    "your_sound_here", 0
gadrysig    =          gadrysig+asndfile*iwetamt
            outs       asndfile*idryamt, asndfile*idryamt
            endin
```

Figure 23.8 Orchestra code for *instr 2307,* a stereo soundfile instrument with scaleable global send levels.

```
            instr     2309        ; REVERB WITH ATTENUATED HI FREQ
irevtime    =         p4
irolloff    =         p6
adelayline  delayr    0.2
amtap1      deltap    0.0430
amtap2      deltap    0.0320
amtap3      deltap    0.1458
amtap4      deltap    0.1423
amtap5      deltap    0.0103
amtap6      deltap    0.0239
amtap7      deltap    0.0446
amtap8      deltap    0.1035
amtap9      deltap    0.1067
amtap10     deltap    0.0087
amtap11     deltap    0.0837
amtap12     deltap    0.1676
            delayw    gadrysig
adiffleft   =         amtap1+amtap2+amtap3+amtap4+amtap5+amtap6
adiffright  =         amtap7+amtap8+amtap9+amtap10+amtap11+amtap12
arevleft    reverb    adiffleft, irevtime
arevright   reverb    adiffright, irevtime
alfo1       oscili    .02, .342, 1
alfo2       oscili    .02, .337, 1, .33
alfo1       =         alfo1+0.025
alfo2       =         alfo2+0.025
achn1dll    delayr    .05
amvleft     deltapi   alfo1
            delayw    arevleft
achn2dll    delayr    .05
amvright    deltapi   alfo2
            delayw    arevright
amvleft     tone      amvleft, irolloff
amvright    tone      amvright, irolloff
            outs      amvleft/6, amvright/6
gadrysig    =         0
            endin
```

Figure 23.9 Orchestra code for *instr 2309,* a stereo global reverb in which tone filters have been added to gradually attenuate the highs.

Reverberator Design Examples: Allpass Models

One of the most important unit generators for reverberator design is the feedback loop or recirculating delay line. Feedback units are ideal for simulating the buildup of reflections in a acoustic space. Just as the reflections of physical sound are recursively reflected, the output of a feedback loop is recirculated back into itself. There are two varieties of feedback loops commonly used in reverberators: **comb** filters and **allpass** filters.

Comb filters are simply a delay line with feedback, generating resonance at harmonics of the loop frequency at a strength specified by the amount of feedback. Allpass filters are slightly modified comb filters that have a uniform frequency response, frequency-specific phase response and similar reverberant characteristics to the comb filter. Allpass filters are often deployed in series, so that the buildup of reflections from one filter is further accumulated in the next filter. By contrast, comb filters are often connected in parallel to avoid accumulating strong resonances. Of course such accumulation can be done for special effect and we will see an example of this later.

A single comb or allpass filter imparts clear reverberant qualities to its input, but is generally too simple and predictable to the ear. Therefore in most reverberators these units are combined in complex networks. Our next reverberator will be built from allpass filters and lowpass filters (see figures 23.10 and 23.11). We will use a simple strategy. The early allpass loops will have shorter reverberation times and the later ones will have gradually longer reverberation times. Also, the cutoff frequency for each successive lowpass filter is gradually lower, simulating the increasing loss of high frequency energy. Notice that the reverberation times are all set relative to the main reverberation time, which is set with *p4*.

We will now build a true stereo reverberator. As it is a bit complex, we will design and listen to it in stages. We begin with two allpass filters in parallel for each channel, run into a time-varying delay (see figures 23.12 and 23.13).

Next we will create some of the background reverb "wash" with three parallel comb filters going into an allpass filter and then a lowpass filter (see figure 23.14).

We will decorrelate this background wash to stereo by running the mono reverberant signal *aglobrev* into two slowly randomly varying delays. Finally, we will mix down a combination of the different reverberant components (see figure 23.15).

Reverberator Design Examples: The Fun House

In our next design we will create a deliberately harsh metallic sounding reverberator that might be appropriate for industrial music applications. In this design we will connect comb filters in sequence to create strong resonances. Since we are driving the reverberator with white noise, all the resonances are generated by the comb filters. Try it on some sampled sounds (voice is a good source) and notice the interaction between the spectral content of the source sound and the resonance of the reverberator (see figure 23.16).

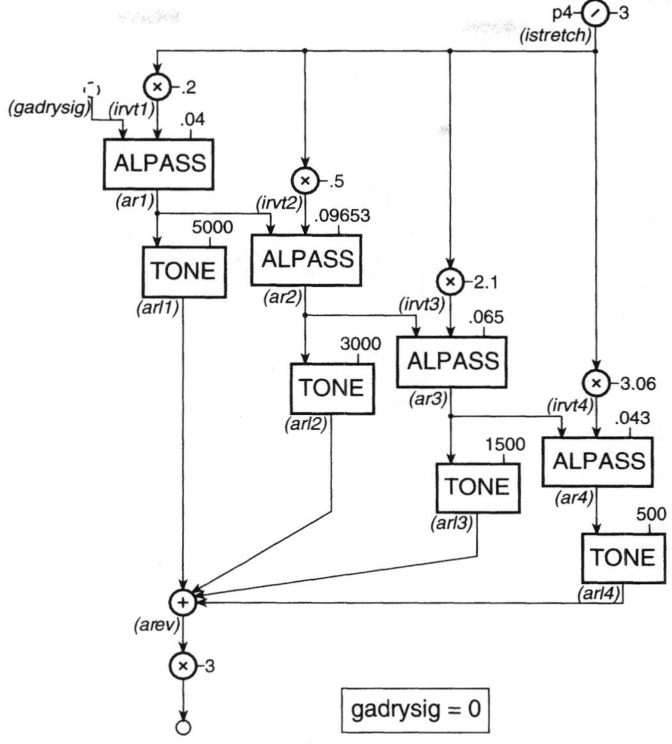

Figure 23.10 Block diagram of *instr 2310,* a series of allpass filters used to progressively accumulate the buildup of reflections and delays following by a tone filter for high frequency damping.

```
           instr    2310     ; ALLPASS FILTERS TO BUILD UP REFLECTIONS
istretch   =        p4/3
irvt1      =        .2*istretch
irvt2      =        .5*istretch
irvt3      =        2.1*istretch
irvt4      =        3.06*istretch
ar1        alpass   gadrysig, irvt1, .04
ar2        alpass   ar1, irvt2, .09653
ar3        alpass   ar2, irvt3, .065
ar4        alpass   ar3, irvt4, .043
arl1       tone     ar1, 5000
arl2       tone     ar2, 3000
arl3       tone     ar3, 1500
arl4       tone     ar4, 500
arev       =        arl1+arl2+arl3+arl4
           out      arev*3
gadrysig   =        0
           endin
```

Figure 23.11 Orchestra code for *instr 2310* as shown in figure 23.10.

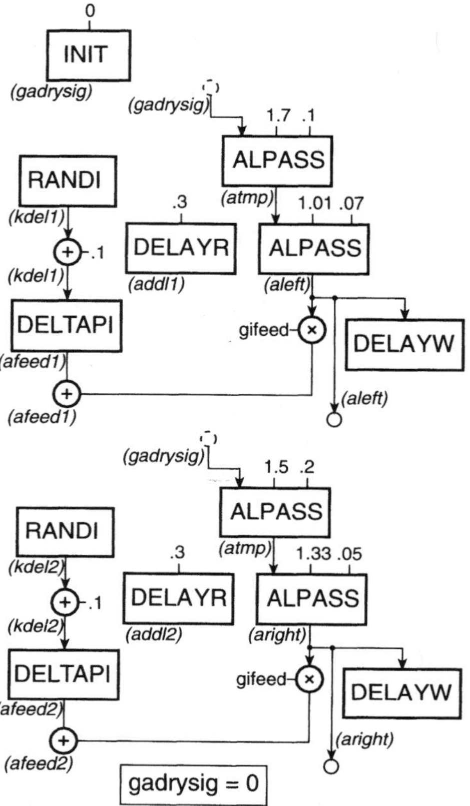

Figure 23.12 Block diagram of *instr 2311,* the preliminary version of a true stereo reverb instrument with 2 parallel allpass filters in each side with random delay times.

Our final example is a bit strange and not a customary reverberation architecture but it builds on the Csound tools and design issues we have already seen. I hope it will suggest the possibilities of creative reverberation design with the purpose of not just replicating familiar reverberation models but also exploring processing architectures that go beyond what fixed-algorithm commercial reverberators can produce (see figure 23.17). The basic idea of this reverberator is to break the input signal into four bands, using Csound's **reson** bandpass filter. Each of these bands is scaled by a slowly changing envelope so we hear the different frequency bands moving in and out of phase.

```
sr        =        44100
kr        =        44100
ksmps     =        1      ; NEEDED FOR SMOOTH DELAY TIME INTERPOLATION
nchnls    =        2

gifeed    =        .5
gilp1     =        1/10
gilp2     =        1/23
gilp3     =        1/41
giroll    =        3000
gadrysig  init     0

          instr    2311   ; 2 PARALLEL ALLPASS FILTERS WITH RANDOM DELAY
atmp      alpass   gadrysig, 1.7, .1
aleft     alpass   atmp, 1.01, .07
atmp      alpass   gadrysig, 1.5, .2
aright    alpass   atmp, 1.33, .05
kdel1     randi    .01, 1, .666
kdel1     =        kdel1+.1
addl1     delayr   .3
afeed1    deltapi  kdel1
afeed1    =        afeed1+gifeed*aleft
          delayw   aleft
kdel2     randi    .01,. 95, .777
kdel2     =        kdel2+.1
addl2     delayr   .3
afeed2    deltapi  kdel2
afeed2    =        afeed2+gifeed*aright
          delayw   aright
          outs     aleft, aright
gadrysig  =        0
          endin
```

Figure 23.13 Orchestra code for *instr 2311,* a stereo reverb as shown in figure 23.12.

```
          instr     2313    ; 3 PARALLEL COMBS INTO AN ALLPASS THEN LOPASS
atmp      alpass    gadrysig, 1.7, .1
aleft     alpass    atmp, 1.01, .07
atmp      alpass    gadrysig, 1.5, .2
aright    alpass    atmp, 1.33, .05
kdel1     randi     .01, 1, .666
kdel1     =         kdel1+.1
addl1     delayr    .3
afeed1    deltapi   kdel1
afeed1    =         afeed1+gifeed*aleft
          delayw    aleft
kdel2     randi     .01,. 95, .777
kdel2     =         kdel2+.1
addl2     delayr    .3
afeed2    deltapi   kdel2
afeed2    =         afeed2+gifeed*aright
          delayw    aright
aglobin   =         (afeed1+afeed2)*.05
atap1     comb      aglobin, 3.3, gilp1
atap2     comb      aglobin, 3.3, gilp2
atap3     comb      aglobin, 3.3, gilp3
aglobrev  alpass    atap1+atap2+atap3, 2.6, .085
aglobrev  tone      aglobrev, giroll
          outs      aglobrev, aglobrev
gadrysig  =         0
          endin
```

Figure 23.14 Orchestra code for *instr 2313,* a global "wash of reverb" achieved with 3 parallel **comb** filters mixed and passed through an **allpass** and **tone** in series for smearing, color and high frequency absorption.

```
          instr     2314        ; GLOBAL REVERB INTO 2 VARYING DELAYS
atmp      alpass    gadrysig, 1.7, .1
aleft     alpass    atmp, 1.01, .07
atmp      alpass    gadrysig, 1.5, .2
aright    alpass    atmp, 1.33, .05
kdel1     randi     .01, 1, .666
kdel1     =         kdel1+.1
addl1     delayr    .3
afeed1    deltapi   kdel1
afeed1    =         afeed1+gifeed*aleft
          delayw    aleft
kdel2     randi     .01,. 95, .777
kdel2     =         kdel2+.1
addl2     delayr    .3
afeed2    deltapi   kdel2
afeed2    =         afeed2+gifeed*aright
          delayw    aright
aglobin   =         (afeed1+afeed2)*.05
atap1     comb      aglobin, 3.3, gilp1
atap2     comb      aglobin, 3.3, gilp2
atap3     comb      aglobin, 3.3, gilp3
aglobrev  alpass    atap1+atap2+atap3, 2.6, .085
aglobrev  tone      aglobrev, giroll
kdel3     randi     .003, 1,. 888
kdel3     =         kdel3+ .05
addl3     delayr    .2
agr1      deltapi   kdel3
          delayw    aglobrev
kdel4     randi     .003, 1, .999
kdel4     =         kdel4+ .05
addl4     delayr    .2
agr2      deltapi   kdel4
          delayw    aglobrev
arevl     =         agr1+afeed1
arevr     =         agr2+afeed2
          outs      arevl, arevr
gadrysig  =         0
          endin
```

Figure 23.15 Orchestra code for *instr 2314,* the final phase of our stereo reverb, which decorrelates the monophonic background "wash of reverb" by passing the signal through two slow randomly varying delays.

```
          instr    2315    ; METALLIC REVERB
ilp1      =        1/p4              ; p4-p9 ARE RESONANCE FREQUENCIES
ilp2      =        1/p5
ilp3      =        1/p6
ilp4      =        1/p7
ilp5      =        1/p8
ilp6      =        1/p9
irvt      =        p10
aecho1    comb     gadrysig, irvt, ilp1
aecho2    comb     gadrysig, irvt, ilp2
aecho1    =        gadrysig+aecho1
aecho2    =        gadrysig+aecho2
aecho3    comb     aecho1, irvt, ilp3
aecho4    comb     aecho1, irvt, ilp4
aecho5    comb     aecho2, irvt, ilp5
aecho6    comb     aecho2, irvt, ilp6
aout1     =        (aecho1+aecho3+aecho5)*.1
aout2     =        (aecho2+aecho4+aecho6)*.1
          outs     aout1, aout2
gadrysig  =        0
          endin
```

Figure 23.16 Orchestra code for *instr 2315,* a metallic sounding reverb. The strong resonances are derived from passing the dry signal through a series of **comb** filters.

```
          instr    2316
iorig     =        .05
irev      =        1.-iorig
igain     =        1.0
ilpgain   =        1.5
icgain    =        .1
ialpgain  =        0.1
ispeed1   =        p4
ispeed2   =        p5
ispeed3   =        p6
ispeed4   =        p7
icf1      =        p8
icf2      =        p9
icf3      =        p10
icf4      =        p11
ifac      =        2
ibw1      =        icf1/ifac
ibw2      =        icf2/ifac
ibw3      =        icf3/ifac
ibw4      =        icf4/ifac
; CYCLIC AMPLITUDE ENVELOPES
aenv1     oscil    igain, ispeed1, 1
aenv2     oscil    igain, ispeed2, 2
aenv3     oscil    igain, ispeed3, 3
aenv4     oscil    igain, ispeed4, 4
; BREAK INTO BANDS
ares1     reson    gadrysig, icf1, ibw1, 1
ares2     reson    gadrysig, icf2, ibw2, 1
ares3     reson    gadrysig, icf3, ibw3, 1
ares4     reson    gadrysig, icf4, ibw4, 1
; SUM THE ENVELOPED BANDS
asum      =        (ares1*aenv1)+(ares2*aenv2)+(ares3*aenv3)+(ares4*aenv4)
; LOWPASS AND COMB SEQUENCE
alp       tone     asum, 1000
adright   delay    alp, .178
adleft    delay    alp, .215
asumr     =        asum+(adright*ilpgain)
asuml     =        asum+(adleft*ilpgain)
acr1      comb     asumr, 2, .063
acr2      comb     acr1+asumr,. 5, .026
acl1      comb     asuml, 2, .059
acl2      comb     acl1+asuml, .5, .031
acsumr    =        asumr+(acr2*icgain)
acsuml    =        asuml+(acl2*icgain)
```

Figure 23.17 Orchestra code for *instr 2316,* a “strange reverb” with shifting resonances.

```
; ALLPASS COMB SEQUENCE
alpo       alpass    asum, 3, 085
alpol      comb      alpo, 2.8, .526
alpor      comb      alpo, 2.8, .746
alol       tone      alpol, 500
alor       tone      alpor, 500
alold      delay     alol, .095
alord      delay     alor, .11
; SUM REVERBERATION COMPONENTS
arevl      =         (alpol*ialpgain)+acsuml+alold
arevr      =         (alpor*ialpgain)+acsumr+alord
aorig      =         gadrysig*iorig
; MIX BACK ORIGINAL SIGNAL
           outs      (arevl*irev)+aorig, (arevr*irev)+aorig
gadrysig   =         0
           endin
```

Figure 23.17 continued

Conclusion

Digital reverberation is an essential tool of the computer musician. Synthetic sounds and sampled sounds recorded in dry environments may seem lifeless without further audio processing to give them a sense of presence and place them in a "space." Like any aspect of sound in the virtual world of the computer, reverberation should be viewed as an attribute to shape and contour, rather than to set and forget. The flexibility of Csound allows the composer to design reverberation processors in any imaginable form. Each sound in a composition may be routed to a reverberator with a different characteristic and reverberators may be designed to gradually change characteristics as a sound evolves. The limitations of commercial hardware (and many software) reverberators simply do not apply here. In Csound, the composer is both liberated and challenged to extend the creative exploration to the vital domain of artificial digital audio environments.

References

Begault, R. 1994. *3-D Sound for Virtual Reality and Multimedia.* New York: AP Professional.

Lucier, A. 1990. "I Am Sitting in a Room." LCD1013, Lovely Music.

Moore, F. R. 1990. *Elements of Computer Music.* Englewood Cliffs, N.J.: Prentice-Hall.

Moorer, J. A. 1979. "About this reverberation business." In C. Roads and J. Strawn eds. 1985. *Foundations of Computer Music.* Cambridge, Mass.: MIT Press.

Roads, C. 1996. *The Computer Music Tutorial.* Cambridge, Mass.: MIT Press.

24 Implementing the Gardner Reverbs in Csound

Hans Mikelson

This chapter describes the implementation of reverbs based on nested allpass filters. Reverberant sound occurs when sound waves are reflected by surfaces repeatedly until the individual reflections merge into a continuous sound. Nested allpass filters proposed by Barry Vercoe and Miller Puckette (1985) can be used to simulate the dense reflections associated with room reverberation. This chapter describes several different types of allpass filters and uses them to implement three different reverbs. The reverbs presented in this section are derived from those developed by Bill Gardner (1992).

The Allpass Filter

An allpass filter is made by adding both a feedback path and a feedforward path to a delay line as shown in figure 24.1. Gain is applied to the feedback path and negative gain is applied to the feedforward path. An allpass filter passes all frequencies unaltered but changes the phase of each frequency. This can be implemented in Csound as follows:

```
adel1   init    0
aout    =       adel1-igain*ain              ; FEEDFORWARD
adel1   delay   ain+igain*aout, itime        ; FEEDBACK
```

The Single Nested Allpass Filter

A single nested allpass filter is implemented by surrounding one allpass filter by a second as shown in figure 24.2.

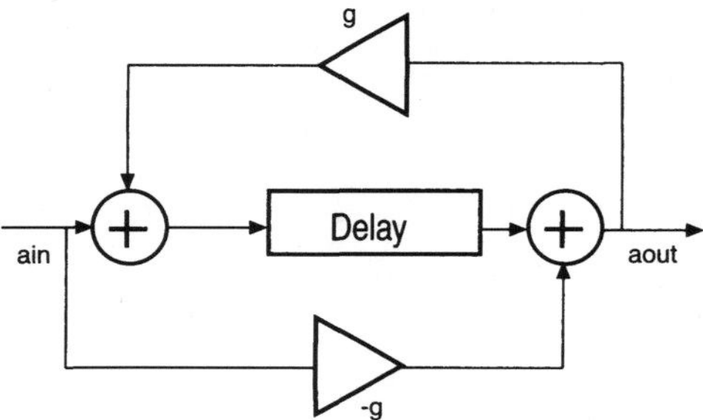

Figure 24.1 Block diagram of a simple allpass filter.

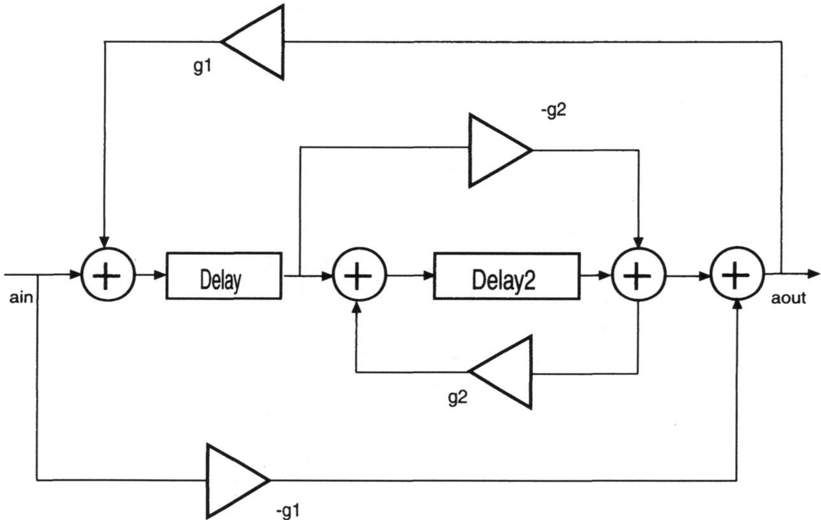

Figure 24.2 Block diagram of a single nested allpass filter.

A simplified representation of the allpass filter presented in figure 24.2 is shown in figure 24.3. The outer delay time *t1* in figure 24.3 is equal to the sum of the *delay1* and *delay2* times of figure 24.2.

This can be implemented in Csound as follows:

```
asum    =       adel2-igain2*adel1            ; FEEDFORWARD
aout    =       asum-igain1*ain               ; FEEDFORWARD
adel1   delay   ain+igain1*aout, itime        ; FEEDBACK
adel2   delay   adel1+igain2*asum, itime2     ; FEEDBACK
```

The Double Nested Allpass Filter

A double nested allpass filter is implemented by surrounding two allpass filters in series by a third allpass filter as shown in figure 24.4.

The simplified version of this is presented in figure 24.5. In this case *t1* in figure 24.5 is the sum of *delay1, delay2* and *delay3* of figure 24.4.

The double nested allpass filter can be implemented in Csound as follows:

```
asum1   =       adel2-igain2*adel1            ; 1ST IN FF
asum2   =       adel3-igain3*asum1            ; 2ND IN FF
aout    =       asum2-igain1*ain              ; OUTER FF
adel1   delay   ain+igain1*aout, itime1       ; OUTER FB
adel2   delay   adel1+igain2*asum1, itime2    ; 1ST IN FB
adel3   delay   asum1+igain3*asum2, itime3    ; 2ND IN FB
```

Small Room Reverberator

The nested allpass filters are now combined to form reverbs. The first reverb presented is for a small room. It consists of a double nested allpass filter followed by a single nested allpass filter. The input is prefiltered at 6 kHz to reduce metallic ringing. An overall feedback path is bandpass filtered and added to the input. The feedback filter also reduces the metallic character of the reverb and reduces DC offset. Another simplified notation is presented in figure 24.6. Delays are indicated by putting the delay time above the signal path; all times in these figures are expressed in milliseconds.

The small room reverb shown in figure 24.6 can be implemented in Csound as shown in figure 24.7.

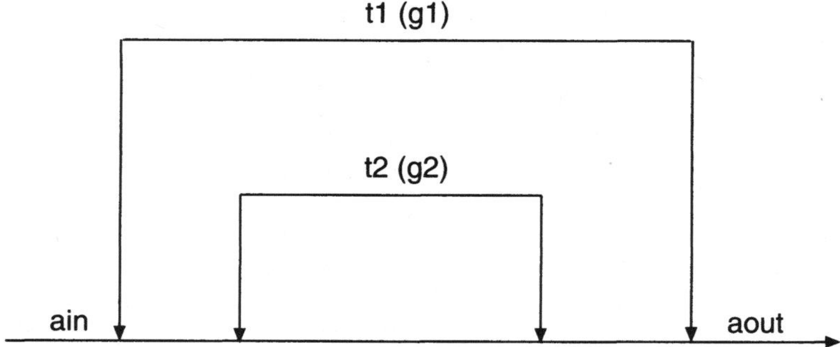

Figure 24.3 Block diagram of a simplified single nested allpass filter.

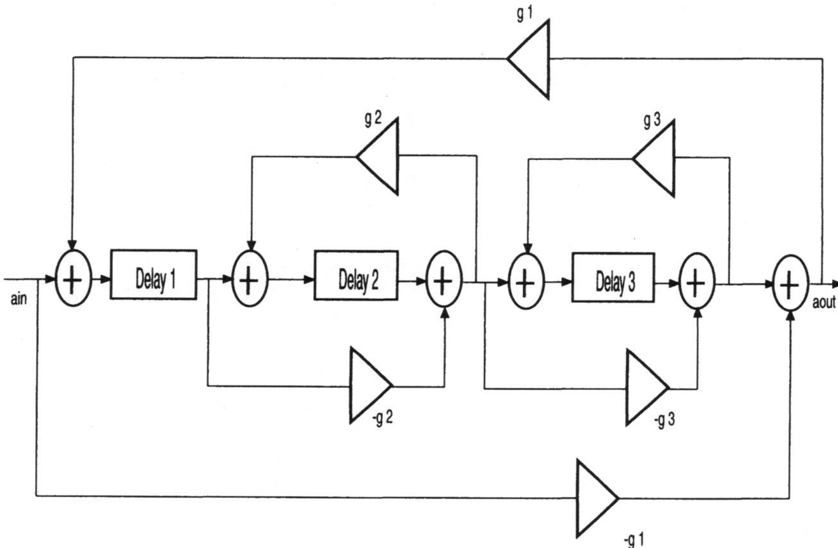

Figure 24.4 Block diagram of double nested allpass filter.

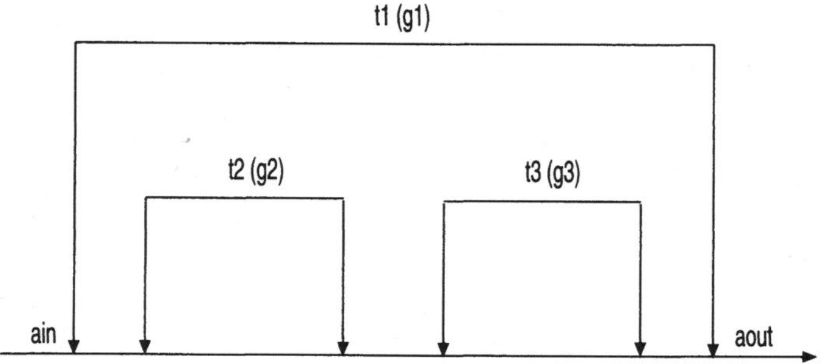

Figure 24.5 Simplified block diagram of a double nested allpass filter.

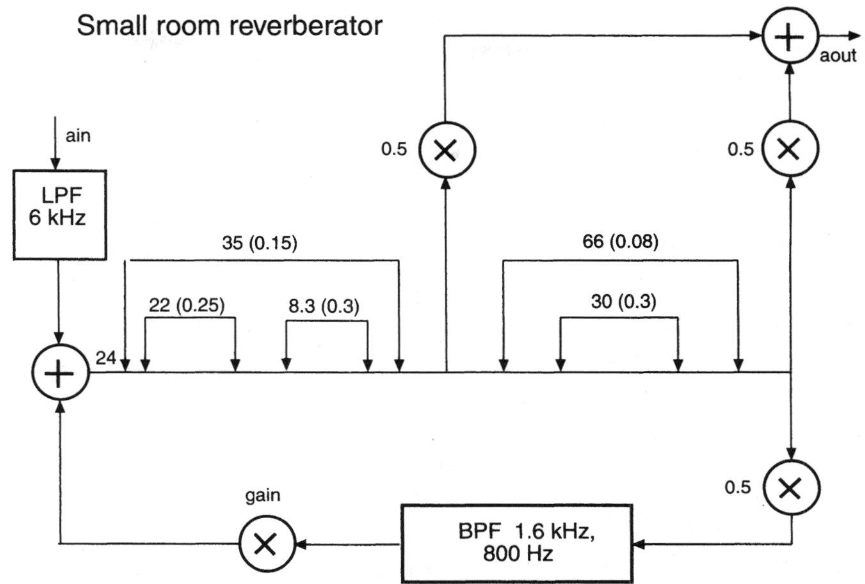

Figure 24.6 Block diagram of small room reverberator.

```
         instr     2402      ; SMALL ROOM REVERB
idur     =         p3
iamp     =         p4
iinch    =         p5
aout41   init      0
adel01   init      0
adel11   init      0
adel21   init      0
adel22   init      0
adel23   init      0
adel41   init      0
adel42   init      0
kdclick  linseg    0, .002, iamp, idur-.004, iamp, .002, 0
; INITIALIZE
asig0    zar       iinch
aflt01   butterlp  asig0, 6000                ; PRE-FILTER
aflt02   butterbp  .5*aout41, 1600, 800       ; FEEDBACK FILTER
asum01   =         aflt01+.5*aflt02           ; INITIAL MIX
; DELAY 1
adel11   delay     asum01, .024
; DOUBLE NESTED ALLPASS
asum21   =         adel22-.25*adel21          ; FIRST INNER FEEDFORWARD
asum22   =         adel23-.30*asum21          ; SECOND INNER FEEDFORWARD
aout21   =         asum22-.15*adel11          ; OUTER FEEDFORWARD
adel21   delay     adel11+.15*aout21, .0047   ; OUTER FEEDBACK
adel22   delay     adel21+.25*asum21, .022    ; FIRST INNER FEEDBACK
adel23   delay     asum21+.30*asum22, .0083   ; SECOND INNER FEEDBACK
; SINGLE NESTED ALLPASS
asum41   =         adel42-.3*adel41           ; INNER FEEDFORWARD
aout41   =         asum41-.08*aout21          ; OUTER FEEDFORWARD
adel41   delay     aout21+.08*aout41, .036    ; OUTER FEEDBACK
adel42   delay     adel41+.3*asum41, .030     ; INNER FEEDBACK
; OUTPUT
aout     =         .6*aout41+.5*aout21
         outs      aout*kdclick, -aout*kdclick
         endin
```

Figure 24.7 Orchestra code for *instr 2402,* a small room reverb.

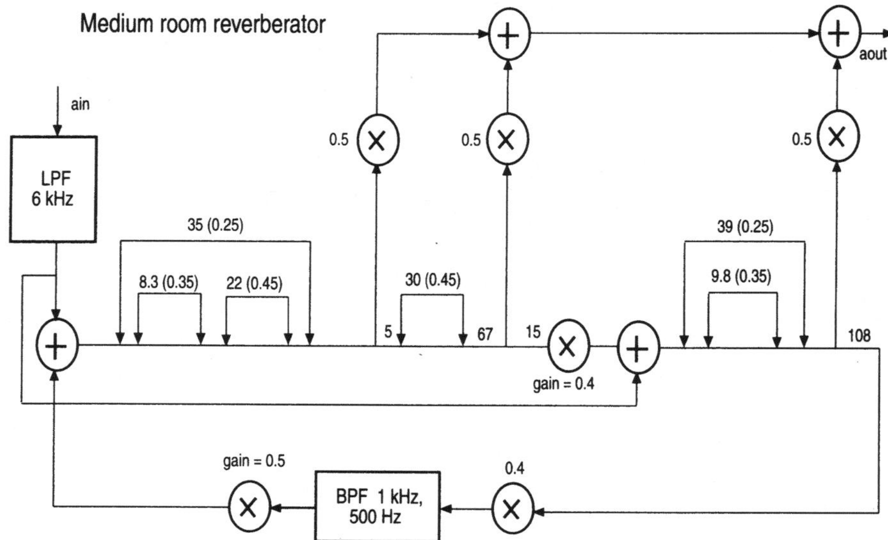

Figure 24.8 Block diagram of medium room reverberator.

Medium Room Reverberator

The next reverb is for a medium room (see figure 24.8). It consists of a double nested allpass filter followed by an allpass filter, followed by a single nested allpass filter. The input is prefiltered at 6 kHz and is introduced at both the beginning and before the final nested allpass filter. Output is taken after each allpass filter section. The overall feedback is bandpass filtered at 1 kHz with a bandwidth of 500 Hz. There are four delays in this reverb. The first delay follows the first output tap. The second and third delays are before and after the second output tap and the third delay precedes the overall feedback. The medium room reverb shown in figure 24.8 can be implemented in Csound as shown in figure 24.9.

Large Room Reverberator

The final reverb considered is for a large room (see figure 24.10). The major elements are two allpass filters in series, followed by a single nested allpass filter and finally a double nested allpass filter. Outputs are taken after the first two allpass filters, after the single nested allpass filter and after the double nested allpass filter. Delays are

```
         instr     2403        ; MEDIUM ROOM REVERB
idur     =         p3
iamp     =         p4
iinch    =         p5
adel71   init      0
adel11   init      0
adel12   init      0
adel13   init      0
adel31   init      0
adel61   init      0
adel62   init      0
kdclick  linseg    0, .002, iamp, idur-.004, iamp, .002, 0
; INITIALIZE
asig0    zar       iinch
aflt01   butterlp  asig0, 6000                   ; PRE-FILTER
aflt02   butterbp  .4*adel71, 1000, 500          ; FEEDBACK FILTER
asum01   =         aflt01+.5*aflt02              ; INITIAL MIX
; DOUBLE NESTED ALLPASS
asum11   =         adel12-.35*adel11             ; FIRST  INNER FEEDFORWARD
asum12   =         adel13-.45*asum11             ; SECOND INNER FEEDFORWARD
aout11   =         asum12-.25*asum01             ; OUTER FEEDFORWARD
adel11   delay     asum01+.25*aout11, .0047      ; OUTER FEEDBACK
adel12   delay     adel11+.35*asum11, .0083      ; FIRST  INNER FEEDBACK
adel13   delay     asum11+.45*asum12, .022       ; SECOND INNER FEEDBACK
adel21   delay     aout11, .005                  ; DELAY 1
; ALLPASS 1
asub31   =         adel31-.45*adel21             ; FEEDFORWARD
adel31   delay     adel21+.45*asub31,.030        ; FEEDBACK
adel41   delay     asub31, .067                  ; DELAY 2
adel51   delay     .4*adel41, .015               ; DELAY 3
aout51   =         aflt01+adel41
; SINGLE NESTED ALLPASS
asum61   =         adel62-.35*adel61             ; INNER FEEDFORWARD
aout61   =         asum61-.25*aout51             ; OUTER FEEDFORWARD
adel61   delay     aout51+.25*aout61, .0292      ; OUTER FEEDBACK
adel62   delay     adel61+.35*asum61, .0098      ; INNER FEEDBACK
; COMBINE OUTPUTS
aout     =         .5*aout11+.5*adel41+.5*aout61
adel71   delay     aout61, .108                  ; DELAY 4
         outs      aout*kdclick, -aout*kdclick   ; FINAL OUTPUT
         endin
```

Figure 24.9 Orchestra code for *instr 2403,* a medium room reverberator.

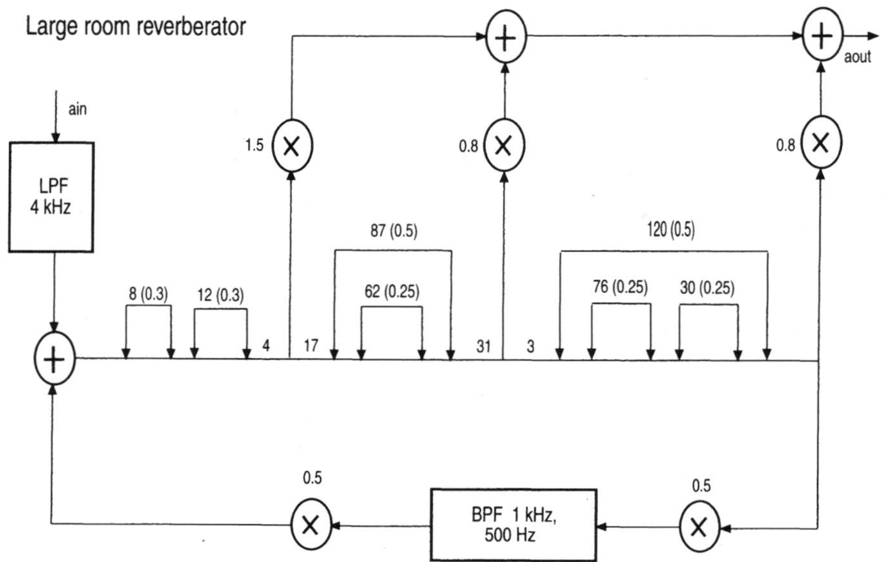

Figure 24.10 Block diagram of large room reverberator.

introduced before and after the first two output taps. The input is again prefiltered and the overall feedback is scaled and bandpass filtered. The large room reverb shown in figure 24.10 can be implemented in Csound as shown in figure 24.11.

Conclusion

The nested allpass filters presented here suggest other configurations of allpass filters. For instance, a third allpass filter could be inserted into the double nested allpass filter for three allpass filters in series. An additional level of nesting could be applied to the nested allpass filters. Many other configurations of nesting could be the subject of future experimentation and many other reverb configurations could be implemented as a result. The final Csound orchestra and score accompanying this chapter, *instr 2405.orc* features a flexible system for experimenting with various reverb configurations. Have fun.

```
         instr     2404        ; LARGE ROOM REVERB
idur     =         p3
iamp     =         p4
iinch    =         p5
aout91   init      0
adel01   init      0
adel11   init      0
adel51   init      0
adel52   init      0
adel91   init      0
adel92   init      0
adel93   init      0
kdclick  linseg    0, .002, iamp, idur-.004, iamp, .002, 0
; INITIALIZE
asig0    zar       iinch
aflt01   butterlp  asig0, 4000                 ; PRE-FILTER
aflt02   butterbp  .5*aout91, 1000, 500        ; FEEDBACK FILTER
asum01   =         aflt01+.5*aflt02            ; INITIAL MIX
; ALLPASS 1
asub01   =         adel01-.3*asum01            ; FEEDFORWARD
adel01   delay     asum01+.3*asub01,.008       ; FEEDBACK
; ALLPASS 2
asub11   =         adel11-.3*asub01            ; FEEDFORWARD
adel11   delay     asub01+.3*asub11,.012       ; FEEDBACK
adel21   delay     asub11, .004                ; DELAY 1
adel41   delay     adel21, .017                ; DELAY 2
; SINGLE NESTED ALLPASS
asum51   =         adel52-.25*adel51           ; INNER FEEDFORWARD
aout51   =         asum51-.5*adel41            ; OUTER FEEDFORWARD
adel51   delay     adel41+.5*aout51,   .025    ; OUTER FEEDBACK
adel52   delay     adel51+.25*asum51,  .062    ; INNER FEEDBACK
adel61   delay     aout51, .031                ; DELAY 3
adel81   delay     adel61, .003                ; DELAY 4
; DOUBLE NESTED ALLPASS
asum91   =         adel92-.25*adel91           ; FIRST  INNER FEEDFORWARD
asum92   =         adel93-.25*asum91           ; SECOND INNER FEEDFORWARD
aout91   =         asum92-.5*adel81            ; OUTER FEEDFORWARD
adel91   delay     adel81+.5*aout91, .120      ; OUTER FEEDBACK
adel92   delay     adel91+.25*asum91, .076     ; FIRST  INNER FEEDBACK
adel93   delay     asum91+.25*asum92, .030     ; SECOND INNER FEEDBACK
; COMBINE OUTPUTS
aout     =         .8*aout91+.8*adel61+1.5*adel21
         outs      aout*kdclick, -aout*kdclick ; FINAL OUTPUT
         endin
```

Figure 24.11 Orchestra code for *instr 2404,* a large room reverb.

References

Gardner, W. G. 1992. *The Virtual Acoustic Room.* Master's thesis, MIT Media Lab.

Vercoe, B., and M. Puckette. 1985. *Synthetic Spaces—Artificial Acoustic Ambiance from Active Boundary Computation.* Unpublished NSF proposal. Cambridge, Mass. Music and Cognition Office at MIT Media Lab.

25 Csound-based Auditory Localization

Elijah Breder and David McIntyre

Within Csound there exist the traditional tools for spatial manipulation—panning and multichannel processing. Both these tools have their limitations. Panning limits the composer to the stereo field, while multichannel processing requires a large and complex arrangement of speakers. In addition, both techniques rely on amplitude relations between channels to create spatial locations. But by incorporating spectral modifications, sound spatialization better approximates the way we hear sounds in the real world.

The **hrtfer** opcode performs these spectral modifications to create the illusion of a three-dimensional auditory space. This space is created by processing a mono signal with Head Related Transfer Functions (HRTFs), producing a left/right pair of audio signals. Although these signals may be presented over speakers, this project was intended for headphone-based listening.

This chapter will first discuss the perceptual and psychophysical issues related to human localization. This will be followed by a general discussion of 3D audio systems. The **hrtfer** unit generator will then be presented along with some examples of its use.

3D Sound

The ability to localize sound in three-dimensional space is an important aspect of real-world auditory perception. It provides for a sense of situational awareness and self-orientation by allowing us to estimate the position of sounds that may be outside the current field of view. The most important cues used in sound localization are interaural time differences (ITDs), interaural intensity differences (IIDs) and spectral changes. Other contributing factors include the precedence or Haas effect, the

Doppler effect and head movement. This section will discuss these various aspects of human localization.

Interaural Time and Intensity Differences

Interaural difference cues are probably the most important localization cues we use to localize sound sources on the horizontal plane. From an evolutionary standpoint, this makes perfect sense: humans are terrain-based animals whose auditory system has been optimized through evolution to deal with terrain-based sound sources, including those sources that are outside the field of view. The horizontal placement of our ears maximizes interaural differences for sound waves emitted by a source on the horizontal plane. Our auditory system has the ability to detect interaural differences in phase, amplitude envelope onset and intensity. By minimizing these differences with head movement, we are able to direct our focal vision to items of interest that may not be in our current field of view.

One of the first people to study and explain binaural localization of sound was Lord Rayleigh who, in 1876, performed experiments to determine his ability to localize sounds of different frequencies (Rossing 1990). He found that lower frequencies were much harder to localize than higher frequencies. His explanation was that sounds coming from one side of the head produced a more intense sound in the ear closer to the source (ipsilateral ear) than in the opposite ear (contralateral ear).

Rayleigh went on to explain that for high frequencies, the head casts a "shadow" on the contralateral ear, thereby reducing a given sound's intensity. This did not occur for lower frequencies because the wavelengths were long enough as to diffract around the head. In 1907, Rayleigh performed a second localization experiment, this time investigating localization of low frequencies. What he discovered was that the sound reached one ear before the other, which resulted in a phase difference between the two ears.

Modern experiments have investigated the role of interaural time and intensity differences and have confirmed Rayleigh's initial findings. Figure 25.1 shows the travel path of sound waves for two sources. We see that for the source directly in front of the listener (source A) the sound waves reach the two ears at the same time. In this case the interaural time and intensity differences are minimized (they are not equal owing to the asymmetry of the human head and ears). The sound waves emitted by the second source to the right of the listener (source B), however, will produce significant interaural differences.

In general, if source B is below approximately 1 kHz, localization will be dependent on the interaural phase or time differences. If the source is greater than about

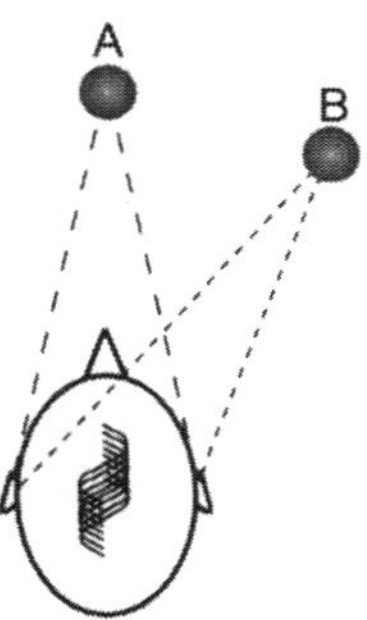

Figure 25.1 Interaural differences.

1.5 kHz (wavelengths are now smaller than the diameter of the head), the interaural intensity differences will be used. This head shadow effect increases with increasing frequency (Middlebrooks and Green 1991).

The use of IIDs and ITDs by the auditory system is commonly referred to as the "duplex" theory of localization. The theory suggests that IIDs and ITDs operate over exclusive frequency regions. Although in the laboratory it is relatively easy to estimate the boundary point (around 1.5 kHz) where the system switches from using ITDs to IIDs, the interaction of the two mechanisms in the real world are not fully understood.

There have been ITD studies that investigated the role of amplitude envelope onset times in the higher frequency region (Begault 1994). In the frequency region above 1.5 kHz, the phase relationship between the two ears leads to an ambiguous situation: it is hard to tell which is the leading soundwave. The studies have shown that if an amplitude envelope is imposed on the test signal, the auditory system is able to detect the difference in envelope onset times, thus providing useful ITD cues.

Sound sources in the real world typically contain frequency components above and below the cutoff (about 1.5 kHz) suggested by the duplex theory. It is quite likely that the auditory system does not really rely on any one mechanism for localization. Rather all available information is used to provide the most suitable answer.

The use of pan pots on conventional stereo mixing boards illustrates how amplitude changes, independent of the sources' frequency content, are sufficient in separating and placing individual sounds on a horizontal plane (the stereo field). Amplitude differences between the left and right channels are interpreted by the listener as various spatial locations. For example, a sound can appear to move across the horizon by continuously varying the amplitude difference of the left and right channels (Begault 1994).

The Precedence Effect

The Precedence effect (other names include the Haas effect and Blauert's "the law of the first wavefront") describes the auditory system's ability to localize a sound source within a reverberant environment. Localization experiments have studied the Precedence effect by delaying one side of a stereo audio signal (either through headphones or loudspeakers) and noting the perceptual effects while varying the delay time. Results show that as the delay time is increased from 1.5 milliseconds to 10 milliseconds the virtual sound position will be associated with the undelayed channel but its width will seem to increase. At some point between 10 milliseconds and 40 milliseconds, depending on the sound source, a distinct echo will be heard coming from the delayed channel. The original event, however, is still perceived as coming from the undelayed channel. In terms of real world localization, the Precedence effect explains how we are able to localize the original sound source (or direct signal) in spite of potentially being confused by reflections and echoes (Begault 1994).

Head Movement in Localization

In real-world perception and localization, our head acts as a pointer, helping us integrate information from both our visual and auditory senses. As already mentioned, we use auditory information to locate and focus on particular objects that may or may not be part of the current visual scene. We use head movements to minimize interaural differences. The following example (adapted from Begault 1994) shows how head movements are used to locate a source at right 150 degrees azimuth, which may be confused with a source at right 30 degrees azimuth.

At first the interaural difference cues suggest that the source is to the right of the listener. As the listener starts turning his or her head toward the right, if the interaural differences are minimized, then the source must be in front. If, on the other hand, the differences increase, then the source is further in the back.

Head movements are also important in front/back disambiguation. Studies have shown that the listener is able to integrate changes in IIDs and ITDs, as well as spectral changes, owing to head movement and use this information in localization judgments (Begault 1994). A simpler example of the importance of quick judgments based on head movements is "if I don't see it but hear it, it must be in the back."

The Doppler Effect

Another important cue that exists in real world human localization is the perceived pitch change of a sound source as it moves past the listener. This is termed the *Doppler effect.*

If, for example, a 100 Hz emitting sound source and listener are stationary, the number of vibrations per second "counted" or heard by the listener will be 100. If, however, the source or listener is moving, the number of vibrations encountered by the listener will differ. If the two are moving away from each other, a drop in pitch will be perceived. If they are moving toward each other, an increase in pitch will be perceived.

Although the Doppler effect has been studied and understood as a perceptual phenomenon, further investigation is necessary to examine its interaction with other localization cues, including cognitive processes such as experience and familiarity.

Spectral Cues

Although IIDs and ITDs are probably the most important cues for localization of sound sources on the horizontal plane, they provide rather ambiguous cues for sources located on the median plane. Although IID and ITD values won't be exactly the same owing to the asymmetrical construction of our head and pinnae, interaural difference values will be minimal along the median plane. This would lead to confusion when trying to determine whether a source is directly in front (0 degrees azimuth) or directly in back (180 degrees azimuth), solely based on interaural difference cues.

The "Cone of Confusion" concept describes how, for any two points on a conical surface extending outward from a listener's ear, identical (hence ambiguous) IID and ITD values may be calculated (points a & b and c & d in figure 25.2). It is in these

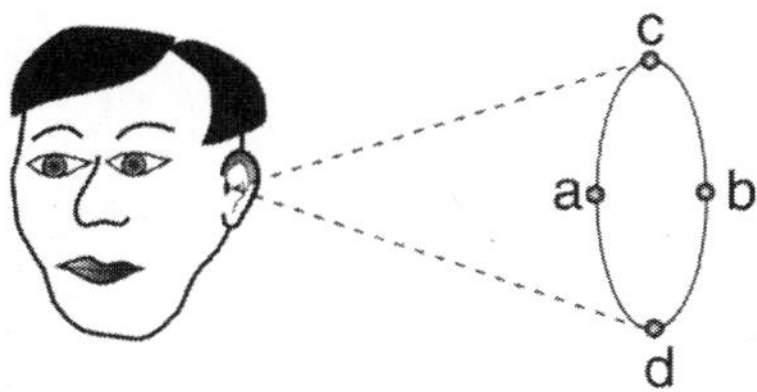

Figure 25.2 Cone of confusion.

situations that spectral cues provide further localization cues and disambiguate front from back and up from down.

The pinnae are responsible for the spectral alterations of incoming soundwaves. They act as directional filters, imposing amplitude and phase changes as a function of sound source location. Most of these spectral alterations are caused by time delays (0–300 μsec.) owing to the complex folds of the pinnae (Begault 1994). Because of the asymmetrical construction of the pinnae, sound coming from different locations will have different spectral changes imposed on it. The listener recognizes these modifications as spatial cues.

The filtering process of the outer ears is most often called the *head related transfer function* (HRTF). Other terms used to describe this process include *head transfer function* (HTF), *pinnae transform, outer ear transfer function* (OETF), and *directional transfer function* (DTF). Modern experiments and studies record, analyze, and simulate HRTFs in order to gain a better understanding of the process of using spectral cues for localization. In general, studies have shown that although different people exhibit different ear impulse responses, or HRTFs, most measurements share similar spectral patterns (Hiranaka and Yamasaki 1982; Asano, Suzuki, and Sone 1990). Although people do better in localization tests when using their own HRTFs, they are able to make quite accurate localization judgments when using HRTFs of others. Some even do better with "foreign" HRTFs than with their own.

Besides the pinnae, other parts of the body can influence the spectrum of an incoming soundwave. These can be broken down into directional and nondirectional spectral modifications. For example, the upper body will cause directionally dependent alterations to the spectrum in the 100 Hz–2 kHz range (Genuit 1984). The ear canal on the other hand, is a nondirectional influence owing to its natural resonance between 2 and 5 kHz.

3D Audio Systems

What Is 3D Audio?

Various audio systems provide sound spatialization techniques that attempt to go beyond the two dimensional plane inherent in stereo recordings. These systems fall into two broad categories: multispeaker surround systems and headphone/two-speaker systems. The former category includes Dolby Surround and Ambisonics, which place virtual sound sources by manipulating volume levels in an array of speakers surrounding the listener. At the heart of headphone/two-speaker systems are filtering techniques that simulate the directional cues used in everyday listening. Many of these systems use HRTF-based filters to approximate the directionally-dependent spectral modifications imposed by our outer ears on incoming soundwaves.

HRTF data sets are obtained by playing an analytical signal at desired locations and measuring the impulse responses with probe microphones placed at, or near, the ear canal of a human or dummy head. Often, the source of the signal is placed at a distance of 1.4 meters to minimize the effects of reverberation on the recording. The output of the microphones is then stored digitally as a series of sample points. These data may then be compressed and post-equalized for the frequency response of the measuring (and possibly the playback) system. An inherent difficulty with HRTFs is that they are discrete measurements of a continuous phenomenon. Obviously an infinite number of measurements would be required to accurately represent the continuous nature of this phenomenon, but this is not practical. This leaves a trade-off between spatial resolution and data size/processing load.

Every individual has his or her own unique set of HRTFs. Since it is not practical to create individualized HRTFs, most systems use generalized data sets. These non-specific HRTFs are created by taking the same measurements on a dummy head that approximates the features of the human ear. The KEMAR mannequin from MIT is an example of one such dummy head. As discussed above, listeners are still able to make accurate localization judgments using these generalized HRTF's.

Most HRTF based 3D audio systems provide better results under binaural (headphone) listening conditions. In transaural (loudspeaker) playback, much of the detail in the spatial imagery is lost because the listening environment and loudspeakers will impose unknown nonlinear transformations on the resulting audio output. Transaural playback may be improved by using techniques such a cross-talk cancellation, but these can only approximate binaural listening conditions.

Unless head-tracking is used, binaural presentation of a sound source placed in a virtual space fails to account for head movements. In a normal listening environment, head movements are used to help pinpoint sound sources outside the field of view. Again owing to practicality, most binaural 3D audio systems do not account for head movements, thus removing one key technique used to localize sound sources.

The HRTFER Unit Generator

In order for any HRTF-based filtering to succeed, a comprehensive set of HRTFs is required. For our implementation of the **hrtfer** unit generator, we chose to use the

MIT HRTFs produced by Bill Gardner and Keith Martin. These data sets were recorded using the KEMAR mannequin, a dummy head and torso that produces a reasonable set of generalized HRTFs. Gardner and Martin have several versions of their HRTFs available. From these, we chose to use the compact set of HRTFs. This is a reduced data set of 128 point symmetrical HRTFs derived from the left ear measurements of their full 512 point set. What this means is that for a given left azimuth of theta, the HRTF used for the right ear would be the measurement for the left ear at 360-q (e.g., left ear = left 45, right ear = left 315). Gardner explains that this was done for efficiency reasons. This, however, eliminates the interaural time differences along the median plane that have been shown to help in vertical localization. Positions on the horizontal plane were sampled at approximately every five degrees, while positions on the median plane were sampled every ten degrees. In addition, elevation data are restricted to the range between forty degrees below the listener to 90 degrees above. It should also be noted that the impulse responses were sampled at 44.1 kHz. In order to use these data at a different sampling rate, the HRTFs must be resampled at the desired sampling rate (Gardner and Martin, documentation for MIT HRTFs).

While the HRTF data sets are sampled in the time domain, the convolution performed by **hrtfer** requires frequency domain data. In order to reduce the computational load of **hrtfer**, the HRTF measurements were preprocessed using the Fast Fourier Transform (FFT) to translate the time domain data into the frequency domain. The **hrtfer** utility program, **hrtfread**, was used to obtain the FFT of the MIT HRTFs and store them in a file. This file is then used by **hrtfer** when processing audio.

The **hrtfer** unit generator takes four arguments and produces two audio signals, a stereo left-right pair. The following is an example of an **hrtfer** call:

```
aleft, aright  hrtfer  asig, kaz, kelev, "HRTFcompact"
```

Where:

- *asig* is a mono audio signal. This can either be a sampled sound or a Csound generated signal. If a sample is used, it must match the sampling rate of the HRTFs (in this case, 44.1 kHz). If a Csound generated signal is used, the sampling rate of the orchestra must match that of the HRTFs.
- *kaz* and *kelev* are the requested azimuth and elevation values in degrees. Positions on the left are negative while positions on the right are positive. Similarly, elevation positions below the listener are negative while positions above the listener are positive. In fact, these values can be k-rate values, allowing for dynamic movement.

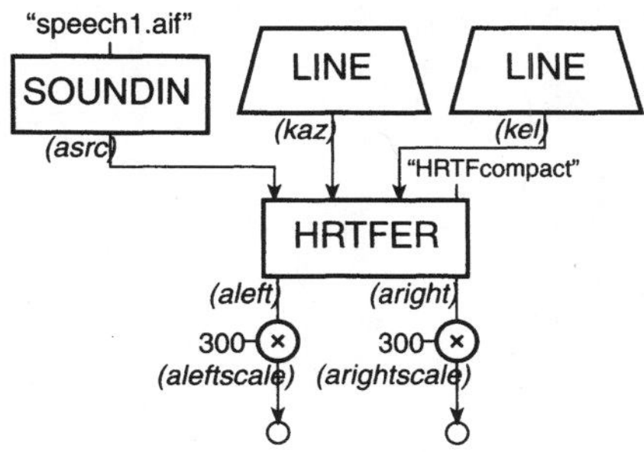

Figure 25.3 Block diagram of *instr 2501,* a 3D audio instrument using the **hrtfer** opcode to localize and move the sound source in virtual space.

- The *HRTFcompact file* for this version of **hrtfer** is literally *HRTFcompact* and needs to reside in Csound's analysis directory.
- *aleft* and *aright* are the resulting audio signals. Note that these signals need to be appropriately scaled before being output.

For example, the following line of Csound code places a sound at hard left and 40 degrees above the listener:

```
aleft, aright  hrtfer  "someSound", -90, 40, "HRTFcompact"
```

A more complicated example might have a sound move around the listener in a circle. Figures 25.3 and 25.4 show examples of Csound orchestra and score files that do just that.

Where:

- Negative values specify positions/movement to the left
- Positive values specify positions/movement to the right
- 0 degrees *azimuth* is directly in front, 180 is directly in back
- HRTFs for elevation range from 40 degrees below (−40) to 90 degrees above (90) the listener
- 0 degrees *azimuth/elevation* specifies the position directly ahead of the listener at a distance of 1.4 meters (the distance used in MIT's HRTFs)

Conclusion

By taking into account spectral modifications and not just amplitude changes, sound spatialization may be made more effective. The **hrtfer** unit generator implements the

```
                instr       2501      ; HRTFER EXAMPLE ORCHESTRA
iazstart        =           p4
iazend          =           p5
ielstart        =           p6
ielend          =           p7
; MOVE THE SOUND HORIZONTALLY FROM IAZSTART TO IAZEND
kaz             line        iazstart, p3, iazend
; MOVE THE SOUND VERTICALLY FROM IELSTART TO IELEND
kel             line        ielstart, p3, ielend
asrc            soundin     "speech1.aif"
aleft, aright   hrtfer      asrc, kaz, kel, "HRTFcompact"
aleftscale      =           aleft*300
arightscale     =           aright*300
                outs        aleftscale, arightscale
                endin

f 1     0       8192    10          1

; ins   start   dur     az start    az end    el start    el end
i 2501  0       7.5     0           360       -45         45
```

Figure 25.4 Orchestra and score code for *instr 2501,* a 3D audio instrument with the ability to move a sound vertically and horizontally in 3D space.

directionally dependent spectral filtering performed by our outer ears. The use of **hrtfer** in orchestras may be complemented by the implementation of Doppler effects, distance attenuation and reverberation through other, more traditional Csound techniques (e.g., pitch manipulations, lowpass filters and reverb unit generators) to create truly vivid listening spaces.

References

Asano, F., Y. Suzuki, and T. Sone. 1990. "Role of spectral cues in median plane localization." *Journal of the Acoustical Society of America.*

Begault, D. R. 1991. "Challenges to the successful implementations of 3-D sound." *Journal of the Audio Engineering Society.*

Begault, D. R. 1994. *3-D Sound for Virtual Reality and Multimedia.* San Diego, Calif.: Academic Press.

Bregman, A. S. 1990. *Auditory Scene Analysis.* Cambridge, Mass.: MIT Press.

Butler, R., and K. Belendiuk. 1976. "Spectral cues utilized in the localization of sound in the median sagittal plane." *Journal of the Acoustical Society of America.*

Gardner, M., and R. Gardner. 1972. "Problem of localization in the median plane: effect of pinnae cavity occlusion." *Journal of the Acoustical Society of America.*

Gardner, M. 1973. "Some monaural and binaural facets of median plane localization." *Journal of the Acoustical Society of America.*

Hiranaka, Y., and H. Yamasaki. "Envelope representations of pinnae impulse responses relating to three-dimensional localization of sound." *Journal of he Acoustical Society of America.*

Kendall, G. S. 1996. "A 3D sound primer." *Computer Music Journal.*

Kendall, G. S., and W. Martens. 1984. "Simulating the cues of spatial hearing in natural environments." *Proceedings of the 1984 International Computer Music Conference.* San Francisco: International Computer Music Association.

Kramer, G. 1994. *Auditory Display: Sonification, Audification, and Auditory Interfaces.* Reading, Mass: Addison Wesley.

Middlebrooks, J. C., and D. M. Green. 1991. "Sound localization by human listeners." *Annual Review of Psychology* 42: 135–159.

Moore, F. R. 1990. *Elements of Computer Music.* Englewood Cliffs, N.J.: Prentice-Hall.

Plenge, G. 1972. "On the differences between localization and lateralization." *Journal of the Acoustical Society of America.*

Rossing, D. 1990. *The Science of Sound.* (second edition). Reading, Mass.: Addison-Wesley.

Working with Csound's Signal Processing Utilities

26 Convolution in Csound: Traditional and Novel Applications

Erik Spjut

Computer music has benefited greatly from the application of long-established signal-processing methods to audio signals. *Convolution* is one such method. This chapter will look briefly at the mathematics of convolution and then examine at some length the aural interpretation of convolution.

The Mathematics

Mathematically, convolution requires two signals, which we will call signal *a* and signal *b*. We will number the samples in signal *a* from 0 to *N* and the samples in signal *b* from 0 to *M*. If we let our sampling variable *n* range from 0 to $N+M$ then the value of signal *a* at time t_n is $a[n]$ and the value of signal *b* is at time t_n is $b[n]$.

To perform a convolution of the two signals we have to pick one of the signals. We can choose either signal and usually (but not always) the shorter one is chosen. We will choose signal *b*. Signal *b* is usually called the *Impulse Response* and signal *a* is usually called the *signal,* the *input signal,* or the *excitation.* Step one is to flip the impulse response, signal *b*, around.

Steps two and three are to slide signal *b* over signal *a* and then multiply the corresponding samples of *a* and *b* and sum the result. If we call the convolution of signals *a* and *b* signal *c*, then:

$$c[n] = \sum_{k=0}^{N+M} a[k]b[n - k] \qquad (26.1)$$

The signal processing texts give the limits of the summation as—from *negative infinity* to *infinity,* but most of us don't have infinitely long soundfiles. Equation 26.1 can be implemented in Csound using the **delay1** opcode. For real-time performance,

```
b[1]  =  0.002177629
b[2]  =  0.032279228
b[3]  =  0.153256114
b[4]  =  0.304044017
b[5]  =  0.304044017
b[6]  =  0.153256114
b[7]  =  0.032279228
b[8]  =  0.002177629
```

Figure 26.1 Signal b for use in direct convolution example from *instr 2601*.

when signal b is quite short, the convolution sum is very fast. The Csound instrument shown in figure 26.3 (*instr 2601.orc*) implements the convolution sum where signal b is shown in figure 26.1. Figure 26.2 is a block diagram of a direct convolution instrument and figure 26.3 is the orchestra code.

When signal b is long or comparable in length to signal a, a mathematically equivalent method is much faster. The equivalent method is to pad signal b with zeros until it is the same length as signal a, pad both of them with zeros to the nearest power-of-two length, take the Fast Fourier Transform (FFT) of both signals, multiply the two FFT's together and take the inverse FFT. Multiplying the FFT's together means that frequencies common to both signals will be emphasized and frequencies in only one or the other will be greatly diminished.

The Csound opcode **convolve** uses a modification of the FFT method that is more suitable when the longer signal won't all fit in memory at once. The Csound instrument in figure 26.4 (*instr 2602.orc*) performs the same convolution as *instr 2601* but by using the **convolve** opcode.

The savings can be enormous. If signal b is 256 samples long, the convolution sum requires *256* multiplications and additions to produce *one* sample in signal c, whereas **convolve** requires about *10* multiplications and additions to produce *one* sample in signal c.

It can be proven mathematically that the convolution of a and b, written $a * b$, is equal to the convolution of b and a, written $b * a$.

$$a * b = b * a \tag{26.2}$$

Mathematically, it does not matter which signal we use for signal b, but because of the way **convolve** is written, it is faster to use the shorter signal for signal b. In addition, the delay before the sound appears (see below) is shorter if the shorter signal is used for signal b.

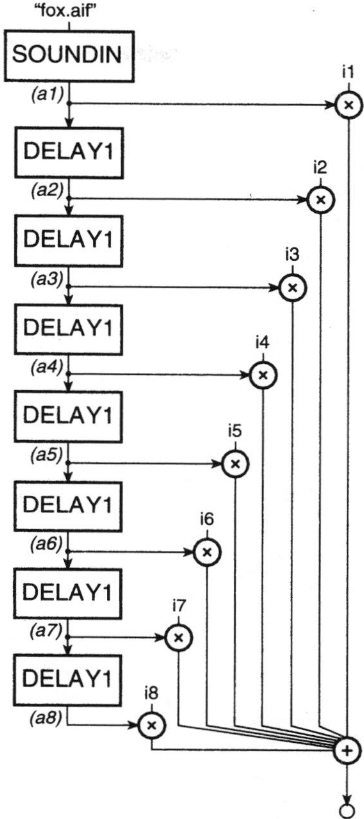

Figure 26.2 Block diagram of *instr 2601,* a direct convolution instrument.

```
     instr    2601         ; DIRECT CONVOLUTION
i1   =        0.002177629              ; SAMPLE 1 OF SIGNAL B
i2   =        0.032279228              ; SAMPLE 2 OF SIGNAL B
i3   =        0.153256114              ; SAMPLE 3 OF SIGNAL B
i4   =        0.304044017              ; SAMPLE 4 OF SIGNAL B
i5   =        0.304044017              ; SAMPLE 5 OF SIGNAL B
i6   =        0.153256114              ; SAMPLE 6 OF SIGNAL B
i7   =        0.032279228              ; SAMPLE 7 OF SIGNAL B
i8   =        0.002177629              ; SAMPLE 8 OF SIGNAL B
a1   soundin  "fox.aif"                ; SIGNAL A
a2   delay1   a1
a3   delay1   a2
a4   delay1   a3
a5   delay1   a4
a6   delay1   a5
a7   delay1   a6
a8   delay1   a7
     out      i1*a1 + i2*a2 + i3*a3 + i4*a4 + i5*a5 + i6*a6 + i7*a7 + i8*a8
     endin
```

Figure 26.3 Orchestra code for *instr 2601,* a direct convolution instrument.

```
    instr     2602        ; FFT CONVOLUTION
a1  soundin   "fox.aif"                    ; SIGNAL A
a2  convolve  a1, "eightPoint.con"         ; SIGNAL B, (USE CVANAL TO MAKE)
    out       a2*p4                        ; P4 IS SCALING FACTOR
    endin
```

Figure 26.4 Orchestra for *instr 2602,* an instrument that performs FFT-based convolution with Csound's **convolve** opcode.

Preparing the Impulse Response Files

In order to use **convolve** in Csound, signal *b* (the impulse response) must be preanalyzed using the sound utility **cvanal**. To use the sound file *oneEcho.aif,* you would type at the command line:

```
csound -Ucvanal oneEcho.aif oneEcho.con
```

Then to convolve *oneEcho.aif* with the audio signal *ain* in Csound, you would write in the body of an instrument:

```
aout        convolve       ain, "oneEcho.con"
```

The demos in this chapter all assume you have the appropriate "*.con*" files in your **SADIR**. The corresponding "*.aif*" files are on the accompanying CD-ROM. The "*.con*" files are machine specific, so you may have to generate them from the "*.aif*" files.

The Csound Instrument

Almost all of the instruments have exactly the same structure. We will use the **strset** opcode to put the filenames in the orchestra and pass them as p-field values from the score. Each subsequent section of this chapter will have its own instrument and score something like those shown in figure 26.5.

Where *iexcite* and *irespond* are replaced with the appropriate **strset** "filename" when referred to by number in *p5* and *p6* and where, via *p4*, *iscale* is the scaling factor to keep the signal in range. In the examples that follow, the shorter file was chosen as signal *b* (the impulse response), purely to decrease computation time. As mentioned above, either file would have worked.

It is important to note that the output from **convolve** is silent for approximately the length of signal *b* (the impulse response). The exact length is given in the *Csound Reference Manual.* For your reference, the lengths of all of the source "*.aif*" files used in this chapter are shown in figure 26.6.

```
            strset     1, "hello.con"
            strset     2, "fox.con"
            strset     3, "oneEcho.aif"
            strset     4, "twoEchos.aif"
            strset     5, "fiveEchos.aif"
            strset     6, "gaussReverb.aif"
            strset     7, "uniformReverb.aif"
            strset     8, "whiteNoise.aif"

            instr      2603          ; ECHO & REVERB DEMOS
iscale      =          p4
iexcite     =          p5
irespond    =          p6
aa          soundin    iexcite
ab          convolve   aa, irespond
            out        ab*iscale
            endin

; INS       STRT       DUR      ISCALE     IEXCITE     IRESPOND
i 2603      0          2.723    1.0000     3           1
i 2603      4.723      2.723    1.0000     4           1
i 2603      8.827      2.723    1.0000     5           1
i 2603      12.931     4.209    0.0384     6           1
i 2603      15.383     8.487    0.0732     6           2
i 2603      25.25      4.209    0.0306     7           1
i 2603      27.702     8.487    0.0542     7           2
i 2603      37.57      4.209    0.0155     8           1
i 2603      40.022     8.487    0.0169     8           2
```

Figure 26.5 Orchestra and score for *instr 2603,* a basic convolution instrument.

This delay is due to the method used to do the convolution. Direct convolution, using equation 26.1, does not have this delay. The nonzero output (the useful signal) runs approximately the sum of the lengths of signal *a* and signal *b* past the initial delay. In the score, *(2603.sco)*, *p3* was chosen as the sum of the delay and the nonzero output length (see figure 26.5). The start time value of *p2* was chosen to add a little space between the examples by accounting for both the end of the previous note and the delay in the present note.

The Sounds of Convolution

Echoes or Scale-and-Translate

The convolution of an audio signal with a single sample gives a copy of the signal scaled by the height of the sample and shifted in time by the position of the sample.

NAME	SIZE (SAMPLES)
388CyclesMidC.aif	65536
5th.aif	129287
a440.aif	65533
altoSax.aif	55296
bassDrum.aif	3872
brass.aif	43987
cymbal.aif	63960
eightPoint.aif	8
fiveCyclesMidC.aif	1024
fiveEchos.aif	65536
fox.aif	121600
gaussReverb.aif	131065
hello.aif	27208
highPass300Hz.aif	255
highPass1kHz.aif	255
highPass3kHz.aif	255
lowPass3kHz.aif	128
lowPass1kHz.aif	128
lowPass300Hz.aif	256
marimba.aif	44228
middleC.aif	65533
oneCycleMidC.aif	256
oneEcho.aif	65536
piano.aif	46406
pluckBass.aif	36013
rimShot.aif	19482
twoEchos.aif	65536
uniformReverb.aif	131065
violin.aif	53429
whiteNoise.aif	131065
wilmTell.aif	64313

Figure 26.6 List of example *.aif* files and their length in samples.

In other words, if signal *b* consists of a single nonzero sample surrounded by a sea of zeros, the convolution of *a* and *b* will be a copy of *a* scaled by the height of the nonzero sample in *b* and shifted in time to correspond to the position of the nonzero sample in *b* as shown in figure 26.7.

If signal *b* consists of two samples of different heights separated by a large amount of time, when we convolve signal *a* with signal *b* we will get two copies of signal *a*, scaled by the relative heights of the samples in signal *b* and separated by the time between the two samples. The result is an echo as shown in figure 26.8. Finally, if we put in three samples, we'll get the original plus two echoes. If the samples in signal *b* are closer together than the length of *a*, the echoes will overlap (see figure

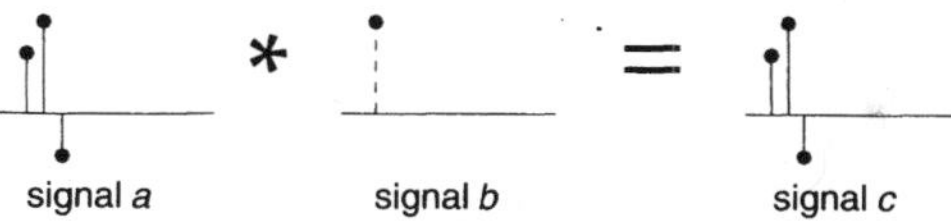

Figure 26.7 Convolution of a signal (a) with a single impulse (b).

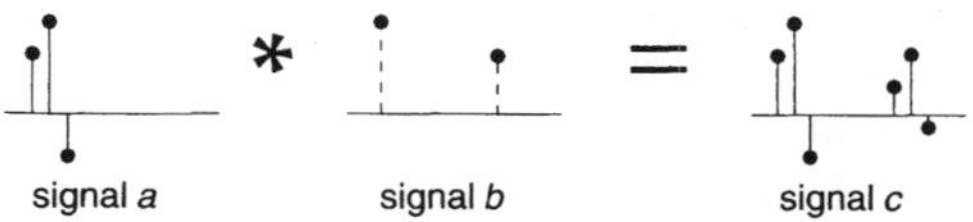

Figure 26.8 Convolution of a signal (a) with two widely spaced impulses (b).

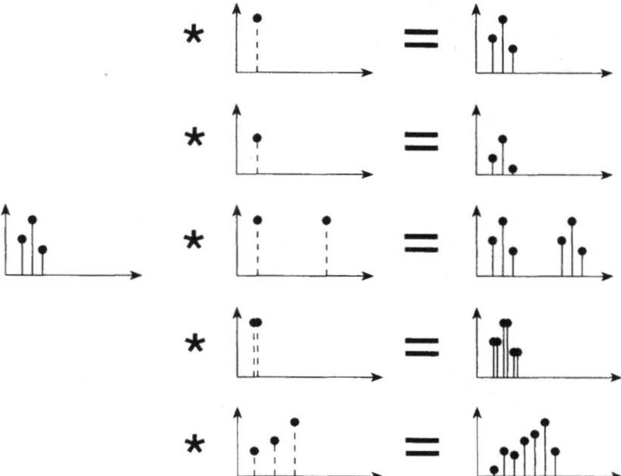

Figure 26.9 Convolution of a signal (a) with a variety of impulses (b).

26.9). If the echoes are dense enough, we end up with reverberation. The set of convolution demos in *2603.orc* and *2603.sco* runs from one echo through a nondecaying reverb.

The file *oneEcho.aif* consists of 65536 samples, but only the first and the last are not zero. The result is an echo 1.5 seconds after the initial sound. The file *twoEchos.aif* has three nonzero entries, one at 0 seconds, one at about 0.7 seconds and one at 1.5 seconds. The result is the signal and two echoes. The file *fiveEchos.aif* has six nonzero entries and gives the signal and five overlapping echoes.

Convolution Reverb

In reverberation, the echoes are dense and randomly placed. The file *gaussReverb.aif* was created with a decaying exponential envelope applied to a random signal generated by **gauss**. The file *uniformReverb.aif* was created with a decaying exponential envelope applied to a random signal generated by **linrand**. The difference between the two is rather subtle, but a Gaussian Reverb is, in theory, a little more realistic. If you have a favorite pattern of echoes, you can create the reverb of your choice. The *whiteNoise.aif* file is a random signal generated by **linrand**. It gives basically a reverb with no decay but a cutoff after 2.9 seconds.

When doing generalized reverberators via convolution, such as the previous set of examples, one wants to control the length of time before the first echo and the relative strengths of the dry signal and the reverb. Of course, it is possible to adjust these in the impulse response file itself, using a soundfile editor, but it is easier to add a few lines in the instrument and leave the file alone. The instrument found in *2604.orc* and illustrated in figure 26.10 has these features and capabilities.

The 2.972789 is the delay calculated by the formula in the Csound manual for *gaussReverb.aif.* Subtracting 20 ms (0.02s) causes the first reverb to appear 20 ms after the main signal. The useful range for the spacing is between 5 ms and 50 ms. The parameter, *irat,* is the ratio of the reverberated signal to the direct sound. For natural-sounding reverbs it should be less than 0.5. The **tone** opcode is used to filter out some of the high frequencies from the reverberated signal, similar to what happens in a large volume of air.

Impulse Response and Filtering

A common application of convolution is for filtering a signal. In fact, the convolution sum, equation 26.1, is also the correct formula for a Finite Impulse Response (FIR) filter where the filter coefficients are the $b[k]$'s. For filtering applications, signal b is usually forced to be symmetric about its midpoint. Extensive literature is available on picking the values of the $b[k]$'s for filtering applications.

If you excite a physical system with a short but intense input (like playing a marimba bar with a mallet) you will cause a response from the system (like a note sounding on the marimba). A short but intense input is known as an *impulse* and the output or response of the system is called the *impulse response.* If you put a short "click" (an impulse) into an audio filter and measure the output you get the impulse response of the filter. Convolving the impulse response of a filter with a signal is mathe-

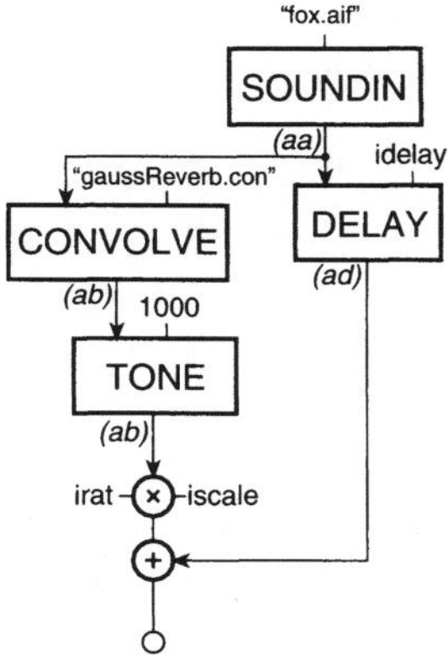

Figure 26.10 Block diagram of *instr 2604,* a convolution-based Gaussian reverberator.

```
strset      9,          "fox.aif"
strset      10,         "gaussReverb.con"

            instr       2604      ; MIX REVERB, DELAY & DARKEN
iscale      =           p4
iexcite     =           p5
irespond    =           p6
idelay      =           2.972789-0.02       ; REVERB STARTS 20 MS AFTER SOUND
irat        =           0.3                 ; RATIO OF REVERB TO DIRECT SOUND
aa          soundin     iexcite
ad          delay       aa, idelay
ab          convolve    aa, irespond
ab          tone        ab, 1000            ; DARKEN (LPF) THE REVERB
            out         ad+ab*iscale*irat
            endin
```

Figure 26.11 Orchestra code for *instr 2604,* a convolution-based Gaussian reverb instrument with delay and tone.

matically (and sonically) the same as sending the signal through the filter. As you may have guessed, the $b[k]$'s can be thought of as the impulse response of a filter.

Lowpass Filters

The next set of demos, found in *2605.orc* and *2605.sco,* demonstrates using convolution for lowpass filtering. The first three files, *lowPass3kHz.aif, lowPass1kHz.aif* and *lowPass300Hz.aif,* are impulse responses for lowpass filters with cutoffs at 3 kHz, 1 kHz and 300 Hz, respectively. If you listen to the files by themselves you will hear a sort of "thunk" sound. But if you listen to their convolution with *hello.aif* and *fox.aif* you'll clearly hear the filtering effect.

The methods for calculating the values in *lowPass3kHz.aif, lowPass1kHz.aif* and *lowPass300Hz.aif* are beyond the scope of this chapter but can be found in any good digital filter text. Note that the files are quite short, either 128 or 256 samples. Reasonably good filters do not have to be huge.

The next two files, *rimShot.aif* and *bassDrum.aif,* are recordings of a snare-drum rim shot and a drum-set kick drum. If you think of them as impulse responses of lowpass filters, you will find that they do a reasonable job of lowpass filtering. The kick drum is, of course, a much better lowpass filter than the snare drum. Notice how much longer these two files are than the first three.

Highpass Filters

The next set of demos, *2606.orc* and *2606.sco,* demonstrates using convolution for highpass filtering. The first three files, *highPass300Hz.aif, highPass1kHz.aif* and *highPass3kHz.aif,* are impulse responses for highpass filters with cutoffs at 300 Hz, 1 kHz and 3 kHz, respectively. If you listen to the files by themselves you will hear a sort of "click" or "snap" sound. But if you listen to their convolution with *hello.aif* you will clearly hear the filtering effect.

The last file, *cymbal.aif,* is a recording of a cymbal crash from a drum set. A cymbal has lots of high frequency content and little or no low frequency content so it works well as a highpass filter.

Smearing and Checking Frequency Content

Another common interpretation of convolution is that the output, signal *c*, is signal *a* "smeared out" by signal *b*. The next set of demos, *2607.orc* and *2607.sco,* show a progression from smearing out one signal with another, to measuring the frequency content at one frequency.

The files, *oneCycleMidC.aif, fiveCyclesMidC.aif* and *388CyclesMidC*.aif contain, respectively, one cycle, five cycles and 388 cycles of a sine wave with a pitch of middle C. The file *oneCycleMidC.aif* smears out *hello.aif* and *fox.aif,* removing any sharp transitions (essentially performing lowpass filtering). The file *fiveCycles-*

MidC.aif smears them even more. The convolution of *388CyclesMidC.aif* with *hello.aif* and with *fox.aif,* however, starts and ends with the smeared versions, but in the middle we just hear Middle C modulated (faintly) by *hello.aif* and *fox.aif.* Sharp transitions (abrupt starts and stops) have lots of high frequency content, so the sudden start and stop of *388CyclesMidC.aif* are what cause the initial and final smeared versions. The middle portion is showing where *hello.aif* or *fox.aif* and *388CyclesMidC.aif* have frequencies in common, which is not that surprising at Middle C.

If we smooth the start and stop, we can decrease the high-frequency content. The file *middleC.aif* and *a440.aif,* both have fade-ins and fade-outs, so they mainly just reveal the frequencies common to *hello.aif* or *fox.aif* and themselves. In the case of *middleC.aif,* that is mainly Middle C and in the case of *a440.aif,* that is mainly the A above Middle C.

People who are into wavelet or granular synthesis and analysis would like to experiment with files like *oneCycleMidC.aif, fiveCyclesMidC.aif* and smoothed versions of the same.

Resonances and Characteristic Sounds

We can use any soundfile we want as an impulse. It is easy to imagine a marimba note or a piano note as an impulse response because something close to an impulse (the mallet or hammer) causes the excitation. Now look closely at a soundfile. It IS just a bunch of impulses.

When we convolve a soundfile of someone speaking with a soundfile of a piano note, it is just like having someone speak (very loudly) into the piano while holding down that specific key and recording the response of the piano. In the physical world, it is hard to do because the excitation (the speaker) is so much louder than the response (the piano strings vibrating). The computer, however, has no such difficulty. The next set of demos, *2608.orc* and *2608.sco,* convolves *hello.aif* and *fox.aif* with recordings of instruments.

The piano and the marimba are easy to picture as impulse responses; but picture, if you will, a strange sort of physical instrument that, when you strike it with a mallet produces the sound of an alto saxophone playing an Eb, or a brass section playing a C. As far as **convolve** is concerned, that's exactly what a recording of a sax or a brass section is. As you listen to the demos, notice that the intelligibility of the voice decreases as you go from the marimba (the most percussive or impulse-like) to the violin (the least percussive or impulse-like). For your reference, the soundfiles are: *marimba.aif* (a marimba), *pluckBass.aif* (a plucked string bass), *piano.aif* (a piano), *brass.aif* (a crummy brass section), *altoSax.aif* (an alto sax) and *violin.aif* (a violin with a little vibrato at the end). Some people have likened this use of convolution to singing through a violin or playing a saxophone through a marimba.

Cross Synthesis

Why should we stop at playing a flute through a clarinet? Why not recite *Hamlet* through Beethoven's "Fifth Symphony?" Most of us do not have the gigabytes of memory that would be required, but we can experiment with some shorter examples. The next set of demos, *2608.orc* and *2608.sco,* convolves *hello.aif* and *fox.aif,* with *5th.aif* (the opening motif from Beethoven's "Fifth Symphony") and *wilmTell.aif* (a short excerpt from Rossini's "William Tell Overture"). This sort of convolution is often called *cross synthesis.* As you listen to these files, try to decide if *hello.aif* and *fox.aif* are playing the music or if the music is playing *hello.aif* and *fox.aif.* The mathematics says either interpretation is correct.

Most natural sounds, such as voice and acoustic instruments, have a limited high-frequency content. The high frequencies that are present give a feeling of brightness or openness to the sound. When we cross-synthesize two natural sounds, the small high frequencies of one are multiplied by the small high frequencies of the other and we get a very small overall high-frequency content. The sparkle sort of disappears from the music. A good recording engineer with a set of parametric equalizers could fix the problem, but Csound does not have a good set of built-in parametric equalizers.

In most filtering applications you want the filter transition (the region where you change from passing frequencies to blocking frequencies) to be as steep as possible. In our case, we need something that will emphasize the high frequencies and de-emphasize the low ones, but we do not want to block out any frequencies completely. The simplest way in Csound is to use the differentiator opcode, **diff**. It works by taking the difference between neighboring sound samples. However the audible effect is to emphasize high frequencies and de-emphasize low ones, just as we wanted.

A steep filter might have a slope of 24 dB per octave or steeper, in the transition band. But the **diff** opcode is an *all* transition band and has a gentle-but-constant upward slope of 6 dB per octave. In other words, for each octave you go up in frequency, you double the amount of emphasis you apply. With **diff** our convolution instrument now becomes as shown in figure 26.12.

The final set of demos, *2610.orc* and *2610.sco,* convolves exactly the same files as *2609.orc* and *2609.sco,* but with the high-frequency emphasis. As you listen to these

```
            instr      2610          ; BRIGHT MUSIC DEMOS
iscale      =          p4
iexcite     =          p5
irespond    =          p6
aa          soundin    iexcite
ab          convolve   aa, irespond
ab          diff       ab
            out        ab*iscale
            endin
```

Figure 26.12 Orchestra code for *instr 2610,* a convolution-resonator with a highpass filter implemented with the **diff** opcode.

files try to decide if *hello.aif* and *fox.aif* are playing the music or if the music is playing *hello.aif* and *fox.aif.* Compare the outputs from *2609.orc* and *2610.orc.* Does your perception of who-is-playing-whom change? Which do you like better?

Summary

We compared direct convolution to FFT convolution and decided that FFT convolution is usually better. We have used convolution to generate echoes and reverberation from individual samples and enveloped random samples. We have performed lowpass and highpass filtering with specifically-generated files and with recordings of *lowpass-ish* and *highpass-ish* percussion instruments (we could have used any arbitrary filter type). We have smeared or spread out sharp transients in a soundfile and examined its frequency content at one frequency. We have used one instrument or a voice to play another instrument. We let the quick brown fox play around in Beethoven's *Fifth Symphony* and we have examined some simple ways to restore the sparkle to cross-synthesized sounds. Even with all this, I have been able to mention only a few of the uses and interpretations of convolution in Csound. But at this point, you should be ready to experiment and convolve all sorts of things with all sorts of other things. You should also have a sense of what you'll get and why. If your interest has been piqued, be sure to check the references.

References

Boulanger, R. C. 1985."The Transformation of Speech into Music: A Musical Interpretation of Two Recent Digital Filtering Techniques." Ph.D. thesis, University of California, San Diego, Department of Music.

Hamming, R. W. 1983. *Digital Filters.* Englewood Cliffs, N.J.: Prentice-Hall.

Oppenheim, A. V., A. S. Willsky, and I. T. Young. 1983. *Signals and Systems.* Englewood Cliffs, N.J.: Prentice-Hall.

Roads, C. 1997. "Sound transformation by convolution." In *Musical Signal Processing.* Roads, C., S. T. Pope, A. Piccialli, and G. De Poli, eds. 1997. Lisse, The Netherlands: Swets & Zeitlinger B.V.

27 Working with Csound's ADSYN, LPREAD, and LPRESON Opcodes

Magdalena Klapper

Csound supports a wide variety of synthesis and processing methods. This chapter is dedicated to the exploration of two powerful analysis/resynthesis algorithms: **adsyn**—based on additive re-synthesis and **lpread/lpreson**—based on linear-predictive-coding. I will present some of the general theory behind these techniques and focus on how they are realized in Csound. Also, I will introduce the exciting world of "morphing" and "cross-synthesis" and show how **adsyn** and **lpread/lpreson** can be used to create hybrid timbres that are clearly a "fused" cross-mutation between two different sound sources.

Additive Synthesis

In the most simple and general sense, additive synthesis creates sound through the summation of other sounds—by adding sounds together. You might even say that "mixing" is a form of additive synthesis, but the distinction here is that when we do additive synthesis, we are creating a single "fused" timbre, not a nice balance of several sounds. Thus, additive synthesis typically implies the summation of harmonic and nonharmonic "partials."

A partial is typically a simple sine function defined by two control functions: the amplitude envelope and the frequency envelope. According to the specific frequency relations, partials can be combined to create harmonic or nonharmonic structures. In fact, when the frequencies of the partials are "tuned" to integer multiples of the fundamental frequency, they are said to be harmonic partials or "harmonics." The definition of additive synthesis may be expressed with the following formula:

$$x(n) = \sum_{k=1}^{N} h_k(n)\sin(nT(k\omega + 2\pi\ f_k(n))) \tag{27.1}$$

where n is the sample number, N is the number of partials, $h_k(n)$ is the amplitude value of the kth partial for the nth sample, ω is the pulsation of fundamental frequency and $f_k(n)$ is the frequency deflection of the kth partial for the nth sample.

Additive synthesis is one of the most general methods of sound synthesis. It enables the precise control of a sound by allowing the sound-designer to directly contour the frequency and amplitude of every partial. The amplitude and frequency control data for this synthesis technique can come from many sources.

In Csound, for instance, you could use **GEN9** or **GEN10** to additively synthesize simple or complex spectra. But these would remain static for the complete duration of the note event. To achieve a dynamic form of additive synthesis, you could use the **linseg** and **expseg** opcodes to control the amplitude and frequency arguments of a bank of **oscili** opcodes that are reading sine waves.

Both of these methods give the user a great deal of control, but they can involve a lot of manual labor. For instance, if the goal were to additively imitate the "pitched" steady-state timbre of an acoustic instrument, such as a clarinet or violin, you would need a lot of sine waves, a lot of points in your envelope generators, a lot of patience and a lot of luck. Csound, however, provides **hetro**, a utility program that automates this process to a large degree.

Csound's heterodyne filter analysis utility, **hetro**, can be used to analyze complex and time-varying sounds into amplitude and frequency pairs that can be read by the **adsyn** opcode to resynthesize this preanalyzed sound.

Heterodyne Filter Analysis

Heterodyne Filter Analysis is used to analyze harmonic or quasi-harmonic sounds. It works by multiplying the sound being analyzed by sine and cosine waveforms at frequencies equal to the given fundamental frequency and then again at each of its harmonics. For each frequency the result of the multiplication is summed to obtain the amplitude and the frequency value. The *orthogonality* characteristic of the sine (cosine) function is of importance here. The orthogonality of two functions $f(x)$ and $g(x)$ within section $[a,b]$ may be defined by the following formula:

$$\int_a^b f(x)g(x)dx = 0 \tag{27.2}$$

Every pair of sine (cosine) functions of different frequencies are orthogonal in a section that holds the complete number of both function periods. The multiplication of a sound (which is considered to be a summation of sine waves, according to Fourier theory) with a sine wave and then summing the result gives us the information about the contribution of this sine in the signal. Differentiation of multiplication with other frequencies is almost equal to zero (because the analyzed section of the sound does not hold the complete number of periods for all frequencies).

When in 1981 James Beauchamp implemented a tracking version of the heterodyne filter, a version that could follow changing frequency and amplitude trajectories of the analyzed tones, the age of additive-resynthesis was born. The major disadvantage of additive synthesis continued to be the problem of dealing with all the data required to accurately model a complex tone additively, particularly given all of the partials involved and the complex nature of each of their frequency and amplitude envelopes. To make this situation more manageable and practical, a form of data-reduction is typically employed, a method in which one uses line-segment approximations of all the frequency and amplitude envelopes.

The Csound Utility Program: HETRO

In Csound, the **hetro** utility program performs the hetrodyne filter analysis of an input signal. It tracks the harmonic spectrum in the sound and can also follow changing frequency trajectories. The specific setting for the analysis are determined either by a set of command-line flags, or via text fields, check-boxes and drop-down menus in your Csound "launcher's" **hetro** dialog box. The meaning of some of these options is explained in figure 27.1.

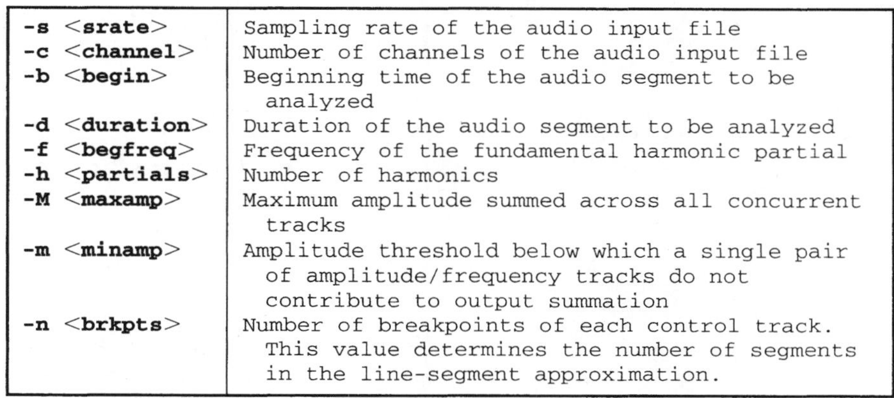

-s <srate>	Sampling rate of the audio input file
-c <channel>	Number of channels of the audio input file
-b <begin>	Beginning time of the audio segment to be analyzed
-d <duration>	Duration of the audio segment to be analyzed
-f <begfreq>	Frequency of the fundamental harmonic partial
-h <partials>	Number of harmonics
-M <maxamp>	Maximum amplitude summed across all concurrent tracks
-m <minamp>	Amplitude threshold below which a single pair of amplitude/frequency tracks do not contribute to output summation
-n <brkpts>	Number of breakpoints of each control track. This value determines the number of segments in the line-segment approximation.

Figure 27.1 The parameters for the **hetro** analysis utility.

Csound's **hetro** utility program creates a file that contains the analysis results, written in a special format. Each component partial is defined by time-sequenced amplitude and frequency values. The information is in the form of breakpoints (time, value, time, value. . .) using 16-bit integers in the range 0–32767. Time is given in milliseconds, frequency in Hertz. The negative value −1 indicates the beginning of an amplitude breakpoint set, the negative value −2 indicates the beginning of a frequency breakpoint set. Each track is ended with the value 32767. And within a composite file, sets may be in any order (amplitude, frequency, amplitude, amplitude, frequency, frequency. . .).

Typically, the **hetro** analysis file provides the input information for Csound's **adsyn** opcode. But in fact, **adsyn** only requires that the analysis file be in the **hetro** format as outlined above, not that it be created by **hetro**. Thus, it would be possible, and interesting, to create a file in the **adsyn** format, but which contains amplitude and frequency information derived from a source other than Heterodyne Filter Analysis.

Resynthesis with Csound

Now that we know how to analyze sounds with the **hetro** utility program, let us focus on how to use the results of the analysis to resynthesize the sounds with Csound. Let's start with the **adsyn** opcode description. Csound's **adsyn** opcode performs the additive synthesis by producing a set of sine functions, whose amplitudes and frequencies are individually controlled. The control signals are derived from the Heterodyne Filter Analysis and data-reduced by using a line-segment approximation method. The **adsyn** opcode reads the control information from the file created by the **hetro** utility program. The **adsyn** opcode is defined as:

```
asig     adsyn     kamod, kfmod, ksmod, ifilcod
```

The **adsyn** opcode requires four input parameters. The first three are the control signals, which determine modifications of the amplitude, frequency and speed of the complete set of harmonics during resynthesis. If these three parameters are set to 1, there is no amplitude, frequency or speed modification. The last input parameter is the name of the file created by the **hetro** program, which supplies the amplitude and frequency envelopes for each harmonic partial.

The first interesting resynthesis possibility is that **adsyn** allows one to transpose the sound and change its duration independently. Transposition is associated with the second input parameter and time-scaling or duration is controlled by the third.

The file *a3.aif* was analyzed with the **hetro** program using the two sets of flags shown in figure 27.2.

flag -f (fundamental frequency)	flag -h (number of harmonics)	adsyn file name
100 200	50 40	a3_1.het a3_2.het

Figure 27.2 Hetro analysis settings for the source file *a3.aif.*

```
          instr     2701        ; BASIC ADDITIVE RESYNTHESIZER
iamod     =         p4
ifmod     =         p5
ismod     =         p6
asig      adsyn     iamod, ifmod, ismod, "a3_1.het"
          out       asig
          endin
```

Figure 27.3 Orchestra code for *instr 2701,* a basic additive resynthesizer.

```
                                AMP,    FREQ,    SPEED,    ANALFILE
2701.orc ← asig    adsyn        1,      1,       1,        "a3_1.het"
2702.orc ← asig    adsyn        1,      1,       1,        "a3_2.het"
2703.orc ← asig    adsyn        1,      1.2,     .5,       "a3_2.het"
```

Figure 27.4 Settings for our first three **adsyn** resynthesis files.

Now we can look at an example of the most basic Csound instrument to resynthesize this sound (see figure 27.3). Both of the control files were used to resynthesize the sound, at first with no modifications (control signals equal to 1) and then with some modifications. The three resynthesized sounds are shown in figure 27.4.

Even a simple instrument like *instr 2701* may be used to create interesting modifications and tone-colors. Clearly, the color of the sound produced by *2701.orc,* which results from the *a3_1.het* analysis file is much duller than *2702.orc,* which resulted from *a3_2.het.* This is caused by the different analysis parameters. In the case of the first example (from *2701.orc*) using *a3_1.het*, the frequency bandwidth is limited to about 5 kHz, whereas the second example (from *2702.orc*), which used *a3_2.het,* has a frequency bandwidth of about 8 kHz. Nevertheless, both of the sounds are quite similar to the source, mainly because of the harmonic character of speech (see figure 27.2).

The third example, *2703.orc,* is an example of resynthesis with a constant modification of frequency (the pitch is 20% higher) and speed (the duration is twice as long). In fact, amplitude, frequency or speed, can be changed dynamically, which is shown in the *2704.orc.*

```
            instr   2704   ; ADDITIVE RESYNTHESIS WITH DYNAMIC FM
iamod       =       p4
ifmodst     =       p5
ifmodnd     =       p6
ismod       =       p7
kfmod       line    ifmodst, p3, ifmodnd
asig        adsyn   iamod, kfmod, ismod, 2
            out     asig
            endin
```

Figure 27.5 Orchestra code for *instr 2704,* an additive resynthesizer instrument with dynamic frequency modulation and variable time and amplitude scaling.

```
2705.orc   ←   asig      adsyn      1, 1, 1, "glass_1.het"
2706.orc   ←   asig      adsyn      1, 1, 1, "glass_2.het"
2707.orc   ←   asig      adsyn      1, 1, 1, "gong1_1.het"
2708.orc   ←   asig      adsyn      1, 1, 1, "gong1_2.het"
```

Figure 27.6 Settings for the resynthesis of nonharmonic timbres breaking glass and cymbal crash.

For the fourth example, then, the static initial value for frequency modification—*ifmod,* is replaced by a control signal as shown in figure 27.5.

The next set of examples show the additive-resynthesis of nonharmonic sounds. The *glass.aif* and *gong1.aif* soundfiles were analyzed with the **hetro** program with the same set of flags as the *a3.aif* sound file (see figure 27.2). As a result, the files *glass_1.het, glass_2.het, gong1_1.het* and *gong1_2.het* were created. Then these files were used to resynthesize the sounds with no modification of amplitude, frequency or speed as shown in figure 27.6.

During the analysis of the sounds of broken glass and gong, there is a significant loss of spectral data. This is because of the settings which limited the number of harmonics to 50, and because of the nonharmonic character of the source files. In case of the broken glass, the tone color of the resynthesized sound is quite different, but, in my opinion, musically attractive.

In the case of the resynthesized gong, another interesting effect appears. Since the control signals of the "harmonic" frequencies created during the analysis move significantly, the resynthesized sound, which is not at all similar to the source, acquires a unique "trembling" character.

Linear Prediction Coding

The method of linear prediction coding (LPC) has been employed a great deal in the signal processing of speech. In principle, this analysis-resynthesis method attempts to approximate a single sample of a signal as a linear combination of previous samples:

$$x(n) \approx \sum_{j=1}^{N} h_j x(n - j) \qquad (27.3)$$

where weights h_j are linear-predictor coefficients.

Based on a speech model, linear prediction allows one to separate the frequency of excitation and the characteristics of the signal spectrum. In the case of speech, the characteristics of the signal spectrum are determined in large part by the characteristics of the vocal tract, which in LPC is modeled with an allpole filter. A filter pole is a point of resonance (a peak or formant region in the spectrum plot). An allpole filter is a kind of filter with several smooth peaks.

The signal is divided into sections or frames, each of which are defined by the following small and efficient set of parameters:

- The average amplitude of the residual and original sound
- The estimated pitch
- The frame duration
- The value that determines whether a sound is voiced or unvoiced
- The group of prediction coefficients (coefficients for the allpole filter)

These data (per frame) are obtained through a four-step analysis process consisting of:

1. A spectrum analysis—in terms of formants.
2. A pitch analysis.
3. An amplitude analysis.
4. A decision about whether the frame was voiced (pitched) or unvoiced (noisy).

The data derived from this analysis may be used as control information in the LPC resynthesis.

-s<srate>	Sampling rate of the audio input file
-c<channel>	Number of channels
-b<begin>	Beginning time of the audio segment to be analyzed
-d<duration>	Duration of the audio segment to be analyzed
-p<npoles>	Number of filter poles
-h<hopsize>	Number of frames per second (in samples), frame length (default value - 200, maximum 500)
-C<string>	Text for the comments field of the .LPC file header
-P<mincps>	Lower frequency range of pitch tracking
-Q<maxcps>	Higher frequency range of pitch tracking

Figure 27.7 The parameters for Csound's **lpanal** LPC analysis utility.

The Csound Utility Program: LPANAL

As mentioned above, control data required for LPC synthesis may be derived from the analysis of natural sounds. For this purpose, the **lpanal** utility program performs LPC and pitch-tracking analysis. The input signal is decomposed into frames, and for each frame a set of information required for the LPC resynthesis is derived. As is the case with the **hetro** analysis utility program, the course of the analysis is determined by the values of a set of command-line flags or menu and "launcher" dialog options as shown in figure 27.7.

It should be noted that the "hopsize", (*-h*), should always be greater than *5*npoles* (*-p*). If not, the filter may be unstable because the precision of the calculation for the filter poles may be too small.

For each frame, the parameters derived from the analysis are averaged. Because the frame length is from 400 to 1000 samples, this averaging may cause a considerable modification of the sound during resynthesis, especially if the source file is changing rapidly.

The **lpanal** program creates a file in a specific format, which contains the results of the LPC and pitch-tracking analysis for use by the LPC family of opcodes. The output file is comprised of an identifiable header plus a set of frames of floating point analysis data. Each frame contains four values of pitch and gain information, followed by *npoles* filter coefficients.

Resynthesis with Csound

The Csound opcodes that perform LPC resynthesis are the **lpread** and **lpreson** opcodes. The **lpread/lpreson** pair are defined as follows:

```
krmsr, krmso, kerr, kcps lpread  ktimpnt, ifilcod[, inpoles[, ifrmate]]
ar                       lpreson asig
```

The reading opcode **lpread** creates four control signals based on the file containing the results of the LPC analysis. These output control signals correspond with the root-mean-square of the residual and original signals (*krmsr* and *krmso*), the normalized error signal (*kerr*) and the pitch (*kcps*). In addition to the name of the file with the LPC analysis results (created by the **lpanal** utility program), **lpread** requires one additional input parameter, a control signal *ktimpnt* (in seconds). This parameter enables time expansion and compression of the resynthesized sound. If it is a linear signal with values from zero to the value of the source file duration, there is no change of duration after resynthesis.

If the LPC analysis file (with the results of the analysis), has no header, two more parameters are required. They must specify the number of filter poles and the frame rate of the analysis.

The **lpreson** opcode then uses the control files, generated by **lpread** to resynthesize the sound. This opcode has one input parameter, an audio signal. For speech synthesis, this audio signal is typically white noise for the "unvoiced phonemes," and a pulse-train for the "voiced phonemes." An evaluation of whether the sound is voiced or unvoiced may be obtained by evaluating the error signal. A value of the error signal of about 0.3 or higher, usually indicates an unvoiced signal. There is also a second form of the **lpreson** opcode in Csound called **lpfreson,** which is a formant-shifted version of **lpreson**.

It should be noted that the input signal for the **lpreson** opcode need not only be noise or a pulse-train. In fact, it can be any audio signal. Given this fact, we can perform a type of cross-synthesis with the LPC method. For now, let us return to the *a3.aif* soundfile and analyze it with **lpanal** using the settings shown in figure 27.8.

flag -p (num poles)	flag -h (hopsize)	flag -P (lowest freq)	flag -Q (highest freq)	LPC file name
50	400	100	2000	a3_1.lpc
40	200	100	2000	a3_2.lpc

Figure 27.8 Two sets of **lpanal** parameters for the analysis of the source file *a3.aif.*

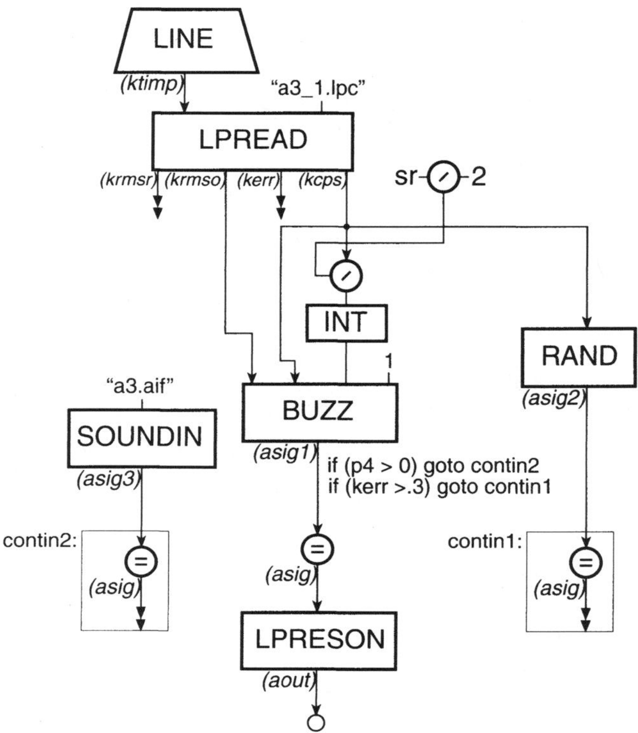

Figure 27.9 Block diagram of *instr 2709,* an LPC speech synthesizer that switches source files between noise, pulse-train and original signal based on a combination of score parameters and the "error" signal analysis from *kerr.*

Figure 27.9 is a block diagram of an LPC speech resynthesizer. This instrument, shown in figure 27.10, offers three different excitation signals: noise, pulse-train, or the original source signal. Which signal is chosen depends on the *iresa3* value (determined by the score) and the error signal (determined by the character of the signal—voiced or unvoiced). In this example, the parameters of the **rand** and **buzz** opcodes are set by control signals passed from the **lpread** opcode. Of course this is only an example and these parameters may be any other signals, but I think it is interesting to join them with the LPC analysis results.

The Csound LPC resynthesis of the *a3.aif* sound was performed with three versions of the **lpreson** input signal (excitation signal): noise, pulse-train and the original sound. There is no modification of the sound duration. After resynthesis, the soundfiles shown in figure 27.11 were obtained. Clearly, the tone color of the sounds after resynthesis has an artificial character, but there is no problem with speech rec-

```
                instr     2709        ; LPC SPEECH RESYNTHESIZER
iosdur          =         p3
iresa3          =         p4
ktimp           line      0, iosdur, .27
krmsr, krmso,   lpread    ktimp, "a3_1.lpc"
kerr, kcps
asig1           buzz      krmso, kcps, int(sr/2/kcps), 1
asig2           rand      kcps
asig3           soundin   "a3.aif"
      if (iresa3 > 0) goto contin2
      if (kerr > .3)  goto contin1
asig            =         asig1
                goto      contin
contin1:
asig            =         asig2
                goto      contin
contin2:
asig            =         asig3
contin:
aout            lpreson   asig
                out       aout
                endin
```

Figure 27.10 Orchestra code for *instr 2709,* an LPC speech resynthesizer that switches the excitation source (asig) based on the "error" signal or p4.

```
2709.orc     ←     a3_1.lpc, asig = asig1 (buzz)
2710.orc     ←     a3_1.lpc, asig = asig2 (rand)
2711.orc     ←     a3_1.lpc, asig = asig3 (soundin)
2712.orc     ←     a3_2.lpc, asig = asig1 (buzz)
```

Figure 27.11 Setting for the initial examples of LPC resynthesis using different source and analysis files for comparison.

ognition. The voice in the *2712.orc* example seems to be a little hoarse. This is because of the particular set of flags used for the analysis, mainly the long frame, and may, in fact, be a desirable effect (see figure 27.8).

In *instr 2709* we can change the duration during resynthesis. Modification of the duration is associated with the value of the *iosdur* parameter. This effect is presented by the three examples shown in figure 27.12 (all of them use the *a3_1.lpc* analysis file and *asig = asig1*).

The first sound is ten times longer than the original, the second sound is two times shorter, and the last sound is two times longer than the original. In this set of examples, a "funny" effect of pitch modulation appears, especially in the longest sound. This effect appears because of the particular **buzz** opcode parameters (*int(sr/2/kcps)*) determining the total number of harmonics requested.

```
2713.orc    ←    iosdur = 2.7
2714.orc    ←    iosdur = .12
2715.orc    ←    iosdur = .55
```

Figure 27.12 Settings for three time-scaled LPC resynthesis examples.

```
2716.orc    ←    asig = asig1    ; glass_1.lpc
2717.orc    ←    asig = asig2    ; glass_1.lpc
2718.orc    ←    asig = asig3    ; glass_1.lpc
2719.orc    ←    asig = asig1    ; gong1_1.lpc
2720.orc    ←    asig = asig2    ; gong1_1.lpc
2721.orc    ←    asig = asig3    ; gong1_1.lpc
```

Figure 27.13 Setting for LPC resynthesis of *gong1.aif* and *glass.aif.*

Next, the sounds of a gong and breaking glass were analyzed with the **lpanal** utility, using the first set of flags from figure 27.8, and the resulting LPC analysis files were named *glass_1.lpc* and *gong1_1.lpc*. The resynthesis was realized with the same three excitation signal options (pulse, noise, source), as employed by **lpreson** for the generation of the *a3.aif* examples above. But the effects of the resynthesis in these cases are quite different. After resynthesis the sound files shown in figure 27.13 were obtained. The resynthesis of these files are not at all similar to the original sounds. In some ways it is difficult to associate them with their sources. Since both the amplitude and spectrum of the original sounds change quickly, some of the information is lost because of the averaging performed by the analysis.

We must remember that the LPC synthesis method is clearly modeled on the synthesis of speech and it imitates the natural way speech originates. The model used for LPC has two components: the input to the filter (the signal of excitation associated with the vocal chords) and the filter shape (the vocal tract), which influences the excitation signal. But quite obviously, the physics and acoustical properties of sounds such as the gong and the breaking glass are quite different than speech. The LPC speech model doesn't fit them at all. The way that the sound of a gong comes into existence is quite different from the way that speech does. Therefore, the LPC method is not suitable for "accurate" resynthesis of sounds like these. But in my opinion, analyzing nonspeech sounds with **lpanal** and resynthesizing them with **lpread/lpreson** is an excellent way to obtain interesting and extraordinary effects. From a musical point of view, I think that the resythesized sounds of the gong and the breaking glass are puzzling, uniquely curious and make for some delicious ear-candy!

Using LPREAD Data to Control Other Csound Opcodes

The **lpread** opcode is an especially useful one. It creates four control signals, which may be used to modify ANY control parameter of any sound we design with Csound. What is more, these control signals are usually derived from natural sounds, so they are usually nonperiodic and have a wonderfully complex nature. Let us examine several examples that show how the **lpread** control signals can be used to modify the sound of plucked strings. For this purpose we have designed an "lpread mapper" instrument (see figures 27.14 and 27.15) that uses a p-field to select from one of four control methods.

The dynamic "controls" for these "acoustically mapped" plucked strings came from the *gong1.aif* file. It was analyzed with **lpanal** using the first set of parameters from figure 27.8. In the case of "method 1" (*2722.orc*), the pitch tracking signal of *gong1_1.lpc* file was used as the frequency control of the string sound. In the case of "method 2" (*2723.orc),* the amplitude of the pluck was controlled by the rms of the original signal. In the case of "method 3" (*2724.orc*), we use a combination of the two methods mentioned above. Finally, in the case of "method 4" (*2725.orc*), a second string was added whose frequency is controlled by the error signal of the analysis file.

These simple sounds are a small example of the great number of possible ways that the **lpread** control signals may be used as dynamic input parameters of other Csound opcodes.

Cross-Synthesis Examples

Cross-synthesis is a technique that uses the characteristics of one sound to modify the characteristics of another sound, based on the analysis of both. Cross-synthesis may have different forms depending on what analysis/resynthesis method is employed (**lpread/lpreson**, **adsyn**, **pvoc**, **cross**, **fog**, etc.). Figure 27.16 shows a block diagram of a simple LPC-based cross-synthesis instrument. In this example we use the analysis data from the singing voice (*a3_1.lpc*) to control the filtering the sound of breaking glass (*glass.aif*).

It is important to understand the meaning of the *idur1* and *idur2* parameters. The *idur1* parameter determines how long the sound coded in *a3_1.lpc* (of *idur2* duration) should be read. Here these values are coded into the instrument, but you could place them in a p-field and modify them on a note by note basis. Two variations of this instrument are presented: one in which the breaking glass is modified by the

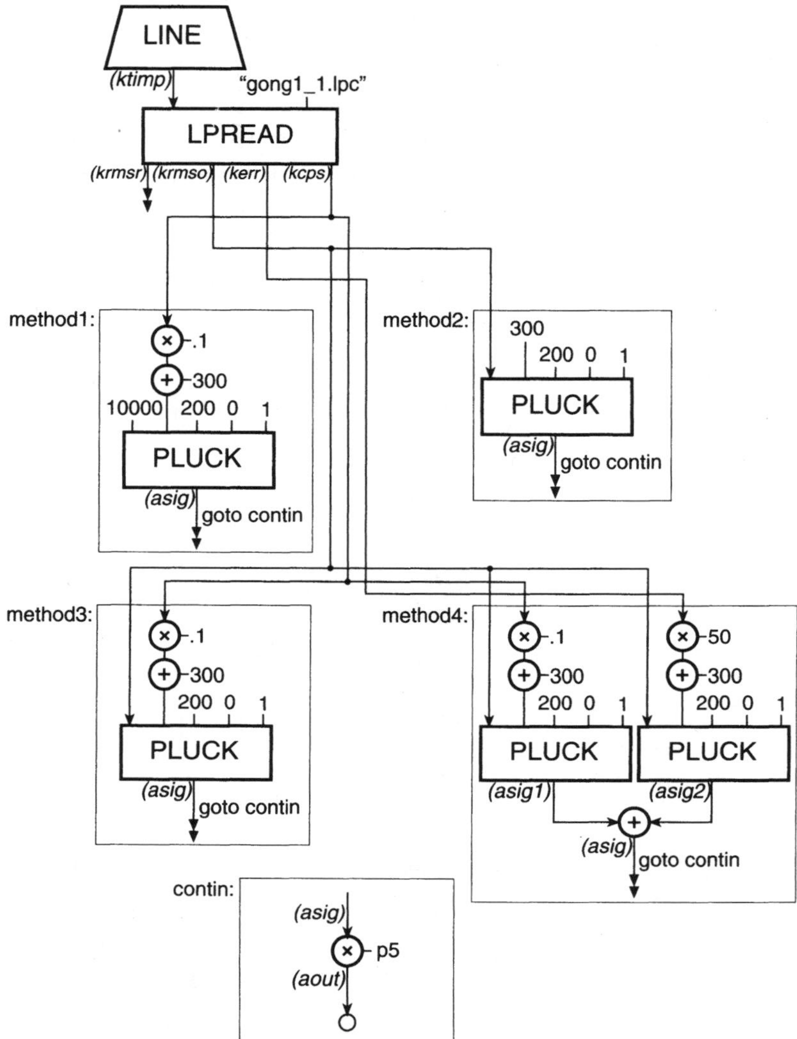

Figure 27.14 Block diagram of *instr 2722,* an instrument that uses p-fields to select a "method" by which the **lpread** control signals will modify the parameters of a synthetic instrument.

```
                  instr       2722          ; LPREAD MAPPER
iosdur            =           p3
imeth             =           p4
ktimpt            line        0, iosdur, iosdur
krmsr, krmso,     lpread      ktimpt, "gong1_1.lpc"
kerr, kcps
      if (imeth == 1) goto method1
      if (imeth == 2) goto method2
      if (imeth == 3) goto method3
      if (imeth == 4) goto method4
method1:
asig              pluck       10000, 300+.1*kcps, 200, 0, 1
                  goto        contin
method2:
asig              pluck       krmso, 300, 200, 0, 1
                  goto        contin
method3:
asig              pluck       krmso, 300+.1*kcps, 200, 0, 1
                  goto        contin
method4:
asig1             pluck       krmso, 300+.1*kcps, 200, 0, 1
asig2             pluck       krmso, 300+50*kerr, 200, 0, 1
asig              =           asig1+asig2
contin:
aout              =           asig*p5
                  out         aout
                  endin
```

Figure 27.15 Orchestra code for *instr 2722,* an instrument that uses the lpread opcode as a way to incorporate complex "natural" control signals into a synthetic instrument.

singing voice (*2726.orc*) and the other where the singing voice is filtered by the analysis data from the breaking glass (*2727.orc*).

Since this chapter is about both additive and LPC resynthesis, let's build two final instruments that will unite both methods. Figure 27.18 shows a block diagram of this cross-synthesis model.

The **lpread** output control signals may be used as the input parameters of the additive resynthesis (to modify the amplitude, pitch or speed). These examples show how the singing voice (*a3.aif*) and the breaking glass (*glass.aif*) may influence each other (see figure 27.19). In the first case (*2728.orc*), the amplitude and frequency of the singing voice (*a3_1.het)* were modified during additive resynthesis by two control signals, derived from the **lpread** of the breaking glass (*glass.lpc).* In the next example (*2729.orc*), the controlling and resynthesizing roles were reversed.

If we compare the cross-synthesis in *instr 2728,* where LPC and additive methods are united (see figure 27.19), with the cross-synthesis in *instr 2726,* where only LPC

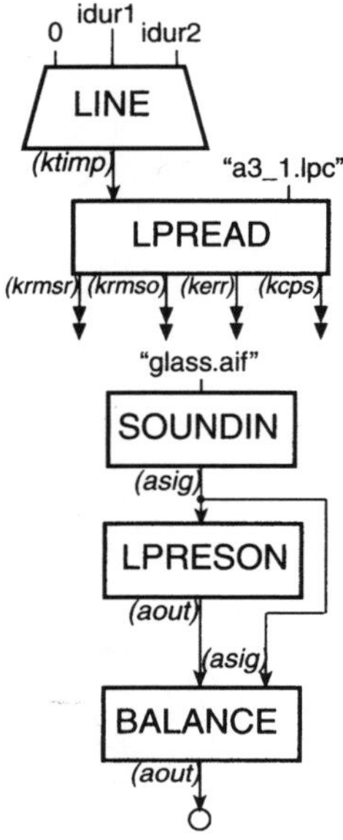

Figure 27.16 Block diagram of *instr 2726,* an LPC-based cross-synthesizer.

```
                instr     2726          ; LPC CROSS-SYNTHESIZER
idur1           =         2.12
idur2           =         .27
ktimp           line      0, idur1, idur2
krmsr, krmso,   lpread    ktimp, "a3_1.lpc"
kerr, kcps
asig            soundin   "glass.aif"
aout            lpreson   asig
aout            balance   aout, asig
                out       aout
                endin
```

Figure 27.17 Orchestra code for *instr 2726,* an LPC-based cross-synthesizer.

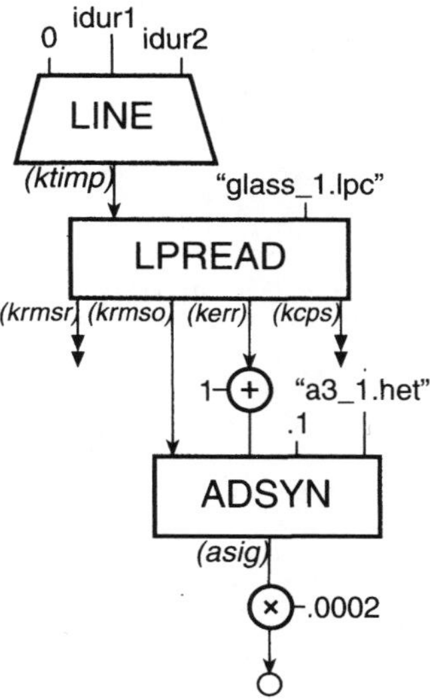

Figure 27.18 Block diagram of *instr 2728,* an instrument combining the **lpread** and **adsyn** opcodes.

```
                instr   2728    ; LPC-ADDITIVE CROSS-SYNTHESIZER
idur1           =       2.7
idur2           =       2.12
ktimp           line    0, idur1, idur2
krmsr, krmso,   lpread  ktimp, "glass_1.lpc"
kerr, kcps
asig            adsyn   krmso, 1+kerr, .1, "a3_1.het"
                out     asig*.0002
                endin
```

Figure 27.19 Orchestra code for *instr 2728,* a combination of an LPC and additive cross-synthesizer.

```
                instr   2730        ; LPC-ADDITIVE FREEZE-FRAME
krmsr,  krmso,  lpread  .3, "glass_1.lpc"
kerr, kcps
asig            adsyn   krmso*.001, 1+kerr, 1, "glass_1.het"
                out     asig
                endin
```

Figure 27.20 Orchestra code for *instr 2730,* a combination of an LPC and additive cross-synthesizer that "freezes" the control spectrum on a single analysis "frame."

was employed (see figure 27.17), we should notice that in *instr 2726,* a change in the shape of the spectrum occurs, whereas in the case of *instr 2728* only modification of amplitude or frequency of the sound are possible.

For our final combined LPC-Additive cross-synthesis instrument (see figure 27.20) the linear input signal of the **lpread** opcode was replaced by a constant value (one point of time). This causes the **lpread** output to be a constant value too because the control signals are read from that particular point in the LPC file. In essence, we "freeze" the control data at that particular "frame" of analysis. In this case also, the input files for the **adsyn** and **lpread** opcodes contain the analysis results of the same file. This algorithm was used to process the breaking glass (*2730.orc*) and the gong (*2731.orc*) and it resulted in two interesting sound effects.

Conclusion

Additive and LPC synthesis are powerful sound design tools. The intermediate analysis stage provides us with important and useful information about the inner structure of the sound we are analyzing. Given this description, we have the possibility to creatively modify and alter the structure of any sound by replacing analysis data from one instrument with analysis data from another. Upon resynthesis we may obtain many wonderful effects that can be extremely useful from a compositional and musical point of view. These analysis/resynthesis methods allow us, for instance, to modify the sound of orchestral instruments creating new hybrid tone colors that are impossible to get from an acoustical instrument. Modification of the tone color of natural sounds is, in my opinion, a great motivation for employing the computer in a composer's work.

We have seen also, that the analysis data may be used, not only to resynthesize and cross-synthesize sounds, but to control parameters of computer generated sounds adding a "natural" level of complexity and bringing the synthetic and acoustic sound worlds closer together.other sounds generated with the computer. It may be used, for instance, to add a natural level of complexity and bringing the synthetic and acoustic sound worlds closer together.

Linear Prediction Coding and Additive Resynthesis are just two examples of the many ways that Csound can be used to make new sounds. The sound design and compositional possibilities of these ways of working can offer the imaginative composer a rich and inspiring area in which to explore, cultivate and harvest.

References

Basztura, C. 1988. *Zrodla, sygnaly i obrazy akustyczne.* Warsaw: WKL.

Jayant, N. S., and P. Noll. 1984. *Digital Coding of Waveforms.* Englewood Cliffs, N.J.: Prentice-Hall.

Kleczkowski, P. 1985. "*The Methods of Digital Sound Synthesis. The Systematic Outline.*" Conference of Mathematics. OSA–85.

Roads, C. 1996. *The Computer Music Tutorial.* Cambridge, Mass.: MIT Press.

Vercoe, B. 1995. *Csound: A Manual for the Audio Processing System and Supporting Programs with Tutorials.* Cambridge, Mass.: MIT Press.

28 Csound's Phase Vocoder and Extensions

Richard Karpen

Phase Vocoder technology, based on Short-Time Fourier Transform (STFT) algorithms, has provided one of the primary methods for "analysis-based-synthesis" in computer music. The term *analysis-based-synthesis* refers to techniques that first derive data describing the time varying *spectra* of an audio signal and then use these data to produce synthetic versions of the original sounds and to produce new sounds based upon the data. The most basic and common use of these techniques is for resynthesizing the original sounds while performing independent time and frequency scaling. For example, one can change the time scale of a sound without effecting the pitch and vice versa. A sound can be stretched in time while its pitch becomes higher.

The data from the analysis process can be used in other ways as well. The technique known as *cross-synthesis* consists of methods for combining aspects of two or more signals, by using more than one set of analysis data in combination. This technique can provide quite powerful ways to create interesting new sounds or even "sound illusions." For example, it is possible to combine recorded speech with another complex sound such that the second sound, while retaining much of its original quality, will speak. More complex and abstract sound hybrids can also be created using these and other related techniques.

This chapter will discuss some of the basics of the phase vocoder as it has been implemented in the Csound opcode **pvoc** as well as some new unit generators that extend the techniques of processing and synthesizing sound using the data from the **pvanal** utility program. The underlying programs that contribute to make **pvanal**, **pvoc** and the new opcodes **pvread**, **vpvoc**, **pvinterp**, and **pvcross** are quite complex and the processes can take an engineer's knowledge to understand completely. The purpose of the present discussion, however, is to provide a user's view, rather than a deeply technical description of the phase vocoder. From this nontechnical vantage point, the phase vocoder is actually one of the easiest computer music techniques to use that can nevertheless yield complex results. Some knowledge of how it all works is helpful, of course, and certain of these details will be discussed in order to shed light on how to use this family of unit generators most effectively.

Phase Vocoder Analysis: PVANAL

The phase vocoder process begins with the analysis of a digital audio signal. Csound has several utility programs that operate with the *-U* option in the Csound command-line. The **pvanal** utility, based upon the Short-Time Fourier Transform (STFT) for the analysis of digital audio signals, is one of those programs. It is executed by the following command-line:

```
csound -U pvanal input_soundfile output_pvocfile
```

where the *input_soundfile* will be the name of the digital audio file that is going to be analyzed and *output_pvocfile* will be the user given name of the phase vocoder data file that will be created by running this utility program. The **pvanal** utility also has a number of optional arguments that can help you *tune* the analysis process. The specific qualities of the *input_soundfile* will sometimes determine how these other arguments are used. Before going into the details of using **pvanal**, a general discussion of how the STFT works on an audio signal and what is in the data that it produces will help in gaining an understanding of how to use this utility.

Jean Baptiste Joseph Fourier (1768–1830) was a mathematician who theorized that any function can be decomposed into a sum of simple harmonic motion (sine waves, for example). The basic premise of Fourier's theory, as applied to sound, is that complex sound waves can be broken down into a collection of pure, sinusoidal components and that by adding these sinusoids together again one can recreate the original sound.

This theory has been put into practice in the phase vocoder and, in general, our ears can accept that it does indeed work for many sounds. In digital signal processing, the Fast Fourier Transform (FFT) is used to *break down* a digital audio signal and produce data that contain the frequencies and amplitudes of a collection of sinusoidal components. By recombining these sinusoids using these data, the audio signal can be reconstructed synthetically. To understand what is happening in this reconstruction it might be useful to think of this process as similar to the way that sine-tone oscillators, with different frequency and amplitude settings, can be combined in *additive synthesis* to create complex sounds.

In order to find the frequencies of the components of a periodic signal and their amplitudes, the FFT operates on segments of the digital sound samples. Each segment has an envelope applied to it, a process called *windowing*. The length of the windowed segment of sound samples is called the *window-size*. In Csound, the window size can be left to a default value in the **pvanal** program, or it can be set according to certain characteristics of the sound being analyzed.

An analogy can be drawn between moving film or video and the segmented FFT process. Movies and video consist of "frames" of individual still pictures that, when played back at a fast enough rate, resolve into what appears to be continuous motion. In the phase vocoder, the FFT is used to take "snap-shots" of the sound and produce frames of data that, when played back, will sound like continuously time-varying sound. The FFT takes these snap-shots and transforms them from time-domain signals into data containing the *average values* for the frequencies and amplitudes of individual sinusoidal components, for the time covered by the window of samples. The FFT analysis of a succession of windowed segments of sound samples produces a series of time-ordered *frames* in a process sometimes referred to as the Short Time Fourier Transform (STFT).

A key to the understanding of how to use the analysis program is to understand the relationship between the window-size and the accurate rendering of the frequency and amplitude values of the spectral components on the one hand and the time-varying qualities of the sound on the other. The general rule of thumb is: *the larger the window-size, the more accurate the frequency data* will tend to be and *the smaller the window-size, the more accurate the time-varying aspects* will be.

A compromise must be found that gives the best possible frequency analysis while capturing, on a frame-by-frame basis, as much of the variation over time in the sound as possible. If the frequency components in each successive window of sound are rather stable, (that is, significant changes are happening at a rate slower than the size of the window), then the variation of the signal over time will be fairly accurately represented by the changes in the values returned by the succession of analyses. But if the window is too large and covers a selection of sound that has significant change, the data will not contain an accurate rendering of this variation in time, since the values in the analysis data are averaged over the entire window.

Remember *that only one value for frequency per spectral component is returned for each window* of sound. So, again, the shorter the window size, the more data frames there will be per second of sound and therefore, the more the process will capture the moment-to-moment changes in the sound. The size of the window, on the other hand, also determines the resolution in the frequency domain and a larger window size will produce data with more individual components and will track their frequencies more accurately.

There is a direct relationship between the size of the window and the number of components derived through the analysis, which is also useful to understand. The

FRAME	**1**	**2**	**3...**
bin1	freqval1 ampval1	freqval2 ampval2	freqval3... ampval3...
bin2	freqval1 ampval1	freqval2 ampval2	freqval3... ampval3...
.			
.			
bin512	freqval1 ampval1	freqval2 ampval2	freqval3... ampval3...

Figure 28.1 Table showing 512 bins of frequency and amplitude channel data per **pvoc** analysis frame.

data in each frame returned by the analysis are separated into *bins*. Each *bin* contains frequency and amplitude values, which may change on a frame by frame basis and can be charted as shown in figure 28.1.

The FFT process actually returns *windowsize* bins of frequency and amplitude, but only half that number will be stored as data and used in the resynthesis process. The window sizes are always powers-of-two in the **pvanal** program, so, for example, a window size of 1024 will return 1024 bins, 512 of which will be used. You can think of these bins as narrow-band filters that are spaced evenly between 0 Hz and the sampling-rate. Only half of the bins are used since only frequencies less than *sr/2* can be used in synthesis.

The bandwidths of the bins overlap slightly, but each bin can only track frequencies that occur within its range. It is important therefore to choose window sizes that produce enough bins to provide as dense a coverage of frequency as needed by particular sounds. A sound with harmonics spaced 100Hz apart, for example, will require the bins to be no more than 100Hz apart. Therefore, at a sampling rate of 44100, it will require a window size of at least 441 (or the length of one period of a 100Hz signal). Since the window size must be power-of-two, the smallest window in this case would be 512.

In practice though, it is better to have windows that are at least two, if not four, times the size of the longest period. Therefore, in the case above, a good choice for the window size would be 1024 or 2048. Once again, we are reminded of the fact that by choosing a larger window size we might end up by loosing crucial information that would represent the variation of the signal in time, but these are tradeoffs we always have to make.

To make this compromise between time and frequency more workable, the selection of samples for the STFT are longer than the increment at which the successive selections are taken. For example, if the FFT size is 1024 samples, the first selection would consist of samples 0–1023. The next selection, instead of containing the next 1024 samples (1024–2047) could instead start at sample 256 and contain samples 256–1279, the selection after that would contain 512–1536 and the one after that would contain 768–1023. The size of the increment by which the selection of samples moves through the sound is sometimes called the *hop-size.* In the case described here, the *hop-size* is 256 while the window size is 1024. Each FFT begins 256 samples further into the sound and each FFT contains 1024 samples to do the analysis. This means that we are overlapping the successive FFT analyses in order to gain the best frequency analysis through the use of a larger FFT size, while capturing more of the time-varying quality of the signal by moving forward through the sound by a smaller increment.

There are two ways of specifying the relationship between the window-size and the *hop-size* in the **pvanal** program. One allows you to specify the exact number of samples in the *window-size* and the exact *hop-size.* The following command-line instruction would cause the analysis to be carried out according to the above description. The number after the *-n* is the *window-size,* the number after the *-h* is the *hop-size.*

```
csound -U pvanal -n 1024 -h 256 input_soundfile output_pvocfile
```

The following would do exactly the same thing. Again the number after the *-n* is the *window-size,* but this instruction uses the *-w* option, which determines how many overlapping analysis windows there will be.

```
csound -U pvanal -n 1024 -w 4 input_soundfile output_pvocfile
```

The **pvanal** utility program allows you to specify either the *hop-size* or the *overlap-amount.* You can remember how to use these by memorizing the following:

```
hop-size = window-size/overlap
overlap = window-size/hop-size
```

The **pvanal** program will analyze only mono soundfiles or channel 1 (usually the left channel) of a soundfile (it is possible that the analysis and the resynthesis processes will eventually allow one to work with multiple audio channels, but as of this writing, only one channel of analysis is possible). Finally, the data produced by the **pvanal** program are stored in binary format in a file on your disk. This file can be large; in fact, it can be larger than the soundfile that is being analyzed. So take care where you are creating and storing these data files. The description above should give you the information you will need to begin making sounds using the Csound phase vocoder.

Phase Vocoder Synthesis: PVOC

Once you have run the **pvanal** program as described above, you will be ready to use the data in a Csound instrument to synthesize sound. The basic unit generator for performing phase vocoder resynthesis is **pvoc**. The manual defines **pvoc** as:

```
ar  pvoc  ktimpnt, kfmod, ifilcod, ifn, ibins[, ibinoffset, ibinincr,
          inextractmode, ifreqlim, iqatefn]
```

The argument *ktimpnt,* is an index value of time, in seconds, into the analysis file. If for example, *ktimpnt* = .5, the **pvoc** opcode will select data from the frame that represents the spectrum at .5 seconds into the original sound. Csound knows how to find that frame because it stores information from the analysis process about how many frames there are per second of sound. If the *hop-size* in the analysis were 256 and the sampling rate were 44100, then there would be approximately 172 frames per second and we might call this the *frame rate.* So, *ktimpnt* = .5 would cause **pvoc** to take its values from around the 86th frame.

Actually, the result of *ktimpnt**framerate is often not an integer value. In this case, **pvoc** will interpolate. For example, if *ktimpnt* = .6 and framerate = 172, then the frame number would be 103.2 and **pvoc** will interpolate the appropriate values along the line between the values in frames 103 and 104. By having *ktimpnt* change over time, **pvoc** can use the successive frames in the analysis file. A simple example instrument shown in figure 28.2 below shows the use of the **line** generator to create a changing time-pointer.

The **line** opcode produces a succession of values from 0 to 1 over the duration. If *p3* is 1 and the sound that was analyzed was for example a 1 second long digitized violin sound, then a resynthesis sounding almost exactly like the original can be achieved. If however, *p3* is 2, so that it takes 2 seconds for the line to go from 0 to 1, then by using the output of that **line** as the time-pointer, the resynthesis would be a version of the original that is twice as long and twice as slow as the original. The pitch of the synthetic sound would remain exactly the same as the original. When the passage through the analysis data is slower than the original sound, more interpo-

```
            instr  2801    ; PVOC RESYNTHESIS WITH DYNAMIC TIME SCALING
ifreqscale  =      1
ispecwp     =      0
ktime       line   0, p3, 1
asig        pvoc   ktime, ifreqscale, "violin.pvc", ispecwp
            out    asig
            endin
```

Figure 28.2 Orchestra code for *instr 2801,* a **pvoc** resynthesizer with dynamic time scaling.

```
bin #1      Freqs:    time1, freq1, time2, freq2, time3, freq3...
             Amps:    time1,  amp1, time2,  amp2, time3,  amp3...

bin #2      Freqs:    time1, freq1, time2, freq2, time3, freq3...
             Amps:    time1,  amp1, time2,  amp2, time3,  amp3...
.
.
.
bin #512    Freqs:    time1, freq1, time2, freq2, time3, freq3...
             Amps:    time1,  amp1, time2,  amp2, time3,  amp3...
```

Figure 28.3 Table of analyses data frames illustrated as a series of breakpoint-functions in which each bin contains a frequency and an amplitude envelope.

lation is performed between the data frames. The Csound **pvoc** opcode will always interpolate values at every k-period. So, even if the frame rate is 172, there will always be **kr** new values per second. It might be useful to think about the data as a series of breakpoint functions (see figure 28.3).

In this representation of the data, you can see clearly that for each bin there is a frequency envelope and an amplitude envelope, where the time values are the *x*-axes and the frequency or amplitude values are the *y*-axes. For some of the extended phase vocoder unit generators, this representation will be useful to return to for reference.

The time-pointer can be derived from any number of Csound unit generators and your own musical and programming imagination. Nor does the time-pointer have to progress in chronological order through the entire length of the **pvoc** file. It can start anywhere between the beginning and the end and it can go forward or backward. You can use linearly or exponentially changing values, a series of line segments, curves, or any shape that you can load into a function table (f-table). You can even use random numbers to access the data. Below are a few examples of some of the ways to create time-pointers. It's worth noting that these can be used in other Csound opcodes (**lpread**, **sndwarp**, **table**) that use indices into data, sound, or f-tables.

To read backward through a sound at a constant speed determined by the length of the note:

```
ibeg    =       0
iend    =       p4                ;p4 = duration of input_sound
ktime   line    iend, p3, ibeg    ;values go from end to beginning
```

To read through the data exponentially from the middle of the data to the end:

```
ktime   expon   (iend*.5), p3, iend
```

To read forward through the data at varying speeds, where the last time-point is specified in the score:

```
iend    =       p4
ktime   linseg  0, .1, .1, p3-.2, iend-.1, .1, iend
```

The above example shows how you can use the time-pointer to preserve the timescale of parts of the sound, in this case the attack portion and the end and alter the timescale of other parts of the sound.

When determining the type of sound, the attack portion can be one of the most important cues to our ears. The attacks of many sounds tend to be around the same length, no matter how long the sound is sustained over time. Sometimes, stretching or compressing the attack portion of a sound using **pvoc** can reveal wonderful new sounds. But sometimes you might want to preserve the timescale of the attack or of any other part of the sound and using the time-pointer with multiple line segments or curves can allow you to move through the sound with extremely fine resolution in time. Try making a time-pointer that stretches the attack of a sound by a large factor but then moves through the rest of the sound at the original speed. In some sounds this can be quite an interesting effect.

At this point it is appropriate to discuss the effects of time-scaling upon the spectra of the sound. Remember that the FFT analysis breaks down the original sound into a representation of frequencies and amplitudes and that the resynthesis process can be thought of as an additive synthesis version of the sound, using the frequencies and amplitudes as settings for the collection of sine tones. Therefore, as you might expect, the phase vocoder analysis/synthesis process works best with sounds that have periodic and harmonically related components.

You will notice, however, that if you analyze a sound that has unpitched parts, such as the consonants in speech, that **pvoc** can do well at synthesizing those sounds under certain circumstances. Since the resynthesis process does not include any noise element, even the consonants must be synthesized with sinusoids. This can be achieved because, in the noisy portions of the sound, the frequency data in each bin will change chaotically from one frame to the next and if the window is large enough, the frequency data will be dense enough to create a noisy signal. But the resynthesis of the noisy part of the signal will not be as successful as you stretch the time-scale by greater and greater amounts. Then, what you will hear are the sinusoids gliding up and down over time, creating a dense inharmonic mess. You might be attracted to this sound at first, but you should also be aware that it has become somewhat cliché and it is immediately recognizable as a phase vocoder trying to synthesize noise while significantly stretching the time-scale.

Sounds that have noise that you want to preserve and sounds that have attacks or particular attributes that need to be synthesized at their original time scale, may require using a time-pointer such as the one above using a **linseg**. Used as a time-pointer into a **pvoc** file, it will preserve the original speed of the first and last .1

seconds of the sound, but expand the length of time during the rest of the sound. In some cases you may need to have functions with many breakpoints, if the sound has many attacks and inharmonic or noisy segments. Speech and singing, for example, can be well synthesized using the phase vocoder with carefully worked out time-pointers that preserve the synthesis speed of the consonants.

Finally, before going onto some of the extended techniques and unit generators based on the Csound phase vocoder, a few words about the other **pvoc** arguments are in order. The *kfmod* argument is simply a frequency scalar on the entire spectrum of the analysis:

```
ifmod     =       1             ; NO CHANGE IN PITCH:
ifmod     =       2             ; PITCH TRANSPOSED UP ONE OCTAVE:
ifmod     =       .5            ; PITCH TRANSPOSED DOWN ONE OCTAVE:
kfreq     line    .5, p3, 2     ; TIME-VARYING PITCH CHANGE
```

As with the time-pointer, the pitch envelope can be as simple or complex as you would like, using any of the many ways to create constant or time-varying values in Csound.

The initialization argument, *ispecwp,* can be used when pitch transpositions are being made to try to preserve the spectral envelope of the original. When you shift the pitch up or down by a significant amount, you are also shifting the entire spectrum up or down. Sounds that rely upon fixed formant areas in their spectra will not retain their unique quality of sound that the formants provide. By setting *ispecwp* to a non-zero value, **pvoc** will attempt to generalize the spectral envelope and rescale the amplitudes across the frequency range to maintain the spectra even when the frequencies of all of the components are being shifted. This effect can be heard clearly on resynthesized speech.

```
ifmod     =       2
ispecwp   =       1                          ; JUST NEEDS TO BE NONZERO
asig      pvoc    ktime, ifmod, "hellorcb.pvc", ispecwp
```

Vocoder Extensions

The use of **pvoc**, as you have seen, is quite straight forward with two basic transformations of the original sound that can be achieved—time and pitch scaling. The data produced by the **pvanal** program lend themselves to a variety of other kinds of processing however and new unit generators have been created to extend the function of the basic Phase Vocoder. These will be discussed below and some examples will be shown to give you some ideas of how to use these opcodes.

PVREAD

The **pvread** opcode is a unit generator that reads from a data file produced by **pvanal** and returns the frequency and amplitude values from a single analysis bin. It is defined in the manual as:

```
kfr, kap    pvread    ktime, ifile, ibin
```

The arguments *ktime* and *ifile* are used exactly as in **pvoc**, but **pvread**, does not perform any synthesis using the data. Recall in figure 28.2 above seeing the bins as time functions with frequency and amplitude values. The **pvread** opcode returns the time-varying values for one bin as specified in the *ibin* argument. These values can be used to synthesize single components, or to create your own additive synthesis instrument using several or many **pvread** opcodes.

In a composition of my own, I analyzed a section of a *Pibroch,* a centuries old Scottish classical bagpipe form. This is quite slow moving music with sudden leaps of pitch, sometimes by an octave or more. These leaps of pitch are present throughout the spectra, of course, since the fundamental changes as do all of the related components. I used **pvread** to take the frequency and amplitude data from two high bins. I transposed the frequencies down to the mid-range and used the values to control the frequency and amplitude of two sine tones in resynthesis. Since the frequencies and amplitudes of each bin change slightly from frame to frame, the effect was an eerie mixture of the expressionlessness of a pure sinusoid with subtle changes in the frame by frame data and sudden shifts of pitch as occurred in the original bagpipe recording (see figures 28.4 and 28.5).

You can use your imagination to find interesting ways using this opcode. The example shown in figures 28.6 and 28.7 illustrate an orchestra and score that uses **pvread** to access one bin of analysis data at a time and to fade in successive components gradually. Added to this is the use of frequency modulation in which, at the beginning, the index of modulation is large enough to produce a significant number of sidebands but later, the index decreases until only sine tones will be produced. Both the time-pointer and the FM index are controlled by global variables in a separate instrument, so that all the notes, no matter when they begin, will have the same values for time and FM index. This is one way to synchronize values between different notes and instruments in Csound.

In this example (see figure 28.7), the sound will begin with single FM sounds at the frequencies and amplitudes of the bins being read by **pvread**. By the end, when many notes are sounding together, the FM index is too small to produce sidebands and there will be a collection of sine tones, each with frequency and amplitude data from a different bin. After 45 seconds the sound should be much like the original

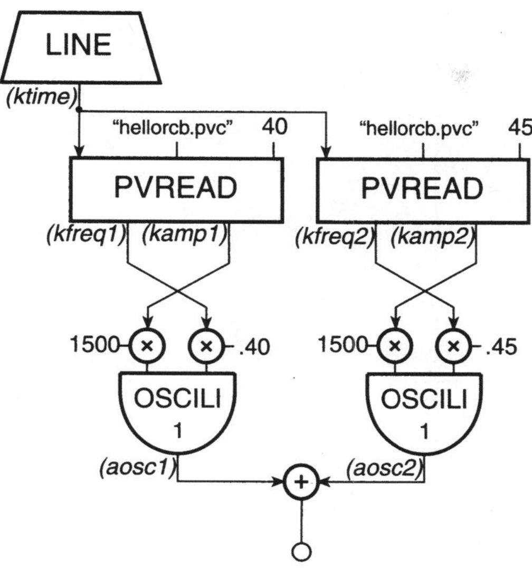

Figure 28.4 Block diagram of *instr 2810,* an instrument that uses **pvread** to generate control functions for the frequency and amplitude arguments of a pair of oscillators.

```
                instr   2810             ; PVREAD: ADDITIVE SYNTHESIS
iend            =       p4
ktime           line    0, p3, iend
kfreq1, kamp1   pvread  ktime, "bagpipe.pvc", 40
kfreq2, kamp2   pvread  ktime, "bagpipe.pvc", 45
aosc1           oscili  kamp1*1500, kfreq1*.40, 1   ; f 1 IS A SINE
aosc2           oscili  kamp2*1500, kfreq2*.45, 1
                out     aosc1+aosc2
                endin
```

Figure 28.5 Orchestra code for *instr 2810,* a **pvread** controlled additive synthesis instrument.

one on which the analysis was based. Here you can see me adding new notes reading from different bins, whenever, and in whichever order seems interesting. Of course, this can be done much more easily if you are using some kind of higher level programming language to produce your score files.

VPVOC, TABLESEG, TABLEXSEG

The **vpvoc** opcode is identical to **pvoc** except that it takes the result of a previous **tableseg** or **tablexseg** and uses the resulting function table, passed internally to the

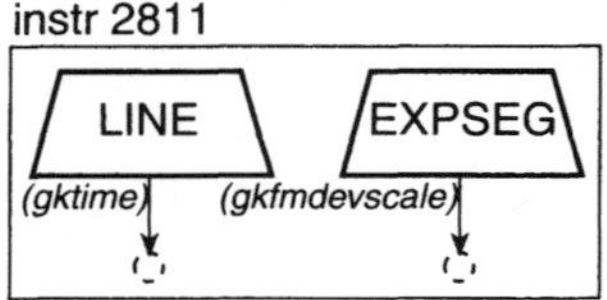

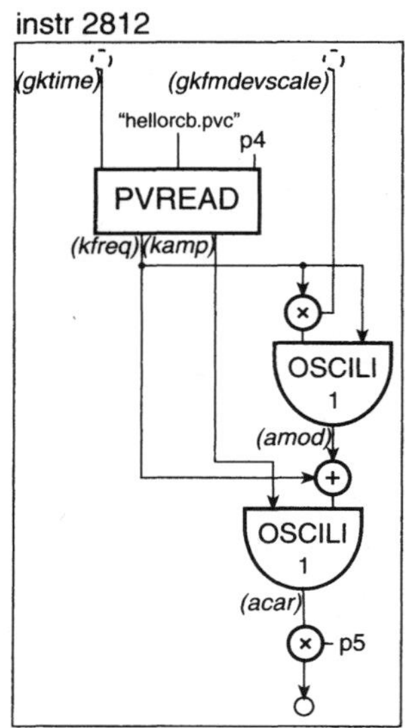

Figure 28.6 Block diagram of *instr 2811* and *2812*, a global control instrument (*2811*) and a **pvread** controlled FM synthesizer (*2812*).

```
                instr   2811            ; GLOBAL TIME POINTER
iend            =       p4                          ; CONTAINS A GLOBAL TIME
gktime          line    0, p3, iend                 ; ...POINTER AND FM INDEX
gkfmdevscale    expon   5, p3*.5, 5, p3*.5, .001 ; ... THAT WILL BE APPLIED
                endin                               ; ...TO ALL OF THE NOTES
                                                    ; ...PRODUCED BY INSTR 2812
                instr   2812 ; GLOBALLY CONTROLLED FM SYNTHESIZER
kfreq, kamp     pvread  gktime, "hellorcb.pvc", p4
amod            oscili  kfreq*gkfmdevscale, kfreq, 1
acar            oscili  kamp, kfreq+amod, 1
                out     acar*p5
                endin

f 1             0       16384           10          1

i 2811          0       25              2.2

i 2812          0       25              8           500
i 2812          1       24              10          300
i 2812          5       20              12          150
i 2812          9       16              14          100
i 2812          13      12              18          100
i 2812          17      8               26          200
i 2812          21      4               43          500
```

Figure 28.7 Orchestra and score code for *instr 2811* and *2812*, featuring a globally controlled FM synthesis instrument, (*instr 2812*), with parameter data from **pvread**.

vpvoc opcode, as an envelope over the magnitudes of the analysis data channels. The result is spectral enveloping. The function size used in the tableseg should be *framesize/2,* where framesize is the number of bins in the phase vocoder analysis file that is being used by the **vpvoc**. Each location in the table will be used to scale a single analysis bin. By using different functions for *ifn1, ifn2,* etc. in the **tableseg**, the spectral envelope becomes a dynamically changing one. For example, take an analysis file with 512 bins (your window size would have been 1024) and you create the f-statement:

```
f 2     0     512   5     1 512 .001                        ; LOWPASS
```

The **vpvoc** opcode can use the successive values stored in this function to scale the amplitudes of the 512 analysis bins. In this case, bin #1 would be scaled by 1 and therefore remain unchanged, bin #2 would be scaled by a value slightly less than one and would therefore be scaled down. This would continue to bin #512, which would be scaled by .001 and would therefore virtually be eliminated from the spectra. The effect would be that of a lowpass filter. The Csound manual defines **vpvoc** as:

```
ar        vpvoc       ktimpnt, kfmod, ifile [, ispecwp]
```

Below are a few more example functions and short descriptions of the effect they would have upon the sound. This function allows frequencies contained in the first 100 bins to be heard, while the rest will have their amplitudes scaled to zero:

```
f 3     0     512      7        1 100 1 1 0 411 0       ; LOWSHELF
```

It acts like a lowpass filter, where the cut-off frequency is a precise demarcation below which all of the signal will be allowed through the filter and above which none of the signal will be heard. This kind of filtering is far more exacting the **reson** filters, which have gradual, curved slopes describing the frequency response. This one creates a bandreject filter centered around bin #256:

```
f 4     0     512   5      .001 256 1 256 .001      ; BANDREJECT
```

An exponential curve is used, making the attenuation closer to that of a simple time-domain bandreject filter.

A bandpass filter effect, with the pass band in the shape of a half-sine and the frequency centered around bin #256, can be achieved by the following:

```
f 5     0     512      9        .5 1 0                  ; BANDPASS
```

The way to use these functions to alter the spectral envelope with **vpvoc** is to use the **tableseg** or **tablexseg** opcodes. These two unit generators are similar in syntax to **linseg** and **expseg**, but instead of interpolating between values over given amounts of time, they interpolate between the values stored in f-tables producing new time-varying functions over time. The **tableseg** opcode does this linearly, while **tablexseg** performs exponential interpolation. They are defined in the manual as:

```
tableseg      ifn1, idur1, ifn2[, idur2, ifn3[, . . .]]
tablexseg     ifn1, idur1, ifn2[, idur2, ifn3[, . . .]]
```

The arguments *ifn1, ifn2, ifn3* and so on, refer to f-table numbers that have been defined in the scorefile. Here *idur1, idur2* and so on, are the amounts of time over which the values of one table are interpolated until they become the values of the next table. To give you an idea of how they work, consider the following simple example:

```
        ktableseg      2, p3, 3
```

Where the functions 2 and 3 are:

```
f 2    0    512    7    1 512 1
f 3    0    512    7    0 512 0
```

The result would be a changing function over time, where all of the values begin at one and gradually, over the duration (*p3*), move to zero. If the two functions were:

```
f 4    0    512    5    1 512 .001
f 5    0    512    7    .001 512 1
```

and the results were applied over time to using **vpvoc** as described above, the sound would begin with a lowpass filter effect and change over the duration, until the effect would be that of a highpass filter.

You may have noticed that **tableseg** and **tablexseg** have no output. The way to use these two unit generators with **vpvoc** is to make sure that they come *before* the **vpvoc** in your instrument. See, for example, figure 28.8.

```
          instr          2815          ; VPVOC
iend      =              p4
ktime     line           0, p3, iend
          tableseg       2, p3*.5, 3, p3*.5, 4
asig      vpvoc          ktime, 1, "hellorcb.pvc"
          out            asig
          endin

f 2       0      512     7       0 100 0 1 1 1 0 410 0
f 3       0      512     5       1 256 .001 256 .001
f 4       0      512     5       1 256 .001 256 1

i 2815    0      10      2.28
```

Figure 28.8 Orchestra code for *instr 2815,* a **vpvoc**-based instrument whose resynthesis spectrum is modified by the tables *f 2, f 3* and *f 4* under the control of **tableseg**.

The result of the above will be a sound that begins with just one sinusoidal component, that of bin #101. Over 5 seconds (*p3*.5*) it will be transformed into a sound that has many components but with a lowpass effect with all frequencies above those in bin #256 being silenced. Then, over the next 5 seconds, a further transformation will take place gradually giving the sound a spectral envelope like that produced by a notch or bandreject filter.

Remember that *ispecwp* also operates on the spectral envelope, but it works to keep the peaks and valleys of the amplitudes of the components in the same frequency range, even when the pitch is being shifted up or down. When using this option in **vpvoc**, the spectral warping is done *after* the work is done using the function table, or the **tableseg/tablexseg** opcodes.

PVBUFREAD, PVCROSS, PVINTERP

These three unit generators make it possible to combine the data from different phase vocoder analysis files in order to create transitions from one sound to another, or to create sound hybrids that mix attributes of the different sounds. The opcodes **pvcross** and **pvinterp**, both of which require a previously defined **pvbufread** in the instrument, offer two ways of performing cross-synthesis. The three unit generators are defined in the manual as:

```
     pvbufread  ktimpnt, ifile
ar   pvcross    ktimpnt, kfmod, ifile, kamp1, kamp2[, ispecwp]
ar   pvinterp   ktimpnt, kfmod, ifile, kfreqscale1,
                kfreqscale2, kampscale1, kampscale2,
                kfreqinterp, kampinterp
```

The opcode **pvbufread** accesses data from a phase vocoder analysis file in the same way that **pvoc** does. But instead of using the data to resynthesize sound, it makes the data available for use in **pvcross** and **pvinterp**. These two opcodes also access data from analysis files in the same way, using a time-pointer to retrieve the time-varying data. The opcode **pvcross** simply allows one to add some amount of the amplitudes contained in the analysis bins of one file to those of another. It allows one to determine how much of the amplitudes of each file will be used and it allows the amounts of the two files' amplitudes to be changed over time.

In the example shown in figure 28.9, the **pvbufread** and **pvcross** opcodes are each reading from separate analysis files using their own time-pointer values. The two values using *kamp* determine the mix of the amplitudes that will be applied to the frequency spectrum contained in the analysis file being read by **pvcross**. When *kamp* is 0, then the amplitudes from *file1.pvc* will be multiplied by 0, while all of the

```
         instr      2816        ; CROSS-SYNTHESIS: PVBUFREAD
ifmod    =          1
ktime1   line       0, p3, 2.28
ktime2   line       0, p3, 1
kamp     line       0, p3, 1
         pvbufread  ktime1, "file1.pvc"
asig     pvcross    ktime2, ifmod, "file2.pvc", kamp, 1-kamp
         out        asig
         endin
```

Figure 28.9 Orchestra code for *instr 2816,* a cross-synthesis instrument using **pvbufread.**

amplitudes of *file2.pvc* will be multiplied by 1. The result should be exactly the same as if a simple **pvoc** had been used with the same file and time-pointer. But as *kamp* changes from 0 to 1 over the duration, the balance between the amplitudes from *file1* and *file2* changes. When *kamp* is .5, then equal amounts of the amplitudes of both files will be added together and then used to scale the frequency spectrum. By the end of the note, *kamp* is equal to 1 and therefore only the amplitudes of *file1* will be used. Through this process the frequencies are always those from *file2,* so that at the end of the note the frequency values are those of *file2,* while the amplitudes are those of *file1.*

Remember that the bins can be thought of as pairs of breakpoint functions, reflecting the time-variation of the frequency and amplitude values in each bin. You can think of **pvcross** as a process that allows you to replace the amplitude breakpoint functions of one sound with those of another, as well as allowing cross-fading between them.

The example shown in figure 28.10 shows how you can use the same analysis file in the **pvbufread** and the **pvcross** opcodes. In **pvcross**, *ktime2* is causing the frames to be read in reverse chronological order. The amplitudes of the backward version of the sound will be applied to the forward version of the frequencies.

As you can see, **pvcross** allows a specific type of cross-synthesis, using just the amplitudes returned by the **pvbufread**. On the other hand, the **pvinterp** opcode is a more powerful unit generator, allowing the same kind of processing as **pvcross**, but with a number of other interesting possibilities. An important difference between **pvcross** and **pvinterp** is that **pvinterp** will interpolate between the frequencies of the two data files, as well as between amplitudes. While the interpolation process is the same for frequencies and amplitudes, the effects are quite different. The instrument shown in figure 28.11 illustrates how **pvinterp** works on the frequencies.

Let's look at a slightly more complex example. Let us assume that we have two sounds, a violin and an alto sax. And further, let's say the two sounds that produced the analysis files were both 1.2 seconds long and that the violin was at the pitch of

```
        instr     2817           ; CROSS-SYNTHESIZER
iamp1   =         1
iamp2   =         0
ifmod   =         1
ktime1  line      0, p3, 2.26
ktime2  line      2.26, p3, 0
        pvbufread ktime1, "hellorcb.pvc"
asig    pvcross   ktime2, 1, "hellorcb.pvc", iamp1, iamp2
        out       asig
        endin
```

Figure 28.10 Orchestra code for *instr 2817,* a cross-synthesizer that reads the amplitude analysis data in reverse and combines it with frequency analysis data that is read in the forward direction.

```
        instr     2818  ; CROSS-SYNTHESIS INTERPOLATES BETWEEN 2 FILES
ifmod   =         1
iamp1   =         1
iamp2   =         2
ifreq1  =         1
ifreq2  =         1
ktime   line      0, p3, 1.2
kinterp line      0, p3, 1
        pvbufread ktime, "violin.pvc"
asig    pvinterp  ktime, ifmod, "marimba.pvc", ifreq1, ifreq2, iamp1,
                  iamp2, kinterp, kinterp
        out       asig
        endin
```

Figure 28.11 Orchestra code for *instr 2818,* a cross-synthesis instrument that interpolates between the frequency data of both files.

c4 (middle-c), while the alto sax was a minor third higher, at the pitch *e-flat4*. Now let's take a look at some of the data in each analysis file. The two lines below show the frequency values for bin #11 in each file covering six frames:

```
 violin:  Bin 11   Freqs   261.626 261.340 261.471 261.389 261.286 261.555
altosax:  Bin 11   Freqs   311.127 311.137 311.715 311.924 311.950 311.708
```

When **pvbufread** reads through the violin file, it will interpolate between consecutive values according to the value of the time-pointer. The **pvinterp** opcode will do the same with the *altosax* file. But **pvinterp** will take the value of *kfreqinterp,* to determine a value between that returned by the **pvbufread** and that found by **pvinterp**. Using the actual values of two analysis bins shown above, you can see that if *kinterp* were 1 in the first frame shown, then the value of bin #11 used for synthesis would be 261.626. If the value of *kinterp* were 0, the value used for bin #11 would be 311.127. If the value of *kinterp* were .5, the frequency for bin #11 would be halfway between 261.626 and 311.127. Since *kinterp* changes over time from 0 to 1, the frequency values will change over time from those of the alto sax to those of the violin. And this will occur for all of the analysis bins. Notice that *kinterp* is also being used for the amplitudes that will cause the interpolation over the same time period between the amplitudes of the alto sax and those of the violin.

Now let us look at the use of the other arguments. Suppose we want a transition between alto sax and violin, as shown above, but we want both to be at the same pitch (remember that the alto sax is at *e-flat4* and the violin is at *c4*). You can use the *kfreqscale2* argument to bring the pitch of the alto sax down to that of the violin:

```
ifreq1    =           1
ifreq2    =           cpspch(8.00)/chspch(8.03)
kinterp   line        1, p3, 0
          pvbufread   ktime, "violin.pvc"
asig      pvinterp    ktime, ifmod, "altosax.pvc", ifreq1,
                      ifreq2, iamp1, iamp2, kinterp, kinterp
```

Or we can scale the violin frequencies up a minor 3rd:

```
ifreq1      =      cpspch(8.03)/cpspch(8.00)
ifreq2      =      1
```

Now let us assume that the amplitudes of the alto sax were much greater than those of the violin, so that when the interpolation is made between them, the amplitudes of the alto sax are still much more prominent in a 50/50 interpolation (when kinterp is .5 for the *kampinterp* argument in this example). We can scale up the violin amplitudes:

```
iamp1       =      2
iamp2       =      1
```

Or we can scale down the sax amplitudes:

```
iamp1       =      1
iamp2       =      2
```

If the amplitudes of the violin get louder over time and those of the alto sax get softer and we want to maintain a somewhat more equal balance over the duration of the sound, we might take advantage of k-rate variables for these arguments and do something like:

```
kamp1  line   0, p3, 1
kamp2  expon  1, p3, 2    ; EXPON, JUST TO HAVE DIFFERENT SLOPE FOR KAMP2
```

Now, let us put this all together into a simple instrument (see figures 28.12 and 28.13). The argument *kfmod* acts to transpose the pitch after the work of *ifreq1* and *ifreq2* is done. In the example below, *ifmod* is equal to .5. The result, when *ifreq1, ifreq2* and *ifmod* are put into play, will be a sound with the pitch *c3* (the alto sax is

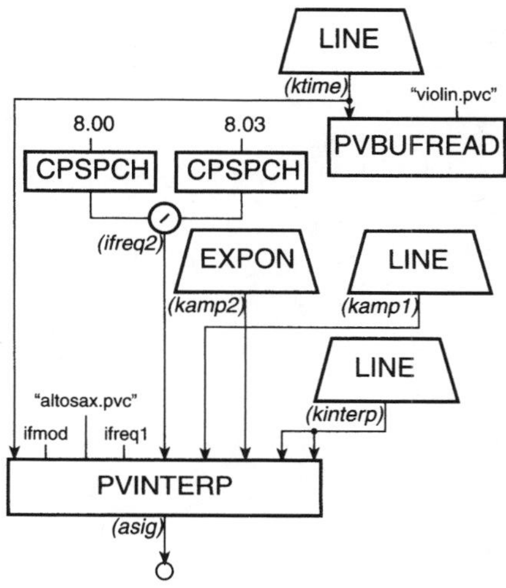

Figure 28.12 Block diagram of *instr 2821,* a flexible cross-synthesis instrument with dynamic control of time, amplitude, and pitch transposition.

```
         instr      2821       ; CROSS-SYNTHESIS: CONTROL OVER AMP & PITCH
ifreq1   =          1
ifreq2   =          cpspch(8.00)/cpspch(8.03)    ; TRANSPOSE DOWN A MINOR 3RD
ifmod    =          .5                           ; TRANSPOSE THE WHOLE THING
kamp1    line       1, p3, 2                     ; ... DOWN AN OCTAVE.
kamp2    expon      2, p3, 3
kinterp  line       0, p3, 1
ktime    line       0, p3, 1
         pvbufread  ktime, "violin.pvc"
asig     pvinterp   ktime, ifmod, "altosax.pvc", ifreq1, ifreq2, kamp1, kamp2,
                    kinterp, kinterp
         out        asig
         endin
```

Figure 28.13 Orchestra code for *instr 2821* as shown in figure 28.12.

first transposed down a minor 3rd and then the whole sound is transposed down an octave), that changes over time from a sax into a violin.

As you can see, there are many different combinations of frequency and amplitude scaling and different ways of combining those two aspects of two analysis files. Since all of the arguments can change over time at the k-rate, there can be innumerable combinations with constantly changing relationships between all of the values. While there are few limits to the kind of transitions that you can do using **pvinterp**, in practice there are some limitations if you want to maintain high quality in your sounds.

```
                instr      2822      ; TALKING MARIMBA/VIOLIN MORPH
ifreq           =          1                  ; READ THROUGH 7.5 SEC.
iamp            =          1                  ; ...OF LPC ANALYZED SPEECH.
kpvtime         line       0, p3, 1
klpctime        line       0, p3, 7.5         ; PVINTERP WILL PRODUCE
kinterp         line       0, p3, 1           ; ...THE MARIMBA-VIOLIN MORPH
krmsr, krmso,   lpread     klpctime, "speech1.lpc"
kerr, kcps
kfmod           =          kcps/cpspch(7.00)
                pvbufread  kpvtime, "violin.pvc"
apv             pvinterp   kpvtime, kfmod, "marimba.pvc", ifreq, ifreq, iamp,
                           2, kinterp, kinterp
alpc            lpreson    apv                ; ...WHICH WILL "SPEAK" WITH
                out        alpc*.0006         ; ...THE PITCHES FROM THE LPC
                endin
```

Figure 28.14 Orchestra code for *instr 2822,* a cross-synthesis instrument in which the **pvinterp** output is used as the input to **lpreson** resulting in a "talking marimba/violin morph."

One of the biggest problems, which you can hear quite well when using **pvinterp**, is making transitions between sounds that have different spectral distributions. Let us say that you want to have a transition between a pitched sound and a noisy one (violin to cymbal). If you do this transition over a fairly short time period, it can produce quite wonderful results. But if you stretch the time frame by using a slowly changing time-pointer, you will hear that during the stage of interpolation that is between the two sounds, it can sound extremely muddy and unfocused. If you try the same thing with a variety of pairs of different sounds, it can sound nearly the same, no matter which two sounds you are using. The reason for this is that, if the spectral distributions are different, all of the different frequency bins might be changing in different ways from one frame to another. The results can therefore be quite chaotic and messy sounding.

Finally, remember that you can combine different synthesis techniques quite easily in Csound and that there is no need to try to make one method do everything. For example, you can use the output from **pvinterp** as shown above as input into an **lpreson** (see figure 28.14).

Conclusion

Use your imagination to guide your experiments with this family of unit generators and then try combining them with other techniques. You will find that you can make original and even amazing sounds that can inspire you as you compose new musical works.

Modeling Commercial Signal Processing Applications

29 Efficient Implementation of Analog Waveshaping in Csound

Michael A. Pocino

Many analog synthesizers and effects have interesting and characteristic sounds that can serve as sources of inspiration for Csound instrument design. In fact, good simulations of analog gear can be based directly on the behavior of the actual circuits. This article is not, however, about circuit analysis. That would take an entire book. Rather, the focus of this chapter will be on several specific analog waveshaping techniques and their efficient implementation in Csound. These techniques will be presented in the context of a couple of example instruments, but are general enough to have a wide variety of uses. While these approximations will not sound exactly like a particular manufacturer's synthesizer or effect, they will provide some of the "classic" sounds and effects of that old analog gear.

The Comparator

The basic waveshaper we will look at is the comparator. An analog comparator compares a signal to a reference voltage and produces a high or low output depending on whether the input is higher or lower than the reference. If an audio waveform were put through a comparator, its output would look like a series of pulses. An example of a guitar signal that is put through a comparator with a reference of 0 can be seen in figure 29.1.

In Csound, a comparator can be made with the following function table (f-table) and the **table** opcode:

```
acomp table asig-aref, 1, 1, 0.5

f 1   0      32 7 -1 16 -1 0 1 16 1
```

This is a table lookup, where the table contains a square wave that goes from −1 to 1. The origin is set at the middle of the table, where the change from −1 to 1

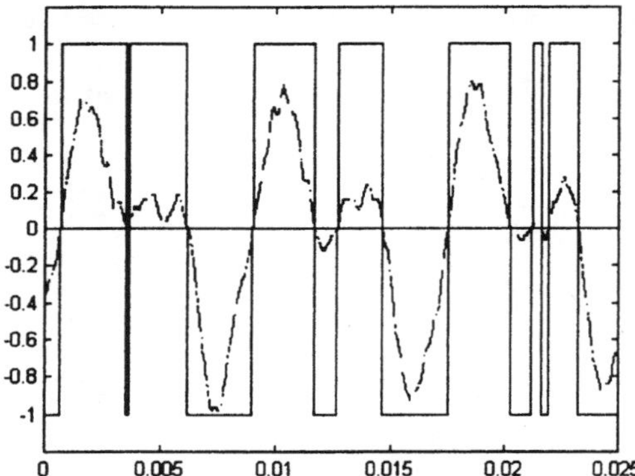

Figure 29.1 A guitar signal (dashed line) is fed through a comparator with reference 0. The output is shown as a solid line.

occurs. If the index to the table is greater than 0, the output will be 1. If it is less than 0, then the output will be -1.

The reference (*aref*) is subtracted from the input signal (*asig*), so that the signal must be greater than the reference for the total to be greater than 0. Thus, the output of the comparator is 1 if the signal is greater than the reference and -1 if it is less. If the reference were fixed at 0 (or simply left out), the comparator would act like a "sign" function. This means that the output would be 1 or -1, when the input is positive or negative, respectively. In general, the reference can change with time and be used for a variety of applications.

The Pulse Wave

One way that comparators can be put to good use is in a pulse oscillator with variable width, a circuit found in many analog synthesizers. This differs from most typical analog oscillators, in that it can not be approximated with just one **oscili** opcode and a corresponding f-table. An analog pulse oscillator is made with a sawtooth oscillator and a comparator. We can do the same thing in Csound with the instrument shown in figure 29.2. Here, a sawtooth wave is generated at the same frequency as the desired pulse wave, using the second wave table. It is likely that a sawtooth wave will already be needed in an analog synth instrument, so this is sort of a freebie. The sawtooth is put through the comparator and it can be used with a varying reference to produce pulses of varying widths.

```
          instr    2901      ; PULSE WAVE WITH MODULATABLE PULSE-WIDTH
iatk      =        .2
idec      =        .1
isus      =        .8
irel      =        .2
istdy     =        1-(iatk+idec+irel)            ; LENGTH OF SUSTAIN LEVEL
alfo      oscili   0.2, p6, 3                    ; p6=LFO RATE
apw       =        alfo+0.25
asaw      oscili   1, p5, 2                      ; p5=FREQ IN HZ
apulse    table    asaw-apw, 1, 1, 0.5
kenv      linseg   0, p3*iatk, 1, p3*idec, isus, p3*istdy, isus,
p3*irel, 0
          out      p4*apulse*kenv
          endin

f 1       0  32    7     -1    16 -1 0 1 16 1     ; TABLE FOR COMPARATOR
f 2       0  256   7     -1    256 1              ; SAWTOOTH WAVEFORM
f 3       0  1024  10    1                        ; SINE WAVE FOR LFO

i 2901    0  6     6000  110   .5
i 2901    0  6     6000  165   .5
i 2901    1  5     6000  55    1
i 2901    1  5     4000  440   1
i 2901    1  5     4000  220   1
i 2901    1  5     4000  660   1
i 2901    1  5     4000  330   1
```

Figure 29.2 Orchestra and score code for *instr 2901,* an instrument that uses a sawtooth waveform and table-lookup comparator to realize a pulse wave with modulatable pulse-width.

In this comparator, *apw* is a time-varying reference that determines the pulse width at any given time. If the reference (*apw*) is zero, we can see that the sawtooth will be greater than zero and less than zero for equal amounts of time, producing a square wave. As *apw* is increased, however, a smaller portion of the sawtooth is above this reference, so the positive portion of the pulse will be shorter than the negative portion.

Figure 29.3 shows how a changing reference changes the pulse width. Notice how the width of the positive parts of the pulses (solid) increases as the reference (dash-dot) increases. Generally, a low frequency oscillator is used to vary the pulse width in a synth. And in *instr 2901,* the only thing the LFO changes is the pulse width, so any LFO sounds you hear are only due to changing pulse width. More full-blown analog synth simulations can be found in *instr 2902* and *instr 2903.*

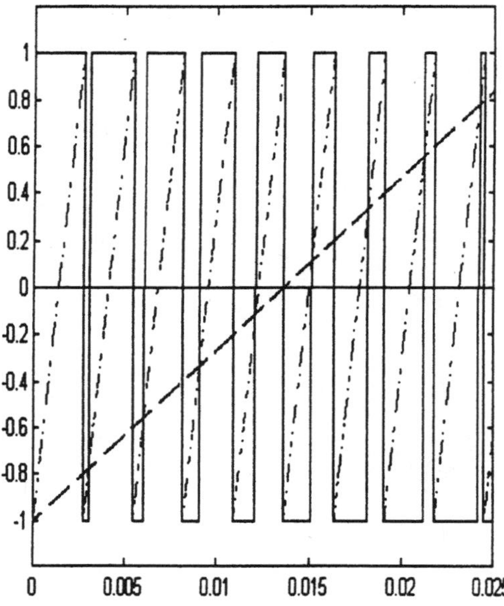

Figure 29.3 A rectangular waveform of varying pulse-width. A sawtooth waveform (dashed) is fed through a comparator with a varying reference (dash-dot) that controls the pulse-width. The output waveform (solid) is a pulse wave.

Audio Rate Comparisons and Logic

Comparisons and logical operations can be useful ways to implement more complicated waveshaping techniques. Unfortunately, the relational and logical operators in Csound, such as >, <, **&&** and ||, will not work with audio rate signals. It is possible, however, to generate the same relational and logical functions using comparators and arithmetic. This allows the use of these functions at audio rates without having to set the control rate equal to the sampling rate. In this case, the comparator will be generating outputs of 1 and 0 (for true and false) instead of 1 and –1 (for the sign of the signal). In this section, the procedure for generating each of these functions will be explained. An example of how these can be used is described in the next section.

The following f-table and **table** opcode make up an "$a > b$" function, which returns 1 if it is true and 0 if it is not:

```
aagtb     table       asiga-asigb, 1, 1, 0.5
f 1  0 32 7 0 16 0 0 1 16 1
```

```
aagtb       table       asiga-asigb, 1, 1, 0.5
acgtd       table       asigc-asigd, 1, 1, 0.5
aand        =           aagtb*acgtd

f 1         0     32    7       0 16 0 0 1 16 1
```

Figure 29.4 Using tables to generate the "and" function "a > b && c > d."

```
aagtb       table       asiga-asigb, 1, 1, 0.5
acgtd       table       asigc-asigd, 1, 1, 0.5
aor1        =           aagtb+acgtd
aor         table       aor1, 1, 1, 0.25

f 1         0     32    7         0 16 0 0 1 16 1
```

Figure 29.5 Using tables to generate the "or" function "a > b || c > d."

In order to generate an "$a < b$" statement, it is probably simplest just to say "$b > a$," or switch the order of the inputs. This way, the same f-table can be used for both relations.

It is also possible to implement "and" and "or" functions with audio rate relational operators using simple arithmetic. Figure 29.4 shows how the statement "$a > b$ && $c > d$" can be generated. In this case, multiplying the two conditions together is equivalent to the "and" operation, because if either of the statements is false (or zero), the output of the "and" function will be zero. If both are true, the output will be 1.

The generation of the "or" function, "a > b || c > d," can be done using addition rather than multiplication as shown in figure 29.5. This simply adds the two conditions together. If either is true, the output will be positive. If both statements are true, the output of *aor1* will be 2. The comparator at the end normalizes this to be either 0 or 1, but is optional. For instance, if you are using the output to be the gate of a **samphold** unit generator, it doesn't matter what the value is, as long as it is positive. In this case you could leave the last opcode out and make the instrument run a little faster.

The Guitar Sub-Octave Generator

The previously explained techniques can all be used in a guitar sub-octave generator. The method we will use inverts the signal during every other cycle, which makes the guitar sound as though it is playing one octave lower. When mixed with the original

```
kpwr           rms          ain
apos           table        ain-ithr*kpwr, 1, 1, 0.5
aneg           table        ithr*kpwr-ain, 1, 1, 0.5
agate          =            apos+aneg
aset           =            apos-aneg
aschmitt       samphold     aset, agate
```

Figure 29.6 Orchestra code excerpt from *instr 2904* for the generation of an adaptive "Schmitt" trigger for counting zero crossings.

guitar signal, this can give a surprisingly clean and natural sound much like a guitar and bass playing in unison.

The first task is to determine where each period of the waveform starts and stops. One way to do this is to find the zero-crossings of the signal. That is, every time the signal crosses zero, one half cycle has occurred. However, a complicated signal may cross zero too many times during a cycle, causing glitches. There is a way to compensate for this; we will use what is called an *adaptive Schmitt trigger.*

Basically, a Schmitt trigger does not count a zero-crossing unless the signal goes far enough past zero. For instance, if the signal is negative, it will not count as going positive until it passes a sufficiently large positive value. It will then count as positive until it passes a large enough negative value and so on. It ignores any part of the signal between these two thresholds, in order to avoid glitches. We can make an adaptive Schmitt trigger by setting this threshold value based on the power of the signal. This way, we can count zero-crossings of loud signals without glitches, while still being able to count zero-crossings of soft signals. The output of the adaptive Schmitt trigger will be a glitchless pulse wave that oscillates between 1 and –1. This function can be generated by the collection of opcodes shown in figure 29.6, and examples of their effects can be seen in figures 29.7 and 29.8.

The power of the signal is found, which is used (when multiplied by *ithr*) as the threshold for the trigger. In figure 29.7, the positive and negative thresholds appear as dash-dot lines. What follows is a logical statement, which is generated using the techniques covered in the previous section. A simplified logical equation for *agate* would be:

```
agate      =      (ain > ithr*kpwr) || (ain < -ithr*kpwr)
```

This equation, however, is implemented as shown in figure 29.6 with the **table** opcodes and sum, in order to work with the audio rate signals. If the signal is greater than the positive threshold or less than the negative threshold, *agate* is true. In other words, any ambiguous case (between the two thresholds), is ignored. A **samphold** unit generator is used to store the current state of the trigger. If *agate* is true,

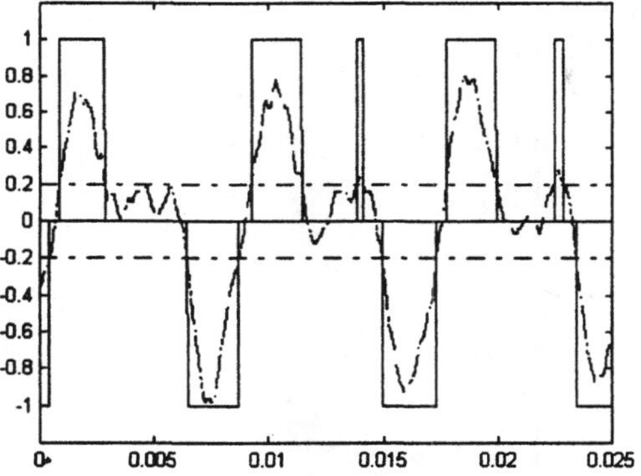

Figure 29.7 A guitar signal (dashed) is passed through the Schmitt trigger. Dash-dot lines designate the thresholds. The output (solid) is only positive or negative during positive or negative parts (respectively) of each cycle.

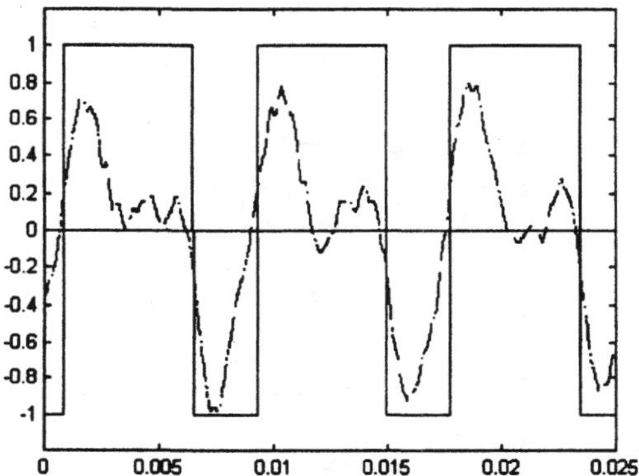

Figure 29.8 The output of the adaptive Schmitt trigger (solid line) is compared to the original guitar

samphold reads in *aset,* which is 1 or –1 depending on the sign of the signal. The solid and variable width pulses in figure 29.7 represent the output of *aset* and *agate* would be the absolute value of this function. The output of *aschmitt* would look like the pulse wave shown in figure 29.8. As you can see, *aschmitt* goes positive the first time *aset* goes positive and stays positive until *aset* goes negative. This new pulse wave in figure 29.8 is clearly much cleaner that the original glitchy one we had in figure 29.7.

Once we have the pulse wave with the same period as the input from the adaptive Schmitt trigger, we need to get a square wave of half the frequency. This can be easily accomplished by using a "divide-by-two-counter." Basically, the output of the divide-by-two-counter changes sign every time the input changes from negative to positive. And detecting a change of sign of the pulse wave is simple.

```
alast        delay1       aschmitt
aedge        =            aschmitt-alast
```

This subtracts the last value of the pulse wave from the current value. If they are the same, the output is zero. If they are different the output is 2 or –2, depending on the direction of the sign change. So, *aedge* has a nonzero value only at the edges of the pulse.

The tricky part is getting a square wave that will work at half this frequency. One solution to this problem uses a **phasor** controlling a **table**.

```
iincr        =            sr/8
aphs         phasor       abs(aedge*iincr)
asub1        table        aphs, 1, 1
```

Every time an edge occurs, *aphs* is incremented by 0.25. This causes one period of the square wave to occur for every 4 edges of the pulse wave (2 positive edges and 2 negative). The output of the divide-by-two-counter can be seen in figure 29.9. Each period of the guitar waveform is contained nicely in one half period of the square wave.

In order to invert every other cycle of the guitar waveform, we can just multiply the original signal by the square wave. This has been done to the signal shown in figure 29.10. Notice how the period is now twice as long as before. It is easiest to see this by finding the first positive peak, which matches up with the peak near the right of the graph. Compare this period to that of the original waveform in figure 29.9. This is the output waveform, which sounds much like a guitar playing one octave lower than the original.

A working guitar sub-octave generator has been included in *instr 2904.orc* (see figure 29.11). A few smoothing filters have been added, but it is basically the same

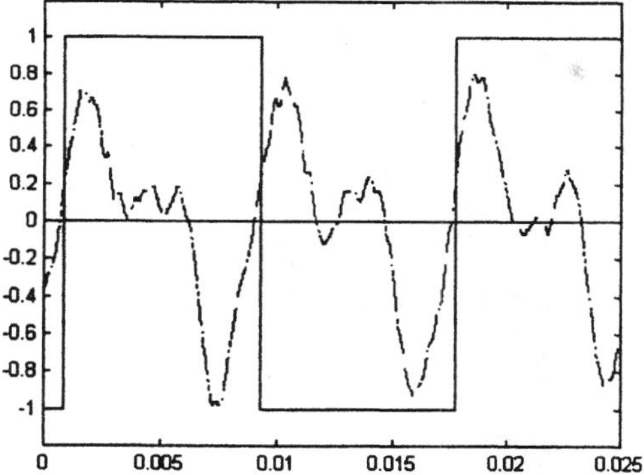

Figure 29.9 The output of the "divide-by-two-counter" compared to the input guitar signal.

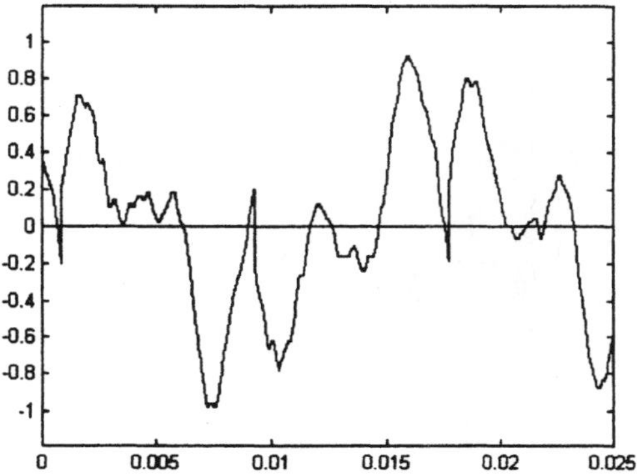

Figure 29.10 The final sub-octave output is the same as the guitar input, but inverted every other cycle. The result sounds one octave lower.

process as outlined above. An example guitar audio file (*guitar1.aif*) has also been included, but you can easily process your own files with the instrument.

Conclusion

Comparators can be extremely useful components of instruments. They are in wide use in analog circuits and are just as useful in Csound. They can be combined to generate complicated waveshaping methods at audio rates and eliminate the need for setting the control rate equal to the sampling rate in many situations. This allows

```
        instr     2904        ; SUB-OCTAVE GENERATOR
idlev   =         1.0             ; DIRECT GUITAR LEVEL
isublev =         0.4             ; SUB-OCTAVE SIGNAL LEVEL
istl    =         0.4             ; SCHMIDTT TRIGGER LEVEL FOR SQUARE WAVE
iincr   =         sr/8            ; FOR INCREMENTING DIVIDE-BY-TWO-COUNTER
ain     soundin   "guitar1.aif"   ; SOUND FILE TO BE PROCESSED
alpf    butterlp  ain, 700        ; 700 HZ LPF
kpwr    rms       alpf
ahigh   table     (alpf-istl*kpwr)/5000+16, 2
alow    table     (-alpf-istl*kpwr)/5000+16, 2
asqr1   samphold  ahigh-alow, ahigh+alow
adela   delay1    asqr1
agate   =         -asqr1+adela
aphs    phasor    abs(agate*iincr)
asub1   table     aphs, 1, 1
asub2   tone      asub1, 3000
asub    =         asub2*ain
aout    butterlp  asub, 600
        out       0.5*(isublev*aout+idlev*ain)
        endin

f 1     0    2    2      -1 1
f 2     0    32   7       0 16 0 0 1 16 1

i 2904  0    15   ; p3 SHOULD BE LONG ENOUGH FOR THE SOUNDIN
```

Figure 29.11 Orchestra and score code for *instr 3404,* a guitar sub-octave generator instrument.

for the modeling of "classic" and "hybrid" instruments, which can be implemented efficiently. While only two example instruments have been given, the complexity of the second should give a good background on the many ways audio rate comparators can be used in your own designs.

Additional Information

Schematics of many effects and synthesizers can be found at the following web sites. They may be useful if you want to analyze other circuits and implement them in Csound.

Music Machines (http://www.hyperreal.com/music/machines) has schematics of several commercial synths and a few home-brew projects. It also has information about synthesizers and quite a few samples.

DMZ Schematics (http://members.aol.com/jorman/schem.html) has many schematics of commercial synths and effects, as well as home-brew projects.

The Synth-DIY Mirror Archive (http://aupe.phys.andrews.edu/diy_archive/) has quite a few schematics of modular synths, vocoders, etc.

Synth Fool (http://www.synthfool.com/) has information about modular synths, some schematics, good links and lots of pictures of drool-inspiring equipment.

References

Horenstein, Mark N. 1996. *Microelectronic Circuits and Devices.* Englewood Cliffs, N.J.: Prentice-Hall.

Thomas, R. E. and A. J. Rosa 1994. *The Analysis and Design of Linear Circuits.* Englewood Cliffs, N.J.: Prentice-Hall.

30 Modeling a Multieffects Processor in Csound

Hans Mikelson

This chapter describes a Csound implementation of a multieffects processor. Several categories of effects are presented including dynamics processing, filtering and pitch effects. Robin Whittle's **zak** opcodes provide a flexible method of routing between the effects routines. The **pluck** opcode is used to demonstrate these effects since many of them are often used with guitars.

The ZAK Opcodes

Communication between effects is handled by the **zak** opcodes. One advantage of the **zak** system over global variables is that communications between instruments may be reconfigured in the score without requiring changes to the orchestra. Using the **zak** opcodes requires that they first be initialized, which is done with the following statement:

```
        zakinit       isizea, isizek
```

where *num-a-rate* and *num-k-rate* are the number of allocated audio rate and control rate channels.

Communication between effects is accomplished using **zaw** and **zar**. To write to an audio channel, one uses:

```
        zaw           asig, kndx
```

To read from an audio channel, one uses:

```
ar      zar           kndx
```

Here, *asig* is the audio signal and *ichannel* is the number of the channel.

The **zawm** opcode mixes the current contents of the audio channel with the new audio data. During a chord, several instances of the pluck instrument are active at

```
        instr   3099            ; ZAK-BASED MIXER
asig1   zar     p4                          ; p4  = CH1 IN
igl1    init    p5*p6                       ; p5  = CH1 GAIN
igr1    init    p5*(1-p6)                   ; p6  = CH1 PAN
asig2   zar     p7                          ; p7  = CH2 IN
igl2    init    p8*p9                       ; p8  = CH2 GAIN
igr2    init    p8*(1-p9)                   ; p9  = CH2 PAN
asig3   zar     p10                         ; p10 = CH3 IN
igl3    init    p11*p12                     ; p11 = CH3 GAIN
igr3    init    p11*(1-p12)                 ; p12 = CH3 PAN
asig4   zar     p13                         ; p13 = CH4 IN
igl4    init    p14*p15                     ; p14 = CH4 GAIN
igr4    init    p14*(1-p15)                 ; p15 = CH4 PAN
asigl   =       asig1*igl1+asig2*igl2+asig3*igl3+asig4*igl4
asigr   =       asig1*igr1+asig2*igr2+asig3*igr3+asig4*igr4
        outs    asigl, asigr
        zacl    0, 30
        endin
```

Figure 30.1 Orchestra code for *instr 3099,* a stereo **zak**-based mixer with four input audio channels.

the same time, so the pluck instrument uses **zawm** to accumulate sound. The audio channels must be cleared every sample period, or the data will continue to accumulate. The mixer is the last instrument in the orchestra and is used to clear audio channels 0–30 with the statement:

```
zacl        0, 30
```

Mixer

The mixer, shown in figure 30.1, reads from four audio channels and provides independent gain and pan control for each channel.

Dynamics Processing

This section describes a compressor, a limiter, a noise gate, a de-esser and a distortion effect (Lehman). These are all related effects that change the dynamics of the sound.

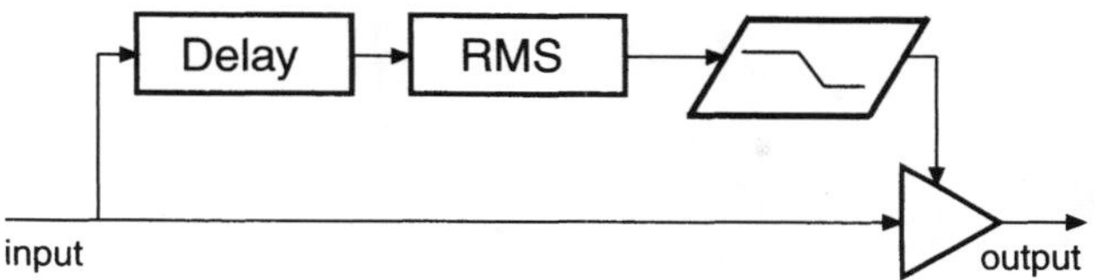

Figure 30.2 Block diagram of compressor/limiter.

```
          instr   3011          ; COMPRESSOR/LIMITER
ifqc      =       1/p4                      ; RMS CALCULATION FREQUENCY
ideltm    =       p5    ; DELAY TIME TO APPLY COMPRESSION TO INITIAL DYNAMICS
itab      =       p6                        ; COMPRESSOR/LIMITER TABLE
ipostgain =       p7                        ; POST GAIN
iinch     =       p8                        ; INPUT CHANNEL
ioutch    =       p9                        ; OUTPUT CHANNEL
kenv      linseg  0,.02,1,p3-.04,1,.02,0    ; AMP ENVELOPE TO DECLICK
asig      zar     iinch                     ; READ INPUT CHANNEL
kamp      rms     asig, ifqc                ; FIND RMS LEVEL
kampn     =       kamp/30000                ; NORMALIZE RMS LEVEL 0-1.
kcomp     tablei  kampn, itab, 1, 0         ; LOOKUP COMPRESS VALUE IN TABLE
adel1     delayr  ideltm                    ; INPUTDELAYTIME,1/IFQC/2 TYPICAL
          delayw  asig                      ; WRITE TO DELAY LINE
acomp     =       kcomp*adel1*ipostgain     ; COMPRESS DELAYED SIG AND POSTGAIN
          zaw     acomp*kenv, ioutch        ; DECLICK AND WRITE TO OUTPUT CHAN
          endin
```

Figure 30.3 Orchestra code excerpt from *instr 3011,* a compressor/limiter.

Compressor

A compressor is used to reduce the dynamic range of a signal. It does this by monitoring the level of an input signal and varying the gain applied to the output signal. Sounds greater than a specified level are reduced in volume. The **rms** opcode can be used to give a time average of the level of the input signal. The output from **rms** is used to reference a table that determines the amount of gain applied to the output signal. A post gain is usually included to restore the level of the output signal after it has been compressed. The **rms** opcode does not respond immediately to changes in level so that sudden attacks are sometimes allowed to pass. To avoid this, the original signal is monitored and compression is applied to a time delayed copy of the signal. In this example a delay time equal to one half of the **rms** averaging time is used (see figure 30.3).

The compressor block diagram is presented in figure 30.2. The amount of compression is given by the compression curve *f 6.* Compression levels of 2:1 and 4:1 are common.

```
f 6     0       1025      7      1 256 1 256 .5 513 .5
```

Limiter

The limiter is merely a compressor with a severe compression curve. Limiters prevent a signal level from going above a specified limit. Limiters commonly use compression levels of 10:1 or 100:1. This can be implemented by simply using a different compression table:

```
f 6      0       1025      7      1 256 1 512 .01 257 .01
```

Noise Gate

Noise gates are used to remove unwanted background noise and hiss from a signal. A noise gate can be implemented by changing the *f 6* table again:

```
f 6      13      1025      7      0 64 0 0 1 448 1 513 1
```

In this case, signals below a certain level are completely silent. Once they exceed that level they are allowed to pass. Noise gates are sometimes criticized for removing playing dynamics. To solve this problem a delayed signal is used to determine the level and the original signal is modified and output. This results in the gate opening just before playing begins. This technique can also be used on a compressor to prevent compression of initial playing dynamics (see figures 30.4 and 30.5).

De-Esser

The next effect considered in this section is the de-esser. When a microphone is used, certain consonant sounds such as "s" and "p" produce loud artifacts. The de-esser, a relative of the compressor, can be used to reduce these artifacts. The de-esser monitors the level of the high frequency component of the signal and applies compression to the signal based on this level. This can be implemented by applying a highpass filter to the input signal and monitoring the level of the filtered signal (see figures 30.6 and 30.7).

Distortion

This section describes a distortion effect. An amplifier can be considered as having two operating ranges: a linear range and a nonlinear range. In the linear range of operation, the output signal is an amplified copy of the input signal. In the nonlinear range of operation, the output signal is a distorted version of the input signal. Early

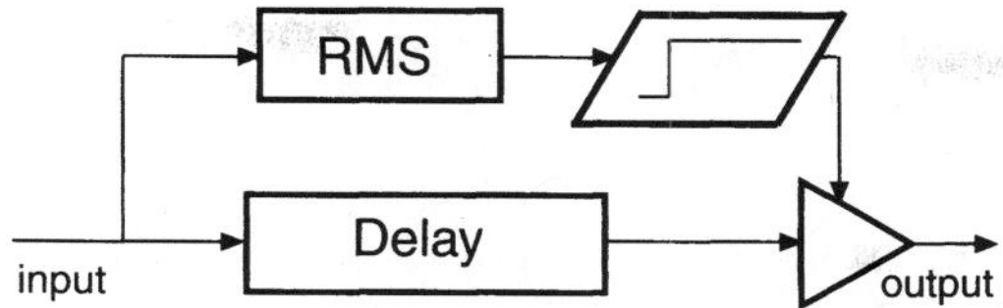

Figure 30.4 Block diagram of a noise gate.

```
            instr     3010          ; NOISE GATE
ifqc        =         1/p4                    ; RMS CALCULATION FREQUENCY
ideltm      =         p5     ; DELAY TIME TO OPEN GATE JUST BEFORE SIGNAL START
itab        =         p6                      ; NOISE GATE TABLE
ipostgain   =         p7                      ; POST GAIN
iinch       =         p8                      ; INPUT CHANNEL
ioutch      =         p9                      ; OUTPUT CHANNEL
kenv        linseg    0,.02,1,p3-.04,1,.02,0  ; DECLICK ENVELOPE
asig        zar       iinch                   ; READ FROM INPUT CHANNEL
adel1       delayr    ideltm                  ; DELAY THE SIGNAL
            delayw    asig
kamp        rms       adel1, ifqc             ; CALCULATE RMS ON DELAYED SIGNAL
kampn       =         kamp/30000              ; NORMALIZE TO 0-1
kcomp       tablei    kampn, itab, 1, 0       ; REFERENCE THE NOISE GATE TABLE
acomp       =         kcomp*asig*ipostgain    ; APPLY NOISEGATE TO ORIG SIGNAL
            zaw       acomp*kenv, ioutch      ; DECLICK AND WRITE TO OUTPUT CHAN
            endin
```

Figure 30.5 Orchestra code for *instr 3010,* a noise gate.

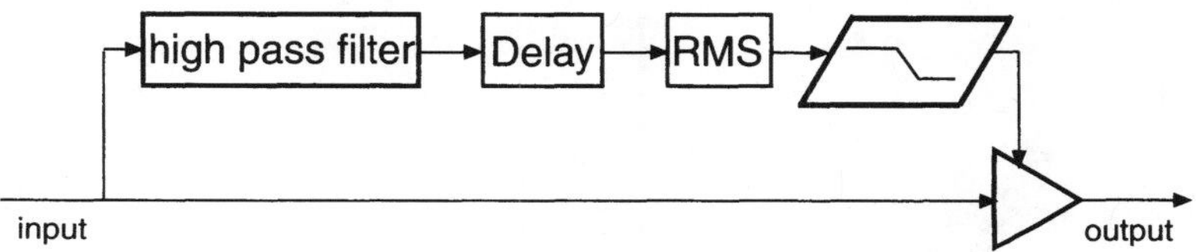

Figure 30.6 Block diagram of a de-esser.

```
            instr     3012          ; DE-ESSER
ifqc        =         1/p4                      ; RMS CALCULATION FREQUENCY
ideltm      =         p5                        ; DELAY TIME IS USUALLY 1/FQC/2
itab        =         p6                        ; DE-ESS TABLE
ifco        =         p7                        ; CUT OFF FREQUENCY
ipostgain   =         p8                        ; POST GAIN
iinch       =         p9                        ; INPUT CHANNEL
ioutch      =         p10                       ; OUTPUT CHANNEL
kenv        linseg    0,.02,1,p3-.04,1,.02,0    ; DECLICK ENVELOPE
asig        zar       iinch                     ; READ INPUT CHANNEL
afilt       butterhp  asig, ifco                ; HIGHPASS FILTER THE SIGNAL
kamp        rms       afilt, ifqc               ; CALCULATE RMS ON HIGHPASS SIG
kampn       =         kamp/30000                ; NORMALIZE RMS 0-1
kcomp       tablei    kampn, itab, 1, 0         ; LOOKUP DE-ESSER VALUE IN TABLE
adel1       delayr    ideltm                    ; DELAY SIGNAL FOR DELAY TIME
            delayw    asig
acomp       =         kcomp*adel1*ipostgain     ; APPLY DE-ESS AND POST GAIN
            zaw       acomp*kenv, ioutch        ; DECLICK AND WRITE TO OUT CHAN
            endin
```

Figure 30.7 Orchestra code for *instr 3012,* a de-esser.

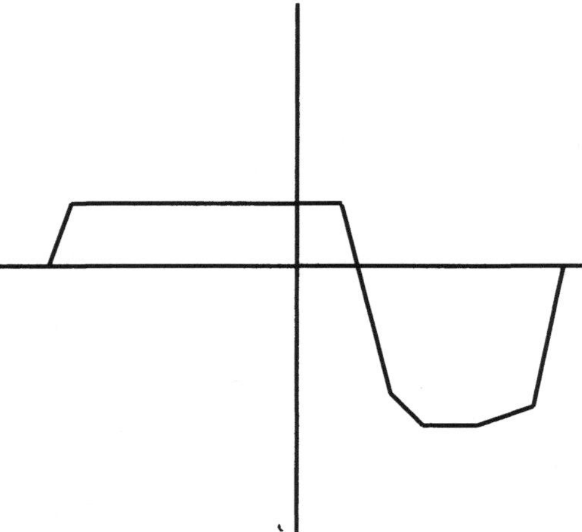

Figure 30.8 Waveform of a sine wave passed through a tube amplifier.

electronic amplifiers were based on vacuum tubes. Vacuum tube distortion is usually described as warmer and more musical than other types of distortion (Hamm 1973).

If a sine wave signal is passed through an overdriven tube amplifier, the resulting waveform differs from the original in several ways. The top of the waveform becomes flattened or clipped. The bottom of the waveform is also flattened although not as much as the top. The duty cycle of the waveform is also shifted so that the upper part of the curve is not the same width as the lower part of the curve. The resulting shape is approximated in figure 30.8.

Waveshaping may be used to reshape an input waveform to resemble figure 30.8. For slight distortion use the following table:

```
f 5  0  8192  8  -.8 336 -.78 800 -.7 5920 .7 800 .78 336 .8
```

And for heavy distortion use the following table:

```
f 5  0  8192  7  -.8 934 -.79 934 -.77 934 -.64 1034 -.48 520 .47 2300 .48 1536 .48
```

A shifted duty cycle can be accomplished by implementing an amplitude dependent delay line (see figures 30.9 and 30.10).

Filtering Effects

This section describes an equalizer, a wah-wah and a resonant lowpass filter.

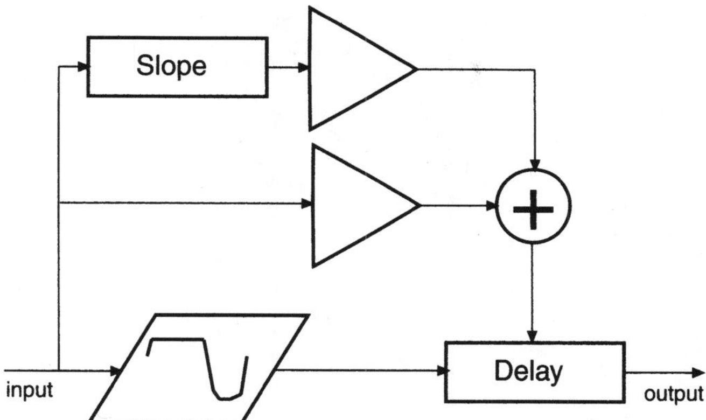

Figure 30.9 Block diagram of distortion processor.

```
          instr     3013          ; DISTORTION
igaini    =         p4                          ; PRE GAIN
igainf    =         p5                          ; POST GAIN
iduty     =         p6                          ; DUTY CYCLE OFFSET
islope    =         p7                          ; SLOPE OFFSET
izin      =         p8                          ; INPUT CHANNEL
izout     =         p9                          ; OUTPUT CHANNEL
asign     init      0                           ; DELAYED SIGNAL
kamp      linseg    0,.002,1,p3-.004,1,.002,0   ; DECLICK
asig      zar       izin                        ; READ INPUT CHANNEL
aold      =         asign                       ; SAVE THE LAST SIGNAL
asign     =         igaini*asig/60000           ; NORMALIZE THE SIGNAL
aclip     tablei    asign, 5, 1, .5             ; READ THE WAVESHAPING TABLE
aclip     =         igainf*aclip*15000          ; RE-AMPLIFY THE SIGNAL
atemp     delayr    .1                          ; AMP AND SLOPE BASED DELAY
aout      deltapi   (2-iduty*asign)/1500+islope*(asign-aold)/300
          delayw    aclip
          zaw       aout, izout                 ; WRITE TO OUTPUT CHANNEL
          endin
```

Figure 30.10 Orchestra code for *instr 3013,* a “tube-amp” distortion processor as shown in figure 30.9.

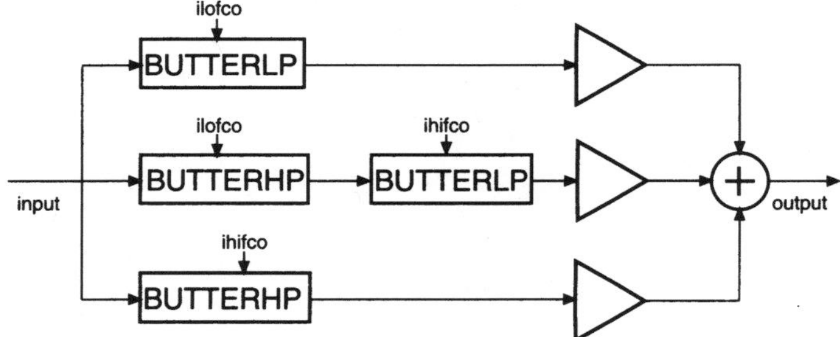

Figure 30.11 Block diagram of a 3-band equalizer.

```
            instr       3018            ; 3 BAND EQ
ilogain     =           p4                              ; LOW GAIN
imidgain    =           p5*1.2                          ; MIDRANGE GAIN
ihigain     =           p6                              ; HIGH GAIN
ilofco      =           p7                              ; LOW FREQUENCY CUT-OFF
ihifco      =           p8                              ; HIGH FREQUENCY CUT-OFF
izin        =           p9                              ; INPUT CHANNEL
izout       =           p10                             ; OUTPUT CHANNEL
asig        zar         izin                            ; READ FROM INPUT CHANNEL
alosig      butterlp    asig, ilofco                    ; LOWPASS FILTER
atmpsig     butterhp    asig, ilofco-ilofco/4           ; HIGHPASS AT LOWFRQ CUT-OFF
amidsig     butterlp    atmpsig, ihifco+ihifco/4        ; THEN LOWPASS @ HIGHFRQCUTOFF
ahisig      butterhp    asig, ihifco                    ; HIPASS FILTER
aout        =           ilogain*alosig + imidgain*amidsig + ihigain*ahisig
            zaw         aout, izout                     ; WRITE TO OUTPUT CHANNEL
            endin
```

Figure 30.12 Orchestra code for *instr 3018,* a 3-band equalizer using Butterworth filters.

Equalizer

An equalizer can be used to increase or decrease the level of different frequencies in a signal. In the example shown in figures 30.11 and 30.12, a three-band equalizer is implemented. The **butterlp** and **butterhp** opcodes are used to isolate the low and high frequency components of the signal. The midrange component is isolated by highpass filtering above the lowpass cut off frequency and lowpass filtering below the highpass cut off frequency. Individual gains are applied to each of the three signal components before they are added together and output.

Wah-Wah

A wah-wah pedal is a type of lowpass filter that incorporates several resonances to give it a unique character. In the example shown in figures 30.13 and 30.14, several resonances derived from the vowel sounds "ahh" and "ooh" are used to add character to the standard lowpass filter sound. The vowel "ahh" has resonances and amplitudes of 730 Hz −1 dB, 1090 Hz −5 dB, 2440 Hz −28 dB. The vowel "ooh" has resonances of 300 Hz −3 dB, 870 Hz −19 dB, 2240 Hz −43 dB. As the frequency is swept from high to low the resonances are swept from "ahh" to "ooh." This wah-wah effect could be take several steps further and developed into a full blown "talk-box" as in *instr 3017*. Check it out!

Resonant Lowpass Filter

Some theory of resonant filters can be found in chapter 10, "Modeling 'Classic' Electronic Keyboards in Csound," and will not be discussed here in detail. This implementation shown in figures 30.15 and 30.16, uses the **nlfilt** opcode, which avoids the need of setting **kr** = **sr** and also provides for simpler code. This filter is designed to resonate for approximately the same amount of time no matter what the cut-off frequency. Filters could also be used to model the resonances of the guitar body such as in *instr 3019*.

Pitch Effects

This section describes vibrato, pitch shifting, chorus and flanging effects. All of these effects make use of delay lines whose delay times are modulated with an oscillator. An interpolating delay tap, **deltapi**, is used to allow continuous variation of the delay time.

Vibrato

Vibrato can be accomplished by modulating a variable delay tap with a sine wave. When the delay tap sweeps forward in the same direction as the signal the pitch is lowered. As the delay tap sweeps backward in the opposite direction of the signal the pitch is raised (see figures 30.17 and 30.18).

Pitch Shifting

A simple type of pitch shifting can be implemented with a variable length interpolating delay tap. The delay time is modulated with a sawtooth wave whose amplitude is equal to the wavelength of the sound. This results in a resampling of the waveform with linear interpolation between successive samples. Lowering the pitch results in

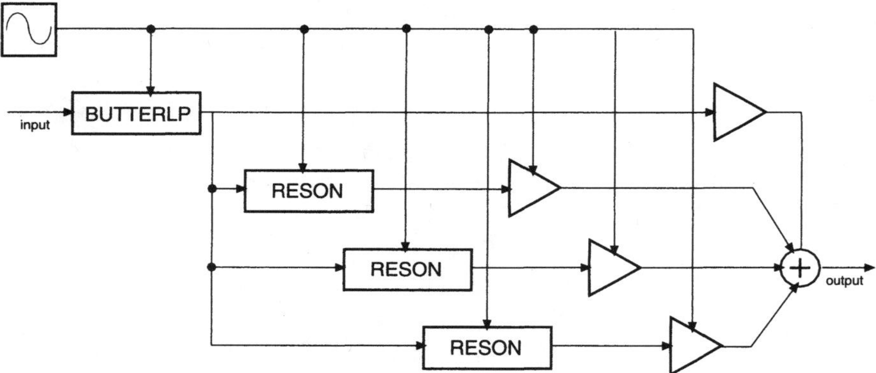

Figure 30.13 Block diagram of *instr 3016*, a wah-wah.

```
            instr      3016            ; WAH-WAH
irate       =          p4                                  ; AUTO WAH RATE
idepth      =          p5                                  ; LOWPASS DEPTH
ilow        =          p6                                  ; MINIMUM FREQUENCY
ifmix       =          p7/1000                             ; FORMANT MIX
itab1       =          p8                                  ; WAVE FORM TABLE
izin        =          p9                                  ; INPUT CHANNEL
izout       =          p10                                 ; OUTPUT CHANNEL
kosc1       oscil      .5, irate, itab1, .25               ; OSCILLATOR
kosc2       =          kosc1 + .5                          ; RESCALE FOR 0-1
kosc3       =          kosc2                               ; FORMANT DEPTH 0-1
klopass     =          idepth*kosc2+ilow                   ; LOWPASS FILTER RANGE
kform1      =          430*kosc2 + 300                     ; FORMANT 1 RANGE
kamp1       =          ampdb(-2*kosc3 + 59)*ifmix          ; FORMANT 1 LEVEL
kform2      =          220*kosc2 + 870                     ; FORMANT 2 RANGE
kamp2       =          ampdb(-14*kosc3 + 55)*ifmix         ; FORMANT 2 LEVEL
kform3      =          200*kosc2 + 2240                    ; FORMANT 3 RANGE
kamp3       =          ampdb(-15*kosc3 + 32)*ifmix         ; FORMANT 3 LEVEL
asig        zar        izin                                ; READ INPUT CHANNEL
afilt       butterlp   asig, klopass                       ; LOWPASS FILTER
ares1       reson      afilt, kform1, kform1/8             ; COMPUTE SOME FORMANTS
ares2       reson      afilt, kform2, kform1/8             ; TO ADD CHARACTER TO THE
ares3       reson      afilt, kform3, kform1/8             ; SOUND
aresbal1    balance    ares1, afilt                        ; ADJUST FORMANT LEVELS
aresbal2    balance    ares2, afilt
aresbal3    balance    ares3, afilt
            zaw        afilt+kamp1*aresbal1+kamp2*aresbal2+kamp3*aresbal3,izout
            endin
```

Figure 30.14 Orchestra code for *instr 3016*, a wah-wah.

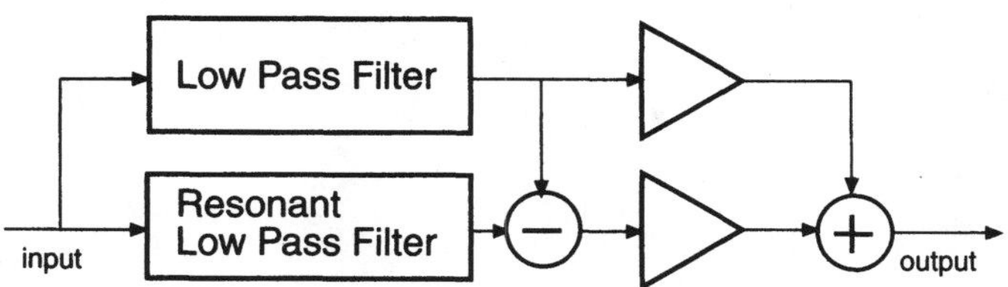

Figure 30.15 Block diagram of resonant lowpass filter.

```
        instr   3015          ; RESONANT LOWPASS FILTER
idur    =       p3
itab1   =       p4                      ; CUT-OFF FREQUENCY
itab2   =       p5                      ; RESONANCE
ilpmix  =       p6                      ; LOWPASS SIGNAL MULTIPLIER
irzmix  =       p7                      ; RESONANCE SIGNAL MULTIPLIER
izin    =       p8                      ; INPUT CHANNEL
izout   =       p9                      ; OUTPUT CHANNEL
kfco    oscil   1, 1/idur, itab1        ; CUT-OFF FREQUENCY ENVELOPE FROM TABLE
kfcort  =       sqrt(kfco)              ; NEEDED FOR THE FILTER
krezo   oscil   1, 1/idur, itab2        ; RESONANCE ENVELOPE FROM TABLE
krez    =       krezo*kfco/500          ; ADD MORE RESONANCE AT HIGH FCO
kamp    linseg  0, .002, 1, p3-.004, 1, .002, 0
axn     zar     izin                    ; READ INPUT CHANNEL
ka1     =       1000/krez/kfco-1        ; COMPUTE FILTER COEFF. A1
ka2     =       100000/kfco/kfco        ; COMPUTE FILTER COEFF. A2
kb      =       1+ka1+ka2               ; COMPUTE FILTER COEFF. B
; USE THE NON-LINEAR FILTER AS AN ORDINARY FILTER.
ay1     nlfilt  axn/kb, (ka1+2*ka2)/kb, -ka2/kb, 0, 0, 1
ay      nlfilt  ay1/kb, (ka1+2*ka2)/kb, -ka2/kb, 0, 0, 1
; RESONANCE OF 1 IS A LOWPASS FILTER
ka1lp   =       1000/kfco-1
ka2lp   =       100000/kfco/kfco
kblp    =       1+ka1lp+ka2lp
; LOWPASS FILTER
ay1lp   nlfilt  axn/kblp, (ka1lp+2*ka2lp)/kblp, -ka2lp/kblp, 0, 0, 1
aylp    nlfilt  ay1lp/kblp, (ka1lp+2*ka2lp)/kblp, -ka2lp/kblp, 0, 0, 1
ayrez   =       ay - aylp               ; EXTRACT THE RESONANCE PART.
ayrz    =       ayrez/kfco              ; USE LOWER AMPLITUDES AT HIGHER FCO
; SCALE THE LOWPASS AND RESONANCE SEPARATELY
ay2     =       aylp*6*ilpmix + ayrz*300*irzmix
        zaw     ay2, izout              ; WRITE TO THE OUTPUT CHANNEL
        endin
```

Figure 30.16 Orchestra code for *instr 3015,* a resonant lowpass design using Csound's nonlinear filter opcode—**nlfilt**.

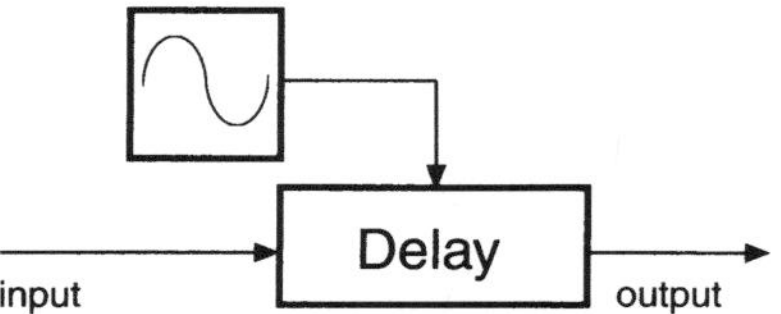

Figure 30.17 Block diagram of simple vibrato algorithm using an oscillator and a delay line.

```
            instr     3020        ; VIBRATO
iamp        =         p4/1000                     ; VIBRATO AMPLITUDE
ifqc        =         p5                          ; VIBRATO FREQUENCY
itabl       =         p6                          ; WAVE SHAPE
iphase      =         p7                          ; PHASE SHIFT
idelay      =         p8                          ; DELAY TIME BEFORE VIBRATO BEGINS
irmptim     =         p9                          ; RAMP TIME FOR VIBRATO
izin        =         p10                         ; INPUT CHANNEL
izout       =         p11                         ; OUTPUT CHANNEL
asig        zar       izin                        ; READ INPUT CHANNEL
                                                  ; DELAY AND RAMP VIBRATO
kramp       linseg    0, idelay, 0, irmptim, 1, p3-idelay-irmptim, 1
kosc        oscil     kramp*iamp, ifqc, itabl     ; LOW FREQUENCY OSCILLATOR
atmp        delayr    3*iamp                      ; DELAY THE SIGNAL
aout        deltapi   kosc+1.5*iamp               ; VARIABLE DELAY TAP
            delayw    asig
            zaw       aout, izout                 ; WRITE TO THE OUTPUT CHANNEL
            endin
```

Figure 30.18 Orchestra code for *instr 3020,* a variable tap-delay vibrato instrument.

cycles being discarded periodically. Raising the pitch results in some cycles being repeated. In order to produce a good quality sample, the wavelength of the sound must be known. In this example it is simply supplied when the instrument is called (see figures 30.19 and 30.20).

Chorus

Chorus is an effect that attempts to make one instrument sound like more than one instrument. The resulting sound is thicker than the original sound. Chorus can be implemented by adding the original signal to a frequency-modulated delayed signal (Cronin 1994). The signal is typically delayed between 20 and 30 msec. Gain is applied to control the amount of mix between the original signal and the delayed signal. Common waveforms used to modulate the signal are sine, triangle and logarithmic waves (see figures 30.21 and 30.22).

Many choruses can be combined with different phases, waveforms and delay times to produce a rich sound. A stereo chorus effect, for example, can be created by having

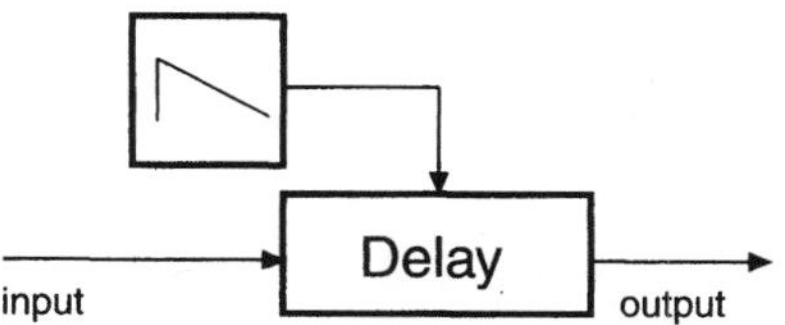

Figure 30.19 Block diagram of a tap-delay pitch shifter.

```
          instr     3022          ; DELAY-BASED PITCH SHIFTER
ipshift   =         (p4<=1 ? p4-1 : p4/2)
itabl     =         p5
izin      =         p6
izout     =         p7
asig      zar       izin
kosc      oscil     1/gifqc, gifqc*ipshift, itabl
atmp      delayr    .1
aout      deltapi   kosc+1/gifqc
          delayw    asig
          zaw       aout, izout
          endin
```

Figure 30.20 Orchestra code for *instr 3022,* a variable delay-based pitch shifter.

two choruses one quarter cycle out of phase with each other and sending the output of each to a separate channel as follows:

```
;        STA  DUR  RATE  DEPTH  WAVE  MIX  DELAY  PHASE  INCH  OUTCH
i 3035   0    1.6  .5    2      1     1    25     0      2     3
i 3035   0    1.6  .5    2      1     1    20     .25    2     4
```

Flanger

Flanging was originally produced by taking two tapes with the same music on them and playing them at the same time. By pushing on the flanges of one of the tape reels, the playback speed of one of the copies of the sound was modulated. This detuning of the signal results in areas of constructive and destructive interference as the different frequencies moved in and out of phase with each other. This produced notches in the audio spectrum. As the frequency of the modulated signal was swept back and forth, these notches moved closer together and farther apart producing the characteristic "jet airplane" effect.

In this implementation, shown in figures 30.23 and 30.24, the original signal is added to a delayed signal. The delay time is modulated by a sine wave, so that the

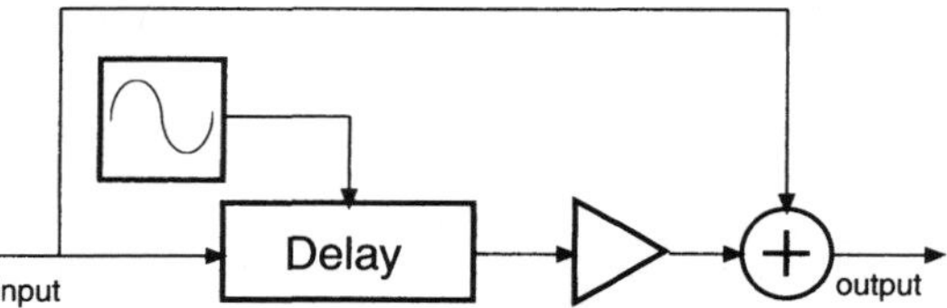

Figure 30.21 Block diagram of a “chorus” effect.

```
          instr     3035                ; CHORUS
irate     =         p4
idepth    =         p5/1000
iwave     =         p6
imix      =         p7
ideloff   =         p8/1000
iphase    =         p9
izin      =         p10
izout     =         p11
kamp      linseg    0, .002, 1, p3-.004, 1, .002, 0
asig      zar       izin
aosc1     oscil     idepth, irate, iwave, iphase
aosc2     =         aosc1+ideloff
atemp     delayr    idepth+ideloff
adel1     deltapi   aosc2
          delayw    asig
aout      =         (adel1*imix+asig)/2*kamp
          zaw       aout, izout
          endin
```

Figure 30.22 Orchestra code for *instr 3035,* a “chorus” instrument.

pitch of the delayed signal is modulated. The combined signal is then fed back into the beginning of the delay path, which makes a more pronounced flanging effect. Typical delay times are 10 msec.

A stereo flanger can be implemented by running two flangers at one quarter cycle out of phase from each other and sending each to a separate channel as follows:

```
;       ST  DUR  RATE  DPTH  WAVE  FEEDBK MIX  DELAY  PHASE  INCH  OUTCH
i 3030  0   1.6  .5    1     1     .8     1    1      0      2     3
i 3030  0   1.6  .5    1     1     .8     1    1      .25    2     4
```

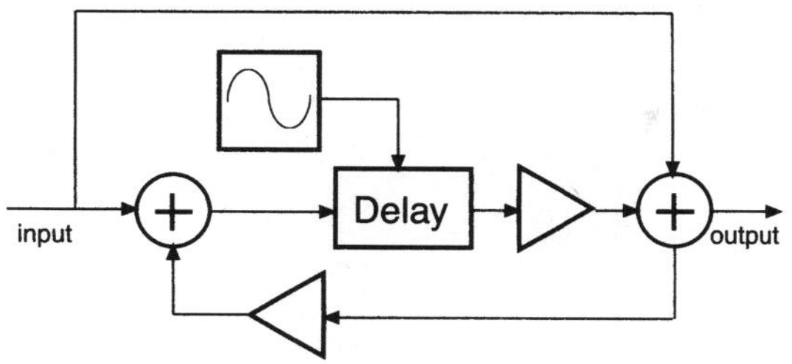

Figure 30.23 Block diagram of a flanger.

```
            instr     3030              ; FLANGER
irate       =         p4
idepth      =         p5/1000
iwave       =         p6
ifdbk       =         p7
imix        =         p8
ideloff     =         p9/1000
iphase      =         p10
izin        =         p11
izout       =         p12
adel1       init      0
kamp        linseg    0, .002, 1, p3-.004, 1, .002, 0
asig        zar       izin
asig1       =         asig+ifdbk*adel1
aosc1       oscil     idepth, irate, iwave, iphase
aosc2       =         aosc1+ideloff
atemp       delayr    idepth+ideloff
adel1       deltapi   aosc2
            delayw    asig1
aout        =         (imix*adel1+asig)/2
            zaw       aout, izout
            endin
```

Figure 30.24 Orchestra code for *instr 3030,* a flanger.

Miscellaneous Effects

This section describes a digital delay, a panner, a tremolo effect and a simple reverb effect.

Stereo Delay

This section describes a stereo delay with cross feedback (see figures 30.25 and 30.26). The **delayr** and **delayw** opcodes provide a straight forward implementation of this. The right and left channels are delayed independently. The delayed signal from each channel may be mixed with the original signal in either channel.

Tremolo

Tremolo is usually considered to be a periodic variation in the volume of a sound. This can be implemented by generating a low frequency oscillating sine wave between 0 and 1 in amplitude and simply multiplying the input signal by this (see figures 30.27 and 30.28). Note that using the same instrument, a square wave can be used to generate an amplitude-gated sound.

Panner

A panner can be implemented by multiplying one channel by a low frequency sine wave and multiplying the other channel by one minus the low frequency sine wave, so that the channels are 180 degrees out of phase with each other. This way, the signal is swept from one channel to the other by the oscillator (see figures 30.29 and 30.30).

Reverb

All sound produces some type of reverberation as the sound waves are reflected and absorbed on surfaces in the listening environment. The type of reverb depends on the size, shape and material of the area in which the sound is produced. A concert hall can produce a rich spacious reverb. Artificial reverb is often added to signals to make them sound as if they were generated in a specific type of area, such as a concert hall. Reverberation can be simulated by using a combination of allpass filters, comb filters and delays. Csound provides the **nreverb** opcode for generating simple reverbs. This is used in the instrument shown in figure 30.31 to create a simple

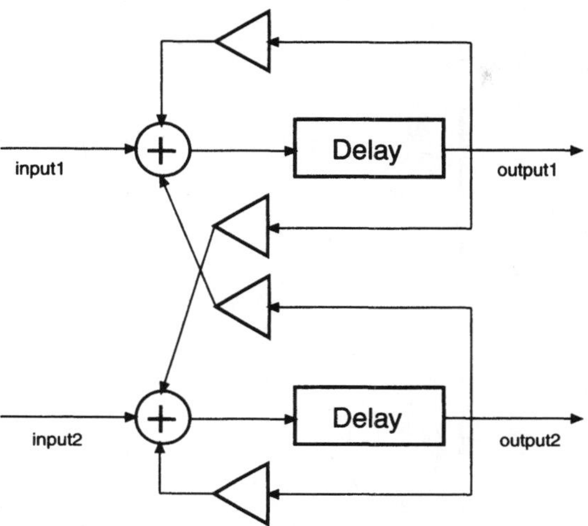

Figure 30.25 Block diagram of a stereo delay.

```
            instr    3040          ; STEREO DELAY
itim1       =        p4
ifdbk1      =        p5
ixfdbk1     =        p6
itim2       =        p7
ifdbk2      =        p8
ixfdbk2     =        p9
izinl       =        p10
izinr       =        p11
izoutl      =        p12
izoutr      =        p13
aoutl       init     0
aoutr       init     0
asigl       zar      izinl
asigr       zar      izinr
aoutl       delayr   itim1                              ; SUM DELAYED SIGNAL...
            delayw   asigl+ifdbk1*aoutl+ixfdbk1*aoutr   ; ...WITH ORIGINAL AND
aoutr       delayr   itim2                              ; ...ADD CROSS-FEEDBACK
            delayw   asigr+ifdbk2*aoutr+ixfdbk2*aoutl   ; ...SIGNAL.
            zaw      aoutl, izoutl
            zaw      aoutr, izoutr
            endin
```

Figure 30.26 Orchestra code for *instr 3040,* a stereo delay with feedback.

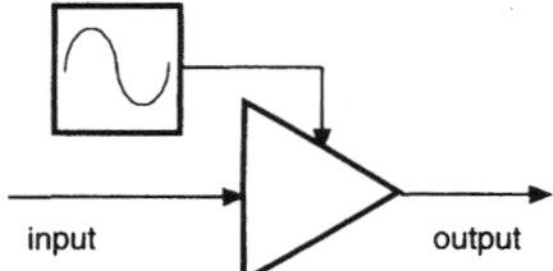

Figure 30.27 Block diagram of a tremolo effect.

```
            instr     3021              ; TREMOLO
iamp        =         p4
ifqc        =         p5
itabl       =         p6
iphase      =         p7
izin        =         p8
izout       =         p9
asig        zar       izin
kosc        oscil     iamp, ifqc, itabl, iphase
aout        =         asig*(kosc+1)/2
            zaw       aout, izout
            endin
```

Figure 30.28 Orchestra code for *instr 3021,* a tremolo/gate effect.

reverb. There are many excellent examples of reverbs available in the Csound archives, which can be modified to work with the system presented in this chapter.

Conclusion

I hope that this section has provided insight into the theory and implementation of many of the most popular sound effects and has provided inspiration for further audio experiments. Some further ideas to try would be to use different waveforms with the pitch-based effects. You might try calling the chorus routine many times with different parameters and waveforms, to produce a dense chorusing effect. Try setting up different types of distortion and then devise an instrument to oscillate between them. Add attack and decay envelopes to the dynamics effects. And if you have a fast computer, one of the first things you may wish to do is to implement real-time input and output for the effects. Effects processing is an important dimension of the sound design process; I hope these instrument models help you get further into it.

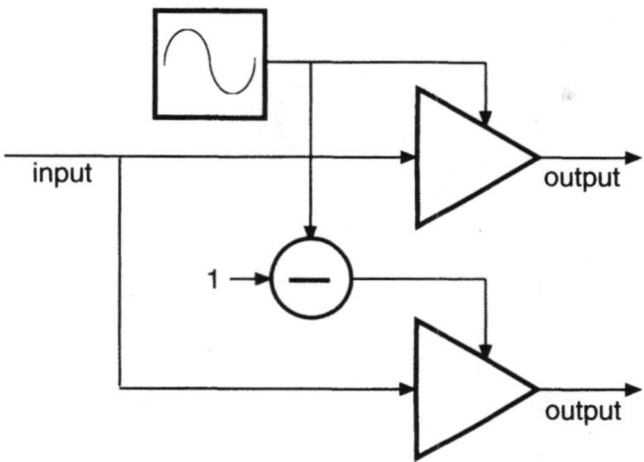

Figure 30.29 Block diagram of an LFO-based auto-panner.

```
            instr    3023            ; AUTO-PANNER
iamp        =        p4
ifqc        =        p5
itab1       =        p6
iphase      =        p7
izin        =        p8
izoutl      =        p9
izoutr      =        p10
asig        zar      izin
kosc        oscil    iamp, ifqc, itab1, iphase
kpanl       =        (kosc+1)/2
kpanr       =        1-kpanl
aoutl       =        asig*kpanl
aoutr       =        asig*kpanr
            zaw      aoutl, izoutl
            zaw      aoutr, izoutr
            endin
```

Figure 30.30 Orchestra code for *instr 3023,* an auto-panner.

```
            instr      3045            ; SIMPLE REVERB
irvtime     =          p4
irvfqc      =          p5
izin        =          p6
izout       =          p7
asig        zar        izin
aout        nreverb    asig, irvtime, irvfqc
            zaw        aout/5, izout
            endin
```

Figure 30.31 Orchestra code for *instr 3045,* a simple reverb instrument.

References

Cronin, D. 1994. “Examining audio DSP programs.” *Dr. Dobb’s Journal.*

Hamm, R., O. 1973. “Tubes versus transistors—is there an audible difference?” *Journal of the Audio Engineering Society.*

Lehman, S. “Effects Explained.” http://www.harmony-central.com/effects/.

Programming

Adding Opcodes

31 Extending Csound

John ffitch

As you begin to master the Csound system, there may come a point when you wish it could do more and a desire may grow to change and extend Csound. In this chapter, a number of pointers are given to start you on this endeavor. Granted, there is a great deal to learn before declaring oneself an expert, but there is no better way than to read the code and improve it.

Csound was originally conceived, designed and coded so that new opcodes could be added by users who were not necessarily experts in all the workings of the system. In practice this facility has been less used than was expected, possibly because the instructions were not sufficiently explicit. Nevertheless, the facilities are there for anyone with a sense of adventure and an idea for a new opcode. This chapter describes the various stages that are necessary to add one's own operations to Csound, drawing on examples of code that have been added by programmers other than the original Csound author.

What Is Needed in a New Opcode

In adding a new opcode to Csound, there are five components that ideally should be provided. They are:

1. New information for *entry.c* to define the syntax of the opcode
2. A header file (*.h*) to define the structure—how the opcode passes information
3. The actual C code (*.c*) that implements the opcode
4. Documentation and a manual page for the opcode
5. An *.orc* and *.sco* example to show how to use your new opcode

Introducing the Syntax

The purpose of the first of these is to make the word used to designate the opcode, known to Csound; to specify the number and types of the opcode's input arguments; and to specify the number and type of the output arguments. These requirements are achieved by a single line in a table defined in the *entry.c* file. Each line of this table gives the complete information for a single opcode.

There are eight entries in the line. The first gives the name of the opcode as a string. For example, in the line for Csound's value converter for generating non–12-note equal-tempered scales, the string **cpsxpch** introduces the word into the language.

```
{ "cpsxpch", S(XENH), 1, "i", "iioo", cpsxpch, NULL, NULL },
```

The second field defines the size of the data area—how large is the argument and workspace. The *S* is a macro for *sizeof* and the name *XENH* is the name of the structure. This is explained in more detail in the next section.

The third field indicates when in performance Csound needs to act on this opcode. There are three possibilities, note initialization time, control rate and audio rate. These are coded as the numbers 1, 2 and 4 and the third field is the addition of the necessary times. In this example the number 1 indicates that it is only required at note initialization time. The number 5 would indicate that this opcode is usable at both initialization and audio time (i.e., 1+4).

The output or "answer" of the opcode is coded in the fourth field. The possible types are i, k, or a, for the i-value, k-value or a-value. It is possible to have no answer (an empty string), or values like "*aa*" to indicate stereo audio answers. Other values, such as m, d, or w are possible but are not common.

Similarly, the fifth field codes the input arguments. In addition to the codes already seen, it is possible to use the following codes:

```
S     String
h     Optional, defaulting to 127
j     Optional, defaulting to -1
m     begins an indefinite list of iargs (any count)
n     begins an indefinite list of iargs (nargs odd)
o     Optional, defaulting to 0
p     Optional, defaulting to 1
q     Optional, defaulting to 10
v     Optional, defaulting to .5
x     a-rate or k-rate
```

Care does need to be taken with optional arguments. They must be at the end and they are interpreted strictly left to right. Any missing argument must be a right-most one. In the example here "*iioo*" means two compulsory initialization time arguments and two optional arguments, which, if missing, take the value zero.

The remaining three entries in the table are the functions that are called at initialization, at control-rate and for audio-rate activities. If any of these is absent then a *NULL* is used, but the third argument has already indicated which of these are to be used. These functions are treated as functions of a *void** argument (which will be the argument and variable structure whose size is given in the second field) which return no answer.

In order to complete the changes to *entry.c,* you need to add prototypes for any new functions, for example for the **cpsxpch** opcode, whose entry is given above, you will find:

```
void cpsxpch(void*);
```

The final stage is to include the header at the start of the file. This defines the new structure in order that the size can be known.

The Header File

The main requirement of the header file is to define the data area for the opcode. This data area is used for the arguments and the "answer," as well as any local variables that are needed. Arguments and the answer(s) are addresses—where to find the floating point number that is the value, or where to find the vector of length **ksamps** in the case of audio arguments or answers. If we consider the opcode above, **cpsxpch**, we see that it has a total of 5 answers and arguments, so there will need to be 5 fields of type *float**. In fact, the structure is:

```
typedef struct {
 OPDS h;
 float *r, *pc, *et, *ref, *cy;
} XENH;
```

The *OPDS* field is needed for organizing the collection of opcodes that make an instrument. For example, it includes chaining of opcodes together so the next performance step can be found and the next initialization step. If one of the arguments is a string it is coded within this header. For most purposes, the user or extender of Csound need not worry about this header information, except to remember to include it at the start of every opcode data definition.

Following the header there are the five pointers to floats that we expected. Notice that there is no intrinsic difference between input and output values, or between single values and audio vectors. It is assumed that the programmer is sufficiently skilled to use the variables correctly.

If the algorithm requires any values that are determined at initialization time and used at performance time, then they should be inside this structure. These additional values can be of any form or type.

A different example is from the nonlinear filter opcode **nlfilt**.

```
typedef struct {
 OPDS h;
 float *ar /* The output */
 float *in, *a, *b, *d, *C, *L; /* The parameters */
 AUXCH delay; /* Buffer for old values */
 int point; /* Pointer to old values */
} NLFILT;
```

Here the opcode has six arguments and generates audio output. As part of the algorithm it is useful to have an offset into a buffer. The offset is maintained between successive calls to the performance function so is coded in the structure. An integer value is sufficient. The buffer however is included via the *AUXCH* structure, which is designed for just such a purpose. There is a function *auxalloc* to allocate space with this structure and in a fashion where space is not lost.

The Code

The code embodies the algorithm for the opcode. There are usually two functions. The first is called at opcode initialization time. Its purpose is typically to check the arguments, calculate important constants and to initialize performance values and buffers.

The creation of buffers is important for delay-lines or similar algorithms. Csound has support for such buffer creation with the structure *AUXCH* and the allocation function *auxalloc*. This function is given the number of bytes required and the address of an *AUXCH* structure. It returns after allocating a buffer of sufficient length. In the process, it records it so the space can be recovered and undertakes other housekeeping activities. It is strongly recommended that this mechanism is used rather than some private method. In the case of the nonlinear filter mentioned above, the initialization is:

```
if (p->delay.auxp == NULL) { /* get new space */
 auxalloc(MAX_DELAY*sizeof(float), &p->delay);
}
```

The first test checks to see if there is already a buffer defined from an earlier use of the structure and if so, it is unnecessary to create a new one. If this test were omitted, the only loss would be in time.

The second function is the one to be called every control period. It can be called either entirely for control or for audio-rate. The latter is the more informative. The structure of the function is usually:

```
void perform_opcode(STRUCTURE *p)
{
 int nsamps = ksmps;
 ...other declarations...
 ...read saved values from structure...
 do {
 ....calculate audio values....
 *ar++ = newvalue;
 } while (--nsmps);
 ...write values back to structure...
}
```

It is worth remarking that the efficiency of the loop in this part of the opcode is what has the largest effect on the efficiency of the opcode in performance. The usual programming advice: "avoid recalculation; avoid structure access; and avoid function calls" cannot be repeated too often.

Of course, the code may include additional functions, or make use of other parts of Csound.

Documentation and Example

Each opcode should have a page of documentation, in the same style as the *Csound Reference Manual.* This ensures that other users can benefit from the work you have done in creating the opcode. In fact, the new hypertext manual is such that it can be easily extended by all opcode creators.

Finally, a small and simple example may significantly help others understand what the opcode does and how it could be used. For this reason, opcode designers are strongly encouraged to produce working examples as models for study.

What Is Needed in a New Table Type

When a table is created at performance time (or indeed at compilation time as a result of the **ftgen** opcode), the action of Csound is first to check that the table number is not already in use and then, to allocate the space for the table. After this, the table is filled by one of the more than 20 Csound GEN routines.

If you want to add a new way of initializing a table, all that is required is to write a function to do the writing of the data and then to extend the table called *gensub* defined in *fgens.c*. Also, you need to increase the constant *GENMAX* as well. The function would look something like the following form:

```
void gennew(void)
{
 float *fp = ftp->ftable;
 float *pp = &e->p[5];
 int nvals = nargs;
 ........
}
```

This fragment demonstrates where the function can find the allocated table (*FUNC *ftp*) and the arguments to the table (*EVTBLK *e*). If the method uses a soundfile, it should be opened with the function *sndgetset(SOUNDIN *)* and read with *getsndin(-int, float *, long, SOUNDIN *)*. For further suggestions it is probably best to read the file *fgens.c*.

Steps in Adding an Opcode

In the following idealized scenario, it is assumed that a new opcode called **chaos** is to be added and this has been correctly coded in the files *chaos.h* and *chaos.c*. This new opcode is assumed to be one to generate audio results from one initialization value (that is, one i-value) and two control-rate values (two k-values), the second of which is optional and defaults to zero.

The first action is to edit *entry.c* in three places:

Step 1: Include Header—At the top of the file there are a number of lines like:

```
#include "butter.h"
#include "grain.h"
#include "grain4.h"
#include "cmath.h"
```

You should add the line:

```
#include "chaos.h"
```

at the end of this list.

Step 2: Add Prototypes—to the next section of the file *entry.c,* which contains forward declarations, of the form:

```
void ihold(void*), turnoff(void*);
void assign(void*), rassign(void*), aassign(void*);
void init(void*), ainit(void*), flwset(void*), follow(void*);
void gt(void*), ge(void*), lt(void*), le(void*), eq(void*);
```

To the end of this list of the prototypes, add the two functions, which we will assume are:

```
void chaosset(void*), chaos(void*);
```

Step 3: Add Syntax—about 3 lines from the end of the *entry.c* file it is necessary to add the definition of the opcode and its arguments for the parser. The new line will look like:

```
{ "chaos", S(CHAOS), 5, "a", "iko", chaosset, NULL, chaos }
};
```

There will be an initialization call and a function to call on every control period (as specified by the *5*) and the two strings encode the answer and argument type.

Step 4: Add to the System—move the files *chaos.c* and *chaos.h* into the base Csound source directory and then add these to the Makefile or the compiler project.

Assuming this has not caused any problems, compile Csound with the compilation method for your system, whether that is an integrated environment or a Makefile. Any compilation errors are user errors at this stage and it is beyond the scope of this chapter to assist in debugging your code. We will assume that all is well.

The only remaining stage is to test the opcode, using the simple example that you will be supplying. Check that the documentation is in the correct format to be added into the manual and then you are ready to disseminate your contribution to the world.

Files in Csound Sources

There are a number of different platforms that support Csound, with the same functionality. Indeed that is the power of the system; orchestras developed on one platform can run on others. The following description comes from the PC and UNIX implementations. It ignores platform-specific user interfaces. Of course on other platforms there may be slight differences, but the global structure will be the same.

In this description, I have divided the sources into eight major sections. In some cases the allocation is a little arbitrary, but this form should provide enough information to enable the Csound programmer to find their way around the sources: either in the case of a certain area is of particular interest, or when one wants to change a component.

The Main Engine

The main engine contains the files that do the general organization and conduct the performance. There are also headers that provide structures throughout the system:

```
Prototyp.h      ANSI C Prototypes
cs.h            The main header file
Main.c          Argument decoding and organization
Insert.c        Insertion of playing events
Insert.h
Musmon.c        Control of performance
midirecv.c      MIDI message receiving; the MIDI Manager
memalloc.c      Memory allocation
memfiles.c      Utility; Loading files into memory
sysdep.h        System dependent declarations
version.h       Current version number and string
filopen.c       Utility; Opening files
opcode.c        Write list of opcodes
auxfd.c         Utility; Various
getstring.c     Localisation of messages to languages
text.h
natben.c        Utility for byte order
one_file.c      .csd format input
argdecode.c     command line arguments
```

Compiling the Orchestra

The reading, compilation and loading of the orchestra is a major component of Csound. The files here organize the process, but do not have information about the opcodes themselves, except the syntax information that is coded in entry.c as described elsewhere.

oload.c	Loading of a translated orchestra
oload.h	
rdorch.c	Reads an orchestra
entry.c	Table of opcodes and actions associated with them
express.c	Expression reading
otran.c	Translation of orchestra

Translating the Score

rdscor.c	Read the basic score
sort.c	Sort score events into order
sort.h	
linevent.c	Handle score events read in real-time
sread.c	Read the revised score
swrite.c	Write the revised score
twarp.c	Warp the time for beats. acceleration etc.
dpwelib.h	

Soundfile Input/Output

sfheader.c	Deal with sound file headers
sfheader.h	
soundin.c	Sound input
soundio.c	Basic sound I/O
soundio.h	
ieee80.c	IEEE80 arithmetic, needed for AIFF
ieee80.h	
aiff.c	AIFF Output format
aiff.h	AIFF Output format
aifc.c	AIFC Output format
ulaw.c	Translation for ulaw encoding
wave.c	WAV Output format
wave.h	

Audio I/O and Real-Time

rtDec.c	Real-time I/O of Dec audio
rtHP.c	Real-time I/O of HP audio
rtSGI.c	Real-time I/O of SGI audio
rtSUN.c	Real-time I/O of SUN audio

rtlinux.c	Real-time I/O of Linux audio
rtmacintosh.c	Real-time I/O of Macintosh audio
rtnext.c	Real-time I/O of Next audio
rtwin32.c	Real-time I/O of Win32 audio
DECaudio.c	For DEC platforms
DECaudio.h	
DECplay.c	
DECplay.h	
HPplay.c	For HP platforms
LINUXaudio.c	For LINUX platforms
SGIplay.c	For SGI platforms
solarisAudio.c	For SUN platforms
solarisAudio.h	

Graphics Code (for Various Systems)

winEPS.c	Postscript printing
winEPS.h	
winSGI.c	SGI pictures
winX11.c	X pictures
winascii.c	ASCII graphics
winbor.c	Borland C graphics
wincwin.c	Windows95 graphics
windin.c	Window input
windin.h	
window.c	Controlled code
window.h	
winfg.c	Flash Graphics
winwat.c	Watcom DOS Graphics

Utilities

cscore.c	Cscore
cscore.h	
cscorfns.c	Cscore support
cscormai.c	
cvanal.c	Convolve analysis
extract.c	Extract parts of a score
lpanal.c	Linear Predictive Coding analysis
lpc.h	
hetro.c	Hetrodyne Analysis
pvanal.c	Phase Vocoder analysis

scot.c	Scot scoring system
scot.h	
scsort.c	Scot Score sorting
scxtract.c	Extract from Scot
sndinfo.c	Sound Info
ustub.h	
pvlook.c	Decode PV files
het_expo.c	Various binary to/from coma-separated translations
het_impo.c	
lpc_expo.c	
pv_expor.c	
pv_impor.c	

Opcode Implementation

3Dug.h	
aops.c	Arithmetic
aops.h	
butter.c	Butterworth filters
butter.h	
cmath.c	Mathematical opcodes
cmath.h	
convolve.h	Convolution
cross2.c	Cross synthesis
dam.c	Dynamics limiter
dam.h	
diskin.c	
diskin.h	
disprep.c	
disprep.h	
dsputil.c	DSP utilities for opcodes
dsputil.h	
dumpf.c	Dump of k-values
dumpf.h	
fft.c	Fast Fourier transforms
fft.h	
fgens.c	Table generators
fhtfun.h	
filter.c	Filter2 opcode
filter.h	
complex.c	Support code for filter
complex.h	

flanger.c	Flanger opcode
flanger.h	
follow.c	Envelope follower
follow.h	
ftgen.h	
grain.c	Granular synthesis
grain.h	
grain4.c	Full granular synthesis
grain4.h	
hrtferX.c	Surround sound
hrtferx.h	
lptrkfns.c	LPC support
midioops.h	MIDI output
midiops.c	MIDI controllers and similar
midiops.h	
midiops2.c	Additional MIDI code
midiops2.h	
midiops3.c	
midiops3.h	
midiout.c	MIDI output
midiout.h	
midisend.c	Low-Level MIDI
nlfilt.c	Non-linear filter
nlfilt.h	
ptrigtbl.h	
pvinterp.c	Phase Vocoder interpolation
pvinterp.h	
pvoc.c	Phase Vocoder
pvoc.h	
pvread.c	
pvread.h	
repluck.c	Physical model plucked and reverberating string
repluck.h	
revsets.h	
sndwarp.c	Sound warping/stretching
sndwarp.h	
spectra.c	Spectral opcodes
spectra.h	
ugens1.c	Basic opcodes from original system
ugens1.h	
ugens2.c	
ugens2.h	
ugens3.c	
ugens3.h	
ugens4.c	
ugens4.h	

```
ugens5.c
ugens5.h
ugens6.c
ugens6.h
ugens7.c
ugens7.h
ugens8.c
ugens8.h
ugens9.c
ugens9.h
ugensa.c       FOG opcode
ugensa.h
ugrw1.c        Zak system
ugrw1.h
ugrw2.c        printk
ugrw2.h
vdelay.c       vdelay opcode and echos
vdelay.h
vpvoc.c        Sound morphing via Phase Vocoder
vpvoc.h
wavegde.c      Waveguide plucked string
wavegde.h
biquad.c       Various filters
biquad.h
physmod.c      Physical model opcodes
bowed.h
brass.h
clarinet.h
flute.h
mandolin.c
mandolin.h
onepole.h
onezero.h
vibraphn.h
physutil.c     Support code for physical models
physutil.h
fm4op.c        FM synthesis models
fm4op.h
dcblockr.c     DC blocking
dcblockr.h
modal4.c       Modal physical models
modal4.h
marimba.h
moog1.c        Mini Moog emulation
moog1.h
```

shaker.c	rattles and shakers
shaker.h	
singwave.c	Singing-like sound
singwave.h	
locsig.c	Locating sounds in space
locsig.h	
space.c	
space.h	
lowpassr.c	
lowpassr.h	
pitch.c	Pitch tracking and other utility opcodes
pitch.h	
pluck.c	Plucked string emulation
pluck.h	
pvadd.c	Phase vocoding operations
pvadd.h	
pvocext.c	
pvocext.h	
schedule.c	Scheduling events from orchestra
schedule.h	
uggab.c	Various opcodes
uggab.h	
ugsc.c	Various filters
ugsc.h	
sndinfUG.c	Information from sound files
sndinfUG.h	
dcblockr.c	
dcblockr.h	
fout.c	Multi-file output
fout.h	
control.c	Generalised instrument controllers
control.h	

References

Kernighan, B., and D. Ritchie. 1988 The C Programming Language. 2d ed. Englewood Cliffs: Prentice Hall

Winsor, P. 1991. Computer Music in C. Blue Ridge Summit: Tab Books.

32 Adding New Unit Generators to Csound

Marc Resibois

Csound is an outstanding tool. From the off-the-net version we have the means to realize a myriad of applications. But still, sometimes we need to optimize a special purpose algorithm, or sometimes the particular synthesis technique that inspires us is not yet implemented. Fortunately, Csound was designed to allow users to expand the language by adding their own opcodes to the basic set.

In this chapter we will learn how to add new functionality to the program by creating our own processing units and then compiling them into the Csound language. First, we will look at the steps involved in building a user-extended Csound from the source code. Then, we will build our own simple unit generator.

Along the way, we'll see the steps and issues involved in this procedure and focus on those issues specific to the Csound environment. Finally, we will build a more complicated opcode that acts as a general purpose compressor/expander unit. This example will allow us to go over the various steps involved in converting a desired unit generator's behavior into actual code that is implemented in Csound.

Quite obviously, this chapter relies on C programming, the language in which Csound was written. Although it is not absolutely required to fully understand this language in order to follow the basics of this chapter, it is assumed that the reader has at least some knowledge of C.

Creating a Csound Executable

Before even thinking of adding any code to the Csound environment, the first task is to make sure you can get the existing code to compile. Although this might sound trivial, it is not always an easy task. If you are familiar with programming, this will probably not take more than a quarter of an hour, but for novices, it can be hard to understand what is going wrong if complications arise.

The Compilation Process

The compilation process is the action that will turn source code (the program text) into a program that will run on your computer platform. Basically, compilation involves two phases: the first is to individually compile each of the required pieces of *source code* (representing the different functionalities of the software) and turn these into *object code*. Then, all the *objects* are *linked* together in order to form a single Csound executable (see figure 32.1).

Compiling for a given platform implies a few strategic decisions. First, you have to select which part of the code is needed for your machine. And even though Csound is known to be cross-platform compatible, the way you address a sound output device on a Silicon Graphics machine is quite different from how you do it on a Macintosh. For each of these platforms, you will need to select a different source code file, implementing the same functionality for the different hardware.

Then you have to activate the right compiler options. The way to specify some actions may differ from compiler to compiler and you need to select the right ones. When it comes to making these choices and determining the correct compiler settings, it is worth noting that all platforms are not equal. For instance, if the source code you grabbed is destined for a PC or a Mac, it is likely that it will contain a *project* file that, assuming you use the same compiler as the creator, already contains all the settings needed. The only thing you have to do is launch your compiler, open the project file and press the *compile* button. If, on the other hand, you work on UNIX machines, you will have to cope with the dreaded *makefile* and edit it in order

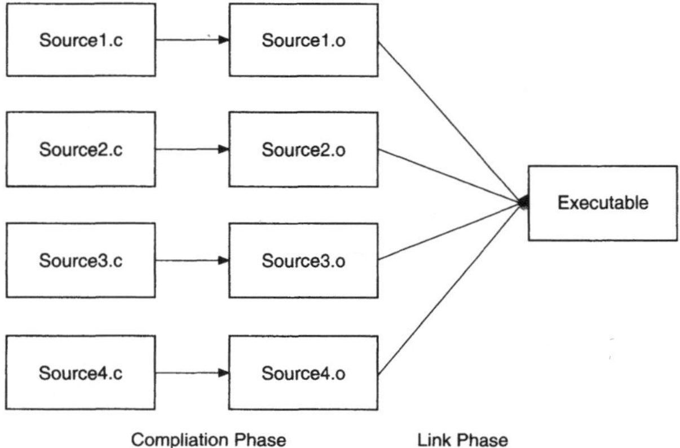

Figure 32.1 An illustration of the compilation and link phases of the compilation process.

to suit your needs. A complete discussion of the makefile syntax is beyond the scope of this chapter. But if you are a novice, I would recommend that you read some documentation and try a few little examples before trying to attack the Csound configuration.

The Basics of Opcode Design: IMPULSE

The addition of opcodes to Csound is not complicated, once the basic principles are known. Generally, the most difficult thing is coming up with a synthesis or processing algorithm that provides relevant and useful results, not its interfacing with Csound. Throughout this section, we will see how to convert a simple process into a Csound opcode that can be used in an instrument definition. This new opcode will only generate one single pulse of a given amplitude. In Csound terms, we would define the following opcode:

```
aout    impulse   iamp
```

Just writing the code from scratch and without worrying about Csound, we might end up with the following bit of C code:

```
void impulse(float amplitude, float *buffer, int bufferLength)
{
 int i ;
 buffer[0]=amplitude ;
 for (i=1; i<bufferLength;i++) {
 buffer[i]=0 ;
 }
}
```

Now, starting from this piece of code, we will need to make it into something compatible with Csound. The first conflict with the code above is that Csound is oriented toward real-time output. Although this has other implications, the main concern here is that Csound cannot afford to compute the whole content of the sound buffer, corresponding to the rendering of an instrument and mix it to the result of the others. Since a note can have an arbitrary length, it has to cut its duration into small chunks that are processed, one after the other and sent regularly to the output device that is selected—either DAC or file.

This means that, if an instrument, consisting of a collection of opcodes (let us suppose *opcode 1, opcode 2, . . . , opcode n*), is allocated for a given time, Csound's sequence of operations doesn't allow all the opcodes to successively compute their entire result. Rather, Csound computes some small block of each opcode in succession. From an implementation point of view, this has a quite big impact. Indeed, our main processing routine, instead of being called once to do all the computing, will be called several times and will have to act on a specified time slice. This means that we will need to be able to recover the state of the processing from one call to the next, so that we can continue computing from the place we left off the last time we called.

Getting back to our example above, it would mean that each time the code is called, we will have to check if the chunk that is currently processed is the first one or not. If the answer is yes, then we generate the impulse. Otherwise, we just fill everything with zeros. In C code, this can lead to something like:

```
for (i=0; i<chunkSize; i++) {
 chunk[i]=0 ;
}
if (isFirstTime) {
 buffer[0]=amplitude ;
}
```

Note that in Csound, the size of those chunks is actually determined by the initialization variable *ksmps,* which tells us how many a-rate samples there are in one k-rate. Essentially, this means that our opcode will be called at each k-time pass. This variable is know globally and can be accessed by including the *cs.h* file.

Since we need to associate some internal state to our opcode, we will have, at some time, to initialize it. This means that, for each opcode, we need to create at least two routines. The first one is an initialization routine—called by the kernel at each new note of an instrument, and the other one is a processing routine—called to process each chunk of *ksmps* samples. In our case, we will name them *impulseinit* and *impulse.* Both of them have to be declared as receiving one argument that is an *opcode data structure* pointer. This opcode data structure is in fact a collection of information relevant to the particular opcode that is used to communicate with Csound. In our case, we will choose the name of this structure to be *impulse* and we can thus declare our routines to be:

```
/* file: impulse.c */

#include "impulse.h" /* declaration of IMPULSE structure */

void impulseinit(void *) {
 /* init code here */
}
 void impulse(void*) {
/* processing code */
}
```

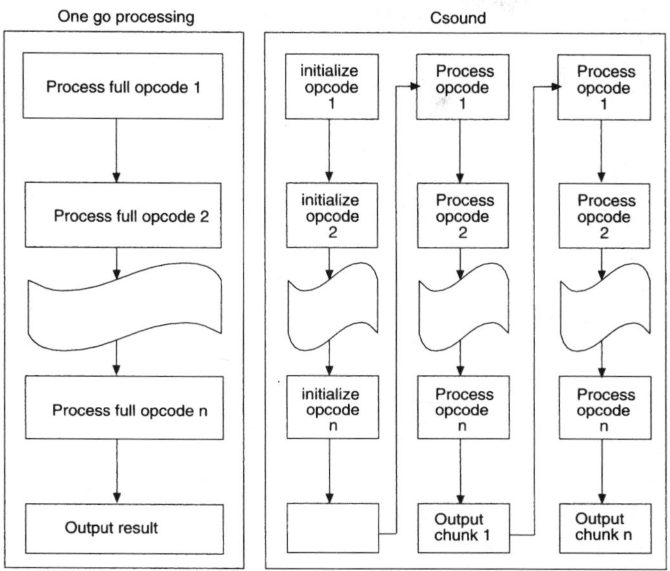

Figure 32.2 Comparison of Csound's "block-processing" to "one go" processing.

Let us get into the detail of what the *impulse* structure must contain. It will act as a communication channel between the Csound kernel and our opcode. It is through these means that we receive current values of the input(s) and send back the output resulting from our processing. This is also the place where we will store the internal state of our opcode, in order to remember where we are when doing the chunk by chunk processing. Indeed, the other option would be to store our opcode state in some global variables, but this would lead us to problems when we have more than one instance of the opcode working at the same time (e.g., when playing two simultaneous notes). Since a new copy of the structure is created for each new instrument's note, it is the perfect place to store anything that might be needed to keep track of our opcode's internal status.

To create this opcode data structure, we need to follow some rules. First, it has to start with an *OPDS* part. This is something we do not really need to know about; it is just needed by Csound to handle the invocation and registration of the various instruments in an uniform way. Since the definition of *OPDS* is located in *cs.h,* we will have to include this file at the beginning of our header file:

```
/* file: impulse.h */

#include "cs.h"

typedef Struct {
 OPDS h ; /* Csound opcode common part */
 ...
} IMPULSE ;
```

Then, we have to declare variables for the output and input (in that order). Note that in Csound, when we communicate a parameter value, it is always through a pointer to a float. Actually, it is because it wants to handle, in an uniform way, the a, k or i-rate variable.

Remember that each time the opcode is called, we have to process one k-rate step and *ksmps* a-rate steps. This means that any a-rate parameter will be passed as a buffer of *ksmps* values while any i and k-rate parameter will be passed as a single value. Using pointers gives a common interface to both situations. In our case, we have one a-rate output and one i-rate input. This gives:

```
typedef Struct {
 OPDS h; /* Csound opcode */
 float *aout ; /* Declare output first */
 float *iamp ; /* Input value */
 ...
} IMPULSE ;
```

After those declarations, we can add whatever variable we find suitable for the good functioning of our opcode. In our case, all we need to know when the processing routine is called is whether it is the first time the opcode has been called or not. We will keep track of this by adding a flag variable to the *impulse* structure that will be properly initialized in *impulseinit.* Our *impulse.h* file finally looks like the following:

```
#include "cs.h"
typedef Struct {
 OPDS h; /* Csound opcode */

 float *aout ; /* Declare output first */
 float *iamp ; /* Input value */

 char isFirstTime ; /* opcode internal state */
} IMPULSE ;
```

Now, having all the pieces together, we can easily write the routine's content. Our *impulse.c* file contains the following lines:

```
/* file: impulse.c */

#include "impulse.h" /* declaration of IMPULSE structure */

/* Initialization code */

void impulseinit(IMPULSE *p) {
 p->isFirstTime= 1 ;
}

/* Processing code: process ksmps samples at a time */
/* the value of ksmps is known through the cs.h file */

void impulse(IMPULSE *p) {
 int i;

 for (i=0;i<ksmps;i++) {
 p->aout[i]=0.0 ;
 }
 if (p->isFirstTime) {
 p->aout[I]=*(p->iamplitude) ;
 p->isFirstTime=0 ;
 }
}
```

The last step we need to complete is to let Csound know that our opcode exists and what its syntax is. The list of all opcodes available is defined in a file called *entry.c*. This is where we'll have to add ours. Since this file will have to know our code, we will need to reference both our opcode data structure and our routine in it. This can all be done by including our *impulse.h* (containing both the *impulse* definition and our function prototypes) at the beginning of the file. All opcodes are declared by means of a big array called *opcodlst*. For each opcode declared in this array, we have to declare the following fields:

- The name of the opcode in the Csound language `[impulse]`
- The size of the opcode data structure `[sizeof(IMPULSE)]`
- When the opcode can be called `[i and a rate]`
- The rate(s) of the output variables `[a]`
- The rate(s) of the input variables `[i]`
- The initialization routine name `[impulseinit]`

- An eventual k-rate routine name [none]
- The a-rate processing routine [impulse]

This gives us the following line that has to be added to the array:

```
OENTRY opcodlst[] = {
 ...
 ...
 { "impulse",S(IMPULSE), 5, "a", "i", impulseinit, 0 , impulse}
} ;
```

Now that our code is complete, we have to produce a new executable of Csound. What we need first is to add the file containing our opcode (the *impulse.c* file) to the list of files to be used for the compilation (this is done via the edition of the makefile, or through a specific project-builder feature) and to ask for a recompilation of all the modified files (*impulse.c* and *entry.c.*) If this compilation is successful, we will now have a customized version of Csound that is able to understand our new opcode.

A Full Opcode Implementation: *Dynamic Amplitude Modifier*

In this section we will construct a new opcode, whose goal is to modify the amplitude of a signal as a function of its power content—a compressor/expander-type unit. It will help us crystallize the notions we have just learned and will demonstrate how we can start from a desired behavior and wind up with an actual Csound implementation. Note that, although the flow of this chapter might suggest the opposite, getting an opcode right is not trivial. Usually, one has to make some suppositions of the opcode's behavior and validate them through the use of a number of model implementations. It turns out regularly that some assumptions were not correct and that the model has to be revised, re-implemented and re-tested. As I said earlier, the most difficult part of adding relevant code to Csound is the modeling itself.

Defining the Model

The first thing to do is to analyze what we want to model. In our case, we would like to build a single opcode that can be used to model a number of compression/expansion/limiting and gating effects found in many commercial recording studio processor boxes. In order to picture the common attributes of this family, we will take a look at them one after the other:

- **Compressors** are used when one wants to reduce the amplitude of the peaks found in a signal, thus making it more uniform. This is achieved by lowering the amplitude of the sound when it is too loud and keeping it unchanged otherwise. Also, a compressor could be used to smooth the transient attack of an acoustic signal such as a bass guitar, for instance, while giving more emphasis to its release.
- **Expanders** are used to increase the dynamics of a signal's tail. It works by keeping the signal unchanged when it is loud and amplifying it when it is quiet. It could be used to lift up an instrument whose release is too fast (on guitar strings or drums, for example) to achieve a *hold* effect.
- **Limiters** ensure that the level of the output signal will not exceed a given value (to avoid hard clipping in digital recording systems, for example.) This effect is obtained by reducing a lot of the signal's amplitude when it is above the given limit and keeping it unchanged when it is under.
- **Noise gates** are used to remove static or system noise when no musical sounds are being produced. This is done by setting the output gain to zero when the sound is under a low threshold level and by leaving the signal unchanged when it is above this threshold.

From this enumeration, we can deduce that what we want from our opcode is a processor that modifies the amplitude of the sound fed into it. In fact, each of the four algorithms described above uses a 'threshold' value to divide the amplitude range of the input signal into two zones and, depending whether the sound's amplitude is over or under this threshold, to amplify the input by the corresponding factors (see figure 32.3).

Let us consider the prerequisites of our unit. First, our opcode should not modify the harmonic content of our signal. This means that the only transformation we can apply to the input signal is a multiplication. Moreover, this multiplication factor has to be the same, no matter if the instantaneous value of the input is above or under the threshold. Failing to do so would introduce modifications in the original waveform and distort the signal. As a consequence, the central part of our opcode has to be something like this:

```
aout(t) = ain(t)*gain(t)
```

Thus, our job will be to properly link or map the value of the gain applied to the input signal with its own loudness characteristics. Again, since we do not want to modify the signal's harmonic content, the variation of the gain will have to be much slower than the frequency content of the signal; we cannot directly link the gain to the value of *ain*. What we need is an average value of the amplitude; that is, we will link the gain to the mean value of the signal's power over a short period of time.

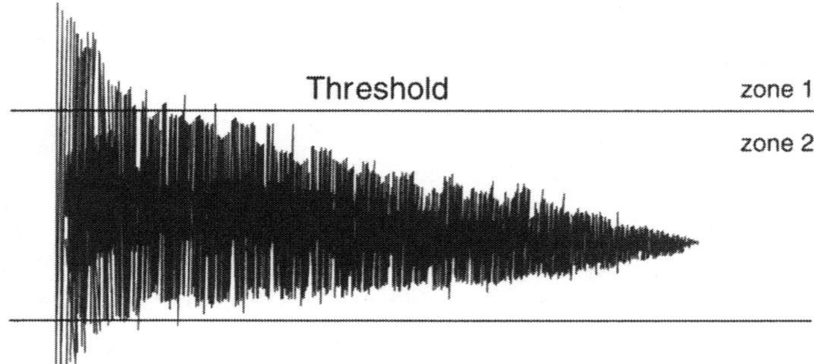

Figure 32.3 A signal divided into two zones by a threshold setting.

Starting from that, we can start to shape the algorithm. We will somehow have to measure an average power value of the signal and compute a resulting gain, depending on whether this value is above the threshold or not (see figure 32.4).

The way the gain is computed in both zones will depend of the settings made by the user of our opcode. Intuitively, we want to allow the user to say how strongly the sound should be amplified or reduced in each region. In order to do this, we will introduce a parameter called *compression ratio* for both zones. With a ratio equal to one, the sound is left unchanged. When greater than one, the sound will be expanded and, when less, it will be compressed.

We now need to establish a relationship that links the compression ratio defined by the user to the gain to be applied to the signal. To do this properly, we have to consider and comply with some additional criteria. First, the application of a change in one of the regions should never send the signal over the other threshold. Indeed, what we want is to control how the sound is modified in a given range, not send it all over the place.

Also, to help us realize a smooth transition between the two zones, no matter what the settings in either, we would like the signal's power left unchanged when it hovers around the threshold value. In order to address these requirements, we will consider power values and, for each zone, define how a given input power value should induce some output power value, given the various compression ratios. The actual gain to be applied to the sound will then be computed by evaluating the ratio of the output power divided by the input power.

Let us first take a look to what happens when the signal is over the threshold. First, we know that the resulting output power should never be under the threshold. Also, for a compression ratio lower than one, we would want the general output power to

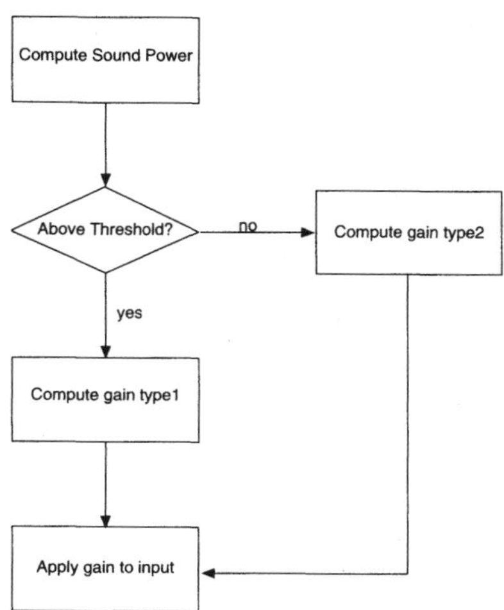

Figure 32.4 A general overview of the compressor algorithm.

be lower than the input power and vice versa. One can easily meet these specifications by having a linear relation between the input and output power. Thus we define a family of lines that passes through the point (threshold,threshold) and have a slope equal to the compression factor as shown in figure 32.5.

Then, on the lower side of the threshold, we have to satisfy one more condition. If the input power is zero, the output power should also be zero. Therefore, the relation between the input and the output has to be a family of curves, always passing by the two points (0,0) and (threshold,threshold). For the compression ratio equal to one, the curve should be a straight line, for values lower than one, the curve should raise slower than this line and for a compression ratio greater than one, it should raise faster. One can achieve this behavior by adopting the family of curves shown in figure 32.6.

Now, for any value of the input signal power, using the curves shown in figure 32.6, we are able to compute what the output power has to be and derive what gain should be applied to the signal.

The last situation we have to account for is if the sound power suddenly changes from region to region. Often we do not want the gain to change drastically and would rather have a smooth change from one behavior to the other. To do so, we will introduce two speeds that describe how fast the gain is allowed to grow and how fast it is allowed to diminish. The full algorithm is shown in figure 32.7.

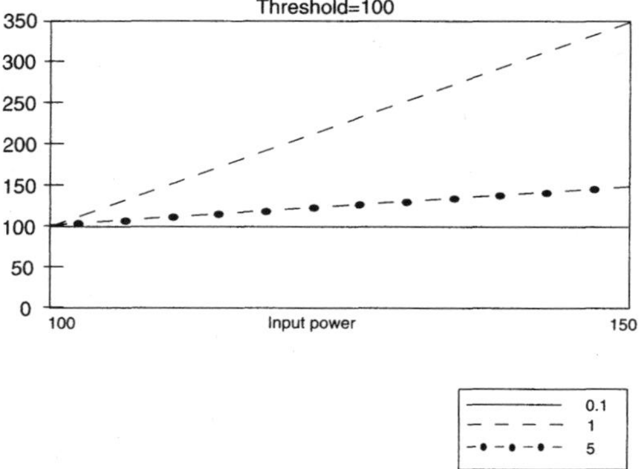

Figure 32.5 Compression curve for threshold = 100.

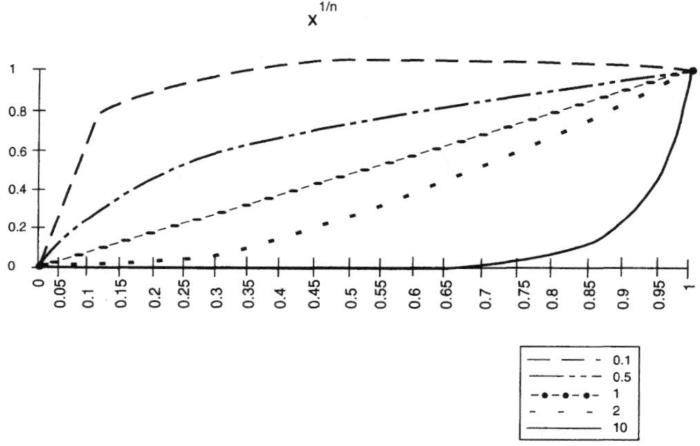

Figure 32.6 Family of compression curves $X^{1/n}$. OutputPower/Threshold = (InputPower/Threshold)(1/CompressionRatio)

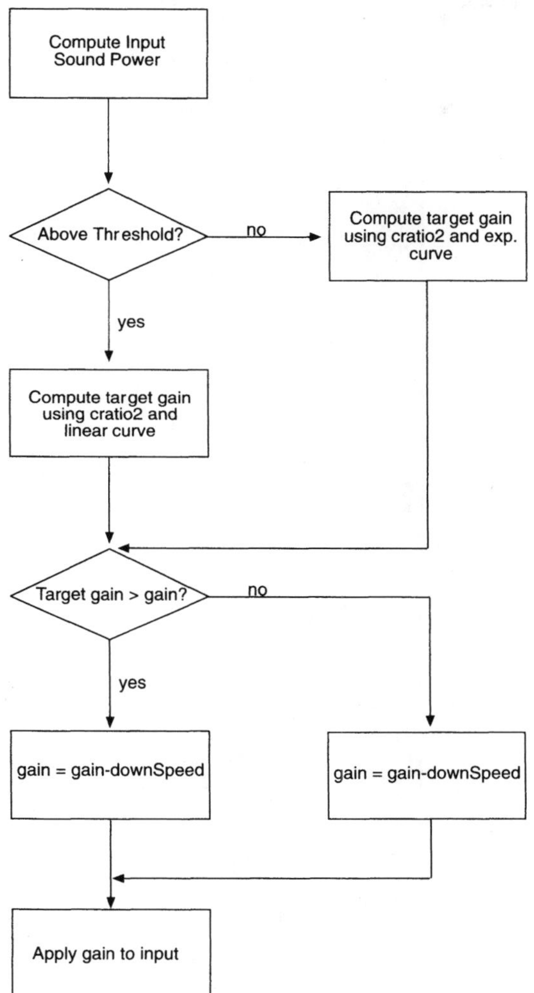

Figure 32.7 Flow chart of the full compressor/limiter algorithm.

Turning the Algorithm into Code

In itself, the processing is not complicated. Each time we have a new sample, we first have to compute the average sound around the current time. Since we are in a real-time oriented environment, we cannot use the future samples and will therefore rely only on past values. One convenient way to implement the power calculation is to have a buffer filled with the n previous values of the samples. Each time we start processing a new sample we add its value to the power and retrieve the oldest one contained in the buffer. Then we drop the oldest value from the buffer and replace it with the newest. This can be represented in the following C code:

```
/* NOTE: powerPos is the current position in the power buffer */
 /* Adds and store value of new sample */

 *powerPos=fabs(ain[i])/(float)POWER_BUFSIZE*sqrt(2.0) ;
 power+=(*powerPos++) ;

/* Look if we reach the end of the buffer */

 if ((powerPos-powerBuffer)== POWER_BUFSIZE) {
 powerPos=p->powerBuffer ;
 }

/* Removes the value of the oldest sample */

power-=(*powerPos) ;
```

Looking at the current value, we see which side of the threshold we are on and, according to the equations described above, deduct a target gain to be reached:

```
/* Looks where the power is related to the threshold
 and compute target gain */

 if (power>threshold) {
 tg=((power-threshold)*comp1+threshold)/power ;
 } else {
 tg=threshold*pow(power/threshold,1/comp2)/power ;
 }
```

Finally, we modify the actual gain value in the direction of the target gain, according to the allowed speed and apply it to the input sound:

```
/* move gain toward target */

 if (gain<tg) {
 gain+=p->rspeed ;
 } else {
     gain-=p->fspeed ;
 }

/* compute output */

 aout[i]=ain[i]*gain ;
```

Implementing the Opcode

We will now follow all the steps needed to introduce our algorithm into the Csound environment. Since we know all the parameters governing our opcode, we can define its syntax in the orchestra:

```
ar  dam   ain, kthreshold, icomp1, icomp2, rtime, ftime
```

With *ar* being the output signal, *ain* the input signal, *kthreshold* the sound level separating the two zones, *icomp1* and *icomp2* their associated compression ratio, *rtime* the time in milliseconds it takes for the gain to rise one unit and *ftime* the time it takes for the gain to drop one unit value.

Opcode Data Structure

As we've seen, the opcode data needs to respect some structure. First, it has to contain the *OPDS* part:

```
/* file dam.h */

#include "cs.h"

typedef Struct {

 OPDS h ; /* Csound opcode */
 ...
} DAM ;
```

Then, we have to declare the output and input variables:

```
typedef struct {
 ...

 float *aout ; /* Declare output array first */
 float *ain ; /* Input array */
 float *kthreshold ;/* sound level threshold */
 float *icomp1 ; /* Compression factors */
 float *icomp2 ;
 float *rtime ; /* Raise/Fall times */
 float *ftime ;

 ...
} DAM ;
```

And after those declarations, we can add all that we need to store the state of our opcode from one call to the other. From the processing code we have just described, we can see that from one call to the other we need to keep track of:

- The current gain
- The current power value
- The power buffer
- The current "store" position in the buffer

Additionally, we will need to derive gain variation speeds (in gain unit per sample) from the time given by the user and the sample rate. Since this conversion is always the same, we'll do it once, at initialization time and store the value in the opcode too. We finally wind up with a complete structure looking like:

```
typedef struct {
 OPDS h ;

 float *aout ; /* Declare output array first */
 float *ain ; /* Input array */
 float *kthreshold ;/* sound level threshold */
 float *icomp1 ; /* Compression factors */
 float *icomp2 ;
 float *rtime ; /* Raise/Fall times */
 float *ftime ;

 float rspeed ;
 float fspeed ;
```

```
 float gain ;
 float power ;
 float powerBuffer[POWER_BUFSIZE] ;
 float *powerPos ;

} DAM ;
```

Initialization Routine

As we saw, this routine is called once every time a new instrument copy is started. It is here that the additional variables representing the internal state of the particular opcode instance have to be set. In our particular case, we need to initialize the current gain value, the power value, the power buffer and compute the two gain speed changes.

```
void daminit(DAM *p)
{
 int i ;

 /* Initialize gain value */

 p->gain=1.0 ;

 /* Compute the gain speed changes from parameter given by
Csound */
 /* the computed values are stored in the opcode data
structure p */
 /* for later use in the main processing */

 p->rspeed=(*p->rtime)/esr*1000.0 ;
 p->fspeed=(*p->ftime)/esr*1000.0 ;

 /* Initialize power value and buffer */

 p->power=*(p->kthreshold) ;
 for (i=0;i<POWER_BUFSIZE;i++) {
 p->powerBuffer[i]=p->power/(float)POWER_BUFSIZE ;
 }

 p->powerPos=p->powerBuffer ;
}
```

The Main Processing Routine

The main routine has to treat *ksmps* samples each time the function is called. According to what we just saw, we have:

```
/*
 * Run-time computation code
 * /

void dam(DAM *p)
{
 int i;
 float *ain,*aout ;
 float threshold ;
 float gain ;
 float comp1,comp2 ;
 float *powerPos ;
 float *powerBuffer ;
 float power ;
 float tg ;

 ain=p->ain ;
 aout=p->aout ;
 threshold=*(p->kthreshold) ;
 gain=p->gain ;
 comp1=*(p->icomp1) ;
 comp2=*(p->icomp2) ;
 powerPos=p->powerPos ;
 powerBuffer=p->powerBuffer ;
 power=p->power ;

 /* Process ksmps samples */

 for (i=0;i<ksmps;i++) {

 /* Estimates the current power level */

 *powerPos=fabs(ain[i])/(float)POWER_BUFSIZE*sqrt(2.0) ;
 power+=(*powerPos++) ;
 if ((powerPos-powerBuffer)==POWER_BUFSIZE) {
     powerPos=p->powerBuffer ;
 }
 power-=(*powerPos) ;
```

```
/* Looks where the power is related to the threshold
     and compute target gain */

if (power>threshold) {
    tg=((power-threshold)*comp1+threshold)/power ;
} else {
    tg=threshold*pow(power/threshold,1/comp2)/power ;
}

/* move gain toward target */

if (gain<tg) {
    gain+=p->rspeed ;
} else {
    gain-=p->fspeed ;
}

/* compute output */

aout[i]=ain[i]*gain ;
}

/* Store the last gain value for next call */

p->gain=gain ;
p->power=power ;
p->powerPos=powerPos ;
}
```

Making the Opcode Known to Csound

To let our opcode be known, we just have to add a new opcode line in the *opcodlst* table. The characteristics of our opcode are:

- Its name
- The size of the opcode data structure
- When can it be called (i- and a-rates)
- The rate of the output variable(s)
- The rate of the input variables (in order)
- Its initialization function

Unit name	Threshold meaning	gain1 value	gain2 value
Compressor	Compression threshold	< 1	1
Expander	Expansion limit	1	> 1
Limiter	Output limit	very small	1
Noise gate	Noise level	1	very small

Figure 32.8 Table of recommended parameter values for the **dam** opcode's various modes of operation.

- No k-rate processing function
- Its a-rate processing function

```
{ "dam", S(DAM), 5, "a", "akiiii", daminit, NULL, dam }
```

Remember, because this line has to know your opcode data and your function prototypes, we will need to include *dam.h* at the beginning of the *entry.c* file.

Using the Opcode

Now that our opcode is created, we can recapitulate the various units described in figure 32.8 and see what parameters need to be used.

In addition to those uses, the opcode can also be turned into a *ducker,* a unit that reduces the loudness of one signal in response to the value of another. In order to do that, one has simply to put the opcode in *limiter* mode and adjust the threshold at k-rate as a function of the master sound level.

Conclusion

As a quick summary of the work needed for adding our opcodes, we've seen that first we had to create two new functions—one for the opcode initialization and one for the run-time code. We have chosen to place those functions in a separate source file—*dam.c,* although we could have put them into an existing one. Then, we had to edit the *entry.c* file in order to let Csound know the presence of our routines. Using our compilation environment, we added the new file to the list of currently included source code, then recompiled the program with all those changes and created a new version of Csound with the new functionality of our **dam** and **impulse** opcodes.

References

Embree, P. M. 1995. *C Algorithms for Real-time DSP.* Englewood Cliffs: Prentice Hall.

Kernighan, B., and D. Ritchie. 1988. *The C Programming Language.* 2nd ed. Englewood Cliffs: Prentice Hall.

Moore, R. F. 1990. *Elements of Computer Music.* New York: Prentice Hall.

Press, W., B. Flannery, S. Tevkolsky, and W. Vetterling. 1993. *Numerical Recipes in C.* 2nd ed. Cambridge, England: Cambridge University Press.

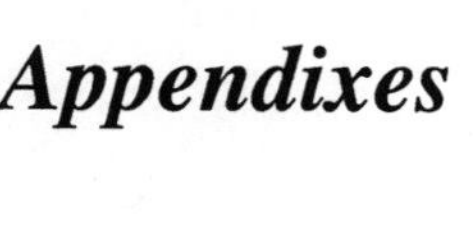

Appendixes

List of the Csound Book Chapter Instruments

1. Introduction to Sound Design in Csound

```
instr 101   ; SIMPLE OSCIL
instr 102   ; SIMPLE FM
instr 103   ; SIMPLE BUZZ
instr 104   ; SIMPLE WAVEGUIDE
instr 105   ; SIMPLE GRANULAR
instr 106   ; SIMPLE WAVETABLE
instr 107   ; P-FIELD OSCIL
instr 108   ; P-FIELD FM
instr 113   ; SIMPLE OSCIL WITH ENVELOPE
instr 115   ; SWEEPING BUZZ WITH ENVELOPE
instr 117   ; GRAINS THROUGH AN ENVELOPE
instr 118   ; LOSCIL WITH OSCIL ENVELOPE
instr 119   ; RETRIGGERING FOSCIL WITH OSCIL ENVELOPE
instr 120   ; SIMPLE CHORUSING
instr 122   ; SIMPLE SPECTRAL FUSION
instr 124   ; SWEEPING AMPLITUDE MODULATION
instr 126   ; SIMPLE DELAYED VIBRATO
instr 128   ; BANDPASS-FILTERED NOISE
instr 129   ; ONE-POLE LOWPASS
instr 130   ; TWO-POLE LOWPASS
instr 131   ; THREE-POLE LOWPASS
instr 132   ; FOUR-POLE LOWPASS
instr 133   ; LOWPASS WITH RESONANCE
instr 135   ; DISKIN ECHO-RESONATOR
instr 136   ; VDELAY FLANGER
instr 137   ; GLOBAL ECHO/REVERB LOSCIL
instr 138   ; SWEEPING FM WITH VIBRATO & DISCRETE PAN
instr 141   ; AMPLITUDE MODULATION LFO PANNER
```

2. Understanding Csound's Function Table GEN Routines

```
instr 201  ; READING A SOUNDFILE USING TABLEI & GEN1
instr 202  ; TABLE-LOOKUP OSCILLATOR - PHASOR/TABLEI
instr 203  ; TABLE-LOOKUP OSCILLATOR - OSCILI
instr 204  ; CPSPCH PITCH CONVERTER
instr 205  ; SIMPLE WAVESHAPING
instr 206  ; WAVESHAPING WITH NORMALIZATION
instr 207  ; PHASE-QUADRATURE WAVESHAPING
instr 208  ; AM/FM
instr 209  ; 12-TONE ROW PLAYER
instr 210  ; 3D WAVE-TERRAIN
```

3. What Happens When You Run a Csound Program

```
instr 301  ; REVERB SEND WITH EXPON AMPLITUDE ENVELOPE
instr 302  ; REVERB SEND WITH GAUSS PITCH ENVELOPE
instr 399  ; SIMPLE REVERB
```

4. Optimizing Your Csound Instruments

```
instr 401  ; SIMPLE (& SLOW) MIDI
instr 402  ; SIMPLE (& SLOW) MIDI
instr 403  ; SIMPLE OPTIMIZED MIDI
instr 404  ; A-RATE VIBRATO
instr 405  ; K-RATE VIBRATO
instr 406  ; INEFFICIENT AMPLITUDE SCALING
instr 407  ; EFFICIENT AMPLITUDE SCALING
instr 408  ; REDUNDANT FM
instr 409  ; OPTIMIZED STATIC FM
instr 410  ; USING FUNCTION CALLS
instr 411  ; USING TABLE-LOOKUP
instr 412  ; USING DIVISION
instr 413  ; USING MULTIPLICATION
instr 414  ; USING UNIQUE A-RATE OUTPUT ARGUMENTS
instr 415  ; REUSES A-RATE OUTPUT ARGUMENTS
instr 416  ; NEEDING USER OPTIMIZATION
```

5. Using Csound's Macro Language Extensions

```
instr 513  ; MACRO EXAMPLE 1
instr 514  ; MACRO EXAMPLE 2
instr 513  ; EXPANDED MACRO 1
```

```
instr 514  ; EXPANDED MACRO 2
instr 515  ; EXPANDED REVERB MACRO 1
instr 516  ; EXPANDED REVERB MACRO 2
```

6. Designing Acoustically Viable Instruments in Csound

```
instr 601  ; PARALLEL BANDPASS FILTER
instr 604  ; AMPLITUDE CONTROLLED TIMBRE MAPPING
instr 606  ; FM WITH MODULATION INDEX MAPPED TO AMPLITUDE
instr 607  ; FM WITH PITCH & AMP MAPPED TO ENVELOPE & SPECTRA
```

7. Designing Legato Instruments in Csound

```
instr 701  ; SIMPLE LEGATO INSTRUMENT
instr 702  ; MORE ELABORATE LEGATO INSTRUMENT
instr 705  ; FULL LEGATO INSTRUMENT WITH "CHIFF"
```

8. Contiguous-Group Wavetable Synthesis of the French Horn in Csound

```
instr 801  ; WAVETABLE FRENCH HORN
instr 899  ; SIMPLE REVERB
```

9. FM Synthesis and Morphing in Csound: from Percussion to Brass

```
instr 901  ; CHOWNING FM
```

10. Modeling "Classic" Electronic Keyboard Instruments in Csound

```
instr 1001 ; GLOBAL INITI: TONE WHEEL/ROTATING SPEAKER
instr 1002 ; THE FOOT SWITCH CONTROLLING ROTOR SPEEDS
instr 1003 ; TONE WHEEL ORGAN
instr 1004 ; ROTATING SPEAKER
instr 1007 ; TB-303 EMULATOR
```

11. A Survey of Classic Synthesis Techniques Implemented in Csound

```
instr 1102 ; SIMPLE OSCILLATOR WITH AMPLITUDE ENVELOPE
instr 1105 ; ENVELOPE-CONTROLLED WHITE NOISE
instr 1106 ; PULSE TRAIN WITH AMPLITUDE ENVELOPE
instr 1109 ; SIMPLE AMPLITUDE MODULATION
instr 1111 ; RING MODULATION
```

```
instr 1112 ; SIMPLE WAVESHAPING
instr 1113 ; DUAL WAVESHAPING
instr 1114 ; SIMPLE STATIC FM
instr 1115 ; FM WITH AMPLITUDE AND SPECTRAL ENVELOPES
```

12. A Guide to FM Implementation in Csound

```
instr 1201 ; SIMPLE CHOWNING FM
instr 1202 ; BETTER SIMPLE FM
instr 1203 ; SIMPLE PHASE MODULATION (PM)
instr 1204 ; PHASE MODULATION WITH MODULATOR STACK
instr 1205 ; DX7 EMULATOR – ALGORITHM 16
```

13. A Guide to Granular Synthesis in Csound

```
instr 1301 ; SIMPLE GRANULAR WITH GRANULE OPCODE
instr 1302 ; STEREO GRANULAR WITH COMMON AMPLITUDE ENVELOPE
instr 1303 ; 220 HZ SINE TONE
instr 1304 ; QUAD GRANULAR
instr 1306 ; SIMPLE GRANULAR WITH GRAIN OPCODE
```

14. Exploring FOF and FOG Synthesis in Csound

```
instr 1401 ; SINGLE FORMANT FOF
instr 1414 ; BASIC FOG
instr 1415 ; DYNAMIC SPEED CHANGE OF FOG PLAYBACK
instr 1416 ; SAMPLE-BASED FOG THAT "DISINTEGRATES"
```

15. Processing Samples with Csound's FOF Opcode

```
instr 1501 ; SIMPLE FOF
instr 1502 ; FOF THAT PROCESSES A TAMBURA SAMPLE
```

16. A Look at Random Numbers, Noise and Chaos with Csound

```
instr 1601 ; FILTERED NOISE WITH "DECLICKING" ENVELOPE
instr 1602 ; ADDITIVE WITH "GAUSSIAN" FREQUENCY DEVIATION
instr 1603 ; BASIC FM "BELL"
instr 1604 ; ENHANCED FM "BELL" WITH NOISE BURSTS
instr 1605 ; CUBIC OSCILLATOR USING THE DUFFING EQUATION
```

17. Constrained Random Event Generation and Retriggering in Csound

```
instr 1701 ; PERIODIC RE-INITIALIZATION
instr 1702 ; AMPLITUDE MODULATION WITH LFO
instr 1703 ; REINIT WITH PHRASE-ENVELOPE
instr 1704 ; A "POPCORN" SIMULATOR
instr 1705 ; 3 PART "GESTURE" INSTRUMENT
instr 1706 ; ALGORITHMIC MUSIC GENERATOR
```

18. Using Global Csound Instruments for Meta-Parameter Control

```
instr 1801 ; SIMPLE PORTAMENTO
instr 1802 ; CONTROLS 1803 FREQUENCY
instr 1803 ; SIMPLE OSCIL 1
instr 1804 ; CONTROLS 1806 FREQUENCY
instr 1805 ; SIMPLE OSCIL 2
instr 1806 ; SIMPLE OSCIL 3
instr 1807 ; GLOBAL LFO
instr 1808 ; GLOBAL ADSR
instr 1809 ; SIMPLE VCO
instr 1811 ; FIXED-FREQUENCY OSCIL FOR SPECTRAL FUSION 1
instr 1812 ; FIXED-FREQUENCY OSCIL FOR SPECTRAL FUSION 2
instr 1813 ; GLOBAL VIBRATO
instr 1814 ; FIXED-FREQUENCY OSCIL FOR SPECTRAL FUSION 3
instr 1815 ; FIXED-FREQUENCY OSCIL FOR SPECTRAL FUSION 4
instr 1816 ; TIME-VARYING STOCHASTIC GENERATOR 1
instr 1817 ; TIME-VARYING STOCHASTIC GENERATOR 2
instr 1818 ; EFFICIENT TIME-VARYING STOCHASTIC GENERATOR 1
instr 1819 ; EFFICIENT TIME-VARYING STOCHASTIC GENERATOR 2
instr 1820 ; SIMPLE FM
instr 1821 ; CONTEXT SENSITIVE GLOBAL RMS
instr 1822 ; PULSED NOISE
instr 1823 ; PASSES DATA TO 1824
instr 1824 ; PASSES DATA TO 1823
instr 1825 ; GLOBAL FEEDBACK
```

19. Mathematical Modeling with Csound: From Waveguides to Chaos

```
instr 1901 ; WAVEGUIDE PLUCKED BASS
instr 1902 ; WAVEGUIDE SLIDE-FLUTE
instr 1903 ; WAVEGUIDE CLARINET
instr 1904 ; DRUM STICK
instr 1905 ; SQUARE DRUM
instr 1908 ; LORENZ ATTRACTOR
```

```
instr 1909 ; ROSSLER'S ATTRACTOR
instr 1910 ; PLANET ORBITING IN BINARY STAR SYSTEM
```

20. An Introduction to Signal Processing with Csound

```
instr 2001 ; 440 HZ SINE WAVE AT FULL AMPLITUDE
instr 2002 ; SIMPLE 440 HZ OSCILLATOR
instr 2003 ; SINGLE IMPULSE
instr 2004 ; PITCHED PULSE TRAIN
instr 2005 ; ALIASING
instr 2006 ; IMPULSE RESPONSE OF RESON FILTER
instr 2007 ; DIRECT IMPLEMENTATION OF CONVOLUTION
instr 2008 ; CONVOLUTION USING CONVOLVE OPCODE
instr 2009 ; FIR FILTER EXAMPLE
instr 2010 ; IIR FILTER EXAMPLE
instr 2011 ; FM SCI-FI VOICE EXAMPLE
instr 2012 ; AM SCI-FI VOICE EXAMPLE
instr 2013 ; PHONE VOICE SCRAMBLER
instr 2014 ; PHONE VOICE DESCRAMBLER
```

21. Understanding Csound's Spectral Data Types

```
instr 2101 ; BEAT TRACKER, TEMPO FOLLOWER
instr 2102 ; PITCH TRACKING HARMONIZER
```

22. Using Csound to Understand Delay Lines and their Applications

```
instr 2201 ; PLUCK WITH ECHOES
instr 2202 ; DRY PLUCK
instr 2203 ; GLOBAL EFFECT
instr 2204 ; VDELAY VIBRATO
instr 2205 ; SOUNDIN 1
instr 2206 ; STEREO FLANGER
instr 2207 ; PITCH SHIFTER
instr 2208 ; SOUNDIN 2
instr 2209 ; HARMONIZER WITH FEEDBACK
```

23. An Introduction to Reverberation Design with Csound

```
instr 2301 ; NOISE BURST
instr 2302 ; REVERB UNIT
instr 2303 ; NOISE BURST WET/DRY
instr 2304 ; REVERB WET/DRY
instr 2305 ; STEREO DIFFUSION OF ECHOES
```

```
instr 2306 ; DOPPLER SHIFT
instr 2307 ; SCALEABLE GLOBAL SEND LEVELS
instr 2309 ; REVERB WITH ATTENUATED HI FREQ
instr 2310 ; ALLPASS FILTERS TO BUILD UP REFLECTIONS
instr 2311 ; 2 PARALLEL ALLPASS FILTERS WITH RANDOM DELAY
instr 2313 ; 3 PARALLEL COMBS INTO AN ALLPASS THEN LOPASS
instr 2314 ; GLOBAL REVERB INTO 2 VARYING DELAYS
instr 2315 ; METALLIC REVERB
```

24. Implementing the Gardner Reverbs in Csound

```
instr 2402 ; SMALL ROOM REVERB
instr 2403 ; MEDIUM ROOM REVERB
instr 2404 ; LARGE ROOM REVERB
```

25. Csound-based Auditory Localization

```
instr 2501 ; HRTFER EXAMPLE ORCHESTRA
```

26. Convolution in Csound: Traditional and Novel Applications

```
instr 2601 ; DIRECT CONVOLUTION
instr 2602 ; FFT CONVOLUTION
instr 2603 ; ECHO & REVERB DEMOS
instr 2604 ; MIX REVERB, DELAY & DARKEN
instr 2610 ; BRIGHT MUSIC DEMOS
```

27. Working with Csound's ADSYN, LPREAD and LPRESON Opcodes

```
instr 2701 ; BASIC ADDITIVE RESYNTHESIZER
instr 2704 ; ADDITIVE RESYNTHESIS WITH DYNAMIC FM
instr 2709 ; LPC SPEECH RESYNTHESIZER
instr 2722 ; LPREAD MAPPER
instr 2726 ; LPC CROSS-SYNTHESIZER
instr 2728 ; LPC-ADDITIVE CROSS-SYNTHESIZER
instr 2730 ; LPC-ADDITIVE FREEZE-FRAME
```

28. Csound's Phase Vocoder and Extensions

```
instr 2801 ; PVOC RESYNTHESIS WITH DYNAMIC TIME SCALING
instr 2810 ; PVREAD: ADDITIVE SYNTHESIS
instr 2811 ; GLOBAL TIME POINTER
```

```
instr 2812 ; GLOBALLY CONTROLLED FM SYNTHESIZER
instr 2815 ; VPVOC
instr 2816 ; CROSS-SYNTHESIS: PVBUFREAD
instr 2817 ; CROSS-SYNTHESIZER
instr 2818 ; CROSS-SYNTHESIS INTERPOLATES BETWEEN 2 FILES
instr 2821 ; CROSS-SYNTHESIS CONTROL OVER AMP & PITCH
instr 2822 ; TALKING MARIMBA/VIOLIN MORPH
```

29. Efficient Implementation of Analog Waveshaping in Csound

```
instr 2901 ; PULSE WAVE WITH MODULATABLE PULSE-WIDTH
instr 2904 ; SUB-OCTAVE GENERATOR
```

30. Modeling a Multi-Effects Processor in Csound

```
instr 3099 ; ZAK-BASED MIXER
instr 3011 ; COMPRESSOR/LIMITER
instr 3010 ; NOISE GATE
instr 3012 ; DE-ESSER
instr 3013 ; DISTORTION
instr 3018 ; 3 BAND EQ
instr 3016 ; WAH-WAH
instr 3015 ; RESONANT LOWPASS FILTER
instr 3020 ; VIBRATO
instr 3022 ; DELAY-BASED PITCH SHIFTER
instr 3035 ; CHORUS
instr 3030 ; FLANGER
instr 3040 ; STEREO DELAY
instr 3021 ; TREMOLO
instr 3023 ; AUTO-PANNER
instr 3045 ; SIMPLE REVERB
```

Recommended Reading

Cage, J. 1976. *Silence.* Middletown, Conn.: Wesleyan University Press.

Chadabe, J. 1997. *Electric Sound: The Past and Promise of Electronic Music.* New York: Prentice Hall.

Cook, P. R. 1999. *Music, Cognition, and Computerized Sound: An Introduction to Psychoacoustics.* Cambridge, Mass.: MIT Press.

De Poli, G., A. Piccialli, and C. Roads. 1991. *Representations of Musical Signals.* Cambridge, Mass.: MIT Press.

De Poli, G., A. Piccialli, S. T. Pope, and C. Roads. 1997. *Musical Signal Processing.* Lisse, The Netherlands: Swets and Zeitlinger.

Dodge, C., and T. Jerse. 1997. *Computer Music.* 2d rev. New York: Schirmer Books.

Eliot, T. S. 1971. *Four Quartets.* New York: Harcourt Brace & Company.

Embree, P. 1995. *C Algorithms for Real-Time DSP.* Englewood Cliffs: Prentice Hall.

Kernighan, B., and D. Ritchie. 1988. *The C Programming Language.* 2d ed. Englewood Cliffs: Prentice Hall.

Mathews, Max V. 1969. *The Technology of Computer Music.* Cambridge, Mass.: MIT Press.

Mathews, Max V., and J. R. Pierce. 1989. *Current Directions in Computer Music Research.* Cambridge, MA: MIT Press.

Moore, R. F. 1990. *Elements of Computer Music.* New York: Prentice Hall.

Oppenheim, A. V., and A. S. Willsky, with S. H. Nawab, 1997. *Signals and Systems.* 2d ed. New Jersey: Prentice Hall.

Pierce, J. R. 1992. *The Science of Musical Sound.* 2d rev. ed. New York: W. H. Freeman.

Pohlmann, Ken C. 1995. *Principles of Digital Audio.* 3d ed. New York: McGraw-Hill.

Press, W., B. Flannery, S. Tevkolsky, and W. Vetterling. 1993. *Numerical Recipes in C.* 2d ed. Cambridge, England: Cambridge University Press.

Roads, C. 1989. *The Music Machine.* Cambridge, Mass.: MIT Press.

Roads, C. 1996. *The Computer Music Tutorial.* Cambridge, Mass.: MIT Press.

Roads, C., and J. Strawn. 1987. *Foundations of Computer Music.* 3d ed. Cambridge, Mass.: MIT Press.

Steiglitz, K. 1996. *A Digital Signal Processing Primer.* Reading, Mass.: Addison-Wesley.

Vonnegut, K. 1987. *Bluebeard.* New York: Delacorte Press.

Winsor, P. 1991. *Computer Music in C.* Blue Ridge Summit: Tab Books.

Recommended Listening

Collections

Dinosaur Music: Chris Chafe, *In a Word;* David Jaffe, *Silicon Valley Breakdown;* and William Schottstaedt, *Dinosaur Music.* Wergo. WER 2016-50.

Electroacoustic Music I: Jean-Claude Risset, *L'Autre Face;* Paul Lansky, *notjustmoreidlechatter;* Daniel Warner, *Delay in Grass;* Richard Boulanger, *from Temporal Silence;* Kaija Saariaho, *Petals;* Charles Dodge, *Profile.* Neuma. 450–73.

Electroacoustic Music II: Jonathan Berger, *An Island of Tears;* Peter Child, *Ensemblance;* James Dashow, *Disclosures;* John Duesenberry, *Agitato (Ergo Sum);* Gerald Shapiro, *Phoenix.* Neuma. 450–75.

Electroacoustic Music Classics: Edgard Varese, *Poeme Electronique;* Milton Babbitt, *Phonemena, Philomel;* Roger Reynolds, *Transfigured Wind IV;* Iannis Xenakis, *Mycenae-Alpha.* Neuma. 450–74.

Music from SEAMUS Vol. 7: Tom Lopez, *Hollow Ground II*, William Rice, *SATX;* Bruce Hamilton, *Interzones;* Jon Christopher Nelson, *They Wash Their Ambassadors in Citrus and Fennel;* Matt Ingalls, *f(Ear);* Glenn Hackbarth, *Passage.* EAM-9801. 278044/45.

Le Chant du Monde Cultures Electroniques Vol. 2: Richard Karpen, *Exchange;* Jonathan Berger, *Meteora;* Julio d'Escrivan, *Sin ti por el Alma Adentro;* Henri Kergomard, *Hapsis;* Georg Katzer, *La Mecanique et les Agents de l'Erosion;* John Rimmer, *Fleeting Images;* Javier Alvarez, *Papalotl;* Josh Levine, *Tel;* Werner Kaegi, *Ritournelles;* Ben Guttman, *Different Attitudes* (2 CDs). LDC 278044/45.

Pioneers of Electronic Music: Arel, *Stereo Electronic Music No.2;* Davidovsky, *Syncronisms No.5;* Luening, *Low Speed, Invention in 12 Tones, Fantasy in Space* and *Moonflight;* Luening and Ussachevsky, *Incantation;* Shields, *Transformation of Ani;* Smiley, *Kolyosa;* Ussachevsky, *Sonic Contours, Piece for Tape Recorder* and *Computer Piece No.1.* CRI. CD 611.

Wergo Computer Music Currents Vol. 4: David Evan Jones, *Scritto;* Michel Decoust, *Interphone;* Charles Dodge, *Roundelay;* Jean-Baptiste Barriere, *Chreode I;* Trevor Wishart, *VOX-5;* Roger Reynolds, *The Vanity of Words.* Wergo. WER 2024-50.

Wergo Computer Music Currents Vol. 9: Gerald Bennett, *Kyotaka;* Joji Yuasa, *Towards the Midnight Sun;* Thomas Delio, *Against the Silence;* William Albright, *Sphaera.* Wergo. WER 2029-2.

Wergo Computer Music Currents Vol. 13: The Historical CD of Digital Sound Synthesis. Newman Guttman, *The Silver Scale* and *Pitch Variations;* John R. Pierce, *Stochatta, Variations in Timbre, Attack, Sea Sounds* and *Eight-Tone Canon;* Max V. Mathews, *Numerology, The Second Law, Bicycle Built for Two, Masquerades,* and *International Lullaby;* David Lewin, *Study No. 1* and *Study No. 2;* James Tenney, *Dialogue;* Ercolino Ferretti, *Pipe and Drum* and *Trio;* James Randal, *Mudgett* and *Monologues for a Mass Murderer.* Wergo. WER 2033-2.

Composers and Groups

Aphex Twin. *I Care Because You Do*. Sire. 61790-2.

Aphex Twin. *Selected Ambient Works, Vol. II*. Sire/Warner Bros. 9 45482-2.

Barron, Louis and Bebe. *Forbidden Planet*. Crescendo. PRD-001.

Byrne, David, and Eno, Brian. *My Life in the Bush of Ghosts*. Sire. 6093-2.

Carlos, Wendy. *Secrets of Synthesis*. CBS. MK 42333.

Carlos, Wendy. *Beauty in the Beast*. Audion/Jem. SYNCD 200.

Cascone, Kim. *"blueCube( )."* Rastermusic.

Chowning, John. *Turenas, Stria, Phone, Sabelithe*. Subharmonic. SD 7017-2.

Cypher 7. *Security.* WER 2012-50.

Dhomont, Francis. *Sous le regard d'un soleil noir.* empreintes DIGITALes. IMED 9633.

DJ Shadow. *Endtroducing*. Mo'Wax/ffrr. 697-124 123-2.

DJ Spooky. *Songs of a Dead Dreamer.* Asphodel. 0961.

Dodge, Charles. *In Celebration, Speech Songs, Story.* CRI. C-348.

Dolby, Thomas. *Retrospectacle*. Capital Records. CDP 7243 8 27642 2 9.

Eno, Brian. *Nerve Net*. Opal/Warner Bros. 9 45033-2.

Fast, Larry. *Computer Experiments Volume 1—Synergy.* Audion/Jem. SYNCD 104.

Fast, Larry. *Synergy—Electronic Realizations for Rock Orchestra*. Chronicles. 314 558 042-2.

Future Sound of London. *Cascade*. Astralwerks. ASW 6175-2.

Future Sound of London. *ISDN*. Astralwerks. ASW 6144-2.

Future Sound of London. *"Lifeforms: paths 1–7" (Maxi-Single)*. Astralwerks. ASW 6114-2.

Future Sound of London. *My Kingdom*. Astralwerks. ASW 6184.

Future Sound of London. *Papua New Guinea*. Hypnotic. CLP 9743-2.

Hancock, Herbie. *Dis is Da Drum*. Mercury. 314 522 681-2.

Heavenly Music Corporation. *Anechoic*. Silent. SR9599.

Heavenly Music Corporation. *Consciousness III*. Silent. SR9458.

Jarre, Jean Michel. *ZooLook*. Dreyfus. FDM 36145-2.

Johnson, Scott. *Rock/Paper/Scissors*. Point Music. 454 053-2.

Kraftwerk. *The Mix*. Elektra. 9 60869-2.

Lansky, Paul. *Fantasies and Tableaux*. CRI. CD 683.

Lansky, Paul. *Homebrew*. Bridge. BCD 9035.

Lansky, Paul. *More than Idle Chatter*. Bridge. BCD 9076.

Lansky, Paul. *Things She Carried*. Bridge. BCD 9050.

Laswell, Bill. *Second Nature*. Submeta. SM-9802-2.

Lucier, Alvin. *I Am Sitting in a Room*. Lovely Music. LCD 1013.

Material. *Seven Souls*. Triloka. 314 534 905-2.

McNabb, Michael. *Invisible Cities*. Wergo. WER 2015-50.

McNabb, Michael. *Computer Music*. Mobile Fidelity Sound Lab. MFCD 818.

Moby. *Into the Blue Remixes*. Mute. LCDMUTE179.

Moby/Voodoo Child. *The End of Everything*. Elektra. 62092-2.

Meat Beat Manifesto. *Subliminal Sandwich*. Interscope.

Nine Inch Nails. *Pretty Hate Machine*. TVT Records. 2610-2.

Nine Inch Nails. *Further Down the Spiral*. Nothing/Interscope. Halo ten. 95811-2.

Nine Inch Nails. *"The Perfect Drug" Versions*. Nothing/Interscope. Halo Eleven. Intdm-95007.

Normandeau, Robert. *Tangram*. empreintes DIGITALes. IMED-9419/20-CD.

The Orb. *Adventures in the Underworld*. Island.

Orbital. *Orbital-2*. FFRR. 162 351 026-2.

Oval. *systemisch*. thrill jockey. thrill032.

Oval. *diskont*. thrill jockey. thrill036.

Oval. *dok*. thrill jockey. thrill046.

Panasonic. *Osasto ep*. BFFP128CD.

Panasonic. *Vakio*. BFFP118CD.

Parmegiani, Bernard. *La Creation du Monde*. INA. C 1002.

Parmerud, Ake. *Grains of Voices*. Caprice. CC103.

PGR. *A Hole of Unknown Depth*. Silent. SR9602.

Pierce, Derek. *Beatsystem*. em:t. em:t2297.

Propellerheads. *Decksandrumsandrockandroll*. DRMD-50031.

Redolfi, Michel. *Too much Sky, Desert Tracks, Pacific Tubular Waves*. INA. C 1005.

Redolfi, Michel. *Sonic Waters #2*. Hat Art. CD 6026.

Redolfi, Michael. *Detours*. Mirage Musical. mm303.

Reynolds, Roger. *Personae, Variation, The Vanity of Words*. Neuma. 450-78.

Risset, Jean-Claude. *Sud, Dialogues, Inharmonique, Mutations*. INA. C 1003.

Risset, Jean-Claude. *Songes, Passages, Little Boy, Sud*. Wergo. WER 2013-50.

Roach, Steve. *The Magnificent Void*. Fathom. HS11062-2.

Seefeel. *CH-VOX*. Warp. 036 CD.

Squarepusher. *Feed Me Wierd Things*. Rephlex. CAT037CD.

Stockhausen, Karlheinz. *Stockhausen 3—Elektronische Musik 1952-1960*. Gemany.

Subotnick, Morton. *Touch, Jacob's Room*. Wergo. WER 2014-50.

Subotnick, Morton. *Silver Apples of the Moon, The Wild Bull*. Wergo. WER 2035-2 282 035-2.

Tenney, James. *Selected Works 1961-1969*. ART. 1007.

The Golden Palominos. *Dead Inside*. Restless. 7 72907-2.

Tomita, Isao. *Tomita's Greatest Hits*. RCA. 5660-2-RC.

Truax, Barry. *Digital Soundscapes*. Wergo. WER 2017-50.

Underworld. *"Born Slippy" (Maxi-Single)*. Wax Trax. TVT 8745-2.

Vangelis. *Themes*. Polydor. 839 518-2.

Varese, Edgar. *Music of Edgar Varese*. One Way Records. A 26791.

Orbital. *Insides*. FFRR. 697-124 087-2.

Vinao, Alejandro. *Son Entero, Triple Concerto*. Wergo. WER 2019-50.

Xenakis. *Electronic Music*. EMF. CD 003.

Sound Intensity and Formants

Sound Intensity Values for a 1000 Hz Tone

Dynamics	**Intensity (W/m²)**	**Level (dB)**
pain	1	120
fff	10^{2}	100
f	10^{4}	80
p	10^{6}	60
ppp	10^{8}	40
threshold	10^{12}	0

Formant Values

SOPRANO "a"	**F1**	**F2**	**F3**	**F4**	**F5**
freq (Hz)	800	1150	2900	3900	4950
amp (dB)	0	-6	-32	-20	-50
bw (Hz)	80	90	120	130	140
SOPRANO "e"	**F1**	**F2**	**F3**	**F4**	**F5**
freq (Hz)	350	2000	2800	3600	4950
amp (dB)	0	-20	-15	-40	-56
bw (Hz)	60	90	100	150	200
SOPRANO "i"	**F1**	**F2**	**F3**	**F4**	**F5**
freq (Hz)	270	2140	2950	3900	4950
amp (dB)	0	-12	-26	-26	-44
bw (Hz)	60	90	100	120	120

SOPRANO "o"	**F1**	**F2**	**F3**	**F4**	**F5**
freq (Hz)	450	800	2830	3800	4950
amp (dB)	0	-11	-22	-22	-50
bw (Hz)	70	80	100	130	135
SOPRANO "u"	**F1**	**F2**	**F3**	**F4**	**F5**
freq (Hz)	325	700	2700	3800	4950
amp (dB)	0	-16	-35	-40	-60
bw (Hz)	50	60	170	180	200

ALTO "a"	**F1**	**F2**	**F3**	**F4**	**F5**
freq (Hz)	800	1150	2800	3500	4950
amp (dB)	0	-4	-20	-36	-60
bw (Hz)	50	60	170	180	200
ALTO "e"	**F1**	**F2**	**F3**	**F4**	**F5**
freq (Hz)	400	1600	2700	3300	4950
amp (dB)	0	-24	-30	-35	-60
bw (Hz)	60	80	120	150	200
ALTO "i"	**F1**	**F2**	**F3**	**F4**	**F5**
freq (Hz)	350	1700	2700	3700	4950
amp (dB)	0	-20	-30	-36	-60
bw (Hz)	50	100	120	150	200
ALTO "o"	**F1**	**F2**	**F3**	**F4**	**F5**
freq (Hz)	450	800	2830	3500	4950
amp (dB)	0	-9	-16	-28	-55
bw (Hz)	70	80	100	130	135
ALTO "u"	**F1**	**F2**	**F3**	**F4**	**F5**
freq (Hz)	325	700	2530	3500	4950
amp (dB)	0	-12	-30	-40	-64
bw (Hz)	50	60	170	180	200

TENOR "a"	**F1**	**F2**	**F3**	**F4**	**F5**
freq (Hz)	650	1080	2650	2900	3250
amp (dB)	0	-6	-7	-8	-22
bw (Hz)	80	90	120	130	140
TENOR "e"	**F1**	**F2**	**F3**	**F4**	**F5**
freq (Hz)	400	1700	2600	3200	3580
amp (dB)	0	-14	-12	-14	-20
bw (Hz)	70	80	100	120	120
TENOR "i"	**F1**	**F2**	**F3**	**F4**	**F5**
freq (Hz)	290	1870	2800	3250	3540
amp (dB)	0	-15	-18	-20	-30
bw (Hz)	40	90	100	120	120

TENOR "o"	F1	F2	F3	F4	F5
freq (Hz)	400	800	2600	2800	3000
amp (dB)	0	-10	-12	-12	-26
bw (Hz)	40	80	100	120	120

TENOR "u"	F1	F2	F3	F4	F5
freq (Hz)	350	600	2700	2900	3300
amp (dB)	0	-20	-17	-14	-26
bw (Hz)	40	60	100	120	120

BASS "a"	F1	F2	F3	F4	F5
freq (Hz)	600	1040	2250	2450	2750
amp (dB)	0	-7	-9	-9	-20
bw (Hz)	60	70	110	120	130

BASS "e"	F1	F2	F3	F4	F5
freq (Hz)	400	1620	2400	2800	3100
amp (dB)	0	-12	-9	-12	-18
bw (Hz)	40	80	100	120	120

BASS "i"	F1	F2	F3	F4	F5
freq (Hz)	250	1750	2600	3050	3340
amp (dB)	0	-30	-16	-22	-28
bw (Hz)	60	90	100	120	120

BASS "o"	F1	F2	F3	F4	F5
freq (Hz)	350	600	2400	2675	2950
amp (dB)	0	-20	-32	-28	-36
bw (Hz)	40	80	100	120	120

COUNTERTENOR "a"	F1	F2	F3	F4	F5
freq (Hz)	660	1120	2750	3000	3350
amp (dB)	0	-6	-23	-24	-38
bw (Hz)	80	90	120	130	140

COUNTERTENOR "e"	F1	F2	F3	F4	F5
freq (Hz)	440	1800	2700	3000	3300
amp (dB)	0	-14	-18	-20	-20
bw (Hz)	70	80	100	120	120

COUNTERTENOR "i"	F1	F2	F3	F4	F5
freq (Hz)	270	1850	2900	3350	3590
amp (dB)	0	-24	-24	-36	-36
bw (Hz)	40	90	100	120	120

COUNTERTENOR "o"	F1	F2	F3	F4	F5
freq (Hz)	430	820	2700	3000	3300
amp (dB)	0	-10	-26	-22	-34
bw (Hz)	40	80	100	120	120

COUNTERTENOR "u"	**F1**	**F2**	**F3**	**F4**	**F5**
freq (Hz)	370	630	2750	3000	3400
amp (dB)	0	-20	-23	-30	-34
bw (Hz)	40	60	100	120	120

Pitch Conversion

NOTE #	CPS	CPSPCH	MIDI
C-1	8.176	3.00	0
C#-1	8.662	3.01	1
D-1	9.177	3.02	2
D#-1	9.723	3.03	3
E-1	10.301	3.04	4
F-1	10.913	3.05	5
F#-1	11.562	3.06	6
G-1	12.250	3.07	7
G#-1	12.978	3.08	8
A-1	13.750	3.09	9
A#-1	14.568	3.10	10
B-1	15.434	3.11	11
C0	16.352	4.00	12
C#0	17.324	4.01	13
D0	18.354	4.02	14
D#0	19.445	4.03	15
E0	20.602	4.04	16
F0	21.827	4.05	17
F#0	23.125	4.06	18

NOTE #	CPS	CPSPCH	MIDI
G0	24.500	4.07	19
G#0	25.957	4.08	20
A0	27.500	4.09	21
A#0	29.135	4.10	22
B0	30.868	4.11	23
C1	32.708	5.00	24
C#1	34.648	5.01	25
D1	36.708	5.02	26
D#1	38.891	5.03	27
E1	41.203	5.04	28
F1	43.654	5.05	29
F#1	46.249	5.06	30
G1	48.999	5.07	31
G#1	51.913	5.08	32
A1	55.000	5.09	33
A#1	58.270	5.10	34
B1	61.735	5.11	35
C2	65.406	6.00	36
C#2	69.296	6.01	37
D2	73.416	6.02	38
D#2	77.782	6.03	39
E2	82.407	6.04	40
F2	87.307	6.05	41
F#2	92.499	6.06	42
G2	97.999	6.07	43
G#2	103.826	6.08	44
A2	110.000	6.09	45
A#2	116.541	6.10	46

NOTE #	CPS	CPSPCH	MIDI
B2	123.471	6.11	47
C3	130.813	7.00	48
C#3	138.591	7.01	49
D3	146.832	7.02	50
D#3	155.563	7.03	51
E3	164.814	7.04	52
F3	174.614	7.05	53
F#3	184.997	7.06	54
G3	195.998	7.07	55
G#3	207.652	7.08	56
A3	220.000	7.09	57
A#3	233.082	7.10	58
B3	246.942	7.11	59
C4	261.626	8.00	60
C#4	277.183	8.01	61
D4	293.665	8.02	62
D#4	311.127	8.03	63
E4	329.628	8.04	64
F4	349.228	8.05	65
F#4	369.994	8.06	66
G4	391.955	8.07	67
G#4	415.305	8.08	68
A4	440.000	8.09	69
A#4	466.164	8.10	70
B4	493.883	8.11	71
C5	523.251	9.00	72
C#5	554.365	9.01	73
D5	587.330	9.02	74

NOTE #	CPS	CPSPCH	MIDI
D#5	622.254	9.03	75
E5	659.255	9.04	76
F5	698.456	9.05	77
F#5	739.989	9.06	78
G5	783.991	9.07	79
G#5	830.609	9.08	80
A5	880.000	9.09	81
A#5	932.328	9.10	82
B5	987.767	9.11	83
C6	1046.502	10.00	84
C#6	1108.731	10.01	85
D6	1174.659	10.02	86
D#6	1244.508	10.03	87
E6	1318.510	10.04	88
F6	1396.913	10.05	89
F#6	1479.978	10.06	90
G6	1567.982	10.07	91
G#6	1661.219	10.08	92
A6	1760.000	10.09	93
A#6	1864.655	10.10	94
B6	1975.533	10.11	95
C7	2093.005	11.00	96
C#7	2217.461	11.01	97
D7	2349.318	11.02	98
D#7	2489.016	11.03	99
E7	2637.020	11.04	100
F7	2793.826	11.05	101
F#7	2959.955	11.06	102

NOTE #	CPS	CPSPCH	MIDI
G7	3135.963	11.07	103
G#7	3322.438	11.08	104
A7	3520.000	11.09	105
A#7	3729.310	11.10	106
B7	3951.066	11.11	107
C8	4186.009	11.12	108
C#8	4434.922	12.00	109
D8	4698.636	12.01	110
D#8	4978.032	12.02	111
E8	5274.041	12.03	112
F8	5587.652	12.02	113
F#8	5919.911	12.06	114
G8	6271.927	12.07	115
G#8	6644.875	12.08	116
A8	7040.000	12.09	117
A#8	7458.620	12.10	118
B8	7902.133	12.11	119
C9	8372.018	13.00	120
C#9	8869.844	13.01	121
D9	9397.273	13.02	122
D#9	9956.063	13.03	123
E9	10548.08	13.04	124
F9	11175.30	13.05	125
F#9	11839.82	13.06	126
G9	12543.85	13.07	127

Csound's Error Messages

Csound is capable of generating about 1000 difference messages. These are not all easy to understand, but they fall generally into 4 catagories.

- **Fatal:** messages of this class cause Csound to stop, as they are irrecoverable.
- **Error:** there messages indicate an error, usually of the user getting something wrong in an opcode. They do not cause Csound to stop but the individual note may stop, or other similar patch-up is taken. Errors in the parsing of the orchestra may cause Csound to refuse to run.
- **Warning:** warning messages are not necessarily errors, but indicate that there may be something wrong. The user should ensure that they are expecting this situation, or correct for later runs.
- **Information:** Csound prints a number of informational messages as it runs. These include the names of the orchestra file, number of instruments and so on. There are mainly for reassurance, but they can also indicate small errors.

The following table contains all the messages that Csound generates. The words in *italics* will be replaced by numbers, strings or characters as indicated. Of course not all error messages relate to all platforms. The list here is sorted in some alphabetical order to make it easier to look up a message.

about to draw graph...type ENTER to continue	Information
active:*integer*	Information
ADSYN cannot load *string*	Error
ADSYN: not initialized	Fatal
AIFF 3-byte samples not supported	Fatal
AIFF does not support *string* encoding *string*	Fatal
AIFF looping file, once through only	Warning
AIFF soundfile	Information

ALAW and ULAW not implemented here	Fatal
ALAW audio_in not yet implemented	Fatal
ALAW bytes	Information
ALAW not yet implemented	Fatal
all channels	Information
allocate owner port	Fatal
allocate port set	Fatal
allocate timer reply port	Fatal
allpadd: not initialized	Fatal
analysis aborted	Fatal
analyzing harmonic #*integer*	Information
analyzing *integer* sample frames (*float*, secs)	Information
arg1 is zero	Fatal
arg2 is zero	Fatal
audio buffered in *integer* sample-frame blocks	Information
audio relational	Fatal
audio samps *integer* exceeds ftsize *integer*	Warning
audio sr = *integer*	Information
audio_in *string* format unclear, deducing *string*	Warning
audio_in *string* has *integer* chnls, orch *integer* chnls	Information
audio_in *string* has sr = *integer*, orch sr = *integer*	Information
auxchfree: illegal auxp lx in chain	Fatal
avail_ports:*integer*	Information
-B *integer* probably too large, suggest <= 2048	Warning
-B *integer* probably too large, suggest 1024	Warning
-B *integer* probably too small, suggest 1024	Warning
-B *integer* probably too small, suggest *integer*	Warning
bad form for aiffReadHeader	Fatal

bad form for wavReadHeader	Fatal
bad header length *integer* in '*string*'	Fatal
balance:*integer*	Information
baseNote	Information
become owner	Fatal
B*float* ..*float* T*float* TT*float* M:*float*	Information
bootfile: *string*	Information
both channels	Information
Buffer memory not allocated!	Fatal
buffer p size *integer*	Information
buffer_size:*integer*	Information
bufsize = *integer* frames	Information
buzz knh <= 0	Error
buzz: not initialized	Fatal
can't find end of file string	Fatal
can't ioctl EXTCLK	Fatal
can't ioctl ITIMER	Error
can't ioctl RS422	Fatal
can't open MIDI device	Error
can't open string, errno = *integer*	Error
can't rewrite header if no header requested	Fatal
can't write AIFF/WAV soundfile with no header	Fatal
can't write header	Fatal
can't write to MIDI device	Error
cannot create cscore.out	Fatal
cannot create output file	Fatal
cannot extract *string*, name conflict	Fatal
cannot get capabilities	Fatal
cannot handle uneven pole count yet	Error

cannot load *string*	Fatal
cannot load *string*, or SADIR undefined	Fatal
cannot open extract file *string*	Fatal
cannot open LoFi	Error
cannot open orch file *string*	Fatal
cannot open PV file	Information
cannot open scorefile *string*	Fatal
cannot open SCOTout score for writing	Fatal
cannot open *string*	Fatal
cannot open *string* for writing	Fatal
cannot open *string*, SFDIR undefined	Fatal
cannot open *string*. Not in cur dir, SSDIR or SFDIR as defined	Fatal
cannot read sformat *string*	Error
cannot read *string*	Error
cannot reopen cscore.out	Fatal
cannot reopen cscore.srt	Fatal
cannot reopen *string*	Fatal
cannot use *string* as MIDI input	Fatal
CHAN *integer* DRUMKEY *integer* not in keylstm PARAM *integer* NOT UPDATED	Warning
channel *integer*	Information
channel *integer* illegal	Fatal
channel must be in the range 1 to 4	Fatal
channel request *integer* illegal	Error
channels:*integer*	Information
characters after not comment	Error
chnl *integer* using instr *integer*	Information
chnl mode msg *integer* not implemented	Information
clockbase = *float*	Information

closed	Information
closing bracket not allowed in context []	Fatal
closing the file ...	Information
coef range: *float* - *float*	Information
coefficients too large(param1 + param2)	Fatal
coeffs not allocated!	Fatal
comb: not initialized	Fatal
command-line srate / krate not integral	Fatal
config : *string*	Information
connect failed	Warning
CONVOLVE: cannot load *string*	Error
CONVOLVE: channel number greater than number of channels in source	Error
CONVOLVE: not initialized	Fatal
CONVOLVE: output channels not equal to number of channels in source	Error
could not find indefinitely playing instr *integer*	Warning
could not get audio information	Fatal
could not open /dev/audio for writing	Fatal
could not set audio information	Fatal
couldn't allocate for initial shape	Fatal
couldn't configure output device	Fatal
couldn't find	Warning
couldn't open space file	Fatal
couldn't write the outfile header	Fatal
Csound Version *integer.integer* (*string*)	Information
ctrl *integer* has no exclus list	Information
currently active instruments may find this disturbing	Information

CVANAL: Error allocating header	Fatal
DECaudio record not available	Fatal
deferred alloc	Information
deferred size for GEN01 only	Fatal
deferred size, but filesize unknown	Fatal
deferred-size ftable *float* illegal here	Fatal
deferred-size ftable *float* load not available at perf time.	Fatal
delay: not initialized	Fatal
delayr: not initialized	Fatal
delayw: not initialized	Fatal
deltap: not initialized	Fatal
deltapi: not initialized	Fatal
destination dft table *float* not found	Error
dev/audio: cannot do AUDIO_GETINFO	Fatal
dev/audio: couldn't write all bytes requested	Warning
dev/dsp: couldn't write all bytes requested	Warning
diskin can't find "*string*" in its search paths	Error
diskin cannot open *string*	Error
diskin read error - during backwards playback	Fatal
diskin seek error: invalid skip time	Fatal
diskin *string* superceded by *string* header format *string*	Information
diskin: illegal no of receiving channels	Error
diskin: not initialized	Warning
dispfft: not initialized	Fatal
display: not initialized	Fatal
displays suppressed	Information
divide by unary minus	Fatal

do not understand block data yet	Error
do not understand symbols	Error
done	Information
DSP device does not support the requested mode (mono/stereo)	Fatal
duplicate *integer: string* (*string,integer*)	Information
duplicate label	Fatal
duration < zero	Warning
early end of file	Information
encoding:*integer*	Information
end of audio_in file	Information
end of lplay event list peak amps:	Information
end of MIDI track in '*string*'	Information
end of MPU401 midifile '*string*'	Information
end of score. overall amps:	Information
end of section *integer* sect peak amps:	Information
end of track in midifile 'string'	Information
envlpx rise func ends with zero	Error
envlpx(krate): not initialized	Fatal
eof:*integer*	Information
error code: already allocated	Fatal
error code: ID is out of range	Fatal
error code: unable to allocate or lock memory	Fatal
error code: unsupported wave format	Fatal
error in coef *integer* : *float* <> *float*	Warning
error in score. illegal opcode *char* (ASCII *integer*)	Error
error line *integer.* unknown label:	Error
error reading format data: is this a compressed file?	Fatal

error reading PVOC file	Information
error reading unknown chunk in WAV file	Fatal
error rewriting sfheader	Fatal
error rewriting WAV header	Fatal
error seeking to start of sound data	Fatal
error skipping unknown chunk in WAV file	Fatal
error trying to loop back to the beginning of the sound file!?!??	Fatal
error while closing sound mixer device	Fatal
error while opening *string*	Fatal
error while reading DSP device for audio input	Fatal
error while rewriting AIFF header	Fatal
error while seeking past AIFF chunk	Fatal
error writing AIFF header	Fatal
error writing PVOC file	Information
error writing size into sfheader	Fatal
error writing WAV header	Fatal
error: follow - zero length!	Fatal
error: illegal character *char*(*hex*) in scoreline:	Error
error: linseg not initialized (krate)	Fatal
error: too many pfields:	Error
error:*integer*	Information
escape event, length *integer*	Information
expression syntax	Fatal
expseg (krate): not initialized	Fatal
extending Floating pool to *integer*	Information
extending Global pool to *integer*	Information
extending instr number to *integer*	Information
extending Local pool to *integer*	Information

extending Polish array length *integer*	Information
extracting ...	Information
-F: stdin previously assigned	Fatal
failed to open DAC	Fatal
failed to open MIDI OUT due to already allocated	Error
failed to open MIDI OUT due to no current MIDI map	Error
failed to open MIDI OUT due to port in map does not exist	Error
failed to open MIDI OUT due to specified device is out of range	Error
failed to open MIDI OUT due to unable to allocate or lock memory	Error
failed to open MIDI OUT due to unknown	Error
failed to open text file	Fatal
failed to set signal	Fatal
failed while querying soundcard about buffer size	Fatal
failed while trying to set soundcard DMA buffer size	Fatal
fcntl failed on *string*	*Fatal*
fdclose: illegal fd *integer* in chain	Fatal
fdclose: no record of fd *integer*	Fatal
file *string* (*integer* bytes) loaded into memory	Information
file *string* bytes are in wrong order	Error
filter cutoff freq. = *float*	Information
filter not inited, can't set	Fatal
floats	Information
FOF needs more overlaps	Error
FOF: not initialized	Fatal
forcing 16bit -s sound format	Information

forcing 8bit -c sound format	Information
form header not type AIFF	Fatal
form header not type WAV	Fatal
foscil: not initialized	Fatal
foscili: not initialized	Fatal
found formant: *string* (number *integer*)	Information
found only *integer* poles...sorry	Fatal
frameSize must be between *integer* &*integer*	Fatal
frameSize=*integer* frameInc=*integer* MinFreq=*float* MaxFreq=*float*	Information
freq est *float*	Information
from timepoint *float*	Information
ftable does not exist	Fatal
ftable *integer* now deleted	Information
ftable *integer* relocating due to size change	Information
ftell error on *string*	Fatal
fterror, ftable *integer: string*	Information
ftgen error	Fatal
ftgen *string* arg not allowed	Fatal
full requested duration not available	Warning
gain:*integer*	Information
gbuzz knh <= 0	Error
gbuzz: not initialized	Fatal
GEN call has illegal x-ordinate values:	Fatal
GEN call has negative segment size:	Fatal
GEN01: early end-of-file	Information
GEN01: read error	Fatal
GEN01: AIFF file truncated by ftable size	Warning
GEN01: input file truncated by ftable size	Warning

GOTOS list is full..extending	Information
grain: not initialized	Fatal
grain4: not initialized	Fatal
granule_set: igap_os must be 0 to 100	Fatal
granule_set: igsize_os must be 0 to 100	Fatal
granule_set: igskip_os must be greater then 0	Fatal
granule_set: Illegal combination of igskip and ilength	Fatal
granule_set: Illegal ithd, must be greater then 0	Fatal
granule_set: Illegal value of iatt and/or idec	Fatal
granule_set: imode must be -1, 0 or +1	Fatal
granule_set: ipitch1 must be greater then zero	Fatal
granule_set: ipitch2 must be greater then zero	Fatal
granule_set: ipitch3 must be greater then zero	Fatal
granule_set: ipitch4 must be greater then zero	Fatal
granule_set: ipshift must be integer between 0 and 4	Fatal
granule_set: iratio must be greater then 0	Fatal
granule_set: kgap must be greater then 0	Fatal
granule_set: kgsize must be greater then 0	Fatal
granule_set: must be positive and smaller than function table length	Fatal
granule_set: not enough voices for the number of pitches	Fatal
granule_set: too many voices	Fatal
granule_set: unable to find function table	Fatal
granule_set: unable to find function table for envelop	Fatal
graphics not supported in this terminal, ascii substituted	Information

graphics suppressed, ascii substituted	Information
h of *integer* too low, reset to 1	Warning
had *integer* init errors	Error
hardware buffers set to *integer* bytes	Information
harmonic #*integer:* amp points *integer,* frq points *integer,* peakamp *integer*	Information
header init errors	Fatal
headersiz *integer,* datasiz *integer* (*integer* sample frames)	Information
hex, reading	Information
high frequency diffusion not in (0, 1)	Fatal
hopsize may be too small, recommend at least poleCount * 5	Warning
HP audio record not available	Fatal
HP write to streamSocket: couldn't write all bytes requested	Warning
hrtfer: not initialized	Fatal
htim ftable must be all-positive	Fatal
-i cannot be stdout	Fatal
-i: stdin previously assigned	Fatal
iatss = 0	Fatal
IEEE80:DoubleToUlong: val < 0	Fatal
ifn table begins with zero	Fatal
ignoring name *string* not in file	Warning
i*integer* pset args != pmax	Warning
ilen > ksmps	Fatal
illegal channel number	Fatal
illegal code *integer* encountered	Error
illegal controller number	Fatal
illegal ctrl no	Fatal
illegal delay time	Fatal

illegal frqratio	Error
illegal ftable number	Fatal
illegal gen number	Fatal
illegal idisprd	Fatal
illegal ihtim	Fatal
illegal imemdur	Fatal
illegal imindur	Fatal
illegal input to getsizformat	Fatal
illegal input val (y <= 0) for gen call, beginning:	Fatal
illegal input vals for gen call, beginning:	Fatal
illegal instr number	Error
illegal iperiod	Fatal
illegal iprd	Fatal
illegal istartempo value	Fatal
illegal itweek	Fatal
illegal loop time	Fatal
illegal MIDI chnl no *integer*	Fatal
illegal mrtmsg argument	Fatal
illegal no of output args	Fatal
illegal no of partials	Fatal
illegal ntracks in '*string*'	Fatal
illegal number of filenames	Fatal
illegal release loop data	Fatal
illegal reson iscl value, *float*	Error
illegal resonk iscl value, *float*	Error
illegal roughness factor(param1) value	Fatal
illegal RT scoreline:	Error
illegal sampframsiz	Fatal

illegal startempo	Fatal
illegal stretch factor(param1) value	Fatal
illegal stretch factor(param2) value	Fatal
illegal strset index	Warning
illegal sustain loop data	Fatal
illegal table length	Fatal
illegal value for iolaps	Fatal
illegal x interval	Fatal
illegal xamp value	Fatal
illegal xint value	Fatal
improper chunksize in '*string*'	Fatal
inactive allocs returned to freespace	Information
incompatible sample/channel/width	Fatal
inconsistent AIFF sizes	Fatal
inconsistent argoff sumcount	Fatal
inconsistent opds total	Fatal
inconsistent sr, kr, ksmps	Fatal
inconsistent strarg sizecount	Fatal
inconsistent WAV size	Fatal
incorrect cond value format	Fatal
incorrect evaluation	Fatal
incorrect logical argumemts	Fatal
incorrect number of filenames	Fatal
increasing number of tables from *integer* to *integer*	Information
index *integer* exceeds ctrl *integer* exclus list	Warning
index out of range	Fatal
indexing overflow error	Fatal
infile error: illegal *string* info in aiff file *string*	Fatal

init error in instr *integer: string*	Information
init error: *string*	Fatal
init phase truncation	Warning
input and begin times cannot be less than zero	Fatal
input arg '*string*' of type *string* not allowed	Fatal
input framesize (inter-frame-offset*2) exceeds maximum allowed	Fatal
instr *integer* expects MIDI event data, can't run from score	Error
instr *integer* had *integer* init errors	Information
instr *integer* now on	Information
instr *integer* p*integer* illegal for MIDI	Warning
instr *integer* pmax = *integer*, note pcnt = *integer*	Warning
instr *integer* redefined	Fatal
instr *integer* seeking MIDI chnl data, no chnl assigned	Warning
instr *integer string*, dft (*string*), *integer* octaves (*float* - *float* Hz):	Information
instr *integer string*, dft (*string*), *integer* octaves (*integer* - *integer* Hz):	Information
instr *integer* tempest:	Information
instr *integer*, signal *string:*	Information
insufficient args	Fatal
insufficient args and no file header	Error
insufficient arguments	Fatal
insufficient gen arguments	Fatal
insufficient sound for analysis	Fatal
insufficient terms	Fatal
integer amp tracks, *integer* freq tracks	Error
integer chans (not 1) in PVOC file *string*	Error

integer errors in performance	Information
integer forced decays, *integer* extra noteoffs	Information
integer infrsize, *integer* infrInc	Information
integer integer-byte soundblks of *format* written to *file* (WAV)	Information
integer integer-byte soundblks of *format* written to *file* (AIFF)	Information
integer integer-byte soundblks of *format* written to *file* (IRCAM)	Information
integer integer-byte soundblks of *string* written to *string string*	Information
integer lpc frames written to *string*	Information
integer memfile *string* deleted	Information
integer opcodes	Information
integer output frames estimated	Information
integer output frames written	Information
integer syntax errors in orchestra. compilation invalid	Information
integer usecs illegal in Tempo event	Warning
integer WAVE IN devices found	Information
integer WAVE OUT devices found	Information
integer(*float*)	Information
integer: File *string* position *integer*	Information
internal error op=*char*	Fatal
interpolation failed	Error
invalid ftable no. *float*	Fatal
invalid ftable no. *float*	Error
invalid switch option	Fatal
ioctl: *integer*	Information
isfinit: cannot open string	Fatal

ival *integer* is zero	Error
ival *integer* sign conflict	Error
ixmod out of range.	Fatal
-J overriding local default AIFF/WAV out	Warning
k rate function table no. *float* < 1	Error
kfn table *integer* not found	Error
kin lopass coef1 *float,* fwd mask coef1 *float*	Information
k-period aligned audio buffering	Information
kperiods/tick = *float*	Information
ksmps of *integer* needs wdw of *integer,* max is *integer* for pv *string*	Error
kstart *integer* is outside table *integer* range 0 to *integer*	Error
-L: stdin fcntl failed	Fatal
-L: with negative p2 illegal	Error
-L: stdin previously assigned	Fatal
LABELS list is full...extending	Information
last argument must be the string 'HRTFcompact' ...correcting.	Information
less sound than expected!	Fatal
linseg: not initialized (arate)	Fatal
linux sound driver does not support floating-point samples	Fatal
linux sound driver does not support long integer samples	Fatal
locscil: sustain defers to non-looping source	Warning
loFi player: timeout at *string*	Fatal
logLin = *integer*	Information
longs	Information
loop terminated	Information

looping endpoint *integer* exceeds ftsize *integer*	Warning
looping with modes *integer, integer*	Information
lpfile srate != orch sr	Warning
lpheader comment:*string*	Information
lpheader overriding inputs	Warning
lpinterpol works only with poles files..	Fatal
lpinterpol: not initialized	Fatal
lpread cannot load *string*	Error
lpread ktimpnt truncated to last frame	Warning
lpread timpnt < 0	Error
lpread: not initialized	Fatal
lpslot number should be less than 20	Fatal
lpslot number should be positive	Fatal
-M: stdin fcntl failed	Fatal
-M: stdin system has no fcntl reading stdin	Warning
-M: stdin previously assigned	Fatal
macro definition for *string*	Information
macro definition for string	Information
macro error	Error
macro *string* undefine	Information
macro *string* undefined	Information
massign: chnl *integer* exists, ctrls now defaults	Information
max found *float*, rel amp *float*	Information
memfiles: cannot allocate for MEMFIL extention	Fatal
memory allocate failure for *integer*	Fatal
memory fault	Error
metrical timing, Qtempo = 120.0, Qticks = *integer*	Information
MIDI channel *integer* using instr *integer*	Information

MIDI init cannot find any instrs	Fatal
MIDI_get_data	Fatal
MIDI_set_proto	Fatal
MIDI_set_sys_ignores	Fatal
MIDIfile console input not implemented	Fatal
minimum frequency too low	Fatal
misplaced relational op	Fatal
missing endin	Fatal
missing fscale table	Fatal
missing htim ftable	Fatal
MIT Csound (BorlandC): *integer.integer*	Information
MIT Csound: *integer*86 with floating point, v*integer.integer*	Information
MIT Csound: *integer*86, v*integer.integer*	Information
MIT Csound: *integer.integer* (*string*)	Information
monaural	Information
mono loscil cannot read from stereo ftable	Fatal
multitap: not initialized	Fatal
name : *string*	Information
name not found	Error
named section >>>*string*<<<	Information
need quoted filename	Fatal
negative rates not allowed!!, correcting	Information
negative segsiz	Fatal
negative time period	Fatal
negative time?	Warning
new alloc for instr *integer:*	Information
NeXT audio record not available	Fatal
NeXT supports nchnls = 2 (stereo) output only	Fatal

nh partials < 1	Fatal
nlfilt: not initialized	Fatal
no amplitude maximum	Fatal
no amplitude minimum	Fatal
no arguments	Fatal
no base frequency for clarinet	Error
no base frequency for flute	Error
no begin time	Fatal
no channel	Fatal
no coefs present	Fatal
no comment string	Fatal
no control rate	Fatal
no duration time	Fatal
no filter cutoff	Fatal
no framesize	Fatal
no fundamental estimate	Fatal
no hardware bufsamps	Fatal
no harmonic count	Fatal
no high frequency	Fatal
no hopsize	Fatal
no infilename	Fatal
no iobufsamps	Fatal
no latch	Fatal
no legal base frequency	Fatal
no linein score device_name	Fatal
no log file	Fatal
no looping	Information
no low frequency	Fatal
no memory for PVOC	Information

no message level	Fatal
no MIDI device available	Error
no MIDI device_name	Fatal
no MIDI output device	Fatal
no MIDI: after_touch(*integer,integer*)	Fatal
no MIDI: control_change(*integer,integer,integer*)	Fatal
no MIDI: note_off(*integer,integer,integer*)	Fatal
no MIDI: note_on(*integer,integer,integer*)	Fatal
no MIDI: openMIDIout()	Fatal
no MIDI: pitch_bend(*integer,integer,integer*)	Fatal
no MIDI: poly_after_touch(*integer,integer,integer*)	Fatal
no MIDI: program_change(*integer,integer*)	Fatal
no MIDI: send_midi_message(*integer,integer,integer*)	Fatal
no MIDIfile name	Fatal
no number of output points	Fatal
no orchestra name	Fatal
no outfilename	Fatal
no output file for trace	Fatal
no pedal threshold	Fatal
no poles	Fatal
no pool for unexpected global name	Fatal
no PV error	Information
no recognizable soundfile header	Warning
no -s and no soundheader, using sr default *integer*	Information
no sample rate	Fatal
no sampling rate	Fatal

no sound capabilities	Fatal
no sound input capabilities	Fatal
no sound written to disk	Information
no soundin header, presuming orchestra sr	Warning
no such window!	Fatal
no table for FM4Op	Error
no table for Agogobell strike	Error
no table for Brass	Error
no table for Clarinet	Error
no table for Flute	Error
no table for FM4Op	Error
no table for Mandolin	Error
no table for Marimba strike	Error
no table for Modal4 case	Error
no table for Singwave	Error
no table for Vibraphone strike	Error
no table for VibWaveato	Error
no table for wgbow vibrato	Error
no tempo value	Fatal
no tuning table *integer*	Fatal
no utility name	Fatal
no verbose level	Fatal
no volume level	Fatal
no windfact	Fatal
no xfilename	Fatal
no za space: zakinit has not been called yet	Fatal
no zk space: zakinit has not been called yet	Fatal
non-deferred ftable *integer* needs size *integer*	Warning

non-positive iatdec	Fatal
not #undef	Error
not writing to sound disk	Information
note aborted	Information
note deleted. i*integer* had *integer* init errors	Information
note deleted. instr *integer*(*integer*) undefined	Information
npoles > MAXPOLES	Error
null iopadr	Fatal
null opadr	Fatal
number not allowed in context []	Fatal
number of output points is too great	Fatal
number of outputs must be the same as the previous locsig;	Fatal
number of samples out of range:	Information
numeric syntax '*string*'	Fatal
-o cannot be stdin	Fatal
object/file not PVOC	Information
oct, reading	Information
offset *float* < 0 or > tablelength	Error
open bracket not allowed in context []	Fatal
open:*integer*	Information
opening AIFF infile *string*, with bytrev	Information
opening AIFF infile *string*, with no bytrev	Information
opening AIFF outfile *string*, with bytrev	Information
opening AIFF outfile *string*, with no bytrev	Information
opening string infile *string*, with bytrev	Information
opening string infile *string*, with no bytrev	Information
opening WAV infile *string*, with bytrev	Information
opening WAV infile *string*, with no bytrev	Information

opening WAV outfile *string*, with bytrev	Information
opening WAV outfile *string*, with no bytrev	Information
openout: illegal dirtyp	Fatal
operator *char* not allowed in context []	Fatal
orch compiler:	Information
orch now loaded	Information
orchestra sampling rate is not compatible with HRTF.	Fatal
orchestra text extended to *integer*	Information
orchname: *string*	Information
oscil(krate): not initialized	Fatal
oscil: not initialized	Fatal
oscil1(krate): not initialized	Fatal
oscil1i(krate): not initialized	Fatal
oscili(krate): not initialized	Fatal
oscili: not initialized	Fatal
osciln: not initialized	Fatal
out contr14 msb:*hex* lsb:*hex*	Information
output arg *string* illegal type	Fatal
output name previously used, type *char* must be uniquely defined	Fatal
output soundfile cannot be both AIFF and WAV	Fatal
output timer port	Fatal
over *integer* harmonics but continuing	Warning
overall samples out of range:	Information
overriding local default WAV out	Warning
padding error	Fatal
pan: not initialized	Fatal
partial count exceeds MAXPTLS	Error
pause:*integer*	Information

pch track range: *float* - *float* Hz	Information
per oct rolloff too steep	Fatal
perf error in instr *integer: string*	Information
perf error: *string*	Fatal
perf-pass statements illegal in header blk	Fatal
Pickup out of range (*float*)	Warning
pitch tracking inhibited	Information
PLAY......................................	Information
playing from cscore.srt	Information
pluck: not initialized	Fatal
PMLqueuesize = *integer*	Information
pole file not supported for this opcode !	Fatal
poles exceeds maximum allowed	Fatal
poles=*integer* hopsize=*integer* begin=*float* duration=*float*	Information
port:*integer*	Information
postScript file *string* cannot be opened	Warning
postScript graphs written to file *string*	Information
precision:*integer*	Information
printks parm 1 was not a "quoted string"	Error
ptlap = p ptlim = p	Error
PV frame *integer* bigger than *integer* in *string*	Error
PV frame *integer* seems too small in *string*	Error
pvadd cannot load *string*	Error
pvadd ktimpnt truncated to last frame	Warning
pvadd timpnt < 0	Error
pvadd not initialized	Fatal
pvanal cannot have both -w and -h	Fatal
pvanal error: *string*	Fatal

pvanal: frameSize must be 2^r	Fatal
pvanal: *integer* is a bad window overlap index	Fatal
pvanal: *string*	Information
pvbufread: not initialized	Fatal
pvcross: not initialized	Fatal
pvinterp: not initialized	Fatal
PVOC cannot load *string*	Error
PVOC debug : one frame gets through	Information
PVOC frame *integer* bigger than *integer* in *string*	Error
PVOC frame *integer* seems too small in *string*	Error
PVOC ktimpnt truncated to last frame	Warning
PVOC not initialized	Fatal
PVOC timpnt < 0	Error
PVOC transpose too high	Error
PVOC transpose too low	Error
PVRdH: wanted *integer* got *integer*	Error
PVRead: wanted *integer* got *integer*	Error
QIOLOFIINFO failed *integer* times, errno = *integer*	Fatal
quad, reading	Information
read error on *string*	Fatal
reading *integer*-byte blks of *string* from *string*	Information
reading sound from *string*, writing lpfile to *string*	Information
reading sys_ex event, length *integer*	Information
realtime performance using dummy numeric scorefile	Information
RECORD.......................................	Information
recv port	Fatal
reflection invalid (*float*)	Warning

release loop	Information
release loop playMode	Information
remainder of line flushed	Information
repeat not at top level; ignored	Error
repeat section (*integer*)	Information
replacing previous ftable *integer*	Information
req chan *integer,* file string has only *integer*	Information
reverb: not intialized	Fatal
reverb2: not initialized	Fatal
revlpsiz inconsistent	Fatal
rise func ends with zero	Fatal
RT MIDI_event Console not implemented	Fatal
rtaudio: illegal dsize	Fatal
rtevent: T*float* TT*float* M:	Information
-s *integer* overriding soundfile sr *integer*	Warning
sample rate overrides: esr = *float,* ekr = *float,* ksmps = *integer*	Information
sample rate set to *integer* (instead of *integer*)	Information
sample_rate:*integer*	Information
samples:*integer*	Information
scorename: *string*	Information
sect *integer* line *integer*	Information
section *integer:*	Information
seeding from current time	Information
seeding with *integer*	Information
seek error while updating AIFF header	Fatal
selecting device *integer*	Information
setting phoneme: *float integer*	Information
SFDIR undefined. using current directory	Information

sfinit: cannot open /dev/audio	Fatal
sfinit: cannot open *string*	Fatal
shorts	Information
Should be *integer*...exiting	fatal
signed chars	Information
Size=*integer* Format=*integer* Rate=*float* Channels=*integer*	Information
skip time larger than audio data,substituting zero	Warning
skipping meta event type *hex*	Information
SMPTE timing, *integer* frames/sec, *integer* ticks/ frame	Information
sndwarp at last sample frame	Warning
sndwarp: not initialized	Fatal
sndwarpst: not initialized	Fatal
socket creation failed	Warning
sort: illegal opcode	Error
sorting cscore.out	Information
sound output format cannot be both -*char* and -*char*	Fatal
soundcard DMA buffer size set to *integer* bytes (instead of *integer*)	Warning
soundcard does not support the requested sample format	Fatal
soundfile header write error. aborting ...	Fatal
soundfile read error	Fatal
soundfile read error, couldn't fill first frame	Fatal
soundfile write returned bytecount of *integer*, not *integer*	Information
soundin can't find "*string*" in its search paths	Error
soundin cannot open *string*	Error

soundin of *string* not implemented	Fatal
soundin seek error	Fatal
soundin *string* superceded by *string* header format *string*	Information
soundin: illegal no of receiving channels	Error
soundin: not initialised	Fatal
soundout can't find *string* in search paths	Error
soundout cannot open *string*	Error
source 1 s1ft table *integer* not found	Error
source sft table *integer* not found	Error
space: not initialized	Fatal
spdist: not initialized	Fatal
specaddm: not initialised	Fatal
specdiff: local buffers not initialized	Fatal
specdiff: not initialised	Fatal
specdisp: not initialised	Fatal
specfilt: local buffers not initialized	Fatal
specfilt: not initialized	Fatal
specptrk: not initialised	Fatal
specscal: local buffer not initialized	Fatal
specscal: not intiialised	Fatal
sr = *float*, kr = *float*, ksmps = *float*	Information
srate 44.1K or 22.05K only. This *integer* playing at *integer*	Warning
srate and krate overrides must occur jointly	Fatal
srate *integer*, hex, *integer* bit *string*, *float* seconds	Information
srate *integer*, monaural, *integer* bit *string*, *float* seconds	Information

srate *integer,* oct, *integer* bit *string, float* seconds	Information
srate *integer,* quad, *integer* bit *string, float* seconds	Information
srate *integer,* stero, *integer* bit *string, float* seconds	Information
srate *integer,* unknown, *integer* bit *string, float* seconds	Information
sread is confused on legal opcodes	Error
sread: text space overrun, increase MARGIN	Fatal
sread: illegal number format, sect *integer* line *integer:* xxx zero substituted.	Warning
sread: illegal opcode *char,* sect *integer* line *integer*	Error
sread: illegal use of carry, sect *integer* line *integer,* 0 substituted	Warning
sread: illegally placed *string,* sect *integer* line *integer*	Error
sread: instr pcount exceeds PMAX	Error
sread: requesting more memory	Information
sread: unexpected char *char,* sect *integer* line *integer*	Error
sread: unmatched quote, sect *integer* line *integer*	Error
starting new frame...	Information
stdin audio not supported	Fatal
stdout audio not supported	Fatal
stereo loscil cannot read from mono ftable	Fatal
stereo, reading	Information
striking three times here!!!	Information
striking twice here!!	Information
string integer points, max *float*	Information
string integer points, max *float string*	Information

string format *string* not yet supported	Error
string has no soundfile header, assuming *string*	Information
string has no soundfile header, reading as *string, integer* chnl*(s)*	Information
string integer pts, max *float*	Information
string nchnls = *integer,* soundin reading as if nchnls = *integer*	Information
string not a CONVOLVE file (magic *integer*)	Error
string not a PVOC file (magic *integer*)	Error
string not a recognized SFOUTYP env setting	Fatal
string sr = *integer,* orch sr = *float*	Information
string: assuming MPU401 MIDIfile format, ticksize = 5 msecs	Information
string: couldn't write all bytes requested	Warning
string: found standard MIDIfile header	Information
string: Midifile format *integer* not supported	Fatal
string's srate = *float,* orch's srate = *float*	Warning
strset index conflict	Warning
SUN audio record not available	Fatal
SUN Solaris audio record not available	Fatal
sustain count still *integer*	Information
sustain level out of range!!, correcting	Information
sustain loop	Information
sustain loop playMode	Information
swrite: output, sect*integer* line*integer* p*integer* has illegal number	Error
swrite: output, sect*integer* line*integer* p*integer* has illegal ramp symbol	Error
swrite: output, sect*integer* line*integer* p*integer* has illegally terminated *string*	Error
swrite: output, sect*integer* line*integer* p*integer* makes illegal reference to xxx. Zero substituted	Warning

swrite: output, sect*integer* line*integer* p*integer* ramp has illegal forward or backward ref	Error
swrite: unexpected opcode, section *integer* line *integer*	Error
syntax error in macro call	Fatal
system exclusive buffer overflow	Warning
table *float* not found	Error
table kfn=*integer* < 1	Error
table kfn=*integer* length *integer* shorter than ksmps *integer*	Error
table no. < 1 dft=*integer* s1ft=*integer* s2ft=*integer*	Error
table no. < 1 dft=*integer* sft=*integer*	Error
table number < 1 dft=*integer* s1ft=*integer* s2ft=*integer*	Error
table size too large	Fatal
table write k rate function table no. *float* < 1	Error
table write offset *float* < 0 or > tablelength	Error
table(krate): not initialized	Fatal
table: not initialized	Fatal
tablei(krate): not initialized	Fatal
tablei: not initialized	Fatal
tabolexseg: not initialized	Fatal
target label '*string*' not found	Fatal
tempest: not initialized	Fatal
term count	Fatal
terminating	Fatal
T*float*	Information
T*float* - note deleted	Information
the pole files have different pole count	Fatal
this Csound needs an 80x87	Fatal

time advanced *float* beats by score request	Information
time values must be in increasing order	Fatal
timeout waiting for DSP to boot	Error
timer start	Fatal
token length extended to *integer*	Information
token storage LENTOT exceeded	Fatal
tokens length extended to *integer*	Information
too few pfields	Error
too few points requested	Fatal
too many allocs	Fatal
too many arguments	Fatal
too many arguments to macro	Error
too many iterations in laguer	Fatal
too many lines...increasing	Information
too many open files	Fatal
too many pfields	Error
too many points requested	Fatal
too many turnons waiting	Warning
tracksize = *integer*	Information
translating Scot score ...	Information
try '-8' or '-s' options	Fatal
try '-c' or '-s' options	Fatal
trying to get solaris audio device...	Information
turnon deleted. instr *integer*	Error
turnon deleted. instr *integer* undefined	Fatal
twarp: illegal opcode	Error
twarp: t has extra or disordered beat value	Error
twarp: t has non-positive tempo	Error
twarp: t segments exceed twarp array	Error

type ENTER to continue...	Information
-U *string* not a valid UTIL name	Fatal
ulaw bytes	Information
unable to close audio device	Fatal
unable to close DSP device	Fatal
unable to configure MIDI port	Error
unable to open MIDI port *string*	Error
unable to open soundcard for audio input	Fatal
unable to open soundcard for audio output	Fatal
unable to open soundcard mixer for setting volume	Fatal
unable to set mode (mono/stereo) on soundcard	Fatal
unable to set output volume on soundcard	Fatal
unable to set requested sample format on soundcard	Fatal
unable to set sample rate on soundcard	Fatal
undefined macro	Error
undefined sys_common msg *hex*	Fatal
undefined sys_common msg *hex*	Warning
undefined sys-realtime msg *hex*	Information
undefined sys-realtime msg *hex*	Warning
undefining undefined macro	Error
undetermined file length, will attempt requested duration	Warning
uneven ctrl pairs	Fatal
uneven number of args	Fatal
unexpected end of '*string*'	Fatal
unexpected global name	Fatal
unknown # option	Error
unknown audio_in format	Fatal

unknown audio_out format	Fatal
unknown csr field	Warning
unknown distribution	Fatal
unknown drum param nos, msb *integer* lsb *integer*	Warning
unknown flag -*char*	Fatal
unknown format request	Fatal
unknown instr	Fatal
unknown kdump format	Fatal
unknown lowest frequency for bowed string	Error
unknown method code	Fatal
unknown nametype	Fatal
unknown NPRN lsb *integer*	Warning
unknown opcode	Fatal
unknown sample format	Fatal
unknown sound format *integer*(0x*hex*)	Fatal
unknown srctable number	Fatal
unlike signs	Fatal
unrecognized flag -*char*	Fatal
unrecognized message type *integer*	Fatal
unrecognized switch option	Fatal
unrecognized sys_common type *integer*	Fatal
unsigned bytes	Information
unsupported CONVOLVE data format *integer* in *string*	Error
unsupported PV data format *integer* in *string*	Error
unsupported PVOC data format *integer* in *string*	Error
usage: cvanal [-d<duration>] [-c<channel>] [-b<begin time>] <input soundfile> <output impulse response FFT file>	Information
using Cscore processing	Information

using filter coefficient storage method	Information
using filter coefficient type of file	Information
using pole storage method	Information
using pole type of file	Information
using previous *string*	Information
value out of range	Fatal
vdelay: not initialized	Fatal
version: *string*	Information
volume must be between 0 and 100	Fatal
vpvoc: not initialized	Fatal
-W overriding local default AIFF out	Warning
waiting:*integer*	Information
warning: High frequency diffusion<0	Warning
warning: High frequency diffusion>1	Warning
warning: Unknown # option	Warning
warning: xdns: zero Density requested	Warning
WAV does not support *string* encoding *string*	Fatal
WAVE IN dev.#*integer* ENABLED (*string*)	Information
WAVE IN device *integer: string*	Information
WAVE OUT device *integer: string*	Information
WAVE OUT unknown wave format	Fatal
WAVE OUT unknown wave format	Information
WAVE soundfile	Information
we're confused. file '*string*' begins with 'MT', but not a legal header chunk	Fatal
window size must be power of two	Fatal
window type =*integer*	Information
winGL:MakeGraph: fmfindfont failed	Information
write error	Fatal

writing *integer*-byte blks of *string* to *string string*	Information
writing text form to file *string*	Information
wrong input count in multitap	Fatal
wrong number of input arguments	Fatal
wrong number of outputs in locsig; must be 2 or 4	Fatal
wrong number of outputs in sndwarpst; must be 2 or 4	Fatal
wrote *integer* bytes to *string*	Information
x coordindate greater than function size:	Fatal
x coordindates must all be in increasing order:	Fatal
xfilename: *string*	Information
zacl first > last. Not clearing	Error
zacl first or last < 0. Not clearing	Error
zacl first or last > isizea. Not clearing	Error
zakinit should only be called once	Fatal
zakinit: both isizea and isizek should be > 0	Fatal
zamod kzamod > isizea. Not writing	Error
zar index < 0. Returning 0	Error
zar index > isizea. Returning 0	Error
zarg index < 0. Returning 0	Error
zarg index > isizea. Returning 0	Error
zaw index < 0. Not writing	Error
zaw index > isizea. Not writing	Error
zero length escape event	Fatal
zero length sys_ex event	Fatal
zir index < 0. Returning 0	Fatal
zir index > isizek. Returning 0	Fatal
ziwm index < 0. Not writing	Fatal

ziwm index > isizek. Not writing	Fatal
zkcl first > last. Not clearing	Error
zkcl first or last < 0. Not clearing	Error
zkcl first or last > isizek. Not clearing	Error
zkmod kzkmod > isizek. Not writing	Error
zkr index < 0. Returning 0	Error
zkr index > isizek. Returning 0	Error
zkw index < 0. Not writing	Error
zkw index > isizek. Not writing	Error
zkwm index < 0. Not writing	Error
zkwm index > isizek. Not writing	Error

Csound Quick Reference (version 4.01)

Orchestra Syntax: Orchestra Header Statements

```
sr                  =            iarg
kr                  =            iarg
ksmps               =            iarg
nchnls              =            iarg
                    strset       iarg, "stringtext"
                    pset         con1, con, ...
                    seed         ival
gir                 ftgen        ifn, itime, isize, igen, iarga[,
                                 iargb, ... iargz]
                    massign      ichnl, insno
                    ctrlinit     ichnkm, ictlno1, ival1[, ictlno2,
                                 ival2[, ictlno3, ival3[, ... ival32]]
```

Orchestra Syntax: Variable Data Types

```
iname         (init variable - initialization only)
kname         (control signal - performance time, control rate)
aname         (audio signal - performance time, audio rate)
giname        (global init variable - initialization only)
gkname        (global control signal - performance time,
              control rate)
ganame        (global audio signal - performance time, audio
              rate)
wname         (spectral data - performance time, control rate)
```

Orchestra Syntax: Instrument Block Statements

```
instr         NN
endin
```

Orchestra Syntax: Variable Initialization

```
i/k/ar      =          iarg
i/k/ar      init       iarg
ir          tival
i/k/ar      divz       ia, ib, isubst
```

Instrument Control: Instrument Invocation

```
            schedule   inst, iwhen, idur[, p4, p5, ... ]
            schedwhen  ktrigger, kinst, kwhen, kdur[, p4, p5,
                       ... ]
            schedkwhen ktrigger, kmintin, kmaxnum, kinsnum,
                       kwhen, kdur[, kp4, kp5, ...]
            turnon     insno[, itime]
```

Instrument Control: Duration Control

```
            ihold
            turnoff
```

Instrument Control: Realtime Performance Control

```
ir          active     insnum
            cpuprc     insnum, ipercent
            maxalloc   insnum, icount
            prealloc   insnum, icount
```

Instrument Control: Time Reading

```
i/kr        timek
i/kr        times
kr          timeinstk
kr          timeinsts
```

Instrument Control: Clock Control

```
            clockon    inum
            clockoff   inum
ir          readclock  inum
```

Instrument Control: Sensing and Control

```
kpitch,    pitch      asig, iupdte, ilo, ihi, idbthresh
kamp                  [, ifrqs, iconf, istrt, iocts, iq,
                      inptls, irolloff, iskip]
kcps,      pitchamdf  asig, imincps, imaxcps[, icps
krms                  [, imedi[, idowns [, iexcps]]]]
ktemp      tempest    kin, iprd, imindur, imemdur, ihp,
                      ithresh, ihtim, ixfdbak, istartempo,
                      ifn[, idisprd, itweek]
kr         follow     asig, idt
kout       trigger    ksig, kthreshold, kmode
k/ar       peak       k/asig
           tempo      ktempo, istartempo
kx, ky     xyin       iprd, ixmin, ixmax, iymin, iymax[,
                      ixinit, iyinit]
```

Instrument Control: Conditional Values

```
(a   >    b   ?   v1   :   v2)
(a   <    b   ?   v1   :   v2)
(a   >=   b   ?   v1   :   v2)
(a   <=   b   ?   v1   :   v2)
(a   ==   b   ?   v1   :   v2)
(a   !=   b   ?   v1   :   v2)
```

Instrument Control: Macros

```
#define     NAME # replacement text #
#define     NAME(a'b'c) # replacement text #
$NAME.
#undef      NAME
#include    "filename"
```

Instrument Control: Program Flow Control

```
                                              igoto    label
                                              tigoto   label
                                              kgoto    label
                                              goto     label
          if        ia       R       ib       igoto    label
          if        ka       R       kb       kgoto    label
          if        ia       R       ib       goto     label
          timout    istrt    idur    label
label     :
```

Instrument Control: Reinitialization

```
reinit     label
rigoto     label
rireturn
```

Mathematical Operations: Arithmetic and Logic Operations

```
- a         (no rate restriction)
+ a         (no rate restriction)
a && b      (logical AND; not audio-rate)
a || b      (logical OR; not audio-rate)
a + b       (no rate restriction)
a - b       (no rate restriction)
a * b       (no rate restriction)
a / b       (no rate restriction)
a ^ b       (b not audio-rate)
a % b       (no rate restriction)
```

Mathematical Operations: Mathematical Functions

```
int(x)        (init-rate or control-rate args only)
frac(x)       (init-rate or control-rate args only)
i(x)          (control-rate args only)
abs(x)        (no rate restriction)
exp(x)        (no rate restriction)
log(x)        (no rate restriction)
log10(x)      (no rate restriction)
sqrt(x)       (no rate restriction)
powoftwo(x)   (init-rate or control-rate args only)
logbtwo(x)    (init-rate or control-rate args only)
```

Mathematical Operations: Trigonometric Functions

```
sin(x)        (no rate restriction)
cos(x)        (no rate restriction)
tan(x)        (no rate restriction)
sininv(x)     (no rate restriction)
cosinv(x)     (no rate restriction)
taninv(x)     (no rate restriction)
sinh(x)       (no rate restriction)
cosh(x)       (no rate restriction)
tanh(x)       (no rate restriction)
```

Mathematical Operations: Amplitude Functions

dbamp(x)	(init-rate or control-rate args only)
ampdb(x)	(no rate restriction)

Mathematical Operations: Random Functions

rnd(x)	(init-rate or control-rate only)
birnd(x)	(init-rate or control-rate only)

Mathematical Operations: Opcode Equivalents of Functions

ar	**sum**	asig1, asig2[,asig3 ... asigN]
ar	**product**	asig1, asig2[,asig3 ... asigN]
i/k/ar	**pow**	i/k/aarg, i/k/pow
i/k/ar	**taninv2**	i/k/ax, i/k/ay
ar	**mac**	asig1, ksig1, asig2, ksig2, asig3, ...
ar	**maca**	asig1, ksig1, asig2, ksig2, asig3, ...

Pitch Converters: Functions

octpch(pch)	(init- or control-rate args only)
pchoct(oct)	(init- or control-rate args only)
cpspch(pch)	(init- or control-rate args only)
octcps(cps)	(init- or control-rate args only)
cpsoct(oct)	(no rate restriction)

Pitch Convertors: Tuning Opcodes

icps	**cps2pch**	ipch, iequal
icps	**cpsxpch**	ipch, iequal, irepeat, ibase

MIDI Support: Converters

ival	**notnum**	
ival	**veloc**	[ilow, ihigh]
icps	**cpsmidi**	
i/kcps	**cpsmidib**	[irange]
icps	**cpstmid**	ifn
ioct	**octmidi**	
i/koct	**octmidib**	[irange]
ipch	**pchmidi**	

i/kpch	**pchmidib**	[irange]
iamp	**ampmidi**	iscal[, ifn]
kaft	**aftouch**	[imin[, imax]]
i/kbend	**pchbend**	[imin[, imax]]
i/kval	**midictrl**	inum[, imin[, imax]]

MIDI Support: Controller Input

	initc7	ichan, ictlno, ivalue
	initc14	ichan, ictlno1, ictlno2, ivalue
	initc21	ichan, ictlno1, ictlno2, ictlno3, ivalue
i/kdest	**midic7**	ictlno, i/kmin, i/kmax[, ifn]
i/kdest	**midic14**	ictlno1, ictlno2, i/kmin, i/kmax[, ifn]
i/kdest	**midic21**	ictlno1, ictlno2, ictlno3, i/kmin, i/kmax[, ifn]
i/kdest	**ctrl7**	ichan, ictlno, i/kmin, i/kmax[, ifn]
i/kdest	**ctrl14**	ichan, ictlno1, ictlno2, i/kmin, i/kmax[, ifn]
i/kdest	**ctrl21**	ichan, ictlno1, ictlno2, ictlno3, i/kmin, i/kmax[, ifn]
i/kval	**chanctrl**	ichnl, ictlno[, ilow, ihigh]

MIDI Support: Slider Banks

i/k1, ... , i/k8	**slider8**	ichan, ictlnum1, imin1, imax1, init1, ifn1, ... , ictlnum8, imin8, imax8, init8, ifn8
i/k1, ... , i/k16	**slider16**	ichan, ictlnum1, imin1, imax1, init1, ifn1, ... , ictlnum16, imin16, imax16, init16, ifn16
i/k1, ... , i/k32	**slider32**	ichan, ictlnum1, imin1, imax1, init1, ifn1, ... , ictlnum32, imin32, imax32, init32, ifn32
i/k1, ... , i/k64	**slider64**	ichan, ictlnum1, imin1, imax1, init1, ifn1, ... , ictlnum64, imin64, imax64, init64, ifn64
k1, ... , k8	**slider8f**	ichan, ictlnum1, imin1, imax1, init1, ifn1, icutoff1, ... , ictlnum8, imin8, imax8, init8, ifn8, icutoff8
k1, ... , k16	**slider16f**	ichan, ictlnum1, imin1, imax1, init1, ifn1, icutoff1, ... , ictlnum16, imin16, imax16, init16, ifn16, icutoff16

k1, ... , k32	**slider32f**	ichan, ictlnum1, imin1, imax1, init1, ifn1, icutoff1, ... , ictlnum32, imin32, imax32, init32, ifn32, icutoff32
k1, ... , k64	**slider64f**	ichan, ictlnum1, imin1, imax1, init1, ifn1, icutoff1, ... , ictlnum64, imin64, imax64, init64, ifn64, icutoff64
i/k1, ... , i/k16	**s16b14**	ichan, ictlno_msb1, ictlno_lsb1, imin1, imax1, initvalue1, ifn1, ... , ictlno_msb16, ictlno_lsb16, imin16, imax16, initvalue16, ifn16
i/k1, ... , i/k32	**s32b14**	ichan, ictlno_msb1, ictlno_lsb1, imin1, imax1, initvalue1, ifn1, ... , ictlno_msb32, ictlno_lsb32, imin32, imax32, initvalue32, ifn32

MIDI Support: Generic I/O

kstatus, kchan, kdata1, kdata2	**midiin**	
	midiout	kstatus, kchan, kdata1, kdata2

MIDI Support: Note-on/Note-off

noteon	ichn, inum, ivel
noteoff	ichn, inum, ivel
noteondur	ichn, inum, ivel, idur
noteondur2	ichn, inum, ivel, idur
moscil	kchn, knum, kvel, kdur, kpause
midion	kchn, knum, kvel
midion2	kchn, knum, kvel, ktrig

MIDI Support: MIDI Message Output

outic	ichn, inum, ivalue, imin, imax
outkc	kchn, knum, kvalue, kmin, kmax
outic14	ichn, imsb, ilsb, ivalue, imin, imax
outkc14	kchn, kmsb, klsb, kvalue, kmin, kmax
outipb	ichn, ivalue, imin, imax
outkpb	kchn, kvalue, kmin, kmax
outiat	ichn, ivalue, imin, imax

	outkat	kchn, kvalue, kmin, kmax
	outipc	ichn, iprog, imin, imax
	outkpc	kchn, kprog, kmin, kmax
	outipat	ichn, inotenum, ivalue, imin, imax
	outkpat	kchn, knotenum, kvalue, kmin, kmax
	nrpn	kchan, kparmnum, kparmvalue
	mdelay	kstatus, kchan, kd1, kd2, kdelay

MIDI Support: Realtime Messages

	mclock	ifreq
	mrtmsg	imsgtype

MIDI Support: MIDI Event Extenders

	xtratim	iextradur
kflag	**release**	

Signal Generators: Linear and Exponential Generators

k/ar	**line**	ia, idur1, ib
k/ar	**expon**	ia, idur1, ib
k/ar	**linseg**	ia, idur1, ib[, idur2, ic[...]]
k/ar	**linsegr**	ia, idur1, ib[, idur2, ic[...]], irel, iz
k/ar	**expseg**	ia, idur1, ib[, idur2, ic[...]]
k/ar	**expsegr**	ia, idur1, ib[, idur2, ic[...]], irel, iz
ar	**expsega**	ia, idur1, ib[, idur2, ic[...]]
k/ar	**adsr**	iatt, idec, islev, irel[, idel]
k/ar	**madsr**	iatt, idec, islev, irel[, idel]
k/ar	**xadsr**	iatt, idec, islev, irel[, idel]
k/ar	**mxadsr**	iatt, idec, islev, irel[, idel]

Signal Generators: Table Access

i/k/ar	**table**	i/k/andx, ifn[, ixmode[, ixoff[, iwrap]]]
i/k/ar	**tablei**	i/k/andx, ifn[, ixmode[, ixoff[, iwrap]]]
i/k/ar	**table3**	i/k/andx, ifn[, ixmode[, ixoff[, iwrap]]]
kr	**oscil1**	idel, kamp, idur, ifn

```
kr          oscil1i     idel, kamp, idur, ifn
ar          osciln      kamp, ifrq, ifn, itimes
```

Signal Generators: Phasors

```
k/ar        phasor      k/xcps[, iphs]
k/ar        phasorbnk   k/xcps, kindx, icnt [, iphs]
```

Signal Generators: Basic Oscillators

```
k/ar        oscil       k/xamp, k/xcps, ifn[, iphs]
k/ar        oscili      k/xamp, k/xcps, ifn[, iphs]
k/ar        oscil3      k/xamp, k/xcps, ifn[, iphs]
k/ar        poscil      kamp, kcps, ift[, iphs]
k/ar        poscil3     kamp, kcps, ift[, iphs]
k/ar        lfo         kamp, kcps[, itype]
```

Signal Generators: Dynamic Spectrum Oscillators

```
ar          buzz        xamp, xcps, knh, ifn[, iphs]
ar          gbuzz       xamp, xcps, knh, klh, kr, ifn[, iphs]
ar          vco         kamp, kfqc, iwave, kpw, ifn, imaxd
```

Signal Generators: Additive Synthesis/Resynthesis

```
ar          adsyn       kamod, kfmod, ksmod, ifilcod
ar          adsynt      kamp, kcps, iwfn, ifreqfn, iampfn,
                        icnt[, iphs]
ar          hsboscil    kamp, ktone, kbrite, ibasfreq, iwfn,
                        ioctfn[, ioctcnt [, iphs]]
```

Signal Generators: FM Synthesis

```
ar          foscil      xamp, kcps, kcar, kmod, kndx, ifn[,
                        iphs]
ar          foscili     xamp, kcps, kcar, kmod, kndx, ifn[,
                        iphs]
ar          fmvoice     kamp, kfreq, kvowel, ktilt, kvibamt,
                        kvibrate, ifn1, ifn2, ifn3, ifn4,
                        ivibfn
ar          fmbell      kamp, kfreq, kc1, kc2, kvdepth,
                        kvrate, ifn1, ifn2, ifn3, ifn4, ivfn
ar          fmrhode     kamp, kfreq, kc1, kc2, kvdepth,
                        kvrate, ifn1, ifn2, ifn3, ifn4, ivfn
```

ar	**fmwurlie**	kamp, kfreq, kc1, kc2, kvdepth, kvrate, ifn1, ifn2, ifn3, ifn4, ivfn
ar	**fmmetal**	kamp, kfreq, kc1, kc2, kvdepth, kvrate, ifn1, ifn2, ifn3, ifn4, ivfn
ar	**fmb3**	kamp, kfreq, kc1, kc2, kvdepth, kvrate, ifn1, ifn2, ifn3, ifn4, ivfn
ar	**fmpercfl**	kamp, kfreq, kc1, kc2, kvdepth, kvrate, ifn1, ifn2, ifn3, ifn4, ivfn

Signal Generators: Sample Playback

ar[, ar2]	**loscil**	xamp, kcps, ifn[, ibas[, imod1, ibeg1, iend1[, imod2, ibeg2, iend2]]]
ar[, ar2]	**loscil3**	xamp, kcps, ifn[, ibas[, imod1, ibeg1, iend1[, imod2, ibeg2, iend2]]]
ar	**lposcil**	kamp, kfreqratio, kloop, kend, ift[, iphs]
ar	**lposcil3**	kamp, kfreqratio, kloop, kend, ift[, iphs]

Signal Generators: Granular Synthesis

ar	**fof**	xamp, xfund, xform, koct, kband, kris, kdur, kdec, iolaps, ifna, ifnb, itotdur[, iphs[, ifmode]]
ar	**fof2**	xamp, xfund, xform, koct, kband, kris, kdur, kdec, iolaps, ifna, ifnb, itotdur, kphs, kgliss
ar	**fog**	xamp, xdens, xtrans, xspd, koct, kband, kris, kdur, kdec, iolaps, ifna, ifnb, itotdur[, iphs[, itmode]]
ar	**grain**	xamp, xpitch, xdens, kampoff, kpitchoff, kgdur, igfn, iwfn, imgdur[, igrnd]
ar	**granule**	xamp, ivoice, iratio, imode, ithd, ifn, ipshift, igskip, igskip_os, ilength, kgap, igap_os, kgsize, igsize_os, iatt, idec[, iseed[, ipitch1[, ipitch2[, ipitch3[, ipitch4[, ifnenv]]]]]]
ar[, ac]	**sndwarp**	xamp, xtimewarp, xresample, ifn1, ibeg, iwsize, irandw, ioverlap, ifn2, itimemode
ar1, ar2	**sndwarpst**	xamp, xtimewarp, xresample, ifn1, ibeg,

[,ac1, ac2]		iwsize, irandw, ioverlap, ifn2, itimemode

Signal Generators: Waveguide Physical Modeling

ar	**pluck**	kamp, kcps, icps, ifn, imeth[, iparm1, iparm2]
ar	**wgpluck**	icps, iamp, kpick, iplk, idamp, ifilt, axcite
ar	**repluck**	iplk, xam, icps, kpick, krefl, axcite
ar	**wgpluck2**	iplk, xam, icps, kpick, krefl
ar	**wgbow**	kamp, kfreq, kpres, krat, kvibf, kvamp, ifn[, iminfreq]
ar	**wgflute**	kamp, kfreq, kjet, iatt, idetk, kngain, kvibf, kvamp, ifn[, iminfreq[, kjetrf[, kendrf]]]
ar	**wgbrass**	kamp, kfreq, iatt, kvibf, kvamp, ifn[, iminfreq]
ar	**wgclar**	kamp, kfreq, kstiff, iatt, idetk, kngain, kvibf, kvamp, ifn[, iminfreq]

Signal Generators: Models and Emulations

ar	**moog**	kamp, kfreq, kfiltq, kfiltrate, kvibf, kvamp, iafn, iwfn, ivfn
ar	**shaker**	kamp, kfreq, kbeans, kdamp, ktimes[, idecay]
ar	**marimba**	kamp, kfreq, ihrd, ipos, imp, kvibf, kvamp, ivibfn, idec
ar	**vibes**	kamp, kfreq, ihrd, ipos, imp, kvibf, kvamp, ivibfn, idec
ar	**mandol**	kamp, kfreq, kpluck, kdetune, kgain, ksize, ifn[, iminfreq]
ar	**gogobel**	kamp, kfreq, ihrd, ipos, imp, kvibf, kvamp, ivibfn
ar	**voice**	kamp, kfreq, kphoneme, kform, kvibf, kvamp, ifn, ivfn
ax, ay, az	**lorenz**	ks, kr, kb, kh, ix, iy, iz, iskip
ax, ay, az	**planet**	kmass1, kmass2, ksep, ix, iy, iz, ivx, ivy, ivz, idelta, ifriction

Signal Generators: STFT Resynthesis (Vocoding)

ar	**pvoc**	ktimpnt, kfmod, ifilcod, ifn, ibins[, ibinoffset, ibinincr, iextractmode, ifreqlim, igatefn]

```
kfr, kap    pvread       ktimpnt, ifile, ibin
            pvbufread    ktimpnt, ifile
ar          pvinterp     ktimpnt, kfmod, ifile, kfreqscale1,
                         kfreqscale2, kampscale1, kampscale2,
                         kfreqinterp, kampinterp
ar          pvcross      ktimpnt, kfmod, ifile, kamp1, kamp2[,
                         ispecwp]
            tableseg     ifn1, idur1, ifn2[, idur2, ifn3[ ... ]]
            tablexseg    ifn1, idur1, ifn2[, idur2, ifn3[ ... ]]
ar          vpvoc        ktimpnt, kfmod, ifile[, ispecwp[, ifn]]
ar          pvadd        ktimpnt, kfmod, ifilcod, ifn, ibins[,
                         ibinoffset, ibinincr, iextractmode,
                         ifreqlim, igatefn]
```

Signal Generators: LPC Resynthesis

```
krmsr,      lpread       ktimpnt, ifilcod[, inpoles[, ifrmrate]]
krmso,
kerr,
kcps
ar          lpreson      asig
ar          lpfreson     asig, kfrqratio
            lpslot       islot
            lpinterp     islot1, islot2, kmix
```

Signal Generators: Random (Noise) Generators

```
k/ar        rand         k/xamp[, iseed[, isize]]
k/ar        randh        k/xamp, k/xcps[, iseed[, isize]]
k/ar        randi        k/xamp, k/xcps[, iseed[, isize]]
i/k/ar      linrand      krange
i/k/ar      trirand      krange
i/k/ar      exprand      krange
i/k/ar      bexprnd      krange
i/k/ar      cauchy       kalpha
i/k/ar      pcauchy      kalpha
i/k/ar      poisson      klambda
i/k/ar      gauss        krange
i/k/ar      weibull      ksigma, ktau
i/k/ar      betarand     krange, kalpha, kbeta
i/k/ar      unirand      krange
```

Function Table Control: Table Queries

	nsamp(x)	(init-rate args only)
	ftlen(x)	(init-rate args only)
	ftlptim(x)	(init-rate args only)
	ftsr(x)	(init-rate args only)
i/kr	**tableng**	i/kfn

Function Table Control: Table Selection

k/ar	**tablekt**	k/xndx, i/kfn[, ixmode[, ixoff[, iwrap]]]
k/ar	**tableikt**	k/xndx, kfn[, ixmode[, ixoff[, iwrap]]]

Function Table Control: Read/Write Operations

	tablew	i/k/asig, i/k/andx, ifn[, ixmode[, ixoff[, iwgmode]]]
	tablewkt	k/asig, k/andx, kfn[, ixmode[, ixoff[, iwgmode]]]
	tableiw	isig, indx, ifn[, ixmode[, ixoff[, iwrap]]]
	tableigpw	ifn
	tablegpw	kfn
	tableimix	idft, idoff, ilen, is1ft, is1off, is1g, is2ft, is2off, is2g
	tablemix	kdft, kdoff, klen, ks1ft, ks1off, ks1g, ks2ft, ks2off, ks2g
	tableicopy	idft, isft
	tablecopy	kdft, ksft
ar	**tablera**	kfn, kstart, koff
kstart	**tablewa**	kfn, asig, koff

Signal Modifiers: Standard Filters

kr	**portk**	ksig, khtim[, isig]
kr	**port**	ksig, ihtim[, isig]
kr	**tonek**	ksig, khp[, iskip]
ar	**tone**	asig, khp[, iskip]
kr	**atonek**	ksig, khp[, iskip]
ar	**atone**	asig, khp[, iskip]
kr	**resonk**	ksig, kcf, kbw[, iscl, iskip]

ar	**reson**	asig, kcf, kbw[, iscl, iskip]
kr	**aresonk**	ksig, kcf, kbw[, iscl, iskip]
ar	**areson**	asig, kcf, kbw[, iscl, iskip]
ar	**tonex**	asig, khp[, inumlayer, iskip]
ar	**atonex**	asig, khp[, inumlayer, iskip]
ar	**resonx**	asig, kcf, kbw[, inumlayer, iscl, iskip]
ar	**resonr**	asig, kcf, kbw[,iscl, iskip]
ar	**resonz**	asig, kcf, kbw[,iscl, iskip]
ar	**resony**	asig, kbf, kbw, inum, ksep[,iscl, iskip]
ar	**lowres**	asig, kcutoff, kresonance[, iskip]
ar	**lowresx**	asig, kcutoff, kresonance[, inumlayer, iskip]
ar	**vlowres**	asig, kfco, kres, iord, ksep
ar	**lowpass2**	asig, kef, kq[, iskip]
ar	**biquad**	asig, kb0, kb1, kb2, ka0, ka1, ka2[, iskip]
ar	**rezzy**	asig, xfco, xres[, imode]
ar	**moogvcf**	asig, xfco, xres[, iscale]
alow, ahigh, aband	**svfilt**	asig, kcf, kq[, iscl]
ar1, ar2	**hilbert**	asig
ar	**butterhp**	asig, kfreq[, iskip]
ar	**butterlp**	asig, kfreq[, iskip]
ar	**butterbp**	asig, kfreq, kband[, iskip]
ar	**butterbr**	asig, kfreq, kband[, iskip]
k/ar	**filter2**	k/asig, iM, iN, ib0, ib1, ... , ibM, ia1, ia2, ... , iaN
ar	**zfilter2**	asig, kdamp, kfreq, iM, iN, ib0, ib1, ... , ibM, ia1, ia2, ... , iaN

Signal Modifiers: Specialized Filters

ar	**nlfilt**	ain, ka, kb, kd, kL, kC
ar	**pareq**	asig, kc, iv, iq, imode
ar	**dcblock**	asig[, ig]

Signal Modifiers: Envelope Modifiers

k/ar	**linen**	k/xamp, irise, idur, idec
k/ar	**linenr**	k/xamp, irise, idec, iatdec
k/ar	**envlpx**	k/xamp, irise, idur, idec, ifn, iatss, iatdec[, ixmod]
k/ar	**envlpxr**	k/xamp, irise, idur, idec, ifn, iatss, iatdec[, ixmod[, irind]]

Signal Modifiers: Amplitude Modifiers

kr	**rms**	asig[, ihp, iskip]
ar	**gain**	asig, krms[, ihp, iskip]
ar	**balance**	asig, acomp[, ihp, iskip]
ar	**dam**	ain, kthreshold, icomp1, icomp2, rtime, ftime

Signal Modifiers: Signal Limiters

i/k/ar	**wrap**	i/k/asig, i/k/klow, i/k/khigh
i/k/ar	**mirror**	i/k/asig, i/k/klow, i/k/khigh
i/k/ar	**limit**	i/k/asig, i/k/klow, i/k/khigh

Signal Modifiers: Delay

ar	**delayr**	idlt[, iskip]
	delayw	asigar
	delay	asig, idlt[, iskip]
ar	**delay1**	asig[, iskip]
ar	**deltap**	kdlt
ar	**deltapi**	xdlt
ar	**deltapn**	xnumsamps
ar	**deltap3**	xdlt
ar	**multitap**	asig, itime1, igain1, itime2, igain2 ...
ar	**vdelay**	asig, adel, imaxdel[, iskip]
ar	**vdelay3**	asig, adel, imaxdel[, iskip]

Signal Modifiers: Reverberation

ar	**reverb**	asig, krvt[, iskip]
ar	**reverb2**	asig, ktime, khdif[, iskip]
ar	**nreverb**	asig, ktime, khdif[, iskip]
ar	**comb**	asig, krvt, ilpt[, iskip]
ar	**alpass**	asig, krvt, ilpt[, iskip]
ar	**nestedap**	asig, imode, imaxdel, idel1, igain1[, idel2, igain2[, idel3, igain3]]

Signal Modifiers: Waveguides

ar	**wguide1**	asig, kfreq, kcutoff, kfeedback
ar	**wguide2**	asig, kfreq1, kfreq2, kcutoff1, kcutoff2, kfeedback1, kfeedback2

```
ar              streson     asig, kfr, ifdbgain
```

Signal Modfiers: Special Effects

```
ar              harmon      asig, kestfrq, kmaxvar, kgenfreq1,
                            kgenfreq2, imode, iminfrq, iprd
ar              flanger     asig, adel, kfeedback[, imaxd]
ar              distort1    asig[, kpregain[, kpostgain[,
                            kshape1[, kshape2]]]]
ar              phaser1     asig, kfreq, iord, kfeedback[, iskip]
ar              phaser2     asig, kfreq, iord, imode, ksep,
                            kfeedback
```

Signal Modifiers: Convolution and Morphing

```
ar1[,ar2[,      convolve    ain, ifilcod, ichannel
ar3[,
ar4]]]
ar              cross2      ain1, ain2, isize, ioverlap, iwin,
                            kbias
```

Signal Modifiers: Panning and Spatialization

```
a1, a2,         pan         asig, kx, ky, ifn[, imode[, ioffset]]
a3, a4
a1, a2          locsig      asig, kdegree, kdistance, kreverbsend
a1, a2,         locsig      asig, kdegree, kdistance, kreverbsend
a3, a4
a1, a2          locsend
a1, a2,         locsend
a3, a4
a1, a2,         space       asig, ifn, ktime, kreverbsend[, kx, ky]
a3, a4
a1, a2,         spsend
a3, a4

k1              spdist      ifn, ktime[, kx, ky]
aleft,          hrtfer      asig, kaz, kelev, "HRTFcompact"
aright
```

Signal Modifiers: Sample Level Operators

```
kr              downsamp    asig[, iwlen]
ar              upsamp      ksig
```

ar	**interp**	ksig[, iskip]
k/ar	**integ**	k/asig[, iskip]
k/ar	**diff**	k/asig[, iskip]
k/ar	**samphold**	x/asig, k/xgate[, ival, ivstor]
i/k/ar	**ntrpol**	i/k/asig1, i/k/asig2, i/k/kpoint[, imin, imax]
ar	**fold**	asig, kincr

Zak Patch System

	zakinit	isizea, isizek
	ziw	isig, indx
	zkw	ksig, kndx
	zaw	asig, kndx
	ziwm	isig, indx[, imix]
	zkwm	ksig, kndx[, kmix]
	zawm	asig, kndx[, kmix]
ir	**zir**	indx
kr	**zkr**	kndx
ar	**zar**	kndx
ar	**zarg**	kndx, kgain
kr	**zkmod**	ksig, kzkmod
ar	**zamod**	asig, kzamod
	zkcl	kfirst, klast
	zacl	kfirst, klast

Operations Using Spectral Data-Types

wsig	**specaddm**	wsig1, wsig2[, imul2]
wsig	**specdiff**	wsigin
wsig	**specscal**	wsigin, ifscale, ifthresh
wsig	**spechist**	wsigin
wsig	**specfilt**	wsigin, ifhtim
koct, kamp	**specptrk**	wsig, kvar, ilo, ihi, istrt, idbthresh, inptls, irolloff[, iodd, iconfs, interp, ifprd, iwtflg]
ksum	**specsum**	wsig[, interp]
	specdisp	wsig, iprd[, iwtflg]
wsig	**spectrum**	xsig, iprd, iocts, ifrqa, iq[, ihann, idbout, idsprd, idsinrs]

Signal Input and Output: Input

a1	**in**	
a1, a2	**ins**	
a1, a2, a3, a4	**inq**	
a1, a2, a3, a4, a5, a6	**inh**	
a1, a2, a3, a4, a5, a6, a7, a8	**ino**	
a1[, a2 [, a3, a4]]	**soundin**	ifilcod[, iskptim[, iformat]]
a1[,a2 [, a3, a4]]	**diskin**	ifilcod, kpitch[, iskiptim[, iwraparound[, iformat]]]

Signal Input and Output: Output

out	asig
outs1	asig
outs2	asig
outs	asig1, asig2
outq1	asig
outq2	asig
outq3	asig
outq4	asig
outq	asig1, asig2, asig3, asig4
outh	asig1, asig2, asig3, asig4, asig5, asig6
outo	asig1, asig2, asig3, asig4, asig5, asig6, asig7, asig8
soundout	asig1, ifilcod[, iformat]
soundouts	asig1, asig2, ifilcod[, iformat]

Signal Input and Output: File I/O

dumpk	ksig, ifilname, iformat, iprd
dumpk2	ksig1, ksig2, ifilname, iformat, iprd
dumpk3	ksig1, ksig2, ksig3, ifilname, iformat, iprd
dumpk4	ksig1, ksig2, ksig3, ksig4, ifilname, iformat, iprd

ksig	**readk**	ifilname, iformat[, ipol]
k1, k2	**readk2**	ifilname, iformat[, ipol]
k1,k2,k3	**readk3**	ifilname, iformat[, ipol]
k1,k2, k3,k4	**readk4**	ifilname, iformat[, ipol]
	fout	"ifilename", iformat, aout1[, aout2, aout3, ...,aoutN]
	foutk	"ifilename", iformat, aout1[, aout2, aout3, ...,aoutN]
	fouti	ihandle, iformat, iflag, iout1[, iout2, iout3, ...,ioutN]
	foutir	ihandle, iformat, iflag, iout1[, iout2, out3, ...,ioutN]
ihandle	**fiopen**	"ifilename",imode
	fin	"ifilename", iskipframes, iformat, ain1[, ain2, ain3, ...,ainN]
	fink	"ifilename", iskipframes, iformat, kin1[, kin2, kin3, ...,kinN]
	fini	"ifilename", iskipframes, iformat, in1[, in2, in3, ...,inN]
	vincr	asig, aincr
	clear	avar1[,avar2, avar3, ... ,avarN]

Signal Input and Output: Sound File Queries

ir	**filelen**	"ifilcod"
ir	**filesr**	"ifilcod"
ir	**filenchnls**	"ifilcod"
ir	**filepeak**	"ifilcod"[, ichnl]

Signal Input and Output: Printing and Display

print	iarg[, iarg, ...]
display	xsig, iprd[, inprds[, iwtflg]]
dispfft	xsig, iprd, iwsiz[, iwtyp[, idbouti[, iwtflg]]]
printk	kval, ispace[, itime]
printks	"txtstring", itime, kval1, kval2, kval3, kval4
printk2	kvar[, numspaces]

Score Syntax: Statements

f	"table number" "action time" "size" "GEN routine" arg1[arg2...arg...]
f0	"action time" (Dummy f-table for padding score sections with silence and reporting on progress of long running jobs).
b	"base clock time" (Effective prior to score sorting. This time base is pre-warped.)
t	0 "initial tempo" "time in beats" "tempo2"["time in beats" "tempo3" "time in...]
a	0 "begin time advance in beats" "duration of time advance in beats"
i	"instrument number" "start" "duration" [p4 p5 p...]
s	(marks end of section and restarts score counting from time 0)
m	"score location name" (marks a score section with a name)
n	"score location name" (named score section is re-read into the score file at this location)
r	"integer repeat count" "a macro name" (begins a new repeating sections)
e	(marks end of score - optional)

Score Syntax: P-Field Substitution

.	(carries same p-field value from preceding "**i**" statement with like instrument #)
+	(determines current start from sum of preceeding durations by adding p2 + p3 from previous "**i**" statement. legal in p2 only.)
^+*x*	(determines current start of instrument from sum of preceeding written event by adding last p2 to *x*. legal in p2 only.)
^-*x*	(determines current start of instrument from sum of preceeding written event by subtracting *x* from last p2. legal in p2 only.)
np*x*	(replace with p-field(x) value from next note statement illegal in p1 p2 p3.)
pp*x*	(replace with p-field(x) value from previous note statement illegal in p1 p2 p3.)
<	(p-field replaced by value derived from linear interpolation between previous and subsequent "anchor" values in same p-field. illegal in p1 p2 p3)

```
>      (p-field replaced by value derived from linear
       interpolation between previous and subsequent "anchor"
       values in same p-field. illegal in p1 p2 p3)
)      (p-field replaced by value derived from exponential
       interpolation between previous and subsequent "anchor"
       values in same p-field. illegal in p1 p2 p3)
(      (p-field replaced by value derived from exponential
       interpolation between previous and subsequent "anchor"
       values in same p-field. illegal in p1 p2 p3)
~      (p-field replaced by value derived from random value in
       the range between previous and subsequent "anchor"
       values in same p-field. illegal in p1 p2 p3)
```

Score Syntax: Expressions

```
[x+y]  (add value x to value y within a p-field. Note
       expressions must be in [brackets])
[x-y]  (subtract value y from value x within a p-field. Note
       expressions must be in [brackets])
[x*y]  (multiply value x by value y within a p-field. Note
       expressions must be in [brackets])
[x/y]  (divide value x by value y within a p-field. Note
       expressions must be in [brackets])
[x%y]  (value x remainder value y within a p-field. Note
       expressions must be in [brackets])
[x^y]  (power of value x to value y within a p-field. Note
       expressions must be in [brackets])
 [@x]  (next power-of-two greater than or equal to x. Note
       expressions must be in [brackets])
[@@x]  (next power-of-two-plus-one greater than or equal to x.
       Note expressions must be in [brackets])
```

Score Syntax: Macros

```
#define     NAME # replacement text #
#define     NAME(a'b'c) # replacement text #
$NAME.
#undef      NAME
#include    "filename"
```

GEN Routines: Sine/Cosine Generators

```
f # time size 9  pna   stra   phsa  pnb   strb phsb ...
f # time size 10 str1  str2   str3  str4  ...
```

```
f # time size 19 pna     stra     phsa    dcoa    pnb    strb phsb dcob
f # time size 11 nh      lh       r
```

GEN Routines: Line/Exponential Segment Generators

```
f # time size 5  a       n1       b       n2      c      ...
f # time size 6  a       n1       b       n2      c      n3   d    ...
f # time size 7  a       n1       b       n2      c      ...
f # time size 8  a       n1       b       n2      c      n3   d    ...
f # time size 25 x1      y1       x2      y2      x3     ...
f # time size 27 x1      y1       x2      y2      x3     ...
```

GEN Routines: File Access

```
f # time size 1  filcod  skiptime format channel
f # time size 23 "filename.txt"
f # time 0    28 filcod
```

GEN Routines: Numeric Value Access

```
f # time size 2  v1      v2       v3      ...
f # time size 17 x1      a        x2      b       x3     c     ...
```

GEN Routines: Window Functions

```
f # time size 20 window  max      op
```

GEN Routines: Random Functions

```
f # time size 21 type    lvl      arg1    arg2
```

GEN Routines: Waveshaping

```
f # time size 3  xval1   xval2    c0      c1      c2     ...  cn
f # time size 13 xint    xamp     h0      h1      h2     ...  hn
f # time size 14 xint    xamp     h0      h1      h2     ...  hn
f # time size 15 xint    xamp     h0      phs0    h1     phs1 h2   phs2
```

GEN Routines: Amplitude Scaling

```
f # time size 4  source# sourcemode
f # time size 12 xint
```

Command Line Flags: Generic

-I	i-time only orch run
-n	no sound onto disk
-i *fnam*	sound input filename *fnam*
-o *fnam*	sound output filename *fnam*
-b *N*	sample frames (or -kprds) per software sound I/O buffer
-B *N*	samples per hardware sound I/O buffer
-A	create an AIFF format output soundfile
-W	create a WAV format output soundfile
-J	create an IRCAM format output soundfile
-h	no header on output soundfile
-c	8-bit signed_char sound samples
-a	alaw sound samples
-8	8-bit unsigned_char sound samples
-u	ulaw sound samples
-s	short_int sound samples
-l	long_int sound samples
-f	float sound samples
-r *N*	orchestra srate override
-k *N*	orchestra krate override
-v	verbose orch translation
-m *N*	tty message level. *N* = Sum of: 1 = note amps, 2 = out-of-range msg, 4 = warnings
-d	suppress all displays
-g	suppress graphics, use ASCII displays
-G	create Postscript displays of any display
-S	score is in Scot format
-x *fnam*	extract from score.srt using extract file *fnam*
-t *N*	use uninterpreted beats of the score, initially at tempo *N*
-L *dnam*	read Line-oriented real-time score events from device *dnam*
-M *dnam*	read MIDI real-time events from device *dnam*
-F *fnam*	read MIDI file event stream from file *fnam*
-P *N*	MIDI sustain pedal threshold (*N* = 0 - 128)
-R	continually rewrite header while writing soundfile (WAV/AIFF)
-H/H1	print a heartbeat character at each soundfile write
-H2	generates a "." every time a buffer is written.
-H3	reports the size in seconds of the output.
-H4	sounds a bell for every buffer of the output written.
-N	notify (ring the bell) when score or MIDI file is done

-T	terminate the performance when MIDI file is done
-D	defer GEN01 soundfile loads until performance time
-z	List opcodes in this version
-z1	List opcodes and arguments in this version
-- ***lognam***	Log all text output to *lognam*
-j fnam	Derive console messages from database *fnam*

Command Line Flags: Utility Invocation

-U sndinfo	run utility program **sndinfo**
-U hetro	run utility program **hetro**
-U lpanal	run utility program **lpanal**
-U pvanal	run utility program **pvanal**
-U cvanal	run utility program **cvanal**
-U pvlook	run utility program **pvlook**
-C	use Cscore processing of scorefile

Command Line Flags: PC and Windows-Specific

-j ***num***	set the number of console text rows (default 25)
-J ***num***	set the number of console text columns (default 80)
-K ***num***	enables MIDI IN. *num* (optional) = MIDI IN port device id number
-q ***num***	WAVE OUT device id number (use only if more WAVE devices are installed)
-p ***num***	number of WAVE OUT buffers (default 4; max. 40)
-O	suppresses all console text output for better real-time performance
-e	allows any sample rate (to use only with WAVE cards supporting this feature)
-y	doesn't wait for keypress on exit
-E	allows graphic display for WCSHELL by Riccardo Bianchini
-Q ***num***	enable MIDI OUT. *num* (optional) = MIDI OUT port device id number
-Y	suppresses real-time WAVE OUT for better MIDI OUT timing performance
-*	yields control to the system until audio output buffer is full

Command Line Flags: Macintosh-Specific

-q ***sampdir***	set the directory for finding samples
-Q ***analdir***	set the directory for finding analyses
-X ***snddir***	set the directory for saving sound files

-V *num*	set screen buffer size
-E *num*	set number of graphs saved
-p	play on finishing
-e *num*	set rescaling factor
-w	set recording of MIDI data
-y *num*	set rate for progress display
-Y *num*	set rate for profile display

Utilities: Analysis File Generation

hetro	-sr *n*	infilename outfilename	Hetrodyne analysis *sample rate*
	-c *n*	infilename outfilename	Hetrodyne analysis *channel number*
	-b *n*	infilename outfilename	Hetrodyne analysis *segment begin time*
	-d *n*	infilename outfilename	Hetrodyne analysis *segment duration*
	-f *n*	infilename outfilename	Hetrodyne analysis *beginning frequency*
	-h *n*	infilename outfilename	Hetrodyne analysis *number of partials*
	-M *n*	infilename outfilename	Hetrodyne analysis *maximum amplitude*
	-m *n*	infilename outfilename	Hetrodyne analysis *minimum amplitude*
	-n *n*	infilename outfilename	Hetrodyne analysis *number of breakpoints*
	-l *n*	infilename outfilename	Hetrodyne analysis use third order low-pass filter with f_c of *n*
lpanal	-a	infilename outfilename	LPC analysis write filter pole instead of coeffecients
	-s *n*	infilename outfilename	LPC analysis *sample rate*
	-c *n*	infilename outfilename	LPC analysis *channel number*
	-b *n*	infilename outfilename	LPC analysis *segment begin time*
	-d *n*	infilename outfilename	LPC analysis *segment duration*
	-p *n*	infilename outfilename	LPC analysis *number of poles*
	-h *n*	infilename outfilename	LPC analysis *hop size* in samples

	-C *s*	infilename outfilename	LPC analysis *text string* for comments
	-P *n*	infilename outfilename	LPC analysis *lowest frequency*
	-Q *n*	infilename outfilename	LPC analysis *highest frequency*
	-v *n*	infilename outfilename	LPC analysis *verbosity level* of terminal messages
pvanal	-s *n*	infilename outfilename	STFT analysis *sample rate*
	-c *n*	infilename outfilename	STFT analysis *channel number*
	-b *n*	infilename outfilename	STFT analysis *segment begin time*
	-d *n*	infilename outfilename	STFT analysis *segment duration*
	-n *n*	infilename outfilename	STFT analysis *frame size*
	-w *n*	infilename outfilename	STFT analysis *window overlap factor*
	-h *n*	infilename outfilename	STFT analysis *hop size* in samples
cvanal	-s *n*	infilename outfilename	FFT analysis *sample rate*
	-c *n*	infilename outfilename	FFT analysis *channel number*
	-b *n*	infilename outfilename	FFT analysis *segment begin time*
	-d *n*	infilename outfilename	FFT analysis *segment duration*

Utilities: File Queries

sndinfo		soundfilename	get info about one or more sound files *soundfilename*
pvlook	-bb *n*	infilename	STFT analysis file formatted text output *beginning bin number*
	-eb *n*	infilename	STFT analysis file formatted text output *ending bin number*
	-bf *n*	infilename	STFT analysis file formatted text output *beginning frame number*
	-ef *n*	infilename	STFT analysis file formatted text output *ending frame number*
	-i	infilename	STFT analysis file formatted text output as integers

Index